CU00687346

THE COMPLETE GUIDE TO FINANCING REAL ESTATE DEVELOPMENTS

THE COMPLETE GUIDE TO FINANCING REAL ESTATE DEVELOPMENTS

IRA W. NACHEM

McGraw-Hill

New York   Chicago   San Francisco   Lisbon   London
Madrid   Mexico City   Milan   New Delhi
San Juan   Seoul   Singapore   Sydney   Toronto

3 4 5 6 7 8 9 0   DOC/DOC   0 9 8

ISBN–13: 978–0–07–147935–6
ISBN–10: 0–07–147935-X

Printed and bound by RR Donnelley.

This publication is designed to provide accurate and authoritative information in regard to the subject matter covered. It is sold with the understanding that neither the author nor the publisher is engaged in rendering legal, accounting, or other professional service. If legal advice or other expert assistance is required, the services of a competent professional person should be sought.

—From a Declaration of Principles jointly adopted by a Committee of the American Bar Association and a Committee of Publishers

McGraw-Hill books are available at special quantity discounts to use as premiums and sales promotions, or for use in corporate training programs. For more information, please write to the Director of Special Sales, Professional Publishing, McGraw-Hill, Two Penn Plaza, New York, NY 10121–2298. Or contact your local bookstore.

This book is printed on acid-free paper.

For my wife, Auden, my children, Jessica and Matthew,
and
In memory of my friend
Matt Vega

CONTENTS

PREFACE

If you want to learn how to obtain a development[1] (construction) loan, who should you go to? The best source is probably not a borrower but a lender. Many books on development lending are written by borrowers, but does a borrower really know what a lender wants? In this book I talk about lenders. I do my best to convey not only what lenders want but who they are—what their pressures, concerns, incentives, and motivations are.

I wrote this book because in my search for a reference on real estate development finance, I was not able to find one that was devoted specifically to that subject. Some were very good, but they addressed real estate development lending broadly, not with the depth and purpose that I needed. I also found several lending institutions' manuals, but they were little more than extensive checklists that contained so many caveats that I was surprised anyone would ever want to consider making a loan. Most disappointing to me, those which described the development financing process took a safe, dry, "this is what you're supposed to do" approach. The crucial and elemental combination of why, when, and how to do something—and why, when, and how *not* to do something—was not explored.

---

[1] Almost anywhere in this book you may substitute the word *development* for *construction* and vice versa. I use the word *development* to emphasize the holistic process of building and/or renovating real estate. Note, however, that in the real estate industry, development financing is referred to commonly as construction financing.

This book is different from the others because although it details the fundamental application of real estate finance, it addresses more practical and often more user-important needs for those who work in the field and those who want to or are considering entering the field.

There are many examples of the book's uniqueness. For instance, I don't think a discussion of a career in construction finance can be found in any published book. I even include estimates of salaries. For the developer, there is guidance on how to make a presentation to a lending institution to get a loan. For a lending officer, there is guidance on how to make a loan presentation to senior management, both orally and in writing. No other book gets into the developer's role as well as the lender's in developing budgets (I have experience as both a developer and a lender). I talk about plagiarism and recommend its use to get things done more quickly and accurately and with less effort. I go over the forms needed to get a loan advance by providing specific examples. I talk about tax credits and tax abatements and their value. I not only talk about the developer's capacity and ability to finish a project but also specifically address more subjective attributes such as the following: Is the developer greedy, cheap, difficult, stubborn, unfocused, secretive, dishonest, or contemptuous of authority? A chapter is devoted to problems: what the lender looks for to make a bad situation better and what a developer should be alert to if he has problems. This book covers everything from a union workers walk-off to a shortage of materials.

With this book, if you're new to real estate lending, you will gain valuable insights into what it's like to be in this multifaceted, intellectual, and mentally rigorous (and even physically demanding) business. If you're currently active in the field, you'll be presented with relevant, usable advice that can be applied readily and immediately to your job.

WHO THIS BOOK IS FOR

- Commercial real estate lending officers and senior managers in commercial banks, savings banks, and investment banks.
- Developers and would-be developers of commercial real estate who depend on financing to fund their projects (virtually all developers).
- Commercial real estate mortgage brokers.

- Construction managers, contractors, and the financial personnel in development firms.
- Commercial real estate loan servicers.
- Professors and students in colleges and universities that offer continuing education, undergraduate, or graduate courses in real estate.

WHAT THIS BOOK WILL DO FOR YOU

If you are a lender, after you read this book, you will benefit in the following ways:

- You will increase your level of personal, professional, and technical confidence.
- You will be more competitive in your industry and your institution.
- You will be more cognizant of the external and internal pressures that shape the goals and motives of your institution's senior management.
- You will have greater technical proficiency.
- You will be able to increase your success in presenting loans and getting them approved.
- You will close more deals.
- You will understand how and when to be flexible and when to be firm to create a loan structure that is a good piece of business for you and your institution.
- You will have a stronger background on which to base credit judgments and career decisions.
- You will make fewer mistakes.

If you are a borrower, after you read this book, you will benefit in the following ways:

- You will be able to avoid many common (and uncommon) pitfalls when asking for a development loan.
- You will have a better sense of institutional requirements so that you can adjust and fine-tune a loan proposal.
- You will be better able to assess how large a loan you will receive and under what terms and know how to argue for a better and more favorable loan structure.

- You will be able to anticipate obstacles and address issues before they become major ones.
- You will be able to channel more energy in the correct and most productive direction and toward the right targets.
- You will be able to help lending officers see the "right" way to structure your loan and do it tactfully.
- You will be better prepared to protect yourself against inexperienced or misinformed lenders who may do you more harm than good.
- You will make fewer mistakes.

If you are a broker, after you read this book, in addition to some of the benefits outlined above, you will

- Be a more knowledgeable and effective deal maker.
- Reap added benefits for your time and efforts by closing on larger and more complex deals as word of your success spreads and referrals keep coming in.

The Complete Guide to Financing Real Estate Developments is not loaded with useless tables, charts, and exhibits. There are no loan amortization schedules, present value tables, or copies of lengthy legal documents. When I discuss present value and amortization tables, it is assumed that you know something about these concepts; if you do not, you can learn about them quickly by reading a basic book on finance or real estate finance. Although this book discusses mortgages and building loan agreements, the discussion is purposely succinct. When a table or exhibit is presented, it is there to introduce a form or document that you should be familiar with, clarify a concept through illustration, or be adapted and used as a guide or template.

Unfortunately, I could not overcome the issue of gender. In using the third person, I have relied on history and convention by using the male rather than the female pronoun. Today, in commercial finance, approximately half the practitioners are female, and so I guess I could have gone either way. Please take this as an up-front apology for my bias. I sincerely hope that if this bothers or offends you, you can see through it to the many benefits this book provides. Also, please note that all names, addresses, telephone numbers, and other details in the examples in this book, unless otherwise noted, are fictitious.

Some of the reviewers of the book thought that I went too far. I received comments in the margins such "Are you sure you want to put this in a book!?" Let me state unequivocally that the comments, observations, and opinions in this book (there may be errors as well) are solely my own. They are based on undisputable facts, current circumstances, and my personal experiences. If I were not honest in stating my beliefs, I would do justice to no one. So be aware that this book is a guide. Your truth may well be different from mine.

This book was written with the objectives of providing information and insights not presented elsewhere and providing real value as a reference and a beginning-to-end read-through. I believe it lives up to those goals, and I'm sure it will make a positive contribution to your commercial real estate career. Good luck and much success!

ACKNOWLEDGMENTS

During the writing of this book, I have been very fortunate to have received a great deal of encouragement, helpful suggestions and invaluable criticism. I am especially grateful to:

Anne Teshima who reviewed my early drafts and as poorly written and full of errors as they were, encouraged me to continue in spite of them.

Robert Liner, Terence Tener, Michael Muroff and Jane Cucchi for their deliberate, thoughtful and very constructive critiques, comments and insights on many of the technical sections of the manuscript.

Auden Grogins, Jessica Nachem and Matt Nachem for their patience and encouragement from beginning to end.

Marilyn and Jack Grogins, Ann and Bill Janowitz, Irene and Ken Nachem, Michele and Dick Popilowki, Philip Pilevsky, Joshua Stein, George Klett, Chris Hooke and LisaMarie Pan for their interest and support.

Paul Fritz, Oisin Clancy, Carolyn Garramone, Jeffrey Kosow and Robert Plotka for their help with illustrations.

Jan Nicholson whose enduring brilliance inspired me to write this book in the first place.

Dianne Wheeler, Stephen Isaacs, Peter McCurdy and Eric Lowenkron for their indefatigable encouragement and effort to get this book from draft form to completion.

CHAPTER 1

The Commercial Real Estate Lender

INTRODUCTION: HISTORY AND PERSPECTIVES

In the mid–1980s, commercial real estate credit became one of the most lucrative activities for lending institutions. Banks with little or no experience or expertise in real estate development suddenly became players in the market. Asked by chief executive officers (CEOs) to increase business to meet yearly budget and yield goals, senior management moved farther and farther into areas where they had little experience or history. For institutions throughout the country, particularly those which were financially troubled, the message was unequivocal: Lend money to real estate developers at high yields with the hope that you will get it back with interest tomorrow. The alternative was to die slowly as the cost of institutional funds overwhelmed loan revenues.[1]

As the lending frenzy grew, the demand for real estate lenders and support staff grew. Because the demand for those people exceeded the supply, the quality of lending officers from the standpoint of experience and education declined. There was plenty of demand for even minimally skilled people. A person with real estate skills, let alone development expertise, was courted by many

---

[1] Because of their higher than average risk, yields on real estate development loans are usually high. Also, lenders almost always fund their own development loan interest and bank charges until a project is refinanced by another lender or becomes income-producing. Since the lending institution is funding all of the borrower's loan costs, at least during the early stages of the loan, the likelihood of the borrower defaulting for financial reasons is very low.

1

headhunters and could expect a great compensation package in the form of a high salary and almost guaranteed yearly bonuses.

The cycle ended abruptly when, presaged by the stock market fall of 1987, real estate markets tumbled. What was obfuscated, set aside, and ignored in the march for institutional profits in soaring markets was the fact that supply had outstripped demand greatly. Of course there were all kinds of related issues, such as exaggeration and fraud, that are discussed in later chapters of this book. However, the major cause of the real estate debacle was the imbalance of supply and demand, something that is clear to anyone who has read the first chapter of a basic economics textbook.

Over the last decade liquidity has returned to the real estate markets, although not in the same quantity or entirely from the same historical sources from which it once flowed. Investment banks and private equity funds have increased their activity dramatically as major players, whereas insurance companies and banks have moved with much greater caution. Helping to increase the supply of funds has been the enhanced ability of borrowers to find permanent lenders to refinance development loans. This is due in large part to the revolution in capital markets in which loans are packaged into pools, rated by private agencies, and sold primarily to institutional investors. For a lender making loans that are secured by existing properties, creativity has diminished significantly, as rating agencies dictate loan terms. However, since development loans continue to be held in the portfolios of lending institutions, a development lender still functions with a good deal of challenge, creativity, and innovation.

With the rapidity of change in the capital markets has come volatility in one's career. Real estate lending, in all its facets but more acutely in development lending, is subject to a host of vagaries and uncertainties that destine it to be unique, often in unfortunate ways. The recent wave of opportunities for development lenders may abate suddenly. If those who will be laid off in the next trough of a cycle return as lenders, they probably will return in a diminished capacity because of industry consolidations and takeovers that have resulted in decreased employment opportunities, less authority, less responsibility, and lower compensation. The emphasis will be on younger, less experienced employees who are more trainable because of their general eagerness to do well and recent educational experiences that some believe make them more receptive to training, a more immediate familiarity with the latest developments in the financial world, and the ability to work for much lower pay. In short, the surface of the employment balloon expands and contracts. Today, achieving longevity in the real estate lending field may be beyond your control. The best you can do to assure your survival is to strive to be the best you can be in your professional endeavors. This book will help you do that.

WHY BE A DEVELOPMENT LENDER?

Development lending is a multidisciplined activity that is intellectually stimulating, challenging, and often exciting. It continually evolves as a result of changes and trends in the real estate, financial, and capital markets; technological advances in the construction and financial industries; changes in management and business philosophies; and national and international economic cycles. For those who like a fast-paced environment and are willing to give up some of the security characteristic of more mundane areas of institutional lending, the rewards can be great. A development lender is recognized as someone who has special expertise in an area that requires creativity and intelligence. With the prestige comes institutional recognition. With recognition comes the opportunity for promotion and greater levels of authority and responsibility. Ultimately, whether you stay in the field of development lending or use your position and experience as leverage to enter other areas of professional activity, your enhanced qualifications will always be an asset on your résumé.

A CAREER IN REAL ESTATE LENDING

It is logical to think that one of the positive aspects of a career in real estate lending with a development specialty is that your skills and experience will remain in demand in both a growing economy and a contracting economy. Since real estate development is a "big ticket" expenditure that requires months or even years of planning, it usually lags at the start of an expansion. Often, larger projects that began during an economic expansion are caught in mid development or are near completion when the economy falls into a contraction.

In an economic expansion, a lending officer is involved in new loan originations; in an economic contraction, he may be involved in the workout of problem loans. Unfortunately for lenders, the movement between origination departments and workout departments is far from perfect. Often, newly hired employees are used to staff a workout area. Lending officers currently employed by the same lending institution are laid off. Even if you are lucky and smart enough to stay with your institution in the workout department, you will be working yourself out of a job as the size of the problem loan portfolio decreases with each successful resolution of a problem loan. An astute lender will realize that although development lending may fall out of favor temporarily, other areas of the real estate lending industry may be doing well. This may occur, for example, at a different lending institution specializing in multifamily loans, a private lender specializing in higher-risk–higher-yielding credits, an opportunity fund that lends and invests in distressed ownerships and properties, or a rating agency that analyzes individual loans for placement in loan pools.

If you manage to survive a complete economic cycle, your career will be enhanced. Employers are much more apt to hire experienced lenders who have worked on both the up and the down sides of the cycle. You will pick up a breadth of perspective and hands-on technical understanding and expertise that is almost impossible to obtain without direct experience. For a development lender, managing to continue a career in real estate lending with development financing knowledge almost certainly will be very exciting, personally satisfying, and financially rewarding.

PERSONAL ATTRIBUTES

To pursue a career as a development lender, you must be above average in intelligence, adaptable to fast-moving conditions, able to tolerate high levels of stress, and accepting of the need to make written and oral reports to higher levels of management regularly. You also must be able to understand the mathematical and technical aspects of a situation as well as its broader aspects; be able to communicate orally and in writing with people of all levels of sophistication, experience, education, and status; be able to multitask; not resent working long hours when deadlines loom; have the ability to stay focused when a deadline is near; be able to tolerate occasional discomfort when visiting construction sites, particularly in cold or inclement weather; and be a bit of an overachiever.

To enhance your chances of being successful, you should be goal-oriented. Knowing where you want to go professionally, including remaining in the real estate lending industry for your full career, even if some of your subgoals and desires change over time is very important. A personal goal orientation will make your job easier and more satisfying, making the time you spend at it more productive.

Education

Today a job candidate must have at least a bachelor of science or bachelor of arts degree, preferably in real estate, economics, architecture, finance, or accounting, or a technical degree in math or engineering. The preference for a particular type of undergraduate degree is not very strong, but persons with majors outside those areas may be at a small disadvantage. For many employers a master's degree in business administration (MBA) is a baseline requirement. It should be a degree in a technical area such as engineering or a business degree in accounting or finance. Surprisingly, a master's degree in real estate does not give you a particular advantage. If you have an MBA, your undergraduate discipline becomes almost irrelevant; if it is in liberal arts, it may be to your advantage since many employers interpret that to mean that you are a candidate with extended educational experience and a broad perspective. In addition to or instead of an MBA, a Member, Appraisal Institute (MAI) or a similar appraiser designation is well perceived in the industry. As in all professional fields, where you went to school can make a significant difference. Your academic achievement in school, though, is seldom an evaluation factor.

Training

Many of the larger banks offer excellent in-house general credit training programs. In those programs, lenders and future lenders are taken "off-line" for several weeks or months and learn fundamentals and advanced concepts and practices in accounting, finance, financial and credit analysis, marketing, writing, and presentation skills. In many of the programs the level of difficulty is high. Some programs are judged by the percentage of people who fail. Since the institution pays students a full-time salary, educational expenses, and often room and board without receiving an immediate benefit, only those perceived as the most motivated, able to compete, and likely to succeed are accepted.

Credit training grew in popularity in the mid–1980s as institutions recognized that in-house training programs provided them with many benefits, such as increased employee productivity, increased employee loyalty, and the attraction of promising job candidates. That proliferation in training unfortunately resulted in a dilution in educational and instructional quality. Newly formed marginal programs often moved away from rigorous intellectual study to the memorization of policies and procedures that were specific to an employee's particular institution. Although the lending officer was "credit-trained," the training had less value for the employee and for future employers. Many smaller institutions today do not have the personnel or the physical and financial resources to provide high-quality programs. Some larger institutions with variable education and training budgets sometimes periodically sacrifice training quality as well.

Despite the variable levels of quality, credit training is a very desirable credential and is a prerequisite for hiring in certain lending positions, including some in real estate. It is a competitive advantage in anyone's career, although it becomes less important as a person's career progresses, with experience becoming the overriding qualifier. In a high-quality program, competing in the classroom with highly motivated people with very good credentials can be daunting and intimidating at first, but long hours, focus, and hard work will help ensure success.

If your institution does not have in-house credit training opportunities, the best thing you can do is begin a self-training regimen by getting a book on real estate investing. Even a basic or elementary book can be very helpful in familiarizing you quickly with terms specific to the real estate industry and your job.

Almost all institutions provide some reimbursement for outside training. Out-of-the-office seminars and instruction are a prerequisite for excelling in development lending as well as other types of credit-related and real estate–related professional activities. They will help you gain an advantage in the competitive environment in your lending institution, provide you with transferable knowledge and skills, and provide you with some educational credentials for your résumé. In larger cities, colleges and universities provide many real estate–related and credit-related courses that can be very helpful and effective.

Experience

As in almost all professional salaried positions, the more experience a person has, the more desirable that person is to employers. This general statement, like all general statements, has exceptions and limitations. Importantly, it does not recognize the balance employers need to establish between experience and the amount of money they are willing to pay for it. Also, it does not recognize the bias of many managers toward hiring younger and less experienced individuals who are perceived as more willing to buy into a manager's way of doing things and an employer's corporate culture.

Currently, an employee with, say, three to five years of real estate lending experience is at peak desirability among employers. It generally is assumed that he has a good idea of the technical fundamentals, can document a track record, can be hired for a lower compensation package than someone with more experience and seniority, is less rigid than a more senior job candidate, and is a better candidate than someone with less experience who will need more time to move up the knowledge and productivity curve.

Those with little or no experience in development lending should consider broadening the initial job search to lending in the real estate field. Since real estate lending will give a newcomer 75 percent of what he needs to know to become a development lender, his background in this broader category is invaluable for moving into the arena of development lending. Also, it is important to realize that development lending per se is a subset of real estate lending that is seldom, if ever, allowed to exist on its own in any company. That is, single-family residential and commercial real estate lending departments can be totally mutually independent under a single institution, but development lending and commercial real estate lending cannot. Almost without question, a development lender will be asked to review all types of real estate credit products, including term and long-term loans that contain few, if any, development components.

For an experienced development lender, the future may turn difficult abruptly. With the emphasis on productivity, there are fewer middle managers and more on-line personnel. Although management structures remain vertical, the span of control (number of people supervised) for each manager generally has doubled. This means that advancement through the ranks of any financial institution will be more a reflection of a title change—from senior account manger to assistant vice president to vice president—than an actual change in job function. The result is that no matter how smart and talented he is, an experienced lender will be required to spend more time on the line. It will take longer to move up to a management position and therefore longer to gain valuable management experience. The track in development lending still can be fast, but the distance has been extended.

SPECIALIZATION

As in most other industries, specialization continues to be the operative movement in lending institutions. This should be less of a concern for a development lender since he already knows most of the parameters for making term or permanent loans. This is because in his analysis of a development loan proposal he will have to address the viability of the project after completion, which includes its value, its revenue-producing capabilities, and its attractiveness to term and permanent lenders. Therefore, the movement from a development specialty to a lending department that concentrates on completed income-generating properties is usually not difficult, assuming, of course, that there are job opportunities available. It should be noted, however, that the commercial mortgage-backed securities (CMBS) market, currently one of the most in-demand and high-paying real estate employment engines, requires some specialized knowledge. The dichotomy between development lending and permanent lending therefore has widened.

TRANSFERABLE SKILLS

In moving from one job or career to another, it is prudent to bear in mind that the job market is ruled by a complex set of dynamics. The objective is not to get caught in a bad situation. Try to keep a job in an employers' market and explore opportunities more aggressively in an employees' market. Real estate development lending is multidisciplined, and skills are readily transferable. In fact, most people who spend time in commercial real estate development lending eventually find themselves in other businesses, including real estate–related disciplines such as brokerage, development, investment, construction, marketing, and management. Through the myriad contacts made during their banking careers, many individuals move into personal finance, which has a strong real estate component; project finance, which has a strong development component; and general business lending, which is heavily reliant on analyses of financial statements and in many cases the evaluation of real assets. The point is that development lending can be a rewarding endeavor either as a career in itself or as part of a multiple career path. If you catch the profession in an upswing, the momentum can catapult you above many of your peers. In a downswing, the skills you will have mastered, if marketed selectively and effectively, may allow you to move more easily into new areas of opportunity.

MONEY

Development lending can be highly lucrative. Real estate department heads can make as much as $300,000 per year at a small commercial or savings bank. In some money center banks and investment banks throughout the United States the yearly salary and bonus figure can be significantly higher, in the millions of dollars. An account manager coming into the field in 2007 could expect to make about $60,000 per year altogether (bonus and salary but not counting other benefits, such as insurance and 401(k) contributions) and three weeks of paid vacation. After only two years of experience, he can expect to be able to earn approximately $80,000 to $100,000 and three to four weeks of paid vacation.[2] Other significant perks can include travel expenses to and from sites, including meals and, if necessary, hotel and airfare. This can be a great opportunity to combine work with vacation if you find yourself traveling to desirable destinations. You also will earn a lot of frequent-flier miles.

Near the office, if you have even a small amount of marketing responsibility, you will be reimbursed for meals and entertainment with prospects and customers. Most institutions realize that although entertainment payback is hard to measure, it is essential in today's business culture. It is also a highly desirable and usually pleasant duty for an employee.[3]

---

[2] Salaries and compensation packages may differ significantly, depending on the individual, the hiring institution's policies and circumstances, and of course the location of employment within the United States. Particularly as a result of competitive employment factors and sometimes significant geographic differences in the cost of living, the salaries noted here should be used only as broad and general benchmarks.

[3] Before you accept a gift, make sure you are aware of your institution's gift policy. Even an innocuous gesture such as accepting a bottle of spirits on Christmas from a prospective borrower or a round of golf from a client with whom you have an existing and strong relationship may violate your employer's policy. Usually, even if the gift is above policy limits, if it is reported properly, senior management will allow you to accept it. Ideally, a lender's policy should be balanced between making sure the gift does not become an incentive to treat the borrower more favorably and avoiding the possible insult or social awkwardness of nonacceptance. Moving too far to the right or left of this balance can cause a deterioration in credit objectivity or in a lender-borrower relationship. In an attempt to strike the right balance, some lenders allow you to accept certain items in excess of stated gift values if they are shared by many (e.g., a fruit basket or box of chocolates put in the department's reception area) or donated to a charity.

You also will get several publications and informational resources for free, and that should help keep you abreast of news, events and advances in the real estate industry as well as related financial professions. Finally, the educational package in the form of seminars, conventions—which are a mix of education, marketing, and having a good time—and school reimbursement programs can be very significant. If you have the opportunity, you should avail yourself of all of them.

JOB SECURITY

As was mentioned above, the rampant consolidations, downsizing, and "rationalization" of corporate America have not spared the world of financial institutions. One of the consequences is that the job world has become a colder and less forgiving place to many out-of-work lenders. However, there is a growing contingent of executives who believe that the paring of the industry is coming to a close and that homeostasis is setting in. Corporations can increase productivity and profits only so much by downsizing. Ultimately, to survive and prosper, an institution must depend less on cost cutting and more on revenue growth. Revenue growth, particularly in financial institutions, can come only from investment in human capital.

During the writing of the first draft of this book, office vacancy rates, particularly on the East Coast and West Coast, were stubbornly high. This caused the market for this type of property to be depressed. Other real estate products, with the exception of single-family homes, also were depressed. However, as this book goes to press, vacancy rates have fallen. As the economy continues to grow, no matter how slowly, demand will increase for all types of products. As these product segments continue to recover and demand begins to outstrip supply, something that will happen because of the lag effect of new supply meeting a more rapid ramp-up in demand, there will be an accelerated demand for new development lenders. The net result, especially for those coming into the job market or looking for a new career, is that this is a very good time to enter the real estate profession. Before everyone else gets there, you will obtain experience and skills that will enhance your chances of rising along with the real estate cycle to a higher position within the industry.

HOURS OF WORK

While this book was being written, U.S. lending institutions overall continued to experience increasing productivity. This has been caused in part by better technology, primarily in computer hardware and software and in the increased standardization of credit procedures, processing, and products. It also has resulted, however, from lending institutions' increased demands on employees. With pressure to expand revenues and increase market share and with increasing competition narrowing profit margins, longer hours are expected almost universally. Compounding the problem of longer hours is the fact that the time required to do the job can be very uneven. For example, a large, complex deal will require you to do extra work when the situation demands it, not necessarily when you are up to doing it. Also, since working on a large and time-consuming deal does not relieve you of your day-to-day loan officer responsibilities, it can take weeks to catch up.[4]

Furthermore, unlike in some other disciplines of lending, you usually are required to visit property sites.[5] An additional dimension comes into play with a development loan. Here, because you are lending against a work in progress, you have to visit the property more often.

As in most white-collar professional positions, you will be among those who at times take work home. This is especially true when a credit presentation to senior management is due. For the majority of lending officers, the extra hours are worth it. Cobbling together a credit solution to a challenging problem and getting an "impossible" deal done under a tight deadline is a tremendously exciting and satisfying endeavor.[6]

---

[4] According to an article in the *New York Times*, in 2002 a U.S. worker put in more work hours per year than a worker in any other country in the world.

[5] This sometimes is best done on weekends, when traffic may be more forgiving and routine office demands are not present.

[6] Unfortunately, your hours may be dictated not by the direct demands made by the volume and complexity of work but by office culture and politics. You can be punished for taking a flexible attitude toward being physically present in the office. Although in the commercial real estate lending business attendance during normal business hours is not strictly required, many senior managers do not understand this. Surprisingly, they continue to believe that a physical presence in the office means a higher level of productivity. Usually, it is not possible to change this perception single-handedly. A lending officer in this position has two choices: live with the culture or move on to another employer or a different area in the institution.

OFFICE POLITICS

To get senior management to focus on your business and respect your convictions, you must develop some political skills. Politically ineffective real estate personnel, particularly an ineffective head of a real estate department, usually reflect negatively on the institution's ability to be competitive, close certain types of real estate transactions, and secure market niches and share. Politically effective real estate personnel are usually savvy about their business, have more authority in the decision-making process, have a strong record of successes, and have helped their institutions make more money.

No matter what type of person you think you are—aggressive, nonaggressive, analytical, nonanalytical—you should use your style to develop ties with key management personnel. If you are the less aggressive type and shun politics, nonetheless you inevitability will be involved in political situations at one time or another. Therefore, you should make it one of your career priorities to develop a better sense of your organization, its hierarchical structure, where the invisible but real lines of influence are on the organizational chart, and who has the power to help you and who does not. If you feel you are not being yourself or being phony, put those reservations aside. For most lending officers, the primary career objective is not to socialize or make new friends or show others how sincere one is; it is to achieve a position that will give them the most authority and latitude to use their training, education, and experience in the most productive and creative ways. With a senior position comes tremendous satisfaction and financial security. If you are not on this path, no matter how good you may be technically in development lending, you may find yourself working harder and being left behind.

For those coming into the business or those with a few years of experience, having a mentor and/or an ally is a tremendous plus in accomplishing one's objectives, both professional and personal. It helps not only in accomplishing your immediate goals—for example, gaining a credit approval—but in elevating your status among senior managers who provide opportunities for promotion, training, and compensation. Always keep an eye out for those in power and learn how they can help you in your career. Remember that politics is bred from competition. Just as your institution must be competitive in the marketplace, you must be competitive within your institution.

MANAGEMENT SKILLS

To be an effective development loan officer, you must have a fairly well developed ability to manage because you cannot do the job alone. At the very least, you will rely on a loan administrator and servicer.

Management skills imply a top-down hierarchy in which the people at the apex of the metaphorical pyramid dictate to those below them. In lending, this type of vertical organization still is dominant. The main reason is that through the ages the top-down approach has worked. This is especially true when loans involve huge amounts of money that require someone with authority as well as ultimate accountability. Within this hierarchical framework, there may be limited opportunities to advance into senior management. A real estate department can originate, manage, and maintain a real estate loan portfolio with a significant amount of development facilities in the hundreds of millions of dollars with only a handful of loan officers. With the span of control for managers increasing, as was mentioned earlier in this chapter, there may be only one management position in an entire real estate department.

It is a fact that real estate lending is a collaborative effort. A good manager must have the ability to work with and alongside people. This is especially true in dealing with educated professionals who usually do not respond well to an authoritarian approach. To be most effective, a manager must act as a guide to move a person or people through a process to accomplish group goals, either explicit or implicit.

Often lending officers continue throughout their careers very successfully as lending officers, or they may move into staff jobs such as credit and review officers. People in these positions can wield tremendous power, authority, and compensation, but there are not many in the industry. If you aspire to move into a staff function, be wary of a short-lived tenure. Today, unless you can obtain a very strong position in the firm, mergers, politics, and quick layoff decisions for staff personnel can leave you highly paid today and jobless tomorrow.

COMPUTER PROFICIENCY

Only a short time ago basic knowledge of a word-processing program and a spreadsheet program put you at a significant competitive advantage in most businesses. Today these basic programs are universally known and used. If you do not have proficiency with Word and Excel, you are at a disadvantage. Other programs that may be useful are ones with specific applications to the real estate industry, such as Argus, which is a real estate investment analysis program. It is easy to learn and is used mostly when an Argus file is sent by a prospective borrower. One of Argus's drawbacks is its price, which makes it impractical for most people first coming into the industry to purchase and practice with.

Almost all loan submissions include spreadsheets. In every case, you will have to enter spreadsheet data into your own template to perform your analysis and include it in your reports. Getting a CD or e-mail with the data in an Excel or Argus format from a borrower can save you a considerable amount of time. It also can be a learning tool. You can take advantage of the spreadsheet efficiencies and techniques incorporated by the borrower's analyst in his data.

HOW TO FIND A JOB IN DEVELOPMENT LENDING

Very few lending institutions look for a development lender. Instead, they seek a commercial real estate lender with experience in development lending. Therefore, if you are looking for your first job in the field, you should target institutions that make development loans. If you get the job, you probably will start by receiving a portfolio of loans for which you will have maintenance responsibility. Those loans probably will include several term or permanent loans as well as some development loans. After gaining some experience on the maintenance side, you can segue into loan origination and then into development lending.

Finding a job in development lending is similar to finding a job in most professional white-collar fields. The most common sources include newspaper classified ads and Internet postings. The results from those sources, however, are not the best because they are used by a large number of job seekers and it is difficult to differentiate oneself from the pack.

For those with some real estate experience, in addition to ads and the Internet, headhunters should be courted because they are often much more effective: They know the job market better then the candidate does, often have a professional and/or personal relationship with some of the hiring decision makers at the lending institutions being targeted, are usually lenient in assessing your skills and qualifications and put a positive spin on them, will sell you more aggressively to an institution, have more credibility with the target institutions, and, if you are not the successful candidate, will let you know quickly. If you fail to get a job, a headhunter sometimes can give you real feedback so that you will be more competitive the next time.

Networking is a job-seeking method that can be effective; however, a good degree of luck is involved. You can do a lot of networking before you find a person who is looking for or knows someone who is looking for a person with your experience and qualifications. However, even if your efforts are not directly fruitful, networking is worth doing. It provides you with information on what is happening in the industry that could be very important at an interview, where you can demonstrate your grasp of current trends, activities, and issues.

The most potent aid in getting a job in almost any field is knowing someone in a position of power who can recommend you or, better yet, hire you. For those coming into the real estate lending field, this may be difficult if not impossible, but during your career it always pays to stay in touch with people in the industry and especially with former coworkers. These people know who you are, what experience you have had, and your true capabilities. They also have contacts in the field. If your career is having problems, sometimes a few phone calls to colleagues can deliver you to a person who, with the added boost of a referral from your colleague, will help you smoothly make the transition to a better job. If you have been laid off from a position, a referral can be a lifesaver.

LARGE INSTITUTIONS OR SMALL INSTITUTIONS

For a person starting a career in real estate lending, a position in a large institution is generally more advantageous. A large institution usually has more training opportunities, has a real estate business that is more diverse, has better product differentiation, employs more peers who can provide support, has a larger capital base that enables it to make larger loans, and usually has better name recognition, which can help you earn greater respect in the industry and perhaps help in your next job search.

The disadvantage of going with a large company is the possible compartmentalization of employees within its real estate lending group. You may be exposed to less underwriting diversity (e.g., shopping centers versus office buildings versus multifamily residential developments) and may find it difficult to move from one area of the real estate lending department to another.

Smaller institutions often have more limited types of loan products, but you may be able to get hands-on experience with more of them, thus increasing your overall job experience. There also may be less competition for promotions, but offsetting this, there will be fewer senior positions available.

Employment stability was once a hallmark in smaller institutions. Recently, though, with mergers and consolidations in the industry and shareholder demands for profits, job security at both large and small institutions is roughly equal. From a future employment perspective, it is generally easier to find a job coming from a large institution than it is coming from a small one. The jump from a small lender to a large lender can be very difficult.

It is suggested that if you are just coming into the field, you should if possible seek employment first at a larger institution and then use your experience there to learn all you can and make important contacts. You may spend the rest of your working life at a large institution. However, if after several years you find your career is stalling, you can leverage your training and skills more easily to get a job elsewhere. This can be a move to a larger or a smaller lender.

If you are moving to a smaller lender, during your tenure you usually can obtain a more senior position in a much shorter period than is the case in a larger firm (a big fish in a small pond). This can be a great career move, but it does have some downside risk. Psychologically, the adjustment from a larger firm to a smaller one can be very disconcerting at first. Also, it is more important to get along with senior managers, since there are fewer of them and they therefore have more authority and power. In addition, there is often less red tape in the layoff process. Smaller institutions tend to have more variable revenue and profit swings. A profitable smaller entity that is in a hiring mode one year can be in a firing mode the next year.

SHRINKING DEPARTMENTS: HOW TO COPE

Since development lending advances and recedes according to economic, political, business, social, and regulatory conditions, at some point in your career you probably will find yourself in an area that is waning in institutional importance. This can be very disheartening. Most likely, when your department is contracting, other real estate departments in other institutions are facing a similar reality. If you are uncomfortable, this state of affairs may exacerbate your anxiety. The question is whether to stay where you are or jump ship. Unfortunately, the answer is never clear. It depends on the uniqueness of your situation. As was noted earlier, in smaller institutions you may be at greater risk, since there is less budgeting and payroll flexibility. In larger institutions you have a better chance to be carried into the next economic cycle, or perhaps you will have the opportunity to relocate to another business area within the institution. Unfortunately, large institutions also have few reservations about issuing JDs (job discontinuances).Therefore, the best strategy is probably to stay put but aggressively look for new job opportunities. If nothing else, this can reduce anxiety because you are actively doing something solely for yourself. If you eventually are laid off, you will never look back regretting that you behaved like a sitting duck.

CHAPTER 2

The Borrower's Information

THE LOAN PROPOSAL

A good loan proposal makes it easy for you, the lending officer, to come to initial conclusions relatively quickly. It helps you get a feel for the financial aspects of the transaction, the physical nature of the existing property and to-be-built improvements, the property's surroundings, the market, the supply and demand characteristics of the finished product, the status of the development process (initial planning stage, governmental approval phase, demolition phase, etc.), the timing of project milestones over the course of the loan, and the borrower's experience and background. Loan proposals vary in size from a single page to over 100 pages. The more prolific developers often produce the weakest proposals.

QUALITY AND ORIGIN OF THE LOAN APPLICATION

The most common reasons loan proposals are substandard are that the borrower has a limited staff, is working under time constraints, or lacks presentation skills.

For small to midsize borrowers, the hiring of a dedicated person to create proposal packages and work exclusively with lending institutions is often not efficient or practical. Firms that size cannot handle enough projects at one time to justify the expense and attention necessary to support a person committed to outside financing.[1] Therefore, the task falls to an individual with less time, experience, and/or expertise.

Even if the borrower is capable of putting together a good package, he may be hard pressed to do so because of time constraints. In the case of a property acquisition, the seller almost always urges the borrower to deposit "hard" (nonrefundable) cash quickly to secure the deal. If the borrower does not have enough time to complete a full loan proposal package and meet the seller's deadline, he may have to feed you the required information as you move through the underwriting process. In many instances, this is a member of the borrower's senior management who may know the proposal inside and out but lack presentation skills such as photography, spreadsheet analysis, word processing, and the ability to use certain software programs.

Even if a loan submission is subpar, the proposed loan may represent a good or even excellent lending opportunity. Although no study has been done to determine the correlation between good submissions of loan proposals and the quality of the resulting loan facilities, they probably are mutually exclusive to a large extent. If you are doing a good job, the facility will be booked on the basis of your standards and the standards of the lending institution, not the quality or completeness of the loan application. You should use your leverage as a lender to get the most relevant and useful information from the prospect but should be flexible so that you do not lose a good piece of business. A balance must be established among your workload, your personal production, and the comprehensiveness and clarity of the borrower's loan submission.

PROPOSAL SIZE AND EFFECTIVENESS

Some proposals can be hundreds of pages long and include maps, charts, graphs, plans, photographs, and government publications. Many potential borrowers believe that if a presentation satisfies the

---

[1] A borrower who owns and/or acquires multiple properties may be able to support a staff person whose primary job is to produce clear and accurate loan proposals. He may also shop for the best source of institutional debt financing. As a result, he often will develop direct and close links to lending officers and/or their institutions. After the loan closes, the day-to-day loan mechanics frequently are turned over to another employee of the borrower.

"weight test"—it contains as much information and material as possible—it will be more effective. Additional information can help you underwrite a loan more quickly and efficiently since you may not have to hunt or ask for as much material. However, large, glossy proposals may diminish the chances of success for several reasons:

- The reviewing loan officer, who usually has a limited amount of time, may be overwhelmed by the amount of information presented. Rather than being reviewed quickly, the presentation can sit on the back burner while he examines loan proposals that are less difficult to comprehend. The insertion of extraneous material may suggest that the borrower is trying too hard to convince the reader that the project is a good one. Superfluous and repetitive material also can mask the omission of information the lending officer needs to complete his underwriting.
- For midsize and smaller projects, an overly lengthy and glossy presentation may seem too slick. Furthermore, the cost to produce the presentation can raise doubts about the borrower's ability and/or desire to be cost effective. It also can call into question his ability as a competent developer and doer versus a marketer and showman.

The most important thing a borrower should keep in mind when writing a proposal is who his target audience is. The best loan proposals are those in which thought is given to the reader: the account officer. Proposals should be well organized, concise, and factual so that he quickly can get a good understanding of the project. Once the loan officer expresses interest, the prospective borrower should anticipate requests for additional information. At that time he can offer to send some of the less important information and let the account officer decide whether he wants to review it.

PROPOSAL OUTLINE

A good loan proposal will contain the following sections in one form or another.

Executive Summary

The executive summary or summary gives the reader a quick overview of the transaction and should include the essentials of the proposal on one or two sheets of paper.

Area Description

The area description should be brief and to the point. The objective should be to relate the description to the subject property with relevant facts and observations. Unfortunately, area descriptions more often than not are lifted out of appraisals, tourist guides, and advertisements and can go on for dozens of pages. The area covered in those narratives is often irrelevantly large, and detail about the more important immediate area is lacking.

Fortunately, it is usually not hard to obtain your own information on an area through the Internet, newspapers, and published information. However, it will take some time to find useful information that the borrower should have provided.

Market Analysis

Generally, a good market analysis will include specific comparables ("comps") of properties that are near and similar to the one that will be collateralized by the loan. Comparisons always should be reviewed with skepticism. Often, even among very reputable developers, market comps will be inflated. For instance, on an office project, the comps may be based on asking rents, not on signed leases. Higher comps inflate cash flows and value, making a loan proposal more attractive. They also make the loan request look more conservative than it is and can lead the lender to make a loan in excess of what is prudent. As is discussed in Chapter 3, an overloan position can allow the borrower to recoup his investment before you get paid down on your loan.

Since the loan almost always is subject to an independent appraisal approved by your institution, if the borrower's comps are off, say, on the high side, the loan commitment, which is subject to a satisfactory appraisal, can be adjusted downward readily. However, since you do not want to spend your time and the time of others in obtaining a loan approval that is based on a faulty market analysis, you always should try to get a good feel for the market. Getting a loan approved and then not being able to fund it because of a low appraisal will not elevate your status within your institution. It also can create "negative goodwill" toward a potential borrower or relationship.

Property Description

The property description should supply a brief description of the property. If there is an existing structure, what will be done with it (demolished, rehabilitated, etc.) should be addressed. Floor plans as well as site plans or whatever else is appropriate may be presented here or referred to in an exhibit section. This is, after all, the collateral against which the lender will be lending.

Financial and Economic Analysis

This section, which may be the most important part of a loan application, tells you how the entire transaction works in terms of dollars. From the day the first dollar goes out of your institution to the day the last dollar comes back in, you should have a complete financial picture. In a permanent loan proposal in which the property already is built and is throwing off a cash flow that presumably can support the loan that has been asked for, a single-page cash-flow statement may be all that is required. On a development project, however, a dynamic process is involved. Funding of the loan usually will be done on a periodic basis, costs will increase over time, and revenues may not be received for several years. The time dimension is best represented through a spreadsheet analysis. If the borrower does not provide you with one, you should consider constructing your own.

Notes to Analysis

As part of the financial economic analysis, the borrower should include explanations of his key assumptions. He also should explain the ambiguities that often crop up when a spreadsheet is complex.

Résumé of the Key Principals of the Borrower

If there is an existing relationship with the key principals of the borrower, the loan proposal may not have to contain additional information. The key principals should retain control of the project and be the general partners or the managing members, depending on the borrower's legal entity. If applicable, the proposal should give some detail about other significant members who will have equity, mezzanine, or subordinate finance positions.

Maps, Photographs, and Exhibits

A map of the area and photographs of the property should be included. For one thing, they are easy to produce. For another, they give the lender an immediate conceptual framework in which to review the proposal. However, in spite of their benefits, you should not allow them to influence you overly. Artist's renderings, which almost always are produced by the project's architect, in particular are inevitably prettier then the actual product.

ADDITIONAL INFORMATION

When you decide to underwrite a loan, you will have to address details and concerns beyond the initial loan proposal in order to make an effective loan presentation and later, if it is approved, close the loan. Make sure the borrower understands that he should be prepared to respond to your requests for information very quickly. Failure by the borrower to provide timely information can delay approval of the loan. If part of the loan is to be used for property acquisition and the borrower is under a contract to purchase on a specific date ("time of the essence"), failure to close on or before that date may result in penalty fees, interest charges, opportunity costs, or, worse, the forfeiture of a substantial down payment. In spite of the borrower's tardiness and sole responsibility for delays, if he loses money, he may blame you and your institution and sue in an attempt to recover his losses.

Although you may not get all the information and material you want, what you do get or do not get can be revealing. The decision to insist on specific information should be tempered by the perceived risk associated with the contemplated loan; the ability, sophistication, and size of the borrower; the scale and nature of the project; and the importance of the relationship to you and your institution.

RELATIONSHIPS

If the borrower has a relationship with a senior manager in your institution, you may find yourself in the uncomfortable position of being second-guessed. The borrower can be talking about you to the senior manager without your direct knowledge. If the borrower is uncooperative, unprepared, and/or unsophisticated, the conversation can be slanted against you. You have to be very careful not to offend him and at the same time get what you need to do your job. If you find this type of situation developing, you should maintain a dialogue with the senior manager to receive his feedback, if any, and be prepared to voice your concerns up front. Ideally, the senior manager will be able to maintain a balanced position between your requests and the borrower's complaints. In all circumstances, when you request information or have substantive conversations with the borrower by telephone, follow up with a note to your file and perhaps a letter or fax to the borrower reiterating your request.

Regardless of the circumstances within your institution concerning the borrower's relationship, when the borrower has laid out up-front money, he has much more to lose than you do. By being firm and reasonable in your requests, you can take advantage of his financial risk. He must realize that if he cannot satisfy your institution's requirements in a timely manner, no matter how hard you try, you will not be able to get his loan approved. If necessary and if used properly, that leverage can be very helpful.

REQUIRED INFORMATION

The following is a general list of information and material that is needed for any development loan. You probably will be able to work off an institutional checklist of required items along with a list from your institution's closing attorney and inspecting engineer. The list here is perhaps more useful to a borrower who will have to prepare and submit the information. Since most of the elements are necessary before the loan can receive final approval and close, the more the borrower is able to prepare, put in order, and have available to send to you as the underwriting process continues, the less pressure he and you will feel later, when the closing date nears.

- Name of borrowing members with addresses, Social Security numbers, borrowing entity, and tax ID number
- Personal financial statements of managing members and significant equity contributors
- Personal and corporate tax returns (minimum of two years)
- A résumé or narrative describing all the principals and key participants

- Financial and trade references from the significant participants
- Copy of the property sales contract or closing statement if already purchased, if applicable
- List of recent capital improvements to the property, if any
- Plans and specifications
- Hard and soft cost budgets
- Schedule of intended use of equity and loan proceeds (sources and uses statement)
- Pro forma operating statement
- Name of attorney or attorneys
- Names of architect and engineers
- Names of construction manager, general contractor, and major subcontractors, with résumés
- Copy of latest real estate tax and water and sewer invoices
- Insurance company and amount and types of insurance
- Recent unit sales and/or leases, if applicable
- Copies of leases or lease abstracts (summaries of lease terms), if applicable, or a few sample ones chosen by you
- If applicable, a current rent roll with square footage, lease terms, clauses, bump-ups, escalations, rent per square foot, names of tenants, expiration dates, arrearages, and significant lease details
- If the property is an existing condominium or cooperative, a copy of the offering prospectus with amendments
- If applicable, at least two years of property operating statements
- Existing mortgage documentation, including balances outstanding
- Recent appraisal and feasibility study, if available
- Recent Phase I environmental report, if available
- Engineering reports, zoning analyses, municipal approvals, and so on, if available

SAMPLE PRESENTATION

The following pages show an initial loan presentation for a construction loan for a substantial rehabilitation and conversion to residential use of a six-story manufacturing building in New York City. Since all projects are unique, there will be substantial differences between what you encounter in your career as a construction lender and this example, which was chosen primarily for two reasons:

First it is not a very large transaction or a very small one. Most lenders will be able to make a loan of this size whether they work in a large or a small institution.

Second it is primarily a residential project. A residential project is in many ways more challenging because it involves more construction elements than, say, a warehouse, which is built basically as open space (there are not as many fit-outs, partitions, kitchens, kitchen details, and so on, in a warehouse as there are in a luxury condominium complex). In addition, it is the type of project that a lender who is new to construction is most likely to encounter. (Note that in the example, headings, text, drawings, and exhibits have been modified for brevity.)

Background

The area where the project is situated was well known to the lender. When the lending officer proceeded to underwrite the loan, the appraiser expanded on the project's feasibility, present and future values, and absorption rates. Note that at the time of the loan submission, the borrower was not sure of the number of apartments that were to be constructed (two on each floor or one large floor-through); the allowable size of the penthouse, which depended on subsequent approvals from municipal regulatory bodies; or the hard and soft cost budgets. They all changed considerably before the loan closed. He also was unsure if the rear wall of the building needed to be reconstructed so that the square footage of each floor would be reduced, but the square footage at the penthouse level, which has a higher sale value, would be increased. Since the borrower was under contract to purchase the building with a time of the essence clause, he had no choice but to apply for the acquisition/construction loan before those elements were more certain. He hinted to the lender that the project as presented in the proposal might change (he knew it would) but played down any changes as insignificant. He did that because he wanted the lender to do as much work as possible on the loan underwriting so that it would have the highest probability of being approved and closed.

100 SoHo Street

Rendering of Completed Building

Executive Summary

ABC Group (ABC) is under contract to purchase a vacant six-story building located at 100 SoHo Street in Manhattan (Block 111, Lot 22). The property is being sold for $8,000,000 by the Good family, which has owned it for several decades, where it housed its manufacturing business. During the last decade, with the acceleration and intensification of overseas competition, the business is no longer viable. The real estate, however, has increased in value as Manhattan, and particularly SoHo (an area bounded by Houston St. to the north, the Hudson River to the west, Broadway to the east, and Canal St. to the south), has experienced a virtual explosion in residential and retail demand. With the historic use of the building no longer viable and its real estate value relatively high, the family is strongly motivated to sell. For ABC, considering the building's location, clean condition, and market characteristics and a very reasonable negotiated price of $8,000,000 ($266 per existing SF), the ownership and development of 100 SoHo Street to residential and retail use is an extremely attractive opportunity. A summary of the transaction follows:

Financial Highlights

Price	$8,000,000
Total Project Cost	$14,546,302
Debt Financing	$11,500,000
Equity Financing	$3,046,302
Loan-to-Cost Ratio	79%
Residential Apts/Square Footage	9/20,603
Aggregate Sales/Per SF	$18,327,650/$890
Total Retail Square Footage	7,000
Retail Income/Per SF	$400,000/$57
Internal Rate of Return on Equity	49%

Structure

The property will be purchased for $8,000,000. Following closing, a one-year period will be required for planning, approvals, coordination, organization, and construction. The result will be the creation of nine residences and 4,500 SF of aboveground retail space. During the second year, it is expected that all of the residential units will be sold. However, for conservatism, eight are forecasted to be sold during the second year and one during the third. The eight sales, grossing over $16MM, will easily pay down the $11.5MM acquisition/construction loan. Also, beginning with the second year, the retail space should be fully leased. Using third-year retail cash flows and applying the discounted cash flow and loan-to-value methods, it is projected that a refinancing will occur in the fourth year for $3.5MM. It is highly likely that the retail space will be sold within a 10-year period.

The Area

100 SoHo Street is located in central SoHo. The area's current character was formed in the 1970s when artists, looking for inexpensive, large open areas

to work and live in, found and occupied many functionally obsolete warehouse and manufacturing buildings. Over the years, as the population of people living in these buildings grew, New York City was forced to recognize their presence. The result was that several laws were passed allowing occupants to remain as tenants in buildings that were until then only legally allowed to be occupied by commercial/manufacturing tenants.

As the New York economy grew, so did demand for housing and retail space in the area. The result is that today, SoHo is the home of many art galleries, furniture galleries, and upscale restaurants. It has become a trendsetting place that is exciting to visit and live in. This desirableness is fueled by the increasingly successful number of New York City workers with the want and ability to live in one of the most dynamic and famous areas in the City. SoHo is known internationally as a New York City destination. After September 11, 2001, residential condominium prices held up well and have grown along with or ahead of the general New York luxury condominium market. They are currently among the highest in the country, both for sales and for rentals.

The Market

With an extremely limited number of old manufacturing loft buildings currently suitable and/or available for conversion to residential and retail use, the demand/supply aspects of housing and retail spaces have made the economics of developing 100 SoHo Street very favorable.

Throughout Manhattan, the condominium sales market remains strong. According to a broad consensus of writers and brokers, with the city's vibrancy and firm economy, at least for the foreseeable future, strong demand for condominium apartments coupled with severe existing supply and new development constraints will continue to push up prices in desirable areas, particularly in dense and amenity-rich areas such as SoHo. According to the XYZ Institute of New York, the median price for Manhattan condominiums is now over $500 per SF, with the lower Manhattan area exhibiting some of the strongest gains in the City. In the SoHo area, condominium prices for penthouse spaces are "routinely" topping out well over $1,000 per SF. For example, at 200 SoHo Street, just north of 100 SoHo Street, the building's eight apartments were sold at an average of $1,051 per SF, with its two penthouses each selling for over $2,100 per SF. Currently, there does not appear to be any abatement in price increases. The projections for 100 SoHo Street are conservatively drawn at an average of $890 per SF. And the fact that 100 SoHo Street is a relatively small, uncomplicated project, that it will be a completed condominium in twelve months, and that, with presales, it can be completely closed out shortly thereafter mitigates market risk significantly.

Concerning comparable retail space in the immediate area, rents dropped precipitously throughout SoHo after the September 11 disaster, but the best locations, including 100 SoHo, still top over $200 per SF and have retained most of their former value. Within the last year, they have actually risen (this comeback in retail demand has been recently reinforced with the opening of a new 100,000-SF Bloomingdales in SoHo). In the analysis for 100 SoHo Street, an average rental of $57 per SF for the total 7,000 SF of leasable retail space was used.

The Existing Property

The building, six stories high and with a full basement, sits on a square parcel of land with a footprint of 50 feet of street frontage and 100 feet of depth. It is an early-twentieth-century red brick structure supported by steel and wood columns joined by solid oak beams that support heavy exposed wood joists. In spite of some evidence of settling, the building overall, because of the necessity to bear heavy dead loads created by fixed machinery, appears to be very sound. A very positive feature of the property is that it has windows on all four sides. This is opposed to many buildings in the area that obtain light only from the front and back. Another attractive feature is the structure's high ceilings, which range from a low of approx. 11 feet to a high of 16 feet, depending on the floor. An inspection of the building, chemical samplings, and a review of the Goods' records, permits, and storage revealed that there are no material environmental hazards on the premises. What little hazardous materials there are (some lead-based paint and asbestos primarily in a small area of the basement) can be easily and inexpensively contained or removed.

Improvements

Demolition, cleanup, and new construction should proceed very smoothly and rapidly because the building will be free of tenants, outer walls are bare, there is no ceiling cover, and the premises will be completely empty upon ABC gaining possession. Also, there are two operable freight elevators, one with a bay leading to the street. This should greatly facilitate the moving of equipment and material.

The redeveloped building will have retail space on its main floor and residential space on the levels above. In order to meet zoning requirements, ABC will decrease the depth of the building from 100 feet to 80 feet on residential floors two through six. The reduction of square footage can be applied to the roof, where a seventh-floor penthouse will be built. It is currently envisioned that a staircase on the seventh floor will open up to a 200-SF enclosed "crow's nest" that will give access to the entire penthouse roof for utilization as a terrace.

The plan to date calls for floors two, three, and four to consist of two units each. The fifth and sixth floors may be either configured as one apartment per floor, two, or perhaps two simplexes and one duplex reaching from the fifth floor to the sixth. The basement will contain approx. 2,500 SF of retail space, about 1,500 SF for residential storage, and 1,000 SF for mechanicals, individual gas-fired heaters, and water heaters. Above the back end of the retail space will be a skylight. The front of the property will remain essentially the same except for the removal of the existing fire escape. Preliminary floor plans and a sectional elevation drawn by Easy Architect Co. are included in this presentation.

100 SoHo Street will house one elevator servicing all apartments. It is tentatively planned to be centrally located so that each tenant will be in his residence as soon as the elevator door opens. Every unit will have at least two bathrooms, probably in stone and mosaic, with stone countertops and top-of-the-line fixtures. Kitchens will showcase items such as Sub Zero

freezers, granite countertops, and again, top-of-the-line fixtures and appliances. Except for kitchens and bathrooms, flooring will be oak throughout. Walls will include high-quality baseboard and crown molding. In order to provide sound insulation and light treatments and provide a smooth, solid-looking surface, the exposed joists will be covered with sheetrock. To lend character, however, original detail such as wooden columns and oak beams will be exposed where possible. As noted above, the building has high ceilings. This should aid in the installation of central AC ductwork; sprinkler and plumbing branch work; and electrical, entertainment, security, and communication wiring.

Particularly since ABC has extensive experience in the maintenance and rehabilitation of dozens of New York City buildings, the execution of finishings and work can be done very effectively and efficiently and at a low cost. The finished work relative to the market will be excellent.

Profitability

100 SoHo Street was analyzed in the accompanying spreadsheets. During the second year following acquisition, with eight apartment sales and retail rent, the project will return a net operating income of $15.7MM. This will be enough, after paying down the acquisition/construction loan, to return $3.4MM in net cash flow. In the third year, with only one residential unit and no debt service, almost all of the $2.4MM in gross revenues falls to the bottom line, with a resulting $2.3MM net cash flow. Subsequent to the third year, the remaining retail portion, throwing off over $400M per year, can be either financed or sold. Assuming net proceeds from the sale of the retail space after 10 years of $1,646M, the initial $3,046M equity investment is projected to yield a very strong 49% internal rate of return.

ABC Group

ABC Company (ABC) was formed in 1990 as a real estate consulting group. The firm initially assisted owners and developers in their negotiations with financial institutions and governmental agencies. This advisory experience coupled with opportunities created by a distressed economic environment enabled the company in late 1991 to begin acquiring properties for its own account from financial institutions and government agencies.

To manage its investments ABC formed an in-house management company that is responsible for operating all of its properties. It also acquired a construction company to improve and maintain ABC's existing properties as well as to advise on and execute new development projects.

ABC's vertical integration has allowed it to successfully acquire under-performing properties and make rapid capital and maintenance improvements, thereby decreasing operating costs and increasing revenues. Its initial focus has been on multifamily apartment buildings in the New York City area. When multifamily opportunities in New York diminished, the firm actively sought to leverage its experience by investing in other classes of real estate. This strategy has been a tremendous success. It has allowed the company to continue to achieve very attractive margins while continuing to contain risk. Notable acquisitions included a 280,000-SF shopping mall in New Jersey and the procurement of a 750,000-SF office building in Connecticut. Within the last two years, ABC has acquired a 12-story office building, a 10-story apartment building, and an 18-story apartment building, all in Manhattan. It also acquired 78 apartments and town houses in Purchase, NY, and a site in the Chelsea area of Manhattan that it newly developed into a residential condominium with retail space.

ABC currently has title to real properties with an aggregate asset value in excess of $600,000,000. It owns and manages over 1,400 rental apartments and over 900,000 square feet of retail and office space.

The company's general policy is to purchase and retain properties for the long term. However, the continued strong domestic and international demand for luxury apartments in Manhattan and the very favorable financial climate have led to the recent production of condominium offering plans on a few of its apartment properties.

ABC's experience and track record have enabled it to finance projects either solely with private investors or with the participation of financial institutions. This financial strength enables it to rapidly and efficiently perform on its contracts and promises. It continues to aggressively seek out real estate opportunities for acquisition, development, and improvement.

Financial Analysis

Sources and Uses Estimates

SOURCES:		
	Member Equity	$3,046,302
	Lender	$11,500,000
	Total Sources	$14,546,302
USES:		
	Purchase Price	$8,000,000
	Broker Fee (Direct Purchase)	$0
	Bank Appraisal	$7,500
	Bank Fee	$115,000
	Pre-closing Prof Fees	$20,000
	Bank Environmental	$3,500
	Bank Engineer	$12,000
	Bank Legal Fee	$25,000
	Members Legal Fee	$20,000
	Mortgage Recording Tax	$316,250
	Deed Recording	$400
	RE Tax	$0
	Other	$20,000
	Construction Costs	$4,853,756
	First Year Working Capital	$1,152,896
	Total Uses	$14,546,302

Project Pro Forma

Location: 100 SoHo Street
Desc: Block 000, Lot 00

	Res	Retail	Tot. Net
Total No. Units	9	1	
Total No. of Net SF	20,603	7,000	27,603
Avg. Sales Price per SF	$890		
Avg. Sales Price per Unit	$2,036,406		
Gross Res. SF			23,200
Gross Total SF			32,700

Use of funds:

Purchase price	$8,000,000	55.00%
Closing Costs	$539,650	3.71%
Capital Improvements	4,853,756	33.37%
Other	0	0.00%
Working Capital	1,152,896	7.93%
	$14,546,302	100.00%

Source of Funds:

			Rate/Year	Term (Years)
Debt Financing	79.1%	$11,500,000	7.000%	2
Equity Financing	20.9%	$3,046,302		
		$14,546,302		

Refinancing Assumptions:

Future Interest Rate	8.000%
Term (Years)	30
Debt Service Coverage Ratio:	1.25
Capitalization Rate:	10.00
Loan to Value Ratio:	80%

Refinancing Possibilities end of Yr 3 based on Projected Yr 3
NOI:

DSCR method:	$3,697,825
LTVR method:	$3,256,000
Rounded Figure:	$3,500,000

	Year 1	2	3	4	5	6	7	8	9	REMARKS
Income										
Commercial Rents	$0 (Construction)	$400,000	$412,000	$424,360	$437,091	$450,204	$463,710	$477,621	$491,950	3.00% Increase per annum
Condominium Sales	0	8	1	0	0	0	0	0	0	9 Apartments Sold
Sales Revenue	$0	$16,291,244	$2,036,406	$0	$0	$0	$0	$0	$0	$18,327,650
Gross Income	$0	$16,691,244	$2,448,406	$424,360	$437,091	$450,204	$463,710	$477,621	$491,950	
Effective Gross Income	$0	$16,691,244	$2,448,406	$424,360	$437,091	$450,204	$463,710	$477,621	$491,950	

Expenses	YEAR 1 per unit	YEAR 1 per Gr SF	Year 1	2	3	4	5	6	7	8	9	REMARKS
Real Estate Taxes	$10,302	$6.00	$92,714	$0	$0	$0	$0	$0	$0	$0	$0	3.00% Increase per annum
Water & Sewer	$644	$0.25	$5,800	$0	$0	$0	$0	$0	$0	$0	$0	3.00% Increase per annum
Professional Fees	$644	$0.25	$2,900	$0	$0	$0	$0	$0	$0	$0	$0	3.00% Increase per annum
Insurance	$1,667	$0.35	$15,000	$0	$0	$0	$0	$0	$0	$0	$0	2.00% Increase per annum
Fuel	$1,488	$0.65	$6,696	$0	$0	$0	$0	$0	$0	$0	$0	0.00% Increase per annum
Utilities	$801	$0.35	$3,606	$0	$0	$0	$0	$0	$0	$0	$0	5.00% Increase per annum
Supplies	$458	$0.20	$2,060	$0	$0	$0	$0	$0	$0	$0	$0	3.00% Increase per annum
Repairs & Maintenance	$916	$0.40	$4,121	$0	$0	$0	$0	$0	$0	$0	$0	3.00% Increase per annum

Item											Note
Management	$1,222	$0.47	$11,000	$1,259	$0	$0	$0	$0	$0	$0	3.00% Increase per annum
Payroll	$6,667	$2.59	$30,000	$7,000	$0	$0	$0	$0	$0	$0	5.00% Increase per annum
Accounting	$556	$0.22	$5,000	$5,000	$2,500	$2,575	$2,652	$2,732	$2,814	$2,898	3.00% Increase per annum
Broker Fees	5.0%	$0	$814,562	$101,820	$5,000						
Marketing / Advertising	$5,000	$1.94	$45,000	$30,000						$0	4.00% Increase per annum
Sales Representative	$3,667	$1.42	$16,500	$17,160	$8,923					$0	4.00% Increase per annum
Administration	$556	$0.22	$2,500	$578						$0	
Legal & Closing Costs @	$6,000	$0	$0	$48,000	$6,000					$0	3.00% Increase per annum
Misc & Res	$11,111	$4.31	$100,000	$22,889						$0	
Other	$556	$0.22	$5,000	$1,111						$0	
Total Expenses	$38,655		$347,896	$964,941	$121,743	$2,500	$2,575	$2,652	$2,732	$2,814	$2,898
Net Operating Income		($347,896)	$2,326,662		$421,860	$434,516	$447,551	$460,978	$474,807	$489,051	
Cumulative Net Operating Income		($347,896)	$15,378,408	$15,726,303	$17,705,070	$18,126,930	$18,561,445	$19,008,997	$19,469,974	$19,944,782	$20,433,833
Debt Service											
Interest @	7.000%	$805,000		$278,943	$276,517	$274,116	$271,288	$268,226	$264,910		
Mortgage Amortization		($0)		$29,238	$31,664	$34,065	$36,893	$39,955	$43,271		
Release	75.00%	$11,500,000		$0	$0	$0	$0	$0	$0		
Total Debt Service		($805,000)	($12,305,000)	($308,181)	($308,181)	($308,181)	($308,181)	($308,181)	($308,181)		
Cum Loan Paydown		$11,500,000	$11,500,000	$11,529,238	$11,560,902	$11,594,968	$11,631,861	$11,671,816	$11,715,087		
CF after Paydown		($1,152,896)	$3,421,303	$2,326,662	$113,679	$126,335	$139,370	$152,797	$166,626	$180,870	
Working Capital & Refi		$1,152,896	0	$3,500,000							
Net Cash Flow		$0	$0	$3,421,303	$2,326,662	$3,613,679	$126,335	$139,370	$152,797	$166,626	$180,870 Net Sale= 10 Cap
Cumulative Net Cash Flow		$0	$3,421,303	$5,747,966	$9,361,644	$9,487,979	$9,627,349	$9,780,146	$9,946,772	$10,127,642	$1,645,677
Cum Return on Total Capital		0.0%	105.7%	121.7%	124.6%	127.6%	130.7%	133.8%	137.1%	140.5%	
Cum Return on Equity		0.0%	112.3%	188.7%	307.3%	311.5%	316.0%	321.0%	326.5%	332.5%	
IRR on Equity	49%										
Net CASH FLOW AFTER DS & WC	($3,046,302.15)	$0	$3,421,303	$2,326,662	$3,613,679	$126,335	$139,370	$152,797	$166,626	$180,870	$1,645,677.47 cap 10.00%

Expected Sales

RESIDENTIAL SALES

UNIT	SQ. FT.	EXP. Price/SF	EXP. SALES PRICE
2E	1838	$800	$1,470,400
2W	1715	$775	$1,329,125
3E	1838	$800	$1,470,400
3W	1715	$775	$1,329,125
4E	1838	$825	$1,516,350
4W	1715	$800	$1,372,000
5E	1838	$875	$1,608,250
5W	1715	$875	$1,500,625
6th	3533	$975	$3,444,675
Penthouse	2858	$1,150	$3,286,700

Totals:		20,603		$18,327,650
COUNT	Apts	9		
Avg Sale/SF	$889.56			
Avg Sale/Unit	$2,036,406			

RETAIL RENTS

No. 1	retail	4,500	$75.00	$337,500.00
No. 2	retail	0		
Bsmt	retail	2,500	$25.00	$62,500.00
Total Retail SF		7,000	Avg Ret/SF	$57.14
	Retail		1	
	Total Rent Monthly:			$33,333.33
	Total Rent Yearly:			$400,000.00

Total Usable SF	27,603

Total Condo Sales:	$18,327,650

Note: Retail rents are triple net. There are no charges whatsoever to the landlord.

Construction Costs

CONSTRUCTION COSTS	Square Feet	Cost / SF	Total Cost
ITEM			
1) Residential (existing)	20,000	$160	$3,200,000
2) Residential Penthouse (new const)	3,200	$225	$720,000
3) Retail inc. 2,500 usable bsmt	7,000	$60	$420,000
4) Remaining Basement	2,500	$25	$62,500
4) General Conditions	5%		$220,125
5) Contingency	5%		$231,131
TOTALS:			$4,853,756
Total Existing SF inc. Bsmt	29,500		
Total Residential Gross SF	23,200		
Total Gross SF	32,700		
Avg. Const. Cost / Total SF	$148.43		
Avg. Const. Cost / SF for Residential	$185.86		

Notes to Analysis
The information below helps explain the spreadsheets.

Residential Market Data:
Residential market data was obtained from public sales records, discussions with real estate brokers from New York Well Known Brokerage Co., CDE Appraisal Co., and ABC's experience.

Retail Market Data:
Retail market data was obtained from New York Well Known Brokerage Co. and CDE Appraisal Co. Concerning lease escalations, a 3 percent number per year was used for conservatism.

Expenses:
Attorney's fees at closing are shown in the sources and uses estimates of this presentation. Closing expenses including attorney's fees connected with condominium sales are calculated at a benchmark of $6,000 per unit based on ABC's experience. Fuel and utilities were taken at $1.00 per square foot. Supplies, repairs, and maintenance aggregate to approx. $0.60 per square foot. Broker fees were calculated at an average of 5 percent of gross sales because ABC will have a salaried sales agent on the premises and will also spend on advertising to encourage direct sales. Payroll is estimated at $60,000 per year with staff being hired after six months from closing. Please note that expenses grow by certain percentages per year as indicated on the right side of the project spreadsheet.

Debt/Equity:

Equity and loan amounts aggregate to $3,046M and $11,500M, respectively. ABC anticipates a rate of about 7% on its loan. The sale of each unit will require a principal paydown equal to 75% of the gross sale amount.

Capital Improvements:

An aggregate of $4,854M was used. This may be higher than what will be experienced and was used as a conservative measure. A line-item budget is currently being compiled by ABC's construction staff.

Property Size:

Building gross and net square footage was calculated from information received from the seller and New York City records.

Preliminary Drawings

Sectional View/South Elevation

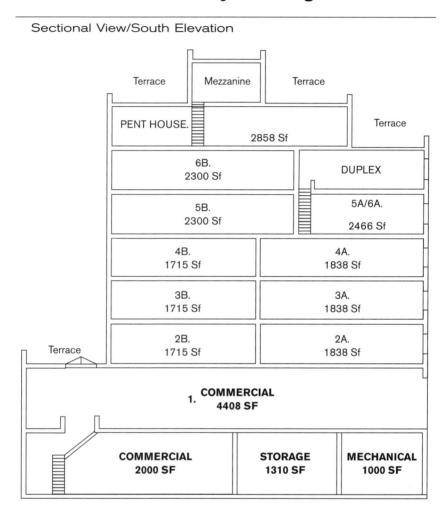

| Terrace | Mezzanine | Terrace |

| PENT HOUSE. 2858 Sf | Terrace |

| 6B. 2300 Sf | DUPLEX |

| 5B. 2300 Sf | 5A/6A. 2466 Sf |

| 4B. 1715 Sf | 4A. 1838 Sf |

| 3B. 1715 Sf | 3A. 1838 Sf |

| Terrace | 2B. 1715 Sf | 2A. 1838 Sf |

1. COMMERCIAL 4408 SF

| **COMMERCIAL 2000 SF** | **STORAGE 1310 SF** | **MECHANICAL 1000 SF** |

Cellar and First Floor

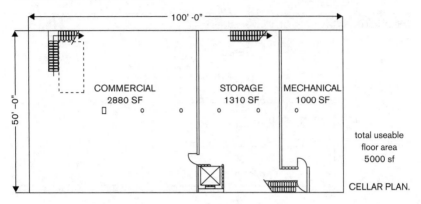

CELLAR PLAN.

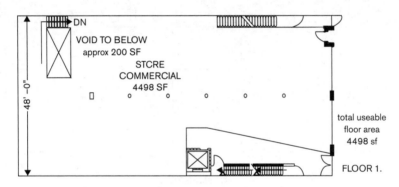

FLOOR 1.

Floors Two through Five

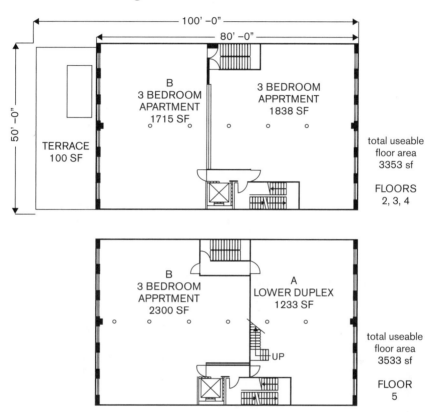

Floors Six and Seven

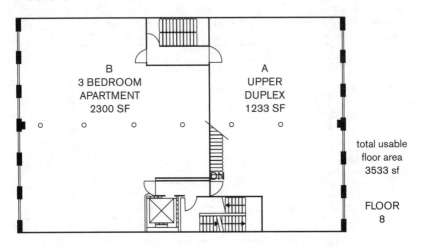

B
3 BEDROOM
APARTMENT
2300 SF

A
UPPER
DUPLEX
1233 SF

DN

total usable
floor area
3533 sf

FLOOR
8

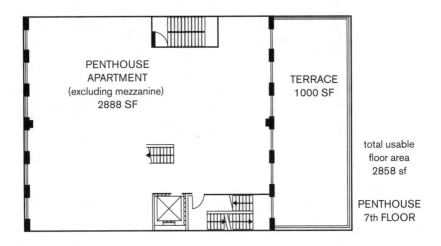

PENTHOUSE
APARTMENT
(excluding mezzanine)
2888 SF

TERRACE
1000 SF

total usable
floor area
2858 sf

PENTHOUSE
7th FLOOR

Mezzanine and Roof

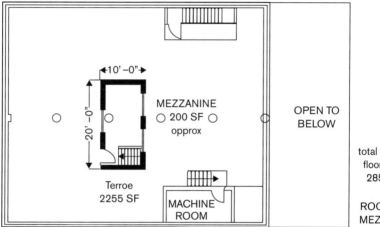

Representative Photos

Facing Building

Frontal View of Lower Portion of Building

Typical interior of 100 SoHo Street

Typical interior of 100 SoHo Street

View from 100 SoHo Street Looking South

View from 100 SoHo Street Looking North

Personal Financial Statement

APPLICANT please typewrite or print clearly Answer all items: if "NONE" so state				Social Security Number		
Name of Borrower Last	First		Middle	Home Phone Number	Business Phone Number	
Present Home Address Number and Street		City		State and Zip Code		Years There

EMPLOYMENT HISTORY

Name of Business or Employer (Present)		Position and Type of Business	Length of Service	Annual Salary (Base) $
Address				Last Bonus
			$	
Name Phone No. of your Accountant:		Name, Phone No. of Your Attorney:		

CO-APPLICANT

Name		Social Security Number		
Present Home Address Number and Street		City	State and Zip Code	Years There

AS OF THE _____ DAY OF _____ , YR _____ .

NOTE: This Statement and any supporting Schedules may be completed jointly by both married and unmarried co-borrowers if their assets and liabilities are sufficiently joined so that this Statement can be meaningfully and fairly presented on a combined basis; otherwise separate Statements and Schedules are required.

Check One: ☐ Completed Jointly   ☐ Not Completed Jointly

Statement of Assets, *Liabilities and Net Worth*

Assets (in whole dollars)			*Liabilities* (in whole dollars)		
1 Cash (Schedule A)	$		16 Loans Payable to Bank-Unsecured (Schedule I)	$	
2 Marketable Securities (Schedule B)			17 Loans Payable to Bank-Secured (Schedule I)		
3 Accounts and Notes Receivable (Schedule C)			18 Loans Payable to Others		
4 Cash Surrender Life Ins. (Schedule D)			19 Mortgage Payable (Schedule J)		
5 Real Estate owned (Market Value) (Schedule E)			20 Installment Contracts Payable		
6 Mortgage Owned (Schedule F)			21 Federal & State Income Taxes Payable		
7 Privately Owned Businesses (Market Value) (Schedule G)			22 Other Taxes & Interest Payable		
8 Invest. Limited Partnership (At Cost) (Schedule H)			23 Loans Against Cash Surrender Value Life Ins.		
9 Pensions, IRA, 401K Keogh			24 Other Liabilities (Schedule J)		
10 Other Assets (Itemize):			25		
11			26		
12			27		
13			28 (add lines 16 and 27) Liabilities		
14			29 (line 15 less line 28) Net Worth		
15 (add lines 1–14) TOTAL ASSETS	$		30 (add lines 28 and 29) TOTAL	$	

Page 2

REMINDER- (If not completed jointly, list only your proportionate interest in any jointly assets and liabilities)

Schedule A   CASH BALANCES

Name and Location of Bank of Financial Institution	Types of Account and Account No.	Signatures on Account	Check (✓) if pledged	Cash Balance
			TOTAL CASH BALANCES $	

Schedule B   MARKETABLE SECURITIES

Name/Description of Securities	Registered in Name (s) of	Number of Shares (Stocks) or face value (Bonds)	Check (✓) if pledged	Market Value
			TOTAL MARKET VALUE $	

Schedule C   ACCOUNTS AND NOTES RECEIVABLE

Due From	Original Amount	Interest Rate	Maturity	Collateral	Annual Payment Collected	Balance
					TOTAL RECEIVABLE BALANCE $	

Schedule D   LIFE INSURANCE

Insurance Company Name	Policy	Type Owner	Face Amount of Policy	Beneficiary	Amount	Net Cash Value Borrowed
					TOTAL NET VALUE $	

Schedule E   REAL ESTATE OWNED

Location / Type of Property	Date Acquired & % Owned	Cost	Annual Gross Rental Income	Annual Net Rental Income (before depreciation)	Market Value
				TOTAL REAL ESTATE OWNED $	

Page 3

Schedule F — MORTGAGES OWNED

Location / Type of Property	Mortgagor	Annual Net Income	Maturity	Check (✓) if assigned	Value Assessed	Value Market
			TOTAL MORTGAGES OWNED $			

Schedule G — PRIVATELY OWNED BUSINESS

Name / Type of Business	Date Acquired	% Owned	Gross Revenue 3 Years	Net Profit 3 Years	Cost	Market Value
METHOD OF DETERMINING MARKET VALUE					TOTAL $	

Schedule H — INVESTMENT IN LIMITED PARTNERSHIP

Title and Description (Real Estate, Oil/Gas etc.)	% Owned	Cost	Cash Distribution Last Year	Cash Distribution This Year	Net Equity
Method of determining market value			TOTAL INVESTMENT $		

Schedule I — LOANS PAYABLE (BANKS)

Name and Location of Bank	Original Amount	Colilateral Description	Interest Rate	Maturity Rate	Monthly Payment	Balance
					TOTAL LOANS PAYABLE $	

Schedule J — MORTGAGES PAYABLE

Name and Location of Creditor	Description	Maturity	Type of Lien (1st, 2nd. etc)	Title in Name of	Mtg. payment Due in One Year	Balance
					TOTAL MORTGAGES PAYABLE $	

Schedule K — OTHER LIABILITIES

Creditor	Description (Taxes, Margin Acct. etc.)	Collateral	Co-Signer	Payments Due in One year	Balance
				TOTAL OTHER LIABILITIES $	

Page 4

In addition to the liabilities listed, I/we am/are contingently liable as a co-signer, endorser or guarantor for the following:

Creditor	Debt in name of	Purpose	Collateral	Maturity	Balance
				Total $	

Income/Expenses My income and expenses for the prior 12 month period ending _____.

Income	Applicant	Co-Applicant	Expenses	Applicant	Co-Applicant
Salary			Personal Living Expenses		
Interest/Dividends			Loans Payable		
Rental Income			Mortgages Payable		
Partnership Income			Partnership Contributions		
Capital Gains			Taxes		
*Other Income			Other (specify below)		
TOTAL INCOME $			TOTAL EXPENSES $		

Specify source of other income: Specify other expenses:

_____   _____

_____   _____

*Alimony, child support or separate maintenance income need not be revealed if you do not wish to have it considered as basis for repaying this obligation.

_____

Have any judgements been entered against you? Are there any legal actions pending against you? _____

_____

_____

Have you ever declared bankruptcy? _____

As of this date, I have not pledged, assigned, hypothecated or transferred title to any of my assets, except as listed on this form or on a supporting schedule, except as follows (give details):

_____

_____

_____

    The information contained in this statement is provided for the purpose of obtaining or maintaining credit with you on my/our behalf or on the behalf of persons, firms, or corporations in whose behalf I/we may, either severally or jointly with others, execute a guaranty in your favor. I/we understand that you are relying on this information (including the designation made as to ownership of property) in deciding to grant or continue credit. I/we represent and warrant that the information provided is true and complete and that you may consider this statement as continuing to be true and correct until a written notice of change is given to you by me/us. I/we agree to notify you promptly of any such change. You are authorized to check the statements made on this form, and to determine my/our creditworthiness. You will tell me/us upon request whether or not a consumer report was requested and, if so, inform me/us of the name and address of the consumer reporting agency. You are authorized to answer questions about your credit experience with me/us. You may order additional consumer reports and otherwise check my/our credit at any time while credit is outstanding in conjunction with an update, renewal, refinance, or extension of such credit or in connection with collection efforts. You may retain this statement whether or not credit is approved.

APPLICANT _____   CO-APPLICANT _____
                  Signature   Signature

Date _____   Date _____

CHAPTER 3

Budgeting

BUDGETING THE PROJECT

The creation of a project budget is an integral part of the project's loan structure. Since a budget is nothing more than an initial forecast that is influenced by the analyst's experience, education, risk preferences, and expectations, it can never be 100 percent right. Variances are normal and can be justifiable viewpoints on the challenges presented by the project. The goal for the analyst is to look back and be able to say that the budgeted expenses came close to or were slightly higher than the final real costs after the project was completed.

THE DEVELOPMENT COST BUDGET

The development cost budget can be broken down into two categories: hard costs and soft costs. It is important to know the differences between them since they always are used as a measure of reasonableness and efficiency in development projects.[1]

---

[1] They also can, by definition, determine which costs are insurable, which are not, what deductions and limitations there will be if an insurance claim is filed because of an unforeseen negative event, and the priority of claims if there is a borrower/owner default.

Hard Costs

Hard costs are the expenses involved in actually building or improving the physical property. They account for all the materials that go into the project and include fixtures such as doorknobs, refrigerators, wine coolers, and washer-driers. Hard costs also include all the labor directly attributed to physical construction. Demolition is considered an improvement to a site and is a hard cost, as is the landscaping of the surrounding grounds or the construction of a parking lot. The amount the developer pays the construction manager or general contractor also is considered a hard cost.

Soft Costs

Soft costs include virtually all costs (except for the purchase price of a property) that are not included in the hard cost category. Examples include legal fees, engineering and architectural fees, surveying costs, real estate and mortgage recording taxes, loan interest, insurance premiums, and brokerage costs.

Be aware that there are gray areas where some professionals will classify an item as a soft cost and others will classify it as a hard cost. Examples include fines, payments to professionals who certify that work that has been completed is in compliance with municipal laws and codes, and some engineering fees.

Once the budget is organized into hard and soft costs and adjustments are made to the gray areas, you can make comparisons of job costs with those on other projects you have underwritten and perhaps others in your department's loan portfolio. Try to make sure that the comparisons are for like line items.

Hard Cost Organization

In the United States hard costs usually are divided into 16 standardized divisions developed by the Construction Specifications Institute (CSI). They are as follows:

1. General requirements
2. Site work
3. Concrete
4. Masonry
5. Metals

6. Wood and plastic
7. Thermal and moisture protection
8. Doors and windows
9. Finishes
10. Specialties
11. Equipment
12. Furnishings
13. Special construction
14. Conveying systems
15. Mechanical
16. Electrical

Within each division are classifications or subdivisions that enable the budget to have as much or as little detail as is needed for each end user. For instance, subdivisions for division 9 may include the following:

9000	Finishes
9100	Furring and lathing
9150	Plastering
9200	Framing
9300	Drywall
9400	Tile
9500	Ceiling systems
9600	Flooring
9650	Carpeting
9800	Painting

Each subdivision can be used as a line item. A line item is a category of work or materials in a budget that is given a dollar cost. Each category is on a row or line that forms a list of costs. The list provides the detail of the project's budget.

There are three hard cost line items that require particular attention: The general conditions line, the contingency line, and the builder's profit line. If these lines have been omitted from the budget, you should ask why.

General Conditions

The general conditions category consists of expenses that are broad in scope, are necessary to get the project done, may not result in the completion of tangible work, and usually cannot be assigned to any single trade. General conditions expenses perhaps can be explained best through examples. They include the costs of a temporary trailer used as a construction office, tool sheds placed on or off site, payroll for the construction manager, and a crew of handymen who work directly for the property developer. General conditions costs also include cleaning, office supplies, telephone and administrative expenses during construction, copying costs, messenger services, and general operating costs. Usually, general conditions are funded through the percentage of completion method based on the entire property budget. They also can be advanced on a monthly basis in equal amounts over the term of the loan (e.g., a 24-month loan with a $1 million general conditions line will advance $41,666 per month: $1 million/24 months = $41,666). [2] The general conditions category usually ranges in the area of 5 to 10 percent of the total hard cost budget. Anything outside that range should be questioned.

Contingency

The contingency line is used to fund unanticipated and/or unidentified future expenses that in the construction industry are called overruns. Anyone who has been to a construction site can appreciate the complexity and dynamic quality of the business. Not to expect changes and overruns even on the smallest projects is naive and not pragmatic.

Overruns can be caused by a multiplicity of events and actions. For instance, in the plans and specifications there can be oversights and omissions of detail because of unfamiliarity with municipal laws and regulations that result in changes and delays; there can be delays resulting from subcontractors not performing in a timely manner; there can be mistakes in coordinating the

---

[2] There are two other types of general conditions that are nonfinancial in nature that you may come across in the development process. One is the general conditions section of project specifications. In project specifications released by an architect or engineer, general conditions will indicate, for example, that all work must be in accordance with federal, state, and local agencies. Another area where general conditions are noted is in a bidding package sent to competing contractors and materialmen. Among other things, it describes the method and requirements for making a bid, the form the bid must be in to be accepted, the deadline for submitting the bid, and other conditions, for example, that the contractor must be bonded and have adequate insurance coverage.

trades and materials that must work together on the job; there can be exchanges of materials and fixtures because of upgrades; there can be design changes simply because of a change of mind about the choice of materials, layouts, or construction details; there can be subcontractors performing inferior work that has to be repaired or replaced; there can be accidents that damage already completed work; there can be materials and fixtures that are delivered late or become unavailable as a result of shortages or unacceptable lead times from order to delivery; and there can be subcontractor fraud, which sometimes occurs when a subcontractor is short of money, takes an advance of funds on his contract, makes some initial appearances, and then fails to show up again.

Most cost overruns and delays are banal in nature, but in the aggregate they can erode a contingency line. Examples of everyday overruns include the addition of a second bathroom mirror that can add thousands of dollars to the cost of a hotel, a local requirement to use heavier sheetrock in a common-way corridor that was not specified in the plans and can be an extremely costly surprise (and one that the developer almost never has any recourse to the architect for except in good faith negotiations), the impossibility of obtaining a specified type of air handler that is out of production and thus must be replaced with an equivalent air handler that is more expensive, the hiring of a security firm as a result of a random vandalism incident, failure to obtain a $300 Saturday work permit that causes a building inspector to issue an order to stop work at the site so that all trades have to leave the job early in the morning, and a window design in a designated landmark building that results in manufacturing delays because the landmark agency repeatedly requires changes to it.

It is important to watch out for requisitions that ask for relatively large amounts under the contingency line even if they appear to be justified. Early or midconstruction overruns can lower the contingency reserve to a level that threatens the loan by putting it out of balance. The best thing to do is listen to the advice of your consulting engineer and use your judgment to limit contingency line drawdowns to avoid its depletion early in the project. Instead of allowing drawdowns from the contingency line, try to force the borrower to use additional equity. Later, if the job is going well and contingency funds appear sufficiently ample to meet future needs, the borrower can be reimbursed partially.

Like the general conditions line, the contingency line should be in the range of 5 to 10 percent of the total hard cost budget.[3]

Builder's Profit

Depending on how the budget is presented and how the work is managed and performed, there may or may not be a line for the builder's profit. If the borrower is also the general contractor, his profit may be incorporated into many of his budgeted line items. In some cases, he will work without a builder's profit. Instead, he will take his profits from earnings when the project generates net sales or lease income. Whether or not it is listed, this is an expense that should be accounted for. If you do not see it, you should ask about it. Like the general conditions and contingency budget lines discussed above, the builder's profit line is in the range of 5 to 10 percent of hard costs.

Closing Costs

With most development loans, at the loan closing you will be making your first advance. If the loan includes a property acquisition component, it is not unusual for that advance, aside from any funds directed toward the property purchase price, to consist entirely of closing costs, which are soft costs.

Closing costs can vary widely, depending on the state and municipality where the property is located. In New York, where expenses are relatively high, closing costs account for a significant portion of the total acquisition costs because taxes and fees are a percentage of the purchase price and the mortgage amount.

A typical New York City closing of a $10 million property purchased with an $8 million mortgage loan will include the following costs:

---

[3] Variations from this norm often can be explained adequately for the contingency and the general conditions budget lines. For instance, some of the general conditions expenses may be incorporated in other budget lines. This is frequently the case for carpentry. On most jobs, the allocation for carpentry accounts for a significant proportion of the development budget and is a logical place to have a 10 percent or more general conditions figure built into it. As a result, the overall budgeted general conditions line may be lower than expected.

Seller Costs

Seller's attorney	$5,000 to $20,000, depending on complexity
New York transfer tax	1.425% up to $499,000 of purchase price
	2.625% for portion of purchase price greater than $500,000
New York state transfer tax	0.4% of purchase price
Closing adjustments	Include taxes in arrears, other owed payments, and agreed-on net debits
Real estate broker fee	0.5 to 5% of the purchase price, depending on price and complexity; usually, the higher the property's sales price, the lower the fee as a percentage of the price, but the greater the complexity, the higher the fee percentage.
Miscellaneous	$1,000

Purchaser Costs

Lender's attorney	$10,000 to $30,000, depending on complexity
Purchaser's attorney	$10,000 to $30,000, depending on complexity
Lender's mortgage fee (points)	0 to 2% of loan amount (usually)[4]
Lender's appraisal fee	$3,500 to $15,000
Lender's engineering	$3,500 to $15,000
Lender's environmental report	$2,000 to $10,000 (or more if contaminants are suspected or found)
Title fees	Around $30,000[5]
Mortgage broker fee	1% to 3% of loan depending on size and complexity; the higher the mortgage amount, usually the lower the fee as percentage of the mortgage; the greater the complexity, usually the higher the fee percentage
Real estate broker fee	1% to 4% of purchase price, depending on price and complexity; the higher the property's sales price, usually the lower the fee as a percentage of the price; the greater the complexity, usually the higher the fee percentage
Mortgage recording tax	2.05% up to $499,000
	2.80% of loan amount at and above $500,000
Recording fees	Approximately $1,000.
Cash reserve (contingency)	$10,000 to $20,000 or more
Closing adjustments	Includes taxes paid in advance, other advance payments, and agreed-on net credits
Working capital reserve	Dependent on expected deficit; however, the reserve often is funded by the lender
Capital improvement reserve	Equity that must go into the project before the lender's construction funding.

---

[4] If a lender offers a loan with no up-front fee (points), he is said to be making the loan at par.

[5] Title fees are regulated in New York and therefore are the same for various title companies. The inelastic commodity structure of pricing results in intense competition among these companies that often, for the benefit of lenders, borrowers, and attorneys, manifests itself in hosting lavish receptions in suites at real estate conventions. Generally, all title companies provide excellent responsiveness and service.

Obviously, the aggregate costs to purchase a property are significantly greater than the contract purchase price agreed on between the buyer and the seller. Using the list above or making your own list on the basis of closings in the areas your institution makes loans in, you can make sure the borrower's preliminary closing projections are reasonably accurate.[6] Below is a sample of a closing statement, which is a summary of the sources and uses of funds that changed hands at a typical closing that included a $16 million acquisition.

PAYMENT OF THE PURCHASE PRICE

SELLER'S CREDITS

Purchase price $16,000,000
Rent $4,253.55

**TOTAL CREDITS
TO SELLER: $16,004,253.55**

PURCHASER'S CREDITS

Down payment $1,600,000

**TOTAL CREDITS
TO PURCHASER: $1,600,000**

BALANCE DUE FROM PURCHASER AT CLOSING: $14,404,253.55

The balance of the purchase price in the amount of $14,404,253.55 was
   paid as follows:

Wire to the account of ZZZ Associates the amount
   of $14,404,253.55 in payment of the balance of
   the purchase price $14,404,253.55
                                                                              $14,404,253.55

DISTRIBUTION OF LOAN PROCEEDS

The proceeds of the loan in the amount of $36,000,000.00 were distributed as follows:

Funds withheld by lender in the amount of $704,167.00 in payment of lender's closing fees:

Loan fee (1.5%)	$525,000.00	
Lender's counsel fee	$45,000.00	
Short-term interest (through 9/30)	$134,167.00	$704,167.00

---

[6] Note that in certain areas of the country, convention or law dictates who pays certain expenses. For instance, in New York the seller always pays the transfer tax. Therefore, it should not show up in the purchaser's closing cost estimate without an explanation.

Funds withheld and wired by lender to SV Services (loan servicer) in the amount of $18,389,320.00 in payment of lender's closing fees:

Real estate tax escrow	$125,000.00	
Insurance escrow	$45,000.00	
Appraisal	$17,013.00	
Environmental	$10,600.00	
Site inspection	$750.00	
Lender expense reimbursement	$957.00	
Interest reserve	$1,278,000.00	
Broker fee	$480,000.00	
Remaining leasehold purchase price	$32,000.00	
Outstanding liens	$800,000.00	
Capital expense deposit escrow	$15,600,000.00	$18,389,320.00

Funds wired by lender to title agency in the amount of $15,906,513.00 in payment of loan proceeds	$15,906,513.00
	$35,000,000.00

DISBURSEMENTS FROM ESCROW
(TITLE AGENCY)

The following disbursements were made from the funds wired into the escrow account of Title Agency in the amount of $15,906,513.00:

Wire from the account of Title Agency in the amount of $434,875.00 made payable to the Estate of Lenora Maxout in payment of the balance of the purchase price for the stock owned by the Estate	$434,875.00
Wire from the account of Title Agency in the amount of $14,404,253.55 made payable to ZZZ Associates in payment of the balance of the purchase price	$14,404,253.55

Wire from the account of Title Agency in the amount of $1,024,634.87 made payable to Agency Title, Inc., in payment of a portion of Purchaser's Title charges:

Mortgage recording tax	$962,500.00
Recording fees	$1,500.00
Title insurance	$49,436.00
Mortgage insurance	$52,827.00
Survey	$875.00
Continuations	$350.00
Departmental searches	$450.00

Vault and water searches	$100.00	
Endorsements	$225.00	$1,024,634.87
	$1,068,263.00	

Wire from the account of Title Agency in the amount of
$42,749.58 made payable to ZZZ Affiliates in payment of
the fee for assignment of Affiliates' interest in the net lease $42,749.58

$15,906,513.00

ADDITIONAL DISBURSEMENTS

Check in the amount of $15,125.00 made payable to Izzy,
Dolby & Roland in payment for New York City and New
York State transfer taxes in connection with the transfer
from the estate of Lenora Maxout $15,125.00

Check in the amount of $50,000.00 made payable to Izzy,
Dolby & Roland in payment of legal fees $50,000.00

Check in the amount of $43,628.13 made payable to
Agency Title, Inc., in payment of the balance of the
title charges $43,628.13

$108,753.13

RECEIPTS

Check no. 148 drawn on the account of ZZZ Associates
made payable to 82nd Street LLC in the amount of
$49,192.42 as a refund of sublease tax escrow $49,192.42

$49,192.42

In this example, at the time the loan closed, the borrower
could not find a commercial bank to make the entire loan because
the project, a run-down hotel in a secondary location, was
perceived to embody too much risk. However, the borrower found
a commercial bank that gave a strong initial indication that it
would make a loan to fund the acquisition of the property but
could not close within the time allowed by the sales contract.
An investment bank, which could react more quickly than the
commercial bank, made the loan. Although it was more expensive,
it still made sense to the borrower.

In the example, a $36 million loan was used to cover part of the property's acquisition cost, closing costs that included the lender's 1.5 percent fee, a construction budget estimated at $15.6 million, and soft costs such as escrows for taxes, insurance, and an interest reserve.

An interesting aspect of this closing statement is that it tells the reader that the entire loan was funded at closing even though the borrower was unable to use a large portion of the funds until actual project costs were incurred. In this case, the capital expense deposit escrow was sent to a loan servicer, an independent company hired by the lender, for later disbursement. The reason the loan was fully funded was to increase the lender's interest revenue. It is noteworthy that the interest reserve came to $1,278,000, well short of the amount required to cover the entire loan. However, the lender and the borrower assumed that the acquisition loan was to be refinanced shortly by the interested commercial bank that would take a first lien position. The investment bank, which expected to be partially paid down, would subordinate to the new lender. (Even if the commercial bank decided not to take out the investment bank's acquisition loan, the borrower's principals had several million dollars in liquid assets and a seven-figure yearly income stream. The investment bank felt comfortable that the borrowers easily could come up with the money out of pocket to make interest payments.)

At first, closing statements are hard to understand, particularly if you are not familiar with the transactions involved. However, after a few closings, they should become more familiar and easier to read. Unfortunately, closing statements are not produced until after the closing, sometimes a few weeks later. Therefore, a closing statement is not a budgeting tool but a reference to see how funds were spent, reimbursed, and escrowed.

Interest Carry

Determining the interest carry is your responsibility. Once you review the closing costs, you should examine how much interest carry is budgeted. Several factors should be considered, such as the amount of the loan that will be outstanding, the time it will take to complete the job and obtain a certificate of occupancy, the time it will take for the project to generate positive operative cash flows, the time it will take for sales and/or rental revenues to pay down the loan, and, if there is a takeout lender, the time it will take to trigger that source of funding. Forecasting interest expense is far from an exact science. The variables are not reliably predictable.

Therefore, considering these variables and referring to the example below to calculate interest carry, a simple rule of thumb is to treat any up-front advances (I) as fully funded from the inception of the loan (property acquisition). Then add 60 percent of the hard and soft cost portions of the loan facility for the first year and 80 percent for the second year (II) since that is usually the average that will be outstanding until completion. Then carry the full loan from the projected completion date until the planned paydown (III) from a sale or takeout. If partial sales or revenues will occur, drop the loan outstanding by the expected percentage decreases in the loan as paydowns occur (50 percent in the example below).

Example Calculation of Interest Carry:

XYZ New Residential Condominium Project

(A) Loan amount: $10,000,000
(B) Acquisition portion $4,000,000
(C) Construction portion $6,000,000
(D) Construction duration   18 months
(E) Paydown duration   Six equal monthly paydowns
                                     through sales
(F) Expected average interest rate   7%

I At loan closing

$(B) \times (D) \times (F) = \$4,000,000 \times 18 \text{ months} \times 7\%/12 \text{ months}$
$= \$420,000$

II Construction phase

First year $[(A) - (B)] \times (D) \times (F) \times 60\%$

Second year $[(A) - (B)] \times (D) \times (F) \times 80\%$

$= (\$10,000,000 - \$4,000,000) \times 60\% \times 7\%$
$= \$252,000$

$= (\$10,000,000 - \$4,000,000) \times 80\% \times 6 \text{ months}$
$\times 7\%/12 \text{ months} = \$168,000$

III From construction completion

(A) × (F) × (E) × ½ = $10,000,000 × 7%/12 months
   × 6 months × ½ = $175,000

Total interest carry = I + II + III = $1,015,000

The simple interest carry should be approximately $1,015,000.[7]

Will the Budget Be under or over Actual Costs?

The borrower has conflicting motives to diminish the cost budget or exaggerate it. Each has merits and risks.

Under Budget

Often, the borrower will forecast a low cost budget so that he can put in less up-front equity. He then can hope that money will arrive during or near the end of the job through expected equity sources, an increase in the loan by the lender, or hoped-for cost savings. Another complementary incentive to submit a low cost budget is that it will result in project forecasts that indicate a higher profit. This will have more attraction for a lender.[8]

Over Budget

In other instances the borrower may inflate the budget so that the project will be eligible for a larger loan. Then, as the job progresses, if there are expenses beyond what was allocated for, there will be funds available from the lender to cover some if not all of them.

Unfortunately, with overbudgeting, less scrupulous borrowers may be able to take out equity through periodic loan advances

---

[7] In development financing, there is no principal amortization. Only interest is collected.

[8] If the credit criteria of a lending institution require a maximum loan to total cost ratio on development projects of 75 percent and the total project is realistically budgeted for $10 million, the lender will lend $7,500,000 and the borrower will need to come up with $2,500,000 in equity or subordinate financing. If the total project budget is artificially reduced to $8 million, the borrower will need to come up with only $2 million, which is $500,000 less. He will, however, have to cover the significant $500,000 budget gap as the project moves forward. Note that in this example, if total revenues are $11 million, a $10 million cost budget results in a total return of only 10 percent. If the borrower instead submits an $8 million cost budget, the total return increases to a much more attractive 37.5 percent. Since the dollar gap is always relatively large when a project is underbudgeted, even though a project's return is more attractive, it is more common to find budgets that are overbudgeted.

buried in line items such as general conditions or contingencies, reducing their risk by effectively reducing their equity. In fact, with an overinflated budget, sometimes by the end of the project a developer will recover all of his equity and even receive a profit.

The Lender's Bias

A common occurrence that many lenders experience is that their institution's senior credit officers have a strong bias toward reducing the underwriter's recommended loan amount on a commercial mortgage in the belief that this approach reduces loan risk. This can occur regardless of the budget's reasonableness or validity. The main reason for their caution is that they are concerned that the borrower will take money out of the project from construction loan advances rather than through profits. Then, if things go wrong, the borrower will have a reduced incentive to focus on, invest in, and work through difficult situations. This raises the possibility that the lender may be caught in an expensive problem loan workout.

This policy may be good for loans secured by existing income-generating properties in which reducing the loan amount typically reduces the loan risk because lending less money increases the borrower's equity and reduces the lender's loan-to-value ratio. Unfortunately, with a development loan, underlending often leads to the unintended effect of higher risk.[9] When the borrower needs some working capital to keep the construction project moving smoothly, he may not have any. The results can be serious if he fails to pay contractors or professionals who, for instance, can stall or even shut down a project. Also, ill will can be created with a borrower who otherwise could generate significant business for the lending institution in the future. The stress put on the borrower-lender relationship by the "arbitrary" loan reduction can foster resentment that may never be bridgeable.

Conversely, with a slight overloan position, the lending institution may be better protected. The borrower is able to focus more

---

[9] Sometimes a sound loan proposal can come up against an overly conservative credit decision, resulting in a reduced loan amount. For whatever reason, the borrower may not have time to get a loan elsewhere (e.g., the borrower must close on a property by a certain time or lose the deal and/or his down payment). The result is that he may have no choice but to accept the loan as is even if he knows it will be a problem later.

on completing the project successfully than on searching for a marginal amount of money. Even with the risk that the borrower may take out some of his equity, it is generally better to err by lending a little more than a little less.

HOW TO EVALUATE THE BORROWER'S BUDGET

After reviewing enough loan proposals, you should start to get a feel for how much in hard costs and soft costs per square foot a project should come to in several geographic areas. If, for example, your institution makes development loans on apartment buildings, office buildings, warehouses, and strip centers, you should learn how much a "typical" apartment building, office building, warehouse, and strip center generally costs per square foot in the geographic areas where you lend and your financial institution does business. Once you have this ability, you can review new proposals more effectively and ask more informed questions. This can prevent you from being overly absorbed in a detailed underwriting analysis on a prospective loan that you later discover does not work. If you believe a prospective deal may be a good one but the costs as projected by the borrower seem unexpectedly high or low, you are in a better position to ask why.

Where to Start

After you form a general opinion, you should review each budget line item for reasonableness, starting with the "easier" known and straightforward calculable items; these items include amounts set aside for the purchase price of the property and closing costs, including those related to the loan. Items such as transfer taxes, mortgage taxes, brokerage fees, and recording fees can be verified without too much difficulty because they are based on a percentage of the loan or the purchase price. Attorney's fees, both your institution's and the borrower's; appraisal fees; and inspecting engineer fees all can be estimated fairly accurately on the basis of your department's past closing experience.

After reviewing the easier closing costs portion of the budget, you should review general operating expenses such as real estate taxes, utility bills, security, management, lease-up or sales costs, and marketing expenses. Benchmarks for these expenses can be obtained readily from a review of past loan proposals and appraisals of similar projects in the area, the municipality where the project is situated (e.g., real estate tax information for larger cities can be found on the Internet), and, if necessary, discussions with appraisers and brokers who practice and work in the area where the property is located. If revenues are expected during construction because of remaining tenancies, new leases, or purchases of a portion of the property, make sure that the expenses related to those revenues are included in the budget (rent abatements for existing tenants during construction, attorney's fees, management fees, utilities, maintenance, brokerage costs, etc.).

The Lender's Consulting Engineer

In the construction lending arena, the lender employs the services of a consulting engineer who has expertise in construction and hard costs. He may be an in-house employee but most often comes from an independent firm specializing in the field.

The written review of the borrower's hard cost numbers by an engineer is the dominant factor in a hard cost budget validation. You should always question a few specific areas of the engineer's review to ensure that he has not just rubber-stamped the developer's original submission. Asking questions also signals to the inspecting engineer and his firm that you expect a high level of professionalism and responsiveness.[10]

How Hard Cost Budgets Are Estimated

In reviewing the borrower's hard cost budget and the engineer's report, you should be aware that developers and contractors use several methods to arrive at cost estimates. All are supported by off-the-shelf software from numerous publishers.

---

[10] The consulting engineer's expertise is the reason you hired him. Since so much reliance is placed on him, choosing the right engineer and knowing what to expect from him and what he should expect from you are very important. Because you are not expected to be a construction expert, if poor hard cost budgeting results in a problem loan, it is usually best to defer engineering and hard cost budgeting to the engineer. If there are disagreements and senior management is looking for someone to blame, let it be the engineer. See Chapter 8 for further discussions of this topic.

At the inception of a project, a top-down method is used to determine the project's feasibility. A broad overall hard cost figure is determined on the basis of past experience with factors such as the proposed building's type, size, general construction, and location. For instance, a residential building in New York City may cost $420 per square foot in hard costs. An office building in that city may only cost $230 per square foot in hard costs because there are fewer bathrooms and kitchens to install, less plumbing to install, and less partitioning. In the first example, if a 100,000-square-foot residential building is to be constructed, the hard costs come to $42 million.

The top-down approach is the method that you will rely on most frequently from the underwriting and loan approval process through the issuance of the commitment letter (one of the conditions of the commitment letter is, of course, to have the borrower submit a thorough and detailed hard cost budget to you and your consulting engineer). The top-down approach is also the primary method used by an appraiser (see Chapter 5).

A more refined estimate carves out components and systems and determines their cost on the basis of the size of the building and each system's function. For instance, a 3,500-square-foot retail space with 14-foot-high ceilings with a 2,500-square-foot cellar with 9-foot-high ceilings and 180 square feet of doors and windows will require a 23-ton-capacity air-conditioning system. The system includes condensers, evaporators, piping, ducting, and electrical work. Each ton of air-conditioning capacity has a cost of $4,000. Therefore, the cost of the air-conditioning system will be $92,000 (23 tons $\times$ $4,000/ton = $92,000).

The most inclusive method is the takeoff method, which, depending on the estimator's purpose, expertise, and software, can have a very high degree of detail. It is used by contractors when the derivation of an accurate cost can be crucial to their profitability. (The developer will have the benefit of contractors who have made bids by using estimates derived from takeoffs. He will determine his final budget on the basis of the final bid.[11]) Units and costs are lumped together into small aggregates that are

---

[11] Experienced developers often specialize in one or two types of real estate projects. They can refer to their most recent projects' final costs to compose or verify a very accurate and detailed hard cost budget.

multiplied to generate a final cost. For example, all the price components that lead up to the installation of a piece of 5/8-inch-thick sheetrock amount to $15.50. The estimator begins with the $15.50 figure and multiplies it by the number of 5/8-inch sheetrock panels that he determines is needed after examining the plans.

Further refinements break down each task into units (linear feet, quantity, capacity, labor, energy, equipment, etc.) and then multiply the number of units by the expected unit cost. Adding all the products results in a total cost. The units are calculated from ("taken off") the plans and then referenced to the specifications that indicate materials and methods. For example, the estimator will determine the price of each 4-inch by 8-inch piece of 5/8-inch-thick sheetrock, the average time (labor) it takes to install each one, and the amount of time (labor) and material cost of taping, sanding, and priming after installation. The total estimated cost, after adding all of these elements, will be $15.50. If, after taking measurements from the plans and calculating waste, it is determined that 1,000 pieces of sheet-rock will be needed, the budget for this item will be $15,500 ($15.50 × 1,000).

The takeoff method is very time-consuming. Although it produces an estimate that is well grounded in data and is defendable, it is not a necessary exercise for the developer. Also, because there are many underlying assumptions (future labor costs, supply costs, etc.), the method can be susceptible to mistakes and manipulation.

THE EVOLUTION OF THE BUDGET

From the approval of the loan to the loan closing and the disbursement of funds, the allocation of the loan amount between and within the hard and soft cost categories frequently changes as a result of refinements of cost estimates.

If the budget declines slightly and there are now "excess funds," they can be reallocated safely to line items such as the interest and contingency categories. Since the lender has control over the release of these excess monies, the risk to the lender does not increase substantially. The borrower has added protection against overruns and will not have to pay interest on the excess funds if he does not requisition for them.[12] However, if the cost of the project declines significantly (which is very unusual), the amount of the loan should be reduced so that it remains within your institution's loan-to-cost ratio.

More often than not, initial budgets increase over time. As more detail is added to and addressed in project planning, complexity and awareness increase. This usually drives up costs. For instance, the cost of drywall may go up because a thicker partition is needed for fire safety, the ventilation system may have to include a "makeup air" unit to avoid air pressure problems, the brands of appliances may have to be upgraded to meet local competition, or a separate sales office with a finished model unit is now deemed indispensable.

THE LOAN AMOUNT

Budget increases are more prevalent among less experienced borrowers, who tend to underestimate a project initially and therefore underbudget it. Those borrowers may not understand that after a loan is approved, it is very difficult, if not close to impossible, to increase the committed loan amount.

This is the case because in most organizations, after the loan has been approved, when a borrower comes back for more money before the loan closes, it raises red flags among senior management and senior credit personnel. For instance, if the borrower is using leverage (mezzanine financing) and is not exceedingly liquid, senior management may become concerned about the ability of the borrower to carry a project to completion financially if additional unexpected costs later surface. Or they may second-guess themselves, your underwriting, and the borrower's construction competence, expertise, budget, and cost containment ability regardless of his financial position. This is especially true if the proposed loan is large and therefore has to be reviewed by the upper reaches of senior management, perhaps needing the approval of a senior credit committee or even an institution's board of directors. When

---

[12] An exception concerns state lien laws. The lender should make sure through his loan administrator or through a knowledgeable real estate attorney (or both) that he can apply excess funds from one budget line to another without jeopardizing the lender's lien position (see Chapter 14 for a discussion of lien law).

it is reintroduced to another round of scrutiny, the original approval may not be sustained. That is, the loan proposal can be killed the second time around. This can be professionally embarrassing for you. In such cases, your resistance to reintroducing a loan for a higher amount may be in the borrower's best interest. Let the borrower know that if budgeted costs increase, the gap must be closed with equity, not debt.[13]

SAMPLE BUDGETS

When you are reviewing a loan proposal, do not assume that because the budget is presented in a form that is not what you are used to, the borrower is not knowledgeable or there is something wrong with it. There are many ways to compose a budget, and styles and details vary. This is especially true at the initial loan proposal stage, when the budget may be composed by the developer or his representative, not by an architect, construction consultant, or estimator. Budget divisions and subdivisions, as was noted earlier in this chapter, often develop along with the project's specifications. With an experienced borrower, the budget may increase considerably in detail but little in composition. To get an idea of budget styles and scope, four examples are presented below that were submitted to lenders, along with narrative loan proposals. They are prefaced with brief project descriptions.

100 SoHo Street

In the loan proposal in Chapter 2, no detail about the derivation of the hard cost budget was provided. As the budget evolved and gained specificity through the methods discussed above, the borrower was able to refine his hard cost numbers and provide them to the lender, who gave them to his inspecting engineer for review. Ultimately, this budget (see Figure 3–1) was used as the template for hard cost advances under the construction loan.

---

[13] You may have to adjust the amount contributed by the borrower so that the loan-to-cost ratio constraint is maintained. Also, with an increased budget, the loan-to-value (LTV) ratio may become a limiting factor in determining the maximum loan amount that will be approved in most lending institutions. If the appraised value at completion does not meet the LTV hurdle of the lender, the loan amount will be reduced until it does. Of course, if the requested loan amount is substantially higher than what was sought originally, the project risk profile may become untenable and may dictate that the loan, and all your work, be abandoned.

FIGURE 3–1

100 SoHo Budget

HARD COST BUDGET

Code	Description	Quantity	Unit	Unit Price	Amount
02050	**Demolition & Shoring**				**$245,650**
	Remove and/or Repair Flooring 1st thru 6th	28,500	sf	$2.50	$71,250
	Dispose of Flooring and Debris	28,500	sf	$2.00	$57,000
	Remove Roof Structure	4,750	sf	$6.00	$28,500
	Remove Rear Masonry Wall	4,200	sf	$6.00	$25,200
	Shore Rear Wall	1	ls	$12,000.00	$12,000
	Shore Masonry Walls for Roof Removal	1	ls	$8,000.00	$8,000
	Remove Slab on Grade	1,300	sf	$7.00	$9,100
	Protect Adjacent Properties	1	ls	$5,000.00	$5,000
	Remove Masonry at Lot Line Windows	20	each	$400.00	$8,000
	Remove Rear Structure Floors 1 thru 6	2,700	sf	$8.00	$21,600
02160	**Excavation & Back Fill**				**$31,125**
	Lower Basement Slab	205	cy	$125.00	$25,625
	Rear Extension Footing	44	cy	$125.00	$5,500
02600	**Site Utilities**				**$25,000**
	Gas	1	ls	$5,000.00	$5,000
	Water	1	ls	$5,000.00	$5,000
	Sewer	1	ls	$15,000.00	$15,000
02800	**Sidewalk Work**				**$53,500**
	Demo Vault	1	ls	$10,000.00	$10,000
	Structure Framing	1	ls	$20,000.00	$20,000
	Double Slab	750	sf	$13.00	$9,750
	Water-Proofing Membrane	750	sf	$15.00	$11,250
	Steel Curb	50	lf	$50.00	$2,500
03100	**Foundations**				**$44,575**
	Underpinning for elevator pit.	1	ls	$14,000.00	$14,000
	Rear Yard Extension	15.5	cy	$650.00	$10,075
	Footing Edge at Dropped Slab	6	cy	$750.00	$4,500
	Slab on Grade	2,000	sf	$8.00	$16,000

(Continued)

Code	Description	Quantity	Unit	Unit Price	Amount
03300	**Concrete Superstructure**				**$109,560**
	Penthouse Floor & Roof Structure	7,000	sf	$14.00	$98,000
	2nd Floor Structure	800	sf	$14.00	$11,200
	Fill in Existing Elevator and stair openings	18	each	$20.00	$360
04000	**Masonry**				**$152,400**
	Clean & Repair Existing Façade	9,150	sf	$10.00	$91,500
	Basement Interior Walls	950	sf	$12.00	$11,400
	Rear Extension Walls	1,750	sf	$12.00	$21,000
	Repair S.M. Cornice	175	sf	$45.00	$7,875
	Replace Stone Sills	15	each	$400.00	$6,000
	Rebuild N & S Parapet @ 6th Floor	450	sf	$32.50	$14,625
05100	**Steel Framing & Metal Deck**				**$154,600**
	Provide New Opening for Stairs	8	ls	$3,000.00	$24,000
	Provide New Opening for Elevator	6	ls	$3,000.00	$18,000
	Penthouse & 2nd Floor	7,800	sf	$12.00	$93,600
	Water Tank Framing	1	ls	$19,000.00	$19,000
05400	**Miscellaneous Iron**				**$154,900**
	Stairs and Railing Typ.	20	Flts.	$3,000.00	$60,000
	Decorative Stairs	1	each	$20,000.00	$20,000
	Decorative Handrail	1	ls	$12,000.00	$12,000
	Guard Rails	405	lf	$80.00	$32,400
	Ladders	3	each	$1,000.00	$3,000
	Loose Lintels	1	ls	$5,000.00	$5,000
	Replace Front Steps	1	ls	$22,500.00	$22,500
06100	**Carpentry & Drywall**				**$829,764**
	Exterior Framing & Gyp. Board	6,300	sf	$18.00	$113,400
	Interior Furn. Wall on Masonry	12,200	sf	$6.00	$73,200
	Interior Gyp. Board on Framing	48,344	sf	$6.00	$290,064
	Interior Shaft Liner Walls	3,220	sf	$8.00	$25,760
	Interior Gyp. Board on Ceilings	30,400	sf	$5.50	$167,200
	Install H.M. Doors	30	each	$200.00	$6,000

	Install Wood Door & Hardware				
	Closets (Double)	48	pair	$200.00	$9,600
	Closets (Single)	10	each	$150.00	$1,500
	Rooms	42	each	$175.00	$7,350
	Apartment Entries	9	each	$200.00	$1,800
	French Doors	17	pair	$500.00	$8,500
	Wood Blocking	1	ls	$10,000.00	$10,000
	Protection	1	ls	$5,000.00	$5,000
	Install Access Doors	1	ls	$8,000.00	$8,000
	Install Accessories & Closet Interiors	9	apts.	$800.00	$7,200
	Trim – Door, Windows & Base	10,020	lf	$9.50	$95,190
					$0
	Millwork				**$326,600**
06200	Kitchen & Bathroom Cabinets	9	apts.	$35,000.00	$315,000
	Closet Interiors (furnish)	58	cls.	$200.00	$11,600
					$0
007500	**Roofing & Flashing**				**$14,000**
	Penthouse Roof	700	sf	$20.00	$14,000
07100	**Waterproofing /Damp Proofing**				**$49,000**
	Terrace Waterproofing	3,500	sf	$12.00	$42,000
	Elevator Pit	1	ls	$2,500.00	$2,500
	Basement extension Perimeter Wall	300	sf	$15.00	$4,500
07200	**Insulation**				**$23,175**
	Walls	22,500	sf	$0.75	$16,875
	Roof	4,200	sf	$1.50	$6,300
07240	**EIFS**				**$113,400**
	Penthouse & Rear Wall	6,300	sf	$18.00	$113,400
07900	**Caulking**				**$15,000**
	Exterior Windows	131	each	$60.00	$7,860
	Interior Finishes	1	ls	$15,000.00	$15,000
08100	**Hollow Metal Door & Frames**				**$8,550**
	H.M. Doors & Frames	38	each	$250.00	$8,550
08200	**Wood Door & Frames**				**$62,100**
	Closets (Double)	48	pair	$250.00	$12,000
	Closets (Single)	10	each	$200.00	$2,000
	Rooms	42	each	$250.00	$10,500
	Apartment Entries	9	each	$400.00	$3,600
	French Doors	17	pair	$2,000.00	$34,000

(Continued)

Code	Description	Quantity	Unit	Unit Price	Amount
08400	**Storefront & Entrance**				**$36,000**
	Replace Timber Doors	6	pair	$4,500.00	$27,000
	Repair Metal Panel	180	sf	$50.00	$9,000
08600	**Windows**				**$162,400**
	Replacement Windows				
	Lot Line	31	each	$800.00	$24,800
	Front	30	each	$1,200.00	$36,000
	Rear	24	each	$1,200.00	$28,800
	New Windows	16	each	$800.00	$12,800
	Skylight @ Penthouse	1	ls	$50,000.00	$50,000
	Skylight @ 2nd Floor	1	ls	$10,000.00	$10,000
08700	**Hardware**				**$57,300**
	H.M. Door	38	each	$150.00	$5,700
	Closet (Double)	48	pair	$200.00	$9,600
	Closet (Single)	10	each	$100.00	$1,000
	Rooms	42	each	$175.00	$7,350
	Apartment Entries	9	each	$300.00	$2,700
	French Doors	17	pair	$600.00	$10,200
	Storefront	4	pair	$1,000.00	$4,000
	Building Entrance	2	pair	$1,000.00	$2,000
	Bathroom Accessories	30	Bthrms	$500.00	$14,750
09680	**Carpet**				**$2,100**
	Public Hallways	60	sy	$35.00	$2,100
09300	**Ceramic Tile & Stone Tile**				**$350,120**
	Terrace Pavers	3,500	sf	$16.00	$56,000
	Floors	1,600	sf	$20.00	$32,000
	Walls	9,340	sf	$18.00	$168,120
	Marble & Saddles	40	each	$100.00	$4,000
	Stone Counters & Backsplashes	9	apts	$10,000.00	$90,000
09550	**Wood Flooring**				**$288,798**
	Subfloor on Existing Structure	12,536	sf	$8.00	$100,288
	Subfloor on New Structure	3,140	sf	$4.00	$12,560
	Hardwood Flooring	14,076	sf	$12.50	$175,950
09900	**Painting**				**$45,000**
	Apartments	9	each	$3,000.00	$27,000
	Scissors Stair	1	ls	$12,000.00	$12,000
	Public Corridors	1	ls	$6,000.00	$6,000

10000	**Specialties**				**$254,500**
	Trash Chute & Compactor	1	ls	$35,000.00	$35,000
	Water Tank on Roof	1	ls	$22,000.00	$22,000
	Fireplaces	9	each	$20,000.00	$180,000
	Signage	1	ls	$12,500.00	$12,500
	Mailboxes	1	ls	$5,000.00	$5,000
11000	**Equipment**				**$182,250**
	Range & Oven	9	each	$8,000.00	$72,000
	Kitchen Hood	9	each	$1,500.00	$13,500
	Dishwasher	9	each	$850.00	$7,650
	MicroWave	9	each	$500.00	$4,500
	Refrigerator	9	each	$7,500.00	$67,500
	Washer	9	each	$950.00	$8,550
	Dryer	9	each	$950.00	$8,550
12000	**Lobby Finishes**				**$80,000**
	Allowance	1	ls	$80,000.00	$80,000
14000	**Vertical Transportation**				**$190,000**
	8 stop traction elevator w/ 2 door/cab	1	ls	$180,000.00	190,000.00
15000	**HVAC**				**$350,000**
15400	**Plumbing**				**$210,000**
15300	**Sprinklers & Fire Protection**				**$120,000**
16000	**Electrical**				**$300,000**
	Subtotal				**$5,041,367**
	General Conditions			8%	**$403,309**
	Contingency			7%	**$352,896**
	Total Construction Costs				**$5,797,572**
	Architect & Engineers				**$190,000**
	Expeditor				**$10,000**
	Permits				**$10,000**
	Reimbursables				**$8,000**
	Survey				**$2,000**
	Subtotal A&E				**$220,000**
	Total Construction and Design Costs				**$6,017,572**

The Harold

The Harold is a to-be-built 157,533-gross-square-foot mixed-use 16-story project consisting of 50 residential condominium units totaling 67,834 square feet, an office complex totaling 47,472 gross square feet, retail space consisting of 11,626 gross square feet, and a community facility consisting of 1,000 gross square feet. Also included is underground garage space for approximately 38 cars. At the time of the loan submission, hard costs were not detailed, but the soft cost budget and the pro forma of revenues and costs were enough for the lender to get a clear understanding of the basic components of the project and its financial aspects. He was able to issue a proposed term sheet to the potential borrower and subsequently, using the budgets shown in Figure 3–2 (with additional supporting information), was able to underwrite the loan.

FIGURE 3-2

The Harold Budget

		% of Total
Permits:		
Building Permits and C of O:	$125,000	1.37%
Subtotal		
Design:		
Architect:	$850,000	9.29%
Interior Design Architect:	$275,000	3.01%
Structural Engineer:	$310,000	3.39%
Mechanical and Electrical Engineer:	$250,000	2.73%
Landscape Architect:	$10,000	0.11%
Soils and Environmental Consultants:	$40,000	0.44%
Security/Telecom Consultants	$20,000	0.22%
Inspection and Testing:	$25,000	0.27%
Miscellaneous Consultants:	$120,000	1.31%
Plan Printing & Disbursements:	$60,000	0.66%
Reimbursables	$60,000	0.66%
Expeditor	$70,000	0.77%
Surveyor:	$15,000	0.16%
Subtotal		
Legal and Administration:		
Borrower's Legal Fees:	$85,000	0.93%
Condominium Legal Fees (includes Tax Abatement Consultants):	$130,000	1.42%
Condominium Conversion Filing Fees:	$50,000	0.55%
Accountant:	$40,000	0.44%
Development Management:	$950,000	10.38%
Insurance:	$250,000	2.73%
Real Property Taxes:	$40,000	0.44%
Subtotal		
Marketing:		
Marketing and Advertisement:	$175,000	1.91%
Subtotal		
Finance:		
Appraisal:	$30,000	0.33%
Lender Environmental & Engineering Consultants:	$20,000	0.22%
Construction Draw Fees & Service Charges:	$25,000	0.27%
Loan Interest and Related Fees:	$3,200,000	34.97%
Mortgage Recording Tax:	$900,000	9.84%
Title Fees:	$100,000	1.09%
Lender's Legal Fees:	$75,000	0.82%
Broker Fee:	$350,000	3.83%
Subtotal		
Contingency:		
Development (Soft Costs) Contingency:	$500,000	5.46%
TOTAL SOFT COSTS:	**$9,150,000**	100.00%

Uptown NYC

The Uptown is a to-be-built 21-story building with 95 residential condominium apartments, street-level retail space, partially underground parking for 88 cars, and, since the seller of the property was a church, as part of the price, a small underground space for community activities. To allow the underwriter to move quickly to finish his analysis and issue the borrower a loan commitment, the construction manager submitted the hard cost budget shown in Figure 3–3. Note that the items were broken down by square footage, making it easy to do a broad comparison of the project's budget with other project budgets. However, the underwriter had to be careful not to make too exact a comparison since garage, retail, and residential spaces all have different costs per square foot.

FIGURE 3-3

Uptown NYC Construction Budget

Assumptions		Total $28,380,000	Per SF
1	General Conditions	$850,000	$5.15
2	Site Work	$350,000	$2.12
3	Excavation & Foundation	$1,800,000	$10.91
4	Concrete	$8,580,000	$52.00
5	Masonry & Waterproofing	$1,250,000	$7.58
6	Metals	$450,000	$2.73
7	Rough Carpentry	$240,000	$1.45
8	Finished Carpentry	$620,000	$3.76
9	Roofing and Insulation	$385,000	$2.33
10	Windows and Glazing	$660,000	$4.00
11	Doors and Hardware	$360,000	$2.18
12	Plastering	$120,000	$0.73
13	Drywall	$850,000	$5.15
14	Ceramic Tile	$295,000	$1.79
15	Flooring	$640,000	$3.88
16	Painting	$350,000	$2.12
17	Specialties	$250,000	$1.52
18	Appliances	$1,340,000	$8.12
19	Furnishings	$60,000	$0.36
20	Special Consideration	$250,000	$1.52
21	Elevators	$500,000	$3.03
22	Heat & Ventilation	$850,000	$5.15
23	Plumbing	$1,200,000	$7.27
24	Electrical	$1,400,000	$8.48
	SUB-TOTAL	$23,650,000	$143.33
CONTRACTOR FEE: 0.10		$2,365,000	$14.33
CONTRACTOR OVERHEAD: 0.10		$2,365,000	$14.33
TOTAL		**$28,380,000**	**$172.00**

The Mega Home

The Mega Home is a 15,000-square-foot to-be-built single-family home in the Westchester County area of New York, one of the most upscale locales in the country. The borrower's hard cost budget (Figure 3–4), along with soft costs directly related to construction, comes to a substantial cost of $477 per square foot, not including the acquisition of 4 acres of land and soft costs. Note that certain "essential" items, such as the lap pool and the golf green costs, were not included, the implication being that they will be provided after completion with borrower's equity.

FIGURE 3 – 4

The Mega Home

THE 13,000 SQUARE FOOT HOME AND ESTATE PRELIMINARY BUDGET

Based on Prelim plans dated 10/9

	Item	
	DIRECT CONSTRUCTION COST	**Budget**
1000	Permits & Fees	17,685.00
1050	Survey	4,050.00
1100	Demolition/Demo Containers	56,700.00
1125	Clearing & Grubbing	13,500.00
1150	Erosion Control	4,050.00
1175	Containers	18,225.00
1200	Excavation & Backfill	108,000.00
1210	Retaining Walls	99,900.00
1230	Blasting	49,950.00
1240	Drainage	10,125.00
1250	Utility Laterals	10,125.00
1260	Fill	33,750.00
1270	Gravel	6,075.00
1300	Septic System	41,175.00
1350	Dewatering System	27,000.00
1400	Landscape Labor	87,750.00
1425	Landscape Material	132,300.00
1450	Central Irrigation System	26,325.00
1470	Driveway	24,300.00
1500	Foundation Labor	58,050.00
1550	Foundation Material	58,050.00
1580	Waterproofing	10,125.00
1600	Fireplace – Chimney	75,600.00
1610	Stone Veneer	471,150.00
1620	Terraces, Stoops & Capping	98,550.00
1660	Stucco – Exterior	17,550.00
1680	Stucco & Plaster Interior	11,475.00
1700	Structural Steel	97,200.00
1750	Ornamental Iron	35,100.00
1800	Framing Labor	184,950.00
1850	Framing Lumber	183,600.00
1900	Plumbing Labor	85,050.00
1925	Plumbing Fixtures	60,750.00
1950	Oil Tank	4,590.00
1975	Bath Hardware	7,425.00

(Continued)

Item		
DIRECT CONSTRUCTION COST		**Budget**
2000	HVAC	160,650.00
2100	Security Systems	21,600.00
2200	Vacuum System	4,725.00
2300	Electric Labor	211,950.00
2320	Electric Fixtures	29,700.00
2330	Exterior Lighting	22,950.00
2350	Lightning Protection	9,720.00
2360	Audio/Visual	43,200.00
2370	Telephone/Computer Systems	11,475.00
2380	Generator	56,700.00
2390	Propane Tanks	7,020.00
3100	Fencing	44,550.00
3150	Entry Gate	33,750.00
3200	Arbors & Trellis	20,250.00
3300	Exterior Trim Labor	24,300.00
3325	Exterior Trim Material	29,700.00
3350	Interior Trim Labor	147,150.00
3375	Interior Trim Material	108,000.00
3400	Interior Doors	59,400.00
3450	Custom Casework	157,950.00
3500	Door Hardware	24,300.00
3550	Cabinet Hardware	2,700.00
3600	Stairs & Rails	75,600.00
3650	Hardwood Floors	63,450.00
3675	Carpeting	5,670.00
3700	Insulation	14,850.00
3750	Drywall	67,500.00
3800	Kitchen Cabinets	58,050.00
3850	Vanity & Laundry Cabinets	11,475.00
3900	Appliances	29,700.00
4000	Roofing Labor	74,250.00
4100	Roofing Material	54,000.00
4200	Siding Labor	10,125.00

4250	Siding Material	10,125.00
4300	Gutters & Leaders	17,550.00
5000	Windows & Patio Doors	191,700.00
5100	Garage Doors	10,125.00
5200	Exterior Doors	17,550.00
6000	Kitchen Countertops	13,500.00
6100	Vanity & Laundry Tops	11,475.00
6200	Hearths – Surrounds	11,475.00
6300	Ceramic & Stone Labor	20,250.00
6400	Ceramic & Stone Material	20,250.00
6450	Deck Stone & Saddles	8,775.00
7000	Shower Doors	7,020.00
7100	Mirrors & Glass	6,075.00
7500	Interior Paint	95,850.00
7550	Exterior Paint	60,750.00
8000	Pool	72,900.00
8050	Lap Pool	–
8075	Pool House	135,000.00
8100	Tennis Court	41,850.00
8150	Golf Greens	–
8200	Sauna	5,670.00
8250	Wine Cellar	25,650.00
8275	Theater & Seating	9,450.00
8300	Awning	–
8400	Elevators	67,500.00
8450	Dam Repairs	199,800.00
8500	General Conditions	747,900.00
	Hard Cost Contingency	527,850.00
	Total Direct Construction Costs:	**6,262,650.00**
	Architecture (Soft Costs)	432,000.00
	Supervision & Staffing (Soft Costs)	189,000.00
	Insurance (Soft Costs)	202,500.00
	Taxes (Soft Costs)	67,500.00
	Total Soft Construction Costs	**891,000.00**
	Total Construction Costs	**7,153,650.00**

Author's Note

Several people and sources will be involved in creating the project budget that will be used in your credit proposal. However, in the end it will be your responsibility to give the approval on budget figures that will affect not only the loan amount but also the amounts of monthly loan advances, whether you have an over or under loan position, and overall loan risk. Make sure you can justify each part of the budget by referring to your outside consulting engineer and using your experience and common sense.

CHAPTER 4

Evaluating the Borrower

THE FIVE Cs OF CREDIT

Almost all experienced lenders have heard of the five Cs of credit: character, capacity, cash flow, capital, and collateral. The five Cs act as reminders so that all the essentials for underwriting a loan proposal are addressed. A surprisingly common mistake (and an often fatal one) occurs when a lender focuses primarily on the deal's structure—the cash flow, capital, and collateral—and not on the borrower—his capacity and character. Particularly in real estate development, in which performance by the borrower and his team is critical, capacity and character are extremely important. First, though, you have to know who the borrower is. This chapter discusses the identity of the borrower and two of the five Cs: the borrower's character and capacity.

THE LEGAL ENTITY OF THE BORROWER

If you have taken a basic law course, a real estate sales person course, or a broker course, you have been introduced to the various forms of legal ownership. In commercial real estate, the usual ownership entities are a limited partnership (LP) and a limited liability company (LLC). A primary reason for these two forms is the limited liability they provide to investors. In an LLC, none of the members are liable beyond their investment. In a limited partnership, the same thing is true except for the general partner, who is usually the developer.

Another important reason is that the investors avoid double taxation on distributions (dividends). Under partnerships and LLCs, profits (and losses) are "passed through" directly to the individual investors. They are not taxed once at the corporate/partnership level and then again at the personal level. Often, LP and LLC profits and losses pass through several legal entities but are recognized only once by each individual partner or member.

SINGLE PURPOSE

To avoid the commingling of funds in various projects, recognize different capital compositions among investors, eliminate tax issues from other ventures, and help in organization and book-keeping, the legal entity that owns the property always is a single-purpose entity. That is, it will be created solely for the project against which you are lending. It is important to get a clear under-standing of who the key people behind the ownership entity are and, most important, who during the course of the loan will be in control of it.

Who Is in Control

The loan proposal comes from the developer. He is the one who, it is assumed, will be in control of the project and is therefore the central figure in your analysis. It is the developer who has the ultimate authority and responsibility for the entire operation of the borrowing entity and who will execute all the tasks that will enable it to complete the project, get the loan paid down, and allow the investors to make a profit.[1]

Who Owns What

The way to discover exactly who the members of an owning entity are and what rights they have is to look at an LLC's operating agreement (or a partnership agreement or a similar type of docu-ment). This document will lay out the legal ownership interests of

---

[1] The developer's day-to-day involvement in a project can vary widely, depending on factors such as his experience, his team, the size and complexity of the development, and the number of projects he is involved in concurrently. No matter how hands-on he is, he remains the CEO of the project and should be competent to carry out his obligations.

the parties, what their duties are, and what their rights are. As in any group that may be called on to reach a consensus, the fewer members involved, the better. You should question the developer about who the members are and what he expects of them throughout the project's life. If the ownership entity has members that are legal entities, find out who owns them and how they will be involved. You then should learn each member's risk-reward relationship.[2]

Risk and Reward

Risk-reward relationships among owning members often do not reflect their monetary contributions. For example, the "money member" may contribute 90 percent of the required equity in return for a deferred simple 10 percent interest on his investment and a 50 percent share of the expected profits. The developer may contribute the remaining 10 percent of equity for the remaining 50 percent of profits (it is unusual but not extraordinary for a developer to contribute no cash equity at all). In this example, the money member is risking his cash. However, his risk is mitigated by the fact that he receives 10 percent simple interest (called a preferred return, or a "pref") before the return of his equity. Equity then can be returned to him first or distributed on a proportional basis (sometimes referred to as a pari passu basis). In this example, on a pari passu basis he would get 90 cents of every dollar of equity returned. If the project falls far short of its expected profit, he still may get back all of his investment plus a return of 10 percent per annum in the form of deferred interest. The developer will get back his 10 percent equity either on a pari passu basis or after the money member gets back 100 percent of his equity.

Usually, only when all the equity is returned to all the investors will the developer receive any profits for his work. However, since the developer may be taking a developer fee, a general contractor fee, a developer profit fee, an overhead fee, or a construction manager fee either directly or indirectly through affiliates or relationships, he may make a good income and recover his equity

---

[2] Sometimes ownership interests, duties, and relationships may change through amendments and side agreements that are apart from the operating agreement and of which you have no way of being aware unless the borrower provides you with the information. It is a good idea always to ask the borrower if the agreement in your hands is the final one.

investment whether or not the project generates any profits or even experiences a loss. In this example, the developer, who may have gotten back his 10 percent of equity already plus some additional funds from fees, may not be very interested in seeing the project through to completion. The money partner, however, can experience a catastrophic loss. Alternatively, a developer may stay involved in a project so that he can continue to receive fees, especially if they are substantial in relation to his net worth.

Additional Capital

When you examine the partnership agreement or the operating agreement, you should review the capital call provision, which dictates who antes up if additional capital is required. Very often, even if the project forecast continues to show a good profit, there can be a shortage of funds along the way to its completion. If the profits will be there, additional equity funding usually will materialize. However, if the investors cannot come up with additional capital, no matter how good the projections are, the lender may be facing a problem loan. To mitigate an adverse situation caused by a developer's lack of funds, it often helps if the lender can get a feel for what is at stake for each member and/or partner. The more that is at stake, usually the more likely it is that money will be found when and if it is needed. Intuitiveness and subjectivity can play an important part in structuring the loan and the loan amount.

The Actual Working Relationship versus the Legal One

Even with a formal delineation of duties, there are times when the developer may not have all the control he appears to have. This is more likely to be true when a well-known, experienced, or strong money partner is an investor in the deal. The developer, who is the weaker financial partner, may be constrained considerably by his dependence on the stronger partner. He may even be dependent to the extent that without the stronger partner, he cannot make a living or sustain his development activities. If there are problems with the project during the course of construction, completion, lease-up, marketing, or sale, the developer may look to the stronger partner for financial, construction, technical, or other help. Whether the problems are due to the developer or to exogenous circumstances, the stronger partner usually will take a more active interest in the day-to-day affairs of the project to offset his higher financial exposure.

Who Is Real?

It is common for developers to form continuing relationships with partners who have invested with them in the past. To an outsider, it may be impossible to decipher exactly what the working relationships among those investors are. A bankruptcy, a criminal record, or a problem with one job that can materially affect the control of another job may force a developer to use a front man who is presented as the head of the development team.[3] The result is that the lender may be dealing with a developer who is not in control of the project to the degree expected.

Getting along with Different Interests

In many real estate deals, there can be interests among owning members that are interdependent but divergent. For instance, it is not uncommon to encounter a joint venture (JV) in which one of the members acts as the developer and the other acts as the general contractor (GC). On the surface, this appears to be a good synergistic relationship. However, if there is a falling out between them, it can be a major problem. They both have the same final goal of finishing the project, but their immediate interests prevent them from doing so. If the GC does not perform as expected, it will be hard or impossible for the developer to fire him.

In another situation, if the JV includes a partner who is a future or current tenant, you should be clear about what the relationship is, particularly what work is going into the tenant's space and who is paying for it. If the tenant is disappointed with the developer's rate of progress or quality of work, what is its recourse and who will bear the penalties in dollars can be serious questions. If the JV partners have strong disagreements, who will dominate? Who will be able to take control?

Of course, what you are trying to ascertain is the following: Given the members and the membership structure, is it good or

---

[3] Especially in a rising real estate market in which investor demand is strong, a straw man posing as a developer is not all that unusual.

bad for the project and the lender? Does it increase or decrease the risk of the loan facility?

Roles of Key Members and/or Partners

Depending on the structure of the borrowing entity, the project may face an adverse situation in which the developer's control is compromised. Therefore, you should know the competency of the major investors as well as their abilities, strengths, and weaknesses. Usually this is not a daunting task because on most projects the developer clearly will be the dominant figure and practically the only one on whom you will be relying. Also, except for financial contributions, limited partners and cash-contributing members often lack the experience, expertise, or desire to take control of a project unless it slides into a very dire condition. In contrast, on larger and more complex deals with several levels of structure or an active JV partner, it may be very important to delve into each member's function and capability.

A key member need not necessarily have extensive development experience. If, for example, a large investment bank is providing mezzanine financing subordinate to your loan, even though it may not have direct construction experience, it will have substantial financial resources to hire the needed skills to complete the job. It also should have ample capital and the unquestioned ability to carry your loan in the short term and be able to pay it down ultimately with its own funds if a refinancing or sale does not occur.

Management Substitution

An important component of the operating agreement is the conditions in which other members can vote to remove the developer as the managing member and put in another member in his place. Unless your attorney addresses this in the loan documents, the developer can be substituted for another without your consent or knowledge.

CAPACITY

Once you know the composition of the borrowing entity (the players), you can focus on its capacity. Capacity can be said to equal ability. After a cursory review of a loan proposal, you sometimes can reject it on the basis of the borrower's capacity. Capacity can become a critical decision point.

Experience with the Proposed Type of Property

The developer and the development team should have verifiable experience in the type of project they are proposing. For example, if the developer has a construction company that has been successful in building freestanding suburban single-family homes, he and his company's experience will have limited value in the development of an urban high-rise office building.

Ordinarily, you should not give a developer a "chance or a break" to work outside his area of expertise. If he has an existing relationship with you or your institution, try not to be influenced by it or by threats that he will move his business to another lender. If the borrower moves to another lender, you and the institution are probably better off. However, there are times when you have no choice but to make a loan to a developer outside his area of experience. This often occurs when the customer is so big that the lack of experience in the particular product type is outweighed by extensive experience in another type (e.g., a large office developer is building a midsize apartment building). It also frequently occurs in a smaller institution in which political concerns outweigh business concerns.

Your challenge is to weigh the sophistication and experience of the developer against the particular project he is proposing and adjust the loan conditions to any additional risks. Some ways to do this are by requiring that the developer augment his team, funding the project in stages if possible, cross-collateralizing the loan, getting personal guarantees, increasing contingency reserves, and requiring more up-front equity.

The Borrower Has Not Been Successful on Past Projects

If you discover that a developer has failed, you should determine the reason through third parties or by asking the developer. Sometimes a developer is making his first proposal to your institution because he has damaged his relationship with another lending institution that holds the developer accountable to some degree for disappointing results. Maybe the borrower did not perform as expected, and the loan's performance, because of the developer, became a real problem. There is no guarantee that he will perform better on his next transaction, which could involve you.

The Developer Is Known as a Paper Tiger

In any business that involves elements of salesmanship, marketing, and promotion, there are borrowers who are better at promoting deals than at working them after closing. These are often, though not always, "big picture" guys who submit beautiful loan proposals that are more dream than reality. If you get a palpable sense that the developer is exaggerating, a feeling that he is too smooth or that the forecasts make the deal look too good, you should be careful in checking his résumé of claimed accomplishments, paying particular attention to his role, contribution, and involvement in past projects. He may have been involved in great things, but only as a small participant.

Political Jurisdiction

The success of even small-scale projects can be influenced strongly by the political jurisdiction in which they are domiciled. Urban areas usually are a labyrinth of regulations, constraints, and politics that can change the size, scope, and character of a development or even kill it. However, in suburban and even rural areas, these factors may take on even more importance because projects have higher visibility and possibly a more substantial impact on the surrounding community. As is discussed throughout this book, a developer working outside his jurisdiction should be expected to have expert, experienced help in navigating the zoning, building, environmental, and other requirements of that jurisdiction. In simple cases, that person can be a local architect. In even slightly complex cases, it can involve several expensive professionals.

Numbers of Projects

Most real estate development firms in the middle market and the higher spheres are dominated by one person or a few individuals who play a very active and authoritarian role in their companies. If the individual is developing several projects at once, the question is how many he can be working on at one time without jeopardizing the successful outcome of the one being lent against.

If the loan is for a project significantly smaller than the borrower's other active projects, he probably will spend more time on the other ones. Since project complexity is not correlated with its size, your project is at a higher risk of not being paid enough attention to. From the opposite viewpoint, if your loan is for a large-scale project, the developer's smaller-scale projects may divert his attention so that the success of the larger one is affected. If his span of control is diluted by too many projects at once, not only will time and attention be diverted, frequently money will be diverted as well.

Many seasoned loan officers are naive enough to believe that the money they advance always goes directly into the project against which they have lent. Usually this is true. However, cost overruns or delays in a loan advance from another lender to another job can result in the borrower using the money you funded to help support his other project. In essence, he makes a loan from a job that is proceeding satisfactorily to one that is in a stressed state. Later, if the other project continues to deteriorate economically, he may not have enough money to continue with your project. Therefore, not only is the number of concurrent projects important, so is their state of financial health.

It is often difficult to determine a developer's ability to work on several projects at one time. An initial impression of how busy the developer and his key employees are and how many projects he can develop can be valuable in determining whether you should be concerned. If you are, you should try to determine whether any of the developer's projects are experiencing trouble that could lead to a need for higher than ordinary levels of cash or attention. Then you must make a judgment call and decide if the developer and his firm have the resources to handle the proposed project at the current time. If you think they do not, have him explain how he is going to handle the project in light of your concerns.

The Borrower's Organization

Related to but not directly connected to the number of projects a developer is involved with at any one time is the type of organization the principal has built around his business.

Look for a strong team or at least one other strong partner who can take over and fill in for him. He also should delegate authority (and responsibility), particularly in areas in which subordinates have more expertise. In construction, without any exceptions, at the very least he should have a representative on the job every day.

The Development Team

Not only is the in-house capacity of personnel important, so is the capacity of outside professionals. Although outside professionals generally are less critical than the developer himself[4] because they usually can be replaced, it is always expensive to do that and in many cases it can jeopardize the project. Material damage to the project, sometimes physical but always financial, will occur when one key professional is replaced with another.

It is not always easy to assess the developer's team, particularly on smaller projects in which professionals are paid lower fees, are less experienced, and may have less extensive track records. At the least, you should get résumés with references from the architect and the general contractor or construction manager. On larger deals, you should ask for the names and résumés of the major subcontractors. Depending on the job, major subcontractors almost always include those performing electrical, plumbing, masonry, superstructure, and carpentry work.

Architects always have résumés, references, and an easily identifiable history. Do not be impressed by a slick brochure, which today is standard in the architectural world. Look to see whether the architect has been involved in projects similar in type, size, and scale to the one being proposed and whether those projects were in the same jurisdiction as yours is. For example, an architect may impress a developer with projects such as a school building, an innovative gymnasium, a courthouse, and a retail center. He may be clueless, though, about the design and construction of and the amenities associated with a hotel or an office building. Size can translate poorly in different types of structures. In assessing

---

[4] There are circumstances in which the developer will hire a general contractor or construction manager to do virtually all the work. If this is the case, the developer takes on more of an investor role and the general contractor or construction manager takes on the role of a developer. In these cases, the general contractor or construction manager should be looked upon as if he were the developer.

an architect's relevant experience, the type of project is a more important criterion.

It is important for the developer to have some experience in the geographic area in which he is building. It is even more important for the architect. Building codes and most regulations can be looked up readily and incorporated into plans and specifications, but almost always some items are overlooked. An architect who already has experienced mistakes and omissions on similar jobs probably will have learned how to avoid making them on yours. With larger architectural firms, this is usually not a problem because a large firm has the experience and resources to hire local professionals to augment its in-house skills. With smaller firms, though, the architect may never be fully cognizant of local requirements, may be spread too thin on several projects, or may be looking for his next job as soon as he has lined up the one he has with your developer. Since the architect may have to interface regularly with local municipal personnel if there are zoning, regulatory, construction, and legal issues, personal familiarity with local officials and employees can be a tremendous advantage by making a tangible quantifiable difference in gaining approvals in the shortest amount of time and with the least expense.[5]

General Contractor or Construction Manager

When you look at the record of the general contractor or construction manager, not only do you want to become familiar with the types, scale, and locations of projects he has completed, it is essential that at least one reference come from the owner of a prior

---

[5] In New York City and New York State, which are known for complex real estate law, rules, and regulations, sometimes professionals are needed to perform tasks that you may not be aware of but that can play a critical financial role in the success of a development. For instance, in a condominium project, a formal offering plan must be created and reviewed by the state attorney general before condominiums can be offered for sale. The plan must pass the test of "full disclosure," which includes a relatively standardized detailed summary of the project from the architect. An architect without experience in producing the synopsis may delay the developer's ability to market condominium units legally, thereby jeopardizing sales, closings, and the project's overall profitability.

project. Without calling on references, it is almost impossible to prove that a contractor actually worked on a particular job and, if he did, the extent of his involvement. Your institution's inspecting engineer also should be consulted to see if he has any insights or knowledge about the key members of the construction team. Since inspecting engineers review projects for a living, they can be a very good source of team reviews.

Bear in mind that while you are doing your due diligence concerning the project's team members, a competent developer probably has done a more thorough job since the team he assembled works for him and will be reporting directly to him. He has a lot at stake. Quite often the developer has used the general contractor or construction manager on prior projects and has experience with most of the major subcontractors. He therefore knows what level of performance to expect. You are performing your due diligence after he has done his. This should provide you with some level of comfort, particularly when you are reviewing the credentials of an experienced builder. However, there are thousands of tales of incompetence in the construction industry, and so it is always important to do at least some due diligence. With an inexperienced or smaller builder, due diligence can be vital to protect your institution and your career.

Financial Capacity

Financial capacity is very hard to gauge even for a publicly traded company. This became especially apparent in the first few years of the twenty-first century, when officers of many publicly traded companies were fined heavily and sentenced to jail for misrepresenting their employers' financial conditions. If they could get away with deception for that long, imagine how many smaller firms are getting away with it now.

The major obstacles to assessing financial strength are inherent in the tools that are used to gauge it. For instance, balance sheets are static glimpses of a company at a point in time. Income statements can show results from year to year, but fund flows can fluctuate widely, particularly in the real estate industry. Bank deposits can evaporate the day after a loan closing. In real estate, you almost always have to rely on unaudited financial statements; even when prepared by an accountant, they can be more fiction than fact.

When you are evaluating the borrower's financial capacity, some of the most important financial aspects to consider are the following:

- Cash flow
- Liquidity
- Overall leverage
- Timing and impact of individual asset refinancings
- Timing and impact of major lease expirations
- Receivables
- Payables
- Net worth
- Contingent liabilities

Be alert for the following:

- A high net worth but a minimal cash position and limited working capital
- The expected timing and quality of cash flows
- Overstated values of real estate assets
- Liabilities that you know exist but that are not listed
- Extremely high leverage

Although it is important to evaluate the borrower's overall financial strength, you will be concentrating more on his performance against the collateralized property, and so his personal financial strength should be scaled appropriately. Also, since the financial information you receive may not be reliable, you should not depend on the borrower's net worth and cash flow as much as on his equity in the transaction.

Equity

A key element in a partnership agreement or operating agreement is the capital call provision. You want to have some confidence that at least one of the partners can and will put capital into the project if it is needed. In most cases, the principal contributor should be the developer because obtaining funds from passive investors is often difficult. Inactive partners ordinarily are not asked for funds until the last minute. They then require time to digest the usually bad news and also may need time to acquire the cash to meet the call. This time delay can jeopardize a project that already is experiencing financial problems. If you feel that the developer will have a problem contributing additional unplanned equity, you may want to consider demanding more equity while keeping the loan amount the same. The additional equity can be put into the project immediately and you can allocate more to the contingency part of the loan budget so that if necessary you can fund overruns through the loan. This gives you some control early on and can help prevent construction delays. Make sure that you control the contingency funds carefully so that they do not run out before project completion.

Land as Equity

A situation to watch out for involves the borrower using the value of his land as the major or sole part of his equity contribution. It is not uncommon for the borrower to have paid very little for land and to have watched it appreciate over the years. The possession of land, even in excess of the usual loan-to-value ratio, will not guarantee that the borrower will have the cash available to complete the project. It also will not guarantee his strong commitment if things get rough. Many borrowers do not feel as strongly about an investment if it is made with highly appreciated land rather than with hard cash.

Intangible Equity

You also should be alert for partners who do not invest cash or invest money that does not go directly into the project. A common example is a deferred broker fee in exchange for an equity interest in the property. The broker, now a partner, does not invest any real out-of-pocket cash funds in the project. Chances are, he will not be able to or want to invest real cash if there is a capital call.

Another situation to be aware of is one in which the developer is or has been working with the same equity partner on several deals. It would seem that the equity partner would put in the majority of up-front funds and, perhaps more important, make further equity contributions if necessary. However, in this case the developer owes the equity partner money that he cannot pay back. Instead, he gives the partner an equity stake in the project against which you are lending. When you do due diligence, you will receive this equity partner's financial statement, and it may be impressive.

However, the partner, not having been paid on his last deal, will be reluctant to put more money in with the developer on this one. If anything, he is looking to get back his capital from the last deal through the one you are lending on and only then to make some profit. In spite of his net worth and liquidity position, a capital call to continue the project may be met with a long delay or a refusal.

PERSONAL CAPACITY OF THE BORROWER

Understanding the personal characteristics of the developer can help you avoid problems down the road.

Health

If the borrower has all the right attributes, including experience, money, and reputation, but has trouble getting around, talks in long tirades about the past, does not appear to be all there when talked to, takes time to orient himself to questions, and so on, perhaps his health has diminished to a level at which he no longer has the capacity to work on a project that is expected to last two or more years before completion and loan repayment. Although this is not common, it is not altogether unusual. Especially in the real estate industry, in which a high proportion of developers are one- or two-man shops or are staffed largely with family members, there is a tendency to fail to recognize or overlook impairments. Several famous and prolific developers have worked well past the time when others would think it would be prudent for them to step down.

If the borrower's health is a question, it is foolish to make a loan without looking into the capabilities of his successor. If something happens to him, does he have anyone to take over? Even if he appears to be in excellent health, it is comforting to know that there is a team in place that can carry on if needed, at least to keep the project moving ahead until the situation can be assessed and addressed.[6]

---

[6] When Washington Roebling began construction of the Brooklyn Bridge after his father, John Roebling, who designed the bridge, died of tetanus, he became afflicted with the bends, a crippling disease that occurs when a person is subject to a rapid decrease in ambient pressure, which can be brought on by surfacing too quickly from deep water. He no longer was able to walk the construction site but instead supervised the bridge's creation by looking out the window of his New York apartment. Importantly, he had crucial help. His wife, Emily Roebling, after studying engineering and mathematics, took over the physical aspects of the bridge's development.

A caveat here is that it may not be legal to turn down a loan request strictly on the basis of health reasons. After all, you are not a doctor, and it can be charged that you or your institution is committing discrimination. If you feel that the borrower's health is a significant risk in the loan analysis that puts the request in the no-go category, you may want to consider using other arguments for rejecting the loan.

If you suspect that the borrower's health can be an issue but are being pressed to move forward and close on the loan, you should look for other areas to strengthen the credit, perhaps by demanding the addition of a project manager or another team member or requiring additional equity to reduce the loan to value to offset the increased risk. As is noted repeatedly in this book, performance on the part of the developer is crucial to the repayment of the loan. If you feel that the borrower is not healthy enough to complete the project and is not backed by others who are healthy and able to take over for him without disruptions, you should not make the loan.

Character

Establishing an objective baseline of the positive and negative attributes that make up a person's character is difficult. Judging a person's character is by nature a subjective call.

With an existing relationship, you or someone in your institution will have firsthand experience with the borrower. Some general questions—Was the borrower easy to get along with? Did he perform as expected? Was he responsive to requests for information? Did he step up to problems? Did he lead his team?—can be illuminating. If he is a new potential borrower, you probably will not pick up on positive traits as much as on potentially harmful negative ones because it is human nature to take positive traits for granted while magnifying negative ones.

It is uncommon to turn down a loan solely because of a potential borrower's character traits. However, it does happen if economic conditions lead to a lender's market or if the borrower is mismatched with the lending institution.

In a strong market, you and your department may be at or near workload capacity, and it could be detrimental to take on loan transactions that can be complicated by a demanding or difficult borrower. Depending on your lending institution's management and reward policies, you may have achieved or exceeded your financial goals as they were given to you by management for a period (a period is almost always one year). Booking more business, particularly with a borrower who you suspect has a character problem that can be a major distraction, can hurt you when a new period begins and a new set of financial goals is handed down. Future performance goals almost always are set at a level higher than that of previous ones. The need to exceed goals by a wide margin in the current period may preclude you from obtaining them in the next.

In a situation in which the borrower has matched his loan request with the wrong type or size of lending institution but there are mitigating circumstances that make the loan attractive, the deciding factor that leads to turning down his request is often character. If his loan is too big or too small in the context of your institution's "sweet spot" (the range in size which most of the institution's loans fall), rather than accommodating him, if he is perceived to have a character problem, you probably should turn him away. Since he is out of your institution's target area, why fight for him? Save the fight for a borrower with a good deal and a good character.

Character Labeling

Sometimes character labeling helps prepare you for what might be less than a smooth lender-borrower relationship. It is a personal way to form a basis on which to react to the developer initially. Some character traits to look out for in a borrower include the following:

> *Greedy*. He always holds out for the impossible deal. He is typically slow to pay and always seems to be squeezing people. He has a "me, me, me" outlook. It is always about him, and it is always about money. This can be a positive attribute sometimes, but usually his negotiations do not result in a win-win situation. They result in a win-lose situation in which he always must be the winner. Resentment from his business partners and his staff can result in compromised performance on the project with delays caused by his one-sided negotiation tactics. Past deals with business partners, brokers, tradesmen, and so on, can earn him a poor reputation in the industry and can breed ill will.

Cheap. This case is similar to greed, but there is less malice involved or none at all. He just hates to spend money to the point where it becomes counterproductive. Completing a job under budget in every category becomes an obsession. His accounts payable are always stretched to the limit no matter how much liquidity he has. His usual targets are subcontractors and materialmen. Ultimately, this trait causes a decrease in motivation on the part of contractors. As contractors get disgusted and lose interest in the job, poor workmanship, physical problems, and delays in completion can develop in spite of retainage being withheld until the job is finished. This also can translate into major headaches for you and can become a major liability if, for instance, there is a takeout lender in place and delays and corrections result in the borrower not being able to satisfy the takeout lender's requirements.

Difficult. Honor does not have much meaning for a difficult borrower. He will seem to make a deal with you but then will decide to change it unilaterally. He does not mind breaking a relationship. He is usually very institutionally savvy and will go behind your back to senior management if you disagree with him. He will try to get his way with no regard for the people he hurts or puts in jeopardy. He seems to question you and may fight with you on even the most innocuous points. He is unpleasant when things are going well. When things are going poorly, his nature often is counterproductive and increases the risk level of the project.

Egotistical. After negotiating a deal, a self-centered borrower will try to renegotiate at the last minute, exploiting any small advantage, often at the cost of alienating those he is negotiating with and those who work for him. He may be very charitable and charming in his personal life, but in his business life his dominant and chief characteristic is the need not only to win but to win at someone else's expense. These people may be very unpleasant, but they are usually very smart, careful, and deliberate. They use their dogged persistence to wear down their opponents.

Stubborn. This trait usually manifests itself in developers with some experience, but sometimes it shows up in relative neophytes as well. It most likely is tied in with a big ego that is based on past experiences that you undoubtedly will hear about. A stubborn borrower may be unable to understand changing conditions and events and their ramifications. Lack of flexibility and inability to see other points of view can lead a project and loan in the wrong direction for too long. Later, when stubbornness gives way to enlightenment, it may be too late. A stubborn person has trouble seeing compromise as a solution. This can be a liability if the project develops problems.

Unfocused. An unfocused person is most likely a big picture guy and could be a paper tiger, as described earlier in this chapter. He comes across as very enthusiastic, is provocative in conversation, and looks like a natural leader. After your initial meeting, you come away impressed by his energy and confidence. After a short period of time, though, you realize that there is little substance behind his ideas. In fact, some of his ideas may be judged as impractical and even illogical. An unfocused developer needs a strong team, and you need a strong point man who can carry out the duties of the borrower.

Unable to expedite things. This type of person is similar to an unfocused individual. This can be a passive trait that, if not countered, can have compounding effects. The construction process is a sequential one in which work on one aspect of the job cannot begin until another aspect is finished. A passive developer may get too far behind to catch up. As with an unfocused borrower, you should look for a strong team and a good point man.

Contemptuous of authority. This individual is usually a self-made developer who "did it his way." He often started up the company and retains an entrepreneurial bent. You also may see this trait in second-generation developers who are eager to establish a name and want to differentiate themselves from their parents. This trait is ordinarily not a problem because in the development process the developer himself is the figure of authority. However, like any trait that is excessive, it can cause serious problems with municipal agencies, for example. A good approach to these types of people is to start with an overt display of respect. However, remain firm in your dealings with them. Try not to equivocate and conduct yourself so that they respect you.

Secretive. With a secretive borrower, you always tend to feel uncomfortable because you never know if things are going well or poorly. If you push for information, you will be rebuffed or, more likely, put on indefinite hold. After the loan closing, you should make sure to have a good inspecting engineer on hand to monitor the project's status and the borrower's performance closely. Also, check up frequently and ask for documentation, material, and information applicable to the project such as copies of permits, newly signed contracts and leases.

Author's Note

All people are dynamic and evolving, with a variety of complex personality traits. Although personal labels with which to form a framework for interaction can be helpful, they can be very detrimental if a person is characterized wrongly or if a label prevents flexible interaction. Use labeling with caution and be willing to change your mind, especially your first impressions, as a relationship develops.

EXAGGERATION, DECEPTION, AND DISHONESTY

Outright deception on the part of a borrower may not be an every-day occurrence, but it is common enough. As in every industry, there are honest people and dishonest people. Finding out who is what is often not possible until you or your institution is a victim.

Who

Deception and even fraud are more prevalent with small to midsize borrowers. However, as seen in the recent excesses, indict-ments, fines, and convictions of large corporations and their offi-cers, they can occur at any level: the heads of Tyco and Enron for false financial reports and tax evasion; Arthur Andersen for faulty audits and consulting; Merrill Lynch, Credit Suisse, First Boston, and Citibank for analysts hyping securities of companies that were clients of their employers; Christie's and Sotheby's auction houses for fixing sellers' commissions and buyers' premiums; insider trading and securities fraud involving ImClone and Computer Associates International—the list goes on and on. Its effects often go undetected for years, especially in a growing economy, and then, in a rapid series of events, lenders, creditors, and investors find themselves with irreparable losses.

Almost always, deception and misrepresentation do not occur as an act of desperation but as an ongoing business practice. Particularly in real estate, in which equity and debt components start in the millions of dollars, there is a strong incentive to lie and exaggerate to get as much money as possible from investors and lenders with the fewest restrictions.

As was discussed earlier, there are several types of borrowers. Although you may and should react differently to different types, none are necessarily more prone to misrepresentation and deception than others. For instance, an "honest" borrower with cash-flow problems can rationalize fraud as a justifiable act. He may face a choice between moving money around from project to project with unrealistic expectations that he will find funds to bail him out later and laying off workers who rely on him for their livelihood. With the common human trait of denial of responsibility operating in conjunction with misplaced ethics, it may seem a better choice to deceive and misrepresent to a faceless lending institution than to fail friends and employees.

Use Your Judgment

In spite of a prospect's misstatements and exaggerations, you should judge the level, materiality, and impact of any deceit carefully. This includes looking for and guarding against discrepancies in information and actions by the borrower that may or may not be intentional. As was discussed earlier, you are part of an institution that consists of many senior individuals who may have needs and objectives that are surprisingly different from yours at any particular time. Since there are gray areas even in ethics, unless he has made egregious outright lies, a borrower should not be ruled out of a loan summarily.

Circumstances within your institution that lead people to overlook factual discrepancies may include the desire of senior management to have the lending institution be a part of a highly visible and well-perceived real estate project, the desire to create a new business relationship with an entity with a prestigious reputation, and a proposed transaction that can stand on its own on the basis of a relatively good return with low risk. (Remember that the former vice president Al Gore claimed to have invented the

Internet. President George W. Bush claimed that the Iraqi government was in the act of procuring nuclear fuel from Africa. This does not necessarily make them uncreditworthy persons.) However, once you can confirm that an individual is dishonest, do not enter into a relationship, or, if you can unwind an existing one, do so. You should alert senior management immediately and document, at least in your personal file, the dishonest action. One caveat: Do your best to make sure that the borrower was indeed dishonest, not mistaken, naive, or in error. Senior management can take the appropriate action, which can range from ignoring the dishonesty but monitoring the situation very closely to alerting law enforcement officials.

There is usually little you can do with a dishonest individual until it is too late. Simple obligatory background checks may come up clean. Even extensive checks may turn up nothing derogatory because many dishonest people are sophisticated con artists who take elaborate measures to execute their plans. A con artist is a chronic criminal. Staying alert and maintaining a degree of skepticism is perhaps the best protection.

Research the Borrower

Typical places to look for truth stretching begin with the borrower's résumé; this should be a part of any loan submission package. Very often, the borrower will exaggerate the time he was in business; the number, size, and complexity of his projects; his net worth statement; and/or his personal accomplishments. Whether this is outright fraud, an exaggeration, or a "mistake," particularly for a new prospective borrower, is important because it may tell you something about the borrower's character.

Perhaps the best time to look for borrower misrepresentation is right before the loan closes. The borrower will have to satisfy a long list of preclosing requirements, one of which is usually the up-front contribution of equity. The closer it is to the closing, the more the borrower has at stake in making sure that the closing goes through. If for some reason he cannot satisfy the cash requirement of the loan at closing, he may forge documents indicating that he has done so. One of the easiest ways to do this is to produce photocopies of checks and claim that they were sent out to the payees. Then, when the loan closes, the money from the closing goes to cover the checks, which then are sent. The project is immediately cash short and out of balance. The borrower's strategy is to continue to delay payables until he can receive cash from outside sources (e.g., from another project or from investors) or until he can effect cost savings that will bring the project more in line.

Standard Checks

You should always check the borrower's history and claims as thoroughly as is practical. This starts with a credit check on the members of the borrowing entity. The loan administration department should do this as a routine matter. They will use one of the common credit services, such as Experian, Equifax, or TransUnion; the cost is less than $10. Concurrently, if the managing members are not well known, you may want to perform standard background checks. This will tell you if they have any felony charges or convictions, the status of their driving records, where they are legally domiciled, if they have ever declared bankruptcy, if they have outstanding or satisfied judgments against them, if they are currently in litigation, and perhaps some of their employment history.

Check the References

You should always ask for references from each of the major players in the borrowing entity and check at least a couple of them. The key members of the borrowing group should give you several references, including business references, financial references that include at least one lender, and personal references from partners and attorneys.

References from contractors usually give high marks to the borrower; especially if the contractors are small, they may depend on the developer for their existence. This is true even if the contractor has had a poor experience with the developer, for instance if the developer owes the contractor money. The contractor may feel that there is little chance of recovery if the developer does not continue to enter into projects that will create new sources of cash flow. By bad-mouthing the developer, even if he is a "bad guy," the contractor can penalize himself indirectly. The same thing is true of suppliers and other business associates.

Lenders are most probably the best source for unbiased information because they are not employed by and are not dependent on the borrower. A key question to ask is what type of banking relationship the prospective borrower has with the lender. If it is not related to real estate, what is the relationship? If it is not apropos of your lending decision, ask for another bank or lender referral. At the least, he should be able to give you an assessment of the potential borrower in professional objective terms. In addition, positive and negative traits, issues, and experiences unique to the lender-borrower relationship have a higher probability of surfacing.

Review Assets, Liabilities, and Cash Flow

The easy way to get financial information is to have the borrower fill out a standard personal financial statement. It should be presented to the borrower as a routine but necessary form in order to move ahead in the loan underwriting process.[7] You should also ask for a few of the borrower's bank account and brokerage statements to make sure they reflect his claimed net worth and check some of the properties that he claims to own for their value and physical condition.

As in any stage of the loan underwriting and approval process, if you do not understand something or are concerned about information you have uncovered, tactfully bring it to the prospective borrower's attention. Often, even when the information looks bad, the borrower may have an explanation that substantially or completely mitigates its negative affect. A common example is a divorce that disrupted the borrower's cash flows and suddenly and substantially reduced his net worth. Balances and liquidity can be affected negatively by a one-time legal settlement, or significant outlays could have been made in fighting a spurious insurance claim.

References

When you ask a potential borrower for references, you should always specify that at least one should come from a lending institution. As was discussed earlier, there are several reasons to talk to

---

[7] You usually can forget about obtaining audited financial statements because in the real estate industry they seldom exist except from larger players. Even audited statements are not often reliable because they mirror past conditions, not present ones.

a previous or current lender.[8] Since there are many subjective elements in determining the creditworthiness and abilities of a potential borrower, there may not be a better source than a fellow professional in your field.

How to Exchange Information

There is always a small risk in the exchange of information: false information, misconstrued information, assumptions taken as facts, erroneous information, and so forth. However, misinformation rarely is conveyed, and if it is, there are ways to check for veracity, including talking directly with the borrower. In spite of the potential for inaccuracies, the exchange of credit information is appropriate and even necessary in light of the large amounts of money and potential risks involved in real estate lending.

If You Are Inquiring

A request for information usually begins by identifying yourself:

> "Hello, my name is John Jones from QRS Bank [if you have to leave a phone mail message, make sure to include your phone number as well]."

Then indicate the purpose of your call:

> "I'm calling concerning Mr. X, who I believe has a relationship with your firm. He gave me your name and number as a reference."

Then briefly and generally indicate what the potential relationship will be between you and the potential borrower:

> "I'm interested in providing him with a commercial mortgage [or a line of credit, a home loan, etc.]."

Then, if the person did not cut in or respond, give him a chance to:

> "Is this a good time to talk? It'll only take a few minutes."

---

[8] One reason not to talk to a lender is that you believe it is or can be a competitor on the transaction. If this is the case, an inquiry can be very counterproductive.

At this point, the person you are calling has all the basic information he needs to understand the nature of your call. He should be able to respond now or be prepared to respond at a later date. If you left a phone message or he said he would get back to you, the chances are good that he will do that within a day or two because the reference ordinarily wants to respond in order to help the borrower (references often call up the borrower to tell him that you called before responding). Unreferred sources such as financial institutions call back if not because of professional courtesy then because that is the policy of their institutions.

Once you get past your introduction and the purpose of your call, the next step is to ask for what you want.

Here are some potential questions:

How do you know the subject?

How long have you known him?

How long has he been in business?

What is your business relationship with him?

If the inquiry includes a loan, what type is it? What is the collateral?

If it is a loan, is he generally performing as expected under the loan terms (better or worse)?

If it is a loan, is he providing a personal guarantee?

Does he make payments on time?

Would you lend to him again?[9]

If the reference is a bank, does he keep balances at the bank?[10]

Is he smart? Is he easy to get along with?

As in any discussion, answers to questions usually lead to other questions. This often results in new information you would not be aware of without an oral exchange.

---

[9] One thing not to ask about is pricing. It can have antitrust implications and does not sit well with competitors.

[10] Generally, bankers give exact numbers when discussing a loan but not when talking about deposit balances. Instead, they give ranges. A banker may tell you that balances are in the four figures (in thousands), five figures (ten thousands), or eight figures (tens of millions). These numbers are broken down into "low," "moderate," and "high" levels. For instance, "balances in the high seven figures" usually means an amount from $7,000,000 up to $9,999,999; "balances in the low seven figures" means an amount from $1,000,000 up to $4,000,000 or $5,000,000.

If You Are Responding

If you are the one responding to an inquiry, be careful. It always pays to be absolutely professional and circumspect in your responses. When you receive an initial request from a stranger, it is best to consult with your institution's policy manual or senior management. To protect confidentiality, get the inquirer's name and telephone number and the name of the institution from which he is calling. Then tell him that you will call him back. If possible, call the general telephone number of his institution and ask to be connected with him. This will verify that he actually works where he says he does. If it is appropriate, call the person he is asking about to verify that your name was given to him as a reference. When you feel prepared and comfortable, call the inquirer back.[11] Whether you are requesting information or giving it, the general rule is to be as factual as possible. State opinions clearly as opinions and try not to go out of your way to help the inquirer form his; he will form his own.

Financial Statements and Written Material:

It is never a good idea to disclose personal or business financial information because the inquirer should be able to get it on his own. Also, you should never send (including by e-mail) written material since it can compromise confidentiality. If the potential borrower asks you to do that, state that as a matter of policy you cannot send out his confidential information but that he, the borrower, should send it directly to the inquirer instead. If the borrower does not have the information in his possession, you can send it to him and he in turn can send it to the inquirer.[12]

The only exception occurs when you are subpoenaed to submit information and material required by a governmental agency or told to do that by your institution's attorney.

---

[11] Let the borrower beware. He most likely will not be notified that someone is discussing his personal and financial profile.

[12] If you have any doubts about making a response, do not respond until you are sure it is appropriate. An inappropriate response, an untrue response, or the disclosure of confidential information either orally or through the dissemination of material can open you and your institution to potential criminal and civil liability. Of course, it can unjustly and perhaps unwittingly harm many people as well.

Author's Note

Most lending officers get excited about a transaction. They see the outline of a completed project, the numbers make sense, a tour of the property and its surroundings goes well, they like the borrower, and they are impressed with his presentation. All these encouraging factors induce the lending officer to put in a lot of time, effort, and personal sacrifice (weekends and overtime) to work on a transaction. Then, when he gets around to checking out the borrower himself, the lending officer encounters disappointing facts that if he had known them at the start would have killed the deal before he did all that work. He then either downplays or ignores the harmful information so that he can get the deal approved or drops the deal and risks the wrath of the potential borrower. The best thing to do is to try not to let either situation occur. Pay attention to the character and capacity of a potential borrower at the beginning of your analysis.

CHAPTER 5

Appraisals

PROJECT VALUE

In today's world it is practically impossible to make a development loan without first obtaining an appraisal report. The appraisal report, using various universally recognized methods, supplies several expectations of the future value of the project at completion and stabilization. (Stabilization is defined as the point in time when the property is at its expected level of utility or usefulness. In real estate, this usually occurs when the property is leased and occupied in a manner that will continue into the future.)

It then "reconciles" those expected values into a single value.

SELECTING AN APPRAISAL FIRM

Once you decide to consider making a loan, one of your tasks is to choose an appraiser and then determine what the appraiser's assignment will be (examine the property as a rental, a condominium, or a leasehold; indicate which existing structures will remain, which new ones will be built, etc.). It is the lending institution's responsibility to choose and hire the appraisal firm. That cannot be done by the borrower except in unusual circumstances (e.g., the loan is relatively small, it entails very little risk, the lending institution is very familiar with the project from prior experience or the lender is very familiar with the appraisal firm and is confident about its integrity and objectivity).[1]

Choosing a firm should not be difficult because most lending institutions have a short list of approved appraisers. Unless there is an extraordinary reason not to do so, you should choose from that list as a practical matter. Later, if there are any questions about an underevaluation or overevaluation or about the appraiser's methodology, thoroughness, or competency with the implication that the appraiser did not produce an appraisal of acceptable quality and standards, any suspicion directed at you in regard to why you chose that appraiser, however remote and unlikely, can be avoided.[2]

With or without an institutional list of approved appraisers, you should select one that has had extensive experience with properties similar to the one against which you expect to lend. This helps ensure the production of an accurate and comprehensive evaluation. For instance, if you are contemplating a loan secured by a warehouse property and past experience with the approved appraisal firms has been with residential and retail properties, there is a greater likelihood that the evaluation will be significantly in error. For more complex types of properties, such as hotels, it is almost always best to secure the services of an appraisal firm with specialized experience in those particular properties. Many lenders segment the approved appraisal list by specialization.

If senior management allows you to choose only from a small universe of firms, selection of the best appraiser may be compromised. Basing lending decisions on appraisals produced by firms that lack experience in evaluating the subject type of property can

---

[1] If you are employed by a bank or a regulated lender, the appraisal firm must be hired by and must work for the lender, not the borrower. Current regulations go so far as to state that if an appraisal was performed on behalf of a potential borrower (not another lender), not only can it not be used by the lender or assigned to the lender, but a new appraisal of the property from the same appraiser cannot be accepted. In effect, the appraiser is precluded from appraising the particular property for purposes of mortgage financing. The regulation is intended to decrease the possibility that the appraiser will be "induced" by the borrower to estimate a higher value than ordinarily would be estimated.

[2] This issue may be moot in instances in which the lending institution prohibits lending officers from choosing an appraiser that is not on a preapproved list. In those institutions, policy dictates that only senior managers or an in-house appraiser can make changes to the list of approved appraisers.

add unnecessary risk. If you have to work with a very limited list and know of a more qualified appraiser for a particular assignment, you should suggest using that appraiser. However, do not resist senior management's decision to stick with the short list. Your job is to use the appraisal as a tool in making your lending decision. Bearing in mind that an appraisal ultimately is based on an opinion, if you believe it is flawed, you should feel free to draw your own conclusions and use them to justify your lending decision. It is not uncommon for a lender to disagree with an appraisal if he can base the disagreement on good arguments. If the appraised value or projected cash flow comes in higher or lower than you believe is justified and if the loan later is compromised, you are on record with your concerns.

ENGAGING THE APPRAISER

Many lenders do little more than telephone an appraiser and give him an assignment orally. That may be all right for a small "simple" property, but for an appraisal of a to-be-built or improved property, there must be some form of engagement letter. This protects the appraiser and particularly the lender from any misunderstandings by putting what is expected from the appraiser in writing. What follows is a sample engagement letter that, with reasonable modifications to fit an individual assignment, can be used by anyone who contracts an appraiser for a commercial development project.[3]

---

[3] There are some practitioners, particularly those with industry designations such as an MAI, who take exception to the idea of sending a letter to an appraiser similar to the one recommended here. They claim that a "nonprofessional" does not know which appraisal, approaches, methods, and practices are appropriate and why and that the letter appears to "spec out the appraisal" without the writer having the professional background or credentials to do that. These claims may be warranted in certain circumstances. However, those practitioners also claim that no qualified and accredited appraiser will allow a letter similar to the one shown here to compromise his professionalism or dictate his approaches, methods, or practices in producing an appraisal report. The purpose of the letter is to establish a written baseline on which the appraiser and customer (lender) form an understanding to move forward. MAI is an acronym for Member, Appraisal Institute. To receive that designation, a candidate must pass eleven examinations that reflect 380 hours of classroom instruction, pass a two-day examination, hold a four-year undergraduate degree from an accredited institution, and receive credit for 6,000 hours of experience, of which 3,000 hours must be directly related to appraisals.

ABC LENDER

Mr. Appraiser
FGH Appraisal, Inc.
Scottsdale, AZ.

Re: 999 Cider Place, Boston, MA.

Dear Mr. Appraiser:

This letter is to acknowledge and confirm your engagement to appraise the above-noted property. You are to provide a complete appraisal in the form of a self-contained report. If additional information is required and when you need to arrange for an inspection of this property, please contact Mr. Prospective Borrower at 212–234–5678 X 007.

You are requested to estimate the Market Value, as defined in the "Specific Appraisal Requirements for ABC Lender" that is attached to this letter. Your appraisal must analyze and report a reasonable marketing period. Whenever you believe that more than one year is necessary for a fair sale of the property, please state the estimated sales period and annual discount rate applied and explain the methodology supporting your conclusion.

The definitions of Market Value as well as the Specific Real Estate Appraisal requirement for the Lender must be included in the appraisal report.

Your appraisal must include a prior sales history for the property going back at least three years and an analysis of market trends in reference to rising or declining values, which might include, for example, increasing vacancy rates, greater use of rent concessions, or declining sales prices.

Your appraisal report must recite all the instructions above.

You are instructed to appraise the property as of the current date and in its actual current condition as of the date of your inspection.

We, of course, assume that all the appraisers or associates who sign the appraisal report have inspected the properties, the neighborhood, and the comparable data.

As agreed, your fee for this assignment will be $XX,000. The amount of the fee is not dependent on the amount of the values reported, nor is the appraisal agreement based on a requested minimum valuation or a specific valuation for the approval for a loan. Delivery of your completed report will be expected within four weeks.

Your report is intended for the exclusive use of the Lender. The contents of the appraisal, the purpose of the report, and the value estimates should not be revealed to anyone other than the Lender. Please submit two signed copies of each report.

Please call Loan Officer at 123–345–5678 if you need further clarification or assistance.

Very Truly Yours,
Account Manager

SPECIFIC APPRAISAL REQUIREMENTS FOR ABC LENDER

1. This engagement letter and the qualifications of all participating appraisers must be included in the appraisal report.
2. For the purpose of this assignment, the definition of "value" must conform to the attached definition of Market Value. Please specify the estimated marketing time for the subject property.
3. You are instructed to appraise the property in its actual state of development, in other words, "As-Is," as of the effective date of the appraisal, unless otherwise directed.
4. Your assignment is to appraise the property interest described. Specifically, define those rights appraised and detail any encumbrances such as title defects, deed restrictions, etc., that are cited in the title information provided. Your value estimate must reflect the impact, if any, of the above-listed items.
5. Your report is intended for the exclusive use of ABC Lender. Neither the content of the appraisal, purpose of the report, or value estimate should be revealed to anyone other than ABC Lender.
6. Our agreement is based on compliance with these instructions. You should not agree to any changes in these instructions without first contacting the undersigned.
7. Appraisals of income-producing properties with existing leases must contain a tenant-by-tenant lease summary. If the current lease rates and occupancy rates are below historical levels because of a temporary imbalance in supply and demand, the appraisal should use a Discounted Cash Flow Analysis, starting at current lease and occupancy rates and adjusting to "normal" market lease and occupancy rates over the time expected to achieve stabilized lease and occupancy. The underlying assumptions used in valuing assets must be fully supported by the appraisal report.
8. The appraisal must also contain a reasonable detailed Highest and Best Use analysis. You must value the property according to what you determine the Highest and Best Use of the subject to be. If you are instructed to appraise the property after planned improvements,

describe what those improvements will be with any qualifications or limits in your information or understanding. Please support your analysis with absorption data and/or sale activity. If your Highest and Best Use presumes a change in zoning, you must explain the likelihood and time frame of such a zoning change.

9. Your appraisal report should be a narrative report with full supporting documentation for your analysis, adjustments, and conclusions. Specifically, it must comply with the minimum requirements of Standard Rule 2–2, Uniform Standard of Professional Appraisal Practices, adopted by the Appraisal Foundation, and the Code of Ethics of the American Institute of Real Estate Appraisers.

10. You should prepare your appraisal in accordance with Guide Note 8 of the Standards of Professional Practice of the American Institute of Real Estate Appraisers, which states, "The Appraiser should note in the report any condition that is observed during the inspection of the subject or becomes known to the appraiser through the normal research involved in performing the appraisal which would lead the appraiser to believe that hazardous substances may be present in or on the subject property or is at variance with information or descriptions provided by others."

11. Your appraisal must include the current assessed value of the property.

12. Estimates to complete essential repairs and to cure violations should be provided, and the appraiser MUST specify whether those expenses (with a breakdown) have already been considered in estimating the property's appraised value.

13. Your appraisal report must contain a statement indicating whether the subject property is situated in a designated flood hazard area.

14. Your appraisal report must include photographs of the subject property and all comparables, location maps for the subject and comparables, and other pertinent exhibits. For comparables on large tracts of land, plats rather than photographs should be shown.

15. Our agreement anticipates that anyone signing the
     appraisal report will have inspected the subject property,
     neighborhood, and comparable market data. This should
     be confirmed in the appraisal report. Any proposed
     exceptions to this must be indicated to the undersigned
     in advance.

PROJECT FEASIBILITY

The feasibility of the project may appear to be a foregone conclusion for the lender for a new development. This is the case because
by the time a loan proposal comes to you, usually a substantial
amount of work has been performed and time and money have
been spent to move the project forward. The developer should be
very familiar with the area; the property; the logic for the development; the demand and supply in the area; natural, marketplace,
and governmental constraints on developments of the type being
proposed; and the overall profitability of the project. Nonetheless,
there are many instances in which the developer's feasibility
assumptions prove to be wrong. That is why you, the lending
officer, especially if you are unfamiliar with the location of the
project or the type of property being proposed, always should
question the feasibility of a project. Many elements necessary to
form an opinion are in the appraisal report and should enable you
to get a feel for the locale quickly. Then, reading more into it, you
can follow the developer's logic, begin to understand how he came
to the conclusion that his project makes sense, and start to make
your own judgments.

REPORT CONTENT

The appraisal report should contain as many facts and statistics as
relevant and practical to back up its narrative, assumptions, and
conclusions. A broad perspective can be used to establish a framework on which to base and organize initial views. However, you
should be cautious about drawing too much significance from the
macro details and numbers. A large proportion of the data is
included as filler and often has little, if any, relevance for drawing
useful conclusions.

For instance, in dense and economically diverse cities such
as Chicago, Los Angeles, San Francisco, and Montreal, overall

citywide statistics may have no bearing on what neighborhood characteristics and trends are. Citywide data may be very misleading. More often, the micro-level section is the most useful. Local aspects usually will have the strongest direct impact on the feasibility of the completed project.

SUPPLY AND DEMAND

In the appraisal report, you should expect to find a local analysis and data section that covers the future supply of similar properties planned or under construction. This often is obtained when the reporter examines the number, type, and location of applications and accepted building permits. Those facts are in the public record. If there is a large amount of building activity in the area around the site that you contemplate lending against, you want to consider its attractiveness carefully in light of the large influx of supply. Developers (and lenders) often see opportunities in the same area at the same time. When several developers finish similar types of properties at the same time, they may create an imbalance in which future supply exceeds future demand. The result is that compared with a completed project in which absorption of space and income are at a certain level that is immediately measurable today, future revenues have a greater possibility of falling and future absorption times have a greater possibility of increasing.

THE LOAN PRESENTATION

A major portion of a lending officer's job consists of creating written reports and loan presentations.[4] In those presentations, sections are devoted to a description of the area in which the project is situated. Regardless of how useful the appraiser's data and narrative content are in shaping your opinions, it is often very helpful to include this information in your loan write-up. Much of it can be copied into your analysis with only minor changes. This adds depth to the loan presentation, is easy to copy, and arguably has value for those who will have to read it and possibly approve the loan. If nothing else, when used judiciously, these facts look good.

---

[4] Loan presentations are the topic of Chapter 6.

THE CONSERVATIVE BIAS OF APPRAISALS

The appraiser tends toward conservatism for several reasons. The primary one is that in contrast to completed properties, the appraiser faces an additional challenge with real estate improvements that are to be constructed: He must make assumptions about and put a value on something that does not yet exist. Therefore, the appraisal of a development project can be at variance with the proven future value of the completed property. Because of the increased uncertainty of the final value, the appraiser most likely will be conservative.

Another reason for conservatism is that the appraiser knows that his appraisal can be an easy target for criticism when a loan gets in trouble. Since he wants or needs to continue to receive work from your lending institution, knowingly producing conservative values is often his best strategy. If the appraised value is lower than the final actual value of the completed project and interest and principal payments are being made as was forecast, the loan will be paid down as planned and no one will pay much attention to the appraisal. The appraisal will become less and less relevant. However, if the project or the market performs below expectations, which can happen when loans are made on properties in "pioneering" neighborhoods where the market cannot be tested reliably, the property's value at completion can be disappointingly lower than what was expected. Because the appraisal was produced conservatively, the appraised value still may come close to the property's final true value.[5]

Other reasons have to do with satisfying the lending institution's credit review officer. Institutional credit review officers want appraisals that contain estimates that are lower than the actual values. Like the appraiser, the credit officer and those who originally contributed to the loan decision want to be perceived as conservative. Since a problem loan is often the result of an overloan position—lending too much money against the value or the cash flow from the property that is the loan's collateral—when a conservative opinion of value is expressed, the result is a smaller, more conservative loan (loan-to-value ratios and debt service coverage ratios are discussed later in this chapter and in Chapter 16).

---

[5] Many practitioners would disagree that appraisers are conservatively biased. They insist that appraisers simply reflect the realities and attitude of the market. If there is a bias, it is a "market bias," not an appraisers' bias.

The risk of overlending therefore is reduced. Furthermore, with a "bad" loan, even unjustifiable blame can hurt or ruin a career. Therefore, through his control of the loan approval process and possible control of an approved appraisers list, the credit officer will encourage the use of conservative appraisers in spite of their track records of consistently forecasting values below actual values as determined at project completion.

For all these reasons, the appraiser may very well make value estimates that are lower than the developer's and perhaps yours. Unlike the credit officer, whose main function is to review loan presentations, the lending officer's main function is to produce loan presentations. It never hurts a lending officer to carry an aura of conservatism, but he shouldn't practice excessive risk avoidance.

INFLUENCING THE APPRAISAL

Since appraisers want to continue to receive assignments, they generally have a desire to satisfy you, their client. You sometimes can play on that desire and get the appraiser to produce a report with values a bit higher (or lower) than he otherwise would report.[6]

If you want to make sure that the appraiser is not undervaluing the property, you should tactfully indicate your concern up front. Once the appraisal has been written and delivered, it is less likely that it will be revised.[7]

Higher Values

One reason to ask the appraiser to review his report is when you are making a loan that involves a strong relationship that is favored by you and by senior management. Rather than make a credit policy exception against a prescribed loan-to-value or debt service coverage ratio, an appraisal that comes in with a higher but fully justifiable value can obviate an exemption.

---

[6] It is very important to bear in mind that the appraiser and you, the underwriter, have an ethical and practical responsibility to be as objective as possible. Your accountability should never be compromised. Any suggestions to an appraiser should be based on firm beliefs. Note, however, that beliefs are not reality. There is almost always some subjectivity in an appraisal, and a pragmatic appraiser will understand this. Therefore, there is often, though certainly not always, room for value adjustments.

[7] If the appraiser agrees to make modifications after the appraisal has been sent to you, he may want to get the original copy back before he sends you the modified one. Therefore, do not throw out the original until it is safe to do so.

Another reason is to give yourself flexibility. Let's say that a lender who believes he has made a prudent loan on a project that experiences problems during construction finds himself with a loan on an unfinished high-risk project. To complete the project and thus reduce risk, he may be called on by the borrower to fund additional costs. If the true unbiased expected value at completion is well in excess of the suggested increased aggregate loan amount, an increase in the loan amount may be the best course of action. Let's say that the appraised value of a completed property is 154 percent of the existing loan commitment, which equals a 65 percent loan-to-value ratio (the reciprocal value of 154 percent is 65 percent). Assuming that the value in fact can be realized, there is a 35 percent margin of comfort before the value of the property is more than the loan amount.[8]

With a loan based on an appraisal that undervalues a property, there is less room or no margin to increase the loan amount. In the example above, if the appraised value, instead of resulting in a 65 percent loan-to-value (LTV) ratio, is unrealistically conservative, resulting in an 80 percent LTV ratio, there is only a perceived 20 percent margin of comfort before the lender will not be able to recover all of its loaned funds. If the lending institution has a maximum 80 percent LTV policy and the loan is increased, a false "overloan" position is created. Although this is not the case (the "more realistic" LTV ratio is 65 percent), the appraisal can result in many adverse and costly consequences. In this case it may preclude or at least delay the lender from advancing additional funds, which arguably is the best strategy for loan recovery. Worse, it can result in an unfinished project with a less than optimal exit plan.

A third reason to go against a conservative valuation involves market conditions and competition among lending institutions. When more lenders are in the market, competition for business increases. This can reduce market share and profits unless individual lending departments (and you) become more aggressive. To be more competitive, loan officers who receive higher appraised values can make larger loans. Larger loans make the lending

---

[8] Note that this example is simplified to address only the appraised value of the property as it relates to the amount of the loan. In real life, the lender would have to review many more credit and business factors, not the least of which is what the total cost of the project will be and what the breakeven value will be for the developer after the inclusion of the added debt.

institution more competitive and help it increase its business. They also, of course, increase risk.[9]

The Right Value

With respect to the discussion above, most often you, the loan officer, will be looking for an appraised value that is as objective as possible. If there is a bias, you want it to be positive rather than negative. A positive bias gives you more personal control of the credit decision because you almost certainly have the most knowledge about the borrower and the transaction. With a low value, your institution's LTV ratio criteria may prevent you from making a larger loan that you firmly support. With a higher value, you have increased flexibility to make a larger loan. However, if you choose to, you still can make a more "conservative" smaller loan with a lower LTV ratio.[10]

EVALUATING THE APPRAISAL

Books and literature on the appraisal process could fill a good-sized library. Fortunately, a standard narrative appraisal will lay out the objective information, state all the appraiser's assumptions, and explain in detail how they were used to derive all of his

---

[9] Particularly in fiduciary institutions that are regulated fairly closely, becoming less conservative is an attitude that is not necessarily displayed or explicitly articulated by credit officers or senior management. It does exist, however, and as competition increases, after an institutional lag time, it often manifests itself in incremental relaxations and modifications of the institution's credit policy.

[10] Sometimes, a potential borrower will "fit" his hard and soft cost budget into what he thinks the value of the project will be at completion. Subsequently, your appraiser will indicate a value for the completed property that is higher than he anticipated. If you decide to give the borrower the loan he asked for, which will be below your institution's maximum LTV ratio (based on its appraised value), you ordinarily should have an easier time getting approval from senior management. However, after the loan is approved, if the borrower learns that the appraisal came in at a higher value, he may ask you to increase his loan and bolster that request by submitting a higher "revised" hard and soft cost budget. You can counter that pressure by indicating that he should have asked for a higher loan amount to begin with. Also, you can explain that taking the proposal back to senior management for a reapproval will raise red flags about his ability to budget realistically (why didn't he ask for more initially?), his ability to fund cost overruns out of additional equity (if he indicated that he had enough capital to complete the project, why is he asking for more?), and the overall feasibility of the project (was the initial loan approval just a platform to ask for more money?). Tell him that if he presses for a loan increase, he risks a reevaluation that can lead to more loan covenants and restrictions or even a rescission of the original approval.

conclusions. You do not have to be an appraiser to have a good understanding of how the appraiser's opinion of value was formed. You just have to read the appraisal.

Remember that the appraiser's opinion is just that: an opinion. Often, all the work was done by a junior nondesignated appraiser and signed off on by the licensed appraiser after a cursory review. No lending officer can know the quality of an appraisal report until he reviews it.

Although you are responsible for examining the appraisal report, particularly its methodology and thoroughness, you may not be able to verify its factual content easily. This should not be a major concern since a licensed appraiser,[11] under the Uniform Standards of Professional Appraisal Practice Promulgated by the Appraisal Standards Board of the Appraisal Foundation and the Guide Notes to the Standards of Professional Appraisal Practice, will state all the facts as he knows them truthfully and accurately. It is the currency, use, and interpretation of facts that should be and can be evaluated.

THE THREE BASIC EVALUATION METHODS

There are three basic valuation methods: the market approach, the income capitalization approach, and the cost approach.[12] The descriptions below are very short because their purpose is to help the reader get a fundamental understanding of or quickly review the basic appraisal methods. The best way to learn more is to read through a few appraisals cover to cover.

Market Approach (Sales Comparison Approach)

The market approach is the most widely known approach, and if it is used appropriately and correctly, it is the best indicator of value for a construction lender's purposes. It is reliable because it is

---

[11] A licensed appraiser will have an MAI or a similar designation that can be obtained only through a rigorous and lengthy process of education, testing, production, and experience (see footnote 3 in this chapter for further discussion).

[12] In construction lending, the cost approach, which is discussed later in this chapter, is of limited use because the lender's consulting engineer will make a more accurate cost estimate. One component of the cost approach is to estimate the property's value before the commencement of construction.; In "ground up" construction it is the land, assuming the developer has a fee simple interest in it. This valuation should be performed regardless of whether the cost approach is used.

based on verifiable data from arm's-length transactions. Since virtually all real estate transactions are recorded in the municipality where the transferred property is situated, going down to the local office of records will give the appraiser instant access to vital statistics such as how much the property sold for, whether there is a mortgage on the property, when the sale occurred, who the seller was, and who the buyer was.[13] The market approach depends on the existence of a reasonable amount of recent sales in the immediate area of properties similar to the one against which you may lend. These sales are called comparable sales, or comps. The appraiser indicates where each property is on a map, shows a picture of each one with some comments, and with the collected data creates a table called a comparable sales grid. Once the data have been obtained, the rule of substitution is applied: An investor will not pay more for a particular property if he can buy a similarly desirable property for less. To apply the rule, the appraiser adds and subtracts from comps on the grid (adjustments) percentages of the recorded sales price that are based on several factors, such as how long ago the sale occurred, the location of the sold property, and its size, configuration, and condition. In effect, adjustments level the playing field by taking into account differences in fairly similar properties.

The market approach can be very accurate if recent local comps are available (at least three). If they are not, a reliable valuation can be compromised because there probably will be a greater number of adjustments, and that increases subjectivity and the chance of error.

A comparable sales grid for a New York City condominium apartment is shown in Figure 5–1.

Comps are shown in the left-hand column, and adjustments are listed along the top row. The "Total Adjust" column is multiplied by the "Unadjusted Sales Price per SF" column and then either added to or subtracted from the "Unadjusted Sales Price per SF" column to arrive at the figure in the column labeled "Adjusted per SF Sales Price."[14]

---

[13] More and more municipalities are putting this public information online.

[14] Note that in Figure 5–1, comp number 1 has a relatively large percentage adjustment (30 percent) and would not be used in most appraisals. The probable accuracy of the final estimate of value is higher if the comps used are more similar to the property being evaluated (they therefore need less adjustment).

FIGURE 5-1

A Comparable Sales Grid

Comp No.	Unadjusted Sales Price Per SF	Financing Terms	Condition of Sales	Market Conditions	Location	Size	Utility	Condition	Total Adjust	Adjusted Per SF Sale Price
1	$1,103	0%	0%	5%	10%	5%	5%	5%	30%	$1,434
2	$1,625	0%	0%	0%	−5%	0%	−5%	0%	−10%	$1,463
3	$1,226	0%	0%	0%	5%	−5%	5%	5%	10%	$1,349
4	$1,599	0%	0%	0%	−5%	0%	5%	0%	0%	$1,599
5	$1,404	0%	0%	0%	0%	0%	5%	0%	5%	$1,474
6	$1,299	0%	0%	0%	5%	−5%	10%	0%	10%	$1,429
	$1,376.00								ADJUSTED AVG =	$1,458

This sales grid shows typical adjustment categories. Brief elaborations of each one follow:

Financing terms. If some of the comparable sales came with favorable financing terms such as a below-rate mortgage from the seller, that must be considered.

Conditions of sale. If sales are less than arm's-length, such as a sale to a relative, they can include unique conditions that could affect the true price of the property.

Market conditions. As the time between comparative sales increases, there is an increasing likelihood that market conditions were different.

Location. Most appraisals make adjustments for location differences, including the prestige of immediate surroundings, views, traffic, and the availability of transportation.

Size. Depending on the location and type of property, smaller structures may sell for more per square foot or less per square foot than larger structures. Adjustments must be based on market facts for the particular type of property, not on intuition.

Utility. This is a determination of the usefulness of the property. For instance, an unfinished retail basement will be less usable than a finished one.

Condition. Age, obsolescence, and wear affect a property's condition. A newly built property usually will be more valuable than an older one. There are exceptions, though, particularly if an older structure has unique and desirable elements.

In the production of a grid, each sale is compared to the property being appraised. A very important factor here is that the direction of adjustments to some people may be counterintuitive. If a comparable is inferior to the subject property, there is a positive adjustment. Conversely, if a comparable is superior to the subject property, there is a negative adjustment.[15]

Income Capitalization Approach

The income capitalization approach is based on a simple formula:

$$\text{Value} = \frac{\text{Net operating income (NOI)}}{\text{capitalization rate (cap rate)}}$$

In the income capitalization approach, if you know the net income of the property being appraised and determine a cap rate, you can establish its value. The net operating income (NOI) of the property will be provided to the appraiser either by the seller if the property is existing and operating at or near stability or by an estimate from the borrower in a construction project in which the

---

[15] Watch out for erroneous comps. A rather drastic example of how an appraisal, relying on inappropriate comps, came up with highly unrealistic results is as follows: In January 2001, an initial appraisal of a lower Manhattan, New York City, to-be-built retail and residential building used a market and income capitalization approach (discussed later in this chapter) to arrive at a completed value for the retail portion of slightly more than $6 million. This was based on an expected gross rent of *$440,000*. Although the space was marketed aggressively, the borrower was unable to lease the space, and it remained vacant well after its completion in mid–2002. This was due almost entirely to the September 11, 2001, World Trade Center disaster that devastated retail businesses in that area. Unable to lease the property, the borrower asked the lender for a term loan secured solely by the retail space. To make the loan, the lender required a new appraisal. The new appraisal, dated October 2002, valued the retail space at $7,500,000 with an expected net rent of *$725,182*. The appraisal was well written and well documented, with details on several current leases of very similar nearby retail spaces used as comps. The appraiser relied on those comps to determine his estimate of value. Nonetheless, both the banker and the borrower were shocked at the new appraised value, which they considered outrageously high. In fact, the borrower had reduced his asking gross rent to *$225,000* and still was unsuccessful. In spite of that reality, the appraiser vigorously defended his opinion. In making his defense, he pointed to the comps as the source and strength of his estimate of value as well as the appraisal's objectivity. The problem, of course (which the appraiser was not willing to admit to), was that all the retail leases had been signed before September 11, 2001. Since the appraisal was completed only one year after that date, none of the current leases used as comps had expired or, to the appraiser's knowledge, had been renegotiated. Unfortunately for the owner, the appraised value was a far cry from the actual value.

property has not been built.[16] Gross income from tenants, vacancy rates, and operating expenses often must be estimated on existing properties, and always on to-be-constructed projects. Revenue and expense data are obtained from other appraisals, records, and owners of comparable buildings in the area being studied. The appraiser then compares the rents and expenses of each property with the one being appraised, which often is referred to in appraisals as the subject. As in the market approach, the appraiser uses a grid that includes factors such as location, size of space, and amenities.

After determining the NOI, the appraiser tries to determine a cap rate that is based on actual sales and NOI statements of like properties in the immediate area. As was mentioned in the discussion on the market approach, the appraiser, by reviewing municipal records, can find recent sales in the area of similar developed properties. He calculates the cap rate by dividing the NOI by the sales price, as shown in the formula above (NOI/purchase price = cap rate). When the cap rate is derived directly from actual transactions, it is usually very accurate. If the NOI is estimated correctly, barring any unforeseen exogenous factors, the value estimate should be very accurate.

An example of deriving a cap rate from actual sales transactions is as follows:

Property	NOI	Price	Cap Rate (NOI/Price)
Office building 1	$575,000	$6,400,000	.0898
Office building 2	$800,000	$13,600,000	.0588
Office building 3	$277,000	$3,000,000	.0923
Office building 4	$1,021,000	$12,500,000	.0817
Office building 5	$847,000	$12,100,000	.0700

The weighted average NOI/price is 0.0739. This equals the cap rate.

Just as in the market approach, the appraiser indicates where each property is on a map, shows a picture of each property with

---

[16] A stabilized property is defined as one where the property reaches its expected level of usage for a period of time such that the concurrent revenues and expenses show the least variability while accounting for inflation and depreciation.

some comments, and makes a comparable lease grid and then adds and subtracts (adjustments).

There are times when the cap rate must be defined by less direct methods. In appraisals, a widely used and relatively simple method (perhaps too simple) uses as variables the proportionate costs of equity and debt. The equity and debt proportions are assumed to be the universal norm for the type of property being appraised. An example of this method, which is called the mortgage equity yield method, is as follows.

Assumptions

Assumed LTV ratio = 70%
Mortgage   = 70%
Equity   = 30%
                              100%

Competitive mortgage interest rate (rate as determined by rates in the marketplace)	8.75%
Amortization period	25 years
Annual mortgage constant[17]	9.98%
Equity dividend rate (rate of return assumed to be required by an investor)	9.00%

Capital Component	Rate Constant	Ratio	Weighted Rate
Mortgage	0.0998	70%	0.0699
Equity	0.0900	30%	0.0270
Overall capitalization rate			0.0969

Adding the two components of capital—equity and debt—by their respective proportions, the overall cap rate comes to. 0969.

Other means of establishing a cap rate include obtaining one or a range of rates from a table provided by institutions such as Price Waterhouse Coopers or the Real Estate Research Corporation.

---

[17] The mortgage constant can be determined easily by using a financial calculator such as the Hewlett-Packard 12C. Punching in 8.75 for I (interest), 25 for N (number of periods), and 1 for PV (one dollar of present value) and then solving for PMT (annual payment), the answer carried to the fifth decimal place is. 09975. With a handheld calculator, mortgage constants can be calculated in a matter of seconds.

The initial cap rate is adjusted by the appraiser to arrive at a final cap rate. For example, the appraiser may subtract from the initial cap rate a percentage estimate of the property's growth of NOI. He also may add a percentage factor for depreciation and obsolescence. The result is a final adjusted cap rate. The formula is

Final capitalization rate = initial rate – expected growth % + obsolescence and depreciation %

Note that when NOI is divided by a lower cap rate, the value of the property comes out higher; when NOI is divided by a higher cap rate, the value of the property comes out lower. If this is confusing, look at it another way: For the same amount of money, an investor generally has a greater risk of loss on his investment when a property is in an untried pioneer area rather than in a well-established one (or a property that has obsolete components versus a property that is modern, etc.). To counter increases in risk in the pioneer area, the investor will want to receive a greater return for his money. Transposing the formula, the cap rate is a simple percentage measured on a yearly basis for a given investment (value). The investor then takes this cap rate and applies it to either the existing NOI, adjusted if necessary to represent the property at stabilization, or the future expected stabilized NOI, which would be the case for a new construction project.

$$\text{Cap rate} = \frac{\text{NOI}}{\text{value (where value equals investment)}}$$

If an investor requires a return of 10 percent and the NOI of the property he is considering buying is $100,000, to receive at least a 10 percent return, he will make a bid on the property of no more than $1 million:

$$\text{Cap rate} = \frac{\text{NOI}}{\text{investment}} = \frac{\$100,000}{\$1,000,000} = 10\%$$

Discounted Cash Flow Method

A variant of the income approach is the discounted cash flow approach, which takes into consideration the dimension of time. It simply takes a property's stream of periodic (periods are usually measured in years) NOIs, including its residual value, which is the assumed sale of the property at the end of the analysis (or cash flows from sales of condominiums in the discounted cash flow sell-out method). Then, using a discount rate, which is similar to a cap rate, the present value is computed. This present value is the value of the property. The discounted cash flow method is particularly useful when NOI or sales activity is anticipated to exhibit fluctuations.

Cost Approach

The cost approach is based on the assumption that anyone buying a completed property will pay no more than the value of the land or fee interest plus the cost of improvements on it, adjusted by an allowance for depreciation and obsolescence.[18] This simply involves adding to the land value all the hard costs and all the soft costs, including estimates for debt costs and builder's profit. Although the cost approach is helpful, it is often not very precise because of the general methods used to calculate hard costs. Fortunately, the construction lender can rely on the inspecting engineer, who is more qualified and experienced in estimating construction costs than the appraiser is. Furthermore, if you have other project proposals that are similar in type and scope to the one you are focused on, you can make your own top-down estimates. Therefore, in the appraisal of a to-be-developed property, the cost approach ordinarily should not be used as a primary estimate of value. It can, however, provide a very useful check by comparing it with the developer's cost estimation (and the inspecting engineer's). A large discrepancy should be questioned, especially if the appraiser's cost estimate is much higher.[19]

Here is an excerpt from the cost method that was used for a Brooklyn, New York, property. Not surprisingly, of the 149 pages making up the appraisal, only 4 were dedicated to the cost method.

---

[18] In new construction, there is essentially no depreciation or obsolescence, and so there are no adjustments.

[19] Large discrepancies are unusual because the developer usually provides the appraiser with his cost estimates. Those estimates are incorporated into the appraisal. Differences almost always are reconciled through discussions between the appraiser and the developer. If the appraiser's estimate is significantly higher, it may be an indication that the developer purposely has lowballed cost estimates to make the project look more profitable or has made unrealistic assumptions that call into question his expertise and ability, or that the appraiser's estimates, which are not as refined, are too high.

123 ABC STREET

Calculator Cost Method

Occupancy		Apartment
Building		
Building class		"B"
Exterior wall		Concrete
Number of stories		Four-story building
Condition		New
	SF	$s
Base cost per square foot (above-grade area)		$140.15
Section 11, Page 15	42,658	$5,978,519
Multistory building adjustment at 0.5% per story		$29,893
Over the third floor 0.5%		
Basement area cost per square foot	10,921	$52.87
Section 11, Page 17		$577,393
Subtotal		$6,585,805
Current cost multiplier—Section 99, page 3		1.05
Local multiplier—Section 99, page 9		1.37
Total replacement cost via calculator cost method		$9,473,680
Per square foot of gross building area	53,579	$176.82

The replacement cost estimate is based on data compiled by Marshall Valuation Service.[20] The costs include labor, materials, supervision, contractor's profit and overhead, architect's plans and specifications, sales taxes, insurance, normal site preparation, and normal interim interest on building funds during construction. Added to the replacement cost figure are amounts associated with buying and assembling the land or any improvement to the land and an estimate of entrepreneurial profit.

Total replacement cost (from above)	$9,473,680
Site improvements (demo of existing structure $9.00 per SF)	$137,000
Development cost prior to land value and entrepreneurial profit	$9,610,680
Entrepreneurial profit at 15%	$1,441,600
Land value	$5,120,000
Total value by cost approach (rounded)	$16,200,000
In this example of the cost approach, the value of the property comes to	$16,200,000.

---

[20] Valuation services such as the Marshall Valuation Service can be a very valuable tool in estimating costs with a top-down approach not only by the appraiser but on occasion by the developer. Often, when there are several bidders for a developable property, there is little or no time to perform more than a rudimentary cost analysis. A valuation service can give a prospective purchaser a handle on how much it will cost to construct the type of building he envisions on the property.

Author's Note

An appraisal report makes assumptions and gives opinions that are based on facts and data that are revealed clearly for the reader's review. It is important never to believe that the appraisal is absolutely objective and infallible. You have an opportunity to form your own opinions.

A common assumption is that lenders, especially those who have been in the business for many years, look only at the summary page of an appraisal. This assumption is understandable among those who have worked in lending environments where appraisal conclusions, no matter how well or badly formulated, are taken as absolute. Fortunately, those conditions are not the norm. You can always learn something new from an appraisal. Quite often you will refer to appraisals in the future for their technique as well as their market intelligence. They are an essential, valuable, and useful source for the lender and the developer.[21]

---

[21] For regulated lenders, they are an absolute requirement.

CHAPTER 6

The Loan Presentation

THE INITIAL PRESENTATION

In almost every lending institution that makes development loans, the first presentation you will make will be an informal conversational one with your supervising manager. Its purpose is to get an initial feel for the desirability of making the loan. At the start, the conversation can be fairly general since the objective is to determine whether it is worthwhile to continue to work on a proposal that could consume a considerable amount of your time and energy.

Depending on his personality and background, the person you report to can exhibit a wide level of expectations about your preparedness even when discussing a potential credit on an informal basis. Since you want to ascertain his interest in the potential transaction as efficiently and effectively as possible, it is important to stress that you want to discuss the potential credit on a preliminary informal basis. However, you must have a grasp of the specific issues, which should include the identity of and some background on the borrower(s); the type of project proposed, its square footage or number of units, and so on; the hard and soft cost estimates; the time from loan inception to completion; the expected profits for the developer; and the capital structure of the proposal, which can simply be the loan amount and the loan-to-value (LTV) ratio.

The level of seniority to initially discuss prospects with depends on the institution's management structure. In some institutions there are weekly meetings in which all new proposals are discussed among the personnel of a real estate unit, with the head of the unit presiding. Everyone at the meeting is free to ask questions and offer suggestions. The unit head then indicates whether he feels the lending officer should proceed or move on to the next proposal. In other institutions, the lending officer pays a visit to the appropriate senior manager or managers for a first round of opinions and suggestions. Whatever the case may be, except for guidance on pricing and basic loan structure, you should not expect too much from these meetings. Getting a go-ahead to proceed is encouraging, but it is far from a formal loan approval. Often, an initial go-ahead can turn into senior management memory loss and denial.

Because he is on the front lines, the lending officer is always performing an initial analysis of potential transactions that will never come to fruition. He is the one who must do all the up-front presentation work, often without institutional feedback. Therefore, if possible, as the lending officer, you should make sure that your immediate senior manager is aware of what you are working on. You should be aware of what his concerns are so that you can stay on track and not waste time.[1] If resistance to the loan proposal increases, the proposal can be worked on to address the resistance or can be abandoned. Either way, you will work more efficiently and effectively and perhaps will gain some esteem when the presentation is made or submitted because after consulting with others, you covered points that you normally would not have considered.[2]

---

[1] Depending on your institution's management climate and your manager's personality, it may not be wise to speak with anyone above his level without talking to him first. With certain managers, that may come across as "double jumping" over his authority.

[2] In one large lending institution, there was a group of real estate lenders who had not gotten a loan approved in several months, not because good deals were not available but because the institution was aggressively whittling down its real estate loan portfolio, which was thought to be out of balance with the rest of the institution's loan assets. In spite of this poor track record of loan approvals, the management of the group did not discourage lending officers from aggressively seeking out new business and making loan presentations. Although almost all the presentations were doomed from the start, the activity was a way to ensure that the department would survive. All the analysis and activity could be presented by the head of the real estate group to senior management in a way that showed high group productivity. In the meantime, the existing portfolio enabled the department to continue to show a positive net operating income. Members of the group hoped to last long enough to retire, find another job within or outside the institution, or wait for personnel and philosophy shifts that would open up opportunities to generate new real estate business. The loan proposal became, in affect, a matter of survival.

OVERSELLING

In almost all institutional situations, the worst course of action is to oversell a proposal because questions about your objectivity can arise. Later, if the loan is made and fails to perform as projected, your integrity can be questioned. Depending on the severity of the problem, the memory and perception by others of how you promoted a loan proposal several months or years earlier can contribute to the loss of your job. You should try to be as objective and professional as possible.

COMMUNICATIONS WITH THE PROSPECTIVE BORROWER

An ever-present danger during the approval process involves your relationship with the prospective borrower. *Never* indicate to a potential borrower that his loan will be or has been approved before it actually is. Unless you are in a senior position, you do not have the power or authority to give a final loan approval. If you receive an oral approval, there is always a chance it will be revoked. Alternatively, the loan may be approved later, but the amount and/or structure will be much different from what you understood it to be.

If you erroneously indicate to the prospect that his loan was or will be approved and his loan proposal subsequently is turned down or changed, you can face unpleasant repercussions. At the very least you will bear the brunt of his justified disappointment and perhaps lose his respect. He may personalize the experience and talk about you negatively in the industry. Worse, he may complain to your institution that you made a commitment to him. Worst of all, he may claim that a loan commitment was made and sue your institution for damages.

Although real estate operates under the statute of frauds,[3] potential borrowers have won cases in court in which a loan officer said that the prospect's loan was approved when in fact it was not. To avoid any of these possibilities, when you are talking to a prospective borrower about the loan approval process and your progress, be as objective as you can.

---

[3] The statute of frauds essentially states that oral contracts in real estate are not binding.

BEGINNING THE UNDERWRITING PROCESS

If there is a high probability that a loan will be approved, you may want to begin writing the loan presentation before you have all the necessary information.[4] If the borrower provided you with a good loan proposal, you should have enough information to write up significant portions of the presentation. If you have some or most of it completed, you can be more confident about being on top of the borrower's deadline. An initial write-up can save you considerable time pressure, frustration, and pain later.[5]

A MOVING TARGET

Being able to hit a moving target is a common underwriting challenge. For instance, you may have to write a presentation before you receive an appraisal, a consulting engineer's report, or an environmental report. If the value of the completed property is not what you anticipated it to be, the engineer's report indicates that the hard cost budget is under or over what the borrower states it will be, or the environmental report indicates significant problems, you may have to rework the presentation. This is a normal risk of the underwriting process and usually results in only minor changes. However, if facts or events that you consider material change, you will have no choice but to rework your presentation or abandon it. Most often, if you receive new information that is substantially detrimental, abandoning a potential transaction, which is especially painful when you have done a lot of work on it, is by far the best course of action. If it is discovered later that you have omitted something major in the write-up, you may need to look for another job.

---

[4] If the borrower does not own the property at the time he makes a loan request, unless there is good reason to make an exception, do not start the formal loan approval process until you are certain he has a sales contract. Otherwise, you may do a lot of work and spend a lot of political capital getting the loan approved only to have the borrower walk away because he could not tie up the property for purchase.

[5] The preliminary write-up usually includes information on the area where the project is located, the borrower's composition, his experience and the experience of his development team, the managing member's financial status, specific known loan terms, and data that will not or are not likely to change.

THE WRITTEN PRESENTATION FORMAT

Generally, every lending institution has its own loan presentation format.

In regard to the underwriting, a defined presentation format imposes a discipline that provides a higher level of credit protection for the lending institution. If a lending officer or a senior reviewer has a positive bias toward making a loan, it may be tempting to leave out negative information or do a less than thorough credit analysis. The lending institution's imposition of a defined format with the objective of producing an all-inclusive loan presentation makes it harder to slant the presentation through omissions. This arguably reduces the number of avoidable bad credit decisions.

One reason for this is that senior credit officers may have to review many presentations in a day, or a loan committee may be presented with many proposals at one meeting. For efficiency, those concerned must know where relevant information is located so that they can find it quickly.

The Cover Page

In almost all lending institutions, a loan presentation usually starts with a cover page (sometimes two or three pages in length) that gives a standardized summary of the proposed transaction. A typical cover page from a commercial bank is shown in Figure 6–1.

COMMERCIAL REAL ESTATE
CREDIT APPROVAL REQUEST

		Date Prepared: Sept. 29, 200	New Request for Credit? ☒ Yes ☐ No

New	X	Modification	Was CRA a Consideration?
Review		Renewal	YES NO ☒
Restructure		Increase	If yes, attach explanation
Extension		Reduction	LINE OF BUSINESS: Real Estate Development & Mgt.
Waiver		Next Review 9/0	RELATIONSHIP SINCE: New
Last Review NA			

Date Request Submitted: 6/24/05		
TAX ID #/SOCIAL SECURITY # 12-2345678		
PHONE #: 123-137-2222	REFER. SOURCE: BBB Brokerage	
NAICS CODE: 531390	CENSUS TRACT: 0000.00	

BORROWER NAME Super Realty, LLC	IN BUSINESS SINCE: Approx. 20 Years
	ACCOUNT OFFICER: James Underwriter / OFFICER #: 239

LEGAL ADDRESS	Anywhere Street 100 North First Avenue New York, NY, 10000	RELATIONSHIP YIELD:
		ACTUAL: NA / PROJECTED: 6.42%

SMSA 35644	UNIT #: 88	
UNIT NAME: COMMERCIAL REAL ESTATE		

Legal Status

S Corp ☐	Partnrshp ☐	NFP ☐
C Corp ☐	LLC / P ☒	Trust ☐
Sole P ☐	PC/ PLLC ☐	Municipality ☐
		Other ☐

OWNERSHIP (with %):
Konan, LLC – RobertJones   – 20%
IWN Group, LLC- Michael Kone   – 7%
IWN Group, LLC – James Lorne – 73%

NAME/BRANCH #:   TBD

1) Loan# New	Type	Original	Recommended	Current	Maturity	
Rating: 3	Facility	Amount	Amount	Outstanding	Current	Proposed
FDIC: 30-300	Construction Loan	$0	$16,100,000	$0		30 months

Terms/Repayment: 30 months, interest only. Repayment from the sale of 31 residential condominium units, one professional unit and 31 parking spaces.
Comments:

2) Loan#	Type	Original	Recommended	Current	Maturity	
Rating:	Facility	Amount	Amount	Outstanding	Current	Proposed
FDIC:						

Terms/Repayment:

Comments:

3) Loan#	Type	Original	Recommended	Current	Maturity	
Rating:	Facility	Amount	Amount	Outstanding	Current	Proposed
FDIC:						

Terms/Repayment:

Comments:

Use of Proceeds and Sources of Repayment	PRICING	DDA A/C TBO

Use: Towards the construction of a new 88,560 gross sf condominium building containing 31 residential units, one community use unit, and 31 garage parking spaces.
SOR: Sale of apartments, community unit and parking spaces.
Bank should be paid down upon the sale of 21 residential units (67% of total).

PRICING: P + 1%

DDA A/C   TBO
☒ Debit A/C   ☐ Other

SUBORDINATIONS: ☒ None   ☐ Std. Form   ☐ Other Form

☒ Prime
☐ Other _____

PAYMENT GUARANTEES
☒ Std. Form   ☐ Other Form   ☐ Secured
☐ None   ☐ Limited (Specify)
Full joint and several personal guarantees of repayment.

☒ Floating   ☐ Fixed   ☐ Monthly
☐ Quarterly
☐ Other:

NAME	PFS DATE	LA	ONW	FICO
RobertJones	9/0	$180M	$2.2MM	749
Michael Kone	9/0	$51M	$4.0MM	765
James Lorne	9/0	$328M	$25.7MM	728

Fees: ☐ None

☒ Facility   1.0 %   ☐ Ext. %   ☐ In Advance
☐ Monthly   ☐ Unused ___ %   ☐ In Arrears
☐ Quarterly   ☐ Other:
☐ Other:

COLLATERAL: ☐ Unsecured   ☒ Secured (specify)

First mortgage on 3000 Elm Avenue, Williamsburg, NY upon which will be built a twelve story condominium building containing 31 apartments, one community facility, and 31 garage spaces.

Assignment of all contracts, deposits, etc.

TOTAL BORROWER EXPOSURE		
PRESENT LIMITS	NEW LIMITS	CURRENT OUSTANDING
$0	$16,100,000	$0

Appraised Value: $ TBD   Effective Date:
Appraisal Firm: The Appraiser Group, Inc.

BORROWER: Super Realty LLC		DATE: September 29, 200			PAGE 2

STANDARD ECR ☒
PREFERRED ECR ☐   DEPOSIT BOOK BALANCES (000'S OMITTED)

	DDA YEAR TO DATE	DDA LAST YEAR	MMA YEAR TO DATE	MMA LAST YEAR	C/D'S	OTHER
BORROWER	$0	0				
GUARANTOR(S)						
AFFILIATED						
TOTAL	$0					

CURRENT MONTH TOTALS: (Sept.)	DDA: $0	MMA:

SUPPORTING BALANCE REQUIREMENTS:
All operating accounts related to property.
All condominium contract deposits.

OTHER BANK & CREDITOR LINES:
None

OTHER NFB BANK SERVICE REQUIREMENTS:
None

OTHER NFB SERVICES PROVIDED:
None

CONDITIONS PRECEDENT TO FUNDING:
Borrower/guarantor OFAC Complete: Yes
Site Inspection Completed: (Y/N) Yes   Date: 07/06/0
Satisfactory Appraisal indicating L/V < = 75%
Satisfactory Phase I environmental report.
Subject to cost review and inspection by engineering consultant.
$300M to be placed in an ABC restricted account prior to closing to be used for interest payments.

KEY FINANCIAL, AFFIRM/NEGATIVE COVENANTS
Construction loan subject to ABC's standard BLA.
Advances based on work in place subject to review by engineering consultant.
10% retainage on advances.
Condominium units released upon the greater of 90% of net sales proceeds or 125% of loan amount apportioned to each unit.
Parking spaces and community space will be released upon the receipt of 90% of net sales proceeds.
Annually: Signed copy of principals' personal tax returns and financial statements.

ACCOUNTANT / FIRM: Tried and True & Assoc.

TYPE OF STATEMENT: ☐ AUDIT ☐ REVIEW ☐ COMPILE ☐ TAX RETURN ☒ INTERNAL ☐ RENT ROLL

AUDITED STATEMENT REQUIRED: ☐ YES ☒ NO

STATEMENT FOR PERIOD ENDING: FISCAL: INTERIM:
RENT ROLL: TAX RETURN:

(000)	Rental Fallback		
GROSS ANNUAL INC.	$1,491		
VACANCY/LOSS	5%		
EFF. GROSS INC.	$1,416		
OPER. EXPENSES	$212		
NET OPER. INC.	$1,204		
DSCR	0.96X		
PROPERTY TAXES	$15 inc tax abate		

EXCEPTIONS TO POLICY   IF NONE, STATE SO
Rental Fallback will not support 1.25 DSCR
Rental Fallback will not support 75% LTV

TOTAL GROUP EXPOSURE

PRESENT LIMITS	NEW LIMITS	CURRENT OUTSTANDING
$0	$16,100,000	$0

IS THE BANK NAMED LOSS PAYEE ON:

FIRE/THEFT/LIABILITY? ☐ N/A ☒ YES ☐ NO ☐ WAIVE

FLOOD INSURANCE? ☒ N/A ☐ YES

KEY MAN LIFE? ☒ N/A ☐ YES ☐ NO ☐ WAIVE
IF YES $

BUSINESS INTER. INS. ☐ N/A ☒ YES ☐ NO ☐ WAIVE

OFFICER DATE:	OFFICER DATE:
SIGNATURE	SIGNATURE
OFFICER: DATE:	OFFICER DATE:
SIGNATURE	SIGNATURE
DATE	OFFICER DATE:
	SIGNATURE
	OFFICER DATE:
	SIGNATURE

The cover page is useful not only for those who will review and approve the loan but also for those who will need to record and administer the loan at and after closing. It provides many of the salient facts, loan terms, pricing, risk rating, institutional codes, and descriptions that have corresponding fields in the lender's management information system. It is also a rapid way for anyone to get a good sense of the transaction.

The Credit Memorandum

The credit memorandum follows the cover page and usually begins with an executive summary. Typical elements of an executive summary include the amount and purpose of the loan—what the funds will be used for; a description of the transaction (e.g., first mortgage secured by property XYZ); a brief project/transaction analysis (usually basic LTV and debt service coverage ratios); the rate, fee, term, and so on, of the proposed transactions; the expected profitability; the names of the borrowers/guarantors, including their backgrounds and capacity; a risk assessment (a listing of major risks); and a summary/recommendation.[6]

The body of the credit memorandum follows the executive summary. Depending on your institution's culture and requirements, its length can be a few pages, say, four or five, or there may be no stated limit. Its purpose is to provide all the relevant data, facts, analysis, assessments, conclusions, and recommendations in an objective manner so that the reader can form his own opinion. The credit memorandum can be viewed as a term paper. A good presentation should be complete and concise. It is almost always written in narrative form with standard sections prescribed by the lending institution.

A credit memorandum will include the proposed terms and conditions of the loan facility; a discussion of the existing property and proposed improvements; its feasibility and market; the financial and professional status, depth, capacity, and relationship of the developer and his team; any environmental issues, jurisdictional

---

[6] Some executive summaries may not include all the elements listed here since they are in the cover sheet or immediately follow the executive summary. The basic thrust of the summary is to introduce and acquaint the reader with the pertinent facts of the proposal. Where applicable, they will be expanded in the body of the presentation.

regulations, or constraints that must be addressed or complied with; the deal structure, including the terms of the proposed loan; a project budget, a comprehensive financial review, and possibly including financial forecasts with a variance analysis for expected and worst cases; an evaluation of the property with or without an appraisal report;[7] a discussion of the borrower's marketing strategy and a discussion of existing and to-be-signed leases from identified tenants; a summary/conclusion section; and exhibits such as pictures, site plans, documents, and detailed budgets.

Depending on the complexity of the transaction and the size and type of real estate being underwritten, credit summaries and memorandums can vary materially from one another even when they are produced within the same institution and lending department (e.g., the construction of a substantially preleased 20,000-square-foot office building should be relatively more simple to analyze than that of a 200,000-square-foot hotel).[8]

PRESENTATION PLAGIARISM

There are lending officers who, in their desire to break out and diffe-rentiate themselves, put a great deal of effort into trying to be creative in their written presentations. Although they may get some satisfaction from this, if their objective is to advance in the organization, they probably are not going about it in the best way. In lending, innovation almost always loses to productivity. If you are respon-sible for attracting new business, writing unnecessarily long or innovative reports will keep you away from your primary responsibility: calling on prospects. If your job function is oriented towards credit analysis, the more deals you can analyze in a succinct and complete manner, the more you will accomplish your productivity objectives and the more time you will have to do other things.

In many industries and professional endeavors, copying or plagiarizing written material is at best frowned on and at worst is illegal. In the lending industry, in contrast, it is a useful and

---

[7] If an appraisal has not been completed, a condition of the loan approval, or at least the loan amount, is the receipt of the appraisal that supports the conclusions of the credit memorandum.

[8] Two samples of credit memoranda appear at the end of this chapter.

acceptable tool. You should rely on the works of others whenever possible. This can save you a large amount of time. You also can learn a lot from studying colleagues' and third parties' material.

What to Copy

As was mentioned in Chapter 5, you can save time by copying sections from appraisal reports. In fact, in most cases the information you will be copying was copied by the appraiser from an industrywide source or from another analyst in the appraiser's shop. You must be careful to use only information that is relevant. The use of too much material may work against you. It can give the reader the impression that your presentation is too unfocused or not well thought out or that material has been included to impress the reader by its volume, not its content.

Other sections may be copied from the potential borrower, his consultant, or the broker submitting the loan proposal. They often create very good income statements, cash flows, sources and uses statements, and financial projections on an Excel spreadsheet or on a real estate–specific program such as Argus. You should try to get their work by e-mail or directly from a disk. Then, instead of spending time re-creating spreadsheets and/or inputting data, you can use the material and modify it to suit your presentation and analysis.

THE POWER OF RELATIONSHIPS

Many experienced real estate lenders listen with interest and a bit of skepticism when a borrower boasts that because of his close personal relationship with a lender, the lender will approve his loan requests on the basis of little more than a word-of-mouth application. Because of a lack of proper institutional controls or theconscious relaxation of those controls for "choice" powerful customers, their claims sometimes have credibility. This is unfortunate, particularly in the construction field, where borrower performance is essential for success and risks are higher than they are in most other areas of lending.

The word *relationship* is used loosely and most often adds very little to the lending analysis and to the likelihood of an ultimate loan approval. A relationship, like a good résumé, may get the prospective borrower in the door but ordinarily will not be much help in getting a better deal or a loan approval that embodies above-average credit risk. [9]

Except in unusual situations, as a general rule, the relationship aspect of a borrower with your financial institution should not be a very important factor in fashioning the loan facility and, of course, in deciding whether to extend a loan. If the loan sours and you are called on to explain why or specify why the loan was made in the first place, the fact that the loan was made because of a strong relationship between the borrower and the lender will not go over well. If internal politicians are looking for someone to blame, the relationship aspect of a loan facility is often the weakest defense. Do not be a scapegoat. Analyze the transaction by using sound lending principles. Put the relationship where it belongs, as a necessary part of your presentation but a noncritical part of your credit decision.

PRESENTATION PRESSURE

In the early 1990s, institutions that made commercial real estate loans were devastated by poor construction lending practices. Deregulation of the savings and loan industry in conjunction with relatively high interest rates on deposits set by supply and demand

---

[9] Despite the fact that relationships usually have little force in a credit approval, there are exceptions. For example, a small commercial bank solely owned by an offshore bank that is the state bank of a foreign country has strong ties to its local ethnic community that sometimes force it to ignore risk and return considerations for political ones, both domestic and offshore. The bank makes several construction loans to churches that practice the state religion of the foreign country. The churches usually request several million dollars to expand, modernize, and enhance existing church property or to build entirely new church structures near the existing ones. The primary concern of the lending institution is, of course, how the loan will be paid back. Almost always, some, if not most, of the money projected for repayment will come from congregational pledges. Since pledges are nothing more than unenforceable promises by members of the congregation, they can be ephemeral when it comes time for actual fulfillment. If the stock market goes down, pledges may not materialize into dollars. Therefore, the risk of nonrepayment is very high.

In light of the significant negative publicity (and concurrent loss of business) a lender may experience when it forecloses on a church or forces it into bankruptcy, the lender may turn quickly from a good guy into a very bad guy. Even if the lender takes possession of the church, which is unlikely, its specific purpose and intended use usually do not give it much commercial value. There is essentially no other way out of the loan than a collective promise to repay. In spite of these risks, loans to churches (of a certain denomination) by this bank are made routinely. The real estate department acts more as a clearinghouse and rubber stamp than as a true critical lender.

market conditions led to intense pressure for lenders to make larger and higher-risk loans to cover deposit costs and expenses. The result was a deterioration in credit analysis and procedures that carried through from the initial application review to final approval and loan funding. Unfortunately, the opportunity to implement poor practices will always be manifest in certain lending institutions, especially those which have subgoals that are not aligned with making profits and reducing risks and losses (e.g., making cons-truction loans to churches of a particular denomination). This also can be pervasive in institutions in which the attempt to gain market share, the desire to attract star borrowers, and the power of senior management's personal friendships are very strong forces.

When these conditions exist, you can come under considerable pressure to make a loan that is based on data with significant omissions or even errors. Senior management, with its own motivations, often will suggest several supposedly compelling arguments for making the loan. It will be your job to produce a presentation with enough fluff that it will look sufficiently good to gain approval.

In situations like these, you have little choice but to recommend the loan facility. Unfortunately, aside from the increased risk to the lending institution, you are putting yourself at considerable career risk because if and when the loan runs into trouble, the ultimate source document will be the loan presentation. Auditors and even the managers who initially approved the loan facility will be critical of your work because, taken out of the context in which it was under-written, it is clearly not up to stated institutional standards. Especially if, from the time the loan was approved to the time it draws attention, new senior management has been put in place, you may find yourself in a precarious situation that can have serious career consequences.

LOAN FILES

You should always keep two files. The first is a working file, an unofficial file that can be used to keep documents, letters, notes, and memorandums for quick reference. The other is the "official" loan file that will be seen by other bank personnel and outside auditors.[10]

---

[10] You should always be careful with the unofficial file—your personal one—because in many lending institutions keeping one is against policy. Although this happens only rarely, you can be subpoenaed to deliver all documents concerning a loan. It is a crime to lose, shred, or not turn over any documents in your possession. Even if there is embarrassing material, unless you have committed fraud (which is beyond the scope of this book), you should turn over everything.

The Official File

As you progress through the approval process, you will be building up a loan file that will consist of elements such as an appraisal report, an environmental report, photos, maps, budgets, credit reports, background checks, and correspondence with the prospect. While you are building the file, you should be careful to limit its content to professional and objective material. Personal notes and memos have no place in a credit file unless they are part of your credit analysis or are factual accounts of events and interactions. This is important because if there are disagreements or charges are brought by the borrower against you or your institution (e.g., claims of discrimination, libel or slanderous statements, or meddling in the borrower's operating business), the file can be used against you. Once this material is in a file, it may be difficult to cull it, and during reviews by internal or external auditors or senior management, items that should not be there could reflect poorly on your professionalism.

The Unofficial File

If you are pressured into making a loan that you think is not a good one, one of your best defenses is to monitor the loan carefully and create and file written reports as to its status. Your first file document should be a brief summary of the additional concerns that were discussed through the approval process and how they were addressed. You should write the summary in a professional and objective manner and, if you can, insert it in the official loan file. If the loan runs into problems, you have documented the file appropriately.

If you cannot insert summaries and file memorandums because of the policy of your institution, you should still write them but keep them in an unofficial file. If the loan performs as planned, you have lost nothing by your diligence. If it develops problems, you have another source of review. If blame becomes an issue, you can defend yourself more effectively by reviewing the notes and memorandums in your unofficial file to refresh and sharpen your recollections.

TWO LOAN PRESENTATIONS

To get a better idea of the thought, effort, and time needed to produce a loan presentation, especially if you have limited or no access to one,[11] two examples, each written by a different author and edited for clarity, are included in this chapter.

Letoha Hotel

The Letoha Hotel project involves the all-new construction of a hotel with office space. It took the loan officer three weeks to write the presentation from start to finish, which is more or less typical. The time frame is primarily a function of the underwriter's workload: his writing speed and ability; the time it takes him to discover the need for and ask for additional information; the time it takes the borrower to supply the necessary information and for the underwriter to incorporate it in his write-up; and the overall complexity of the transaction.

Letoha Associates, LLC Presentation

CREDIT MEMORANDUM[12]

Letoha Associates, LLC.

Executive Summary

Background:

On October 25, Letoha Street Associates, LLC **("Letoha"),** a single-purpose entity, purchased a 22,223-SF [square foot] site on the southwest corner of 68th Street and Madison Avenue. At sale, the property housed a single-story parking garage. It has since been demolished and removed along with all environmental hazards (which will be reconfirmed by a QRS consultant before any advance of Bank funds). The site has been divided into two lots: The interior lot, approx. 100 feet east of Madison Avenue, is slated to be developed into a 15-story 226-room hotel with 40,000 SF of office space. The corner lot is in the early stages of development into a 196-unit, 32-story luxury residential rental building with street-level restaurant space.

---

[11] This would include those considering a career as a commercial real estate lender, developers with no experience with or access to a lending institution's loan approval process, and a contractor getting ready to submit his first request for construction financing.

[12] Names, locations, and so on, have been changed from the original memorandum. Certain descriptions have been omitted for the sake of confidentiality. However, those modifications should not detract from the informational and instructional benefits of this example.

Proposal:

This memorandum proposes a **$32MM, 36-month construction loan** against the hotel/office project. The loan will fund based on work in place after $8.1MM of equity and $14.5M of mezzanine financing have been advanced. The total project cost of approx. $54MM results in an L/C ratio of 59% and, with a projected hotel market value by HRSW Appraisers, Inc ("HRSW"), of $61,100M eighteen to twenty-four months after completion, an L/V ratio of 52%. On the hotel reaching stabilized occupancy and generating an average 1.3X DSCR over a consecutive six-month period, among other conditions, the borrower will have the option for a 1% fee of converting the construction loan into an QRS five-year term loan. The hotel will be managed by the Melissa Management Corporation under the Melissa Imperial brand. The management contract is for a term of 20 years.

Before closing the loan, the borrower must have a signed contract with a school (the Good Children School) for the sale of approx. 16,500 of the 40,000 SF of office space. On its completion and the consummation of the sale, QRS will release the space in exchange for $4MM of cash collateral. An additional $2.0MM will be substituted as collateral for the release of the remaining office space. All net proceeds of office space sales above the aforementioned amounts to QRS must be used to pay down the $14,500M mezzanine facility. It is expected that the sale of the office space will net approximately $13.5MM in total.

Ownership:

Letoha's managing member is **Ben Glock**. Under an agreement between him and **Sylvia Rush**, Letoha and Ms. Rush will each receive a 50% ownership interest in the project. Ben Glock has an 80% interest in Letoha, and Sheila Carmine, an employee of Mr. Glock under his company, Wave Properties, retains a 20% interest. Mr. Glock will give up 5% of Letoha to another of his associates, Carol Willis.

The net effect is that Sylvia Rush will have a 50% interest, Ben Glock will have a 37.5% interest, Sheila Carmine will have a 10% interest, and Carol Willis will have a 2.5% interest in the project.

Transaction:

Mr. Glock will handle all of the development aspects of the project. Ms. Rush will oversee the hotel's financial, management, and business operations after its completion. Ms. Rush will invest $5.5MM and Mr. Glock's group will invest $2.6MM before or at closing. Of this amount, approximately $8.1MM will be used to pay down existing first and second mortgages on the project site.

Senior to Letoha's equity will be a $14,500M mezzanine loan from **Mezzanine, Inc. ("MEZ")**. MEZ will advance as work is in place, will take a 12% interest rate on its funds outstanding payable in arrears, and will require a 15% IRR [internal rate of return] on its loan by maturity, which is six years from closing. MEZ, founded in 1997, is a private company that specializes in mezzanine financing secured by commercial real estate.

QRS will not fund any money until all of the $8.1MM of equity and $14,500M of the mezzanine financing has been advanced. QRS will then begin to fund its $32,000,000, 36-month construction loan that on project completion and a DSCR of 1.3X will fund into a five-year QRS term loan.

Guarantors:
Neither Mr. Glock nor Ms. Rush is an existing QRS borrower, but since May, Ms. Rush has established a substantial deposit relation with QRS's Branch No. 68.

Ben Glock heads up a real estate firm that has been in the high-end real estate development business for over 50 years. He has substantial experience in completing large scale, high-end, often difficult projects in Manhattan. Notable buildings of which he was directly involved include [ ].

The proposed hotel/office project should be readily manageable by him and his development and construction teams. Mr. Glock claims a current net worth of $[ ], with liquid assets of approx. $[ ]. The writer believes that his actual adjusted net worth is more in the $[ ] range.

Sylvia Rush, along with her family, owns several hotels in Ireland. In the United States she manages several of her family's apartment buildings through her firm [ ] Properties. During the construction of the hotel, she will take a relatively passive role. On hotel completion, Mr. Glock will step back and Ms. Rush will take over by overseeing hotel management. Ms. Rush is known as a knowledgeable investor. She currently maintains over $[ ] at QRS in a DDA account and over $[ ] in a QRS managed bond portfolio. She claims a net worth of $[ ]MM.

Terms and Conditions

This proposal recommends a $32MM 36-month construction loan funding into a 5-year term loan based on the following terms and conditions.

Borrower:
Letoha Street Associates, LLC.

CONSTRUCTION LOAN

Loan Amount:
$32,000,000, but no greater than 60% of the appraised market value at completion or the total cost of land and improvements, whichever is less.

Purpose:
Financing for the new construction of an approximately 134,000 gross square foot fifteen-story building consisting of a 226 room hotel and 40,000 square feet of rentable/saleable office space located at 165 East 68th Street, New York, NY.

Collateral:
1st Mortgage on land and all improvements thereon.
Assignment of all leases, rents, deposits, contracts, etc.

Term
36 months from closing. Two six-month extension options provided that hotel is completed evidenced by a C of O or a
T C of O.

Amortization:
Interest only – No amortization.

Interest Rate:
QRS Prime plus $1\frac{1}{2}$ %

Fee:
1% of commitment amount ($320,000)
$\frac{1}{2}$ % per each six-month extension if exercised.

Guarantors:
Ms. Sylvia Rush and Mr. Ben Glock.

Recourse:
100% joint and several of completion and repayment.

Initial Advance:
Prior to QRS making any advances under its senior Loan:
Borrower must provide proof satisfactory to QRS that it has invested at least $8,100,000 in cash equity into the project.
Mezzanine, Inc. (MEZ) must have advanced under its loan $14,500,000 into the project.

Subordinate Financing:
Except for $14,500,000 of financing provided by MEZ, whose loan terms, conditions and documentation must be satisfactory to QRS in its sole discretion, subordinate financing will be prohibited.

Mezzanine Advances
All MEZ fundings shall be advanced first into an QRS account. QRS will then advance funds to Borrower based upon funds schedule approved by MEZ and QRS.

Appraisal:
Full Review of HRSW Appraisers, Inc's October 9th appraisal by QRS approved firm – Super Valuation Company.

Environmental Audit:
Bank to engage environmental consultant to review all matters with respect to the subject site including, but not limited to, review of completed Phase I Environmental Assessment. Approval of report by QRS is at its sole discretion and the Bank may require additional site testing.

Transferability:
The Loan will be due upon the sale or transfer of the property.

Accounts:
All deposit, escrow, construction and operating accounts must be maintained at QRS.

Condition of Title:
The decision of the Bank, or its counsel, on title, marketability, encumbrances, use and condition of the property, requirement of all necessary permits, inspection of plans, specifications and sufficiency of all documents incidental to the closing of the proposed loan shall be final and conclusive.

Commitment Period:
The Loan is to close within forty-five (45) days from the issuance of a commitment.

Closing:
At the offices of QRS or at its attorney's office.

Brokerage Fees:
The Borrower shall hold the Bank harmless from all brokerage claims, if any, which may be made in connection with this transaction and under no circumstances is the Bank to be liable in any way for any brokerage fees or commissions. This provision will survive the closing, at which time borrower shall pay all and any commissions and/or compensation due its authorized broker.

Prepayment:
Borrower has the right to prepay the principal in multiples of $50,000 with interest computed to the last day of the month in which prepayment is made subject to "Walkaway Fee" as described below.

Partial Substitution of Collateral:
The Bank will allow the release of up to 17,000 square feet of leaseable/sellable office space upon the sale of said space to a single entity and upon the receipt of $4,000,000 to be applied to an interest bearing escrow account held by QRS as additional collateral. All additional proceeds from the sale must be used to paydown the MEZ loan.

Release of Collateral:
With the exception of the sale of up to 17,000 square feet of leaseable/sellable office space as noted above, any additional leaseable/sellable office space will be released as collateral for a sum equal to 90% of the net sales proceeds or a minimum of $325 per square foot, whichever is greater; until such sum aggregates to $2,000,000. This amount will be applied to an interest bearing escrow account held by QRS as additional collateral.
All proceeds from the sale of office space above $6MM must be used to paydown the MEZ loan.

Repayment:
Remaining balance due upon maturity or refinancing by QRS or another source.

Other Conditions:
- All advances under the Construction Loan are subject to completion of a Plan, Specification and Cost Review by QRS and an engineering consultant chosen by QRS stating that the budget, plans and specifications are acceptable.
- All construction advances will be subject to on-site inspections of work in place by the Bank's engineering consultant.
- All construction advances are subject to QRS's Building Loan Agreement which requirements include only advancing for work in place and a 10% retainage.
- Advances for required deposits for FF&E prior to manufacture and delivery are limited to $1,000M in the aggregate. Further advances only upon FF&E delivered and installed, if necessary, on-site.
- Subject to receipt of a signed contract by The Good Children School to purchase up to 17,000 sf of to-be-built office space for a price of at least $6MM. Contract deposit to be held in an escrow account at QRS.
- Satisfactory inter-creditor and recognition agreements with MEZ and Borrower.
- Any default under the MEZ loan will be a default under QRS's Loan.

TERM LOAN

Loan Amount:
Up to the amount of the Construction Loan outstanding at the time of closing or 70% of the appraised market value of the completed property, whichever is less.

Interest Rate:
Five year treasury index plus 2.50%.

Term:
Up to five years:
No greater than six months before the maturity of the MEZ loan
-or-
Five years if the MEZ loan is paid down in full at least six months before its maturity.

Amortization:
25 Year Schedule.

Fee:
1% of Loan amount payable at closing.

Collateral:
Same as Construction Loan.

Debt Service Coverage Ratio (DSCR):
Minimum average of 1.3X for a six-month consecutive period.

Recourse:
100% joint and several of repayment. Upon the DSCR equal to or exceeding an average of 1.5X for a consecutive 12 month period, recourse will be reduced to 50%. Upon DSCR equal to or exceeding an average of 1.5X for a consecutive 24 month period, the loan will become non-recourse except as to standard carve-outs for fraud, misrepresentation and environmental matters.

Walkaway Fee:
If the Borrower meets the requirements of the Term Loan, but chooses not to draw down on it for any reason, or if the amount of the Term Loan is less than the amount of the Construction Loan outstanding at closing, a fee of $1/4$ % of the difference between the Construction Loan outstanding and the amount of Term Loan will be due and payable.

Appraisal:
New or update of original appraisal, at the Bank's sole discretion, prior to closing.

Transferability:
The Loan will be due upon the sale or transfer of the property.

Prepayment:
Borrower shall have the right to prepay the principal in multiples of $50,000 with interest computed to the last day of the month in which prepayment is made; provided, however if prepayment is made during the first year, Borrower shall pay a prepayment penalty equal to 5% of the amount of principal prepaid, reducing by 1% in each subsequent year to a minimum prepayment penalty of 1% of the amount of principal prepaid. A 60 day window prior to maturity will be provided without penalty.

Other Conditions:
- Same as under Construction Loan whenever applicable plus additional conditions noted, but not limited to those below:
- Closing subject to issuance of a Temporary Certificate of Occupancy for all hotel and commercial spaces. Permanent C of O to be in place no later than one year following issuance of a Temporary C of O.
- QRS, at is sole discretion, may collect monthly escrow payments for real estate taxes, insurance, and water and sewer charges.

Project Description:

The Property:

The developer plans to construct on a 14,502-SF lot a 15-story hotel consisting of 226 rooms and 40,000 SF of office space. With the transfer of 10,540 SF of air rights from adjacent parcels and the obtainment of 32,172 SF from New York City's community use zoning, the building will comprise a total of 115,222 square feet above grade. An additional 14,500 SF of below-grade space plus allowances for mechanical areas will result in a total structure of approx. 134,000 SF. The below-grade space will include a 7,000-SF health club with exercise equipment, sauna, whirlpool, and massage facilities and a 50-linear-foot indoor pool and approx.1,800 SF of meeting space. The street level will have 4,500 SF of office space and two separate entrances and lobbies, one for the hotel component and one for the office component. Office space will be located on floors two through four. The fifth through fifteenth floors will house guest rooms. In addition, the fifteenth floor will offer 3,000 SF of outdoor space for special events (please note Exhibit I of this memorandum for pictures and renderings provided by Letoha).

Hotel:

The hotel, to be named the Auden, will be targeted toward transient guests. It will consist of 139 rooms with king-size beds, 70 rooms with double queen-size beds, sixteen $2\frac{1}{2}$-room suites with king-size beds, and one room with two double beds.

Floors five through fourteen will be identical. Each will have one suite, 13 rooms with king-size beds, and 7 with double queen-size beds. The fifteenth floor will contain six suites with terraces, nine rooms with king-size beds, and one with two double beds. The large number of suites and rooms with double queens will be a competitive advantage.

The Auden will fly under the Melissa Imperial flag (its management contract is detailed below). To compete more effectively with hotels closer to the city's midtown core, the level of design and materials in mechanicals, public areas, and room finishes will be above average, especially for the Melissa Imperial brand. For instance, mechanicals include a roof makeup air system and a ducted HVAC system. The design will include a 70-foot-long mural from the basement pool area up to the second floor. All suites have wet bars, refrigerators, and microwaves.

Office Space:

The office space will have a separate entrance and lobby as well as separate utilities and mechanicals. Except for approx. 16,500 SF that is expected to be delivered in a white box condition to the Good Children School, a nonprofit group, for a net price of $375 per SF or $6,225,000 (the school will pay for its own improvements, which will be executed by the developer), the remaining 23,500 SF of space will be sold raw. The office space and the hotel, under a commercial condominium status, will have separate tax lot numbers and will operate autonomously. The developer is planning to receive a TCO [temporary certificate of occupancy] on the office space before receiving one covering the entire building in order to be able to sell the space as soon as possible.

Office Space Rationale

The 40,000-SF office space was built in order to receive the additional 32,172 SF of buildable square footage. The developers claim that the space will sell at a net $375 SF. The writer attributes its marginal all-in cost at roughly $300 per SF. This results in a $75 per SF, or $3,000M, net profit. However, its real value is that it creates a four-story base that enables the guest rooms to be raised above surrounding buildings. This translates into greater light and air penetration and broader street visibility.

In return for the increased square footage, New York City requires that the facility be occupied by an entity that contributes community value. To satisfy this requirement, the developer will target sales toward nonprofit groups. Since nonprofit entities, as owners, do not have to pay real estate taxes, they save considerably over leasing. Under a lease, irrespective of the tenant's tax status, the landlord is required to pay real estate taxes that then are passed on to tenants in the form of higher monthly charges.

For the borrower, the advantages of selling the space versus leasing it are that it can quickly pay down a portion of QRS's loan and, more importantly, the higher-cost mezzanine loan. Also, it can keep its focus directly on opening and operating the hotel. Of note is that, based on the Good Children School preconstruction sale, the space appears in demand at the $375/SF price point. According to a representative of OB Brokerage, which will be the sales agent on the space, the property will feature the largest contiguous modern office space in the Murray Hill area.

Adjacent Residential Property:
Along with the development of 165 East 68th Street, Wave Properties entered into a joint venture with a San Francisco entity, the Newbold Co., to develop the adjacent corner site at 155 East 68th Street into a 28-story 178-unit residential rental building with a corner restaurant. The residential property and the hotel/office building will be developed more or less at the same time, but with mutually exclusive design and construction teams. For the residential building, Newbold will be responsible for development and project management through completion. Wave Properties will have almost no day-to-day involvement.

Although each building will be completely separate and distinct, for a minimal fee, residents of the rental property will have access to the hotel pool and health club. The restaurant lease will require that it provide service to the hotel, and hotel guests will have direct access to the restaurant through the hotel lobby. A space into the hotel adjacent to the restaurant will be a breakfast/meeting area. The restaurant must provide Melissa with its kitchen facilities so that hotel guests can be served the "Melissa Breakfast," one of the branded services provided by Melissa.

Hotel Management Agreement:
The developers have entered into a 20-year contract with Melissa Management Corporation. The terms call for a management fee of 5 percent of gross revenues for the first two years and 6 percent thereafter. Also, there is an incentive fee of 25 percent of the operating cash flow before debt service above $6MM, which, after ten years, increases by an additional $50,000 until the management contract expires. The $6MM incentive fee floor is expected to be reached by the developer, Melissa, and HRSW during the hotel's fourth year of operations. The writer's projections are more conservative, as noted in the cash flow section later in this credit proposal.

The Area:

The Upper East Side is defined by a two-square-mile area bounded by 59th St. to the south, 96th St. to the north, Fifth Ave. to the west, and the East River to the east. According to the 2000 census, its population of 210,880 has grown by 3.2 percent from the 1990 estimate. With the large number of new residential developments in the ensuing fourteen years, it is believed the figure today is significantly higher. The growing population and the relatively low number of immediate hotel competitors, due in great part to the difficulty of creating an assemblage in the area with as-of-right zoning for hotel use, make the 68th St. site, in the writer's opinion, very conducive to hotel development.

Convenience:
165 East 68th Street benefits from its proximity to the FDR Drive (68th Street leads directly onto the northbound and southbound FDR entrances) and First Avenue, which suffers less from traffic congestion then more westerly south-north Manhattan traffic arteries. The location is easily accessible to automobile traffic. Uptown bus service is

located on the corner of First Avenue, and downtown service is a block east on Second Avenue. The hotel's high visibility from First Avenue, coupled with identifying Melissa signage, should be a significant marketing benefit. Management intends to take advantage of the FDR's proximity by promoting the hotel as the closest, most accessible Manhattan hotel from LaGuardia Airport.

Unfortunately, with the nearest subway stations located at 53rd Street and 42nd Street on Lexington Avenue, service is not convenient. The writer does not see this as a significant negative factor as the hotel's target markets include significant proportions of guests with ties to local area residents and nearby hospitals.

Residential and Hospital Target Segments:
Even for Manhattan, the area immediately surrounding 165 East 68th Street is unique in that it exhibits a high density of housing and hospitals.

Residential:
Residential properties in the immediate area consist of prewar 5-story buildings interspersed with much larger, newer luxury-style buildings under rental, cooperative, and condominium ownership. Just north of the site is the Eagle Watch Housing complex, spanning from 69th through 72nd Streets on First Avenue. This five 25-story building complex contains 1,137 low- to moderate-income rental apartments. The development would ordinarily preclude the construction of a hotel at the level of a Melissa. However, the soaring incomes and demand for upper- to high-end housing have grown rapidly in Manhattan, particularly on the Upper East Side, which over the last decade has solidly expanded its luxury residential product. Since the neighborhood has become very desirable and expensive, apartment turnover is very low. The high degree of tenant stability has helped to make it, along with submarket rents, a very sought-after place to live. In essence, the area's new and existing housing occupied by upper-income households has overtaken this complex.

Direct evidence of this luxury housing expansion is manifested by many relatively new upscale residential buildings within a few blocks of the complex. Rental properties include the SailWell House, 150 units on 68th St. and 2nd Ave.; the Clinton, 300 units on 66th St. and York Ave.; the Brittany, 300 units on 92nd St. and York Ave.; Century Tower, 150 units on 90th St. and 1st Ave; the Speers, 250 units on 70th St and 1st Ave; and several more. Now under construction is the Melody Building, a 160-unit building on 73rd St. and Lexington Ave., and, of course, 155 East 68th Street, the building adjacent to the Auden. Typical rents in these buildings reach into the $50 and better per square foot range. Furthermore, sales in the immediate area are routinely over $1,000 per SF. The fact that people will invest in the purchase of apartments at high prices or will sign leases at high rents with the intention of living in them for many years is an excellent market indication of the desirability of and demand for housing in the area. This should carry over to the Auden, where, for rates below much of the Upper East Side, a guest can get a modern room in a hotel with a recognized and reliable management brand.

Hospitals:
Hospitals, in order of their rough proximity to the Auden are as follows:

Beth Israel (89th St. and East End Ave.), Metropolitan Hospital (97th St. and 1st Ave.), Mt. Sinai (98th–102nd and Madison Ave.), New York-Presbyterian (68th–70th Sts. and York Ave.), Memorial Sloan-Kettering Center (68th St. and 1st Ave.), Lenox Hill Hospital (77th St. and Lexington Ave.), Hospital for Special Surgery (70th St. and FDR Drive), and Manhattan Eye and Ear (65th St. bet. 2nd and 3rd Aves.). The hospitals are expected to generate a significant proportion of the hotel's occupancy. The commercial and hospital segments will be discussed in detail in the following section of this presentation.

The Manhattan Hotel Market:

The Manhattan-wide hotel market rose during the mid to late 1990s, peaking in 2000 with average occupancy greater than 80 percent, average daily rates (ADRs) exceeding $220, and revenue per available room (RevPAR) greater than $180. In 2001, the Sept. 11 tragedy decimated the business, particularly with the tourist and group segments. However, the upper Manhattan hotel market, of which the Auden is a part, experienced less stress than many other areas. In 2003, upper Manhattan hotel occupancies increased 2 percent to 70 percent while ADRs declined by only 4 percent to $263. HRSW's October 9, 2005, appraisal conservatively estimated a meager 2005 Manhattan-wide increase in the occupancy rate by 1.4 percent and an average ADR of $186. The appraisal attributes the weak showing to the military buildup and war with Iraq and a weak economy that gave few signs, particularly at the year's beginning, of imminent improvement. In the writer's opinion, for 2006 and beyond, with the elimination or abatement of the aforementioned issues, and especially the strengthening U.S. economy and the weaker U.S. dollar, the hotel business should improve at a markedly accelerated rate.

Market for the Auden:

The Auden will be directly competitive with five hotels listed below.

Name	Address	# of Rms	Meeting Space SF	Market Segmentation			
				Comm	Group	Leisure	Hospital
Melissa Times Sq. South	434 West 44th St.	244	650	63%	10%	27%	0%
The Murray	184 East 97th St.	48	None	0%	45%	55%	0%
Hotel Fresca	Madison Ave. bet. 102nd & 103rd Sts.	87	None	10%	10%	70%	10%
The Moore	160 East 83rd St.	306	None	25%	0%	50%	25%
BMW Hotel	600 East 52nd St.	197	None	50%	20%	0%	30%
TOT/AVGs		882		38%	11%	35%	16%

The first hotel is included because it is a Melissa.* In spite of its distance from the Auden (over 30 blocks southeast), it is expected that there will be some cannibalization due to the sharing of the Melissa reservation system.

---

* A Melissa Imperial hotel much closer to and more competitive with the Auden, on Third Avenue between 32nd and 33rd Streets, is scheduled to close its doors before the Auden becomes operational. The owner believes that the highest and best use of the property is as a residential condominium building. It is estimated that approx. 60% of its occupancy was from the Melissa reservation system. The closing of this 308-room hotel should directly benefit the Auden.

In 2004, according to PWC, the Melissa reservation system for Melissa Hotels (236 in sample) was responsible for generating an average occupancy of 47%. The West 44th St. hotel derives approx. 70% of its occupancy from the Melissa reservation system. Certainly, the flag is a significant revenue driver. Working against the potential for the dilution of Melissa's reservation business is the Auden's location in a very underserved area of Manhattan. Specific to its location is the character of surrounding residences and its proximity to major hospitals, two segments that are certainly not major strengths for the 44th St. hotel.

The remaining four hotels display significant variances in the quality of their accommodations and their occupancy segmentation. In this competitive group, none have nationally recognized reservations systems and none have meeting space. Noting each one, the BMW, because of its location at the lip of the FDR and its unattractive facade, has a virtually zero share of the leisure market. Built in the 1930s, the Murray, the closest competitor to the Auden, has only 48 rooms and has experienced obsolescence due to its small room sizes. The Hotel Fresca, which was recently sold and is undergoing extensive renovations, relies on approx. 70% of its occupancy from the leisure segment that, similar to the Auden, consists of a large number of guests with relationships to nearby residents. The Moore (the old Cathy) has recently been renovated and offers a good mix of room sizes. It is also near the subway system and has a relationship with the open-to-the-public Muscle fitness center, which is housed in the hotel. This hotel attracts a good number of hospital-related visitors but has no group business and receives only 25% of its bookings from business and commercial guests.

With regard to these four hotels, the Auden will be at an advantage due to the following:

- It will be the only hotel in the competition with an internationally recognized brand name as well as an international reservation system. Its competitors are all run by boutique, independent management.
- It will be the newest product in the area. It will be modern and clean and not suffer from deferred maintenance.
- It will have a full-service health club and indoor pool.
- It will have a restaurant with direct access for guests.
- It will have meeting space and roof terrace space for private functions.
- It is easily accessible to New York's Kennedy and LaGuardia airports.

The Auden's disadvantages with respect to its competition are:

- It is several blocks from subway stations.
- Potential guests may prefer hotels nearer to the midtown and downtown sections of Manhattan.

The Auden's Expected Market
The Auden's expected market segmentation is as follows.

Name	Address	# of Rms	Meeting Space SF	Market Segmentation				
				Comm	Group	Leisure	Hospital	
The Auden First year of stabilization	Occupied Rooms	226	1,800 + 3,000	35,313	6,528	16,232	8,076	66,149
	% of Total Occ			52%	10%	26%	12%	100%

Commercial business will be attracted by the Melissa brand as well as representatives from companies and consultants doing business with the area's hospitals and medical offices.

The **Group** segment will include business from pharmaceutical companies and off-site doctor meetings and seminars.

The **Leisure** segment will consist predominantly of those visiting relatives in the area, those who like the on-site health club facilities, and those who want to be in Manhattan at a flag hotel without the midtown hotel prices.

The **Hospital** business includes patients before or after surgery or who are undergoing medical treatment and family members and friends visiting patients. It is anticipated that the hotel will attract business due to the unsatisfied demand in the Upper East Side. However, from time to time, it should benefit from group bookings and from downtown hotel spillover.

ADRs and RevPARs:
The average daily rates and revenues per available room of the six-hotel competitive set are listed below.

Name	Address	Occupancy	ADR	RevPAR
Melissa Times Sq. South	114 East 40th St.	85% - 89%	$192	$169
The Murray	164 East 87th St.	75% - 79%	$147	$116
Hotel Fresca	Madison Ave. bet. 92nd & 93rd Sts.	75% - 79%	$212	$162
The Moore	140 East 63rd St.	65% - 69%	$177	$121
BMW Hotel	500 East 62nd St.	70% - 74%	$147	$107
TOT/AVGs		75%	$176	$135

During the first year of stabilized hotel operations, which is projected by the writer to occur in 2006, the Auden is expected to achieve 79% average occupancy, ADRs of $205, and a RevPAR of $162. Except for the Hotel Fresca and Melissa Times Square South, these are significantly above the competitive averages (note that the hotel market has improved markedly since the above figures were derived in October 2004; the occupancy, ADR, and RevPAR almost certainly improved as well). However, noting the general inferiority of the Murray and the BMW; the high level of leisure business at the Moore and Fresca, which will be similar at the Auden; the Auden's location, which is significantly removed from the 306-room Moore; and the generally nearer location to hospitals and New York airports, the writer believes that the projections are realistic and achievable.

Financial Analysis

The income and expense projections below were submitted by the appraiser and adjusted by the underwriter based on experience and discussions with other hotel operators.

Year	2006	2007	2008	2009	2010
Number of Rooms	226	226	226	226	226
Rms Available	78,366	81,665	81,665	81,665	81,665
Occupied Rms	57,207	64,515	66,149	66,149	66,149
% Occupancy	73%	79%	81%	81%	81%
ADR	$191	$205	$210	$214	$222
REVPAR	$139	$162	$170	$173	$180
REVENUES					
Room	$10,926,502	$13,225,663	$13,891,234	$14,155,828	$14,685,018
Tel & Other	$757,000	$824,000	$863,000	$888,000	$915,000
Tot. Revenues	**$11,683,502**	**$14,049,663**	**$14,754,234**	**$15,043,828**	**$15,600,018**
Dept. Costs (Rm & Tel)	$2,897,508	$3,259,522	$3,275,440	$3,339,730	$3,463,204
Undistributed Exp.	$3,401,000	$3,747,000	$4,147,000	$4,272,000	$4,399,000
Income Before Fixed Charges	$5,384,993	$7,043,141	$7,331,794	$7,432,099	$7,737,814
Fixed Charges*	$1,216,500	$1,914,000	$2,152,000	$2,217,000	$2,450,000
NOI Before QRS DS	**$4,168,493**	**$5,129,141**	**$5,179,794**	**$5,215,099**	**$5,287,814**
QRS Debt Service ($32MM, T+2.5% =6.5%, 25Yr)**	$2,623,407	$2,623,407	$2,623,407	$2,623,407	$2,623,407
NET INC. AFTER DEBT SERVICE	**$1,545,086**	**$2,505,734**	**$2,556,386**	**$2,591,691**	**$2,664,407**
Mezz					
DSCR X	**1.6**	**2.0**	**2.0**	**2.0**	**2.0**
Break Even Dependent on Occupancy	59%	60%	62%	62%	62%
Break Even Dependent on ADR	$155	$155	$161	$164	$171
DSCR at Occ & Rate Bet. Expected & BE (see below)	1.0X%	1.1X%	1.1X%	1.1X%	1.1X%
Midpt Occ Bet Exp&BE	66%	70%	72%	72%	72%
Midpt ADR Bet Exp&BE	$173.00	$180.00	$185.50	$189.00	$196.50

* Assumes first year property taxes of $630M. After assessment, taxes should increase second year to +/− $1,260M.

** Using 2007 as first stabilized year, the interest rate on QRS's loan would have to reach 15.9% before CF turns negative.

Of all the assumptions, the most critical are the occupancy rate and the ADR. The first full year of stabilized operations shows an occupancy rate of 79% at an ADR of $205, resulting in room revenues of $13,226M. With telephone and other charges (laundry, meeting room, terrace events, movies, etc.) total revenues are projected at $14,050M. Subtracting out variable room expenses of $3,260M, undistributed expenses (which include utilities, administrative costs, Melissa fees, and system costs) and fixed costs (real estate taxes, insurance, and, importantly, a reserve for replacement), total expenses come in at $8,921M. This leaves a net operating income of $5,129M.

To achieve a breakeven operation, a minimum NOI of $2,623M is required given a fixed interest rate of 6.5% and a 25-year amortization schedule. Using the assumptions above and adjusting for each variable, ADRs would have to drop off by 25% from forecast to a rate of $156. Leaving ADRs at their current projections, the vacancy rate would have to drop by 26 to 58%. Both of these situations are extremely unlikely.

To get a better idea of exposure in a market downturn (a worse-case scenario), the writer moved the ADR and occupancy rates to a midpoint between each year's BE figure and forecast. As noted, DSCR still produces some comfort at 1.1X.

In a worst case, the hotel will fail to achieve a 1.3X DSCR and QRS's term loan will never be funded. In this situation, the $6MM cash collateral accounts will reduce the bank's net loan exposure to $26MM. At this level of outstanding principal, breakeven points are very low. At a 6.5% interest rate and a 25-year amortization schedule, the annual mortgage payment is $2,131,519. The breakeven occupancy and ADR rates are shown in the table below.

QRS Debt Service ($26MM, T+2.5%= 6.5%, 25Yr)*	$2,131,519	$2,131,519	$2,131,519	$2,131,519	$2,131,519
Break Even Dependent on Occupancy	55%	56%	58%	58%	58%
Break Even Dependent on ADR	$144	$145	$151	$154	$161
DSCR at Occ & Rate Bet. Expected & BE (see below)	1.1X%	1.1X%	1.1X%	1.1X%	1.1X%
Midpt Occ Bet Exp&BE	64%	68%	70%	70%	70%
Midpt ADR Bet Exp&BE	$167.50	$175.00	$180.50	$184.00	$191.50

* In this scenario, default rates are not considered. The table merely illustrates the level of reduced occupancy rates and ADRs as compared to the prior breakeven table. Both use the same interest rate and amortization schedule.

As was mentioned in an earlier section, the net income from office sales should be around $13.5MM. Subtracting $6MM of this amount as the source of QRS's cash collateral, the remaining $7.5MM must be used, under QRS's loan terms, to pay down the MEZ mezzanine loan principal. This leaves MEZ with $7.0MM of its principal outstanding. The hotel would have to perform extremely poorly for **both** the developer (with at least $8.1MM invested) and the mezzanine lender to walk away from their respective investments.

Sources and Uses

A summary of project costs and expenses and how they will be funded is as follows.

Initial Project Cost Statement

Items of Cost/Use

BUILDING COSTS	Total Costs	Initial Loan Budget Amounts	Borrower's Equity Paid In	Borrower's Equity Due
HARD COSTS				
Construction Costs	$29,550,000	$25,050,000		$4,500,000
Tenant Improvements (Office)	$250,000			$250,000
FF&E	$4,500,000	$4,500,000		
Subtotal (Hard Costs)	$34,300,000	$29,550,000	$0	$4,750,000
SOFT COSTS				
Real Estate Taxes	$817,096	$187,596		$629,500
Interest on QRS Loan	$2,290,200	$2,262,404		$27,796
Appraisal Fee/ Environmental Fee	$90,000			$90,000
Commitment Fee	$320,000			$320,000
Lender's Construction Consultant	$15,000			$15,000
Lender's Counsel	$45,000			$45,000
Interest on Mezz. Loan	$1,950,000			$1,950,000
Recording Documents	$1,000			$1,000
Borrower's Architect/ Engineering	$500,000			$500,000
Title Policies	$189,000			$189,000
Builder's Risk Insurance	$500,000			$500,000
Mtge Rec Tax	$1,056,000			$1,056,000
Expeditor, Permits	$125,000			$125,000
Subtotal (Soft Cost)	$7,898,296	$2,450,000	$0	$5,448,296
TOTAL BUILDING COSTS	$42,198,296	$32,000,000	$0	$10,198,296
OTHER COSTS				
Land Acquisition	$8,100,000			$8,100,000
Marketing & Advertising	$130,000			$130,000
Sales Costs	$140,000			$140,000
Brokers	$600,000			$600,000
Accounting	$50,000			$50,000
Developer Fee	$900,000			$900,000
Contingency	$1,000,000			$1,000,000
Operating Reserve	$600,000			$600,000
Borrower's Attorney	$300,000			$300,000
Misc.	$581,704			$581,704
Subtotal (Subor. Soft Cost)	$12,401,704	$0	$0	$12,401,704
TOTAL BLDG AND SUBORD. SOFT COST	$54,600,000	$32,000,000 58.6%	$0 0.0%	$22,600,000 41.4%

The land is currently encumbered with two mortgages aggregating to $8.5MM. The first mortgage is for $5.5MM from Hurl Bank at a rate of 7%, maturing on 4/30/04. The second is a $3MM loan ($2,150M OS) at 15% from ZYX, which also matures on 4/30/04.

At closing the borrower's equity will pay down in full the Hurl Bank's $5.5MM Loan and ZYX's outstanding $2.1MM balance. The remaining $500M in equity will be used to pay for closing costs, fees, etc. All equity will be confirmed by QRS before it advances any funds.

When QRS becomes involved, since it is advancing after $22,600M in verifiable cash has gone into the project, many of the most problematic and time-delaying activities will have already taken place (such as the obtainment of approved DOB plans and specifications, the buying out of the job, the commencement of construction, and supervisory coordination). Therefore, the potential for delays and overruns is significantly abated. This helps ensure that the bank's loan will remain in balance throughout its term.

Note that in an August 1 appraisal performed by TA Quirk, an approved QRS appraisal firm that was contracted by the developer, the hotel land parcel, cleared of all structures, was valued at $15,500,000. This is significantly above the $8,100,000 cost allocated to the land in the above budget. The $15.5MM figure should at least provide some comfort that the land has not been overvalued by the borrower in order to gain credit under the proposed loan for additional equity that was not contributed to the project.

The Development Team

Wave Properties, LLC: Developer:

Members of the project team have been assembled by Ben Glock with his wholly owned company Wave Properties, LLC. In the writer's opinion, he has assembled an experienced, knowledgeable, and capable team. Backgrounds on the firm's key associates are as follows:

Ben Glock has been involved with all aspects of commercial real estate finance, development, and management. Projects of particular note are 1011 Sixth Avenue, an 890,000-SF office building, and 531 East 55th Street, a 475,000-SF office building. He recently was responsible for the site assemblage and development of 1962 Broadway (now the "X"), a 55-story 562-key hotel.

George Win has worked for Wave Properties for 23 years. Before that he worked on several joint venture projects, including a major hotel expansion project, during his nine-year tenure with Common Insurance Co. Mr. Win will act in a broad supervisory role.

Gloria Sorres has been involved in hotel development in England and the United States for over 20 years. In the United States she worked with Mr. Glock on 1962 Broadway as project overseer and owner representative. She has direct experience with all aspects of hotel design, including working with architects, interior designers, builders, contractors, and purchasing agents. She also was general manager at the New York New York Club and the Gardener Hotel. Ms. Sorres will be the project representative for the Auden.

Carol Willis has over 30 years of large residential development experience, including ownership, finance, and management. On the firm's commercial real estate projects, she is responsible for arranging and following through on equity and debt portions of project finance as well as tax credits and abatements. She also heads up a brokerage company owned by Wave Properties.

Sylvia Rush: Investor/Consultant:

Sylvia Rush is a native of France. She has studied there as well as in Germany and the United States and has earned a degree from NYU in international studies and finance. She is fluent in French, German, and English. In 1983 she worked for a year in Düsseldorf, Germany, reportedly responsible for constructing an office building. From 1988 to the present, she has headed up NYRE Management, a real estate management company that manages 76 apartments in several buildings in Manhattan. These properties are owned by her and her family. In discussions with the writer, she claims that most of her wealth is derived from her father and that his family owns several hotels in France and Brussels. Through her family, she is channeling liquid assets into the United States for investment. Ms. Rush's familiarity with the immediate Upper East Side area, her experience with hotel operations, and her real estate management experience add depth to the development team. Her main expertise will, however, be in overseeing Melissa's management of the new hotel. She will contribute $5.5MM of equity into the project before or at loan closing in exchange for a 50% ownership interest in the project.

Architect

Steven Handle has been the project architect on such notable and complex projects as the Hadley Castle Hotel (which, incidentally, QRS has a first mortgage loan against) and the Opra Hotel.

Construction Manager

Caloway is a 100+-year-old company with 200 employees in New York and South Carolina. Caloway works in tandem with Intertone Inc., which has an international presence with over 1,300 employees in twenty-one cities. Caloway is responsible for development of the base, core, and shell of the Auden. Intertone Inc. will manage the interior fitting and finish work. Caloway and Intertone's résumé includes a plethora of building experience with a good concentration of projects in New York City. This is particularly important since having a practical knowledge of New York City's often overlapping and confusing laws, rules, regulations, and manners of getting things done reduces construction risk considerably.

Mezzanine Lender

Mezzanine (MEZ) was formed in 1997 as a vehicle for Asian capital to be invested in North American real estate. The company is headed by Lenny Forest (39), who before forming MEZ claims to have invested over $300MM in real estate assets on behalf of his family trust. The company's primary business is commercial real estate mezzanine lending, with expertise in specialized areas such as shopping centers, hotels, and golf courses. Its competitive advantage is primarily its ability to react quickly with a relatively high level of flexibility due to its being a privately held firm apparently closely controlled by Mr. Forest. Since its inception, it has claimed to have been involved in transactions exceeding $3,400MM. Based on the writer's discussions with Mr. Forest concerning his firm and, in particular, the proposed Auden hotel, he appears to be an astute hands-on investor with a strong knowledge of the development process and the New York hotel market. MEZ has one office in New York City and one in San Francisco. Under the terms of the proposed facility, MEZ will periodically advance $14.5MM based on the QRS approved project budget. Advances will be controlled by QRS to ensure that funds are properly applied. Only after MEZ has advanced all of its $14.5MM facility will any advances be made by QRS.

Guarantor Analysis

The borrowing entity is newly formed and has no significant assets, liabilities, income, or expenses other than those related to the start-up of this project. Annual financial statements and tax returns will be required during the term of the loan.

The guarantors are Ben Glock and Sylvia Rush. Mr. Glock has submitted his tax returns and his personal financial statement on QRS form. Mrs. Rush has submitted her 2000 and 2001 tax returns. Mrs. Rush is in the process of a divorce with her husband of twenty years. Due to the litigation involved, she was advised not to give us her personal financial statement. Instead, she has given us a letter from Jeffrey Slavet, a CPA, declaring that her net worth exceeds $[ ].

Ben Glock

Mr. Glock's signed January 29 statement indicates a net worth of $[ ]M consisting primarily of real estate–related investments that he values at $[ ]M. He reports cash balances in checking accounts in excess of $[ ]M, which will be confirmed before closing by submission of bank account statements. The bulk of his real estate asset value is related to the 68th Street property. The hotel site is valued at a net $8,250M. To date, he has invested an additional $4.5MM of cash into it. $[ ]MM is his anticipated share in the adjacent apartment building after completion and stabilization. Other assets include a $[ ]MM interest in a hotel on Spruce and Greene Streets, a $[ ]MM land contract in Southport, CT, a $[ ]M real estate brokerage firm, and $[ ]M in receivables (development fees from the 165 East 68th St. apartment building). On the liability side, a $[ ]MM loan is payable to one of his business associates, Jerome Knudson.

Mr. Glock's tax returns show a negative AGI of $[ ]M in 2000, an AGI of $[ ]M in 2001, and a negative AGI of $[ ]M in 2002. His large 2001 income was from the sale of his interest in the 1962 Broadway hotel property. His ordinary income and expenses are the result of passing through costs from

Wave Properties. Since Mr. Glock's net worth statement is based to a large degree on illiquid assts that are not yet fully developed, the writer believes that his net worth is considerably less than stated, perhaps in the $[ ]MM area. However, Mr. Glock's net worth and cash flows are still ample, and he should be able to easily cover any significant project cost overruns.

Mr. Glock is well known to the writer, who made two low-seven-figure real estate secured loans to him in the late 1990s at a different lending institution. They both performed satisfactorily. He has exhibited a thorough knowledge of the Manhattan market and has verifiable experience in the development of major New York City properties.

Sylvia Rush

Sylvia Rush's claimed $[ ]MM net worth consists of substantial assets held outside the United States. Her family owns several hotels, all in France and Belgium, including a Melissa and a Hyatt. They also own the residential properties she manages in the United States. A letter from Bank de Paris (followed up with a telephone conversation) states that she has had a relationship with that bank since 1989 and that she and her family are well known in the French hotel business. Ms. Rush currently has a secured (not real estate) borrowing relationship that is in the mid-seven-figure range.

Ms. Rush's 2000 and 2001 tax returns show a salary from her management company of $[ ]M and $[ ]M, respectively. In spite of her comparatively modest income, Ms. Rush can apparently access large amounts of money. This ability is demonstrated by her $[ ]MM+ investment and deposit accounts at QRS.

The writer believes Ms. Rush has the capacity to readily increase her equity contribution to the 68th Street project if required. In conversations, she appears to be very knowledgeable about the NYC real estate market and its business conditions, the hotel industry, and various classes of investments. Jay Owens of QRS's private banking area described Ms. Rush as a hands-on knowledgeable investor.

Personal Credit Reports

Ms. Rush's credit report was clean. Mr. Glock's credit was also clean, but his report displayed several unsatisfied judgments totaling $[ ]. In a discussion with him, he was not aware of their existence. Before closing, all outstanding judgments will be satisfied.

Risks and Mitigants

The greatest risks to the proposed credit are the inability to complete the project on time and within budget and the lack of adequate occupancy or RevPARs to bring the hotel up to a positive cash flow that is able to support a QRS or alternative permanent takeout loan. These concerns are addressed below.

Project Completion:

As noted, Ben Glock has been in the development business all of his adult life. Importantly, he and his family have developed signature buildings in

Manhattan that have left a significant imprint on its skyline. The Auden and the adjacent residential building are certainly not projects where he or his development team is overreaching. From a construction and development perspective, the project is relatively straightforward. The architect, engineers, designers, and contractors are not constructing a tall, innovative, or complex building that may be difficult to execute but one that functions well and fits the Melissa image. Mr. Glock's experience with New York City developments of larger size and scope should transfer well to this project. Furthermore, his in-house project team appears capable and experienced. In the writer's opinion, the budgeted $220 per SF appears reasonable for a New York City construction project. QRS's facility will be dependent on a cost review by its engineering consultant. The Bank along with its consultant will review the Guaranteed Maximum Price (GMP) contract between the developer and Caloway, the construction manager, before funding.

Occupancy and Rates:
Since the hotel will be new and will have amenities and FFE above the standards of Melissa and its immediate competition, the level of product quality should not be an issue. The most influential and least controllable variable affecting the achievement of operational stability will be the condition of the New York, the United States, and, indeed, the global economies. A downturn in tourism or a national economic downturn curtailing business travelers can negatively affect ADRs and occupancies. Against this possibility is the fact that the Auden will offer rates below the high-end competition, will have the advantages of a recognized brand name and reservation system, and is in a location recognized for being underserved. Furthermore, competition is unlikely to increase any time soon due to the difficulty and lead time necessary to locate and assemble hotel sites in Manhattan. Also, discrete exogenous shocks such as a health epidemic or terrorist attack can have costly consequences. Concerning these types of events, the hotel is not deemed to be in a target location, and a large portion of its clientele will continue to be attracted to the surrounding medical industry or residents in the immediate area.

As detailed under the financial analysis section of this proposal, the breakeven income level of $2.6MM can be achieved with an occupancy rate of around 60% or with ADRs in the $155 to $171 range. These are well below the developer's, Auden's, and Price Play's projected occupancies of approx. 80% and ADRs exceeding $200. The spread offers the Bank a good margin of safety. Furthermore, for the release of the office space, QRS's exposure will be reduced by $6MM from $32MM to $26MM until takeout by it or another permanent lender.

Loan Grade:
The loan proposed herein is rated a "C." The principals are experienced in real estate development, management, and finance with a demonstrable track record. Their personal assets, in part represented by Mrs. Rush's

current QRS deposit balances, indicate a very good depth of liquidity. A strong and experienced mezzanine lender provides additional protection. Revenue, expense, and occupancy projections are well within reason, and the hotel management concern is well known and experienced. The overall feasibility of the project will be reconfirmed by an independent appraisal firm hired by the Bank with expertise in the hotel field.

Profitability:

The bank's deposit and private banking relationship with Mrs. Rush has been very satisfactory. Current DDAs are substantial at $6.2MM. With Mrs. Rush's equity contribution to the Auden, deposits will be reduced by $5.5MM, leaving a net balance of about $700M. However, these balances should rise as she and her family continue to reserve cash for other acquisitions. The first-year earnings on this facility are anticipated to be $1,143M and yield a healthy 6.03%. During the second year, earnings should increase as the full facility will be drawn down and escrow and working capital deposits will increase by an estimated minimum of $5MM.

Exhibits:

Site pictures
Melissa 10-year forecasts
Some examples of Wave Properties' past projects

100 SoHo

Whereas Letoha Hotel entails totally new construction, 100 SoHo Street involves a substantial renovation and the conversion of an existing manufacturing building to a residential one with street-level retail space. The presentation is the result of a loan request that was shown in Chapter 2. Note that from the time the loan proposal was presented to the lender to the time he wrote his presentation, several assumptions, including the project budget, changed because of the fluid environment that is common in development projects.

100 SoHo Presentation

CREDIT APROVAL MEMORANDUM

100 SoHo St. LLC

Executive Summary

100 SoHo St., LLC ("SoHo"), is a single-purpose entity formed to acquire title to and then convert and expand an existing six-story, 29,144-SF building at the same address in Manhattan's SoHo district. The property is on the west side of SoHo between Prince and Spring Streets. The Good Manufacturing Co., Inc., currently occupies the loft building in question. The name for the new development will be "The Good Building."

Member 1 and his frequent real estate venture partner, Member 2, currently own SoHo 50/50. Member 3, a friend and occasional business associate, is being brought in as an investor before acquisition of the property. Member 3 is a partner in Member 3 Associates, a NYC-based real estate brokerage firm.

Messrs. Member 1 and Member 2 are the principals in a larger entity called the ABC Group ("ABC"), which is a residential and commercial property management company headquartered in Manhattan. Through this entity they currently manage, while personally having made investments in, 35 apartment buildings, all but one of which (an apartment building being converted to condo ownership) are in Manhattan. Their historical holdings have varied because they have been very active in converting former commercial loft buildings and residential rentals to condos. They have disposed of several properties over the past year upon sellout.

QRS Bank's $7,250M November 1 mortgage loan to an affiliated entity, 42 West 89th Street LLC, is one such property. This 16-story property had been operating as a 218-unit apartment building since the 1970s. After their acquisition, the owners installed new windows, repointed the entire structure, overhauled the heating system and elevator controls, and renovated several apartments. Since the principals were in process of vacating and renovating apartments, a $650M reserve has been held by QRS since closing. Member 1 reports that he now has offers from two potential purchasers for over $20MM each. He expects to close one of these within six months. The bank's original appraisal value was $9,800M.

Their investments, in the aggregate, contain over 1,600 residential apartments. They also control nearly 200,000 SF of commercial and retail space in the various properties.

The current plan to redevelop the property at 100 SoHo Street calls for adding two stories to create a seventh- and eighth-floor two-story penthouse with terraces at both levels. Retail/commercial space will comprise the first floor at grade and a portion of the cellar below grade. This will result in nine residential condominium units on the second through eighth floors. They have asked QRS to provide acquisition and construction financing. We have agreed to recommend approval [loan (1)] but also have elected to offer permanent financing should the property not generate the sales required [loan (2)] or should the principals retain the ownership interest in the commercial space for income generation purposes [loan (3)].

Credit Proposal—Loan (1): Acquisition and Construction

Loan Amount	For acquisition and construction up to an aggregate of $11,500,000, but no greater than the lesser of 80% of the stabilized appraised rental value or 80% of the total project cost (currently estimated at $14,818M on the "Initial Project Cost Statement" attached). A $5,994M sublimit "Project Loan" for acquisition ($5,676M at closing) and interest carry (up to $318M drawn monthly) will be available before receipt of formal approvals and building permits, which will not be obtained by the time of the essence closing date of September 21.
Borrower's Cash Equity	$2,932M in cash for preclosing, acquisition, and closing costs. Subsequent cash equity due is estimated at $386M.
Collateral	First mortgage on the property and improvements at 100 SoHo Street, assignment of leases and rents, and UCC filings on all personal property and equipment on the property.
Term	Two years from closing.
Repayment	Interest only monthly at prime rate floating plus 1% by autodebit
Fee	1% of Loan Amount
Guarantors:	Joint and several guarantees of completion and repayment from Member 1, Member 2, and Member 3.

Appraised Values	As-is land value to be no less than $7,993M (75% LTV of Project Loan portion). Stabilized rental value to be no less than $14,375M to advance up to $11,500M.
Environmental Audit	Phase I received; borrower and guarantors to perform all tasks recommended in Phase I report before initial construction loan advance (see Addendum for listing of items). Closing of Project Loan permitted before performance of tasks.
Construction/Consulting Engineer	Initial construction advance subject to completion of a Plan and Cost Review by a bank engineer stating that the budget and plans are adequate. Subsequent construction advances will be subject to inspection of work in place by the bank's engineer.
Prepayment	Borrower has the right to prepay the principal in multiples of $25,000 with interest computed to the last day of the month in which prepayment is made subject to payment of "Walkaway Fee" (see below).
Release Prices	Residential and commercial units will be released for a consideration equal to the greater of 80% of the net sales proceeds per unit or $1,150,000. Any sales proceeds in excess of 80% will be deposited in a QRS money market account to be designated solely for the purpose of future project expenses. These funds will be released on payment in full of all principal, interest, late fees, and other out-of-pocket fees due under this proposed facility or, if necessary, applied to reduce the final amount of loan (3) to no more than a 75% LTV and a 1.25X DSC ratio based on signed leases at the time of closing.[13]
Transferability	Due on sale or transfer of any ownership interest other than sales of individual condominium units to bona fide third-party occupants or investors.

---

[13] The provision requiring "excess" proceeds to be deposited with the lender, QRS, was dropped because it was not competitive in the marketplace and the borrower threatened to take his business elsewhere.

Subordinate Financing	Prohibited.
Brokerage Fees	The Borrower shall hold the Bank harmless from all brokerage claims, if any, which may be made in connection with this transaction, and under no circumstances is the Bank to be liable in any way for any brokerage fees or commissions. This provision will survive the closing, at which time Borrower shall pay all and any commission and/or compensation due to its authorized broker.
Other Conditions	During the term of the Loan and any extension thereof, the Borrower will be required to maintain all operating accounts, sales contract escrow accounts, and/or tenant lease security accounts at the Bank.

Credit Proposal—Loan (2): Permanent Loan for Entire Building as Rental[14]

Loan Amount	Up to $11,500M, but no greater than 80% of the "as-stabilized" appraised value from a current appraisal based on market rents and leases at the time of conversion from construction loan.
Term	Five years from closing with one 5-year extension option.
Collateral	Same as Loan (1).
Amortization	Fixed monthly principal and interest payments on a 25-year payout basis during the first five-year term; a 20-year payout basis during extension term.
Interest Rate	5-year Treasury Bill rate plus 225 basis points.
Fee	1% of the Loan Amount unless the Construction Loan converts to a Permanent Loan within 15 months of closing of the construction loan, in which case this fee will be reduced to ½ %.

---

[14] For a property that will be sold as a condominium, it is very unusual for a credit presentation to suggest a loan facility with specific terms if the sales plan fails and a rental situation develops. The rental scenario usually is addressed and analyzed, as it is later in this presentation, but specific terms are not discussed or put in the loan commitment or loan documents. Why lock in terms under a very hypothetical situation that has a low probability of occurrence? If the project fails as a condominium, with the threat of calling the loan, the lender has tremendous flexibility and leverage to negotiate without being constrained by terms that were devised when market conditions and circumstances were probably very different.

Guarantors/Recourse	If residential tenant leases generate 75% or more of actual aggregate rental income, nonrecourse except as to standard carve-outs for fraud, misrepresentation, and environmental matters.
	If residential tenant leases generate less than 75% of actual aggregate rental income, Member 1, Member 2, and Member 3 will be required to execute joint and several guarantees for any principal amount in excess of 50% of the appraised rental value.
Appraisal	Update of original appraisal to be obtained.
Prepayment and Right of Assumption	5–4–3–2–1 repeating during extension period. Sixty (60)-day windows before the original or any extended maturity to repay without penalty. Borrower to be permitted an opportunity to sell the property, after conversion to permanent status, with the purchaser assuming the mortgage debt subject to payment of a fee of 1% of the then principal outstanding and the Bank's approval of the creditworthiness, character, and capacity of the proposed purchaser.
Subordinated Financing	Prohibited.
Other Conditions	Closing subject to a review of the then current tenants' leases by the Bank and its counsel, which review will determine if the Leases support the Loan, at the Bank's sole discretion.
	Net operating income from leases in effect at the time of conversion must be adequate to provide a minimum Debt Service Coverage Ratio of 1.2X during the term of the Permanent Loan.
	Closing subject to issuance of final Certificate of Occupancy for all residential and commercial spaces.
	Bank will collect monthly escrow payments for real estate taxes, insurance, and water and sewer charges (if not metered).
	All operating accounts and tenant lease security accounts to be maintained at the Bank.
Extension Option	A default under any related Borrower or Guarantor loan at the Bank will be a default under this loan.

An additional five-year term available subject to compliance with the following:

The Bank must receive written notice of the Borrower's desire to exercise the extension option no less than ninety (90) days before the initial Loan Maturity Date.

Maximum LTV Ratio to be 75% as determined by the Bank in its sole discretion, based on leases then in effect.

Minimum DSC Ratio to be no less than 1.2X based on leases then in effect.

Payment of an extension fee of 1.0% of the then outstanding loan amount payable on submission of the written notification of the Borrower's intention to extend.

Rate to be reset at the five-year Treasury bill rate index as of ninety (90) days before the initial Loan Maturity plus 250 basis points.

All payments during the prior term must have been made in a satisfactory manner and no events of default can have occurred whether declared or undeclared.

Credit Proposal—Loan (3): Permanent Loan—Retail Condominium Unit Only

Loan Amount

Up to $3,200M, but no greater than 75% of the "as-stabilized" appraised value from an updated appraisal based on market rents and leases at the time of conversion from construction loan.

Term

5 years from closing with one 5-year extension option.

Collateral

First mortgage on commercial condominium space of approximately 6,000 SF, assignment of leases and rents, and UCC filings on all personal property and equipment on the Property.

Appraised Value

A stabilized value of the commercial space to be no less than $4,300M to advance up to $3,200M as determined by the bank in its sole

	discre-tion, based on leases in effect at the time of conversion.
Amortization	Fixed monthly principal and interest payments on a 25-year payout basis during the first five-year term; a 20-year payout basis during extension term.
Interest Rate	5-year Treasury bill rate plus 225 basis points.
Fee	1% of the Loan Amount; however, if the Construction Loan converts to this Permanent Loan within 15 months of closing of the construction loan, this fee will be reduced to ½ %.
Guarantors	Member 1, Member 2, and Member 3 to execute joint and several guarantees of repayment of 100% of loan.
Prepayment and Right of Assumption	5–4–3–2–1 repeating during extension period. Sixty (60)-day window before the original or any extended maturity to repay without penalty.
Transferability	Borrower to be permitted one opportunity to sell the property with the purchaser assuming the mortgage debt subject to a payment of a fee of 1% of the then principal outstanding and the Bank's approval of the creditworthiness, character, and capacity of the proposed purchaser.
Subordinated Financing	Prohibited.
Other Conditions	Net operating income from leases in effect at the time of conversion must be adequate to provide a minimum Debt Service Coverage of 1.25X during the term of the Permanent Loan.
	Closing subject to the issuance of a final Certificate of Occupancy.
	Monthly escrow payments for real estate taxes, insurance, and water and sewer charges (if not metered).
	All operating accounts and tenant lease security accounts to be maintained at the Bank.
	A default under any related Borrower or Guarantor loan at the Bank will be a default under this loan.

The Borrower will have the right to extend the Loan for an additional five-year term subject to compliance with the following conditions:

- The Bank must receive written notice of the Borrower's desire to exercise the extension option no less than ninety (90) days before the initial Loan Maturity Date.
- Maximum LTV Ratio to be 75% as determined by the bank at its sole discretion, based on leases then in effect.
- Minimum DSC Ratio to be no less than 1.25X based on leases then in effect.
- Payment of an Extension Fee of ½ % of the then outstanding loan amount payable on written notification of the Borrower's request to extend.
- Rate to be reset at the five-year Treasury bill rate index as of ninety (90) days before the initial Loan Maturity plus 250 basis points.
- All payments during the prior term must have been made in a satisfactory manner, and no events of default can have occurred whether declared or undeclared.

Project Description

The property will be delivered vacant at closing. The contract to buy the property is being assumed by the borrower at the same $8,000M price that the original contract states. Closing can be no later than September 21, with time of the essence.

The site encompasses one building, 100 SoHo Street. It is currently improved with a six-story plus basement turn-of-the-century building between Prince and Spring Streets in SoHo. It is believed that two small mortgages totaling $155M are outstanding which will be paid off at closing, but will likely continue to remain recorded to save mortgage recording tax.[15] The Project Cost Statement will be adjusted at closing to move any savings based on the assignment to another equity item.

The lot size is 50 feet by 100 feet, or 5,000 SF. As currently proposed, the redevelopment will result in a total gross building area of 35,833 SF including common area of approximately 5,796 SF (16% loss factor) and usable

---

[15] By keeping the mortgages recorded, under the New York City tax system, the borrowers can save $4,340 in mortgage recording tax.

space of 30,042SF including terrace space totaling 3,399SF. The plan calls for adding two stories of approximately 12 feet each to create a seventh-floor two-story penthouse with terraces at both levels. The net residential living area will total 24,042 SF. Retail/commercial space at and below grade will be approximately 6,000 SF of gross space. There will be 9 residential units. On completion, the building will contain a partially leasable cellar, ground floor retail/commercial space, 8 finished residential spaces on the second through sixth floors, and one penthouse above. Electric, gas, water, and boiler utility rooms plus 10 individual storage rooms will take up approximately 50% of the cellar, with the balance being usable retail storage space. The first floor will be open for retail or other commercial uses. The ceiling height will be approximately 15 feet, which is normal for these typical converted SoHo loft buildings.

The second through fourth floors will each contain two apartments, one consisting of 1,817 SF and one of 1,636 SF. These will be completely finished and will contain two bedrooms, two baths, a kitchen, living room/dining area, and, depending on the options chosen, a study area. The rear second floor unit will also have a 700-SF terrace. The fifth and sixth floors will be single full floor finished units. Each will consist of 3 bedrooms, 2 ½ baths, kitchen, living room/dining area, study, and large walk-in closets. Total living space will be 3,550 SF.

The penthouse to be erected will consist of a 3,184-SF duplex unit. It will feature an aggregate of 2,699 SF of terrace space on the seventh and eighth floors. The seventh floor will contain three bedrooms, the kitchen, and the living room/dining area. There will be an open space to the eighth floor from which light from a large skylight will be available. This floor will also contain 2 ½ baths. The eighth floor will consist of a 25 ½ -foot × 16-foot family room. However, the use attributed to it depends on the purchaser.

Major features of the renovated premises will be residential unit ceiling heights of no less than 10 ft., the above-noted large terraces for the second floor and penthouse units, a complete security and intercom system, sprinklers throughout the building, new hardwood floors, and a modern elevator opening directly into each apartment. Certain existing interior architectural features will be retained to preserve the character of the building. These consist primarily of open wood beams, structural joists, bolts, etc. The exterior façade will be repaired or replaced with upgraded materials, but its general features will be essentially retained. The availability of sidewalk vault space of approximately 250 SF permits utility rooms to extend under the sidewalk. The plans also call for lowering the cellar floor by 2 ft.

100 SoHo Street
INITIAL PROJECT COST STATEMENT

Items of Cost/Uses	Total Costs	Initial Loan Budget Amounts	Borrower's Equity Paid In	Borrower's Equity Due	
CONSTRUCTION LOAN					
Hard Costs:					
Building/Site Hard Costs (see attached budget)	$4,333,561	$4,333,561			Per Hard Cost Estimate Sheet Provided
General Conditions	$346,685	$346,685			Per Hard Cost Estimate Sheet Provided
Contingency	$303,346	$303,346			Per Hard Cost Estimate Sheet Provided
Subtotal—Hard Costs	$4,983,592	$4,983,592	$0	$0	Per Hard Cost Estimate Sheet Provided
Soft Costs:					
Real Estate Taxes	$60,000	60,000			1st year taxes only
Interest on Loan	$231,000	$231,000			Building Loan, interest only
Appraisal Fee/ Environmental Fee	$10,200	$10,200			Appraisal @ $8,500; Ph I @ $1,700
Commitment Fee	$100,000		$100,000		1% of $10MM
Lender's Construction Consultant	$15,000	$5,000		$10,000	Plan & Cost $5M; Inspections @ $10M
Lender's Counsel	$25,000		$25,000		Bank Estimate
Recording Documents	$155,680	$75,000	$80,680		2.75% on Building Loan Total + $400 Deed Fee
Architect/Engineer/ Expeditor	$220,000	$80,787	$88,149	$51,064	Per Hard Cost Estimate Sheet Provided
Title Policies	$35,000		$35,000		Borrower Estimate
Builder's Risk Insurance	$60,000	$60,000			Borrower Estimate
Surveys and Permits/Other	$10,000			$10,000	Borrower's "Other"
Subtotal—Soft Costs	$921,880	$521,987	$328,829	$71,064	
TOTAL BUILDING LOAN COSTS	$5,905,472	$5,505,579	$328,829	$71,064	
PROJECT LOAN: Land Acquisition	$8,000,000	$5,676,208	$2,323,792		
Condominium Offering Plan	$70,000		50,000	$20,000	Borrower Estimate
Marketing & Sales	$40,000			$40,000	Borrower Estimate
Fuel, Utility, Water & Sewer	$16,160			$16,160	Borrower Estimate
Sales and Leasing Broker In-house	$81,196			$81,196	Borrower Estimate
Mortgage Broker	$50,000		$50,000		Borrower Estimate
Acctg, Mgt, Payroll, Office, Maint. Supplies	$54,708			$54,708	Borrower Estimate
Professional Fees	$23,020		$20,000	$3,020	Borrower Estimate
Contingency/Misc. & Reserve	$120,000		$20,000	$100,000	Borrower Estimate
Borrower's Attorney	$20,000		$20,000		Borrower Estimate
Project Loan Closing Costs	$119,720		$119,720		2.75% on Project Loan Total + $400 Deed Rec.
Interest on Project Loan	$318,213	$318,213			Project Loan Interest Only - see next page
SUBTOTAL—PROJECT LOAN	$8,913,017	$5,994,421	$2,603,512	$315,084	
TOTAL BUILDING AND PROJECT LOAN	$14,818,489	$11,500,000	$2,932,341	$386,148	
	100.00%	77.6%	19.8%	2.6%	

The Initial Project Cost Statement breaks down the aggregate cost to acquire and convert the property based on the plans outlined above. To date, no subcontracts have been signed as the plans have not been accepted for issuance of a building permit by the city. Excluding the $8,000M land cost, completion is expected to require hard costs of $4,984M and total soft costs of $1,835M. Hard costs are explained by trade line item on the "Estimate Sheet" attached to the Cost Statement. The hard cost per SF, excluding contingency, is projected to be $130 per SF. The bank has engaged Construction Associates as its construction engineer to evaluate the adequacy of the hard costs proposed. The psf cost does not seem higher than other cost estimates, but each of these projects is unique to the property being converted.

The engineer is best qualified to do the final cost evaluation. The plan and cost review will be required before funding the initial hard cost construction advance.

Soft costs have been carefully reviewed with the developer. The bank has already requested modifications in the original budget to reflect certain items that are now properly accounted for. The estimates are believed to be conservative.

As noted on the Cost Statement, the bank's loan will approximate 78% of the total cost. The borrower will be required to contribute no less than $2,932M toward acquisition and closing costs. This equates to 20% of total costs. Additional potential equity required totals $386M. It will be demonstrated that the borrower and guarantors have the ability to provide such funds in the financial statement analysis below.

Project Sales Prices

The borrower as sponsor does not currently expect to sell the commercial space. The present plan is to continue ownership of that space for cash flow–generating purposes. The borrower's projected gross residential sales proceeds totals $18,292M, or an average of $886 psf. Projected prices for each apartment are as follows.

UNIT	SF	TERRACE SF	SALES PRICE	PRICE PSF Excluding Terraces	PROPOSED RELEASE PRICE (Lower of 80% of net or 1MM) (Assumes Net at 94% of Gross)
2A	1,817	700	$1,470,400	$809	$1,382,176X80%=$1,105,741/ $1,150,000
2B	1,636		$1,329,125	$812	$1,249,378X80%=$999,502/ $1,150,000
3A	1,817		$1,470,400	$809	$1,382,176X80%=$1,105,741/ $1,150,000
3B	1,636		$1,329,125	$812	$1,249,378X80%=$999,502/ $1,150,000
4A	1,817		$1,516,350	$835	$1,425,369X80%=$1,140-,295/ $1,1500,000
4B	1,636		$1,372,000	$838	$1,289,680X80%=$1,031,744/ $1,1500,000
5	3,550		$3,216,500	$906	$3,023,293X80%=$2,418,808/ $1,150,000
6	3,550		$3,301,375	$930	$3,103,293X80%=$2,482,634/ $1,150,000
PENTHSE 7	2,538	1055			
PENTHSE 8	646	1644			
PENTHOUSE TOTAL	3,184	2,699	$3,286,700	$1,075	$3,089,498X80%=$2,482,634/ $1,150,000
TOTALS	20,643	3,399	$18,291,975	$886	$13,755,565/$11,500,000=120%
BANK BREAK-EVEN IF RETAIL AT $3,200M PERMANENT			$8,300,000	$402	REPAYMENT POSSIBLE FROM AS FEW AS 4 BUT COULD BE UP TO 7 UNITS
BANK BREAK-EVEN IF REPAYMENT FROM RES. ONLY			$11,500,000	$557	REPAYMENT POSSIBLE FROM AS FEW AS 7 BUT COULD BE UP TO 9 UNITS

This project and the loan could evolve under three scenarios:

The residential and commercial units are accepted for sale by the market and sold by the sponsor;

Only the residential units are sold by the sponsor who retains the commercial unit; or

None are accepted by the market and remain as rentals for the sponsor to manage (worst case).

One possibility—that the residential units remain as rental and the commercial unit is sold—is not factored into the analysis because this is believed to be very unlikely to develop.

The above scenarios are accounted for by the three loans proposed herein. Loan (1) allows the project to be developed as planned. Loan (2) addresses the possibility that the project is not accepted on a for-sale basis, is marketed as a rental, and requires a permanent loan on stabilization of rental income. Loan (3) recognizes the borrower's plan to maintain ownership of the commercial space.

The bank's construction loan will be repaid under either of the successful sale scenarios from proceeds of residential unit closings and/or the refinancing of the stabilized commercial unit. A loan value of approximately $3,200M has been allocated to the commercial unit. Refinancing the unit at the loan amount would require a payment of total release prices from residential sales of $8,300M. The minimum price psf on the residential units to repay such a loan would be $402 psf.

If the commercial unit did not justify a $3,200M loan (at a 75% LTV, the value required would be $4,300M), loan (1) could be repaid in full if the residential units sold for $557 psf. Both of these prices are well below those proposed and well within the demonstrated market prices of SoHo conversions over the last 12 to 18 months. [This circumstance does not factor in the fact that sales proceeds in excess of the release price will be held by the bank and can be used to further reduce loan (3) if it does not achieve a minimum appraised value of $4,300M. The approximate difference between 94 percent of net sales proceeds and the 80 percent minimum release price is $3,439,000.]

Typical sales comps are attached, as is a segment of a recent first quarter Manhattan market survey. These reports provide evidence of the very strong trends in condominium construction and sales over the prior two years. Contract prices in SoHo and Tribeca (and the West Village as we know) are averaging anywhere from $800 psf to $1,400 psf. The bank's residential loan department is approving loans on condo units at upward of $1,100 psf. The prices in the market justify the prices being projected by the borrower. Most importantly, QRS's breakeven under either scenario above is at the very low end or well below the market comps. An inability to achieve QRS's breakeven would require market price declines of no less than 50%.

Rental Estimates

A fallback position should sales prices diminish or the project not be accepted by the market is to rent the units. In such a case, the residential rents would average $60 psf and commercial rents would be $80 psf for floor space and $20 for storage space. A projected cash flow follows.

Projected Cash Flow	($M)
Commercial Rent–4,400 SF floor space @ $80 psf	352.0
Commercial Rent–1,600 SF storage space @ 20 psf	32.0
Total Potential Commercial Rent [average $64]	384.0
Residential Rents–20,610 SF @ $60 psf	1,236.6
Total Potential Rent	1,620.6
Less 10% commercial vacant/collection loss	35.2
Less 5% residential vacant/collection loss	61.8
Effective Gross Revenue	1,523.6
Real Estate Taxes	100.0
Water & Sewer	6.0
Insurance	15.9
Fuel/Utilities	23.5
Repair/Maintenance	20.7
Management @ 5%	81.0
Administration/Accounting/Other Professional Fees	23.4
Other	15.0
Total Operating Expense	285.5
Net Operating Income	1,238.1
Estimated Value at 8% cap rate	15,476.3
LTV @ maximum $11,500,000 loan	74%
Annual Debt Service–$11,500,000 @ 7%/25 years	975.4
Debt Service Coverage Ratio	1.27X

The income and expense projections above are a combination of those submitted by the borrower and adjustments made by the bank. Retail rents for storefront space ranging from $65 psf to $105 psf can be easily documented. The assumptions above assume retail rents are triple net, which is not uncommon, but may also be adjusted as leases are negotiated.

Of all the assumptions, the most critical is the residential rental income assumption at $60 psf per annum. The bank's appraiser has found that rental levels in this area are continuing to rise as they are in other, less desirable locations in lower Manhattan. Recent direct evidence of the trend in rents is a bank financed project on 4th Street between First and Second Avenues in the East Village. This very modest but newly constructed 12-unit apartment building is being leased for $52 psf. 100 SoHo's location and overall appeal are clearly more desirable and likely to be more expensive than those of the East Village.

To achieve a breakeven operating and DSC ratio level, a minimum effective gross revenue of $1,260.9M is required. Using the assumptions above for commercial rents, the average residential net rent would have to be only $48 psf to generate the minimum $944.1M of revenue required. This is well below the current market.

Commercial Unit Cash Flow Projection

Using the projection above, estimated income from the commercial space would be $384.0M. This assumes a triple net rent of $64 psf. With a 10% vacancy allowance, net income is $348.8M. A cap rate of 8% would be required to achieve the necessary valuation for the $3,200M proposed loan. The proposal herein limits that loan to 75% based on rents at that time. The additional proceeds from closings to be held by the bank provide a cushion should the commercial space not justify the full $3,200M loan.

Principal's Financial Condition

The borrowing entity is newly formed and has no significant assets, liabilities, income, or expenses other than those related to the start-up of this project. Annual financial statements or tax returns will be required during the term of each respective loan.

The principals of the borrower have submitted individual personal financial statements, their most recent respective tax returns, and a schedule of cash flows and debt service requirements on properties owned by their affiliated entities. The statements presented and attached will have to be resubmitted on the bank's form before closing.

Member 1 reports his net worth to be $67,739M. It consists primarily of real estate investments valued at $53,950M. He also reports liquid assets of $1,763M, which will be confirmed before closing by submission of bank account and broker statements. His real estate consists of varying interest in 21 Manhattan properties managed by ABC. Most of these are owned in common with Member 2 as well as other partners. Member 2 reports a net worth of $50,612M consisting almost exclusively of real estate and business investments. He reports no cash or other liquid assets. He has justified this by reporting that all cash is left or used in the various real estate entities. On a combined basis, their reported net equity in real estate is $98,454M.

Based on information submitted by the borrower with the application package, a schedule summarizing cash flows and bank estimated net property values was derived and is included in this package. In summary, the properties listed report the following aggregates:

Category	($M)
Gross Rental Income	42,113.3
Operating Expenses	19,600.5
Net Cash Flow Before Debt Service	22,512.8
Annual Regular Prin. & Int.	12,749.9
Net Cash Flow After Debt Service	9,762.9
Member 1 / Member 2 Shares of Net Cash Flow After Debt Service (NCFADS)	5,271.5
Estimated Aggregate Property Value	333,474.0
Aggregate Mortgage Debt	191,244.0
Net Equity in Real Estate	142,230.0
Member 1 / Member 2 Shares of Net Equity in Real Estate	78,203.2

Based on the bank's analysis, their reported values are approximately 26% greater than the bank's estimate. However, the net value of $78MM+ is still very substantial. Their aggregate LTV ratio is a very acceptable 57.3% as well.

On an aggregate basis, the cash flow from their investments covers debt service payments by 1.77 times. Their allocated portions of net cash flow after debt service are a very substantial $5,271M.

Credit References/Personal Credit Reports

Telephone credit checks were made to Institution A and Institution B, both of which have large mortgage exposures on properties owned by the partners. Both entities reported excellent experience with the group after several years and several transactions. It was stated that the partners could very easily handle this type of project.

Member 1's credit report was spotless. Member 2's was not. His report showed several past-due collection and charge-off credit card items. These were all small and totaled approximately $5M. Member 2 has been asked to provide a written explanation of each item at or before closing. It has been preliminarily reported that such items show up frequently but are usually found to belong to others with his very common name.

Finally, ABC's litigation and lien report contained several small items, including typical slip and fall cases and modest mechanic's liens. The borrower's attorney is preparing a response to our request for information regarding these that will also be a requirement for closing.

None of the above items were believed to be serious enough or appeared to represent such a significant pattern of bad debts that we might be precluded from making these loans.

Risks and Mitigants

The major issues regarding the risk in this credit are the inability to complete the redevelopment and the inability to sell the residential units. Leasing the commercial unit is important, but the loan could still be repaid from sale of residential units only.

The ABC members are well known to the bank. Their performance on existing debt has been as agreed, and they have exhibited a thorough knowledge of the Manhattan market. They have a strong track record of acquisition and redevelopment of property that is verified by reviewing the asset schedules submitted. Credit references indicate that they have an excellent development track record.

Further protecting our exposure will be the fact that the bulk of the cash equity required will be due at closing. Up-front contribution of this equity, which is approximately 20% of the total estimated cost, means that there is minimal risk associated with an inability to support the job if it develops as planned. If it develops with overruns or delays, the outside cash flow strength of the principal and guarantors is more than adequate to continue financial support. It is equally protective if unanticipated delays occur in the approval process as our initial investment will be limited to 69% of the costs of acquisition and closing.

The inability to sell units is the overriding risk to be overcome. Any serious downturn in market conditions would have a ripple effect at some level on condo sales in Manhattan. These units, however, are clearly high-end units in an area that was a major attraction even in the early 1990s, when other market areas were still in disarray. It is believed that the sale of nine well-developed and well-conceived units in this location will remain attractive to buyers whose income levels would be less affected by economic slowdown than more middle-class developments. As noted earlier, the breakeven sale levels of $402 or $557 psf are well below market norms today and are believed to be an adequate cushion for the bank's investment.

If sales are not achieved at an adequate level, the prospect of renting the project's units is still viable. Again as noted, the ability of the borrower and its principals to generate rents at a level to sustain a 1.2 DSC ratio would be an issue if not for the prime location and appeal of this neighborhood. Even at lower levels of rent, there is adequate income to maintain operations and debt service payments.

The fact that we will hold excess sales proceeds to protect until the construction loan is repaid and against unforeseen circumstances relating to the leasing and value of the commercial unit further mitigates the rental risk related to that portion of the property.

Loan Grade

The three loans proposed herein are all rated as "C," Good Quality. The principals are competent builder-developers with a satisfactory operating history. The project in question has at least satisfactory sales and/or rental prospects. In this case, the loans have elements of high quality as well in that the builder-developers have very significant business and personal resources, significant initial equity in the project, conservative cost estimates, and an estimated absorption period of less than 18 months.

Profitability

The bank's relationship with this group has resulted in a good yield estimated at 4.56% over the past 12 months. Average deposits have been steadily increasing, and the credits in question are both well secured and performing as agreed. The interest rate on the largest currently outstanding loan is a well-priced 6.25% as well.

The yield is projected to increase due to the currently high level of prime, which results in a projected spread of 4.0% on the new construction loan in question. Although average loan outstandings will rise significantly, deposit balances are expected to increase based on recent increases and the needs of the project in question. Given size and types of properties managed by ABC, assuming an additional level of deposits is not unreasonable.

CHAPTER 7

The Loan Closing, Legal Documentation, and Guarantees

TERMS, PRECLOSINGS, AND CLOSINGS

Once the underwriting is complete and the loan has been approved, the process to and through the loan closing can take on a life of its own. Depending on the institution, the lender may have a lot of control or very little but almost certainly will not have the level of control he had before. For the uninitiated, the many necessary and seemingly esoteric tasks leading up to and including the closing almost certainly will be confusing at first. In fact, it probably will take several loan closings before a loan officer starts to feel comfortable, let alone understands what is happening. Depending on the complexity of the transaction, the municipality where the closing occurs, and where the property is situated, even the closing attorneys may have a hard time grasping all the legal and procedural nuances.

With a fairly complex transaction in New York, for instance, it is not unusual to involve, and have attending a closing, fifteen or more people. At a "simple closing" there probably will be a minimum of eight attendees.[1] The closing room, filled with accordion

---

[1] For example, at a recent closing of a sale of a building in New York City, in attendance was the purchaser (borrower) and his attorney, the seller and his attorney, a title company representative, the lending institution's attorney, the lender's loan administrator, and the lender. This does not include typical additional attendees, including partners of the buyer and seller and assistants to the attorneys.

files containing documents, makes things even more crowded and confusing. This chapter helps clarify the closing process, the purpose of certain documents, and the usefulness of guarantees.

WHAT IS A CLOSING?

A closing is the assembling of several people in one place to close (complete) a transaction. Although a closing can be achieved with a telephone, fax machine, overnight mail, and perhaps e-mail, using these methods the process almost certainly would take days instead of hours.[2] When all the participants meet face to face, questions can be answered immediately; concerns can be addressed; changes, additions, and subtractions to documents can be taken care of more easily; last-minute negotiations can be entered into on the spot; and misunderstandings can surface and be corrected quickly. Therefore, for the sake of efficiency, the centralization of expertise, personal and professional support, and to overcome unexpected problems, a closing, particularly with regard to a devel- opment loan, virtually always takes place at a specific time and place usually chosen by the lender.

CHOOSING THE RIGHT LENDER'S ATTORNEY

Real property law is so complex that in the real estate arena there are attorneys who only write and review commercial leases, those who work solely on residential landlord-tenant law, those who limit their practice to tax abatements and tax credits, those who focus on environmental issues, those who only do closings, those who litigate in court, those who only write construction managers' and contractors' contracts, and those who specialize in several other areas. In light of the depth and scope of knowledge and experience required, to protect the lending institution, especially in crafting the documentation for a development loan, no matter how overtly simple the project appears to be, a qualified experienced attorney is a must.

---

[2] Most commercial real estate closings take several hours but can last a day or longer.

Too often, a senior officer of a small lending institution will require his real estate lenders to hire a law firm on the basis of a personal relationship he has with one or more of that firm's attorneys or his experience with the firm in another field of credit. If things go well, the attorney will continue to work on real estate transactions. If things go poorly, though, the attorney's mistakes and/or omissions may cause major problems. Choosing the right attorney is not difficult but it does have a subjective component and, like a job interview, can lead to a top candidate who after a short period reveals himself to be less capable than originally thought. The following checklist is a good basis on which to select a qualified attorney:

- The law practice should have at least three attorneys solely involved in real estate.
- The lead attorney should have no less than seven years of practice in real property law.
- The practice should have closed on multiple development and construction loans.
- References from other lenders and borrowers should be checked out carefully.
- The firm should have a reputation for working around the clock. Someone should always be available.
- If a particular credit involves special experience, such as with environmental, landmark, or condominium issues, the firm must be thoroughly experienced in the special area and be able to prove it.
- The law practice's offices should look good. Since closings and meetings will occur there, they will be perceived as an extension of your lending institution.
- The attorneys should be personable but professional and resolute when necessary. They will be representing and protecting you through their negotiating abilities.
- The attorneys should take the time and be articulate in explaining legal points and business points to you and your colleagues.
- Cost should not be a major factor (although it requires some consideration) since all legal costs ultimately will be borne by the borrower.

Occasionally, it makes sense to hire more than one attorney, depending on the type of credit. For instance, you may need an environmental attorney to review certain issues and a closing attorney to book a loan. Often, larger firms have all the experience and the attorneys you will need under one roof.

The most important thing to remember is that no matter how much you know or think you know, you are not an attorney who has the specialized and detailed knowledge necessary to practice real estate law. However, this will not preclude you before and at the closing from making business decisions and suggestions to your attorney or to a senior loan officer who has the authority to make decisions that affect the closing and possibly the structure of the loan. These decisions include renegotiating some of the loan terms at the closing and possibly interpreting the intentions of your institution's senior credit officer in approving the loan's final terms and conditions. Therefore, it is important that you review the loan approval memorandums and your notes to memorize the salient points of the facility. Then, if called on, you will be prepared to answer questions and make decisions about the terms and character of the deal. If you are not prepared, you could face embarrassment and possibly make a poor decision that will come back to haunt you.

GETTING IT TOGETHER

After the lending officer has completed his underwriting and gained his institution's final approval, aside from appraisal, environmental, and consulting engineer matters, the preclosing process generally does not involve him. It involves his attorney, the borrower's attorney, and the borrower. To make sure everyone does what he is supposed to do and to assign specific responsibilities, a checklist usually is produced by the lender's attorney. A checklist of closing documents, responsibilities, and status for the new ground-up construction of a condominium consisting of hotel, office, and school space in Manhattan follows.

PRELIMINARY CLOSING AGENDA

$32,000,000 Financing
provided by QRS Bank to
Letoh Associates, LLC

Parties

Letoh Associates, LLC	Borrower
By:	
Ben Glock	Guarantors
Sylvia Rush	
QRS Bank	Lender ("QRS")
By: Melvin Vangwork	
Senior Vice President	
Jay Benito	
Vice President	
Brothman & Bowman, P.C.	Counsel for Lender ("BB")
By: Barry C. Brothman, Esq.	
Cargel & Jacobson, P.C.	Counsel for Borrower and Guarantors ("CJ")
By: Auden Grogins, Esq.	
Mezzanine Inc.	Mezzanine Lender
("MEZ")	
By:	
Arlo & Smith LLP	Counsel to Mezzanine
Lender	
By: Zackery Malabu, Esq.	("AS")
Liberty Abstract, New York LLC	Title Company
By: Paul Orien, Esq.	

INDEX OF DOCUMENTS

DOCUMENT	RESPONSIBILITY	STATUS
QRS FINANCING DOCUMENTATION		
1. QRS Commitment Letter	BB	Final
2. Building Loan Mortgage Note	BB	Revised
3. Building Loan Mortgage, Assignment of Leases and Rents and Security Agreement	BB	Revised
4. Project Loan Mortgage Note	BB	Open
5. Project Loan Mortgage, Assignment of Leases and Rents and Security Agreement	BB	Open
6. Building Loan and Project Loan Agreement	BB	Revised
7. Assignment of Plans, Permits and Contracts	BB	Revised
8. Guaranty of Payment	BB	Revised
9. Guaranty of Completion	BB	Revised

10. Environmental Indemnity	BB	Revised
11. UCC-1 Financing Statements	BB	Open

CONSTRUCTION DOCUMENTS

12. Architect's Agreement	CJ	Received
13. Architect's Certificate	BB/CJ	Received
14. Construction Manager's Agreement	CJ	Received
15. Construction Manager's Certificate	BB/CJ	Draft
16. Major Trade Contracts	CJ	Open
17. Trade Contractor's Certificates	BB/CJ	Draft
Other Design Contracts		
18. (a) Structural Engineer	CJ	Received
(b) Consulting Engineer		
Interior Designer		
Other Design Professionals' Certificates		
19. (a) Structural Engineer	CJ	Received
(b) Consulting Engineer		
Interior Designer		
20. Building Permits and Municipal Approvals	CJ	Open
21. Construction Budget and Project Cost Statement	QRS	Preliminary
22. Construction Consultant Plan & Cost Review	QRS	Preliminary
23. Payment and Performance Bonds	CJ	Open
24. Hotel Manager Plan and Specifications Consent	CJ	Received

PROJECT DOCUMENTS

25. Hotel Management Agreement and Amendments Condominium Documents	CJ	Received
26. (a) Declaration	CJ	Draft
(b) By-Laws		Draft
No-Action Letter		Received
27. School Unit Sales Contract and Amendment	CJ	Received
28. Direction Letter re: School Unit Deposit	BB	Draft
29. Air Rights/Development Rights Acquisition Documents	CJ	Received
30. Hotel Management Agreement SNDA	BB	Final
31. Hotel Manager Estoppel Letter	BB/CJ	Final
32. Kitchen Facilities Easement Agreement	CJ	Received
33. Residential Developer Estoppel Letter	BB/CJ	Received
34. Option Agreement	CJ	Received
35. Optionee Estoppel Letter	BB/CJ	Received

Note that of the 58 items, only 3 are required from the lender (QRS). They are the Construction Budget and Project Cost Statement (doc. # 21), the Construction Consultant Plan and Cost Review (doc. # 22), and the QRS Closing Statement (doc. # 57). The Construction Budget and Project Cost Statement is a breakdown of the total development cost and the portion of the loan allocated to each cost item. It was completed by the lending officer in his credit memorandum and, subject to possible straightforward adjustments, requires no additional work other than copying or e-mailing it to the attorney (see Chapter 6 for a sample). The Plan and Cost Review is a report written by the lender's consulting engineer. After its review and perhaps making adjustments to the Construction Budget and Project Cost Statement previously noted, all the lending officer has to do is deliver a copy (see Chapter 8 for a sample Plan and Cost Review).[3]

The QRS Closing Statement is a document that is worked up by the loan administrator. It then is submitted to the attorney, who, often in collaboration with the administrator, will finalize the statement, which is a list of sources and uses of funds that will occur at the closing. In the list above, the lending officer has little to do between the loan approval and the loan closing. He may be asked from time to time to make business, credit, and operating decisions, but those decisions are basically reactive and usually not difficult.

THE CLOSING DOCUMENTS

A simple closing in New York City that involved the rehabilitation and conversion of a factory building into residential condominiums and retail space had the following index of documents in the closing binder:[4]

---

[3] If at the time of the loan closing a plan and cost review has not been completed, which is not unusual in development loans that have a site acquisition component and a construction component, a closing can take place without the advancement of funds toward construction costs. The loan documents will indicate that advances under the construction portion of the loan will occur only on the receipt of a plan and cost review that must be reviewed and approved by the lender. Ultimate approval to advance funds under the loan may occur after changes are made to the borrower's budget and the lender's construction budget and project cost statement.

[4] A closing binder consists of all the documents generated from a real estate transaction. They are bound together in book form. The binder with the original documents is kept in a secure place with the attorney or the lender, depending on the lending institution's policy.

Index of Closing Documents

1. Contract of Sale for Purchase of Property
2. Notice of Assignment of Contract to Property Owner
3. Assignment and Assumption of Contract of Sale
4. Contract Extension Letters
5. Bargain and Sale Deed with Covenants
6. New York City Real Property Transfer Tax Return
7. Combined Real Estate Transfer Tax Return
8. Seller's Certification as to Vacancy of the Property
9. Seller's Certification of Nonforeign Status
10. Seller's Certification as to Resolution and Corporate Incumbency
11. New York City HPD Affidavit in Lieu of Registration Statement
12. Smoke Detecting Alarm Affidavit
13. Adjustments and Related Notes and Invoices
14. Holdback Postclosing Letter
15. Loan Commitment—Bank
16. Loan Mortgage Note
17. Land Mortgage and Security Agreement
18. First Building Loan Mortgage Note
19. First Building Loan Mortgage and Security Agreement
20. First Building Loan Agreement
21. Second Building Loan Mortgage Note
22. Second Building Loan Mortgage and Security Agreement
23. Second Building Loan Agreement
24. Section 235 Tax Affidavit
25. Completion Guaranty
26. Hazardous Material Guaranty of Payment and Carry
27. Unlimited Guaranty
28. ADA Guaranty and Indemnification Agreement
29. Security Agreement
30. UCC–1 Financing Statements
31. Assignment of Leases and Rents
32. Assignment of Contracts, Management Agreements
33. Legal Opinion of Borrower's Counsel
34. Undertaking

35. Inducement Letter
36. Buyer: Consent of Members with Certificates and Operating Agreement
37. I Member of Buyer: Consent of Members with Certificates and Operating Agreement
38. II Member of Buyer: Consent of Members with Certificates and Operating Agreement
39. III Member of Buyer: Consent of Members with Certificates and Operating Agreement
40. Hazard and Liability Insurance Certificate
41. Title Escrow Letter
42. Market Title Binder

Clearly, even a simple development loan closing is not really simple (or inexpensive). At this closing table there were three members from the buying entity, two members from the seller, the loan officer and his assistant, attorneys for the buyer and lender, an attorney's assistant for the seller, a representative from the prior mortgagee, and a title company representative. In all there were twelve people at the closing. Because of delays caused by disagreements and a lack of documentation, the closing took seven hours.

DRAFT A PERSONAL SUMMARY

Since even a simple development loan generates so much paper, it is a good idea just after the closing to create a one-page "cheat sheet" of the significant loan terms along with any unique operational requirements. You can refer to it easily and memorize or rememorize the salient loan terms when the need arises. It is almost guaranteed that a year into the loan you will be unsure of even its most fundamental aspects. Although most lending institutions require that a loan file begin with a one-page summary of the loan proposal, it is usually more concerned with the credit aspects of the transaction, not the operational part of the credit (see Figure 6.1). Your summary sheet also can include subjective and personal notes. It is for your reference only.[5]

---

[5] It also can be useful many years later when, say, for a job interview, you can do a quick review of each of the transactions in which you were involved.

LOOKING UP TERMS, CONDITIONS, INSTRUCTIONS, AND "RULES"

Most of the legal documents in a closing binder are straightforward and easy to understand. Once you read them even cursorily, you understand what they mean and why they are included. There are, however, a few key basic documents in a loan binder that every professional should be knowledgeable about if for no other reason than to know where to find information about the loan. For a development lender, the three that are the most important to understand are the note, the mortgage, and the building loan agreement (BLA). The descriptions below focus concisely on these documents from an operational perspective.

The Note

The note, which rarely exceeds 10 pages and often, regardless of the loan's size, consists of no more than 4 or 5, is a promise by the borrower to pay back the lender. It states basic terms such as the name of the borrower, the name of the lender, the principal amount of the loan, the interest rate and how it is calculated, when the loan matures, default rates and late charges, and fundamental conditions such as loan extension options (if any), the jurisdiction under which the documents apply (New York, New Jersey, Ohio, or any other state), and waivers by the borrower such as a trial by jury (lenders as a general rule do not like juries, which tend to favor borrowers). Legally, it is proof of a debt. From an operational perspective, it is good for a quick lookup of the basics. Often, because of its brevity, it is bound with the mortgage document.

The Mortgage

The mortgage, which can run 50 pages or more, is the rules and regulations manual of the loan. If you want to find the interest rate on the loan, look at the note first. If you want to know what happens if there is damage to the property by fire or flood, if there is a property condemnation, if an escrow fund has been set up to collect real property taxes and how it works, if rental achievements are not met, if there is a newly discovered environmental issue, when to obtain estoppel certificates from tenants, what rights a second mortgagee has, when to file operating statements with the lender, how to send notices and to whom, what the events of default are, and other rules, regulations, and covenants[6] pertaining to the loan, you should look at the mortgage. Legally, the mortgage is proof of an interest in the property as collateral for the debt. Its priority against other present and future claims on the property is established after its recording at the proper municipal office.[7]

The Building Loan Agreement

Whereas the note and the mortgage are standard on all loans secured by real estate, the building loan agreement[8] is unique to a development loan. It is the instruction manual that provides specific information on the administration of the loan, including, of course, the requirements and method of making loan advances up to and including project completion.

Since the BLA is unique to the development loan, every development lender should become at least somewhat familiar with it. Almost all BLAs start with a definitions section that can be very helpful in understanding a complex transaction. Even for those who have been in the development lending business for many years, reading through this initial definition portion (there are further definitions throughout the document) can be a good learning experience. An initial definition portion taken from the Letoha example (see Chapter 6) follows.[9]

---

[6] Restrictions and requirements placed on the borrower.

[7] In several states, a deed of trust is used instead of a mortgage (some states use both mortgages and deeds of trust). A deed of trust still involves the lender (called the bene-ficiary) and the borrower (called the trustor) but also incorporates a third party, usually an attorney or title company (called the trustee). If there is a loan default, the lender may instruct the trustee to sell the property to satisfy the loan obligation. Unlike a mortgage, the property can be sold without the necessity of going through the court.

[8] The building loan agreement may go under various names, such as the construction loan agreement and the project loan agreement. They are all the same, just differently titled.

[9] In the preface to this book, it was promised that *The Complete Guide to Financing Real Estate Developments* would not contain "useless exhibits." What follows are portions taken from a BLA that are not, at least in the writer's opinion, useless. Their purpose is to give the reader an appreciation of the scope of the BLA and the information it contains. Several of the definitions in the example are deal-specific.

BLA DEFINITIONS

"Architect": ABCDE P.C. or such other architect as may be engaged by the Borrower with the Lender's prior written approval (such approval not to be unreasonably withheld) to design the Improvements.

"Architect's Agreement": The Architect's Agreement, dated November 1, between the Borrower and the Architect, providing for architectural services in connection with the design and construction of the Improvements, as the same may be amended, supplemented, or otherwise modified or replaced from time to time in accordance with the provisions of this Agreement.

"Architect's and Other Design Professionals' Certificates": Certificates by the Architect and the Other Design Professionals in substantially the forms of Exhibits F–1 through F–4 attached hereto.

"Borrower": As defined in the preamble to this Agreement.

"Borrowing Date": The day on which an advance shall be made pursuant to Section 4.1 hereof.

"Budget": The Building Loan Budget and the Project Loan Budget, collectively.

"Budget Line": A Building Loan Budget Line or a Project Loan Budget Line.

"Building Loan": The loan to be made as provided in Section 2.1(a) hereof.

"Building Loan Budget": The budget for the Building Loan that has been delivered by the Borrower to, and approved by, the Lender, as it may be amended from time to time in accordance with this Agreement.

"Building Loan Budget Line": An individual line item shown on the Building Loan Budget.

"Building Loan Commitment": The Lender's obligation hereunder to make the Building Loan to the Borrower.

"Building Loan Costs": Costs of Improvement to be funded using proceeds of the Building Loan as shown in the Building Loan Budget.

"Building Loan Mortgage": The Building Loan Mortgage, Assignment of Leases and Rents, and Security Agreement, dated the date hereof, in the principal amount of the Building Loan, as the same may be hereafter modified, amended, or supplemented from time to time.

"Building Loan Note": The Building Loan Mortgage Note, dated the date hereof, executed and delivered by the Borrower in favor of the Lender, in the principal amount of the Building Loan, as the same may be hereafter modified, amended, or supplemented from time to time.

"Business Day": Any day other than a Saturday, Sunday, or other day on which the Lender is authorized or permitted to close.

"Closing Date": July ___, 200_.

"Collateral": The Borrower's interest in the Premises (including the Borrower's interest in any development rights), the Improvements, the

Tangible Personal Property, the Construction Documents, and the other property encumbered by the Collateral Documents, collectively.

"Collateral Documents": The Mortgage, the Guaranty, the UCC Financing Statements, and all other documents and instruments from time to time evidencing or securing the Loan or any obligation for payment thereof or performance of the Borrower's obligations hereunder.

"Commitment": The Building Loan Commitment and the Project Loan Commitment, collectively.

"Commitment Letter": The Commitment Letter dated April 2, 200_, issued by the Lender to the Borrower, as amended.

"Community Facility Unit": As defined in the Mortgage.

"Completion of the Project": As defined in Section 9.2 hereof.

"Condominium": As defined in the Mortgage.

"Condominium Act": As defined in the Mortgage.

"Condominium Documents": As defined in the Mortgage.

"Construction Consultant": UGE, Ltd., or such other architectural or engineering consultant as the Lender may engage, subject to the terms of Section 4.1(c) of this Agreement, to examine the Plans, the Building Loan Budget, the Construction Schedule, and requests for Building Loan advances, to monitor construction of the Improvements, and to advise and render reports to the Lender concerning the same.

"Construction Documents": The Architect's Agreement, the Other Design Contracts, the Construction Manager's Agreement, the Trade Contracts, the Plans and the Permits, collectively.

"Construction Manager": Workaholic, Inc., or such other general contractor or construction manager as may be engaged by the Borrower, with the Lender's prior written approval (such approval not to be unreasonably withheld), to coordinate, oversee, and perform the construction of the Improvements in accordance with the Plans.

"Construction Manager's Agreement": The Construction Management Agreement dated as of June 2, 200_, between the Borrower and the Construction Manager, as the same may be amended, supplemented, or otherwise modified from time to time in accordance with the provisions of this Agreement.

"Construction Manager's Certificate": A certificate of the Construction Manager in substantially the form of Exhibit G attached hereto.

"Construction Schedule": A construction schedule, in form and substance satisfactory to the Lender, showing the anticipated scheduling of the Project as proposed from time to time by the Construction Manager.

"Cost(s) of Improvement": "Cost of improvement" as defined in Section 2 of the Lien Law, as such definition applies to the Project.

"Debt": Shall have the meaning ascribed to such term in the Mortgage.

"Declaration": As defined in the Mortgage.

"Default": Any of the events specified in Section 10.1, whether or not any requirement for the giving of notice, the lapse of time, or both, or any other condition, provided for therein has been satisfied.

"Default Rate": As defined in the Mortgage.

"Deficiency": As defined in Section 3.1 hereof.

"Equity Requirement": As defined in Section 6.11 hereof.

"Event of Default": Any of the events specified in Section 10.1, provided that any requirement for the giving of notice, the lapse of time, including, without limitation, the expiration of any cure period, or both, or any other condition provided for therein, has been satisfied.

"Force Majeure Delay": Any delay caused by any condition beyond the reasonable control of the Borrower, such as an act of God, fire or, other casualty, any unanticipated governmental restriction, regulation, control, or other delay caused by any Governmental Authority unrelated to any act or failure to act by the Borrower, any strike, lockout, or other general unavailability of labor, utilities, or materials, a military invasion by an enemy of the United States, a civil riot, adverse weather conditions, acts of a public enemy, acts of terrorism, epidemics, quarantines, or any other similar event reasonably determined by the Lender not to be within the reasonable control of the Borrower (not including the insolvency or financial condition of the Borrower or the Guarantor or any member or partner of the Borrower or any other affiliate of the Borrower), provided that such delay shall be considered a "Force Majeure Delay" only if the Borrower has notified the Lender of the existence of such delay within three (3) Business Days after the event causing the delay occurs.

"Governmental Authority": Any nation or government, any state or other political subdivision thereof, any other entity exercising executive, judicial, regulatory, or administrative functions of or pertaining to government and any corporation or other entity owned or controlled (through stock or capital ownership or otherwise) by any of the foregoing, whose consent or approval is required as a prerequisite to the commencement of the construction of the Improvements or to the operation and occupancy of the Real Property, or to the performance of any act or obligation or the observance of any agreement, provision, or condition of whatsoever nature herein contained.

"Guarantor": Jointly and severally, Alan Principal and Betty Principal.

"Guaranty": Collectively, the Completion Guaranty made by Guarantor to the Lender, the Environmental Indemnity made by Guarantor and the Borrower to the Lender, and the Guaranty of Payment made by Guarantor to the Lender, each dated as of the date hereof, as the same may hereafter be amended, modified, or supplemented from time to time.

"Hard Costs": The costs of the Project paid by the Borrower pursuant to the Construction Manager's Agreement and the Trade Contracts and any contingency therefor.

"Hotel": The approximately 226-key Letoha Hotel to be constructed on the Premises by the Borrower and operated by the Hotel Manager.

"Hotel Manager": Courtyard Management Corporation, a Delaware corporation.

"Hotel Manager Estoppel Letter": An estoppel letter, in form and substance satisfactory to the Lender, in favor of the Lender, to be duly executed and delivered by the Hotel Manager prior to the Closing Date.

"Hotel Management Agreement": The Management Agreement, dated as of October 7, 200_, by and between the Borrower and the Hotel Manager with respect to the management and operation of the Hotel, as the same may be hereafter amended, modified, or supplemented from time to time, to the extent permitted by the Loan Documents.

"Hotel SNDA": The Subordination, Nondisturbance, and Attornment Agreement, by and among the Lender, the Borrower, and the Hotel Manager, as the same may hereafter be amended, modified, or supplemented from time to time.

"Hotel Unit": As defined in the Mortgage.

"Improvements": The structures, fixtures, equipment, and other improvements, including, without limitation, the Tangible Personal Property, to be constructed on the Premises in accordance with the Plans.

"Intercreditor Agreement": The Intercreditor and Subordination Agreement, dated the date hereof, by and between the Lender and Mezz. LLC, as the same may be hereafter amended, modified, or supplemented from time to time.

"Kitchen Facilities Easement Agreement": The Easement Agreement, dated as of October 25, 200_, by and between the Residential Developer and the Borrower, and duly recorded in the New York County Register's office on December 24, 200_, at Reel 3456, Page 202.

"Leases": All leases and subleases of the Improvements, whether now existing or hereafter executed.

"Lender": As defined in the preamble to this Agreement.

"Lien": Any mortgage, pledge, hypothecation, assignment, deposit arrangement, encumbrance, lien (statutory or other), preference, priority, or other security agreement or preferential arrangement of any kind or nature whatsoever (including, without limitation, any conditional sale or other title retention agreement, any financing lease having substantially the same economic effect as any of the foregoing, and the filing of any financing statement under the Uniform Commercial Code or comparable law of any jurisdiction), but excluding the Mortgage, the UCC Financing Statements, and any and all other Loan Documents.

"Lien Law": The Lien Law of the State of New York.

"Loan": The Building Loan and the Project Loan, collectively.

"Loan Documents": This Agreement, the Guaranty, the Note, and the Collateral Documents.

"Major Contract": Any Trade Contract of $_____ or more.

"Mezzanine Loan": The loan in the principal amount of up to $14,500,000 made on the date hereof by Mezz. LLC to the Borrower and evidenced, advanced, and secured by the Mezzanine Loan Documents.

"Mezzanine Loan Documents": As the same may hereafter be amended, modified, or supplemented from time to time, to the extent permitted by the Intercreditor Agreement.

"Mortgage": Collectively, the Building Loan Mortgage and the Project Loan Mortgage.

"Note": Collectively, the Building Loan Note and the Project Loan Note.

"Option Agreement": The Option Agreement, dated as of October 25, 200_, by and between the Borrower and the Optionee, a memorandum of which was recorded in the New York County Register's Office on December 24, 200_, at Reel 3456, Page 222.

"Optionee": Danforth/2nd L.L.C., a Delaware limited liability company.

"Optionee Estoppel Letter": An estoppel letter, in form and substance satisfactory to the Lender, in favor of the Lender, to be duly executed and delivered by the Optionee to the Lender prior to the Closing Date.

"Other Building Loan Costs": Building Loan Costs other than Hard Costs.

"Other Design Contracts": The contracts (i) dated February 10, 200_, with K&B Associates, structural engineer, (ii) dated March 10, 200_, with Hark Associates, consulting engineer, and (iii) dated October 17, 200_, with Jon Gun Design, interior designer, as each of the same may be amended, supplemented, or otherwise modified in accordance with the provisions of this Agreement, as well as any other contracts with Other Design Professionals approved by the Lender (such approval not to be unreasonably withheld).

"Other Design Professionals": (i) K&B Associates, structural engineer, (ii) Hark Associates, consulting engineer, and (iii) Jon Gun, interior designer, and/or such other design professionals as may be engaged by the Borrower with the Lender's prior written approval in connection with the Project (such approval not to be unreasonably withheld).

"Mezz LLC": Mezz. LLC, a Delaware limited liability company.

"Permits": All authorizations, consents, licenses, approvals and permits required for the construction, completion, occupancy, and operation of the Improvements in accordance with all Requirements of Law affecting the Real Property.

"Permitted Exceptions": All liens, encumbrances, restrictions, and other matters affecting the Borrower's title to the Real Property that are set forth as title exceptions in the title insurance policies (or binders) of even date herewith issued by the Title Company insuring the Mortgage, and approved by the Lender, the Liens of the Collateral Documents, and any

Liens that have at any time been consented to in writing by the Lender or otherwise permitted under the Loan Documents, including the Liens of the Mezzanine Loan Documents, subject to the Intercreditor Agreement.

"Person": An individual, partnership, corporation, business trust, joint stock company, trust, unincorporated association, joint venture, Governmental Authority, limited liability company, or other entity of whatever nature.

"Plans": The complete plans and specifications for the construction of the Improvements, including, without limitation, sidewalks, gutters, landscaping, utility connections (whether on or off the Premises), and including all fixtures and equipment necessary for construction, operation, and occupancy of the Improvements, prepared or to be prepared by the Architect, including such amendments thereto as may from time to time be made by the Borrower and approved by the Lender (such approval not to be unreasonably withheld).

"Premises": As defined in the recitals to this Agreement.

"Project": Construction of the Improvements and the acquisition and installation of the Tangible Personal Property.

"Project Loan": The loan to be made as provided in Subsection 2.1(b) hereof.

"Project Loan Budget": The budget for the Project Loan that has been delivered by the Borrower to, and approved by, the Lender, as it may be amended from time to time in accordance with this Agreement.

"Project Loan Budget Line": An individual line item shown on the Project Loan Budget.

"Project Loan Commitment": The Lender's obligation hereunder to make the Project Loan to the Borrower.

"Project Loan Costs": Costs to be funded using proceeds of the Project Loan as shown in the Project Loan Budget.

"Project Loan Mortgage": The Project Loan Mortgage, Assignment of Leases and Rents, and Security Agreement, dated the date hereof, executed and delivered by the Borrower in favor of the Lender, in the amount of the Project Loan, as the same may be hereafter amended, modified, or supplemented from time to time.

"Project Loan Note": The Project Loan Mortgage Note, dated the date hereof, executed and delivered by the Borrower in favor of the Lender, in the amount of the Project Loan, as the same may be hereafter amended, modified, or supplemented from time to time.

"Punchlist Items": Collectively, minor or insubstantial details of construction, decoration, mechanical adjustment, or installation.

"Real Property": The Premises and the Improvements and any other real property encumbered by the Collateral Documents.

"Requirement of Law": As to any Person, the certificate of incorporation and by-laws, partnership agreement, or limited partnership agreement and certificate of limited partnership or other organization or governing documents of such Person, and any law, treaty, rule or regulation, or determination of an arbitrator or a court or other Governmental Authority, in each case applicable to or binding upon such Person or any of its property or to which such Person or any of its property is subject; and, as to the Real Property, any applicable environmental, zoning, building, and/or land use laws, ordinances, rules, or regulations of any Governmental Authority, and any applicable covenants and restrictions.

"Residential Developer": First Residential Tower, LLC, a Delaware limited liability company.

"Residential Developer Estoppel Letter": An estoppel letter, in form and substance satisfactory to the Lender, in favor of the Lender, duly executed and delivered by the Residential Developer to the Lender prior to the Closing Date.

"Responsible Officer": The managing member of the Borrower or its duly appointed officer or agent.

"Retainage": The total amount actually held back by or on behalf of the Borrower from the Construction Manager with respect to the value of the work in place and performed by each Trade Contractor, which shall not be less at any time than (i) ten (10%) percent of the aggregate Hard Costs actually incurred by the Borrower with respect to such Trade Contractor for work in place performed by such Trade Contractor, as verified from time to time by the Construction Consultant pursuant to the provisions of this Agreement, until fifty (50%) percent of the Project has been completed, and (ii) thereafter, five (5%) percent of the aggregate Hard Costs actually incurred by the Borrower with respect to such Trade Contractor for work in place performed by such Trade Contractor, as verified from time to time by the Construction Consultant pursuant to the provisions of this Agreement. The portion of the Retainage that relates to work or materials supplied by any Trade Contractor in connection with the Project will, upon request, be disbursed to the Borrower (but will not be disbursed to the Borrower until and unless the following are complied with or the Lender agrees otherwise), whether before or after the Completion of the Project, provided that (a) no Event of Default has occurred and is continuing under the Loan Documents, (b) the Construction Consultant verifies to the Lender that such Trade Contractor has completed 100% of all work, except for Punchlist Items, and has supplied 100% of all materials, except for Punchlist Items, in substantial compliance with such Trade Contractor's Trade Contract and in substantial conformity with the Plans, (c) such Trade Contractor will be paid in full upon the release of such portion of the Retainage, subject to Retainage for Punchlist Items, and (d) such Trade Contractor executes and delivers all lien waivers that may be reasonably requested or required by the Lender or by the Title Company to induce the Title Company to insure the lien of the

Mortgage against any mechanic's or materialman's lien that may be filed against the Real Property by such Trade Contractor or any Person claiming through such Trade Contractor. Notwithstanding the foregoing, at the Lender's option, once the Construction Consultant verifies that such Trade Contractor is substantially complete pursuant to its Trade Contract, the Lender, in its reasonable discretion, may release all or any portion of the Retainage applicable to such Trade Contractor upon such conditions as the Lender shall reasonably impose at that time.

"Scheduled Completion Date": July __, 200_, subject to (i) the Extension Options (as defined in the Note) and (ii) extension, for not more than 45 days, by one day for each day of Force Majeure Delay, as the same may be further extended by the agreement of the parties hereto (it being understood that the Lender shall have no obligation to agree to any such further extension).

"School": The Old School, a New York education corporation.

"School Unit": Shall have the meaning ascribed to such term in the Mortgage.

"School Unit Contract": The Agreement for Sale and Purchase of Property, dated as of May 7, 200_, by and between the Borrower and the School for the sale of the School Unit, as amended by letter agreement dated July 7, 200_.

"Tangible Personal Property": Any and all equipment, furniture, furnishings, and other tangible personal property to be acquired by the Borrower in connection with the development and occupancy of the Improvements.

"Title Company": Planet Abstract of New York LLC, as agent for (i) New Jersey Title Insurance Company and (ii) Loyal Title Insurance Company.

"Trade Contract": Any agreement (other than the Construction Manager's Agreement, the Architect's Agreement, and the Other Design Contracts) entered into by the Borrower, or by the Construction Manager directly with a Trade Contractor, providing for the provision by the Trade Contractor thereunder of labor and/or materials in connection with the construction of the Improvements or the installation of the Tangible Personal Property.

"Trade Contractor": The contractor or vendor under any Trade Contract.

"Trade Contractor's Certificate": A certificate of each Trade Contractor, in substantially the form of Exhibit H attached hereto, with respect to each Major Contract or a form previously approved by the Agent.

"UCC Financing Statements": The UCC-l Financing Statements executed by the Borrower as debtor with the Lender as Secured Party in respect of the tangible and intangible personal property comprising part of the Collateral.
"Units": As defined in the Mortgage.

THE BORROWER'S DEPENDENCE ON THIRD PARTIES BEFORE CLOSING

Within the building loan agreement, there are copies of documents that must be completed before the first loan advance. These documents involve attestations, warranties, and pledges by third parties and typically are brought to the closing.

Unfortunately, on smaller projects with inexperienced development teams, there are often borrowers who do not understand the complexity and interdependency that a construction loan entails. Not only is there an ongoing and active relationship between the borrower and the lender in a development loan, but to varying degrees there is a relationship between the lender and the borrower's architect, engineer(s), construction manager, general contractor, and others.[10]

---

[10] The architect and/or engineer should be signing off on monthly requisitions as well. General contractors and subcontractors must sign for their requisitions. The lender's engineering consultant reviews the requisitions and makes recommendations to the lender.

ARCHITECT'S CERTIFICATE

_____, 200_

XYZ Bank
Anywhere Road
New York, New York 10001

Re: 620 East 32nd Street, New York, New York

Dear Sirs:

The undersigned (the "Architect") understands that XYZ Bank (the "Lender") is about to make certain loans in the maximum aggregate principal amount of $32,000,000 (collectively, the "Loan") to the borrower referred to in Exhibit A attached hereto (the "Borrower"), which Loan will be used, among other things, to finance the construction by the Borrower of the improvements described in Exhibit A (the "Improvements") on the premises described in Exhibit A pursuant to the provisions of a building loan agreement and project loan agreement (the "Loan Agreement") to be entered into between the Lender and the Borrower and to fund certain soft costs in connection with the completion of the Improvements. The Architect has prepared certain plans and specifications (the "Plans") for use in connection with the construction of the Improvements, as more particularly described in Exhibit B attached hereto. In addition, the Architect has been engaged by the Borrower to act as the architect for the Improvements pursuant to the provisions of a certain contract described in Exhibit A, a copy of which is attached hereto as Exhibit C (the "Contract").[11]

The Architect represents and warrants to the Lender that (i) the Improvements, upon completion in accordance with the Plans, and their contemplated use, will comply with all applicable enviøronmental laws, building codes and zoning resolutions, and all other applicable governmental rules, laws and regulations relating to their construction and use, (ii) all permits, licenses, and other approvals required for the construction of the Improvements in accordance with the Plans have been obtained from the appropriate governmental authorities, (iii) all electricity, gas, water, sewage disposal, and other utilities required for the use and operation of the Improvements will be available upon completion of the Improvements in accordance with the Plans, (iv) the maximum contract price for performing all work as architect for the Improvements under the Contract is $400,000, (v) the Contract is in full force and effect and has not been modified or amended, except as specifically set forth in Exhibit A attached hereto, and (vi) the Architect has not sent or received any notice of default or any notice for the purpose of terminating the Contract, nor is there any existing circumstance or event which, but for the lapse of time or otherwise, would constitute a default by the Architect or the Borrower under the Contract.

---

[11] The exhibits referred to as A, B, and C have been omitted.

In addition, the Architect hereby agrees with the Lender as follows:

1. The Architect will not agree to any amendment, modification, release, or discharge (in whole or in part) of the Contract, nor waive or claim any waiver in respect of any provision thereof, without first obtaining the prior written consent of the Lender, and no such amendment, modification, release, discharge, or waiver, without such consent, shall be binding upon the Lender.

2. The Architect will send to the Lender copies of all notices of default sent by the Architect to the Borrower pursuant to the Contract, and no such notice shall be effective for any purpose unless and until a copy thereof shall have been received by the Lender.

3. If the Borrower shall default under the Contract, the Architect will not exercise any remedies, including, but not limited to, any right to terminate the Contract, until and unless the Architect shall give notice of intention to do so to the Lender, and the Lender, for a period of 60 days after receipt of such notice, shall fail to either remedy the default of the Borrower or deliver to the Architect an undertaking to remedy such default at the sole cost and expense of the Lender, within such reasonable time as may be appropriate, taking into account the nature of the default.

4. If the Borrower defaults under the Loan Agreement, or if there is a foreclosure of the mortgages securing the Loan, or if the Borrower becomes insolvent, the Lender, its nominee, or wholly owned subsidiary shall have the use of the Plans at no additional charge or expense, and the Architect will, at the election and option of the Lender, complete its obligations under the Contract for a contract price calculated pursuant to the Contract for the benefit of and with no additional charge or expense to the Lender, its nominee, or wholly owned subsidiary, it being agreed that such contract price shall in no event exceed the maximum price stipulated (as provided for in the first page of this letter) in the Contract. The Architect hereby consents to the assignment of the Contract given by the Borrower to the Lender in connection with the Loan.

5. The Architect will send all notices to the Lender, as required by this letter, to the address of the Lender set forth above, by registered or certified mail, return receipt requested; copies of all such notices shall be sent in like manner, addressed to XYZ Bank, Anywhere Road, New York, NY 10001, Attention: Mr. Ira Nachem, with a copy to Law, Law & Law, P.C., 444 East 42nd Street, New York, New York 10022, Attention: Ted Attorney, Esq.

6. The provisions set forth in this letter shall be binding on the Architect and its successors and assigns and shall inure to the benefit of the Lender and its successors and assigns.

Very truly yours,

By:_____
Name:

TRADE CONTRACTOR'S CERTIFICATE

_____, 200_

XYZ Bank
Anywhere Road
New York, New York 10001

Re: 620 East 32nd Street, New York, New York

Dear Sirs:

The undersigned (the "Trade Contractor") understands that XYZ Bank (the "Lender") is about to make certain loans in the maximum aggregate principal amount of $32,000,000 (the "Loan") to the borrower described in Exhibit A attached hereto (the "Borrower"), the proceeds of which Loan will be used, among other things, to finance the construction by the Borrower of the improvements described in Exhibit A (the "Improvements") on the premises described in Exhibit A pursuant to the provisions of a building loan agreement and project loan agreement (the "Loan Agreement") to be entered into between the Lender and the Borrower and to fund certain soft costs in connection with the completion of the Improvements. The Trade Contractor has been engaged by the Borrower as a trade contractor for the construction of the Improvements pursuant to the provisions of a certain contract described in Exhibit A, a copy of which is annexed hereto as Exhibit B (the "Trade Contract").[12]

The Trade Contractor represents and warrants to the Lender that (i) the Trade Contractor has reviewed and approved in all respects the plans and specifications for the Improvements, (ii) the Trade Contract is in full force and effect and has not been modified or amended, except as specifically set forth in Exhibit A attached hereto, (iii) the maximum contract price for performing all work and supplying all materials under the Trade Contract in connection with the construction of the Improvements is $1,600,598, and, except as specifically set forth to the contrary in Exhibit A attached hereto, no change orders have been agreed to that would increase or decrease the amount payable to contractor under the Trade Contract, and (iv) the Trade Contractor has not sent or received any notice of default or any notice for the purpose of terminating the Trade Contract, nor is there any existing circumstance or event which, but for the lapse of time or otherwise, would constitute a default by the Trade Contractor or the Borrower under the Trade Contract.

In addition, the Trade Contractor hereby agrees with the Lender as follows:

1. The Trade Contractor will not agree to any amendment, modification, release, or discharge (in whole or in part) of the Trade Contract, nor waive or claim any waiver in respect of any provision thereof, without first obtaining the prior written consent of the Lender, and no such amendment, modification, release, discharge, or waiver, without such consent, shall be binding upon the Lender.

2. The Trade Contractor will send to the Lender copies of all notices of default sent by the Trade Contractor to the Borrower pursuant to

---

[12] The exhibits referred to as A and B have been omitted (a sample of a trade contract, "Exhibit B," is included in Chapter 8).

the Trade Contract, and no such notice shall be effective for any purpose unless and until a copy thereof shall have been received by the Lender.

3. If the Borrower shall default under the Trade Contract, the Trade Contractor will not exercise any remedies, including, but not limited to, any right to terminate the Trade Contract, until and unless the Trade Contractor shall give notice of intention to do so to the Lender, and the Lender, for a period of 60 days after receipt of such notice, shall fail either to remedy the default of the Borrower or to deliver to the Trade Contractor an undertaking to remedy such default at the sole cost and expense of the Lender, within such reasonable time as may be appropriate, taking into account the nature of the default.

4. If the Borrower defaults under the Loan Agreement, or if there is a foreclosure of the mortgage securing the Loan, or if the Borrower becomes insolvent, the Trade Contractor will, at the election and option of the Lender, complete its obligations under the Trade Cont-ract for a contract price calculated pursuant to the Trade Contract for the benefit of and with no additional charge or expense to the Lender, its nominee, or its wholly owned subsidiary, it being agreed that such contract price shall in no event exceed the maximum price stipulated (as provided for in the first page of this letter) in the Trade Contract. The Trade Contractor hereby consents to the assignment of the Trade Contract given by the Borrower to the Lender in connection with the Loan.

5. The Trade Contractor will not perform, or permit any subcontractor to perform, any work pursuant to any change order of any nature whatsoever unless the Trade Contractor has obtained the specific prior written approval of the Lender to such change order and agrees that if the Trade Contractor does not obtain the specific prior written approval of the Lender to any such change order, the Trade Contractor shall not have any right, and hereby expressly waives the right, to file any mechanic's or materialman's lien against the construction site for any work performed or any material supplied pursuant to any such change order.

The Trade Contractor will send all notices to the Lender, as required by this letter, to the address of the Lender set forth above by registered or certified mail, return receipt requested; copies of all such notices shall be sent in like manner, addressed to XYZ Bank, Anywhere Road, New York, New York 10001 Attention: Mr. Ira Nachem, with a copy to Law, Law & Law, P.C., 444 East 42nd Street, New York, New York 10022, Attention: Ted Attorney, Esq..

6. The provisions set forth in this letter shall be binding upon the Trade Contractor and the Trade Contractor's successors and assigns and shall inure to the benefit of the Lender and its successors and assigns.

Very truly yours,

TRADE CONTRACTOR

By:_____

Name:

Title:

Following are two samples of certifications. The first is made by an obvious player—the project architect—and the second by perhaps a not so obvious one—a contractor. Both are typical of the few certifications and affidavits included in a closing package. Your attorney will dictate the form and terms of the documents to the borrower's attorney, who then will give them to the borrower so that he can have them completed and returned.

Author's Note
The BLA, mortgage, and note should provide you with essentially all the mechanics and specifics of a loan. Since these three documents virtually mirror the loan presentation, most lenders do not make copies of them. They prefer instead to refer to the approved loan presentation they authored as well as a summary sheet they drafted for themselves after the loan closed. This usually works just as well.[13]

SIMPLE BUT COMPLEX

To this point the discussions in this chapter have focused on the loan closing: attorneys; assembling information, materials, and documentation; participants' general responsibilities; the usefulness and scope of the note, mortgage, and BLA; and dependence on third parties.

The remainder of the chapter explores a particular document: the guarantee, or guaranty. The guarantee can be a very important element in a development loan. However, as with other concepts in real estate, an intuitive sense of what it is may not be the correct one. A guarantee can have several meanings that can result in very different legal and business outcomes. Therefore, like many other loan documents, a guarantee should be negotiated knowledgably and crafted by a skilled attorney. As was mentioned earlier, real property law is complex. A good example of legal complexity is the "simple" guarantee.

---

[13] There are always at least two sets of "legal files." One is kept by the closing attorney, and the other is kept by the lending institution. The lender keeps its legal files for active loans either at the work area of the loan administrator or, if space is limited or security is a concern, at an off-site storage location. After a legal file is requested from a storage facility, it should be shipped back to the office in no longer than a day or two. In anything but a crisis situation (which should be rare), the time to get the physical file is not a problem. If it is needed more quickly, a call to the closing attorney should get prompt results. The closing attorney should be able to read, discuss, or send to you copies of the documentation you require within a single day of your request.

GUARANTEES

Guarantees are one of the most misunderstood concepts in the lending industry. Most lenders, harking back to the last recession (and the one before that and the one before that), are adamant about obtaining one. Borrowers, similarly impressed with economic downturns, are equally resolute about not giving one. The reality is that in almost all but the most unusual circumstances the guarantor never will be compelled to "honor" his guarantee, so why should the lender ask for it? The answer is, Why not?

TYPES OF GUARANTEES

Before you can ask yourself what kinds of guarantees you want and what kinds you can get, you must be familiar with the basic types of guarantees, which are described below.

Repayment (Takeout) Guarantee

The repayment guarantee is arguably the strongest for the lender and therefore offers the least protection for the borrower. With this type of guarantee, the borrower is stating that if for any reason, including circumstances beyond his control, the cash generated from the project, either as originally intended or from other sources, is not sufficient to repay the lender's principal and interest, the borrower must do so out of his own pocket. As a result of the broad nature of the conditions that can result in the triggering of the guarantee, a repayment guarantee may be hard to obtain.

Completion Guarantee

A completion guarantee states that if the project is not completed per the plans and specifications within a reasonable period, the borrower will pay to the lending institution the funds necessary to complete the project. With this guarantee, the borrower is limiting his exposure to the completion of the job. He is not obligated to pay down the lender's loan, pay interest in arrears, or pay the lender. However, since there will be work stoppages before the lending institution steps in and because the lending institution almost certainly will not be as efficient or price-conscious as the borrower, the costs to the guarantor will be higher than they would be if he had the ability to complete the job himself. In spite of market conditions and the viability of the project, once the project is complete, the guarantor is under no further obligation.

Soft Cost Guarantee

Depending upon the loan's structure, many soft costs often are not funded through the construction loan and therefore are the sole responsibility of the borrower. If a lender can get a soft cost guarantee, it will have negotiated powerful loan protection since soft costs continue even after the completion of construction. These costs include large line items such as taxes and insurance and the largest line item of all: your loan interest. If they are required to give a guarantee on soft costs, most developers will insist that a limit (cap) be provided. Otherwise, without the direct ability to control these costs, they theoretically can be paying forever.

Minimum Sales Price Guarantee

In a condominium project, there is usually a minimum release price. This is the lowest amount necessary to be paid to the lender before it will release a condominium unit from its collateral. A sale for an amount under this price is not possible unless the borrower supplements the sale price with his own funds. Coupled with the release of units can be a soft cost guarantee for a period of time. The soft costs guaranteed are often the condominium association charges, insurance and real estate taxes. They are essentially the carrying costs of the property excluding debt service.

Minimum Guarantees

Today, when a borrower and/or a lender tell you that the terms of a construction loan are without any recourse, that simply is not true. There is always a "bad boy" clause and almost always an environmental indemnification. These are the baselines of any development loan.

The Bad Boy or Carve-Out Clause

The bad boy or carve-out clause simply states that the borrower will guarantee the lender against losses incurred on its loan resulting from willful material misstatements of fact, fraud, or embezzlement (stealing). It is very difficult for a borrower to argue with this form of guarantee since without it, the obvious implication is that he may lie or steal.

Environmental Indemnification

Environmental indemnifications (guarantees) are almost always nonnegotiable because they have become such an important part of the public, legal, and lending landscape during the last 20 or so years. If the borrower will not give him an environmental guarantee, the lender will not make the loan.

Today, obtaining an environmental guarantee is almost never an issue because most development loans dictate that the first construction advance will not occur until all environmental matters have been taken care of and proof to the lender has been provided. On the few loans in which some or all of the environmental costs are advanced by the borrower or the lender during development, the borrower still must provide an environmental guarantee. However, his contingent liability should be contained because he has (or should have) addressed the project's environmental issues and costs fully. As additional confirmation, his estimations are substantiated by the lender's environmental consultant. If contaminates are discovered later, for example, in the course of excavation or, in a rehabilitation project, after the tearing down of partitions, they should be of a size and scope that are cost-manageable relative to the project's financial scope. The borrower should be able to pay any cost overruns just as he would for any other budget item.

Nonetheless, it should not be forgotten that if there is a major unfortunate discovery, it can be catastrophic to the economic feasibility of the project. Therefore, environmental matters should not be taken lightly.[14]

GUARANTEE VARIATIONS

Partial Guarantees/Limited Guarantees

The partial or limited guarantee arises out of negotiations between the lender and the borrower and can involve soft costs, hard costs, or

---

[14] Many developers still view environmental testing as an unnecessary expense required by lenders. A guarantee forces the borrower to take environmental issues seriously. The lender also should take environmental issues seriously. If, for example, the lender comes into ownership of the property though a foreclosure, it may be completely and singly liable for the cleanup.

specific items such as interest payments. Like other indeterminate contingent monetary liabilities, it can be based on a percentage, an absolute cost, a period of time, or a combination of all three. For instance, the borrower may promise to pay 50 percent of the loan principal outstanding, agree to cover up to $1 million of the lending institution's losses, be liable for loan interest from the time of the loan default until the property is foreclosed on and title is conveyed to the lender or a third party,[15] or pay up to a certain dollar amount (cap) of a percentage of soft costs and hard costs.

Anything Else

Depending on the lender, the borrower, the transaction, and the variables that surround them, such as real estate supply and demand conditions and the competition level among lenders, guarantees can be negotiable. It is up to the strength and imaginations of the borrower and lender.

Who Guarantees

When you send out your letter of interest[16] in response to a loan proposal, it always should indicate the types of guarantees required (or asked for) and who should give them. Since your letter is often the opening gambit for negotiations, the types and identities of the guarantors should be broad. Later, during give-and-take discussions between you and the borrower (possibly with consultations with your senior management), the question of what types of guarantees are obtained and who is doing the guaranteeing will become better defined. At the least, it will be the developer himself (the "key man") who provides the guarantees because he is the one the lender (and his investors) will be depending on to translate the initial investment into a profit.

---

[15] If you cannot obtain a repayment guarantee, you should try to receive an interest guarantee from the time of a monetary default until the time you gain possession of the property. This partial guarantee should not be as difficult to negotiate since the borrower probably stated to you many times how little risk the loan embodies and will guarantee interest to prove it. This puts some limit on the borrower's contingent liability and gives him a real incentive to resolve a bad situation quickly to stop the interest clock.

[16] A letter of interest also is called a term letter, a summary of terms letter, and so on. It is indicated clearly in the letter that it is not a commitment.

Since he is the one who has primary authority and responsibility to get the project completed, rented, and/or sold, he should be the one on the hook. Each type of legal entity has its own protections and exposures in regard to its individual members. In a general partnership, for instance, the general partners are the ones who are directly liable for losses incurred in the ordinary course of business. They usually are also directly involved with the development team. In a limited liability corporation, though, none of the members are personally liable. Their maximum potential loss is limited to their capital contributions.

As a result of the various ownership forms and agreements among investors, the legal entity and the agreement between members may preclude certain individuals from guaranteeing without changing their ownership rights and interests. It is not always necessary to get a guarantee from the wealthiest participant, but you always should get one from the person who is in control.

Joint and Several Guarantees

If there is more than one player on the borrowing team, you should try to obtain joint and several guarantees. This allows you to go against all or any one of the guarantors for the entire loan. For instance, if there are three guarantors who each put up $2 million for a one-third interest in a project and the lender provided $24 million of financing, under a joint and several guarantee, each one is contingently liable for the entire $24 million. This is equal to 12 times each one's investment. If there is trouble with the loan, the joint and several aspects can give you considerably more negotiating strength.

The Value of a Guarantee

For development loans, the borrower has so many legal defenses in a proceeding against his guarantee that the lender almost always loses in court. Some of these defenses sound very unfair, but a good borrower's attorney invariably can make them work. For example, if the lender is perceived as dictating to the borrower what to do to correct a problem situation, the lender can be cast as meddling in the borrower's business and thus as a contributor to the default of the loan. If the lender did not make a loan advance because the borrower did not satisfy the advance requirements, the court may agree with the borrower's defense that the lender should have made the advance and that because it did not, the project's progress was damaged.

If the lender had another way out of the problem, for instance, through a takeout lender or through an insurance bond, that did not materialize because of the lender's error, the borrower no longer can be held responsible for loan repayment. If there was an immaterial lender's administrative error, it can be inflated to a material error. Even if the lender overadvanced money, a situation most borrowers would not object to, the lender could be deemed to have acted irresponsibly by not leaving enough funds available to advance in the latter stages of the job.

Since the lender probably will have trouble in court, the developer is probably not financially strong, and the legal process can take years during which time the asset will be deteriorating, the lender, if there is a choice between going against the borrower and going against the property, should go against the property first. (In fact, in New York and many other states, the lender cannot proceed against the property and the borrower at once but must make a choice and proceed against one or the other.) The question then is, Why take a guarantee?

Why Take a Guarantee?

The main reason for insisting on a guarantee as part of a development loan is to trade the guarantee for the borrower's performance. With a guarantee there is always an implicit threat that the lender can pursue its claim through the courts directly against the borrower's personal assets.[17] Because of this contingent exposure, if there is a problem situation, the borrower usually will work with the lender harder and longer to try to correct it.

If the situation deteriorates to a point where the best course of action is for the lender to force a foreclosure sale and perhaps take possession of the asset, the lender can bargain for the release of the borrower from his guarantee in return for the deed to the property. The result is that the property can be conveyed to the lender in a much shorter period, saving additional costs because it will be

---

[17] Or at least restrict his ability to enter into the credit markets any time soon.

delivered in better condition. It also lets the lender avoid going through a lengthy and costly foreclosure process.

For the borrower, trading on his guarantee has several advantages. He no longer faces the possibility of spending a good deal of time and incurring considerable attorney and court costs. If the potential liability relative to his net worth is substantial, he can avoid the possibility, however remote, of severe irreparable loss and bankruptcy. Depending on the times, the market, and the lender's negotiating skills, he may be able to trade his property and the full release of his guarantee for a cash buyout. That is, the lender will pay him some money if he gives up the deed in lieu of foreclosure. Also, he probably can negotiate the deal by which this remains confidential. No one will be the wiser about his or the project's problems. He then can get on with his business and pursue a new deal with another lender. With all the potential incentives, conveying the property to the lender in lieu of foreclosure can be an attractive option.

What Guarantee Can the Lender Get?

If you have lending criteria that dictate what types of guarantees are required to make a development loan, you at least know what your institution's minimum requirements are. Depending on the risk of the transaction, the sophistication and financial strength of the borrower, the needs of the borrower, and what the competition is requiring, you can determine whether you should ask for more than the minimum. Obviously, if you can get a repayment, completion, and soft cost guarantee, you will have pretty much everything you want.

Small to Midsize Loans

Currently, on small to midsize development loans (up to $25 million), almost all lending institutions require a completion guarantee and may require a repayment guarantee as well. A guarantee is more meaningful in loans of this size because many borrowers have the financial worth to fund them in full if they are called on to do so. Because lenders in the competitive market for midsize loans require these guarantees, the borrower has few if any options.

Large Loans

For lending institutions with the capital capability to make large loans ($40 million or more), guarantees range from nonexistent to partial. One reason for this is that the larger amounts of money involved heighten the unwillingness or inability of even major developers to have such a large contingent liability on their balance sheet. This is particularly true if the developer is a public company.

The lending institution's rationale for waiving a guarantee on a large project is that the developer would not be able to procure the resources to do large projects unless it had a strong track record and was very able, experienced, and financially sound. There is some basis to this. However, from a practical standpoint because of lender competition, it would be difficult or impossible for a lender to do large quality development financing if full or substantial guarantees were required.

At the time of this writing, it is not difficult to obtain a completion guarantee regardless of loan size because completion is perceived by the borrower to be in his control. A repayment guarantee is not so easy to obtain. The borrower's valid negotiating point is that although he usually can control completion, a downturn in the overall real estate market at the time of project completion is beyond anyone's control. Therefore, he and the lender should share the risk.

Make Sure Your Intentions Are Documented Properly

Your closing attorney is ultimately responsible for translating the loan's terms and conditions into legal documentation. It is your responsibility to enunciate clearly the type of guarantee that is being stipulated. If there is any doubt on your part, based on the form of ownership and the language of the guarantee, you should ask the attorney for a clear answer.

Author's Note

Although calling on a guarantee is a remote possibility, a guarantee can have considerable power. In a deteriorating situation, it may be used by the lender to influence the borrower to his advantage. It can provide an incentive for the borrower to stay focused and perform, and if necessary, it can be a critical factor in taking control of a property in lieu of foreclosure.

The borrower, of course, at least initially should try to give the least he can. Knowing that the likelihood of a guarantee being exercised is remote, the borrower can afford to give more, but not without negotiating for something in return. Using the guarantee as a bargaining chip may get him better loan terms, including a better interest rate.

CHAPTER 8

Preparing for the Funding Process

BASICS YOU SHOULD KNOW ABOUT

To exploit opportunities for new business, underwrite more complex transactions, and control risk, every lender should know some of the basics of development planning, organization, and coordination. This chapter discusses concepts that should help you understand and adapt to surprises that require knowledgeable decisions and actions.

PLANS AND SPECIFICATIONS

For every construction loan, every lender and/or the lender's engineering consultant should receive a set of plans and specifications. It is important to know that plans and specifications are not the same thing, although often, especially on smaller jobs, the specifications are printed on the same paper as part of the plans. Together, they are ideally the instruction manual for building the entire project.

Plans

Plans are nothing more than drawings. The ones most useful to a lender are fitted to a scale and put on large sheets of paper. Others, including all schematics, are not to scale but are used in conjunction with those which are. Working scales vary depending on the amount of detail necessary and the part of the project under view. The scales most often used are one-quarter of an inch and three-eighths of an inch equals one foot.

Since the project will be built using plans, they must be detailed and accurate. There are several sets of plans, depending on the intended use. For instance, there are architectural plans that show the layout and structure of the project (for loan underwriting purposes, these are the most useful and usually the only ones reviewed by the lending officer); electrical plans that show wiring, lighting, electrical panels, and so on; heating, ventilation, and air-conditioning (HVAC) plans; sprinkler and standpipe plans; plumbing plans; elevator plans; demolition plans; excavation plans; and any other plans necessary to build the project. On the lower right-hand corner they are indexed according to their type. "A," for example, means that the viewer is looking at architectural plans; "E" means that the viewer is looking at electrical plans.

Also, there are several types of plan drawings. If you know about them, you can ask for and refer to specific views that can aid your comprehension of the project. The views are the plan view, the elevation view, the sectional view, the detail view, the isometric view, and the schematic view. The plan view looks at the project from straight down, as if from the sky (it sometimes is referred to as the bird's-eye view). The elevation view looks at the project perpendicular to one of its sides (north, east, south, or west). The sectional view looks at a slice of the project that can reveal hidden features. The detail view is a close-up of a particular section that shows more intricate elements where required, such as a method of attachment or the layering of the materials that make up a wall. An isometric view is a three-dimensional view looking up (or down) at the object from a 30-degree angle (there is also an axonometric view, which is from a 45-degree angle). A schematic is a line drawing that most often uses symbols when flows are involved: liquids, electricity, air, and the like (see Figures 8–1 through 8–6).

FIGURE 8-1

Plan View

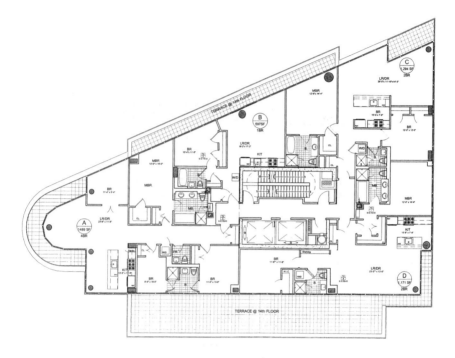

FIGURE 8–2

Elevation View

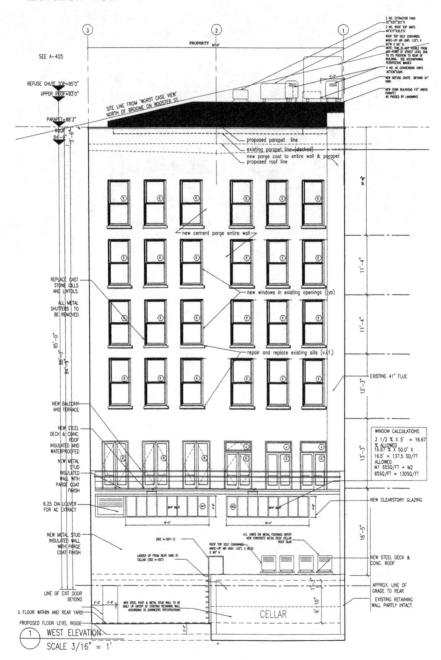

1 WEST ELEVATION
SCALE 3/16" = 1'

FIGURE 8–3

Sectional View

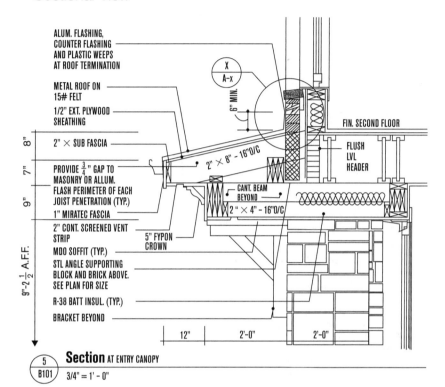

ALUM. FLASHING, COUNTER FLASHING AND PLASTIC WEEPS AT ROOF TERMINATION

METAL ROOF ON 15# FELT

1/2" EXT. PLYWOOD SHEATHING

2" × SUB FASCIA

PROVIDE $\frac{3}{4}$" GAP TO MASONRY OR ALLUM. FLASH PERIMETER OF EACH JOIST PENETRATION (TYP.)

1" MIRATEC FASCIA

2" CONT. SCREENED VENT STRIP

MDO SOFFIT (TYP.)

STL ANGLE SUPPORTING BLOCK AND BRICK ABOVE. SEE PLAN FOR SIZE

R-38 BATT INSUL. (TYP.)

BRACKET BEYOND

X
A-x

6" MIN.

2" × 8" - 16"O/C

FIN. SECOND FLOOR

FLUSH LVL HEADER

CANT. BEAM BEYOND

2" × 4" - 16"O/C

5" FYPON CROWN

8"

7"

9"

9"-2$\frac{1}{2}$ A.F.F.

12"   2'-0"   2'-0"

5
B101   **Section** AT ENTRY CANOPY
       3/4" = 1' - 0"

F I G U R E   8 – 4

Detail View

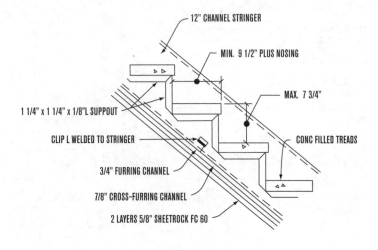

12" CHANNEL STRINGER

MIN. 9 1/2" PLUS NOSING

MAX. 7 3/4"

1 1/4" x 1 1/4" x 1/8"L SUPPOUT

CLIP L WELDED TO STRINGER

CONC FILLED TREADS

3/4" FURRING CHANNEL

7/8" CROSS-FURRING CHANNEL

2 LAYERS 5/8" SHEETROCK FC 60

TYPICAL STEEL STAIR DETAILS

SCALE: 1' = 1'– 0'

F I G U R E   8 – 5

Isometric (30-Degree) View

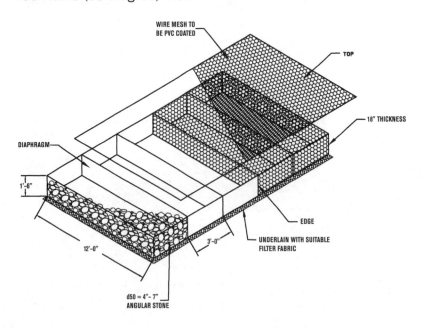

WIRE MESH TO
BE PVC COATED

TOP

18" THICKNESS

DIAPHRAGM

1'-6"

EDGE

UNDERLAIN WITH SUITABLE
FILTER FABRIC

12'-0"

3'-0"

d50 = 4"- 7"
ANGULAR STONE

FIGURE 8-6

Schematic View

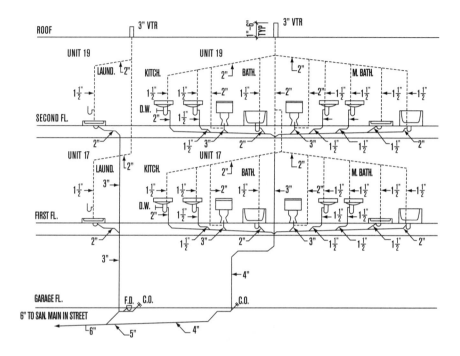

During the loan approval process, accuracy and detail are usually not available in plans to the extent where they can be used to commence construction. This is the case because today even basic structures have a high degree of complexity. Building requires regulatory compliance, and so the procedure takes a considerable amount of time.

If the loan transaction accompanies the purchase of the property, which it often does, the architect may not have done much more than draw a few preliminary floor plans and some renderings of the envisioned building. Also, the developer may want to hedge the risk of paying for and agonizing over a set of plans and specifications only to find that the seller has balked on the sale if there is no signed sales contract or if he cannot obtain financing (including an acquisition and/or construction loan). Therefore, the initial architectural plans often will be used for conceptual purposes and as a baseline for project evolution. Later, assuming that the project is a go, the plans and specifications will be developed in earnest.

Specifications

Specifications always come with plans. They can be printed on paper of the size used for plan drawings or, often on larger projects, kept in a separate book. Whereas plans provide a visual guide for how to proceed, specifications indicate in writing which materials and methods are required. Asking for a buildable or detailed set of plans implies the inclusion of specifications. Specifications must accompany plans for the plans to have any usefulness other than for a broad initial conceptual approach.

Since specifications can be several hundred pages long, having a system of organization is important. Under an industry group, the Construction Specifications Institute (CSI), a standard system has been adapted. Using the system, specifications are organized into divisions, with each division broken down into subdivisions. The divisions are identified by five-digit codes, with the first digit (or the second one after a zero) denoting the division and the remainder denoting subdivisions.[1] For quick reference, the divisions are listed below:

01000	General Requirements
02000	Sitework
03000	Concrete
04000	Masonry
05000	Metals
06000	Wood and Plastics
07000	Thermal and Moisture Protection
08000	Doors and Windows
09000	Finishes
10000	Specialties
11000	Equipment
12000	Furnishings
13000	Special Construction
14000	Conveying Systems
15000	Mechanical
16000	Electrical

---

[1] See Chapter 3 for samples of construction budgets. Note that the division numbers in the left-hand column may not be identical to the ones given by the CSI, but the system is similar (this is often the case when a lender first receives a hard cost budget that is estimated by someone without engineering and architectural experience).

PROJECT DESIGN, CONTROL, AND CONSTRUCTION

There are four basic recognized approaches by which a developer can proceed in the designing and building of a project. These approaches are not inseparable and often overlap. Elements of each one are common on any job from a subtrade level up to the entire job.

Construction Management Approach

In the best-known approach, the architect, hired by the developer, produces a set of plans and specifications in biddable form. The plans and specifications then are given to the owner's construction manager to distribute to prospective bidders. Winners are chosen on the basis of criteria such as price, experience, track record, availability, and references. Contracts are made between the contractors and the owner. The architect maintains direct involvement in the building process by overseeing the work through a continuing dialogue with the contractor or manager and periodic progress inspections. With this method, cost overruns are borne by the developer.

Construction Management At-Risk Approach

This approach is the same as the construction management approach except that in lieu of an independent construction manager, the general contractor takes on that function. Since the general contractor has additional control (contracts are between the contractors and the general contractor, not the owner), its contract provides that it will absorb budget overruns caused by necessary[2] change orders. In both the construction management and the construction management at-risk approaches, the architect works for the developer, who takes an active role in the design of the project.

Design Bid Build Approach

This method differs from the previous one in that the architect serves as the construction manager. With this approach, the architect has the most control, but because of the nature of the industry,

---

[2] Necessary change orders include, for example, the substitution of quarter-inch-thick drywall for five-eighths-inch-thick drywall to satisfy building codes. A change order exchanging tile kitchen countertops with granite ones is not a necessary one, and therefore the cost overrun will be paid for by the developer, not by the general contractor.

the developer usually is stuck with the overruns. The design bid build method may give the architect too much authority. Without enough outside control, if he is not competent in all areas of the architectural and construction management processes, the developer may face serious overruns that are hard to explain. Therefore, this is the least popular method in commercial construction.

Design Build Approach

The design build approach is growing rapidly in popularity because when it works properly, it reduces the time to begin and complete a project, provides a higher degree of on-site flexibility, and reduces up-front costs. With design build, the developer, architect, and general contractor work together on the conceptual design but the architect reports to the general contractor, not the owner.[3] The contractor is responsible for cost overruns. Unlike the construction management and construction management at-risk approaches, in which design, bid, and work are performed linearly, the design build process allows all three to proceed simultaneously. The general contractor will begin work before all the project plans and specifications are finalized (plans and specifications will be filed with all the applicable municipalities in stages). Because functions are performed in parallel rather than serially, the project is completed more quickly.

A potential issue in the design build approach is a higher likelihood that the general contractor will cut corners on quality to push down costs and earn a larger profit. With the architect under the general contractor's control, a valuable check and balance may be compromised. Abuses are most prone to materialize in workmanship and components such as security and HVAC where quality and capacity are traded off for less expensive systems that subsequently may fail, require extra maintenance, or need upgrading.[4]

Also, the more complex and/or unique a project is, the less likely it is that the design build method will be successful because

---

[3] The architect is actually under the employ or under a contract with the general contractor, not the developer.

[4] An example of cutting corners that has become a prevalent problem involves poorly installed EIFS (exterior insulated finishing systems). The "system" is essentially an inexpensive material and building method for exterior walls. When it is installed properly, it is an attractive and durable application. When it is installed improperly, water becomes trapped between the inner wall and the outer wall and over time causes significant damage and may create health problems.

with complexity, the interrelationship among trades, materials, structure, and function grows exponentially. This results in a greater chance that a critical aspect will be overlooked or not considered fully. A major determining factor in the success of the design build method is the general contractor's experience with building similar projects.

THE CONSTRUCTION CONTRACT

Except for simple, routine, or minor work, there can be an extensive process before a construction contract is drafted in its final form and signed. Generally, the order of events goes something like the following description.

As the plans and specs evolve from the conceptual stage, they eventually reach a level at which they contain a good deal of detail and certainty. At or just before this point, copies are produced and sent to contractors so that each one can evaluate his portion of the total project. This usually is followed by a contractors' meeting at which the architect, engineer, owner's representative, construction manager, and general contractor go over the bidding process and answer general questions. At or near the same time, depending on the job, contractors may get a tour of the property to review the work area firsthand.[5] After a meeting and a site visit, there are usually more in-depth questions and suggestions covering the plans, specs, method of bidding, time frames, and the like. Many times, the dialogue will result in improved plans and specifications, cost savings, and the beginning of a productive collaborative working relationship. As exchanges develop with several contractors, the developer (or a general contractor, a construction manager, or whoever is in charge of the process) gets a better feel for each contractor and an idea of which one most likely will work best with him and others on the job. Therefore, the lowest bid is often not the winning bid.

Figure 8–7 shows a worksheet that was created by a consultant specializing in facade work. A developer hired the consultant to evaluate three bidders for work to be performed on the envelope of an 80-year-old building in New York City.

---

[5] On a rehabilitation project, a site visit is practically a must so that the contractor can examine and note potential efficiencies or problems. On a new ground-up construction project, since there may not be anything to see for many of the bidding trades, a site visit may be irrelevant.

FIGURE 8-7

Table Showing Three Bids

Ye Old Hotel, 888 Madison Avennue, NYC

Bid Evaluation – Actual Bids

				Contractor A		Contractor B		Contractor C	
I	**General Conditions:**								
	A. Permits, Inspections, Stages, etc.	100%		$15,000	N/A	$15,000	N/A	$47,500	N/A
	B. Sidewalk Protection.	100%		$0	N/A	$10,000	N/A	$0	N/A
II	**Cleaning All Masonry:**								
	A. Cleaning.	100%		$107,652	N/A	$239,000	N/A	$148,800	N/A
	B. Window Protection	100%		$0	N/A	$33,000	N/A	$40,400	N/A
III	**Air Conditioning. Sleeves**	500	units	$600,000	$1,200.00	$250,000	$500.00	$378,300	$756.60
IV	**Masonry Repairs:**								
	A. Tuck Pointing (Face).	13,000	SF	$78,000	$6.00	$87,750	$6.75	$79,200	$6.09
	B. Tuck Pointing (Rear).	7,000	SF	$38,500	$5.50	$43,750	$6.25	$42,600	$6.09
	C. Tuck Pointing (Sills, Copings, etc.)	100%		$20,000	N/A	$15,000	N/A	$34,300	N/A
	D. Brick Replacement (Face).	10,000	SF	$400,000	$40.00	$450,000	$45.00	$449,500	$44.95
	E. Brick Replacement (Rear).	5,000	SF	$175,000	$35.00	$210,000	$42.00	$210,300	$42.06
	F. Brick Replacement (Backup).	3,000	SF	$90,000	$30.00	$108,000	$36.00	$104,400	$34.80
	G. Steel Lintel Replacement.	5,000	LF	$400,000	$80.00	$175,000	$35.00	$315,000	$63.00
	H. Column Repair.	500	LF	$75,000	$150.00	$20,000	$40.00	$5,100	$10.20
	I. Sill Replacement (concrete).	40	units	$4,800	$120.00	$6,400	$160.00	$7,100	$177.50
	J. Sill Replacement (terra cotta).	20	units	$4,000	$200.00	$7,600	$380.00	$4,900	$245.00
	K. Resetting Copings.	100	units	$8,000	$80.00	$15,000	$150.00	$16,700	$167.00
TOTAL LUMP SUM BID				**$2,015,952**		**$1,685,500**		**$1,884,100**	
				Contractor A		Contractor B		Contractor C	
a. Everything else seems to be similar for all contractors.				Josh Cacin		Rick Angrodello		Benjamin Taubman	
				123 Fifty fifth Ave		234 East 130th St.		923 Dice Street	
				Brooklyn, N.Y.		New York, N.Y.		New York, N.Y.	
				Tel: 718-395-2222		Tel: 212-345-6789		Tel: 212-222-8765	
				Fax: 718-395-1111		Fax: 212-987-6543		Fax: 212-222-0344	

Once a bidder is chosen, the successful contractor or the developer draws up a contract that, perhaps after some additional negotiations and a revision or two, is signed by both parties.

An example of a simple contract is shown in Figure 8–8. It was drafted for the renovation of one floor of an operating budget-style boutique hotel in which the owner and the contractor had worked together before and knew each other well. The renovation took place while the hotel was open for business. Because visitors were prevented from entering the floor where construction was being performed, the work could be done without disturbing the other floors of the hotel, which could continue to generate revenue. Since this book is concerned with development finance and not with construction or contract law, the contract shown in the figure is used only for illustration. On higher-level agreements with, for example, a general contractor and an owner and on larger jobs, more complex jobs, more expensive jobs, and jobs in which the parties are not familiar with one another and therefore want complete protection, a contract can run well over 100 pages.

Standard Form Contract

This contract is entered into at New York, New York on the date set forth below, between **ABC, LLC.,** ("Owner), a New York corporation, acting as general contractor, and **DEF Construction**(Contractor").

Contractor's License #_____CL – 12345 _____   Tax ID # _____98-76543 _____

Contractor's Address:

Regular Phone:_ 631-123-7654 _____   Emergency Phone: 917-321-4567 _____

Contractor is a : X   Corporation _____ Sole Proprietorship _____ General Partnership

Contract Sum: **$ 208,400.00**

Project Site: **Existing Hotel**

Date of Contract: March 22, 200-

Day of the Month to Submit Invoices: 1st

Owner's Address: 700 East 58th Street
                                           New York, New York   10022
                                           Phone: (212) 345-6789
                                           Fax: (212) 222-2222

Work to be performed on the following floor:

Fourteenth Floor

Brief Description of Work To Be Performed:

General   Demolition/removal/disposal of all existing carpets, floors, windows, doors, doorframes, ceilings, lighting, cabinets, kitchen cabinets, wall coverings including wallpaper, paint and tiles, and selected interior walls. Dispose of all debris.

Bathroom

Shower Room

Water Closet   Remove/dispose of all tiles, fixtures, wall coverings and light fixtures from all bathrooms, rooms with showers and rooms with toilets.

Frame out all bathroom areas providing access for all plumbing, electrical and communication connections and fittings, cover with waterproof board, and soundproof where required.

Prepare surface areas and install new tile as specified or marble and mosaic strips from floor to ceilings as specified in all bathrooms, rooms with showers and rooms with toilets.

Finish and paint all ceilings and exposed wall areas.

Install new marble saddles for bathroom, shower and tub entrances.

Install all new bathroom fixtures (soap dish, toilet paper holder, tooth brush holder, towel rod and shower soap dish, wall and door hooks, etc.).

Install bathtub glass doors and shower curtain rods.

Windows   All windows will be replaced with double hung aluminum windows. Installation will be "brick to brick". Upon removing existing windows, opening will be cleaned and reframed with weather treated wood and will be properly insulated. Outside of window will be properly caulked to brick and inside perimeter will be completely sealed and finished for painting and /or wallpapering.

Floor   Remove all floor coverings throughout rooms.

Level all floors and remove imperfections.

Room Surfaces   Remove all existing wallpaper from rooms and dispose of debris.

Patch all walls and ceilings where holes, cavities and imperfections exist.

Scrape all wall and ceiling surfaces and skim coat.

Refinished all walls throughout room, taping, spackling and refinishing.

Prime ceiling and walls with base and second coat of primer.

Paint or prepare for wallpapering all ceilings and walls.

Doors   Remove existing core doors and existing metal door frames and saddle from each room and dispose.

Build up, frame and true door area.

Install new metal door frames.

Install all new metal doors.

Install one security latch to each outside door.

Install peepholes where necessary.

Other   Install new track, studding, and partitions as per plans and owner's specifications..

Ceiling and all walls common to adjacent apartments and / or hallways will receive one layer of Homisote board for sound proofing plus insulation or two layers of sheetrock with insulation between walls. Soundproofing will extend from floor slab to ceiling slab.

Install mirror above each sink using locking attachments provided.

Install large hallway mirrors using locking attachments provided.

Install three pictures in each room using locking attachments on top and bottom as provided. Sheetrock rooms where required using fire code sheet rock.

Install hallway baseboards (one or two pieces) and ceiling moldings.

Notes

The expense and responsibility of filing and obtaining a construction permit will be that of the Owner's.

This job is scheduled to be completed in approx. 4-5 weeks.

Any changes or additional work to be included as part of this project must be submitted in writing, and price to be discussed and approved.

Insurance Hold Harmless—Contractor shall maintain in full force and effect a workers' compensation insurance policy, auto insurance policy, and comprehensive general liability insurance policy with limits of no less than $500,000 or such other amounts as Owner shall deem adequate. Said policy shall not be canceled without 30 days prior written notice to the Owner.

Contract Sum—This is a fixed fee contract. Owner shall pay Contractor the Contract Sum shown on the first page of this Contract. The Contract Sum is the total amount payable by Owner to Contractor for performance of the work under the contract documents. This includes all labor, services and equipment required to complete the work under this contract and also includes all sales, use and other taxes for labor, materials or equipment.

Invoices for Completed Work—Contractor should submit invoices for completed work once per month. Invoices for work that is not completed will only be paid upon completion of work and at the next disbursement date. No payment shall be made unless Contractor's rate of progress, work done, and materials furnished are as herein agreed upon.

Retention—A retention of 10% shall be withheld from each invoice. This retention shall be paid thirty (30) days after payment of the last and final invoice for all work covered under this Contract. The purpose of this retention is to ensure faithful performance of the work under this Contract and to ensure that there are sufficient funds to cover any corrective work that may be required. If corrective work is required, the retention may be withheld until the corrective work is completed.

Building Codes, Laws, Industry Standards—Contractor agrees to perform all work in accordance with applicable laws, regulations, and governmental agency requirements, and in accordance with industry standards. Should there be any variance between the contract documents and the building codes, laws, ordinances, requirements or regulations of governmental agencies of industry standards, the most stringent requirements will govern.

Contractor Has Applicable Licenses—Contractor has and shall maintain a current Contractor's License and a current business license form the city and/or county in which the work is to be performed.

Indemnity—To the fullest extent permitted by law, Contractor shall defend, indemnify and hold harmless Owner and each of their respective agents and employees from and against claims, damages, losses and expenses, including, but not limited to, attorneys' fees, arising out of or resulting from performance of the work, to the extent caused in whole or in part by negligent acts or omissions of the Contractor, anyone directly or indirectly employed by him or anyone for whose acts he may be liable, regardless of whether or not such claim, damage, loss or expense is caused in part by a party indemnified hereunder. The coverage of this indemnity shall include, without limitation, all liability, loss, claims, demands, damages, expenses, costs and attorneys' fees arising out of any failure of Contractor to perform and observe the requirements of the Contract documents, of any law, regulation, code or ordinance relating to the work, unless caused solely by the negligence of Owner. This indemnity shall not be construed to negate, abridge or reduce other rights or obligations of indemnity which would otherwise be available to Owner or any other indemnified party.

Modifications—No modifications of the contract price shall be made and no work of lesser value than that called for shall be accepted without a written change order signed by the Owner.

Assignment—The Contractor shall not assign this Agreement, nor sublet or subcontract any portion of his work hereunder, without the prior written consent of the Owner.

Cleanup—The Contractor agrees to clean up and remove his debris, rubbish, and surplus materials as the work progresses, and to keep his work protected from the elements and from damage occasioned by construction work and to protect all other parts of the work from damage likely to be caused by the Subcontractor's work. Should any such damage be so caused, Contractor agrees immediately to repair same. Any default of the Contractor in any such cleaning, protection or repairs may be remedied by the Owner and the cost deducted from the Contractor's compensation.

Failure to Perform—If, in the opinion of the Owner, the Contractor fails to perform his work in accordance with this Agreement, and should such failure continue for twenty-four (24) consecutive hours after service of a written notice upon the Contractor (specifying the particulars of such failure) served personally or mailed to the Contractor, then such failure shall constitute a breach of this Agreement by the Contractor, which shall entitle the Owner to terminate this Agreement and complete the work himself, or cause the work to be completed by others and the Contractor agrees immediately to repay all costs and damages sustained by the Owner on account of such failure.

Arbitration—If the parties hereto fail to promptly adjust and determine any controversy or claim arising out of this Agreement, the written orders of the Owner shall be followed and such controversy of claim shall be settled by arbitration after completion of the work in accordance with the rules of the American Arbitration Association, and judgment upon award may be entered in any court having jurisdiction thereof.

Responsibility for Material/Workmanship—Neither the final payment nor any provision in
the contract documents shall relieve the Contractor of responsibility for faulty materials or workmanship and, unless otherwise specified, he shall remedy any defects and pay for any damage to other work resulting there from which shall appear within one year of acceptance of the work by Owner.

Hazardous Materials—Contractor shall comply with all government agency regulations and requirements regarding hazardous materials communication standards. Contractor shall provide Owner with Material Safety Data Sheets (MSDS) on all hazardous materials brought on the site.

Attorneys' Fees—If any action is brought by any party against another under this Contract, the prevailing party shall be entitled to recover an amount as the Court may adjudge to be a reasonable attorneys' fee, in addition to costs and other fees.

There are no understandings or agreements except as herein expressly stated.

IN WITNESS WHEREOF, the parties have executed this Contract by their proper officers duly authorized therein.

Dated this _____ day of _____ , 19 _____ .

ABC, LLC

By

_____

DEF Construction

BY_____

Involving the Development Lender

While the developer and his team are refining plans and specifications and reviewing, hiring, and contracting trades (commonly called buying or buying out the job), the developer should send the lender and/or the lender's consulting engineer the information necessary to evaluate the project.

The Consulting Engineer

One of the tools the development lender uses is the consulting engineer (also called the inspecting engineer, engineer, construction consultant, or engineering consultant). In most institutions senior management composes a short list of approved engineers (architects may be used as consultants as well) on the basis of past experience from which the loan officer can choose. The outside consultant is hired from the list on a transaction-by-transaction basis. In large institutions that make many construction loans, there may be an in-house engineer who is responsible for reviewing the outside consulting engineer and monitoring his work. He also may be responsible for hiring the engineering consultant.

What the Consulting Engineer Asks For

Before a construction loan commitment is signed or shortly afterward, the engineering consultant will contact the potential borrower directly with requests for specific information. Figure 8–9 shows some of the items that may be asked for.[6] Checklists like these go out all the time and are a good way to gauge the responsiveness and often the readiness of the borrower.

---

[6] Note that the list is broad. It is unlikely that all the items would be requested for any single transaction.

FIGURE 8-9

Document Request

Dear Mr. Collins:

Please be advised that we have been retained by QRS Bank as Lender's construction consultant on the above-referenced project. Preparatory to our beginning our review process, we will need the following checked documents.

DRAWINGS

☐ Civil/Site   ☐ Mechanical   ☐ Fire Protection

☐ Architectural   ☐ Electrical   ☐ Landscaping

☐ Structural   ☐ Plumbing   ☐ Life Safety Plan

DOCUMENTS

☐ Specifications   ☐ Soils Report & Foundation Recommendations

☐ Property Survey   ☐ Owner/Contractor Agreement(s)

☐ Utility Agreements   ☐ Major Sub-Contractor Agreements

   a – electric/gas   ☐ Cost Breakdown

   b – water   ☐ Progress Schedule

   c – sewer   ☐ Cash Flow Schedule

   d – telephone   ☐ Engineer's Energy Certification/Calculations

☐ Zoning Approval   ☐ Architect's Certification of Code & ADA
                                             Compliance

☐ Building Permits   ☐ Flood Plain Map Delineation

☐ Special Permits (as required)   ☐ Threshold Inspector Certificate

☐ Concurrency Approval Certificate   ☐ Structural Inspection Plan

☐ Tenant Work letter   ☐ Builder's Risk Insurance Certificate

☐ Architect/Engineer Agreement

Our normal procedure requires a minimum of two weeks for review (or more, depending on size and complexity of project), therefore your prompt attention will be appreciated. Please feel free to contact our office should you have any questions.

Very truly yours,

XYZ Construction Consultants

The Engineering Consultant's Responsibilities

The engineering firm's duties begin with an initial comprehensive review that includes an examination of the plans and specifications in regard to their scope and completeness, a perusal of major trade contracts, and a review of the construction budget against the scope of work (note the checklist in Figure 8–9). An opinion then is provided about the feasibility of the construction in light of the work to be done and the money and time allocated to do it. If the engineering firm has concerns, they should be relayed to the borrower and addressed.

During an average development lending career, a loan officer will review several initial inspection reports and receive dozens, if not hundreds, of periodic inspection reports. If you are not familiar with this kind of report, a quick read-through should give you a good idea of what to expect. Figure 8–10 shows a slightly abbreviated report on a substantial (gut) rehabilitation of a vacant manufacturing building into an apartment building with street-level retail space.

Plan and Cost Review

for

100 Black Street
New York, NY

TABLE OF CONTENTS

I. EXECUTIVE SUMMARY

A. INTRODUCTION

The site is located in Manhattan on the west side of Black Street. The total lot area is 5,010 SF (0.11 acres). An existing 6 story building occupies most of the site. This area is zoned M1-5B. This is a Light Manufacturing District allowing for commercial uses. New residential development is excluded except for Use Group 17D, joint living work quarters for artists. Approval must be granted by the New York City Building Department for conversion of the building. The existing building does not comply with zoning regulations for bulk. No increase in degree of non-compliance is proposed.

The project consists of a 26,010 sq. ft. rectangular apartment building with commercial space on the ground floor. The existing building will be increased to 7 stories plus penthouse. The apartments are to be constructed "adaptable" as required by the Federal Fair Housing Act; however, many of the doors in the cellar and exit stairways are not designed to be accessible.

The cellar contains individual locker rooms, retail storage, and mechanical rooms. The apartment building entrance from the sidewalk leads to a corridor to the elevator and exit stair access. A second entrance leads to the egress stair from the cellar and a third to the exit stair from the second floor. The entrance to the retail space is up a set of stairs; there is also access to the retail space from the third apartment building entrance via a wheel chair lift.

The upper apartment floors are accessed by the elevator and 2 fire egress stairs. There are two apartments per floor on the 2nd, 3rd and 4th floors and one apartment per floor on the 5th and 6th floors. The 7th floor apartment is a floor-through with a family room in the penthouse. There are a total of 9 apartments: 6 two bedrooms and 3 three bedrooms.

The existing front facade is cast iron at the first floor and brick above. Above the 6th floor the new construction is brick on cmu. The new rear construction is called out as stucco on metal studs. The penthouse floor appears to consist of a glass skylight across the front facade and a stucco and stud structure at the sides and back utilizing curvilinear shapes at the roof line. We were informed that the NYC Landmarks Preservation Commission requires a mockup of the penthouse before giving final approval.

Heating for the apartment spaces is provided by hot water fin tube baseboard radiators located at the perimeter of the building. Hot water is generated by gas-fired modular boilers located in the cellar. Apartments are cooled via split system air handler units. The building is provided with a combined fire standpipe and sprinkler reserve tank on the roof with a com-bined total capacity of 10,010 gallons. The building is designed for a wet sprinkler system. Fire hose racks are specified at each floor.

B. DOCUMENTS

The documents presented to us appear to be preliminary. They are not signed. The documents are acceptable for loan purposes, subject to the satisfactory resolution of the issues in the Comments and Recommendations section of this report.

C. CONSTRUCTION COSTS

The Estimate Sheet states a Hard Cost Budget of $4,983,592. The gross square footage of the building is approximately 26,010 SF. The budget represents an overall hard cost of approximately $192 per gross square foot of building. This is on the high side of the range of current New York City prices for apartment construction; however, given the preliminary nature of the documents and the many unknowns, the amount is appropriate.

The estimate includes Contractor's General Conditions at $346,685 (8%). This percentage is reasonable. General Conditions of 5% is more common. Contractor's Contingency is indicated as $303,349 (7%). This is reasonable as renovation projects invariably encounter conditions unforeseen in the initial planning and budgeting, hence significant contingencies are recommended. We recommend an additional 5% owner's contingency.

D. CONTRACT AND SCHEDULE

We have not received a copy of the contract or schedule.

II. PROJECT DESCRIPTION

A. SITE DESCRIPTION

1. General

   The proposed site is lot number 21 in block 475 on the NY City Tax Map 1 2a. It is located in Manhattan on the west side of Black Street approximately 95' south of Broome Street. The street address is 101 Black Street.

   The lot has 50 feet of frontage on Black Street. It is rectangular shaped and 101'-0" deep. An existing 6-story building occupies most of the site with a small areaway in the rear. There are existing buildings on either side which share party walls with the project building. The total lot area is 5010 SF (0.11 acres). There is a 5-foot areaway at the rear of the building.

   This area is zoned M1-5B on Zoning Resolution Map 12a. This is a Light Manufacturing District allowing for commercial uses. New residential development is excluded except for Use Group 17D, joint living work quarters for artists. Approval must be granted by the New York City Building Department for conversion of the building to joint living work quarters for artists in conformance with section 43-17 of the Zoning Regulations. Restrictions include that the building lot coverage may not be more than 3,601 sq. ft. per lot. Uses of the ground floor are also restricted. The ground floor will be Use Group 9, retail. The existing building does not comply with zoning regulations for bulk. No increase in degree of non-compliance is proposed.

2. Site Utilities
   Typical of Manhattan, buried utilities exist in the street.

3. Site Drainage
   A duplex sump pump in the cellar removes water from the cellar, but no area drain is indicated.

4. Parking
   Off street parking will not be provided.

B. BUILDING DESCRIPTION

The project consists of a 26,010 sq. ft. rectangular apartment building with commercial space on the ground floor. The existing building is a 6 story manufacturing structure that will be increased to 7 stories plus penthouse. The construction class of the existing building was not provided. The building will be equipped with a sprinkler and standpipe system. The Occupancy Group is J2 with secondary occupancies of C (retail), B-2 (storage) and D-2 (mechanical space). The apartments appear to meet requirements for light and ventilation.

The building is to comply with Multiple Dwelling Law 277. Shafts are to have a 2 hour fire resistance rating. No rating is required for interior partitions. Columns are to be 3 hour rated. Demising partitions between apartments are required to have a 1 hour rating. Lot line windows are to be sprinklered.

Handicap details indicating disabled accessibility design for the apartments to conform to Local Law 58 were provided. We did not note any designated fully accessible apartments; however, the apartments are to be constructed "adaptable" as required by the Federal Fair Housing Act. Many of the doors in the cellar and in the exit stairways are not designed to be accessible; there is inadequate space on the latch side of the door.

The renovated building is 87'-1 1" to the roof of the 7th floor. The height to the penthouse roof is an additional 1 2 feet. The building is set back 20'-0" at the 7th floor in the front. It is set back 1 9'-6" above the first floor in the rear.

Though no demolition drawings were provided it appears that all interior partitions are to be removed. Existing timber columns and wood floors will remain. Exterior walls will remain with the exception of the rear wall. The building will be reduced by approximately 10 feet in rear above the first floor.

The cellar contains individual locker rooms, retail storage, boiler room, electric service room, sprinkler room, water/gas meter room, compacter room, elevator machine room. The various rooms are separated from adjacent rooms by walls providing 2 hour separation.

An enclosed exit stair leads from the cellar up to the 1st floor lobby and to the exterior. A second cellar stair in an enclosed exit passageway leads to the exterior via a vestibule on the 1st floor. There is a third enclosed stair that provides egress from the second and upper floors to the cellar and from there through the exit passage way to the second exit stair back up to the street, bypassing the first floor entirely. Provisions have been made for an open stair from the retail space to the cellar storage. There is an open atrium at this stair. Verify that the surrounding spaces have adequate fire separation protection. The elevator also accesses the cellar.

The apartment building entrance from the sidewalk leads to a corridor to the elevator and exit stair access. A second entrance leads to the egress stair from the cellar and a third to the exit stair from the second floor. The entrance to the retail space is up a set of stairs; there is also access to the retail space from the third apartment building entrance via a wheel chair lift. A skylight is to be constructed at the rear of building.

The upper apartment floors are accessed by the elevator and 2 fire egress stairs. The enclosed exit stairs form a scissor configuration. There are two apartments per floor on the 2nd 3rd and 4th floors and one apartment per floor on the 5th and 6th floors. The 7th floor apartment is a floor-through with a family room in the penthouse. There are a total of 9 apartments: 6 two bedrooms and 3 three bedrooms. The apartments are adequately laid out and generous in size and floor area for the most part. The layouts of all the apartments are similar. The apartments up to the fourth floor are 1,676 sq. ft. (rear) or 1,756 sq. ft. (front) and the fifth and sixth floor apartments are 3,531 sq. ft. The penthouse apartment is approximately 3,601 sq. ft. net.

The apartments are entered directly from the elevator. The apartments can also be entered /exited from the stair enclosure. Note that occupants leaving the apartments through one of the two stairs will only be able to exit the building via the cellar. There is a garbage chute located off the stair enclosure. The fire separation is not given.

Each apartment typically includes a hall closet, a living room/ dining area, an open kitchen which includes a dishwasher and microwave, a washer/dryer closet, 2 or 4 bathrooms and 2 or 3 bedrooms with closets. The master bedrooms on the 5th and 6th floor have access to a large dressing area with a window.

The penthouse apartment has 3 bedrooms and 3 bathrooms on the 7th floor and one on the penthouse floor. There is a kitchenette on the penthouse floor. The 7th floor is setback at the front and the apartment has access to a 20'-0" roof terrace. The penthouse floor is setback on the front, rear and north side and has access to terraces. The front of the penthouse is a greenhouse.

The elevator bulkhead is located on the roof of the 7th floor. A fire water tower is indicated on the fire protection drawings but not located on the architecturals. One stairway extends to the roof of the 7th floor.

C. ARCHITECTURAL SYSTEMS

1. Exterior

   The existing front facade is cast iron at the first floor and brick above. The brick is to be sandblasted and repointed as required. The existing stone lintels, window sills, and banding are to be stripped and sand blasted. The window sills will be replaced as needed. New windows are to be provided. Metal panels at the first floor level are to be replaced or repaired as needed to match existing. Above the 6th floor the new con-struction is brick on cmu. The cornice is shown as existing on the elevations and new on the sections. Details are incomplete.

   The exposed sides of the building appear to be existing brick. The new rear con-struction is called out as stucco on metal studs; however, the drawings indicate stucco on cmu. Cast stone parapets are called out but, metal parapets are drawn.

   The penthouse floor appears to consist of a glass skylight across the front facade and a stucco and stud structure at the sides and back utilizing curvilinear shapes at the roof line. We were informed that the NYC Landmarks Preservation Commission requires a mockup of the penthouse before giving final approval.

   The roof is a concrete and metal deck construction sloped 1/4" to drains. The finish is a EPDM system on rigid insulation over a vapor barrier.

2. Interior

   The interior face of the exterior walls is furred out with 5/8" type X gypsum wall board on 1 5/8" metal stud framing with batt insulation. Stud framing is indicated as 1 6" on center and 24" on center. Batt insulation is noted as 31/2". Please verify. Type X, 5/8" gypsum wall board partitions are used throughout. Metal stud dimensions are typically 1 5/8" at 1 6" on center. Elevator shaft walls are indicated as 2 hour rated. Other fire separation assemblies are not consistently indicated. Stairs details are not provided.

The elevator is to be a traction elevator with two doors. Elevator specifications were not provided.

New floor construction appears to be concrete on metal deck. New hardwood plank flooring is provided on plywood subfloor. Bathroom walls are ceramic tile and are to incorporate reinforcement for future grab bars. Apartment entry doors are hollow metal. Interior apartment doors are wood. Handicap adaptable base kitchen cabinets are to be provided for disabled accessibility.

D. STRUCTURAL SYSTEMS

1. Substructure
   Structural drawings were not provided.
   The existing foundation is to remain in the front half of the building. The building substructure in the rear is to be lowered 2'-0".
2. Superstructure
   The existing superstructure includes brick piers and/or cylindrical steel columns in the cellar and first floor and 1'x1' timber columns at the upper levels. The existing floor structure appears to consist of wood joists. Fire resistive rating of structural members is not indicated. There is no note whether the wood is to be fire-retardant treated.
   Support framing for the cooling towers on roof is not indicated.
   The sidewalk vaults will be cleaned and made water tight. No details are provided.

E. MECHANICAL SYSTEMS

1. Heating ,Ventilation, and Air Conditioning
   Heating for the apartment spaces is provided by hot water fin tube baseboard radiators located at the perimeter of the building. All supply and return lines are equipped with air vents. Hot water is generated by three gas-fired modular boilers located in the cellar. The specified manufacturer is Slant/Fin model GGHT-901E. The boilers are equipped with a 1 6-inch diameter flue. An expansion tank and 2 circulator pumps are provided.
   The lobby is cooled by a self contained packaged air conditioning unit. Apartments are cooled via split system air handler units. The air handler units are suspended from the floor/ceiling slab at each floor. Cooling capacities range from 3 to 5 tons per unit. All air cooled condensing units are located on the rear 2nd floor terrace or penthouse roof. Self contained packaged air conditioning units are to be provided in the retail space by the tenant.
   Five exhaust fans for toilet, dryer and kitchen exhaust located on the roof are rated from 601 cfm to 3601 cfm. A 101% outside air make up unit is also located on the roof.
   The cellar areas are provided with a de-humidifier. The condensing unit is located on the 2nd floor setback. The elevator machine room is provided with a fan coil unit. The trash compactor room is exhausted to the rear of the building.
   The apartments are shown furnished with fire places. Flues are not indicated.
   The mechanical systems are adequately designed per the submitted drawings.
2. Plumbing
   An existing 4" domestic water line was indicated to provide service to the building through a new 4" approved water meter in the cellar. A 4" RPZ backflow preventer is provided. A duplex booster pump system rated at 71/2 H.P. and 150 gpm at 60 PSI is specified to ensure appropriate pressure for domestic water. One domestic hot water heater and one hot water storage tank located in the cellar will provide domestic hot water for the building. The water heater is gas fired and has 250 cfh imput.

A new combined 8"sanitary /storm sewer is provided for the building with house and running traps. Water collected from 4" roof drains flows into the combined sewer drain through internal leaders. A duplex sump pump removes water from cellar floor drains. All plumbing drains are tied into 4" vent stacks through the roof.

An existing 3" gas service is specified for service to the boilers, make up air unit, hot water heater and tenant ranges. Tenant apartments are metered separately.

The plumbing systems are adequately designed per drawings.

3. Fire Protection

The building is provided with a combined fire standpipe and sprinkler reserve tank on the roof with a combined total capacity of 10,010 gallons. An electric immersion heater is provided. The tank is filled via duplex house fill pumps located in the cellar with a capacity of 101 GPM each.

The building is designed for a wet sprinkler system with 6 to 32 sprinkler heads per floor including trash chute. A special service fire booster pump capacity 250 GPM at 130 foot head and an attendant jockey pump is provided.

Fire hose racks are specified at each floor with 125 foot hose each. A Siamese connection is provided facing Black Street. The Siamese connection is served by a 6" water line.

Fire/smoke detectors are specified for the elevator shaft, elevator machine room, boiler room, electric room , and telephone closet. Water flow alarm switches and valve tamper switches are provided for the sprinkler system. An alarm panel is provided on the first floor.

The fire protection system is adequately designed per drawings.

F. ELECTRICAL SYSTEMS

Power is supplied to the building below ground by Consolidated Edison to the 801 amp, 120/208V, 3 phase, 4 wire house C/T cabinet. Power is further distributed to a 601 amp house Distribution Panel (DP) and a dedicated line direct to the fire pump. Power is also supplied by Consolidated Edison to a 601 amp, 3 phase, 4 wire retail metering cabinet and to a meter bank that provides 201 amp, 120/208V, 3 phase, 4 wire service to each apartment. Each apartment is metered individually.

A sprinkler alarm/smoke detection system is provided which includes smoke detectors in the electrical room, telephone closet, elevator machine room, pump room, and top of elevator shaft and a heat detector in the boiler room. Water flow alarm switches and valve tamper switches are provided and an outdoor sprinkler alarm bell is located on the face of the building. The alarm panel is located on the first floor.

A low voltage riser system is provided for an audio/visual intercom system. Incoming telephone and cable TV conduit is provided.

The electrical systems are adequately designed per drawings.

III. ANALYSIS OF COSTS

A. BUDGET DOCUMENTATION

Our cost analysis is based upon the following documents:
1. The Plans listed in Section VI of this report.
2. An Estimate Sheet dated 8/23.

B. METHODOLOGY

We have reviewed the Construction Hard Costs using the following methods:
1. Parameter estimating, comparing each trade with other buildings of similar type that we have monitored. Parameter estimating involves the quantifying of the

major physical features of a building and applying known average unit costs, for a given geographical area, to these quantities.

2. Spot quantity survey and pricing of some of the major trades, taking off significant items of the trades and applying unit prices that, according to our experience and research, are applicable in that area.

We use whichever one or combination of the above procedures is most applicable to the project and the material with which we are furnished. A comparison is then made between the cost breakdown submitted by the Borrower and the results of our own cost study. We then discuss the comparison in our cost report. If we find any major discrepancies for any trade, we attempt to reconcile the differences by discussions with the Borrower or its General Contractor.

We do not make a complete quantity survey as is typically done in bidding a construction job, because this is not within the scope of our assignment. Since there is no one "right" cost for any job, we attempt to examine whether the price appears reasonable.

C. FINDINGS AND CONCLUSIONS

The Estimate Sheet states a Hard Cost Budget of $4,983,592 of which $4,333,558 is the Direct Trade Cost. The gross square footage of the building is approximately 26,010 SF. The budget represents an overall hard cost of approximately $192 per gross square foot of building. This is within the range of current New York City prices for apartment construction. Of the Direct Trade Cost, $301,875 is for Demolition, Excavation, and Sitework. The remaining cost is $4,681,717 for building construction. Of the remaining cost, this works out to be about $181 per square foot. Given the preliminary nature of the documents and the many unknowns, the amount is appropriate.

The estimate includes Contractor's General Conditions at $346,685 (8%). This percentage is reasonable. General Conditions of 5% is more common. Contractor's Contingency is indicated as $303,349 (7%). This is reasonable as renovation projects invariably encounter conditions unforeseen in the initial planning and budgeting, hence significant contingencies are recommended. We recommend an additional 5% owner's contingency.

The line-by-line breakdown of the overall budget is not supported by any proposals from subcontractors. We require subcontracts supporting these values in order to evaluate their validity.

Our estimates were based on broad assumptions and approximated quantity take-offs of the scope of the work. When we checked readily quantifiable items on a unit cost basis, we found most were acceptable.

ABC Group (ABC)
130 East Street
New York, NY 10122

BUDGET

Demolition, Excavation, Sitework	$301,875.01
Hard Costs less Demolition, Excavation, Sitework	$4,031,683.01
Subtotal	$4,333,558.01
General Conditions (8%)	$346,685.01
Contingency (7%)	$303,349.01
Project Total	$4,983,592.01
Design Costs	$220,010.01
Total	$5,203,592.01

D. COST ANALYSIS ASSUMPTIONS

Our review of the hard costs assumes that:
- Good budgetary control will be applied to all General Conditions costs.
- Local market conditions do not create subcontractor or manpower shortages that will adversely affect the project.
- No work will be performed on a time and materials basis by the Developer, Construction Manager, or General Contractor. Work handled in this manner can easily cause cost overruns.
- All equipment, materials, and finishes are assumed to be selected at average value unless specifically and clearly indicated in the construction documents.
- Contingency Hard Costs funds shall only be allocated for the listed line items and standard work, and not for upgrading of materials or other excluded costs, until such time as final costs are determined with a good amount of certainty.
- Normal, prudent cost controls and practices will be followed in all purchases, subcontracts, and payments.

Allowances are accepted as established, but may be a source of future variation in cost.
Our budget review assumes that none of the following are included in the Hard Costs submitted:

1) Overtime or premium costs
2) Early completion bonuses
3) Tenant giveaways or upgradings not currently indicated in the plans or specifications, or specifically delineated in the budget
4) Furniture, fixtures, or equipment
5) Special costs relating to fast-tracking the project
6) Any special equipment, finishes, or other Hard Cost items not clearly required by the plans or specifications.

E. CONTRACT ANALYSIS

We have not received a construction contract.

IV. CONSTRUCTION SCHEDULE

We have not received a construction schedule.

V. COMMENTS AND RECOMMENDATIONS

A. SITE

1. Provide documentation that approval has been granted by the New York City Building Department for conversion of the buildings to joint living work quarters for artists in conformance with section 43-17 of the Zoning Regulations.
2. Indicate whether the sidewalks will be reconstructed.
3. A duplex sump pump in the cellar removes water from the cellar, but no area drain is indicated. Verify.

B. ARCHITECTURAL

1. Provide the new and existing construction types.
2. Provide the fire resistance ratings for the exit stairs, exit passageways, corridors and shafts, interior partitions, floors and beams, and demising partitions between apartments.
3. Many of the doors in the exit stairway are not designed to be accessible; there is inadequate space on the latch side of the door.

4. Provisions have been made for an open stair from the retail space to the cellar storage. There is an open atrium at this stair. Verify that the surrounding spaces have adequate fire separation protection.
5. The architectural details are incomplete and inconsistent. Please revise.

C. STRUCTURAL SYSTEMS

1. Structural systems are not detailed.

D. MECHANICAL SYSTEMS

1. Provide the cooling requirements for the retail space.
2. The apartments are shown furnished with fireplaces. Flues are not indicated.

E. ELECTRICAL SYSTEMS

No comments.

F. GENERAL

1. Provide proposals from subcontractors to support the line-by-line breakdown of the overall budget. We require subcontracts supporting these values in order to evaluate their validity. A review of the components in the breakdown will be necessary before a reasonable appraisal of the budget can be made.
2. Provide the construction contract.
3. A detailed construction schedule should be submitted.
4. Signed and sealed documents should be provided.

VI. DOCUMENTATION

A. DRAWING LIST

	ARCHITECTURAL	Date
A-1	CELLAR + FIRST FLOOR PLAN-OPTION 208/01/01	
A-2	SECTION	07/18
A-210	2ND& 3RD / 4TH FLOOR PLAN	08/02
A-220	5TH & 6TH FLOOR PLAN	08/02
A-230	7TH & MEZZANINE PLAN	08/02
A-S 10	NEW WINDOW DETAILS	08/03
A-530	EXISTING ELEVATION	08/01
A-540	SOUTH & NORTH ELEVATIONS	08/01
A-101	GENERAL NOTES	10/09
A-102	SITE PLAN	10/09
A-103	(ACCESSIBILITY)	10/09
A-104	AREA CALCULATIONS	10/09
A-201	CELLAR PLAN	11/15
A-202	FIRST FLOOR PLAN	11/15
A-203	SECOND FLOOR PLAN	11/11
A-204	3RD & 4TH FLOOR PLAN	11/15
A-205	5TH FLOOR PLAN	11/15
A-206	6th FLOOR PLAN	11/15

A-207	7TH FLOOR PLAN	11/15
A-209	ROOF PLAN	11/15
A-301	SECTION A-A	11/09
A-302	SECTION A-A AND SECTION B-B	11/09
A-401	EAST & WEST ELEVATION	11/09
A-402	NORTH & SOUTH ELEVATION	11/09
A-501	STOREFRONT ELEVATION DETAIL	09/30
A-503	WALL SECTIONS	10/09
A-601	PARTITION TYPES	10/09
A-602	DOOR & WINDOW SCHEDULES	09/30
A-603	KITCHEN-FLOORS 2-6	09/25
A-604	KITCHEN-PENTHOUSE FLOOR	09/25
A-605	TYPICAL BATHROOMS	09/30

STRUCTURAL
MECHANICAL

H-1	HOT WATER RISER DIAGRAM & AIR RISER DIAGRAM	07/18
H-2	AC UNIT SCHEDULE	07/18
H-3	AIR DISTRIBUTION PLAN (TYPICAL) AND HVAC RISER LOCATION PLAN	07/18
H-1	CELLAR LEVEL HVAC PLAN	10/20
H-2	FIRST FLOOR HVAC PLAN	10/20
H-3	2ND, 3RD & 4TH FLOORS HVAC PLAN	10/20
H-4	5TH & 6th FLOORS HVAC PLAN	10/20
H-S	HOT WATER RISER DIAGRAM	10/20
H-6	AIR RISER DIAGRAM & EQUIPMENT SCHEDULE	10/20
H-7	AC UNIT SCHEDULE	10/20
H-8	HVAC DETAIL	10/20

ELECTRICAL

E-1	LIGHT AND POWER RISER DIAGRAM	07/18
E-2	AUDIO/VISUAL APARTMENT/DOOR INTERCOM SYSTEM AND SPRINKLER ALARM/SMOKE DETECTION SYSTEM RISER DIAGRAMS	07/18
E-3	PANEL SCHEDULES	07/18
E-1	CELLAR LEVEL-ELECTRICAL PLAN	10/20
E-2	FIRST FLOOR-ELECTRICAL PLAN	10/20
E-3	2ND, 3RD & 4TH FLOOR-ELECTRICAL PLAN	10/20
E-4	5TH & 6th FLOORS-ELECTRICAL PLAN	10/20
E-8	LIGHT AND POWER RISER DIAGRAM	10/20
E-9	AUDIO/VISUAL/DOOR INTERCOM SYSTEM & SPRINKLER ALARM/SMOKE DETECTION RISER DIAGRAMS	10/20
E-10	PANEL SCHEDULES AND ELECTRICAL LEGEND	10/20

PLUMBING

P-1	PLUMBING RISER DIAGRAM	07/18
P-2	GAS AND STORM RISER	07/18
P-3	PLUMBING RISER LOCATION PLAN	07/18
P-4	FIRE STANDPIPE RISER DIAGRAM, DETAILS & NOTES	07/18
P-1	CELLAR LEVEL PLUMBING PLAN	10/20
P-2	PLUMBING RISER DIAGRAM	10/20
P-3	GAS RISER DIAGRAM	10/20
P-4	FIRE STANDPIPE RISER DIAGRAM	10/20
P-5	PLUMBING DETAILS	10/20

FIRE PROTECTION

SP-1	SPRINKLER RISER DIAGRAM, DETAILS & NOTES	07/18
SP-1	CELLAR LEVEL - SPRINKLER PLAN	10/20
SP-2	FIRST FLOOR- SPRINKLER PLAN	10/20
SP~3	2ND, 3RD & 4TH FLOORS - SPRINKLER PLAN	10/20
SP~4	5TH & 6TH FLOORS - SPRINKLER PLAN	10/20
SP-7	SPRINKLER RISER DIAGRAM	10/20
SP-7A	SPRINKLER RISER DIAGRAM	10/20

B. OTHER DOCUMENTS

In accordance with the EA Checklist of Required Information, we have received the following documents:
1. Drawings and Specifications (see drawing list)
2. Estimate sheet dated 8/23.

We have NOT received the following documents, which were requested in the EA Checklist of Required Information:
1. Copies of Government Agency approval.
2. Construction Cost Trade Breakdown.
3. Copy of Construction Loan Agreement.
4. Copy of Building Permit including evidence of amount of permit fee.
5. Anticipated Progress Schedule.
6. Copy of Architect/Owner Contract.
7. Copy of contract with General Contractor and/or Construction Manager.

VII. FINAL STATEMENT

The drawings that we received were generally well prepared and adequately describe the overall scope and intent of construction. The submitted documents are acceptable for loan purposes, subject to the satisfactory resolution of the issues in the Comments and Recommendations section of this report.

It is understood that we are not a guarantor or insurer of the adequacy or sufficiency of the plans and specifications and that our services are being rendered solely as an advisor and that we do not assume the role of the design professional(s).

This review has been prepared with reasonable skill and care and may be relied upon by you in connection with the loan, but it is not to be relied upon by any other party or for any other purpose.

Very truly yours,

ENGINEER ASSOCIATES, INC.

What to Do with the Initial Plan and Cost Review

On the surface, the purpose of the plan and cost review is to do the following:

- Provide some assurance that the engineer did a responsible review of the project (measured by its extent and comprehensiveness)
- Provide an overall description of the project
- Brings up questions and/or concerns that need to be addressed further before construction funding can proceed
- Give an opinion about the reasonableness of the developer's budget
- Give an opinion about the reasonableness of the developer's time frame
- Address any areas of concern or that require the receipt of more information and the need for further investigation and analysis

From a practical viewpoint, for a lender, the usefulness of the plan and cost review lies first and foremost in the review of the developer's budget. To make any loan advances, the budget generally must be sanctioned by the engineer. If it is not and you cannot get the engineer and the borrower to reconcile their estimates, you have several options which include overriding the engineer's recommendation (usually not a wise idea), rearranging the distribution of costs and expenses within the borrower's budget (e.g., reduce some soft cost expenses if possible and increase hard costs by a like amount), reducing the amount of the loan, and/or requiring the borrower to contribute more equity.[7]

Performance and Quality

Consulting engineering firms occasionally are able to get away with substandard work. Lack of satisfaction with inspecting engineers has become more pronounced in recent years because of a

---

[7] Occasionally a consulting engineer will have older, outdated plans and specifications. This can occur particularly if the size or scope of the project has changed (e.g., a project's initial plans included a penthouse; subsequently, the penthouse was omitted because of limitations imposed by jurisdictional height and/or bulk restrictions at the project's location).

rise in construction activity. Demand for engineering consulting services has allowed for the hiring of many marginally trained and uncredentialed individuals. Although the owner of the firm may be highly qualified, those under him may not be. Unfortunately, in these circumstances, the lending officer is relying on the consultant for his expertise and may be too time-pressured to pay close attention to his performance. He may not be aware of potential problems early on because the borrower is unlikely to complain as long as the consultant is in general agreement with his budget and his monthly requisitions are honored. Later, when there are large imbalances between the amount of money necessary to complete the project and the amount of money available, both you and the borrower may suffer.

The Consulting Engineer's Contract

To avoid or at least mitigate poor-quality service by a consulting engineering firm, a signed agreement between the consultant and the lender should be entered into. This usually begins with a review of the engineer's written proposal. It should be as specific and comprehensive as possible and delineate the duties of the consultant from the initial project review through loan advances. Make sure that the engineer knows what is expected of him. He should know that if he does not perform satisfactorily for you, his client, you will alert your institution of your dissatisfaction and possibly remove him from the job.

Figure 8–11 shows a typical contract between a lender and its consultant.[8]

---

[8] The contractual agreement should always be between the lender and the consultant, never with the borrower.

FIGURE 8-11

Consulting Contract

Super Consultants
Construction Consultants
512 Eleventh Avenue
Pelham NY 241034204

March 30,

QRS Bank
222 Eighth Avenue
New York, NY 10001

Attention: Administrative Person

Re: Two Luxury Home Project
    Westchester, NY

Dear Mr. Admin:

Super Consultants, Inc. (hereinafter sometimes referred to as "we", "us", "our", or SC) hereby agree to represent QRS Bank (the Lender) as consultants for the above referenced project.

I. We will perform the following services:

    A. See "Scope of Services and Procedures" (Article D):
        Section 1: Review Phase

        1) Review applicable documents listed in Section One (1) of the attached "Scope of Services and Procedures" as supplied by the Lender and/or Lender's customer ("Borrower"). Plans and specifications should be final, complete working drawings stamped and sealed by the Architect and/or Engineer of Record. We will include our opinion and comments with respect to the conformity of the plans and specifications to generally accepted building construction practices subject to the limitations and qualifications described therein.

           Our report will also include our opinion with respect to compliance of the plans and specifications with governing codes. It is expressly understood that our report and the opinions and comments contained therein represent our professional opinion only and that actual compliance with plans and specifications, governing cods, zoning regulations and other applicable laws and regulations are the responsibility of the Architect and/.or Engineer of Record and we assume nor responsibility therefor.

        2) Review and comment upon the construction budget submitted by the Borrower. Our review and comments are based upon what we believe are reasonable costs and time frames under the circumstances but we cannot guarantee that the builder or contractor can or will actually perform the work within budgeted costs or stated time frames.

    B. See "Scope of Services and Procedures" (Article D):
        Sections 2 & 3: Site Inspection Phase

1) Conduct periodic site inspections (once per month, unless directed otherwise by the Lender) in order to evaluate the progress of construction and basic conformance with plans and specifications submitted to us. Further, we will review other relevant documentation supplied during the construction process per Article "D" we will observe workmanship and endeavor to note any deficiencies.

2) Review application for construction draws by the Borrower. Check relevant back-up material supplied by the Borrower as requested in Section 3 of the" Scope of Services and Procedures". Review change orders and back-up material supplied to us and submit any comments or recommendations we may have to the Lender.

3) Submit a single written report of our observations to the Lender found under our "Scope of Services and Procedures" as set forth in Article D, with one set of photographs and copies of relevant material.

It is understood that the inspection service contemplated by this agreement is an on-site inspection report as specified in Section 3 of the "Scope of Services and Procedures". We do not warrant that discrepancies or variations do not or will not exist between the work in place as observed by us during the course of our inspections, and the approved plans and specifications since the frequency of our inspections are limited, as contemplated by this agreement.

II. Our obligations and responsibilities are subject to the following:

A. All reports, both oral and written, prepared and submitted by us pursuant to this agreement are for the sole benefit of the Lender. Our review, inspections, reports, analyses, recommendations, comments and related work, both written and oral, may not be exhibited or made available to or relied upon by any party other than the Lender and are not substitutes for or prepared in lieu of the work required by the Borrower's agents (Architects, Engineers, Construction Manager, et al.).

Under no circumstances do we assume the responsibilities of the Design Architect or Engineers, Contractors, Construction Manager, or any agent of the Borrower, in either their design or supervisory capacity. We do not warrant the completion of the Project.

We do not assume any responsibility to provide supervision of construction methods or processes. We are not responsible for and do not warrant compliance of the Project or any aspect thereof with any rules or regulations of any Federal, State, or local governmental or quasi-governmental agencies or any other organization having jurisdiction over the Project or any aspect thereof.

B. Neither we nor any of our employees or authorized agents will be required to sign any waiver of liability for claims or similar document when entering a construction site. If we or any of our employees or agents are barred from the site, the cost of a return trip will be charged as another inspection.

C. General Conditions:

1. Neither party may assign its rights and obligations under this agreement without the written consent of the other party.

2. This Agreement may be terminated, for any reason, by either party upon not less than 15 days prior written notice to the other party. In the event of such termination, we will be entitled to be compensated for all work performed by us to the date of termination.

3. This contract will be considered in force and binding upon both parties if we begin our work as instructed by the Lender, either verbally or in writing, or if we are paid our first payment, whether or not this document is signed by the Lender.

4. If requested by the lender, we will request, pick-up, and transmit to the Lender, copies of required "Waiver of Lien" forms. We are not responsible for the

content or execution of such forms and Lender is advised to consult its attorney or title insurance company.

5. This contract is governed by the laws of the State of New York applicable to agreements to be preformed entirely therein.

6. It is understood that we are not retained to advise or assist in any way with regard to, and we assume no responsibility for any professional services relating to, the existence, removal or effects of asbestos or other pollutants or hazardous or toxic materials. We have advised Lender that we have no expertise or any liability (errors and omissions) insurance covering any claims arising out of performance or failure to perform any professional services related to asbestos, other pollutants or hazardous or toxic materials. Accordingly, the Lender agrees to bring no claim suits or proceedings against us and to hold us, our principals, employees, and agents harmless, and will defend any claims that may be brought by third parties against us with respect to any matters involving asbestos, pollutants, and toxic or hazardous materials related to the Project.

D. This agreement together with

Article A: Project Participants
Article B: Project Data
Article C: Compensation Schedule
Article D: Scope of Services and Procedures

will constitute the entire agreement between the parties and there are no representations, warrantees, or understandings except as set forth herein. This agreement may not be amended except by an agreement in writing signed by both parties.

Will you kindly indicate your approval of the foregoing by signing and returning one copy of this agreement for our file.

Super Consultants, Inc.   Agreed to and accepted:
                                                     QRS Bank

_____   By: _____
                                                     Title: _____
                                                     Dated: _____

Article C COMPENSATION SCHEDULE

A: BASIC FEE:

For the work as described under this agreement, compensation will be:

Review   – $6,500

Inspection   – $1,100 per inspection

Please note that our review fee assumes that a complete document package will be available when the review effort is initiated. We will not initiate our review until all requested documents are available, unless you otherwise direct. If it is necessary to initiate a review of incomplete documents or if there are substantive revisions to the documents during the course of our review, our fee will be adjusted based on the additional time spent in completing the work.

B: EXTRA SERVICES: beyond the scope of this contract include but are not limited to:

1. Kick-off meeting unless it is a regular inspection.
2. Preliminary review submitted prior to full review if it cannot be incorporated into final review.

3. Re-reviews; Supplemental Review; Reviews of Tenant Work; Review of Furniture, Fixtures and/or Equipment; Inspections of Tenant Work and FF&E unless specifically called for in this contract; Special Investigations.
4. Off-site analysis of change orders which cannot be reviewed during the normal course of our inspections.
5. Extra meetings and special inspections.
6. Off-site inspections of stored material.
7. Inspection of Furniture, Fixtures and Specialty equipment unless specifically called for in this contract.
8. Additional copies of reports and photographs.
9. Other services as may be requested by the Lender and not covered in this basic contact.

Compensation for extra services is calculated as follows plus expenses:

Principal	:	$175 per hour
Professional Staff	:	$145 per hour
Administrative	:	$ 65 per hour
Additional copies of reports	:	$ 40/each

Note: These rates are valid through March 30, 200

C: GENERAL CONDITIONS:

1. Construction shall commence within 6 months of the projected commencement date.
2. Fees are to be remitted within 30 days of invoicing. After 30 days interest will accrue at the rate of 1% per month compounded.
3. If the scope of the project or if our services are changed materially, the amount of compensations shall be equitably adjusted.
4. If the project requires inspections beyond the "Estimated Construction Period" in Article B, we will be entitled to a 10% increase in our inspection fee.

Problems between the Consultant and the Borrower

At an early stage, it is important for you to remain in communication with the engineering consultant and the borrower to make sure both are doing their jobs. Most of the time, when issues arise before or at the onset of a loan, it is the borrower's fault. There are many possible reasons: The borrower may believe that he now has your institution committed to fund the loan and moves his attention elsewhere. He may be resentful of the engineer, who he believes is second-guessing his work. He may feel that the engineer is not appreciative of his considerable risk exposure and that he has spent a great amount of time and money on the project before the engineer got involved. He also knows that he will be paying the engineer's bills through the lending institution regardless of the quality of the engineer's services. The engineering firm, without taking on any risk or expense, in his opinion, is contributing nothing to the project except an additional cost.

If you suspect that the borrower is not cooperating or is indifferent to the engineer for any of these reasons, you should make it clear to the borrower that your institution requires that the engineer be satisfied before you can make any loan advances. Tardy responses to the engineer's requests can result in delays in funding that can increase the borrower's costs. More seriously, early friction between the borrower and the engineer can be indicative of a borrower's lax or sloppy preparation or, worse (although highly unlikely), an apparent lack of the competency necessary to perform and complete the proposed construction project. If you suspect this to be the case, you have major decisions to make.

If the loan has not yet closed, you may, of course, not enter into it. More often, you may, with approval from senior management, require additional conditions, such as the hiring of a construction manager or a general contractor whose credentials satisfy the lender, thus reducing development risk. In either case, since a legal commitment was entered into between your lending institution and the borrower, the risk of litigation is high.

After the loan closes, you might need to consider what the consequences will be if the borrower and engineer have not formed a satisfactory working relationship. If you have the flexibility and authority, you can override the engineering firm and fund the project without your engineer's full concurrence. This is a very risky course of action and should be considered carefully.[9] You may be making a bad situation worse by funding a job that is already in trouble. You also may be open to legal liability later if you decide to stop funding because your loan may have been advanced partially outside the agreed-on loan documents. This provides a precedent that the borrower can use in his defense.

On the positive side, depending on the specifics of a situation, when your inspecting engineer cannot cooperate or communicate

---

[9] It is even more risky to you if you take action unilaterally without having the required authority. Weigh the potential personal dangers and benefits carefully.

with your borrower, by working directly with the borrower to keep the job moving, you or the borrower can correct the underlying problem, neutralizing a potentially serious situation.[10,11]

The Borrower's Architect[12] and Your Consulting Engineer

As was discussed in Chapter 4, the borrower's development team is the most important factor in ensuring a successful project outcome. The architect has tremendous power in the construction process, especially at its commencement. Initially, he is perhaps the most critical team member.

Generally, 80 percent or more of the architect's work is done before above-ground construction begins. However, the consulting engineer usually will request more detail than the architect is able to provide since the plans and specifications still are being refined. An experienced architect working with an experienced consultant will be able to work on a premise of reasonableness. There should not be a problem getting started and funding construction costs without finalized plans (although they must be at least at a level at

---

[10] If the engineer in your opinion is being uncooperative with the borrower, which most often occurs in situations in which the size and scope of the project are relatively small and the borrower has extensive experience, you should make it known to the engineer that he still should be critical and voice concerns but be more tactful. You may want to ask the engineer to relay concerns and criticisms to you first. You then can make judgments about their relevancy and importance; they should be detailed and clear enough for you to understand. From your perspective, you may have broader concerns and needs than the engineer regarding the borrower and his relationship to you and your institution.

[11] In very rare situations, it may be in the best interests of all (particularly and foremost your intuition) to replace the engineering consultant with a new one from a different firm. The problems with this approach include the need for the new consultant to become familiar with the project and perform his own complete and independent evaluation as soon as possible. After this is done, be prepared for the opinions of the new consultant and the deposed consultant to be very much the same. The result is that if you substitute one consultant for another, time and money may be spent verify a problem instead of solving it.

[12] Depending on the type of project and its location, an architect may be substituted for an engineering firm that will perform all the architectural work, including the production of plans, specifications, project monitoring, and the like. A development incorporating manufactured housing is a good example. Although an architect may be used, frequently engineering firms will perform all the work, including site development, which accounts for a much larger proportion of the on-site work since much of the home construction is performed off-site in controlled factory conditions.

which they can be reviewed by the local applicable authorities and fully approved for construction).

However, an inexperienced or unprepared architect may have trouble meeting the demands of your engineer. Also, an inexperienced or inflexible inspecting engineer will expect too much from an architect.

If there is friction between the two, you initially should favor your consultant because, after all, you hired him. He is the one who is officially on your side. Convey to the borrower that he should motivate his architect to do his best to provide the engineer with as much of the requested material as possible.

In practically all cases, what the engineer is asking for is not extraordinary. It is, though, a one-sided relationship because the engineer asks and reviews but the architect does the initial hard work to provide. The cause of the architect's resistance to requests is often the time involved in honoring them and their labor-intensive nature. However, this can be a sign that the architect is not fully cognizant of local requirements, is spread too thin on several projects, or is looking for his next job. As a result, the developer—and you—can suffer.

Project Scheduling and Coordination

One of the words used most frequently by a construction manager is *coordination*. Coordination is the organization of all project tasks by trade and materials delivered and/or installed in a specific sequence and at a specific time. Using some of the dedicated and inexpensive computer programs on the market that help coordinate and track activities, many development teams create a table and a chart that map the construction process from beginning to end.

The Bar Chart: Milestones

The chart typically employed is a bar chart that lists the tasks in the left-hand column (y axis) and dates, usually in months, along the top row (x axis). Lines (bars) are drawn to the right of each task, starting from the date when the task will begin and running up to the date when the task will be completed.

As the job progresses, on a regular periodic basis (weekly or monthly), there will be several adjustments that reflect the interdependency of each task with the others. For instance, floors cannot be laid until floor joists are in place; plumbing, HVAC, electrical work, security work, communications work, and so on, cannot be roughed in until framing is constructed; and interior painting cannot begin until the sheetrock has been properly joined and prepared. This interdependency means that there must be a realistic and carefully thought out sequence of planned events because a delay in one task can set off a chain reaction that affects many others. Whenever possible, there should be some overlap between trades so that as soon as one trade finishes a portion of the work, another trade can start work immediately. By following the trade sequence, the chart is very useful in defining the project's critical path. Some developers regularly update the chart with new lines indicating revised estimates for each task's completion.[13]

You should ask the borrower or your consulting engineer for a copy of the chart. Then, during the construction process, you can refer to it from time to time to see to which stage work has progressed in relation to the original chart. Be aware that the original chart will never match the reality of the project and in some cases may show considerable variance.[14]

A portion of a bar chart is shown in Figure 8–12.

---

[13] The lines may be shown with the original estimates, allowing the actual progress of the job to be measured graphically against the initial forecasts.

[14] Variances are a normal part of the construction process. They can, however, point to problems, particularly concerning completion delays, and delays inevitably result in higher construction and carrying costs. Sometimes delays are unavoidable. There may be problems obtaining materials because of shortages or transportation delays, because specified products and materials are not as readily available as expected, or as a result of inclement weather that precludes outdoor work. At other times, of course, delays are not inevitable. One hopes that they are not major and are the result of discrete, nonrepeatable, and correctible incidents.

FIGURE 8–12

Sample Bar Chart

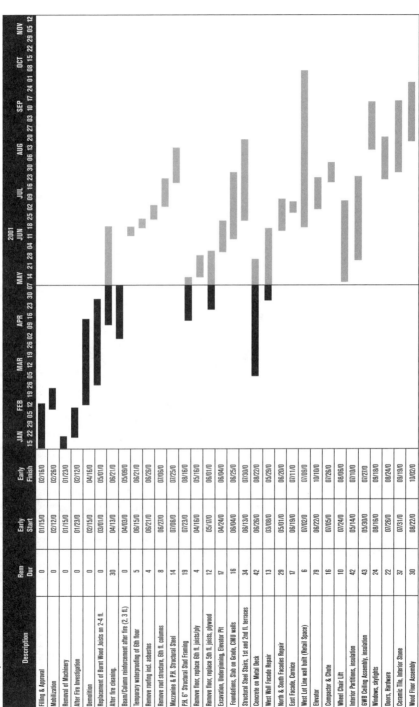

Description	Rem Dur	Early Start	Early Finish
Filling & Approval	0	01/15/0	02/16/0
Mobilization	0	02/12/0	02/26/0
Removal of Machinery	0	01/15/0	01/23/0
After Fire Investigation	0	01/23/0	02/12/0
Demolition	0	02/15/0	04/16/0
Replacement of Burnt Wood Joists on 2-4 fl.	0	03/01/0	05/01/0
After fire cleaning.	30	04/13/0	06/21/0
Beam/Column reinforcement after fire (2, 3 fl.)	0	04/03/0	05/09/0
Temporary waterproofing of 6th floor	5	06/15/0	06/21/0
Remove roofing incl. asbestos	4	06/21/0	06/26/0
Remove roof structure, 6th fl. columns	8	06/27/0	07/06/0
Mezzanine & P.H. Structural Steel	14	07/06/0	07/25/0
P.H. 6" Structural Stud Framing	19	07/23/0	08/16/0
Remove floor, replace 6th fl. joists/ply	4	04/16/0	05/16/0
Remove floor, replace 5th fl. joists, plywood	12	05/17/0	06/01/0
Excavation, Underpinning, Elevator Pit	17	04/24/0	06/04/0
Foundations, Slab on Grade, CMU walls	16	06/04/0	06/25/0
Structural Steel Stairs, 1st and 2nd fl. terraces	34	06/13/0	07/30/0
Concrete on Metal Deck	42	06/26/0	08/22/0
West Wall Facade Repair	13	03/08/0	05/29/0
North & South Facades Repair	29	05/01/0	06/20/0
East Facade, Cornice	17	06/19/0	07/11/0
West Lot Line wall built (Retail Space)	6	07/02/0	07/09/0
Elevator	79	06/22/0	10/10/0
Compactor & Chute	16	07/05/0	07/26/0
Wheel Chair Lift	10	07/24/0	08/06/0
Interior Partitions, insulation	42	05/14/0	07/10/0
GWB Ceiling Assembly, insulation	43	05/30/0	07/27/0
Windows, skylights	24	08/16/0	09/18/0
Doors, Hardware	22	07/26/0	08/24/0
Ceramic Tile, Interior Stone	37	07/31/0	09/19/0
Wood Floor Assembly	30	08/22/0	10/02/0

263

Environmental Report

Concurrent with the consulting engineer's review of the property, cost estimates, permits, contracts, plans specifications, and the like, a Phase I environmental report must be ordered from a third-party environmental inspection firm.[15] As will be discussed in Chapter 18, it is important that an environmental survey (Phase I report) be completed before the issuance of a loan commitment. However, if this is not possible, the loan commitment should indicate clearly that the loan is subject to a satisfactory environmental study of the property for existing, suspected, and potential hazards. The material in Figure 8–13 was taken from a construction loan commitment issued by a commercial bank.

FIGURE 8–13

The obligation of the Bank to make the Loan is conditioned upon the receipt by the Bank of the following site assessments conducted by an independent qualified consultant(s):

(a) an environmental audit which shall include a visual survey, assessing the presence of hazardous or toxic wastes or substances, asbestos, PCBs or storage tanks or other hazardous material at the Premises, the results of checking with governmental agencies, and the identities of previous owners and users of the Premises; and

(b) such further site assessments as Bank may reasonably require due to the results obtained in (a) above. The consultants, their qualifications, the scope and methodology of their investigations, their reports and recommendations and the form, scope and substance of their certifications to Bank shall be acceptable to Bank and its counsel in all respects. Bank reserves the right to condition its closing of the Loan on (i) Borrower's compliance with the recommendations of the consultant(s) and requirements of law and (ii) evidence reasonably satisfactory to Bank of Borrower's financial ability to so comply. In addition, the Loan Documents shall provide that the Bank shall have the right, at any time, to require additional site assessments of the Premises, at the Borrower's sole cost and expense, during the term of the Loan.

---

[15] If a Phase I report (and subsequent testing if required) was completed by a consultant hired by the developer, it must be reviewed by an environmental consultant hired by the lender.

There are a few reasons to perform the environmental survey as early as you can:

- The obvious reason is to assess as soon as possible whether there are any major problems you and/or the developer were unaware of.
- A second reason is to determine the potential costs of removal or remediation if the property requires it. In most cases, if there is a problem, estimating the cost is a simple procedure. Since common environmental problems are discovered on properties almost every day, there are many licensed and experienced competing companies in the field. A line item on the budget for the removal of some asbestos or an underground oil tank may be all that is required. In other cases, however, the discovery of hazards that require a major cleanup may flip a project into a status of unfeasibility.
- A third reason is to factor in the time it will take to address environmental contamination. If there is a significant environmental problem, most lending institutions will not want to get involved in the project until the problem has been addressed fully. (This is done to avoid the potential liability of the lender to bear the cost of cleanup, however remote that possibility is.) Delays after closing can be costly or even catastrophic if they result in a takeout lender or a tenant walking away when its agreement expires. It may be better to delay the closing until the timing issues become clearer. Then, when a construction loan closing occurs, there will be more than a reasonable assurance that the requirements of a takeout lender or future tenant will be met before the clock runs out on its commitment.
- A fourth reason is to allow your environmental consultant, your consulting engineer and you time to review the planned method of remediation and/or removal and factor it into the cost, scheduling, and timing of the project.

Author's Note

Although on the surface preparing for the funding process seems complex, confusing, dependent on several third parties, and fraught with potential obstacles and problems, it is a routine process that occurs with every development loan. The rule is to put some trust in others. It is impossible for any person to know everything about the process, and even if there were such a person, it would be impossible for him to do all the things that have to be done not only within a short period but often simultaneously. That is why the lender works in concert with many highly trained, specialized, and qualified people. An equally important rule is to remain as calm as possible.

Stay focused, take advice, and use your intelligence and judgment.

CHAPTER 9

Loan Mechanics after Closing

After a loan closes, the loan mechanics are primarily the responsibility of the loan administrator, who acts in accordance with a strict set of rules for loan administration. Depending on their nature, the policies of the lending institution, and the level of authority required, exceptions to those rules are approved by the loan officer, a senior loan administrator, or senior management.

Typically, development loans are funded partially at closing to cover a portion of property acquisition costs if there is a purchase involved and agreed-on closing and previously paid hard and soft costs. Then, usually monthly, funds are advanced on the basis of a draw request that follows a defined set of rules to cover hard costs and verifiable soft costs. The loan's interest expense, which usually is part of the loan budget, also is included in each draw request.

REQUIREMENTS BEFORE THE FIRST ADVANCE

Before the first construction loan advance, which ordinarily occurs at or shortly after the loan closing, the following list of materials and information typically is required:[1]

- The contract between the developer and the general contractor and/or the construction manager.

---

[1] Many items on the list probably have been submitted before the closing, such as a budget, plans, and specifications.

- The project budget.
- A complete set of plans and specifications.
- Worker's compensation certificates from the developer, the general contractor, and major subcontractors.
- Current liability insurance certificates from the developer and subcontractors.
- Licenses for each trade as required by the municipality.
- A copy of the developer's builder's risk insurance certificate.
- Copies of surety bonds if required for the total job from the general contractor and/or the major subcontractors.
- Invoices before the first requisition that are older than 45 days should be accompanied by copies of canceled checks.[2]

REQUIREMENTS FOR ALL CONSTRUCTION ADVANCES

The requirements for the initial advance and each subsequent advance are detailed specifically in the building loan agreement (BLA). The normal loan advance process, with minor variations, begins with the borrower submitting a hard and soft cost requisition to the lending officer or the assigned loan servicer. The requisition should be received at least one week before the date of the expected loan disbursement. Concurrently, the hard cost part of the requisition is sent to the lender's inspecting engineer. To save time, it usually is sent directly by the borrower, but a few lenders prefer that the borrower send the requisition only to the loan servicer, who then, certain that there is a fairly complete requisition package, will send the hard cost portion to the inspecting engineer (see Chapter 8 for a discussion of the inspecting engineer, also commonly called the engineering consultant or construction consultant).

The requisition consists of documents agreed on and referred to in the legal loan documentation. They should include forms similar or equivalent to an application and certification for payment (AIA 702) and a continuation sheet (AIA 703), copies of

---

[2] The list of items can seem daunting at first, but most developers and contractors know what to expect and are comfortable with the process.

invoices and/or proof of payments, lien waivers, and other forms the lending institution requires.[3] The requisition package also may contain additional material, such as copies of invoices or proof of payment for items such as insurance, taxes, and other costs that the engineering consultant is not responsible for reviewing.

The standard letter from a lender's engineering consultant shown in Figure 9–1 spells out what material and information on hard costs is required.

FIGURE 9–1

Letter from an Engineering Consultant

Dear Ms. Developer:

In order to facilitate a reasonable turn around on pay applications, Construction Consultants, Inc. requests that the following documents be assembled for each requisition package in the following order:

1. A complete application form (G702 or similar form). The form MUST be certified by the architect and endorsed by a Notary Public.
2. Complete continuation sheets (G703 or similar form) providing a complete schedule of values identifying the scopes of work and the subcontractor for each scope. This will allow us to tie the work back to the contract price of the job.
3. A separate change order summary for all changes in plans or scopes. This is used to track changes in the job's progress.
4. A "billing detail listing" identifying all subcontractors' invoices in the same progression as the schedule of values on the continuation sheet.
5. All the invoices relevant to each pay application request should be behind the billing detail. Invoices must be properly sequenced in order to be able to track them on the continuation sheet.
6. Supporting the invoices should be the owners and contractor's affidavits for the construction progress. These should list the location of the property, its legal address and avow that on a specific day of a certain month, the owner and contractor swear the work was done satisfactorily. It should also state that the owner has paid the general contractor and the general contractor is providing a partial lien waiver with his package. It should further avow that there are no unknown or additional liens or encumbrances on the property with regard to this draw requisition, and the affidavit should be signed by both parties and should be notarized.

(Continued)

---

[3] AIA forms are produced by the American Institute of Architects. Forms similar to AIA forms are shown in this chapter.

7. Underneath the owner's affidavit, there shall be all partial and final lien waivers provided by the subcontractors and vendors, indicating that they have been paid the money dispersed from the previous requisition or from the owner's own sources. Each of the lien waivers must be signed by a CFO, CEO or President, and they must be notarized.

With each requisition package, assembled in the proper sequencing, Construction Consultants, Inc. will be able to facilitate the draw request in a timely manner without delays.

Please note that I have listed material and additional documents we need prior to the first advance along with several of our forms needed to be filled out with each requisition.

Please feel free to contact me at your earliest convenience if you have any questions or need more information.

Sincerely,
J.D. Consultant
Construction Consultants, Inc.

Note that several levels of paperwork are necessary for each loan advance. At one level, each subcontractor will submit his requisition to the general contractor or construction manager for review. After the review, it becomes part of the total requisition package that is given to the lender and/or its consulting engineer for review as the basis for funding. In the discussion below, the focus will be on the higher-level requisition: the requisition the lender receives from the borrower that includes summations of all project costs. This is done because a full requisition package can exceed 100 pages.

An application and certificate for payment or a similar form is a summary page that includes the original hard cost budget agreed on between the lender and the borrower plus net changes to the budget approved by the lender. It states the contractor's claim of the dollar amount of total work performed (and materials stored, if applicable) as of the requisition date. Subtracted from this is a percentage, initially determined in the closing loan documents and perhaps modified by the lender as the project progresses, called retainage (there is further discussion of retainage later in this chapter). Aggregate previous advances are subtracted from that amount. The result is the amount to be funded by the lender for hard costs. Soft costs, if any, are added to determine the total amount to be advanced under the requisition. The form is signed by the borrower, the contractor, and the architect. Figure 9–2 shows a completed application and certificate for payment form.

APPLICATION and CERTIFICATION for PAYMENT

****
****

Borrower: ABCDE Developers

Premises: 100 White Street

Period From: 6/01/0_   To: 7/01/0_

Contractor: Right Build Inc.   Application No: 15
****
****

The undersigned hereby requests QRS Bank for an advance of $ **226,913** pursuant to its BLA with QRS Bank and, in connection therewith, hereby represents and warrants as follows:

1) The amounts set forth in the schedules attached

     hereto are true and correct.

2) All change orders, actual and proposed, for the project have been submitted to QRS's architect or engineer.

Sworn to this   th   day of   July,   200_

By: _____
     Borrower

       _____
       NOTARY PUBLIC

The undersigned hereby certifies that he is the Architect who prepared the plans and specifications for the above project; that he has inspected the above project as of __7_/200_   ; that all construction completed and materials supplied to that date are in accordance with the $5,092,868 plans and specifications prepared by me and approved by QRS Bank and that the percentage of completion of the above project is approximately 90% percent.

Sworn to this   day of   July   , 200_

By: _____
     Architect

       _____
       NOTARY PUBLIC

The undersigned Contractor certifies that the work covered by this Application for Payment has been completed in accordance with the contract documents, that Schedule A attached hereto is true and correct, that all amounts have been paid by him for work and/or materials for which previous Certificates for Payment were issued and that he has

received all monies due him under his contractual arrangement with the Owner up to and including the period covered by the last preceding Certificate for Payment.

CONTRACTOR: **Right Build Inc.**

BY: _____   DATE:

Original Scheduled Value	$4,983,592
Net Change by Change Orders	$ 751,651
Revised Value	$5,735,243
Total Completed & Stored to Date	$5,321,353
Less Retainage	$ 228,485
Total Completed Less Retainage	
Less: Equity & Previous Payments	$4,913,831
CURRENT PAYMENT DUE TO CONTRACTOR	$ 179,037
Plus interest Costs - This Application	$ 47,876
Plus Soft Costs - This Application	$ 0
TOTAL THIS DRAW	**$ 226,913**

271

The form is relatively simple and straightforward. In Figure 9–2, the original budgeted hard cost work was $4,983,592. As work proceeded, there were changes that increased the budget to $5,735,243. As of the date of the requisition, $5,321,353 of work had been completed. Subtracting retainage of $228,485, the net amount that the requisition states should be advanced from the beginning of the project to the requisition date from the lender and from owner equity is $5,092,868. As a result of prior advances, $4,913,831 already has been funded. Therefore, for the current requisition, if approved, the borrower should receive $179,037 for hard costs. Adding loan interest of $47,876, the total advance requested by the borrower is $226,913.

A continuation sheet or a similar form provides backup detail for the application and certificate for payment form. It lists the work by divisions (see Chapter 3), subtrades, and/or specific contractors. A sample of this form is shown in Figure 9–3. Note that all the figures necessary to fill in the hard costs on the application and certification for payment form are taken from the continuation sheet (the continuation sheets in Figures 9–3 through 9–5 were used to complete the application and certification for payment form in Figure 9–2).[4]

---

[4] The form was used in a substantial (gut) renovation project in which an existing industrial building was being converted into a residential building with street-level retail space. Shortly after the loan closed, a devastating fire spread through the existing structure. Fortunately, not much new construction had been performed; as a result, the increased costs that resulted from the fire damage were not as great as they would have been if the fire had occurred later. Nonetheless, since the breadth and scope of the work changed, many line item costs had to be adjusted while the original loan amount was retained. The borrower funded the net increased costs through equity (increased costs that were paid from insurance proceeds were stripped out of the example for clarity). Demolition costs, for instance, were lowered because the fire "demoed" much of the building. Costs for carpentry and drywall, however, increased significantly as a result of the collapse of ceilings and floors. This illustrates the need to be flexible in allocating and sometimes reallocating funds to various trades. In this example, with the increase in the borrower's equity, the loan remained in balance and the project was completed successfully. In spite of the increased costs, it remained economically viable, and the loan was paid down in full through residential condominium sales.

QRS BANK
CONTINUATION SHEET HARD COST REQUISITION

Borrower's Name: ABCDE Developers
Premises: 100 White Street
LOAN #1

Date: 7/6/200-
Application 15

Description of Work	code #	Estimated Cost	Additions (Deductions) or Change Orders	Actual Construction Cost	Bank Budget (a)	Equity Costs	Previous App. (b)	Work In Place This App. (c)	Stored Materials (d)	Total Completed & Stored To Date (e) (b+c+d)	Previous Retainage	This Application	Total To Date	(a-e) Balance To Complete
Building & Site Costs:														
Demolition & Shoring	2050	212,150	(128,741)	83,409	72,139	11,270	72,139	0		72,139	3,607	0	3,607	0
Excavation & Back Fill	2160	31,125	(4,790)	26,335	26,335	0	26,335	0		26,335	1,317	0	1,317	0
Site Utilities	2600	25,000	(20,933)	4,067	4,067	0	4,067	0		4,067	203	0	203	0
Sidewalk Work	2800	33,600	(25,000)	8,600	8,600	0	8,600	0		8,600	430	0	430	0
Foundations	3100	37,130	23,002	60,132	45,321	14,811	45,321	0		45,321	2,266	0	2,266	(0)
Concrete Superstructure	3300	78,360	48,280	126,640	126,640	0	95,640	0		95,640	4,782	0	4,782	31,000
Masonry	4000	180,850	126,932	307,782	295,473	12,309	280,060	0		280,060	14,003	0	14,003	15,413
Steel Framing & metal deck	5100	132,000	59,748	191,748	167,324	24,424	167,324	0		167,324	8,366	0	8,366	0
Miscellaneous Iron	5400	129,725	(68,068)	61,657	43,432	18,225	29,174	14,258		43,432	1,459	713	2,172	0
Carpentry & Drywall	6100	800,564	708,064	1,508,628	1,192,182	316,446	1,145,895	43,714		1,189,609	57,295	2,186	59,480	2,573
Millwork	6200	236,600		236,600	236,600	0	230,400	0		230,400	11,520	0	11,520	6,200
Roofing & Flashing	7500	14,000	92,075	106,075	50,775	55,300	34,057	0		34,057	1,703	0	1,703	16,718
EIFS	7240	113,400	(83,050)	30,350	30,350	0	18,800	0		18,800	940	0	940	11,550
Hollow Metal Door & Frames	6100	55,300	100,260	155,560	55,300	100,260	0	0		0	0	0	0	55,300
Wood Door & Frames	8200	55,300		55,300	55,300	0	35,033	0		35,033	1,752	0	1,752	20,267
Storefront & Entrance	8400	27,000		27,000	27,000	0	21,000	0		21,000	1,050	0	1,050	6,000
Windows	8600	146,200		146,200	146,200	0	146,200	0		146,200	7,310	0	7,310	0
Hardware	8700	52,330	(31,000)	21,330	21,330	0	16,768	0		16,768	838	0	838	4,562
Carpet	9680	2,100		2,100	2,100	0		0		0	0	0	0	2,100
Ceramic Tile & Stone tile	9300	293,020	(83,751)	209,269	203,869	5,400	150,360	53,432		203,792	7,518	2,672	10,190	77
Wood Flooring	9550	201,154	32,310	233,464	201,154	32,310	187,274	4,311		191,585	9,364	216	9,579	9,569
Painting	9900	45,000		45,000	45,000	0	33,740	0		33,740	1,687	0	1,687	11,260
Specialties	10000	202,500	(100,000)	102,500	102,500	0	87,000	6,147		93,147	4,350	307	4,657	9,353
Equipment	11000	138,150	(68,500)	69,650	38,150	31,500	30,000	0		30,000	1,500	0	1,500	8,150
Lobby Finishes	12000	70,000	(30,000)	40,000	40,000	0	0	0		0	0	0	0	40,000
Vertical Transportation	14000	165,000	51,877	216,877	212,377	4,500	192,827	0		192,827	9,641	0	9,641	19,550
HVAC	15000	300,000	(66,954)	233,046	229,546	3,500	221,000	8,500		229,500	11,050	425	11,475	46
Plumbing	15400	180,000	55,500	235,500	203,000	32,500	187,600	5,000		192,600	9,380	250	9,630	10,400
Sprinklers & fire protection	15300	111,000	85,454	196,454	156,454	40,000	141,454	15,000		156,454	7,073	750	7,823	7,610
Electrical	16000	250,000	(30,420)	219,580	200,000	19,580	179,291	13,099		192,390	8,965	655	9,620	7,610
Sidewalk Bridge	17000	15,000	29,316	44,316	15,000	29,316	1850	0		1,850	93	0	93	13,150
SUB - TOTAL		4,333,558	671,611	5,005,169	4,253,518	751,651	3,789,209	163,461		3,952,670	189,460	8,173	197,634	300,848
General Conditions		346,685	30,000	376,685	376,685	0	330,555	25,000		355,555	16,528	1,250	17,778	21,130
Contingency		303,349	50,040	353,389	353,389	0	261,478	0		261,478	13,074	0	13,074	91,911
TOTAL 1ST & 2ND HARD		4,983,592	751,651	5,735,243	4,983,592	751,651	4,381,242	188,461		4,569,703	219,062	9,423.05	228,485	413,889

current retaing -9,423

Net Funding 179,038

Work In Place This App.: 188,461 / -9,423 / 179,038

This Application: 9,423.05

Total To Date: 228,485 — 4,569,703

Total Gross 4,569,703

Tot. Net OS 4,341,218

273

QRS Bank
CONTINUATION SHEET SOFT COST REQUISITION

Borrower's Name: ABCDE Developers

Location: 100 White Street

LOAN #1

DATE: 7/6/200-

Req. #: 15

ITEM	ESTIMATED COST	REVISIONS ADD (DEDUCT)	ACTUAL COST	BANK BUDGET	PRIOR REQUEST	CURRENT REQUEST	TOTAL TO DATE	BALANCE REMAINING
Real Estate Taxes	60,000		60,000	0			0	0
Interest Reserve	261,639		261,639	161,639	72,905	47,876	120,781	40,858
Appraisal & Environmental Fees	5,200		5,200	5,200	5,200		5,200	0
Commitment Fee	100,000		100,000	100,000	100,000		100,000	0
Lender's Construction Consultant	15,000		15,000	5,000	5,000		5,000	0
Lender's Counsel	25,000		25,000	0			0	0
Recording Documents	155,680		155,680	0			0	0
Architect/Engineer/Expediator/Permit/Surv	220,000		220,000	0			0	0
Title Policies	35,000		35,000	0			0	0
Builder's Risk Insurance	15,000		15,000	15,000	15,000		15,000	0
Surveys & Permits/Other	10,000		10,000	0			0	0
							0	0
							0	0
							0	0
TOTAL	902,519	0	902,519	286,839	198,105	47,876	245,981	40,858

274

QRS Bank
CONTINUATION SHEET ACQUSIITHON LOAN REQUISITION

Borrower's Name: ABCDE Developers

Location: 100 White Street
LOAN #2

DATE: 7/6/200-

Req. #: 15

ITEM	ESTIMATED COST	REVISIONS ADD (DEDUCT)	ACTUAL COST	BANK BUDGET	PRIOR REQUEST	CURRENT REQUEST	TOTAL TO DATE	BALANCE REMAINING
Land Acquisition	7,000,000			4,351,208	4,351,208		4,351,208	0
Interest Reserve - Project Loan	378,361			378,361	378,361		378,361	0
TOTAL	7,378,361	0	0	4,729,569	4,729,569	0	4,729,569	0

Lien Waiver

As part of the requisition package, the borrower also submits partial and final lien waivers from the major contractors and subcontractors. A lien waiver is an attestation by a contractor that up to and including the date of the waiver, he has not filed any mechanic's liens against the property.[5] Partial lien waivers are submitted as the contracted work progresses. A final lien waiver is submitted at the completion of the work. A sample lien waiver is shown in Figure 9–6.

---

[5] Often there is confusion about the lien waiver and title insurance. Even if a borrower (or contractor) signs a lien waiver, he still may have filed a lien. If that is the case, the lien has priority over the loan advance until it is addressed properly (see Chapter 14 for a discussion of liens). Furthermore, a subcontractor who has filed a lien probably will not have any paperwork included in the borrower's requisition package, and therefore the lack of an accompanying lien waiver will not be noticed. A lien waiver does not substitute for continuation of title insurance, which is an integral part of the advance procedure.

FIGURE 9-6

PARTIAL WAIVER OF LIEN

Owner	ABCDE Developers
Project	The Good Building
Address	100 White Street, New York, NY
Block 456	Lot 4
General Contractor	Right Build Inc.
Requisition	15
Date of Requisition	7/01/0_

Listed below is the information regarding the above contract:

Contract Price:	_____$4,983,592_____
Net Extras and Deductions:	_____751,651_____
Adjusted Contract Price:	_____$5,735,243_____
Payments received to Date:	_____$4,913,831___ ____
Work completed through:	_____7/01/0_____

The undersigned subcontractor for One Dollar ($1.00) and other good and valuable consideration received by it, hereby waives and releases all liens or rights of lien now existing for work or labor performed or for materials furnished through 7/01/200_, the date of the requisition identified above, with respect to the above designated project. The undersigned subcontractor further covenants and agrees that it shall not in any way claim or file a mechanics or other lien against the premises of the above designated project, or any part thereof, or against any fund applicable thereto for any of the work or labor performed or materials heretofore furnished by it in connection with the improvement of said premises.

This lien waiver is executed and delivered simultaneously with or after payment of the labor performed or materials furnished to the date of the above requisition.

IN WITNESS WHEREOF, we have hereunto set our hand and seal this_____day of _____ , 200_

STATE OF:
COUNTY OF   : SS.:

On this day, of 200_ before me came_____ to me known to be the individual described in, and who executed, the foregoing instrument, and acknowledged that he executed the same.

Borrower Affidavit

The borrower also must submit additional forms required by the lender. These forms vary by lender but almost always include an affidavit or certificate type of form like the one shown in Figure 9–7.

FIGURE 9 – 7

BORROWER'S AFFIDAVIT

STATE OF NEW YORK   )
) ss.:
COUNTY OF   )

Jeffrey Holande , being duly sworn, deposes and says:

That affiant is the Managing Member_of ABCDE Developers (the "Borrower"), and has made due investigation as to matters hereinafter set forth and does hereby certify the following to induce QRS (comment – this change is a must) Bank (the "Lender") to make and advance the sum of Two hundred twenty six thousand, nine hundred thirteen dollars ($__$226,913_) to the Borrower pursuant to the terms of a Building Loan Agreement, dated ___3/01/0_, 200_ between the Lender and the Borrower, and Request for Advance number ___15__, dated __7/01/0 , 200_, the day on which this Affidavit is sworn to by affiant, being submitted to the Lender herewith:

1. All representations and warranties contained in the Building Loan Agreement are true and accurate in all material respects as of the date hereof.

2. No Event of Default exists under the Building Loan Agreement, the Note, the Mortgage, the Guaranty or under any other security document, and no event or condition has occurred and is continuing or existing or would result from the advance about to be made which, with the lapse of time or the giving of notice, or both, would constitute such an Event of Default.

3. Construction of the Improvements has been carried on with reasonable dispatch and has not been discontinued at any time for a period of Unavoidable Delay for reasons within the control of the Borrower, the Improvements have not been damaged by fire or other casualty, and no part of the Premises has been taken by eminent domain and no proceedings or negotiations therefore are pending or threatened.

4. Construction of the Improvements is progressing in such manner so as to insure completion thereof in substantial accordance with the Plans on or before the Completion Date.

5. All funds received from the Lender previously as advances under the Building Loan Agreement have been expended or are being held in trust for the sole purpose of paying costs of construction ("Costs") previously certified to the Lender in Requests for Advances; and no part of

said funds has been used, and the funds to be received pursuant to the Request for Advance submitted herewith shall not be used, for any other purpose. No item of Costs previously certified to the Lender in a Request for Advance remains unpaid as of the date of this Affidavit.

6. All of the statements and information set forth in the Request for Advance being submitted to the Lender herewith are true and correct in every material respect at the date hereof, and all Costs certified to the Lender in said Request in Advance accurately reflect the precise amounts due, or where such Costs have not yet been billed to the Borrower, the same accurately reflect the Borrower's best estimates of the amounts that will become due and owing during the period covered by said Request for Advance. All the funds to be received pursuant to said Request for Advance shall be solely for the purpose of paying the items of cost specified therein or for reimbursing the Borrower for such items previously paid by the Borrower.

7. Nothing has occurred subsequent to the date of the Building Loan Agreement which has or may result in the creation of any lien, charge or encumbrance upon the Premises or the Improvements or any part thereof, or anything affixed to or used in connection therewith or which has or may substantially and adversely impair the ability of the Borrower to make all payments of principal and interest on the Note, the ability of the Borrower to meet its obligations under the Building Loan Agreement or to the best of its knowledge, the ability of the Guarantor to meet obligations under the Guaranty.

8. None of the labor, materials, overhead or other items of expenses specified in the Request for Advance submitted herewith have previously been made the basis of any Request for Advance by the Borrower or of any payment by the Lender.

9. The status of construction of the Improvements is as follows:

10. The estimated aggregate cost of completing the Improvements including but not limited to labor, materials, architectural and engineering fees, management, financial and other overhead costs and expenses, does not exceed $6,637,762.

All conditions to the advance referred to above and to be made in accordance with the Request for Advance submitted herewith in addition to those to which reference is made in this Affidavit have been met in accordance will the terms of the Building Loan Agreement.

The Capitalized terms used herein have the meaning given thereto in the building Loan Agreement.

_____

Jeffrey Holande

Sworn to before me this day of , 200__

_____
Notary Public

Other affidavits typically are required before the first advance and are obtained at or before the loan closing (by the architect, engineer, and major contractors) but usually not on each subsequent advance.[6]

Additional Material

When necessary, which can be often, change order forms are included in the full requisition package. They are accompanied by documentation supporting the change such as an invoice or contract that details the work to be performed (depending on the change, detail can be general or quite specific and can include a materials list, shop drawings, and so on). An abbreviated sample of a change order is shown in Figure 9–8.

---

[6] However, there are cases in which lenders require affidavits (sometimes called certificates) for large trade contracts as a component of each requisition package.

FIGURE 9-8

Sample Change Order

From
> Right Build Inc.
> Charles Avenue
> New York, NY 10005

To
> ABCDE Developers
> Charles Avenue
> New York, NY 10005

Project Name 135 Bliss Street   Date   Oct 20, 200_

Contract For Exterior waterproofing   Change Order Number   3.00

Subcontractor A to Z waterproofing

The above referenced contract for this project is hereby adjusted as described herein

Description of work being changed

New Contract to reflect new scope of work determined after construction loan closing. Scope of work in addition to approved plans and specifications to comply with the recommendation of Consulting corp. [fa?cade consultants] in order to insure adequate waterproofing of the building exterior. A to Z will apply EP Primo Air Block/Blue Skin to completely seal the Glass sheathing, will apply Kemper chemical sealant to the exposed concrete slabs and will supply and install stainless steel shelf angles throughout. See attached drawings reflective of the scope.

Original Contract Amount	$0.00
Approved Change Orders issued to date	$181,404
Contract Sum To Date	$181,404
Subcontract is hereby (increased) by this change	
Total Contract Sum To Date	$181,404

The time for completion of this subcontract is hereby (increased) (decreased)_0____days by issuance of this change order

Approvals

            Owner   Architect   Contractor

(Continued)

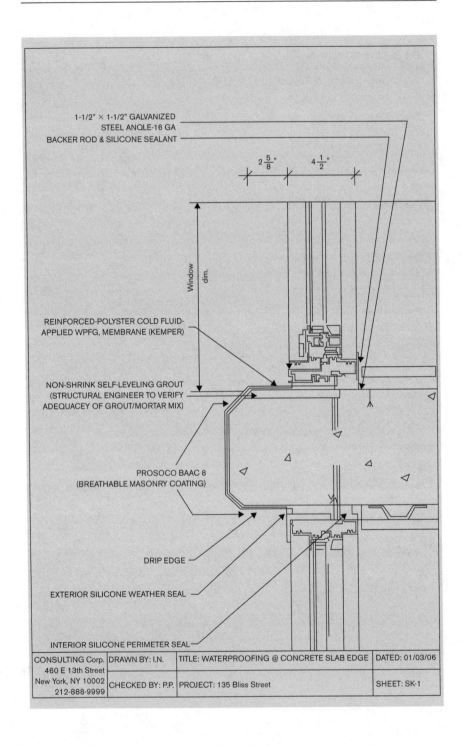

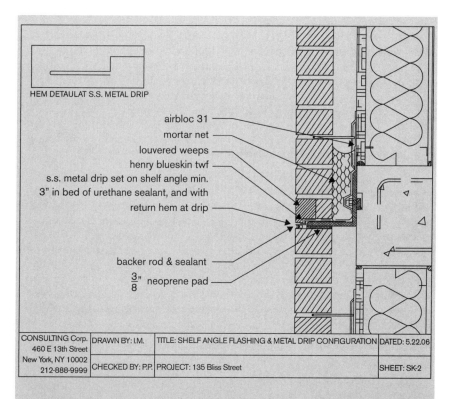

HEM DETAULAT S.S. METAL DRIP

airbloc 31
mortar net
louvered weeps
henry blueskin twf
s.s. metal drip set on shelf angle min.
3" in bed of urethane sealant, and with
return hem at drip

backer rod & sealant

$\frac{3}{8}$" neoprene pad

CONSULTING Corp. 460 E 13th Street New York, NY 10002 212-888-9999	DRAWN BY: I.M.	TITLE: SHELF ANGLE FLASHING & METAL DRIP CONFIGURATION	DATED: 5.22.06
	CHECKED BY: P.P.	PROJECT: 135 Bliss Street	SHEET: SK-2

AGREEMENT

AGREEMENT, made as of the 25th day of May, 200__ between ABCDE Developers, and A to Z waterproofing ("Contractor").

1. SCOPE OF WORK

1.01 Contractor shall provide and furnish all labor, materials, appliances, appurtenances supplies and services of every kind and nature for the installation of all work as more particularly described in Contractor's Scope of Work, **Exhibit "A,"** and in accordance with the Insurance Requirements attached hereto as **Exhibit "B,"** and specifications attached hereto as **Exhibit "C,"** and in accordance with the drawings attached hereto as **Exhibit "D,"** and with the work pursuant to Article 15 (the work and changes are hereinafter collectively referred to as the "Work") in connection with construction of 135 Bliss Street (the "Project").

1.02 Contractor represents that (i) it has fully acquainted itself with the scope of the work, as reflected in the Construction Documents, and (ii) it has visited and inspected the Project Site and examined all existing conditions, including the location of adjacent structures and utilities, and access to the Project Site and is fully familiar with the general condition of the Project.

(Continued)

1.03 Contractor warrants and represents that all materials and equipment incorporated in the Work shall be new and that the Work shall be of good quality, free from improper workmanship and defective materials and in strict conformance with the Contract Documents, and all applicable laws, rules, requirements and regulations of any governmental authorities having jurisdiction over the Work, including the requirements of the Board of Fire Underwriters or any successor thereto. All Work not conforming to these requirements, including substitutions not properly approved and authorized, may be considered defective.

1.04 Contractor hereby guarantees all Work for a period of one (1) year after Final Completion of the Work, or such longer period of time as may be prescribed by law or by the terms of any special warranty required by the Contract Documents or any of the Subcontracts. In the event the Work or any portion thereof is found defective or not in accordance with the Contract Documents, within such time period, Contractor shall correct it or cause it to be corrected, at Contractor's sole cost and expense, promptly after written notice from Owner to do so unless Owner has previously given written acceptance of such defective condition or Owner otherwise releases Contractor of such requirement by the mutual written agreement of the parties.

2. CONTRACT SUM

2.01 As consideration for the full and complete performance of the Work and all of Contractor's obligations hereunder, Owner shall pay to Contractor the Contract lump sum of One Hundred Eighty One Thousand, Four Hundred Four Dollars ($181,404) Payments, subject to additions and deductions as provided in Article 9, Payments to Contractor.

2.02 Based upon Applications for Payment submitted to the Owner by Contractor, the Owner shall make progress payment on account of the Contract Sum to Contractor as provided elsewhere in Article 9.

20.12 Prohibited Interests. No principal, officer, shareholder, family member, employee, agent or consultant of Contractor who, on behalf of Contractor, negotiates, makes, accepts, or approves, or takes part in negotiating, making, accepting, or approving any Subcontract or other agreement entered into by Contractor in connection with the Work, shall become directly or indirectly interested personally in the Subcontract or such other agreement.

20.13 Integrity and Ethical Conduct. Contractor acknowledges and understands that Owner is committed to have the Work performed in accordance with the highest ethical standards applicable to, or governing, the conduct of construction practices. In furtherance thereof, Contractor hereby agrees to comply with and observe all applicable Federal, State and local laws, rules, regulations, requirements, trade standards and ethical guidelines governing said conduct.

3. MISCELLANEOUS

21.01 This Agreement shall be construed without regard to any presumption or other rule requiring construction against the party causing this Agreement to be drafted.

21.02 This Agreement shall not be recorded, and any recording thereof shall constitute a default hereunder.

1.03 Owner shall not be bound by any of the provisions of this Agreement unless and until counterparts thereof, signed by both parties, have been exchanged between the parties or their Attorneys.

IN WITNESS WHEREOF, the parties hereto have executed this Agreement as of the day and year first above written.

By:

President, ABCDE Developers

By:

President A to Z waterproofing

Be aware that change orders do not change the original budgeted loan amount, which is fixed at closing. If overruns on a particular budget line cannot be funded from a contingency or miscellaneous line or a line elsewhere in the lender's budget where there are cost savings (this must be substantiated with evidence to the lender's consulting engineer), the money to finance the increased amount needed to complete the project must come from developer sources.[7]

On the continuation sheet, increases and decreases in the construction budget are a result of a combination of change orders and reallocations. A summary of the changes which in the aggregate were indicated in Figure 9–2 is shown in Figure 9–9 (the summary

---

[7] With the usual exception of the contingency line, when a borrower wants to move funds from one line that has experienced cost savings to a line that will experience an overrun, the lender almost always has the final say, as stated in the loan documents. This is the case because the lender needs to know that there is enough money to complete the project (the loan remains "in balance"). Also, perhaps even more important, in some locales, a reallocation of line item amounts can have an adverse effect on the lender's priority of its mortgage lien. For instance, a seemingly innocuous movement of funds from a hard to a soft cost budget line can result in the loan taking a junior position to mechanic's liens (Chapter 14) and ultimately, if there is a foreclosure, an unexpected and significant loss of interest and principal.

should be submitted by the borrower as part of each requisition and tracked independently by the loan administrator). Note that items with vendor names are the result of change orders, whereas others, noted as adjustments, were made by the borrower in conjunction with the lender without a change order.

FIGURE 9-9

Summary of Changes

	Additions (Deductions)	7/6/200__
	Borrower's Name:	ABCDE Developers
	Premises:	100 White St.

Requisition	Description of Work	Additions (Deductions) or Change Orders
1	A&Z Waterproofing	18,704
2	MAN Carpentry	147,655
3	Q&R Metals	240,944
4	General Conditions	(48,640)
5	MAN Carpentry	29,625
6	CRR	6,500
6	SRD	3,500
6	A&Z Waterproofing	11,270
6 Total		**21,270**
7	CRR	3,000
7	MAN Carpentry	27,880
7 Total		**30,880**
8	CRR	8,640
8	MAN Carpentry	10,536
8	Plumbimg	32,500
8 Total		**51,676**
9	MAN Carpentry	4,000
9	Peter Electric	8,500
9	Concrete Adjustment	5,640
9	Contingency Adjustment	(105,078)
9	Electrical Adjustment	(8,500)
9	Carpentry Adjustment	(4,000)
9 Total		**(99,438)**
10	MAN Carpentry	5,940
10	A&Z Waterproofing	181,404
10	Steel Enterprises	24,424
10	CRR	8,321

10	Peter Electric	3,500
10	Demo & Shoring Adjustment	(140,011)
10	Excavation & Backfill Adjustment	(4,790)
10	Foundations	8,191
10	Steel Framing & metal deck	35,324
10	Roofing & Flashing	18,000
10	Contingency	83,286
Total 10		**223,589**
11	CRR	4,500
11	MAN Carpentry	31,925
Total 11		**36,425**
12	Steel Enterprises	15,975
12	MAN Carpentry	10,057
12	Plumbimg	18,600
12	Communications/Security	2,060
12	CRR	8,028
12	Peter Electric	8,000
12	Common Area Panels	1,800
Total 12		**64,520**
13	MAN Carpentry	5,161
13	Common Area Panels	5,400
13	Lobby	(30,000)
13	General Conditions	30,000
Total 13		**10,561**
14	Steel Enterprises	2,250
14	Common Area Panels	5,400
14	Flooring	4,650
14	Plumbimg	3,500
14	Peter Electric	8,080
Total 14		**23,880**
15	Sidewalk Bridge Adjustment	(12,562)
15	Sprinkler & Fire Protect Adjustment	12,562
Total 15		**0**
	TOTAL	**751,651**

In addition to the material described so far, the lending institution may require other forms or spreadsheets. Many lenders ask that they be in a Word or Excel format so that they can be updated, copied, and e-mailed easily between the borrower and the loan administrator.

INSPECTING ENGINEER'S REPORT

A few days before or right after a requisition submission, the borrower will ask that the lender's inspecting engineer come to the project to review the work performed and verify the presence of stored materials. The engineer then creates a report to the lender summarizing what he saw, what his concerns are, and what, if any, recommendations and suggestions he has. At an agreed-on time the inspecting engineer will visit the site and tour it with the borrower or a borrower's representative who is usually a representative of the developer or the construction manager. During the inspection, they may go over the requisition paperwork so that the inspector can have his questions answered firsthand as the site is toured. The inspecting engineer is concerned primarily with the progress of the job. He verifies the improvements completed and the type, amount, and security of stored materials at the time of his visit.

He reviews and often modifies the amounts requisitioned by the borrower and recommends the hard cost amounts to be funded. He estimates whether the project is on track to be completed on schedule on the basis of current conditions and progress to date. The report should include photographs documenting the project's status at the time of the visit. Here are excerpts from a typical inspection report.[8]

The engineering consultant has been retained by the lender, not by the borrower. Therefore, the report is the lending institution's property, not the borrower's. There is no reason for the lender to offer the borrower a copy; doing so can be counterproductive. Since the consultant will never recommend that the borrower receive more money than he requisitioned for but often will cut the amount asked for to what he perceives to be the actual amount of work completed and materials stored, he can be a target for criticism. When budgets are tight, there is a natural tendency for tension to exist between the borrower and the consultant. On occasion this can put the lending officer in the difficult position of defending his consultant and most likely himself as well.

The best thing the lending officer can do if the borrower asks for a report is to tell him that the policy of the lending institution is to not release any reports in any circumstances. The lender can argue that since the borrower is on the job site along with the inspecting engineer, he can address issues with the engineer face to

---

[8] Reports can vary in their order of presentation, length, and style, but all basically provide the same amount of information to determine the hard cost portion of each loan advance.

SITE OBSERVATION REPORT NO. 15

ENGINEER ASSOCIATES, INC.
Fifth Avenue
New York, NY

100 White Street	Site Observation Report No. 15
New York, NY	July 11, 200_
LRA# 0101	Page 1

PROJECT	100 White Street
	New York, NY
REPORT PREPARED FOR	QRS Bank
	New York, NY
Attn:	Mr. Loan Officer
	212–987–6543
DATE OF OBSERVATION	July 7, 200_
OBSERVATION AND REPORT BY	Ira Observer, P.E.
PRESENT DURING OBSERVATION	Rod West, ABCDE Developers
	Debra East, ABCDE Developers
DATE OF PREVIOUS OBSERVATION	June 10, 200_
DATE OF NEXT OBSERVATION	To be scheduled.
OWNER	ABCDE Developers (ABCDE)
	Charles Avenue
	New York, NY Att: Leslie Winston
CONTRACTOR	Right Build, Inc.
	Charles Avenue
	New York, NY
DATE OF REPORT	July 11, 200_

HIGHLIGHTS OF THIS REPORT

1. APPLICATION FOR PAYMENT:
   A copy of the Application for Payment #15 by ABCDE Developers, for the period ending July 1, 200_, was reviewed during my site visit of July 7, 200_. Based on the Bank Budget of $4,983,592, the Application shows a Total Completed to Date (Gross) of $4,569,703, a retainage of $228,485, and a Current Payment Due (Net) of $179,038. We concur with the Current Request of $179,038.

(Continued)

2. CONSTRUCTION STATUS:
    The restoration work is substantially completed, and Apartment 3-West is displayed as the Model Apartment. Gypsum board installation and taping of the joints were completed in the cellar through the 6th floor. Reportedly, the 6th floor cannot be completed until the Landmark Preservation Commission approves the parapet wall and its surroundings at the penthouse. Painting was substantially completed on the 2nd through 5th floors. Installations of the kitchen cabinets, wood flooring, the limestone on the kitchen floors, and the marble in the bathrooms were completed on the 2nd through 5th floors. Window installation was substantially completed on all floors. Restoration of the face brick along White Street will start as soon as the Landmark Preservation Commission approves one of the several brick samples that have been built in the facade.

    Reportedly, the elevators were inspected and the operating permit was issued. Installations of the domestic water, the fire alarm, the HVAC, and the electrical systems were substantially completed. The project was operating on permanent power.

3. PROGRESS SCHEDULE:
    The Contractor was expecting to obtain the Temporary Certificate of Occupancy (T.C.O.) in mid-August, 200_. He is now trying to obtain the T.C.O. for the 2nd through 5th floors by September 30, 200_. Reportedly, the interior work on the 6th floor and the brick restoration at the facade cannot be completed until the Landmark Preservation Commission issues the necessary approvals. As of June 1, 200_, the project was 93 percent completed, an increase of only 4 percent during the last period.

4. LIEN RELEASES:
    A copy of the Partial Waiver of Lien is attached.

5. CHANGE ORDERS:
    As of July 1, 200_, the Contractor has issued fourteen (14) change orders in the aggregate amount of $751,651. It is our understanding that all the costs beyond the Bank Budget of $4,983,592 will be paid through Equity.

SECTION I–PROJECT SCOPE AND DESCRIPTION

The 5,000-square-foot site is located in Manhattan on the west side of 100 White Street. The project consists of the renovation of the existing 6-story building with cellar into an apartment building with the commercial space on the ground floor. The sixth floor will include two mezzanine/penthouses. There are two apartments per floor, for a total of ten apartments. The building is served by two stairs and an elevator. The apartments can be entered directly from the elevator.

The front facade is decorative metal paneling at the first floor and brick above. The rear and sides of the building are existing brick. The superstructure consists of brick piers, round cast iron columns, and timber beams and columns on the upper floors that have to be reinforced. The apartments are heated by hot water baseboard via three gas-fired modular boilers and cooled via split system air handler units. The building has a combined fire standpipe and sprinkler system. The apartments are furnished with fireplaces.

SECTION II–SCOPE OF CONSTRUCTION CONSULTING SERVICES

A. Engineer Associates, Inc. Format: B–3
B. Outline of B–3 Format services (See Agreement for complete details):
1. Inspect project at construction site once per month for progress, construction quality, and general conformance with the plans and specifications.
2. Review progress of work and developer/contractor. Application for Payment based on percentage of completion of trades in accordance with the schedule of values presented on the application.
3. Review construction progress in relation to Developer/Contractor anticipated schedule and completion date.
4. Prepare written report with photographs indicating our findings based on the above work.

SECTION III–PROGRESS AND APPLICATION FOR PAYMENT A.

Progress Statement:

1. The job was active at the time of our site visit. Reportedly, the work on the 6th floor and on the brick restoration at the facade cannot be completed until the Landmark Preservation Commission approvals are in place.
2. The workmanship and materials, by visual inspection, appear to conform to accepted construction practices and are in general accordance with the plans and specification.
3. The manpower and resources committed to the project appeared to be less than is expected at this stage of construction.
4. Construction was approximately 93% complete, an increase of only 4% during the last period.
A. Budget I Cost to Complete
The Actual Construction Cost calculated by us to be $5,735,243 contains the following items:

(Continued)

Actual Construction Cost

Line Item	Amount
Building & Site Costs	$4,333,558
General Conditions	$346,685
Contingency	$303,349
Sub-Total; Scheduled Value / Bank Budget	$4,983,592
Equity, Change Orders	$751,651
Contractor's Contract Sum	$5,735,243

B. Application for Payment:
   The following is a summary of Application for Payment #15, based on the Bank's Budget and our recommendation for Payment.

The Bank has agreed to the transfer of funds between various line items, with the understanding that the cost will remain within the original QRS construction budget of $4,983,592. In this requisition, $12,562 was transferred from the Sidewalk Bridge (Item 1700) to Sprinkler & Fire Protection (Item 15300).

	Application # 15	Recommendation
Scheduled Value - Bank Budget	$4,983,592	$4,983,592
Net Change by Change Orders	$751,651	$751,651
Revised Value	$5,735,243	$5,735,243
Total Completed and Stored (Gross)	$5,321,353	$5,321,353
Less Retainage	$(228,485)	$(228,485)
Total Earned Less Retainage (Net)	$5,092,868	$5,092,868
Less Previous Payments (Net)	$4,913,831	$4,913,831
Current Payment Due (Net)	$179,037	$179,037

SECTION IV–CONSTRUCTION STATUS AND ACTIVITY

A. Construction Progress
   General: The restoration work is substantially completed, and Apartment 3-West is displayed as the Model Apartment. The field office for Right Build is located in the cellar, with a full-time Project Manager assigned to the project.
   Asbestos Abatement, Demolition, and Excavation were completed.

Concrete: Underpinning of the adjacent buildings, pouring of the slab on grade, and placing of concrete on the new composite slabs were completed.

Masonry: Restoration of the existing masonry, erection of the concrete masonry unit walls, and application of stucco were completed. Restoration of the face brick along 100 White Street will start as soon as the Landmark Preservation Commission approves one of the several brick samples that have been built in the facade.

Structural: This building was damaged by fire. All the structural steel framing and the replacement of the burnt wood joists have been completed. The existing timber beams and columns were reinforced by placing flitch plates on both sides of the members.

Drywall: Gypsum board installation and taping of the joints were substantially completed on all the floors. Reportedly, the interior work on the 6th floor cannot be completed until the Landmark Preservation Commission approves the parapet wall and its surroundings at the penthouse.

Painting: Painting was substantially completed on the 2nd through 5th floors.

Wood Flooring: Installation of the subflooring was completed on all floors, and the wood flooring was placed on the 2nd through 5th floors.

Kitchen Cabinets: Installation of the cabinets was substantially completed on the 2nd through 5th floors.

Windows: Window installation was substantially completed on all floors.

Ceramic Tiles: Installations of the limestone on the kitchen floors and marble in the bathrooms were substantially completed on the 2nd through 5th floors.

Roofing: The waterproofing membrane was placed on the main roof and on the 1st and 2nd floor terraces. Precast pavers were placed on the 2nd floor terrace.

Elevator: Reportedly, the elevators were inspected and the operating permit was issued.

Plumbing: Installations of water heaters, waste and vent stacks, and water risers were substantially completed, including the roughing. Plumbing fixtures were installed through the 5th floor. The water and the sewer lines were connected to the municipal lines.

Fire Protection: Installations of the fire stand pipe, pumps, sprinkler lines, and sprinkler heads were completed.

HVAC: Installation of the HVAC system was substantially completed. The boilers, hot water lines, metal ducts, the air handling units in the apartments, fireplaces, A.C. units, and the heating elements were all in place.

Electrical: Installation of the electrical system was substantially completed. Roughing for the intercom and the card reader was completed.

(Continued)

Work was in progress on fire alarm system. The project was operating on permanent power.

B. Stored Material
Kitchen cabinets, wood flooring, appliances, tiles, and the wheelchair lift were stored securely on the job site.

C. Job Staffing
Reportedly, a full-time Project Manager has been assigned to this project.

D. Tests and Certifications
We have received copies of the Permits issued by the Department of Buildings and by the Landmark Preservation Commission. We have asked for copies of the Technical Reports, Temporary Certificate of Occupancy, Architect's Certificate of Substantial Completion, and the Architect's punchlist, as soon as they become available.

E. Photographs
Photographs taken at the time of our site observation, showing the status of the construction, are attached.

SECTION V–PROGRESS SCHEDULE AND COMPLETION DATE

The Contractor was expecting to obtain the Temporary Certificate of Occupancy (T.C.O.) in mid August 200_. He is now trying to obtain the T.C.O. for the 2nd through 5th floors by September 30, 200_. Reportedly, the interior work on the 6th floor cannot be completed until the Landmark Preservation Commission approves the parapet wall and its surroundings at the penthouse. As of July 7, 200_, the project was 93% completed, an increase of only 4% during the last period.

SECTION VI–CONTRACT AND SUBCONTRACT STATUS

A. General Contract
We have received the following material: An executed copy of the General Construction Agreement between the ABCDE Developers and Right Build; a copy of the executed Agreement, dated August 29, 200_, between ABCDE and Architect Inc.; and an executed copy of the Building Loan Agreement, dated March 1, 200_, between QRS Bank and ABCDE Developers.[9]

B. Lien Waivers/Change Orders
Lien Waivers: A copy of the Partial Waiver of Lien is attached.
Change Orders: As of July 1, 200_, the Contractor has issued fifteen (15) change orders in the aggregate amount of $,751,651. It is our understanding that all the costs beyond the Bank Budget of $4,983,592 will be paid through Equity. A copy of Change Order #15 is attached. Copies of

---

[9] Ordinarily, most consultants do not receive and therefore do not review the building loan agreement. It is the responsibility of the loan administrator to make sure that the terms of the BLA are adhered to by the borrower.

the previous change orders were submitted as attachments to our previous reports.

SECTION VII–SPECIAL PROJECT/JOB CONDITIONS

Reportedly, the interior work on the 6th floor and the brick restoration at the facade cannot be completed until the Landmark Preservation Commission issues the necessary approvals.

SECTION VIII–PLAN AND COST REVIEW STATUS

Our Plan and Cost Review, dated May 14, 200_, was forwarded to QRS Bank.

SECTION IX–ATTACHMENTS

A. Contractor's Application for Payment #15 and the Lien Waiver.
B. Copies of Change Order #15 and the Change Orders summary sheet.
C. Photographs.

SECTION X–FINAL STATEMENT

Any and all reports, certificates, and recommendations have been provided with reasonable skill and care and may be relied on by you in connection with the construction loan for this project. They are not to be relied on by any other party or for any other purpose, nor shall they increase or expand either our or your duties or obligations, as stated in our consultant agreement with you or your construction loan with the borrower. Since our visits to the project are made on a very limited basis (once per month), we can only report on what can be observed at the time of our visits.

We trust that this report provides you with the information you require. If you have any questions please do not hesitate to call.

Very truly yours,

ENGINEER ASSOCIATES, INC.

face, and since he receives revised requisitions indicating exactly which lines were funded and by how much (for guidance on his next requisition), he is already aware of exactly what conclusions the engineer has made without the need of a written report.

Finally, it is important to remember that the engineering consultant has no power or authority to make any decisions or to give any approvals that can be binding on the lender. It is the lending officer's and, depending on his level of authority, senior management's job to make any and all loan, credit, and administrative decisions. In fact, the lender can replace the construction consultant with another consultant at any time. The point is that the lender is the one with the authority and therefore retains control and responsibility. The engineering consultant is just that: a consultant.

Reviewing the Requisition

In all lending institutions, there is some division of labor between the credit and the loan administration functions. In large investment firms, the division is generally the greatest. The lending officer is effectively responsible for only loan originations. Once the loan closes, the responsibility shifts to the loan-servicing department. After delivery by the borrower, the requisition often begins and ends its journey at the loan administrator's desk.[10]

There are, of course, advantages and disadvantages with this division of responsibility. The main advantage is a higher degree of objectivity and processing efficiency. The disadvantages are reduced flexibility in working out problems and the possibility of ill will inadvertently being generated between the service department and the borrower. This may compromise the total business relationship and affect repeat business. To mitigate these disadvantages, most lending institutions prefer that the lending officer be involved at some level with the loan until it is paid down fully. An effective step you can take regardless of your institution's functional organization is to review the continuation sheet or sheets in the monthly requisitions to see if the project generally is on track. Also, personally check in now and then with the loan servicer and the borrower to monitor how the requisition and funding processes are progressing.

ADVANCES

Hard Costs

Hard costs are requisitioned and advanced on a budget-line-by-budget-line basis that reflects the owner's or general contractor's

---

[10] In many active lending institutions, because of institutional cost pressures, the administrator is assigned an inordinate number of construction loan accounts. Most, if not all, of the time the administrator will examine only the first few pages of a requisition because there is too much material in a package to look at it more closely. Also, each borrower is submitting a requisition roughly at the same time—the third week of the month—and so several packages have to be looked at in a short period.

legal agreement with each trade contractor. That in turn is reflected in the aggregate budget (including change orders) necessary to finish the job. After adjusting for the amount of work completed (including any credit for materials stored, etc.) and deducting for retainage, the hard cost amount to be advanced is determined. It is not the job of the administrative person to go over each hard cost line item for each requisition because the consulting engineer supposedly already did this. The administrative person's first responsibility is to do a cross-check of the forms to make sure they add up and are in agreement (e.g., the application and certificate for payment form foots to the continuation sheets). Almost always, they will be, but if they are not, the administrator must highlight the discrepancies and investigate them. Most of the time, by comparing the current requisition with the previous one that was approved and funded, the administrator can spot differences easily, particularly if the borrower has made surprise changes in the budget. If there are still questions, he should call the borrower and ask for clarification. This not only saves him time he otherwise might spend puzzling over paperwork, it also alerts the borrower or the borrower's staff responsible for creating the requisition to do things differently the next time to avoid confusion and possible errors.

Soft Costs

Soft costs require more of the administrator's attention because they are costs that usually are not reviewed by the consulting engineer. Interest costs are one obvious line that is calculated and checked by the administrator. Others are fees and expenses that can be documented with paid invoices and copies of checks (not necessarily copies of canceled checks since the time to receive back proof of payment is usually after the requisition has been submitted).

OTHER ENTITIES WITH INTERESTS THAT AFFECT YOUR LOAN

Depending on the financial structure of the project, there may be other entities involved, such as a mezzanine lender, a loan participant, a public or governmental agency, and a takeout lender (for discussions on mezzanine lenders, forms of takeouts, and loan participants, see Chapters 15 and 20). This can require, on the basis of loan documentation, that the administrator distribute duplicate requisitions to one or more outside parties.

The senior lead lender does not need third-party permission to fund unless there is a significant overrun or change order.[11] However, failing to follow the loan documents pertaining to these parties can result in potential liability and loss if the loan or project experiences problems. Even if the loan officer does not expect any problems with other interested parties or the borrower, he can be unpleasantly surprised. Unforeseen negative events such as a falloff in demand in the leasing or sales markets, key personnel changes, cost overruns, and institutional pressures may encourage participants and/or takeout lenders to try to get out of their obligations. This is why it is very important to follow the loan documentation carefully. With other parties, never take anything for granted and always follow the rules.

CONTINUATION OF TITLE

Once the administrator is satisfied with the requisition package, he must make sure that all the funds that have been advanced will continue to remain in a senior position relative to other claims. This is done by the administrator, who calls the title company to make sure that no liens have been posted. If liens have been posted, they must be bonded, discharged, or insured over by the title company. No matter how the liens are taken care of, the administrator must receive a notice of title continuation or an endorsement to the title insurance policy, dated as of the applicable advance date, indicating that since the preceding advance there have been no changes in the status of title.[12]

---

[11] Conditions of notifications and approvals are spelled out in intercreditor agreements, recognition agreements, and other legal documents with various names that ordinarily are agreed on before the loan closing. It is rare for a participant to come into a deal after the loan closes.

[12] Sometimes a construction lender may make advances directly to third-party contractors, materialmen, the construction manager, or others instead of to the developer. This can occur if there are disputes and mistrust between a developer or general contractor and a subcontractor or subcontractors. To keep the job moving along, the lender makes payments directly to the subcontractor, providing the lender some assurance that there will be money available as work continues on the project. Direct advances also can be made after the occurrence of a borrower default. Often, by making direct payments, the lender not only is adding some protection for itself but also, in spite of the borrower's unsatisfactory performance, helping to protect the borrower as well.

THINGS TO CONSIDER

Retainage

Retainage almost always is calculated as a percentage (usually 10 percent) of the hard costs requisitioned by the borrower for work completed. To allow the borrower to pay off contractors who finish their tasks well before project completion (initial tasks such as site clearing, excavation, foundation work, and superstructure), after a certain period passes or a certain overall percentage of completion takes place, it is common practice to reduce the loan's hard cost retainage amount. Two common approaches used to trigger a retainage reduction are reaching a certain completion level for the overall job and releasing retainage on a contractor-by-contractor basis.

With the percentage of completion approach, when project completion reaches an overall percentage determined by the construction consultant (often measured by the release of half or more of the dollars under the lender's construction budget), an overall reduction in retainage is allowed. For instance, if the loan requires 10 percent retainage until 50 percent of the work is completed and then a reduction to 5 percent is allowed on the remaining 50 percent, the overall retainage is reduced to 7.5 percent ($10\% \times 50\% + 5\% \times 50\% = 7.5\%$). Alternatively, the loan requirement can be a 10 percent retainage amount until 50 percent of the work is completed and then a reduction to 5 percent is allowed for the entire project. Under this approach, the borrower has some latitude in negotiating and reducing the retainage under individual trade contracts. As long as he maintains the overall retainage amount—either 7.5 percent or 5 percent in the examples above—he can keep, for instance, 10 percent retainage with some contractors, 5 percent with some, and zero with others.

In the contractor-by-contractor approach, reductions usually mirror specific retainage reductions as stated in each construction contract. For example, if the foundation contractor finishes its work and the work is free of defects, errors, and the like, after a period of time as specified in its contract (usually 45 or 90 days), the retainage is released.

In either approach, the overall retainage amount the lender is holding back will not drop suddenly but will settle down gradually as the project progresses and various trades complete their work.[13] Note that the reduction of retainage does not create available funds that go into the borrower's pocket. Instead, those funds go directly to contractors who have completed their work, as verified by the lender's consulting engineer.

Importantly, in all cases, before there are any retainage reductions, the contractor should be required to execute a lien waiver, and on completion, before the final payment that includes all retainage held, the contractor must execute a final lien waiver. With the waiver, the developer and the lender are protected against any future claims, just or unjust, by the contractor. [14]

A final point to consider in making modifications of construction draws, including a retainage reduction, is the necessity of making sure the consulting engineer is aware of them before he visits the site or interfaces with the borrower.

On-Site Stored Materials

On the continuation sheet there is a column for stored materials. Some lenders allow advances for stored materials; others do not. There are a few reasons for the difference. The most obvious is that materials that have not been used or installed into the structure can "walk" (due to theft) from the job site. Another is that to receive a bigger advance, the developer may overorder materials that will be stored on the site only until the engineering consultant's inspection has been completed. Then much of the material may be reallocated to another site the borrower is developing.

To guard against these added risks, if the lender is funding for stored materials, it should advance funds only under certain conditions. Those conditions include having the materials contained in a

---

[13] Most lenders recognize completion as occurring when the construction consultant verifies to the lender that the contractor has completed 100 percent of all work, except for punchlist items, and has supplied 100 percent of all materials, except for punchlist items, in substantial compliance with the contractor's contract and in substantial conformity with the plans.

[14] Especially among small and/or inexperienced contractors with poor bookkeeping, after several change orders have gone into effect, there are times when a contractor can lose track of exactly what he is owed by the developer (or hiring contractor). Sometimes, if the contractor underbills, is paid 100 percent on the basis of his billings, and then submits a final lien waiver, he ordinarily does not have any practical recourse to the additional funds to which he is "rightfully" entitled. If the developer is honest and/or there is a continuing relationship between them, this is usually not a problem. Alternatively, if the developer makes a mistake and overfunds after completion, the money he overfunded may be nonrecoverable.

secured area, if possible under lock and key or with a security guard present 24 hours a day. Most lenders require that they also be stored at the job site, not in a remote warehouse or at another job site where they can be stolen, can be used elsewhere, and are hard to verify. Other specific conditions include that they be clearly marked to indicate that they are the property of borrower; that the bills of sale and contracts under which such materials are being provided are satisfactory to the lender and the construction consultant; that they are insured against casualty, loss, and theft; that the lending institution is listed as a named insured and loss payee; that the borrower owns or will own the materials after the payment of invoices free and clear of all liens; and that it delivers to the lender UCC–1s.

Off-Site Stored Materials

In addition to the risks of funding for materials on the job site, you may be asked and compelled to fund materials that are not at the job site or perhaps do not exist. Those materials routinely include specially fabricated items and assemblies that are manufactured off-site or suppliers who require deposits and down payments before the ordering of materials for fabrication and/or delivery. The manufacture of windows and that of curtain walls are two common items that require an up-front deposit to the vendor. A window contract may necessitate a 20 percent down payment to engage the vendor and create shop drawings, an additional 50 percent of the contract amount to be paid before fabrication, and the remaining 30 percent to be paid at delivery of the finished windows to the site. Off-site materials usually have more conditions attached to their physical and financial security than on-site materials before a lender will fund against them.

During the creation of the initial loan documentation, many lenders create an allowance for deposits and off-site materials. Other lenders have policies that forbid any advancement of money for deposits and stored materials. Without an allowance, if the borrower must fund for materials not yet used or stored off-site, he must pay for them out of his own pocket. When they are installed on the job, the borrower is reimbursed.

What to Do

On large jobs that are well secured, it may be essential that you fund against stored materials. One reason for this is that the amount of money for materials laid out by the borrower on a routine basis can be very high. If the borrower does not have the sometimes sizable sums necessary to pay for materials and contracts, the job can be delayed. Also, on large projects, the competition usually is willing to fund on these items. Thus, to stay in the marketplace, the lender may not have a choice. Mitigating the risks, large projects are better guarded and materials are usually stored more securely, making it harder (but not impossible) to steal or misplace inventory.

On smaller projects, a decision not to fund against stored materials is the norm. Usually, the amounts of materials and dollar amounts are not so large that they cannot be absorbed by the developer. In many cases, if the borrower is reputable and has a good credit record with his suppliers, payment for the materials can be delayed at least partially until they are put to use and then requisitioned for. He therefore is not overly burdened by purchasing materials before he is able to requisition your institution for them. Also, security in relation to a smaller project budget may be too expensive. Therefore, the project site often lacks the benefits of a watchman and strong, lockable, and secure containment structures. As a result, the risk of theft increases.

Common Sense

Making periodic funds available on any construction loan involves a degree of common sense. The lender should not be pressured by a borrower into funding stored materials. If the lending officer is not comfortable and decides not to fund, the chances are that the developer will be resourceful and find money or work out a deal with the supplier or contractor. In any event, the lender should not fund just to please the developer. However, regardless of the lending institution's policy, there are times when it makes sense to advance against materials stored on the project site. In these instances, there should be a logical reason why materials were delivered to the site when they were and when they will be used. The materials should be relatively nonportable.

OVERFUNDING VERSUS UNDERFUNDING

Lenders have a bias toward underfunding. This is expected in light of the fact that senior management at most lending institutions has a broad aversion to risk. Less money advanced means less money at risk. Unfortunately, the conservatism that leads to underfunding may increase risk. If a lack of adequate funds forces the developer to be slow in making payments or to make only partial payments to contractors, materialmen, municipalities, and the like, the project has a significantly greater chance of being affected by delays, poor workmanship, higher contractor and trade costs, fines and late charges, an increase in loan exposure resulting from a possible increase in the loan amount to cover budget overruns, delays in sign-offs, and ultimately even noncompletion.

Conversely, slightly overfunding on requisitions very often reduces risk since it can make the job run more smoothly, improving the chance that a project will be completed as scheduled. Obviously, a completed project has substantially more value than does a nearly completed one.

Keeping The Loan In Balance: Budget Increases

Keeping a loan in balance simply means that there is always enough money from equity and debt sources to complete the development as planned. Whenever there is a deficiency in the development budget, the loan is out of balance. Overruns that are caused by construction delays, the replacement of original materials or fixtures by more expensive ones, or misjudgment at the time of the original budgeting process usually are not a problem for the borrower, assuming that he has sufficient available equity and liquidity to invest more money in the job. However, sometimes, particularly if the borrower is thinly capitalized, he will disagree with the lender's (or anyone else's) assessment that there are deficiencies even if it is clear that there are. In this case he does not have the luxury of using more of his capital to fund the project or does not want to part with any more of it.

If the administrator, the engineering consultant, or the lending officer determines that the portion of the loan allocated to a budget line is inadequate, before an advance is approved, the lending officer may consider requiring the borrower to invest the amount of the perceived deficiency in the project, change the budget line allocations by moving funds from areas where there appears to be an overbudgeted line to the deficient line (this includes moving amounts from the contingency line if adequate funds are available), or, in atypical instances, deposit an amount into an account (usually interest-bearing) controlled by the lender that is sufficient to eliminate the deficiency. With regard to a deposit, the funds are disbursed to the borrower on the basis of requisitions. If it is determined later that the amount deposited is in excess of what is needed or there are cost savings on other line items (for instance, the job is moving along faster than anticipated and the interest line therefore appears to contain excess funds that can be used for other purposes), the amount remaining can be released back to the borrower.

THE REQUISITION CYCLE: A CONTINUING ONE

Almost always, by the time the borrower has submitted a requisition, he is in great need of the funds because the process for submitting one takes time and is tedious. On fair-sized jobs, it can take at least a week for subcontractors to prepare and submit their requisitions to the general contractor or construction manager and for the general contractor or construction manager to review the submissions and make changes and then assemble and submit a final requisition package to the lender. Since it could take another week for the lender's inspecting engineer to arrange an inspection at the project site and another week for the loan administrator to review all the documentation and go through the procedures to fund, two to three weeks will go by before the lender advances on the loan. In just one more week it is time to begin the process all over again. Note that except for the borrower, each participant in the process has control and/or responsibility for only a limited portion of the requisition cycle. The borrower must be able to orchestrate the procedure from beginning to end. This brings to light two important points.

The borrower knows that there is always a chance that the lender will fund less than he is asking for; there is, practically speaking, no chance that the lender will volunteer to fund more. This creates a bias for the borrower to ask for more funds than he is strictly entitled to in every requisition. Additionally, by the time the inspecting engineer visits the site, possibly one week to two weeks of work has been completed. Since the borrower and the subcontractors know this, they usually project ahead two weeks of work and stored materials in their requisitions. They will be compensated at least partially for the lead time from the origination of the requisition to the receipt of funds. A problem, of course, is that projections may not equal reality, and more likely than not the error will be on the long side (contractors will requisition for a higher percentage of work than actually was performed).

In light of this bias, coupled with the lead time in the process, which naturally requires estimation, the lender should not be overly concerned if the borrower is requesting more than what he or the inspecting engineer considers the right amount. Only if the amounts are unreasonably and chronically excessive is there real cause for concern.

The second point is that the lender should be careful about making a loan to an inexperienced borrower who submits poor paperwork. On many small construction jobs, the borrower is ill prepared to go through repeated requisition cycles because of thin administrative staffing. The result can be a deteriorating relationship between the lender and the borrower that can increase loan risk. On a moderate-size project, it is not unusual for each requisition sent to a lender to exceed 75 pages. If the paperwork is substandard, the lender must do extra due diligence, which can delay an advance. On a larger and/or more complicated project, the amount of paperwork can be truly onerous and often requires a substantial amount of time. Subcontractors' requisitions must be reviewed by a member of the borrower's construction team and then summarized and put in an acceptable package for the lender by an employee solely dedicated to the task.

Author's Note

Most of the time, loan mechanics after closing proceed in a smooth and routine manner. However, if a project is experiencing problems, perhaps because of unanticipated delays, cost overruns, or friction between the borrower's personnel and the lender's, it can become a difficult process. Often the relationship quickly becomes adversarial. This occurs with "sophisticated" people as well as inexperienced people regardless of the size or reputation of their institution, business, or organization. No matter how well or badly things are going, it is always in the lending officer's interest to try to maintain professionalism and objectivity. He should not let the situation become personal. This can hurt the loan and, more important, the lending officer's esteem, reputation, and career.

CHAPTER 10

Project Completion

PROJECT COMPLETION

Completion means different things to different people. If its meaning is not specified or understood, that can lead to protracted and expensive conflicts that may affect the construction lender.

For a contractor, completing its portion of work can be an issue when a contract's documents lack detail or when there are discrepancies or contradictions in the contract's language, the plans, or the specifications. Since most contractors' contracts do not involve an attorney, there are often specificity issues that allow too great a degree of interpretation. The most common disputes involve missed completion dates, quality, workmanship, and material and equipment substitutions. Those disputes often come to a head at the end of the job, when the contractor files its last requisition for final payment and the developer rejects it. The developer wants items replaced or repaired, and the contractor refuses to do so. Most of the time, an agreement is reached that results in the contractor doing some, if not all, of the work in order to get paid, but with a "negotiated" larger final payment made by the developer (by less scrupulous contractors, this is akin to blackmail). In some cases, though, the dispute will linger and the developer will bring in a new contractor to finish or "correct" the subcontractor's work, almost always at a significantly higher cost than would be the case if the original contractor had remained on the job.

The relationship between a developer and a lender requires a more inclusive definition. The physical completion of the property is only part of the story. Basically, the project must be at a level where it can legally fulfill its intended use. That is, it must be in a condition in which it can be occupied safely. Unfortunately, this basic requirement can be interpreted differently and can become complex. For instance, are punchlist items included?[1] If the building is intended for multiuse purposes, do all of its components have to be completed? For instance, does an office space have to be fitted out in a primarily multifamily rental building? Does an office building need a certificate of occupancy for 70 percent of its floor space or 100 percent?

If a takeout lender is involved, the construction lender and the developer may have to deal with additional conditions. As discussed in the material on takeout loans in Chapter 15, buy-sell documentation has to be airtight. A failure to define completion carefully can mean that if the project's ongoing success is in doubt or the economic environment is clouded, the takeout lender may use whatever means it has available to walk away from its commitment. The result is a construction loan that may not be repaid.

Other interests that have a stake in the definition of completion include prospective tenants with unique requirements, developer's employees who may receive a bonus payment on completion, passive investors who may receive a distribution, and a real estate broker who may receive payment at completion. Definitions can vary with the parties involved.

For the construction lender, when there is no loan takeout, the definition of completion, which always is drafted by a lender's attorney in a legal document generally known as the building loan agreement (BLA), is as follows:[2]

> Completion. "Completion of the Project" shall be deemed to have occurred for purposes of this Agreement when all of the following conditions shall have been satisfied:
>
> (a) the Improvements shall have, in the reasonable opinion of the Lender and the Construction Consultant, been completed (exclusive of the seasonal, punchlist, and other items described in clause (d) of this section) substantially in accordance with the Plans, and the Architect shall have so certified to the Lender;

---

[1] A punchlist is a list of relatively minor work that still has to be done.

[2] The defining of completion given here is "typical" standard language taken from a BLA for a residential condominium construction project in New York City.

(b) the Improvements shall contain all Tangible Personal Property required for the use and operation of the Improvements or that may be required by any Governmental Authority or by any Requirement of Law;

(c) all temporary certificates of occupancy and all other Permits required for the use and operation of the Improvements shall have been issued by or obtained from the appropriate Governmental Authorities for all portions of the Improvements;

(d) all costs and expenses incurred in connection with the Project (other than (i) Hard Costs and other costs and expenses that will be incurred in completing Punchlist Items, landscaping, and other minor work with respect to the Improvements, which in the aggregate shall not in the opinion of the Lender and the Construction Consultant exceed $200,000, and (ii) the remaining balance of the Retainage, if any) shall have been paid in full; and

(e) an as-built survey of the Project shall have been provided to and shall be reasonably acceptable to the Lender.

OCCUPANCY OF A PROJECT

Completion almost always is defined as the obtainment of a certificate of occupancy: either a permanent one (CO or C of O) or a temporary one (TCO). The reason for defining completion in this way is that a CO allows the building to be occupied and used, which in turn enables it to generate revenue. Without a CO, the property is a wasting asset, burdened by operating expenses that include at a minimum taxes, maintenance, and utilities costs plus continued construction loan interest and possibly even obsolescence.[3]

Certificate of Occupancy

To obtain a certificate of occupancy, the developer must complete the project in conformity with the plans and specifications that were filed with the municipality (and any other applicable agencies) and approved before the start of construction.[4] This provides

---

[3] A specific-use property is most at risk for rapid functional obsolescence if the intended tenant fails to occupy it and demand for the specific use falls off sharply. A dramatic example is provided by the "telco hotels" that were built for telecommunication apparatus that, as a result of overcapacity in the industry for those companies' services, were never occupied fully.

[4] In some jurisdictions, most notably to accommodate "design build" delivery systems, which are discussed in Chapter 8, fully approved plans are not necessary before construction can commence.

assurance that the finished structure at least meets the minimum construction requirements that are listed in the municipal building codes.[5]

As straightforward as this seems, for an inexperienced developer or an experienced one without local experience, there almost always are delays in receiving a CO because of failure to make the proper filings on time, failure to have the necessary ongoing inspections performed, and failure to get the required sign-offs from the applicable municipal departments and agencies.

One area that can cause delays and needless repetition of work is fire protection. Requirements are similar throughout the country but are not uniform and can be technical as well as labor-intensive. For example, all spaces between vertical penetrations and floor and ceilings such as open chases (vertical spaces that allow pipes, wires, and ductwork to penetrate from floor to ceiling) have to be firestopped. That is, the joints, cracks, or openings between the penetration and the floor or ceiling must be sealed with an approved compound. In ductwork, there have to be doors capable of closing automatically when there is a fire. On steel columns and beams, an insulating coating must be applied to prevent failure in case of a fire. If finished floors are laid, columns and beams are closed in, or walls are sheetrocked, floor and ceiling penetrations, ductwork, and insulation cannot be inspected. This means that the floors and ceiling must be "opened" up for inspection, a potentially costly process that can cause inspection and construction delays.

To gain more control of the inspection process and therefore increase efficiency, the developer may hire an inspection company that is licensed and authorized to make the necessary ongoing field inspections. This can save a considerable amount of time because the developer is paying for the inspection company, which responds by being available to make inspections and often to give guidance and advice. In some jurisdictions, in regard to certain work or at particular stages in the construction process, an inspection company cannot perform field inspections that will be recognized by the local authority. Instead, a municipal employee must

---

[5] In the southeastern United States a roof system does not have to be able to withstand a load of evenly dispersed or shifting snow but may have to be able to withstand great winds from hurricane forces.

perform the inspections before the developer can continue. Failure to schedule ahead of time with the proper municipal inspector can result in costly delays. As was mentioned previously, failure to plan ahead can result in deconstruction of work in place because a required inspection was not noticed or disregarded.

Final Inspections

When the physical work is completed, a final inspection must be made by the municipal inspector.[6] Even on modest-size projects, it is not unusual for a project to fail its first "final" inspection because of the complexity of real estate development. The inspector will be looking for small things such as the misplacement or absence of an exit sign, a door that does not swing in the proper direction, and a wall that does not show up on filed plans, among other possibilities. Sometimes, if there are small exceptions, errors, or omissions, a letter from the project architect, engineer, or contractor stating that corrections have been made will satisfy the inspector. At other times, the inspector may wish to come back for a reinspection. In some areas, because of the limited number of inspectors and their large workload, it can take several weeks before one can show up again at the project.

As was mentioned above, if the developer does not schedule an inspection in advance, he can experience an expensive delay. However, scheduling too far in advance also imposes risks. If the work is anticipated to be completed but is not completed by the time the inspector comes, a new inspection must be scheduled. This can add a few weeks to the project. Obviously, experience with construction and the jurisdiction where the project is located is very important. Not only does it help one to know the local codes and requirements, but prior knowledge of what is required and

---

[6] Because of strained budgets and limited numbers of inspectors, many areas allow "self-certifications" by plumbers and electricians with a recognized level of license obtained on the basis of benchmarks of experience, education, and testing. This helps the contractor as well as the developer because the trade can do its own report, file it with the proper authority, retain a copy at the project site, and not have to worry about inspection scheduling that can upset the contractor's and developer's timing and coordination. If a particular subcontractor does not have a person with the required level of license, to take advantage of self-certifications, it must hire one who does have that level of license.

when can aid in the coordination process of trades so that areas for inspection are available at optimal times. Scheduling can be done with greater confidence if one knows, for instance, the average or typical lead time required for an inspector to come to the site after an inspection has been requested. Successful builders have done their research and have hands-on experience.

RECORDS: PAPERWORK

In addition to knowing when and what needs to be inspected, it is vital that the developer keep a proper paper trail. Paperwork can be daunting because of local politics, customs, and municipal bureaucracies. For instance, a municipal building department usually has several subdivisions, including one for plumbing, one for electrical, and one for structural work. Each will have its own inspectors who have specific knowledge in their fields, its own specific forms, and its own unique filing system. Since one trade or department (including nonbuilding entities such as the fire department) is often dependent on another, an inspector may ask for documentation from multiple sources. It is always incumbent on the developer, not the municipality, to collate and organize paperwork. In a complicated project, there will be many files on the site and the developer probably will have to hire an administrator to take care of the paperwork and filing requirements. As the project progresses, the administrator becomes an increasingly critical part of the team.

The required paperwork must be in order and always be on hand for the inspector to see. This can be a challenge, especially when the inspector is arrogant, and many of them are. By the time the project manager finds what is being asked for, the inspector may be out the door and unavailable to come back for several days or even weeks.

Before he tours the project, the inspector will look at documents such as earlier sign-offs and inspection reports to make sure work was done properly. He also may look at the approved plans and specifications to make sure the actual construction work agrees with them. Often, seemingly simple and innocuous omissions can take on tremendous significance, especially in terms of obtaining the final sign-off for completion. Examples include the height of a parapet exceeding or being below code by less than an inch and the addition or removal of a water tank without the proper permitting and notifications. Mislabeled or obsolete items are also common nuisances. For example, a water heater does not have to be inspected. If it is improperly designated as a boiler, however, it will need a separate boiler inspection. Similarly, if a building was on the site previously, an old boiler that was removed from the site many years earlier still may be listed as present by the municipality. The inspector can ask for proof of a current boiler inspection even though there is no boiler to inspect.

Because of the nuances and characteristics of each locale, the construction team, including the architect, engineer, and contractors and particularly the project manager, must be cognizant of inspection requirements and required paperwork on a daily basis. If they are not or if there is a weak link on the team, it can cost the developer significant time, money, and aggravation. In this area in particular, experience counts.

Unfortunately, many project managers and contractors do a wonderful job in the physical construction of the project but are weak on understanding the paperwork requirements. They are often not aware of many municipal requirements. They are also not aware of the significant consequences of and penalties for not following even esoteric regulations. The developer, although not necessarily knowing all the rules and regulations, must be sensitive to regulatory issues. He is often the one who will pay the cost of a contractor's ignorance. He can mitigate the risk of noncompliance with municipal requirements and of inspection delays by asking the right questions and hiring the right people.

POLITICS AND DOING BUSINESS

Examples of political influence in real estate abound because most municipalities appoint senior employees, including inspectors, who are sympathetic to the local political groups that appointed them. A borrower always should try to understand the political picture because it may include a negative bias toward or an ongoing controversy involving his project. If this is the case, even minor variances from regulations can cause serious delays.

Included in the political landscape can be environmental groups, neighborhood groups, community boards, chambers of commerce, landmark boards, and very politically oriented zoning boards. The lender and the developer may perceive the world as a level playing field, but in real estate development very often it is not. "It's not what you know but who you know" is true all too often. Having the right architect, engineer, and construction manager can be a real asset. Since they have personal relationships with higher-level members of various municipal departments, they have access and influence that are impossible for an outsider to obtain.[7]

Assuming that a project is going well, it is very important for the borrower to pay courteous attention to inspectors. On the inspector level, a good personal rapport can have palpable benefits. A good owner's representative or construction manager will learn what the inspectors in each department want when they come to the site. If he does not know what their wants are, the project can get a bad reputation. This usually occurs early and is caused by an inexperienced project manager or poor organization of paperwork. The result can be delays in getting an inspector to come to the project site or, more commonly, an inspector who "follows the book" to an extent that borders on unreasonableness. Inspectors appreciate good work. A job that is going well makes an inspector's job easier. Mutual appreciation and general respect will mean a better response from the inspector.[8]

LENDER PROTECTION

In light of all the inspection work and paperwork involved, how can you protect your loan and the developer from errors and delays? The answer is that in most cases you cannot. However, you

---

[7] If a developer gets in trouble with final inspections, hiring someone known to the departments that are responsible for giving final project approvals, even in the late stages of a project's development, is almost always worth the cost. This is the case because near the end of the job, the carrying costs of the property are usually higher (interest expense) and therefore delays are more expensive.

[8] Bribery and kickbacks sometimes get inspectors to a site and/or get them to approve work that ordinarily would not be approved. Of course, it is a felony to offer a bribe to an inspector. However, if an inspector is dishonest, he may go out of his way to find some minor offense that will hold up an approval. The developer often feels that he has no choice but to pay. In fact, when a lot of money is involved in a project, he may feel that that is the best course of action. After all, the economics of a project can involve dozens of lives (investors, future occupants, lenders, etc.). Unfortunately, there are often no simple answers. The developer should be very careful because extortion situations can go on for years before they are detected. This is evidenced by the periodic roundups, indictments, and convictions of inspectors every few years in some major U.S. city. The surprising aspect is that these situations continue for a relatively long period and sometimes involve a remarkable number of people.

can take a step toward protecting yourself by asking either directly or through your inspecting engineer if the required inspections
are being performed. If you have a good consulting engineer who
has experience in the municipality, he can be a real help to the
developer. Asking for copies of inspections can help reveal deficiencies that can be corrected before there are serious consequences. This can alert the development team to get the necessary
inspections done. It also elevates the inspecting engineer's status
with the borrower which can be helpful later if there are other
problems. It gives you, the lender, more leverage in making sure
that the borrower is completing the processes properly. Although
this would be an extremely rare situation, you could threaten not
to make any advances until the inspection reports required by your
inspecting engineer, are produced.

TEMPORARY CERTIFICATE OF OCCUPANCY

Even if the developer has completed the construction work properly, has made sure the proper inspections were done, and has had
the required paperwork signed off on by the proper individuals,
the structure still may not get a permanent certificate of occupancy
but instead receive only a temporary certificate of occupancy. In
fact, the objective of many experienced developers is to receive a
TCO first and a CO later; in many situations a property may not
receive a CO until a year or more has gone by.

A TCO means that the municipality has determined that the
structure is safe and habitable for occupancy and can be used for
its intended purpose but has not been completed. The work that
still needs to be performed is listed by the municipality and put by
the developer on a punchlist, which is a list of items that need to be
completed before a permanent CO can be issued. Examples include
finishing insulation and molding around windows, replacing
brick, applying a final stucco coat to an external wall, installing a
ceiling fixture, and hanging a door.

A TCO has several advantages: It allows part or all of the
structure to become useful at an earlier date, thus generating
revenue; it may be a trigger in the construction loan documentation
for additional fundings, often in the form of a retainage reduction;
it may be all that is required for a takeout lender to fund, thus
possibly increasing the developer's leverage (a bigger loan) or

reducing the cost of debt; and it gives the developer a focused list of things that have to be done to receive a permanent CO.[9]

For you, the lender, the TCO is an indication that the structure is fundamentally complete. It has made the transition from an asset incapable of generating revenue to one in which major construction is no longer on the critical path toward project profitability. This means that its value has increased substantially from that of its former incomplete status. The TCO does involve risk, however. Because it is temporary, the TCO has to be renewed periodically. This usually involves only the submission of an application with a renewal fee. However, depending on the municipality, renewals may last only for a year or two. After that, there can be substantial costs involved, including fines, the submission of added amounts of paperwork with concurrent fees, and expenses for professionals who may be needed to manage and navigate the process.

FROM TCO TO CO: FINISHING THE WORK

After the issuance of a TCO, work still has to be done. However, once the TCO is in place, the pace of work almost always slows down. There are a few reasons for this. From the developer's point of view, the property is generating income or, in the case of a property's sale, already has generated income. In the first situation, it may be practical to wait as long as possible to tackle the items on the

---

[9] In certain areas, a CO must be issued for an entire building but a TCO can be issued for a portion of the building. In certain instances, it may be detrimental to receive a CO if the developer is not sure how all the space in the building will be completed. This often occurs when a future tenant will construct and finish its own interior space; this is often the case with high-end retailers and restaurants. A case in which a partial TCO is advantageous occurs when offices are constructed on the upper floors of a building and retail spaces are partially constructed on the first floor and the basement of a building. Most of the office space, which makes up the bulk of the building, has been preleased (a typical requirement in most construction loans). By obtaining a TCO for the office space as soon as possible, the owner enables tenants with leasing commitments to take occupancy and thus accelerate cash inflows. The retail space, though, may remain unleased, perhaps because of softness in demand. The developer does not want to put in additional work and expense until he has a signed tenant. If he, for example, puts in a staircase leading from the first floor to the basement, installs an ADA (Americans with Disabilities Act)-compliant elevator at a particular point, and finishes the floors in order to get a CO, he may have wasted his money. The new retail tenant may find the staircase unsuitable, the elevator in the wrong place, and the floors not consonant with its theme. The owner spent time and money on elements that essentially, because they were replaced, had no value to him or the new tenant. It would have been better to obtain a CO after the tenant's work was completed.

punchlist. Instead of the developer spending out of pocket, income from the property is used pay for the final work. With the second scenario, once the money from a sale is received, it may be psychologically difficult and economically imprudent to put it back into the property immediately. The developer already has made his full potential return. He may want to hold on to funds earmarked for punchlist items as long as possible and earn interest on that money.[10]

Another reason for a slowdown is a redirection of the developer's attention. For instance, if the property is not fully occupied, he is probably under pressure to spend time and money aggressively on marketing vacant space rather than spend it on punchlist items. This is understandable since the developer will want to cut his monthly carrying expense and perhaps begin to realize a profit. If a TCO time horizon is up to two years, the desire for a permanent CO often falls by the wayside. He also may be working on other projects that demand more immediate attention.

Another reason for delays in completing the remaining work can be that the amount and level of the work are minor. Getting a contractor back on the job, particularly if he has received all his money, can be difficult. In some cases, the developer may have to search for and hire a new contractor to do the work. This can be time-consuming and expensive.

Furthermore, if the work includes occupied space, progress can be impeded if tenants get in the way. It is much harder to complete certain kinds of work because of its disruptive nature. Safety for tenants and workers alike, security, and liability become much bigger issues, as do scheduling, noise, and cleanup. Tenants have to be accommodated. Gaining access to the work area during normal business hours and even during very early hours can be difficult or impossible.

LENDER RISK

The slowdown and the logistics involved in getting a permanent CO after the receipt of a TCO can impose additional risk. If the takeout lender will get you out of the loan with a TCO, it is

---

[10] This situation is very unlikely, but it does occur from time to time. Usually the purchase price is adjusted downward by the buyer to take into consideration the punchlist items' costs, or the funds needed to obtain a CO are placed in an escrow account as a condition of the sale (see the end of this chapter for a discussion).

not your problem. Obviously, you should strive in your buy-sell agreement (see Chapter 15) to make the TCO one of the takeout triggers. If the takeout commitment requires a permanent CO, the construction loan may have to be extended. In the worst case, if a CO is required under the takeout lender's commitment and the commitment expires, there no longer will be any permanent financing. The construction loan will have to remain in place until another takeout is found, or the construction lender may have to restructure the loan with a longer term (e.g., a bridge loan, a term loan, or a permanent loan).

If there is no takeout because the project will be sold, for instance as condominium units, or is a build-to-suit building, the developer may have trouble selling or leasing the property because it does not have a permanent CO. This may not be a problem with commercial occupants whose concerns about a CO are overridden by business considerations such as location and rents, but it can be a major concern with residential purchasers and their closing attorneys. Individuals who do not understand or are not willing to understand the bridge between a TCO and a CO may decide to buy elsewhere. This slows the absorption period, and that delays revenues and increases expenses.

C OF O HOLDBACK GUARANTEE

Even an inexperienced purchaser or lessee (if not personally then through his attorney) will ask for some guarantee that the property eventually will receive a permanent CO. This usually comes in the form of an escrow deposit or a letter of credit. Its amount should always be higher than the estimate of the cost for the work to be completed (which should include a healthy contingency line for unexpected or overlooked expenses and cost overruns on identified budgeted line items). If the escrowed amount is below the cost to complete, the purchaser takes on the risk that the developer may save time and money by walking away. Keeping more money than necessary tied up in the project until full completion is a powerful incentive to keep the borrower committed to completing the project. You should make sure that if there is money left in the project and your loan has not been paid down yet, you will have control over its release. This way, you can make sure that the work will be done by the borrower, and if it is not, you or the takeout lender will have enough funds to complete the work. In a condominium project, if the release provision was thought out properly at loan origination, the lender will be paid down through sales before the escrow deposit becomes the lender's problem. It always pays to remember that ultimately the most important objective for a construction lender is to get the construction loan paid down to zero as soon as possible after construction has been completed.

WHAT THE LENDER SHOULD DO

Near the end of the job, the lender must pay some attention to the review of the final work to be done. You do not need to monitor the process carefully unless there is a problem. However, you should understand the process so that you will not underreact or overreact. Ask when a TCO or CO will be obtained. Ask why there are delays. Ask about the target date for occupancy. Ask about sales, signed lease contracts, and so forth. Do not be taken by surprise. If you can anticipate specific problems or the likelihood of their arising, you can prepare yourself to adjust and react. From a career perspective, there is nothing like being prepared.

CHAPTER 11

The Development Process from the Borrower's Perspective

Very often the lending officer has an unfocused understanding of what the borrower must do to construct a building that ultimately will provide the funds that pay down the development loan. This is understandable because the loan officer probably was trained in general finance, accounting, and credit. He has been working long hours, especially after the recent wave of institutional consolidations and the trend toward an increased portfolio size for lending officers, and the press of day-to-day operations makes it extremely difficult to learn even the rudiments of the development process. Also, he may have career path goals that include being in development lending for only a short period. Since those around him may have similar backgrounds, experiences, and constraints, there is little opportunity to learn about the process from interaction with colleagues.

Even in sophisticated real estate departments, if the lending officer wants to learn more, he may be blocked by his organization's structure. To increase efficiency, many organizations have compartmentalized the real estate credit business by having one area for lending and origination, one for administration, one for reviews, one for workouts, and perhaps several for specialized types of properties (large malls, multifamily projects, etc.), along with separate departments for in-house appraisals and in-house engineers. This decreases opportunities to learn and to get a holistic picture of the commercial real estate credit business. In fact, most lending institutions do not acknowledge the shortcomings in lending officers' understanding of the development process and how it affects the dynamics of a development loan.

This chapter provides a brief overview of the development process from the borrower's perspective. It begins at the point where the borrower has done his preliminary work and purchased a site to build on or has it under contract. The description is brief because throughout the book many of the points discussed here are considered in more depth as they apply to development financing. Familiarity with the process can help the lender make more informed and better decisions that can be applied to situations for the benefit of the lending institution, the borrower, and the loan officer.

THE PLAYERS

Here are brief definitions of the players most important in real estate development. The descriptions may differ slightly from textbook definitions because they are from the borrower's perspective.

Developer	Refers to one or two people who head up the development entity and team. The developer is the point man and the one ultimately held responsible for the project. His level of involvement in the construction process can vary tremendously. For instance, he may be a general contractor, can act as his own construction manager, or can distance himself from construction to any degree desired by hiring a general contractor or a construction manager.
Investor	Most often, the investor is an inactive partner who, depending on his relationship and track record with the developer, may become progressively more involved in the project by putting pressure on the developer if the project is not going smoothly. Pressure usually comes in the form of requesting more frequent progress reports, sitting in on meetings, and second-guessing decisions.
Lender	This is the construction lender who makes a loan, usually after the developer-investor puts

in most or all of its equity. A smart developer will have a friendly but firm relationship with the lender. He may need some concessions in the loan parameters as the project progresses, such as a decrease in retainage, a loan extension, or a deferral of interest. He also may need the lender for a referral and/or as a source of funds on his next project.

Mezzanine lender
The mezzanine lender is an institution that puts its money in concurrently with the developer or after the developer but before the construction lender. For the construction lender, this usually is considered equity. For the developer, it is viewed as an institutional equity partner that is sophisticated, silent, expensive, and necessary. The mezzanine lender sometimes is structured into the project as an owner, most likely as a member of a limited liability corporation (LLC). More often though, it takes a pledge and security interest in the LLC membership or partnership interests with a side agreement delineating its interest. It therefore has potentially more control over the developer since under the operating (ownership) agreement or the agreement pledging an interest, the mezzanine lender can take control of the ownership entity in adverse circumstances and depose the developer without foreclosing, as would be the case if the lender made a conventional second mortgage. The mezzanine lender is a sleeping giant. A smart developer always answers the telephone when the mezzanine lender's representative is on the line, tries to give him information and reports to him with a convincing but positive spin whenever possible, and continually assures him that things are going as well as possible.

Architect
At the beginning of any construction project, the architect is a key player who can make or

break the project. Not only must he design it, he must have a practical sense of costs in relation to anticipated returns as well as a good knowledge and understanding of local laws and requirements. Often a poor architectural job will show up later, when things cannot be assembled or built as planned. This always translates into higher costs. Since the architect is paid on a fee basis and not on a performance basis and since under his standard contract with the developer he cannot be sued except in extreme circumstances, he is more or less immune to financial loss. If things go well, the developer can be certain that the architect will be quick to take credit for "his" creation. If the project goes poorly and the architect is a major factor in the poor performance, when the project finally is completed, the architect still will take credit for "his creation."

Engineer
Structural, electrical, and mechanical engineers take the architect's drawings and work out the "nerves" of the building. Engineers may know more about actual construction processes than the architect does. Like architects, they are paid on a fee basis and almost never suffer financially for their mistakes, which are rare. When they do occur, they usually are confined to problems with local codes and regulations that are exposed by inspectors.

Construction manager and general contractor
The construction manager (CM) is a consultant who works directly for the developer. Contracts are between the developer and the contractors. He has varying control over the general contractor and the subcontractors, depending on his assignment. Often, as an incentive to save money, the developer will offer a bonus to the CM if he can keep costs at or below a specified ceiling and/or complete the project ahead of schedule.

The general contractor (GC) contracts directly with the subcontractors (subcontractors do not contract with the developer). He often negotiates a fixed-price contract with the developer for the entire project. Any cost savings are therefore his. If the developer makes subsequent changes voluntarily or involuntarily, that often provides an opportunity for the GC to make additional money through markups.

Both are responsible for making sure that all the work is coordinated, done within the framework of the plans and specifications, done according to all governmental regulations, finished on time, and finished within budget. They both work in the construction trenches, more or less taking over the day-to-day construction decisions and headaches on behalf of the developer. The developer, though, is ultimately responsible for the project.

Subcontractor A subcontractor is a contractor who reports directly to another contractor. A subcontractor is responsible for a narrower scope of work (a trade or subtrade) than is the hiring contractor. The hiring contactor needs the subcontractor to perform its work so that the hiring contractor can complete all the work under its own contract.

Materialman Materialmen supply and usually deliver all types of products to the site for use and installation. Those materials can include kitchen cabinets, toilets, stoves, bricks, and marble tile. Since the construction lender almost always will not fund until work is in place or inventory is at least stored on-site, the developer and/or contractor must maintain a good relationship with materialmen so that they receive some form of credit. For certain items, the developer or contractor will have to pay all cash on delivery and perhaps post an initial deposit. He must have the working capital to do so or the project can be slowed.

Inspectors   Inspectors can be employed by the municipality where the project is located or can be independent contractors licensed by the municipality and hired by the developer. Qualified inspectors are most often architects and engineers with the proper certifications. They make periodic inspections at critical intervals to certify that construction is being performed in accordance with the approved plans, specifications, and local laws. Inspections are performed for a wide variety of work that typically varies between local jurisdictions. Examples include examinations of fire stopping (sealing areas to prevent fire from spreading from one area of the building to another), foundation placement, smoke testing (ventilation systems and chimneys), steel bolts and welding (to make sure they meet the strength, type, material, and torque requirements listed in the specifications and the building codes), shoring (the use of temporary materials to keep structures from shifting), underpinning (the permanent strengthening of foundations in the structure and adjacent structures to keep improvements from shifting), concrete (strength and other tests), and foundation (making sure the foundation is being constructed according to specifications and building codes). An inspector's work is clear-cut since codes and requirements are detailed and unequivocal. The general contractor or construction manager is usually the point man responsible for scheduling inspections and working with inspectors.[1]

---

[1] As a result of manpower and budget constraints, "self-inspections" are allowed in some municipalities. During construction, the developer's engineers and architect or qualified contractors can submit self-inspection documentation periodically as required. Later, the municipality will do its own inspection by sending a licensed inspector whom it employs to the site.

Inspecting engineer	The inspecting engineer works for the construction lender. He is extremely influential in determining whether there will be a reduction in the requisitioned amount submitted by the developer. Therefore, the developer and the project manager will give him access to virtually all parts of the project, but one or the other will ordinarily follow him around to answer any questions; if there are any doubts on the part of the engineer about the amount of work completed, the developer will try to dispel them. Construction funding is based on the amount of work completed. An inspector who gives a developer the benefit of the doubt or who can be flexible can be very valuable.[2]
Public agency	A public agency is any federal, state, or local government agency, department, or division that has to be notified, have paperwork filed with, and be consulted with. These agencies include but are not limited to zoning boards, community boards, environmental agencies, multiple divisions of building departments, fire departments, traffic departments, utility companies, and telephone companies. Most people in the industry appreciate the need for many of these entities, but often developers experience their negative aspects. They can be bureaucratic, overbearing, inflexible, expensive, and even discriminatory. A developer or a development team that is not experienced with the local government can have serious problems. In extreme cases, the cost to correct and be in compliance can eat up the owner's profits and equity.
End user	The end user is the one who leases or buys the finished space. The entire feasibility of the project rests with the end user. If the project is built "on spec" (without any or with only a

---

[2] The inspecting engineer is discussed in more detail in Chapter 9.

few identified leasees or purchasers), particularly during the design process, there is a lot of guesstimating about what will reap the highest overall return at the lowest overall cost. The developer has a high degree of independence in determining what the final product will be.

If there is preleasing or presales before the commencement of construction, the developer may have to consult with end users (and investors and lenders) continually. Since they probably will not be as familiar with the limitations and constraints on construction and development, he has to be instructive, persuasive, and diplomatic. Above all, he must make sure that the contract he entered into with the end user or end users will remain in full force and effect on completion, particularly if the project is designed and built with many custom and specialized features. If the relationship breaks down or if the end user's needs or financial health changes, the developer has every right to worry that a situation may materialize in which the end user will refuse or not be able to take possession of the space at completion.

THE PROCESS

The Beginning

The architect, with input from the developer and the members of his team, which can include engineers, construction managers, contractors, cost estimators, and marketing consultants, draws up preliminary plans, views, and renderings of the project. As their collective conceptualization evolves, a process that can take many months, a consensus on what the new structure will be begins to form. During the process mechanical, electrical, and structural engineers will be called in to identify and design the structure as well as review technical points as they arise. The architect then produces plans and completes the initial specifications for the project.

Schematic diagrams that overlay the architect's plans are drawn by engineers for sprinkler systems, plumbing, HVAC, electrical systems, and other crucial systems and components. The plans and specifications then are redone and arranged in a logical and orderly fashion so that users can locate areas for study easily and efficiently. Then the plans are reviewed by the developer for approval and sign-off. On the basis of the plans and specifications, costs are estimated, various portions of the project are bought out, and the lender receives a completed hard cost budget and construction schedule.

Filing Plans and Specifications

Once all this has been agreed on, before work can begin, the developer must authorize the architect to file plans and specifications with the proper municipal authorities (often plans and specifications are referred to only as plans in the field; specifications are expected to accompany plans). Plans and specifications are required for all types of work from electrical, plumbing, and demolition to general construction. The process for filing varies considerably from municipality to municipality and is dependent upon such factors as the size of the population in the area; the level of automation, manpower, and the competence of the personnel in the municipal offices where filings are made.[3]

Offices that must be filed with can include a zoning board, a community board, the fire department, the plumbing department, the buildings department, and special agencies such as a landmarks commission if the project is in a designated landmark area or the building has landmark status. The approval process almost always takes months, and full approvals for large projects often take a year or longer.

Often, to speed up the process, certain sections of the plans are submitted for approval while the others are being finalized. For instance, a demolition plan or a foundation plan can be approved early so that that work can begin as soon as possible while the rest

---

[3] Filing can be much more difficult, time-consuming, and expensive in urban centers than in rural areas. In New York City, for instance, almost all developers hire middlemen called expeditors. Expeditors specialize in dealing with city government on a developer's behalf. Among other things, they manage the bureaucracy to obtain construction approvals and, later, the various inspections and sign-offs needed to get a certificate of occupancy.

of the project continues to be designed and later presented to the proper authorities.[4]

The Cost

Concurrent with and a critical part of the planning process is the developer's project cost budget. This budget is different from the one that may have been given to the construction lender, the mezzanine lender, and the investors because this is the "real working budget." As the project progresses through the conceptual stages, previously omitted details, amenities, and systems are added and sometimes subtracted; this almost always increases total costs. The developer must reconcile his budget with the wish list of items and features dictated to him by others: his architect (who, working on a fee basis, cares more about how the building will look and function than about what it will cost), his investment group (which usually wants to have some input into the design in recognition of its monetary contribution), his technical staff members (who often fall in love with higher-quality, more expensive products and methods), and outside brokers and marketing staff members (who find it easier to sell or lease the finished product the more attractive and feature-laden it is). He must do what needs to be done to complete the structure with limited financial resources so that it can produce the required return in a competitive marketplace. This is a very tough job. The developer must balance the needs and wants of these often disparate groups while maintaining working relationships with them.

The developer, with the help of an estimator, the construction manager, or another individual with experience in the field or by himself if he has the expertise, will make as precise an estimate of costs as possible. The estimating process is a technical one that may involve the use of several methods (see Chapter 3). If the developer has the luxury of time, this will be done before the financing (investors, lenders, etc.) is put together. Often, though, because of the up-front at-risk expense involved in this process, an accurate costing out of the project will occur only after the financial players

---

[4] This happened on a large scale in New York City at a time when, to receive real estate tax abatements, foundations had to be in place before a certain deadline. Many developers put in foundations to get the tax advantage. Then the delay in filing final plans and commencing above-ground construction often spanned a year or more.

have made a commitment and the property is under the developer's control.[5]

Buying Out the Job

Once the architect's and engineers' plans and specifications have firmed up, the project manager or general contractor will begin to solicit bids from various contractors and subcontractors by giving them plans and specifications pertaining to each trade's portion of the project.

During the review, bidding, and selection process, contractors can be a valuable source of information about the completeness of the plans and specifications, their feasibility, the construction methods used, materials, and cost containment because they are specialists in their fields of work. Experience and repetition have given them insights that often cannot be gotten from other sources. Their suggestions may result in a restudy of the construction details and an updated solicitation to contractors for bids. Generally, of course, the contractor who makes the best suggestion for saving costs is more likely to win the job.

After bid proposals have been evaluated—as in any hiring (contract) process, this has subjective and objective elements—one bidder is selected to perform the work. This process of selecting and contracting is called buying out the job. The lead time for this process is not always easy to determine because there are several players involved besides the developer (e.g., the architect, engineers, the general contractor, several subcontractors). When there is a high degree of technical expertise and/or workmanship, the winning bidder may have to complete shop drawings, usually at its own expense, before being allowed to begin work. Common examples of elements that require shop drawings include manufactured windows, millwork, cabinetry, and elevator cabs. After a review by the contractor or the project manager, the architect and/or engineer will review and approve the shop drawings by signing them, depending on the type of work required. Then the

---

[5] From the developer's point of view, the hiring of an architect and engineers to draw up plans and specifications for a to-be-built project on a site that he has no signed sales contract for or control over is very costly. Unless he has a lot of faith or is certain that he will gain control, he will do only the minimum amount of work necessary to move along the process until he "ties up the sales contract."

drawings may have to be reviewed by technical experts and municipal agencies before full approval is given and work can begin. The objective is to make sure that the contractor builds what the architect, who is considered the expert, intended.

Getting Ready to Begin Work

Once the plans and specifications are on file, permits must be obtained (pulled) and posted in a conspicuous place on the job site. Permits are pulled by the contractors that will perform the work. Therefore, although the architect and the engineers file the plans and specifications, permits will not be obtained until a portion of the job is bought out and a contractor is identified and under contract.[6] After the permits are pulled, they are reviewed carefully by the general contractor or construction manager to make sure that in the space labeled "description of work" they are sufficiently broad in scope that they encompass all the work described in the subcontractor's contract. Often headaches occur because the space on the permit that describes the allowed work omits a crucial element or part, such as a floor or area of the building or a necessary task. Then the developer and the subcontractor involved have to decide whether to go ahead with work without a properly filled out permit or wait until a new one is received. If the omission is not very significant, the risk of proceeding may not be high. If the permit is in substantial error or if there is no permit, the risks are of course higher. Exactly how much higher is hard to assess because the developer has to be "caught." If an inspector does not come around and the developer gets a correct permit in a couple of days, he has gained two days of progress and avoided possibly substantial opportunity costs from delays. If an inspector does come around, depending on the severity of the error or omission, the developer can receive a fine, or, much worse, the inspector may stop a portion of or the entire job. Since the developer worked with a deficient permit or without a permit, the municipality issuing the permit may penalize the developer unofficially by dragging its feet on issuing a new permit. This could mean that all the workers, not just those whose work is related to the missing permit, will have to

---

[6] Permits are great for municipal governments because they bring in, especially in small municipalities, good fee income. They are required for everything from street closings and sewer connections to putting a trash container on the site.

leave the project until a proper permit is obtained and posted on the job site. For many developers and general contractors, this gamble is part of normal job stress.[7]

Scheduling and Coordinating

Before pulling permits, the project manager should produce a schedule of the work to be performed by each contractor and trade. The scheduling process is extremely important and if done haphazardly or improperly almost always causes delays and cost overruns. Just as important—and interdependent with scheduling—is the coordination process. The construction manager and general contractor must know not only what has to be done by whom and in what order but which trades need to do their work before other trades can do theirs, which jobs are dependent and which are exclusive, which can be performed in parallel, and which can be performed only in a serial fashion.

Sometimes, particularly at the beginning of a job, scheduling and coordinating are easy because there are relatively few trades on the site. This is true, for example, when new construction involves excavation or when a gut renovation of an existing property initially requires extensive demolition. Later, as the job progresses, the complexity of scheduling and coordination grows exponentially because certain things must be done before other things can be done. For instance, before HVAC, plumbing, sprinkler, electrical, security, and communications trades can work, the carpenter must frame the area and block (reinforce) critical points. Along the way, there is always the possibility of delays as problems occur. Those delays can be caused by elements that do not fit into the structure properly, the delivery of damaged materials, workmanship imperfections, and misplaced or missing components

---

[7] Note that it is the GC's and/or the CM's job to make sure the contractors doing the work are qualified. That is, if the laws require it, they must be licensed in the state where the project is situated. This has obvious benefits. An electrician, for example, must have a license to practice his trade. If he is not licensed, he may put himself and all the work on the project in danger if, for example, his actions cause a fire or an electrocution. Without the baseline of a license, there is no objective way to know whether the electrician is properly trained and/or competent. The developer and the members of his team also must be cognizant of the nuances in the local area. In some areas, the use of a licensed professional is required in unlikely circumstances. For example, in certain areas of New York, the owner must use a licensed plumber to change a toilet bowl.

such as wires, connection boxes and fixtures or ones that are not in agreement with the plans and specs. Because of these ongoing problems, the schedule and coordination have to be reviewed and modified constantly, sometimes weekly or even daily, to keep the job moving along efficiently.

The Positive Bias of Scheduling

The loan officer should be aware that the scheduling process has a built in positive bias because the developer and his general contractor or construction manager are under pressure to show a project that will be completed relatively quickly and at a relatively low cost. If the project is scheduled conservatively, stated costs increase. This makes the development less appealing to investors and lenders and in extreme cases may raise fundamental questions about the project's overall economic feasibility. Therefore, the CM or GC will submit a schedule that the developer desires (or needs), which will be submitted to his investors and the construction lender's consulting engineer. Later, when financing is in place, the actual working project schedule can be modified to fit the project's circumstances more accurately. Ideally, there will be enough money to complete the job through an ample budget, savings on budgeted line items, and greater efficiencies than were projected.

Closing Comes First

Sometimes the lender's consulting engineer will not receive a schedule because the time for purchasing the property comes very shortly after a loan is approved. The developer may be scrambling to close because the sales contract is expiring and the seller will not grant an extension under a time of the essence clause. To meet the seller's deadline, the developer may be especially interested in the lender and the lending institutions' ability to fund the acquisition part of the loan in time to meet the closing deadline. With contract deposit money at risk, he will be less intent on producing and reviewing a construction project schedule.

This should not be a problem for the lender at this early stage because the closing will involve the acquisition of the property and the developer will have contributed most or all of his required equity. Therefore, the loan-to-value ratio as well as the loan risk will be relatively low.[8] Once the loan closes, a condition of the first construction advance can be the submission of a schedule to the inspecting engineer.

Since the schedule is essentially a forecast, it always undergoes revisions. Most projects become very dynamic in a surprisingly short period. Very soon, much of the detail in the initial schedule received by the lender may become irrelevant.

Controlled Inspections

Periodically, qualified inspectors must be brought onto the site to view work in place. Depending on the municipality, inspectors are qualified differently. In some areas, self-inspections are allowed on work by the architect or one of the critical trades, such as a plumber. In other areas, outside independent certified inspectors may be allowed to make inspections in exchange for fees paid for by the developer. In other locations and at the completion of a project, municipal employees usually must do the inspections.

As the job progresses, the municipal agencies responsible for sewer, water, electric service, and gas must be contacted so that they can perform the work needed to bring services to the site or, if the services are already available, to inspect and sign off that the connection work has been completed satisfactorily. The municipality then will issue the respective certificates.

Scheduling inspections and installations by the municipality or utility is very important. If an inspection is late in coming, the whole project can be delayed. Therefore, the construction manager has to make sure that inspections are scheduled in advance with as much accuracy as possible.

Testing

Coupled with inspection is testing. Perhaps the most frequently tested material is concrete. Depending on the type of construction

---

[8] For example, a project with a total cost of $25 million includes $10 million for the property's acquisition (including all closing costs) and $15 million for hard and soft costs. The lender, adhering to a policy of lending up to 80 percent of the project costs, commits to the borrower a $20 million acquisition and construction loan consisting of a $5 million acquisition component and a $15 million hard and soft cost component. At closing, the borrower puts in his $5 million of equity and the lender puts in $5 million of loan funds. At that time, the loan-to-value ratio is only 50 percent.

and the concrete's use, concrete may be tested right after mixing, before it is poured or applied, during its curing, and after it has hardened and is fully cured. Tests include material composition, material ratios, water content and, after hardening, a compression test at an off-site lab. The tests must be performed during certain set intervals within clearly recognized parameters. All tests must be recorded.

Nearing Completion

As the project progresses and moves past the 50 percent mark for each trade, there is a rising comfort level that results from familiarity with the technical and spatial aspects of the job, the general contractor, the construction manager, and the trade personnel. This increased job familiarity can result in a smoothing of operations and an increase in efficiency; in isolated instances it can foster inattention and a lack of focus that cause slowdowns, mistakes, and accidents.

As the job continues past the 75 percent mark, however, like the developer, the contractors, and their workers and perhaps architects, engineers, and consultants may have begun to dedicate some attention and time to finding the next project. Unless the developer has another job for his subcontractors and his development team to move into, he does not have much leverage to keep them working at maximum capacity. If a contractor is successful in booking another job, there may be some overlap between the current job and the new one. Not surprisingly, his subcontractors may have moved some personnel to the new job, slowing down this one. Conversely, booking a new job can result in a speedup of work so that the contractor can finish the current job in time to start the next one; however, this can complicate coordination and compromise workmanship.[9]

The developer's skills are challenged here. He must maintain an acceptable level of attention to his project. At the onset,

---

[9] If there is negligence on the part of a contractor in finishing the job, at the later stages of construction the general rule is that it is more costly and time-consuming to fire a contractor and replace him with a new one. The net amount will be higher because of the time it will take to find a new contractor, sign a contract, mobilize new men on the job, and begin work. This can take months at a time when interest costs and possibly other costs are at their highest (a security force, heating expenses, etc.), and the coordination between trades can be impaired. However, in certain circumstances, the developer may have no choice.

developers with good track records and good reputations have a much better chance of assembling a dynamic team. They do better at the final stages of a project because contractors enjoy working with them and know that down the line they probably will have more work, possibly at a time when a contractor does not have the next job lined up.

Close to Completion

Toward the end of the job, the developer may get increasingly uncomfortable as the pressure to finish the project increases. One of his most common concerns is financing. He becomes increasingly squeezed for money as the project moves toward its end even if his budget was realistic because there is less money available. If he initially underbudgeted the project or experienced significant cost overruns, unless he takes some action, he will have to put more money from his own pocket into the project. This can cause friction in the lending relationship because he will be seeking concessions from the original loan documents and approvals. Almost always, this includes the release of a greater percentage of retainage. He also may request a larger advance from the general conditions and contingencies lines. In his requisitions, his percentages of completion may be overly optimistic or he will ask to move money from one trade where there is a greater amount that has not been funded to another trade where the funding is almost exhausted. This movement may be coupled with claims of equity payments and payments to subcontractors that may not be backed up with documentation. A project that is 1 percent away from receiving a temporary certificate of occupancy is 100 percent unusable and therefore unable to generate any revenue.

To complete his project, a weak developer may do one or more of the following: First, he will stop paying, pay only a portion, or significantly delay making payments to subcontractors, the general contractor, the architect, and the engineer. Later, he may ask them to wait for full payment until he receives the TCO or CO and the project generates some income. As was mentioned above, he may apply some of the construction loan funds to other trades that will not continue to work without receiving the full amounts of their requisitions. He may also ask the construction lender for a loan increase although this is usually time-consuming and costly because it necessitates another closing.

If he cannot cover the gap between costs and his remaining funds, he will have to go to his investors with a capital call. This is often a last resort on the part of developers because it has negative repercussions, including the following:

- Embarrassment and blame for mismanaging the project, whether justified or not
- Possibly a tremendous expenditure of energy and time to explain and justify the situation, particularly if the investors are not knowledgeable about commercial real estate investments or if some of the investors have no more funds to give
- The dilution of the developer's profits and/or equity stake
- The closer scrutiny and possible loss of autonomy that the developer may have to bear
- The possibility of losing control as the manager of the owning entity
- Unfavorable word of mouth exposure that can hurt the developer with investors and lenders on his next project

When the developer gets close, he almost always will find the resources to finish the job.

The TCO and the CO

When the job nears completion, the developer or a member of his team asks for an inspection to obtain a TCO. This allows the building to be occupied, but the developer recognizes that there are still items to be completed or corrected before a permanent CO can be issued. Often there will be two or more inspections before a TCO or CO is granted. After the receipt of a TCO, although the building may be occupied, there still can be many things that have to be done to complete the project. These things are listed on a punchlist. Punchlist items can include putting doorstops on the floors so that swinging doors do not bang into and damage walls, repositioning some electrical outlets, rebalancing the building's hydronics, and finishing external facade work. These items do not affect the health and safety of occupants in the building or directly or significantly affect the ability of the tenants to enjoy the use and functionality of the structure. However, a TCO is temporary. Eventually, no more extensions are available from the municipality.

If the owner does not obtain a CO within an allotted time, he probably will be fined repeatedly until the work is performed and the CO is granted. If time drags on, the tenants or the municipality may finish the work by hiring a contractor; in almost every case this will be more costly than it would be for the developer to do the work himself. Since the focus often moves away from a project as it nears completion and especially after the receipt of a TCO, when the rush to complete the project for immediate occupancy is no longer an issue, it can be costly for the developer to finish the work needed. If he has an in-house construction staff, the process from TCO to CO is much easier and much less expensive since most of the items that need correction can be handled by unspecialized staff that also can call in and manage individual specialized contractors when needed.[10]

MARKETING, SALES, AND LEASES

The developer must have established a plan to market the property and successfully lease or sell it to pay down all his obligations and make a profit.

If the property is an office building and 65 percent of the leaseable space had to be presold before a loan could begin to fund and construction could start, the marketing and sales effort probably began well before construction or perhaps even owner-ship of the property. If warehouse and flex space is built, there is a high probability that the space was leased or sold early on, since that is the usual way of building in that industry segment.

More often, however, while construction is continuing, there is some space that has not been sold or leased. This puts the devel-oper under pressure to lease or sell the remaining space at better than the projected rents or sales as soon as possible and concur-rently to complete the project within the projected budget as soon as possible so as to obtain a return quickly. In order to sell, he has to decide how much of the marketing and sales functions he wants to retain and how much he will contract out to third parties. Depending on a variety of factors, such as the size and breadth of his in-house staff, his experience with marketing, leasing and sell-ing, the sophistication of his immediate competitors, the supply

---

[10] See Chapter 10 for more on TCOs and COs.

and demand for his finished product, and the overall economy, the time and money he will need to spend can vary widely.

If he retains the marketing and sales function for a large luxury apartment building, for instance, he may be able to save a considerable amount of money on brokerage fees and retain control and flexibility during the sales process. This makes sense since costs that include a dedicated salaried or commissioned sales staff; specialists such as photographers, models, and graphic artists; and advertising can be spread over a large number of salable units. On smaller projects with limited marketing, it can make sense for the developer to take over the marketing and sales functions because he may be able to act as his own listing broker and save some brokerage costs. Also, on smaller projects, marketing and sales agencies may not give the project the attention necessary to optimize sales. Having a dedicated salesperson can be very important because that person becomes better acquainted with all the features of the product, including not only details such as the square footages of rooms, the types of floor or wall treatments available, and the choices or advantages of appliances but also where the nearest schools are, where the nearest supermarket and dry cleaners are, what forms of transportation are available, and what nearby community amenities and features exist.

Many developers, however, do not have the capacity or will to keep the marketing and sales functions in-house. Instead, they use an outside company. A major attraction of this approach is that marketing services often are provided for free or at a relatively low cost in exchange for the company being named the project's listing broker.[11] This may be worth the cost in effective revenues since the marketing-brokerage company is made up of professionals who often have the knowledge, established marketing channels, and experience to do a better job than the developer can.

For the lender, it is important to know who will be handling the marketing and sales activities when the project is still in the loan proposal stage because if the developer intends to perform those tasks in-house, he must budget for them. Alternatively, if he plans to use outside resources and lists high costs for those tasks, he may be padding his overall budget to obtain more financing. Another

---

[11] There are almost always some costs for marketing and sales even when one uses a full-service marketing-sales agency because the developer often wants to add and pay for things such as more ad space. Also, costs never paid for by the marketing firm, such as the furnishing of model units, may be included in the marketing budget.

potential issue to consider when these functions are handled in-house is that if during the course of the development he finds himself on an increasingly tight budget, a precarious situation may develop in which to finish the job, which is his top priority, he will have to shortchange the marketing effort. In a rising market in which demand is strong, the negative affects can be minimal. In a falling market, however, the results can be catastrophic.

TRANSITION TO MANAGEMENT

As a building becomes tenanted, the developer must make the transition from builder to building manager. On commercial properties, this usually is not difficult. The occupants are often responsible for constructing much of their own interior space, the list and severity of punchlist items[12] ordinarily is not too great, the occupants' dependency on many buildingwide systems is not as critical (hot water in the rest rooms is only used sporadically for washing hands, not taking showers or cleaning dishes), hand-holding often is not required because tenants are concentrating on their businesses, and, perhaps most important, all the occupants go home at night. For apartment buildings, town houses, and the like, management can be much more of a headache because the tenants have paid or are leasing with money out of their own pockets, services must work day and night, and the range of emotion is usually wider and more volatile. On top of this, with residential rental properties the tenants may have a bias against landlords, and with condominiums there can be a bias against the developer turned sponsor. Even if the developer plans to transfer management to a separate company, there can be tension and issues that must be overcome.

Author's Note

With all the work, risk, capital, time, tension, and aggravation, why develop? Whatever the reasons are, it can be helpful to know which ones appear to be dominant so that the lender can interact with the developer more effectively. It could be the satisfaction of having a part in the conception of something that is relatively permanent and lasting, the fulfillment of a creative drive, the sense of power in motivating scores of people to achieve a result, a need to bring art to the process, a compulsion to be

---

[12] See Chapter 10 for a definition and discussion of punchlists.

challenged, a manic need to keep busy, a need to remain professionally relevant, the fun of hanging out with guys who "do construction," the drive toward altruism by keeping people employed in a development company, and of course the desire to make a lot of money. This is only a partial list of motivations. In interviews with developers, there is never a single answer. Even the world's richest people are involved, and certainly there are thousands who do not need the extra money. It is not an evasion of the question to state that there is no single or right reason why people develop real estate. It's just a good thing that they do.

CHAPTER 12

Constraints on and Incentives for Development

A TALL BUILDING AND THE LAW

Local laws and constraints involving real estate are almost always unyielding even when applied to the most prominent structures. When it was completed in 1989, Cityspire was the world's second highest structural concrete building and the tallest mixed-use building in New York City (it remains among that city's 10 tallest buildings). With 23 floors of office and commercial space and 353 luxury apartments above for a total of 72 stories, it towers 814 feet above street level. Unfortunately, its height created a problem under New York City zoning law because it was 11 feet higher than was allowed. Apparently, that was not intentional but was due to an accumulation of small errors in measurement. Since the height difference was so small that not even the most discerning bird would notice, many zoning experts expected the slightly higher building to be approved. However, there was speculation among some that New York City would "ask" the developer to deconstruct the tower, and that is exactly what happened. The settlement also involved the construction, with all costs borne by the developer, of a multi-million-dollar community center. In spite of its physical prominence, New York City made Cityspire an example of the fact that zoning laws are for everyone.

ZONING AND RESTRICTIONS

Zoning and use restrictions can be defined as the regulation of land and buildings by use, size, type, and character within a delineated area called a zone. There are very few places in the United States that do not have some type of zoning and use restriction laws. The borrower's expert and ally in dealing with zoning and use compliance is his architect. In dense urban areas where regulations can be complex and confusing, the architect's expertise may be supplemented with that of a zoning specialist. Since the architect and the developer closely review use restrictions, it is unlikely that the lender will encounter a problem with a construction loan. However, from time to time problems do occur.

DO NOT TAKE ZONING FOR GRANTED

In most cases, if a project proposal appears to make sense and the area surrounding the property is populated with improvements similar to the one being planned, the proposed structure will be in conformity with zoning requirements. However, notably in upscale areas, the developer and the lender can be unpleasantly surprised. In many cities there are multiple zoning regulations that affect a building site that are reflective of changing times and changing needs. Sometimes obsolete zoning requirements remain in effect but are overlaid with newer regulations.[1] Those changes and overlays have distinct boundaries. Sometimes what is allowed on one side of a street is not allowed on the other.[2]

Because use laws can be complicated, you should always receive some assurance from the developer about what he can or have reason to think he can build on the property against which you are lending. Quite often a developer will lack a firm answer to

---

[1] Overlays can be understood as zones within zones. For instance, if an area originally was zoned for manufacturing and over a period of time the character and the demands of the population of that area change, a portion or all of the area may receive additional zoning requirements, either more restrictive or less restrictive, such as an allowance for office or residential space.

[2] Examples of this are found in older manufacturing areas where privately financed revitalization has occurred. Developers replace or renovate manufacturing buildings and warehouses with retail, office, and residential properties. On one side of a popular street in the SoHo area of New York City, one of the most upscale residential and retail centers in the world, a developer can, as of right, create street-level retail space. On the other side of that same street, it commonly takes over a year and costs over $50,000 to effect a change in use from manufacturing to retail. The zoning boundary runs down the middle of the street.

this basic question, especially if the loan includes an acquisition component. If a site allows multiple uses (e.g., commercial, residential, or a combination of the two), the advantages of each type and how they might be combined to maximize value may not have been calculated. If the developer is lobbying for a variance from existing zoning restrictions or if the requirements are unclear or conflicting, he may have more than one development scenario. A lender may choose to fund the acquisition part of the loan and then set the amount of the development part depending on the approvals that are granted.

Figure 12–1 shows a letter from a borrower's consultant indicating various use choices for a site in New York.

FIGURE 12–1

Alex Xela
Architect and Interior Designer
4404 Fayerweather Street
Brooklyn, NY 12345

August 29, 200_

Zoning Analysis
Block 4444
Lots: 888 & 999

To Whom It May Concern:

This is an analysis of the Zoning Regulations governing the development of lots 888 and 999 on Block 4444, Brooklyn, New York. The analysis was done to determine the maximum number of square feet of building that can be built, as-of-right, on these lots. The combined area of the two lots is 111,740 square feet. The zoning is defined on Map 13C of the Brooklyn zoning map. Both lots are zoned C4–2, Commercial.

The C4–2 Zoning District permits commercial buildings, community facility buildings, residential buildings and buildings which combine these different uses. The permitted Floor Area Ratio, FAR, varies depending on the use of the building constructed. By use, the permitted FAR is as follows:

- Commercial Building – Maximum FAR is 3.4 – 379,916 SF.
- Community Facility and Commercial Building – Maximum FAR is 4.8 – 536,532 SF.
- Residential Building – Maximum FAR is 2.43 with a height factor of 13 – 271,529 SF.
- Mixed Building – Community, Commercial and Residential Building – Maximum FAR is 4.8 – 536,532 SF.

The maximum floor area of a development on this site is 111,740 SF X 4.8 = 536,352 SF. This floor area may be used as 271,529 SF residential and 265,003 for commercial and community facilities space. By the zoning regulations, the residential portion of the development cannot exceed 271,529 SF and the commercial portion of the development cannot exceed 379,916 SF.

If you have any questions, please do not hesitate to call me at 123–999–1010.

Sincerely,

Alex Xela

Rules and regulations governing the size, type, style, systems and materials of improvements can vary substantially between different locales and may change with little notice. For a developer unfamiliar with an area or proposing a project with a size or features that require municipal or agency approval, an outside expert is a must. That expert not only has specialized knowledge and experience but also has the relationships with agencies and government personnel needed to get a developer through the process with efficiency and relative certainty. If the stakes are high, which they usually are, particularly on large-scale projects, an expert's opinion is vital.

WHAT THE LENDER CAN DO

As the lender, your major resources are your attorney and your consulting engineer. Loan documents prepared and reviewed by your institution's attorney should have attestations by the borrower's architect and/or engineer that the proposed improvements will be in conformity with all rules and regulations and that if they are not, evidence of approvals will be forthcoming when they are. Furthermore, loan documents should require that before any advances under the development loan are made, regulatory approvals must be submitted to the lender showing that any work performed was permitted. Your inspecting engineer should review those approvals. He should be familiar with those which are required in the geographic area in which he works. However, he may be more knowledgeable about the construction aspects of a job than about the required approval paperwork. If you have any doubt about paperwork, you should turn over approval documentation to your attorney and/or a consultant familiar with the process for his review and opinion.

Remember that even after a careful review, there are innumerable instances in which zoning and use laws have been skirted through lack of awareness or intentionally only to cause problems later. Neither the developer nor the lender should take unnecessary chances.

LANDMARK AND SPECIAL DISTRICT CONCERNS

In addition to zoning regulations, there are other legal constraints imposed by controlling entities that you may need to take into consideration. Examples of these entities common throughout the United States include local and federal landmark boards, commissions, and agencies.[3] Depending on where a construction project is located, the landmark status of a building as well as the landmark status given to an area can have very significant consequences. From the developer's and lender's perspective, those consequences are almost always negative.

In most municipalities, the body responsible for preserving and maintaining landmarks and landmarked areas has very broad powers. Being a partly independent and partly public entity with limited accountability and in most cases a lot of political power, these agencies often rule in what appears to be a subjective and at times arbitrary manner.

A developer can be ensnared in costly delays and revisions because of frequently vague directions, the agency's bureaucratic nature, and the political landscape of the municipality. Furthermore, the landmark agency often provides little guidance about what is necessary to gain its approval. The onus is on the development team to meet its demands. Since landmark agencies have police power, failure to follow their mandates can result in the issuance of fines and stop-work orders that may not be lifted for several weeks or even months. This holds true even after the developer complies by making the necessary changes.

In light of the fact that the process can result in backlogs that can last several months,[4] after an initial formal meeting, many landmark agencies allow the process to continue at the less formal "staff level." This can save the developer considerable time. However, it also gives the staff considerable power by allowing it to interpret the agency's policies and guidelines. If the staff is not responsive or cooperative, the developer can be stalled for a long and expensive amount of time.

Perhaps counterintuitively, when local and regional economies are growing and a developer would expect landmark agency

---

[3] Although the following discussion is centered on landmark regulators, it also applies to other authoritative bodies, such as environmental agencies.

[4] Causes for delays include the necessity of filing proper forms, paperwork, illustrations, and visuals of exactly the right size, all within a certain period, to be eligible to present them at one of a limited number of meetings. Missing a deadline can cause an applicant to be rescheduled near the back of the line.

cooperation to be good, the opposite can occur. This is the case because agencies typically are understaffed and strained when there are high levels of development activity. Necessary approvals may extend out several times longer than expected. Worse, a proposal may have a higher probability of being turned down. If this is the case, the developer as a general rule has little or no recourse but to comply with the rejection and make the necessary construction changes.

CHALLENGES AND RECOURSE

Experienced developers are aware that challenging a regulatory agency in court is almost always impractical before or during construction. One reason, as was noted above, is that most agencies have limited accountability. Agencies and their personnel are not under the same time pressure as the developer and ordinarily do not have much at stake, either personally or professionally, if they later lose a legal suit. Even if the developer is absolutely right, fighting the issue usually requires a lot of expertise, time, and money. Meanwhile, the project is languishing and eating up dollars in taxes, loan interest, and so on. Additionally, pursuing a legal remedy while the project is at the mercy of the agency may have subtle negative consequences such as a delay in its response time. Since a final resolution can take years, the developer has no option but to comply with the agency and pursue legal remedies after or near project completion. Furthermore, depending on the merits of the case, there is always a risk that the developer will lose.

The lender usually becomes aware of disputes with regulatory agencies after delays in construction or change order submissions. However, disputes are the developer's business, not the lender's. It is the developer's responsibility to comply with all regulations. If he does not, you should examine the situation with your institution's senior management and real estate attorney. If advisable (with your attorney's concurrence), advances may be limited or funded selectively until the developer is in compliance.

COST CONSIDERATIONS

You should be reasonably confident that the borrower has budgeted amply for expenses related to local regulations and restrictions.

Usually, those expenses will be part of the architect's expense line and include allowances for drawings, illustrations, printing and mounting, computer-aided renderings, drafting time, after-hours meetings, and public speaking time. If you have any doubts, a call to the developer should satisfy you that these additional expenses were considered.

Regulatory costs frequently are reflected in a project budget on a separate professional/consulting fee line.[5] On a project involving a landmark building, for instance, depending on the work involved, it is often a requirement that laboratory and experts' reports be prepared indicating that analysis was performed on elements such as mortar, brickwork, cornices, building color, and windows. Those reports must be submitted to the landmark agency before work can proceed.[6] A good first-glance rule is that if the costs do not look high, they are probably too low and the project will experience regulatory compliance overruns.

INCENTIVES

Bonuses and Exceptions

In most large cities, to encourage certain types of development or increase growth in particular areas, bonuses periodically are available to developers who add buildable square footage. The developer usually is not required to apply, but the economic incentives of the bonus usually far outweigh the benefits of not participating. Ultimately, the local government allows the bonus to expire, be renewed in its existing form or in a modified form, or be

---

[5] The technical aspects of agency compliance have created many lucrative industries. For landmark compliance there are craftsmen, real property historians, real property forensic specialists, and contractors who specialize in historic restorations. Their limited number leaves the developer with little choice among players, pushing up prices. Also, the ambiguity of directives, regulations, restrictions, and decisions has resulted in the birth of a thriving industry of lobbyists and attorneys. They often charge a great deal of money, but with no guarantee of a successful outcome.

[6] As was noted above, approval delays can be very expensive. This is especially true near the end of the project because it can delay the obtainment of a certificate of occupancy (CO), postponing the generation of revenue. Also, mortgage interest costs will be at a high level since most of the loan funds will have been advanced.

legislated away. In certain circumstances the economic benefits of a bonus are no longer attractive or relevant. Often, to take full advantage of a bonus, the developer must use outside consultants with specific knowledge of municipal opportunities, regulations, and laws. Incentives can be very complicated and very advantageous, as is described in the following example.

Inclusionary Zoning

A bonus available in New York City is called inclusionary zoning (similar programs exist throughout the United States). A recent and well-known project named One Beacon Court that used this bonus sits on a rectangular block between 58th and 59th streets and Lexington and Third avenues in Manhattan. The property, with a footprint of 84,300 square feet, under its existing zoning has a floor-to-air ratio (FAR) of 10:1. This means that as of right, a developer could construct an 843,000-square-foot structure. However, with the use of the inclusionary zoning program, the FAR increased to a 12:1 ratio, resulting in a building of over 1 million square feet. The newly completed building consists of retail and office space on its lower floors. The top 24 floors contain 105 luxury residential condominiums. Thirteen of the 24 floors were built as a direct result of inclusionary bonuses.

To erect such a large building, up to 20 percent larger than it would be under as-of-right zoning, the developer had to participate in the construction of "affordable housing" within the immediate area (not within the building itself). Under the program, for every square foot of affordable-income housing produced, up to 4 square feet of conventional housing can be transferred to a market-rate residential project. A developer of affordable housing can take a construction and development fee, build a rental apartment building, give the building to a nonprofit group to own and manage and thus take a tax deduction, and make a profit on the sale of the 4-for–1 bonus square footage. At One Beacon Court, the developer bought bonus square footage from a few affordable housing developers and, to add more square footage, built its own affordable housing in the area as well.

In the One Beacon Court case, the marginal benefits were particularly valuable since the higher residential floors commanded strikingly high prices. Penthouses in the building sold at over $3,000 per square foot.[7,8]

Coordination

As was noted in Chapter 10, it is very important for the developer to control paperwork and submissions to avoid problems later in the job. This can be difficult because plans, specifications, tests, applications, approvals, and waivers must be submitted to and received from several municipal authorities at different times. When one is working in areas with more complex regulations and more than one regulatory body that must review and approve the same work, coordination among them requires a higher degree of attention to paperwork to avoid costly errors. A situation that can lead to higher costs and delays is discussed below.

It starts when the architect files a set of plans and specifications with a municipality's buildings department. After approval, contractors pull permits and begin construction work. Then, many months later, as the project evolves, a different set of plans is submitted to another regulatory body such as a landmark agency. Sometimes this is not a problem because agencies recognize that there can frequently be small non-material changes as a project progresses. Rather than continually submit minor plan revisions, a set of plans can be submitted with cumulative changes at or near the end of the project. When significant changes occur, however, or

---

[7] In the inclusionary zoning program, the conventional developer benefits, the developer of affordable housing benefits, and of course the moderate-income occupants benefit. Concerning the latter, the lucky tenants who qualify usually are picked by lottery from a pool of candidates that exceeds by several times the number of available apartments (there is virtually no market risk for the housing developer). This allows for quick occupancy, enabling the moderate-income building to support all its expenses quickly. Since the program trades on square footage–4 square feet of market rate housing produced for every 1 square foot of affordable housing-the newly created affordable units are often large and well laid out. This contrasts with programs that promote affordable housing on the basis of room count, in which to maximize program benefits, the developer is encouraged to create as many small rooms, often with difficult layouts, as he can.

[8] Another New York City program allows additional square footage if the developer incorporates community space in the building. In the Letoha hotel example in Chapter 6, the developer was able to add approximately 40,000 square feet of space to his building. This allowed him to build a 10-story hotel starting on the fifth floor, above surrounding low-rise buildings, enhancing the desirability of the hotel rooms by providing more light and better views. In addition, although the 40,000 square feet had to be used for community purposes, it could be rented or sold at a profit.

when there is friction between the developer and a particular government agency, the lack of coordination can become serious. The question becomes, Which set of plans and specifications was approved? Since a property can be physically completed in only one way, which set of plans will match the completed project? Your inspecting engineer should follow up from time to time when multiple authorities are involved to make sure all approvals are consistent with the actual project.

Quid Pro Quo Costs

When a developer requests a variance from existing use laws, he often is forced to give something in return. That can entail renovating a train station, renovating a landmark theater, building a new street, installing more expensive windows, performing landscaping, planting sea grass, providing a public easement, or setting aside land for public use. When you encounter a project that will involve wetlands, virgin land, landmarked structures, and the like, you should ask the developer what regulatory agencies require from him in return. Depending on where he is in the approval process, he may not know or may have only an idea. If this is the case, repeat the question later so that you can get a grasp of the net financial benefits (or net costs) of obtaining all the necessary approvals.

Funding before Approval of a Variance or Exception

Zoning, use, and building regulations typically remain in place for relatively long periods. In areas whose character is changing rapidly, approvals for the development of new property or a change in use of an existing property become more frequent, cause delays, and take time. In light of the political nature and wide discretion of regulatory agencies, from one day to the next and from one block to the next, it can never be taken for granted that the borrower will be successful in receiving approvals or will get them on a timely basis that will fit within the framework of the loan. For instance, if part of the loan is for the acquisition of a property to be developed and it includes a soft cost line to fund loan interest, a delay in approvals will slow the project to a point where the amount of budgeted interest will not be enough for the term of the loan. Furthermore, if approvals cannot be obtained, the value of the collateral will be affected immediately.

With competitive pressures among lenders, coupled with a high level of confidence in a particular borrower's ability to move through the approval process, it often makes sense to fund development loans before approvals are in place. The most common method is a holdback of funds until the variance is approved, as evidenced by full and proper documentation. Then, after the approvals have been received, the borrower can be reimbursed for his outlay since the property's value will be higher. For example, you can satisfy the borrower by helping him acquire the property, say, with a 60 percent loan-to-land-cost ratio. Then, after approvals are in place, you can increase the loan-to-land-cost ratio to 80 percent as part of the development loan. The borrower is being competitively funded, and you have reduced your loan risk.

If you are proposing a loan that is based on a hoped-for approval, that should be addressed clearly in your underwriting proposal. This frequently occurs when a loan has a property acquisition component. The lender is at more risk because at the time of acquisition it is often the case that not all approvals are in place. This adds uncertainty. At worst, if the developer works without the proper approvals, when the project is finished, a CO may not be issued until the violations are corrected. This can be devastating. Not only will it be impossible to derive income from the property while physical corrections are made and the approval process runs its course, but significant additional costs will be incurred to correct the violations. Furthermore, delays in completion can negate a takeout (refinancing) of the construction loan, lead to the expiration or breakage of lease commitments, cause liquidated damages,[9] and lead to the loss of prospective desirable tenants in need of immediately available space.

If the project is forecasted with a significant bonus or an exception, in the underwriting analysis you should consider working out two forecasts to see if the project will be viable with and without it. Assuming that the project initially appears economically feasible either way, it should be looked at with attention to costs and construction. The underwriter should not assume that he can apply the average cost per square foot of a larger building to a smaller one. For instance, if a building of a certain size (which includes additional approvals) is needed to justify a project with

---

[9] Liquidated damages are fines stipulated in a contract or lease for late completion or delivery.

substantial up-front costs (e.g., an uneven site that requires columns for foundation support, an environmentally challenged site that must be cleaned up, a nearby hill prone to rock and earth slides that requires the construction a retaining wall), a smaller building's projected income may not justify construction if approvals for a larger building are not obtained.

Up-front costs normally make a larger building less expensive per square foot because the costs are spread over a greater area, but this assumption does not always hold. In tall buildings, for instance, the added expense of construction on the higher floors can offset the value benefits. Therefore, on a deal in which the size of the structure is critical, in addition to taking a good look at the market value of the additional space, you should try to ascertain the additional costs. If you do several forecasts (a sensitivity analysis), make them meaningful.

TAX ABATEMENTS AND TAX CREDITS

So far in this chapter the discussion has centered on what can or cannot be built or modified physically. It is only a matter of time before you receive a proposal for a project that will be eligible to receive tax abatements or tax credits.

In real estate, a tax abatement applies to local real estate taxes, which are reduced for a certain period. The tax abatement formula typically incorporates variables such as the type of property, its location, its use, the nature and extent of improvements, and their cost. A tax credit also bestows benefits that are based on specific formulas. However, a tax credit, in contrast to a tax abatement, will offset income taxes dollar for dollar (it differs from a tax deduction, which allows only a portion of each deducted dollar to be applied against taxes, based on the taxpayer's marginal tax rate).

Tax Credits

The most common form of tax credit available to developers comes from the federal tax credit program, which is used to encourage the rehabilitation and preservation of certain buildings and structures by the federal government.[10] On landmark-designated buildings,

---

[10] Tax credits for real estate are mostly on the federal level but also can originate from the state and local levels.

all hard and soft costs, including construction loan interest, are eligible for a 20 percent tax credit. For nonresidential buildings built before 1936 that are not historic, the owners are entitled to a 10 percent tax credit. The credit under current regulations can be carried back 1 year and carried forward for 20 years.

Many developers promote tax credit eligibility as an income-producing aspect rather than as an offset to future tax expense because tax credits have a definite market value and can be "sold" at a discount, usually to large corporations, for an up-front or staged cash payment. There are strict rules, which include the fact that the "buyer" must have an ownership interest in the real property before completion of the construction work. A standard checklist that was given to a prospective seller by a tax credit consultant with regard to a multinational corporation interested in purchasing federal tax credits is shown below.[11]

Unless the proper ownership structure is set up first, the developer cannot finish the project and then look to "sell" the credits. There are also recapture provisions, and so the ownership structure must remain in place for at least five years.[12]

A seller can benefit almost immediately after a building is placed back in service with a large up-front cash infusion. At the time this book was being written, a purchase scenario might work out something like this:

> When construction is completed and the building is placed in service, the seller can receive from 88 to 98 cents for each dollar of tax credit sold. This is considered equity in the property. For the next five years, the seller will pay (back) the purchaser 3 percent of the amount of equity paid for the credits. After five years, the seller must pay the purchaser an additional amount equal to between 17 percent and 22

---

[11] This simple checklist was written at the beginning of a $2 million sale of federal tax credits from a $20 million hotel rehabilitation project in New York City to a multinational corporation with an office on the West Coast. The transaction also involved the seller's consultant in New Jersey, the corporation's attorney in Colorado, and the corporation's accountant in Washington, DC. The deal took almost 90 days to complete and cost the tax credit seller almost $100,000 in accounting, attorney, and consulting fees.

[12] The recapture provision is for 100 percent the first year, declining by 20 percent each subsequent year. To avoid recapture, the legal entity and its ownership of the underlying real estate asset must remain in existence for at least five years. If, for example, there is a foreclosure in year 4 and ownership of the asset by the entity ceases, only 80 percent of the credit is deemed earned and if 100 percent of the credit was taken, the owning entity must pay the federal government back 20 percent of the face value of the credits.

Tax Credit Checklist

1. Most Recent Development Budget, showing financing sources (e.g., amount, interest rate, and terms) and development costs. In addition, the underlying financing costs should be distinguished between costs associated with construction versus permanent financing.

2. Detailed Breakdown of All Expenditures for the Official Cost Certification, such as general ledger journal entries with descriptions (otherwise, invoices may be required).

3. Official Documentation confirming that each structure was originally built prior to 1936. For example, a copy of Original Building Certificate or Title Report would be sufficient.

4. Current Ownership Structure, including shareholders, partners, and percentage ownership. Please identify any entities that are not U.S. taxpayers (i.e., REITs, pension funds, nonprofits, foreign investors, etc). In the case of the subject (which is a leasehold estate), provide a copy of the long-term lease.

5. Owner's Aggregate Adjusted Basis Calculation (Substantial Rehabilitation Test Verification). A substantial rehabilitation means that a taxpayer's rehabilitation expenditures during a 24-month or 60-month period must exceed the aggregate "adjusted basis" of the building. The adjusted basis is generally defined as the purchase price, minus the value (or cost) of the land, plus the value of any capital improvements made since the building acquisition, minus any depreciation already claimed. In the case of a leasehold interest, such as your hotel, the leasehold improvements must exceed the owner's adjusted basis in the building at the start of the 24-month measuring period.

6. Construction Start and Completion Dates.

7. Placed "In Service" Date (the date on which a new certificate of occupancy will be issued, building will be reopened for business, and/or rehabilitation construction will be completed).

8. Architect's Certificate from a qualified third party that confirms that the project meets the requirements of the Internal Revenue Code's "Wall Retention Test."

percent of the purchaser's equity, thereby effectively completing the transaction. The net effect is that without allowing for the time value of money (present value), the seller receives about 65 cents for every dollar of tax credits sold.[13]

Unfortunately, the sale of tax credits is complex and typically costs $50,000 to $100,000 in legal and accounting expenses alone. The costs and effort that go into a sale make it feasible only for larger projects. For the developer to sell the credits, the lender will have to cooperate to allow the creation of a legal entity that includes the tax credit purchaser and must make sure that the loan remains properly collateralized with its existing lien priority, with all guarantees in place, and so on.

In evaluating a loan proposal whose feasibility is based on the inclusion of credits or in which the credits will contribute to the paydown of the loan, especially with a developer with limited experience in the locality of the project, you should have a high level of confidence that he is cognizant of what he has to do and when. If the funds from a tax credit sale are to be used to pay down part of the development loan, you should make sure that your institution is recognized in the transaction so that proceeds are funded directly to your institution. In almost all cases, the developer should employ an outside attorney or consultant with a tax credit background. You should know who the developer's consultant is so that if you have doubts about the success of obtaining benefits or if you need more information (perhaps during an annual review of the loan), you can call him.

Tax Abatements

Tax abatements are very popular on the local level and are used, sometimes aggressively, by various municipalities to attract and retain business and development. In regard to the development and rehabilitation of real property, most tax abatement programs work the same way. The developer submits the eligible costs of new construction or capital improvements to the appropriate

---

[13] Depending on the strength of the seller, an interest-bearing escrow account may be set up to help ensure that money will be available to pay the purchaser, particularly after the five-year term.

agency. After a sometimes lengthy review and a large amount of paperwork, the agency multiplies the agreed-on sum of eligible construction costs by a percentage. The product is the amount of the tax abatement that is available for a specific period. During that period, the tax abatement benefits may decline on a yearly or biyearly basis.

An analysis of a New York City tax abatement performed by an appraisal firm is shown in Figure 12–2. Note that the present value of the benefits adds value to the proposed project.

FIGURE 12-2

Tax Abatement Program Analysis for a Project in New York City

421(A) TAX BENEFIT ANALYSIS

YEAR 1: 200_ / 200_

EXEMPTION

BASE ASSESSED VALUE:	$223,650
START DATE:	200_ / 200_
LENGTH OF TERM:	15 YEARS

ASSUMPTIONS

FUTURE TAXES PSF:	$4.75
GROSS BUILDING AREA (SF):	114,000
FULL YEAR 1 TAXES:	$541,500
200_ / 200_ CLASS 2 TAX RATE:	0.12396
PROJECTED 200_ / 200_ CLASS 2 TAX RATE:	0.12520
ANNUAL ASSESSED VALUE GROWTH:	2%
ANNUAL TAX RATE GROWTH:	1%

Year	Projected A.V.	Base A.V.	% of Exemption Allowed (Phase Out)	Allowable Exemption (Increase in A.V. Over Base)	Taxable A.V.	Tax Rate	Full Taxes	Tax Payable	Tax Savings
Year 0	$223,650	$223,650	N/A	N/A	$223,650	0.12396	$27,724	$27,724	$0
Year 1	$4,325,094	$223,650	100%	$4,101,444	$223,650	0.12520	$541,500	$28,001	$513,499
Year 2	$4,411,596	$223,650	100%	$4,187,946	$223,650	0.12645	$557,853	$28,281	$529,572
Year 3	$4,499,827	$223,650	100%	$4,276,177	$223,650	0.12772	$574,700	$28,564	$546,137
Year 4	$4,589,824	$223,650	100%	$4,366,174	$223,650	0.12899	$592,056	$28,849	$563,207
Year 5	$4,681,621	$223,650	100%	$4,457,971	$223,650	0.13028	$609,937	$29,138	$580,799
Year 6	$4,775,253	$223,650	100%	$4,551,603	$223,650	0.13159	$628,357	$29,429	$598,927
Year 7	$4,870,758	$223,650	100%	$4,647,108	$223,650	0.13290	$647,333	$29,724	$617,609
Year 8	$4,968,173	$223,650	100%	$4,744,523	$223,650	0.13423	$666,892	$30,021	$636,862
Year 9	$5,067,537	$223,650	100%	$4,843,887	$223,650	0.13557	$687,022	$30,321	$656,701
Year 10	$5,168,887	$223,650	100%	$4,945,237	$223,650	0.13693	$707,770	$30,624	$677,146
Year 11	$5,272,265	$223,650	100%	$5,048,615	$223,650	0.13830	$729,145	$30,930	$698,215
Year 12	$5,377,710	$223,650	80%	$4,123,248	$1,254,462	0.13968	$751,165	$175,225	$575,940
Year 13	$5,485,265	$223,650	60%	$3,156,969	$2,328,296	0.14108	$773,850	$328,471	$445,379
Year 14	$5,594,970	$223,650	40%	$2,148,528	$3,446,442	0.14249	$797,221	$491,079	$306,141
Year 15	$5,706,869	$223,650	20%	$1,096,644	$4,610,225	0.14391	$821,297	$663,475	$157,822

PROSPECTIVE VALUE OF TOTAL TAX SAVINGS @8% RATE	$4,390,953
ROUNDED	$4,400,000

How to Find Out about Incentives

In large urban areas and affluent suburbs, the best way to learn all the rules for incentives, including tax credits and tax abatements, is to use the Internet. Almost all municipalities produce summaries that describe their programs, where to obtain more information and forms, and how to apply. Most often the borrower will need the services of a professional, frequently an attorney, who specializes in those programs. The cost of this professional should show up in the overall project budget along with the abatement or tax credit's expected expense reduction or, in the case of the sale of tax credits, revenues.

When Earned

Tax credits and abatements are recognized after the completion of a project but in certain circumstances can be received during construction if the process is phased. An example is the rehabilitation of an office building. If building and tenant logistics make it possible, the owner, by rehabilitating one floor or a few floors at a time, can stage the work over several years. That way he can get his tax benefits before he has rehabilitated the entire structure. He also gains cumulative experience and efficiencies for subsequent filings. The disadvantage is the additional time and expense of multiple filings.

A Question of Value: Are Incentives Real?

Should you lend against the cost of bonuses? Should you fund the up-front costs of purchasing or producing tax credits and tax abatements? Will each extra square foot purchased with the lender's money from an inclusionary zoning type of program make the loan safer? Is it prudent to make a construction loan to build an affordable housing project that will be given away for nothing after completion? The answer to all these questions is a qualified yes.

In regard to bonus programs, if it can be shown that there is tangible demonstrable value such that for every dollar spent there will be a marginal increase in the completed project's return, lending against those incentives is justifiable. For instance, using averages, if a borrower's land cost per buildable square foot (SF) comes to $125 and his hard and soft costs are $275, his total projected cost is $400 per buildable SF. If he is able to sell 80 percent of the completed project as residential condominiums (20 percent of the space is not salable because it is used for things such as elevators, common hallways, and mechanical rooms) at a price of $700 per SF, his profit will average $200 per SF (a cost of $400 per buildable SF/80% = a cost of $500 per salable SF). If he is able to buy additional buildable square footage at a price of $100 per SF and his cost to build the additional space is $300 per SF, his costs still will total $400 per SF on the additional space or $500 per SF for the space that is sellable. However, since the additional space will be used for more desirable higher-priced penthouse space selling for $900 per SF, he will have created $400 per SF in marginal profit.

Situations like this are very common in dense urban areas and make every extra square foot important to the overall profitability of the project. Note that the lender's loan-to-value and loan-to-cost ratios will decrease since the overall spread between cost and average sale price will have increased. With respect to taxes, the value of both abatements that reduce property taxes and credits that reduce income taxes can increase the value of the finished property significantly by reducing its final cost and/or operating expenses.

The Right Team

Unfortunately, many developers, architects, attorneys, and lenders' inspecting engineers have little or no knowledge about what municipalities' and agencies' requirements, constraints and benefits are.

With regard to requirements, constraints and benefits, the presence of an inexperienced development team in a highly regulated environment can be a good reason to turn down a loan proposal. The prospective borrower may have built comparable or even more physically complex projects in other places, but if he underestimates regulatory controls in the new locale he is considering building in even slightly, there can be consequences that jeopardize his own and your institution's positions.[14]

On most straightforward projects, the chief liaison between the developer and local zoning, special use, community, and landmark agencies is the architect. In fact, there are municipalities and agencies that do not allow a developer to represent his project

---

[14] This can occur in different neighborhoods in the same city.

during a presentation. Only the architect or another recognized expert may file plans, renderings, displays, and so on, with the proper agencies and give presentations to gain their approval. When there are potentially complex issues, having an architect without prior agency experience can be disastrous. Since the right team is an essential factor in controlling risk, particularly in real estate development with its dependency on experience, education, and performance, you should review the credentials and experience of the proposed architect, any consultants, and the borrower's top-level construction team (at least the general contractor or the construction manager) carefully.

Although your lending institution's inspecting engineer generally addresses concerns from a construction standpoint, not a financial benefit standpoint, he should nonetheless be cognizant of the importance of approvals and approval agencies. Unfortunately, as was discussed in Chapter 8, the quality of inspecting engineers varies widely, and so it should not be assumed that he will be an effective monitor on compliance issues; certainly he cannot be responsible for legal issues. It is up to you to remind the inspecting engineer from time to time to address compliance issues and, if you have any concerns, consult with your attorney.

Author's Note

Adhering to constraints and taking advantage of benefits are the borrower's responsibility. Calling him and responsible members of his team from time to time is a good way to remain comfortable that they are doing what is necessary; if they are not, your telephone call should keep them alert and help ensure that they do what they are supposed to do.

CHAPTER 13

Insurance and Bonding

INSURANCE

Insurance is an esoteric part of development finance about which many lending officers know little more than that it must be in place before or at closing. For some, that is all the knowledge they need. However, even if it never is used, if you do not know at least the basics of insurance, you can compromise your position as a knowledgeable professional.

If there is an occurrence that results in a claim, insurance can be the major variable that determines a successful loan paydown or a situation filled with litigation and finger-pointing. This chapter will provide enough information for you to ask the right questions and understand broad insurance issues.

THE INSURANCE CONSULTANT

Although purchasing insurance is not overly complex, so much is at stake if there is a loss that all lending institutions should have an in-house insurance department or an insurance consultant. The insurance consultant may be an independent professional who works on retainer or on a fee basis with your institution or may be the real estate department's closing attorney. His job is basically threefold:

- To review and recommend the types of insurance required
- To review and recommend the amounts of coverage
- To review and approve the actual binders and policies

YOUR CLOSING ATTORNEY

Although you may receive insurance material directly from the borrower or its insurance agent, you are equally likely to receive it from your closing attorney. It is your attorney's responsibility to follow up and make sure that all the insurance material is received before closing.

Experienced attorneys will have closed dozens of real estate loans and probably will have hundreds of closing binders to which to refer. They should be able to make suggestions about the amount of coverage that is desirable. Many smaller lending institutions that cannot afford to carry an insurance specialist use the closing attorney as the insurance consultant. However, since the closing attorney is probably not an insurance expert, if things go wrong, he will not take responsibility for omissions or errors.

You always should make sure that your attorney either tells you about or sends you insurance information for your approval. You in turn always should consult with and obtain the approval of your insurance consultant before closing. Whether your consultant is an actual expert in the field or an attorney (including a closing attorney), you should document conversations with him in your working file in case there is a loss and the policy does not cover it adequately. If you work for a smaller institution, it may be your responsibility to make sure that the borrower has in place the right types and amounts of insurance.

INSURANCE BINDER

The process of obtaining insurance starts when the borrower calls his insurance agent and discusses the property's acquisition, the broad aspects of the construction project, the anticipated hard and soft cost budgets, the amount of equity and debt, the construction period, and a description of the final completed project. The insurance agent will make suggestions to the borrower about the type of policy needed, its structure, and the amounts of coverage. He then will find an insurance company that will underwrite the policy and call back the borrower with the insurer's terms and the premium costs, including installment payment options. This will be followed up with a letter describing the types and amounts of coverage. Often closings are postponed for weeks, months, or even years. As a result, the borrower may not know exactly when he will own the property and when it will be necessary to purchase insurance.[1]

Since the acquisition of a property is very likely to be indeterminate, it is not exceptional for the borrower not to have an insurance policy to present at the closing. Instead, the borrower will present to you or your closing attorney a two- or three-page binder. A binder is used because the insurance policy can be hundreds of pages long and thus can take weeks to produce by the insurance company before it can be delivered to the borrower.

Even though the insurance agent creates the insurance binder, it is binding on the insurance company. That is, if there is any loss or claim from the time the binder was produced, the named insurance company will be liable for any legitimate claim. The binder should be on a standard recognized form.[2]

An insurance binder often surprises the uninitiated because only a few sheets of paper can represent huge amounts of coverage. However, binders are taken as a matter of course at closings and should not be cause for major concern. Most lenders have a policy by which after the closing the borrower will undertake to deliver a full insurance policy within 60 days or it will not receive its next loan advance.

The Problem with a Binder

The apparent problem with a binder is that it is impossible to distill a large policy into a few pages. Therefore, in the event of a claim there is a level of ambiguity that translates into a higher degree of risk. Something that will be clear in a policy may not show up in the binder.[3] Mitigating that risk is the fact that it is unlikely that there

---

[1] As discussed elsewhere in this book, reasons for delays can include the discovery of environmental problems, an unclear title, a delay in the seller's vacating of the property if it is occupied, discrepancies in the property description that force the seller and the buyer to renegotiate, and delays in the lender's approval process.

[2] Accord Corporation, for example, provides a form that is widely recognized and often used as evidence of insurance.

[3] Note that even after the receipt of an insurance policy or policies, there can be unintentional ambiguity. A famous case involves the destruction of the World Trade Center (WTC) in New York City. The leasee of the WTC, Larry Silverstein, claimed that there were two separate attacks since separate planes hit the two towers at different times. Those attacks were, he contended, two separate occurrences. The insurance companies stated that the incident was a well-coordinated single attack and therefore should be considered as only one occurrence. On December 6, 2004, after eleven days of deliberation, a federal jury agreed with Silverstein's interpretation. The difference was extraordinary. Mr. Silverstein could collect up to $2.2 billion, twice as much as the insurance companies claimed they owed him. The decision is under appeal.

will be a major claim in the short period between the issuance of the binder and the receipt of the policy. Also, as was noted above, the binder is a legal contract that binds the insurance company to the types and amounts of insurance specified. If there is a loss occurrence, the insurance company by law must act in good faith.

INSURABLE VALUE

Insurable value is the replacement cost or actual cash value of a project. The replacement cost value is the cost to replace the property with a functionally equivalent structure of comparable material and quality. In other words, it is the hard cost and soft cost of all the improvements. The actual cash value is the same as the replacement cost value but includes a deduction for depreciation. Since depreciation can be interpreted differently (physical depreciation, obsolescence, etc.), when part of the project involves an existing structure, such as the construction of an addition to an existing building, it is better to obtain a replacement cost policy. Replacement value should not be confused with reproduction value. Reproduction is essentially the reconstruction of a replica of the existing structure. For an existing building, this may not be feasible.

For instance, an old residential walk-up apartment building would not be reproduced today. It would be replaced with a modern walk-up or elevator apartment building with newer materials, perhaps a better design, and more safety features not only because of market demand but to satisfy modern building codes (e.g. a building wide sprinkler system, fire-rated walls between apartments and common areas, a ramp for handicap access, and so on). The result is that replacement costs, since they lack a deduction for depreciation and obsolescence, can be considerably more than the functional value of the existing building.

In cases in which part or all of an existing structure will remain as a component of a new project and the existing structure is older and is not in conformity with current laws, you should ask about ordinance coverage. Ordinance coverage is necessary to insure against an occurrence in which a substantial portion of an older structure is destroyed. In these cases, when part of the structure still stands, local laws may require that this remaining portion of the building be torn down. Ordinance coverage will pay for the loss of the entire building and the cost of demolition. If the structure is repaired or rebuilt, additional costs incurred to comply with modern codes and requirements will be covered as well. Without ordinance coverage, there could be a significant difference between coverage and costs.

THE RIGHT VALUE

As will be discussed below, arriving at the right value for a property is a very important factor in purchasing insurance. Being under-insured can be catastrophic to both the borrower and the lender. When a construction loan will fund a renovation of an existing structure that has considerable value in relation to the construction costs, the borrower's policy should be for an amount equal to at least the future value of the property with improvements as indicated in your appraisal. For a new construction project, the best method of valuation is the amount of the hard cost budget as reviewed by your inspecting engineer (additional insurance to cover soft costs and noneligible hard costs will be discussed below).

If the buyer values the property too high or buys too much insurance, he will pay a higher premium. If he values the property too low or buys too little insurance, he will pay a lower premium. However, no matter how much insurance he buys, if there is a casualty, he will be able to collect only up to the loss. Furthermore, if the loss exceeds his insurance limit, he will be able to collect only up to his limit.

Let's say that a property was purchased for $4 million. Since the property is in an excellent location and the building on it is obsolete, the land was attributed a value of $3 million (land is not insurable since it is assumed to be not damageable) and the building was attributed a value of $1 million. The owner planned to perform a major rehabilitation and upgrade, incorporating the existing building into the project, with anticipated construction costs of another $5 million. The borrower therefore obtained a policy for $6 million (the value of the existing building plus construction costs) with a $100,000 deductible. After the borrower closed on the purchase of the property, a fire destroyed it. The fire occurred right after the property was purchased, and no new construction was performed. Although the borrower attributed a value to the existing building of only $1 million (the shell), after the fire both the insurance company's adjuster and the borrower's adjuster (whom the borrower hired) indicated that the replacement cost value of the shell was $3 million.

Subsequently, the borrower received $2,900,000 from his insurance company. This was $1,900,000 more than what he considered the building's value to be. In this example, not considering soft cost expenses, the fire actually benefited him, at least from his valuation standpoint, by $1,900,000. If the borrower had had a policy with a sublimit, the outcome would have been different.

Sublimits

In the example above, the borrower had a total of $6 million in insurance: $1 million to cover the existing building and $5 million to cover construction. Modifying the example, let's say that on his $6 million policy the borrower asked his insurance agent to limit the amount of coverage on the building to a maximum of $1 million (a sublimit). That, his insurance agent told him, would reduce his premium costs substantially. The borrower, believing that the value of the building was only $1 million and that the likelihood of a loss was very low, decided to take the sublimit. After the fire occurred, even though both adjusters put a $3 million value on what it would cost to replace the building, the borrower received only $900,000 (the $1 million minus the $100,000 deductible). The sublimit cost the borrower $2 million.

As a lender, you should be very careful when you see sublimits. They are usually there to save the borrower money, but not always. It is not uncommon for the insurance company to demand a sublimit to place a ceiling on its maximum potential payout. Whatever a the origin of a sublimit is, if there is a loss, it can compromise your position as well as the borrower's by underfunding the costs involved in a casualty. There is nothing wrong with establishing sublimits as long as they are high enough to protect you and the borrower.

COINSURANCE

Coinsurance can have two meanings. One meaning refers to a situation in which two or more insurance companies share the risk on a single transaction or group of transactions. This can be important to the lender and the owner when the value of the property is very high and there is some doubt that if there is a loss, one individual insurance company will be able to cover it all. Insurers also may seek other insurers to spread the risk. The World Trade Center, for example, involved over 20 insurance companies.

The more common meaning of coinsurance, and therefore the more important one for the lender and the borrower, comes into play when the borrower, for a reduced premium, increases his risk to bear a larger and sometimes very substantial portion of a potential loss.[4] The real danger of coinsurance is that it is not well understood. Most lending officers and many purchasers understand coinsurance as simply the sharing of risk between the insured and the insurance company. They believe that if the purchaser has 80 percent coinsurance (80 percent is the standard), for any loss up to the amount of the policy, the insurance company will pay out 80 percent of the loss. Unfortunately, that belief is often wrong. In the event of a loss, the insured can receive substantially less than the 80 percent to which he thought he was entitled.

The Value

The important consideration in coinsurance is the value of the property. If the insured purchases coverage for less than the product of the coinsurance percentage and the "true" property value, the insured may not recover all of his loss. This occurs because the insurance company takes the amount of insurance bought and divides it by what it contends the purchaser should have bought (the coinsurance percentage multiplied by the true property value). This ratio then is multiplied by the actual loss. The result can be that the insured receives insurance proceeds that are considerably below his actual dollar loss. The best way to understand coinsurance is by illustration. The following examples show how coinsurance works.

Coinsurance Example 1

A. Let's say your borrower wanted to insure a $10 million building. He bought a policy with an 80 percent coinsurance clause and thus bought $8 million of insurance ($10,000,000 × 80% = $8,000,000). There is a $100,000 deductible in the policy.

Later, there is a fire in the building that results in $3,000,000 of damage. The borrower will get back $2,900,000 because he bought the amount necessary to satisfy the 80 percent coinsurance requirement.

---

[4] Coinsurance often is written into policies by the insurer, with no choice given to the purchaser. The variable is not whether to take it but what the percentage will be. Sometimes an insurer will require that less than 100 percent of the value be purchased if the risks of loss are deemed too high.

In this case, the insurance company actually funded 96.7 percent of the loss (100 percent minus the deductible), which is well above the 80 percent expected by an unknowledgeable observer.

B. Using the same example, if the fire results in $4 million in damage, the borrower will get back $3,900,000.

C. Using the same example, if the fire results in $9 million in damage, the borrower will get back only $7,900,000 because the limit of his policy is $8 million with a $100,000 deductible.

Coinsurance Example 2

Using Example 1A, this time the borrower valued the building at $7 million and purchased $5,600,000 of coverage ($7,000,000 × 80% = $5,600,000). After the fire, the insurance company valued the property at $10 million. Even though the $5,600,000 of insurance coverage is higher than the $3 million loss, the maximum amount he can receive from his insurance is reduced significantly:

True value of property	$10,000,000
Coinsurance percentage	80%
Amount of insurance that "should have" been purchased	$8,000,000
Amount of insurance purchased	$5,600,000
Deductible	$100,000

The borrower purchased only 70 percent of the coinsurance amount ($5,600,000/$8,000,000 = 70%). Therefore, he is eligible to receive only $2 million:

Amount of casualty	$3,000,000
Percentage of loss allowable	70%
70% of $3,000,000 =	$2,100,000
Deductible	$100,000
Insurance company's payout	$2,000,000

Now the borrower receives only 67 percent of the loss (70 percent less the deductible), which is significantly below the 77 percent expected by an unknowledgeable observer.

Using Example 1B but changing the coverage again to $5,600,000, the result will be an insurance payout of only $2,700,000, $1,200,000 below what the insured would have received if he had based his coverage on the building's true value ([($5,600,000/ $8,000,000) × $4,000,000] –$100,000 = $2,700,000).

Whenever your borrower uses coinsurance, your insurance consultant should make sure that you are protected adequately. On the surface, coinsurance may reduce costs considerably by decreasing the insurance premium, but it has its dangers. If the amount of the insurance proceeds is well below the loss, will the borrower have the capital and liquidity to cover the difference? If he was naive or knowingly took on too much risk to avoid paying a higher insurance premium, he and the lender may face a loss that could have been prevented.

Keeping Value Current

In a policy with a coinsurance clause, the value of a property at the time of an occurrence is extremely important. Unfortunately, it is the insured, not the insurance agent or the insurance company, who is responsible for making sure that the property's value does not outpace its insurance coverage. There are three basic ways this can be prevented:

1. A third-party appraisal is performed by a qualified appraisal firm.
2. The value of any existing improvements is agreed on, and then the actual construction costs of the project are added.
3. A value is set by the insurance company.

With the third option, the insurance agent should try to find a company willing to agree to include a clause by which the insurance company recognizes that the amount of insurance purchased is the amount that should be carried. On new construction projects, it should not be difficult to agree on value since, especially on a replacement cost basis, there will be no subtractions for depreciation or obsolescence.

If the development loan funds into a term loan, you and the borrower will have to review the value of the property periodically. You also may want to encourage the borrower to purchase optional coverage that takes inflation into account. Usually the insurance company will multiply the property value by an inflation index such as the CPI (consumer price index), increasing coverage each year. In this way, the property value increases automatically and is fully covered. This lets you avoid any shortage that may occur under the coinsurance clause.

COVERAGE OF SOFT COSTS

The discussion so far has dealt primarily with hard costs. Soft cost losses also can be painfully high; this is true particularly as the project progresses because monthly loan advances increase the principal outstanding and therefore interest costs. Taxes also can be a large expense factor.[5] To cover soft costs, the borrower should have soft cost insurance with a limit calculated on the basis of a worst-case scenario. An example of a worst-case scenario is when the entire loan principal is outstanding and interest will have to be covered for at least eight months. Often it is assumed that if the property cannot be rebuilt to its state before a casualty within 8 to 12 months (this assumes full interest costs), insurance proceeds will be used to pay down the development loan. With soft cost insurance, if the decision to rebuild is made, construction loan interest, taxes, and other fixed costs will be covered as construction proceeds. Soft cost insurance is similar to rental insurance for occupied properties. Its primary purpose is to cover fixed costs, which mostly consist of interest and taxes.

FLOOD INSURANCE

Flood insurance is a product that is expensive and sometimes hard to obtain in areas that are prone to periods of flooding. In areas that are designated flood zones but where there is almost no likelihood of a flood, almost all lenders require flood insurance because their lending policy dictates it. Actually, flood insurance is the responsibility of the developer and, regardless of its cost or the likelihood of a flood, should be a requirement if the property is in a flood zone. Only in very limited circumstances can it be waived.[6]

HAZARD AND GENERAL LIABILITY INSURANCE

Hazard insurance covers occurrences of fire, vandalism, and some natural events. It is a must on virtually all real property:

---

[5] If the project is an existing building that is experiencing major improvements or if the project consists entirely of new construction, taxes usually will be relatively low until the project is complete and the property is reassessed.

[6] One example occurred in New York City, where there is a flood zone within a landlocked area because of an underground spring that no longer exists. In this case, the construction lender waived the flood insurance requirement. A condominium apartment building was built on the site, and end loan lenders (those which made loans to individuals who bought the condominium apartments) also waived that requirement.

new developments as well as existing properties. In addition, the borrower must have coverage for liability and for personal property.

UMBRELLA COVERAGE

An umbrella policy raises the limits of one or more existing general liability insurance policies and may provide additional protections that the existing policies lack. The first reason is almost always the one that motivates its purchase. If there is a loss, the umbrella policy will fund the difference between what the underlying insurance amount covers and what the actual loss is. As a simple example, a real property owner purchased an underlying policy with a limit of $1 million and an umbrella policy with a limit of $2 million. Subsequently, a fire caused $2 million in damage. The underlying policy would pay out $1 million (excluding deductibles), and the umbrella would pay out the additional $1 million. Umbrella policies almost always are purchased on the recommendation of the borrower's insurance agent. The coverage they provide above that provided by the underlying policy is relatively inexpensive. Umbrella policies have two important features: self-insured retention (SIR) and exclusions and limitations.

SELF-INSURED RETENTION

Self-insured retention (SIR) is similar to a deductible, and most umbrella policies have it. Let's assume that a boiler leaks and flooding causes $100,000 in damage. The insured has a policy that will cover $50,000 in water damage and a $250,000 umbrella policy with a $25,000 SIR that will cover water damage. The result is that the underlying policy will pay $50,000 and the umbrella will pay the remaining $50,000 (the SIR under the umbrella was covered by the underlying policy). If the scenario is changed slightly so that the underlying policy does not cover water damage, the insured will have to pay $25,000 and the umbrella policy will cover the remaining $75,000. With SIR, in the event of a loss, if the underlying policy covers the loss in an amount equal to or greater than the SIR, the umbrella policy will cover any additional loss amounts up to its limit. If the loss is not covered by an underlying policy, the insured will have to cover his loss up to the retention amount before the umbrella policy will cover any additional amounts.

Exclusions and Limitations

Exclusions and limitations are used extensively in an umbrella policy to prevent the insurance company from taking undue risk without compensation. One way to accomplish this is for the insurance company to make the policy a "following form" one. With this policy, the types and exclusions in the underlying policy follow the same form in the umbrella. The umbrella policy therefore is purchased primarily to increase coverage amounts, not to plug up uninsured areas of the underlying policy.

BLANKET POLICY

The term *blanket policy* can have two meanings. Most often it is insurance that covers two or more properties. Under the blanket policy, there is usually a lump sum of coverage (a dollar amount that covers all insured properties but with no specific dollar amount allocated to any one). For an owner with coinsurance, this can be an advantage since the value of each property covered can be argued over. The property that experienced the loss can be claimed to be insured for the maximum percentage of its value. Often, under a blanket policy, there is a single limit of liability for all types of properties at all the locations covered by the policy. Alternatively, each of the properties covered can be assigned an agreed-to value. This can help prevent ambiguity. However, assigning a dollar number can hurt if the value assigned to a particular property is below (or above if coinsurance exists) the actual value of that property if it experiences a loss.

Another meaning that is used less often is operative when a blanket policy insures both a building and its contents. Usually, each is underwritten in a separate policy: one for the building and one for its contents.

WORKER'S COMPENSATION

Worker's compensation insurance is required in all states except Texas. It is relied on if a worker has an accident that causes injury or a health problem that resulted from his job. Each state has its own regulations. In some states, worker's compensation is needed even if the employer has only one employee. In other states, it is required only when the developer reaches a threshold of a few employees (e.g., three or more). The insurance is no-fault, which means that regardless of whether the employee received an injury or became ill solely through his own action or inaction, the employer is financially liable. In return for this ongoing potential liability, the employer avoids the time and expense of litigation and the effort needed to defend against spurious claims and possible long-term costs in the event of an accident or illness. All premiums are paid by the employer. The insurance is free to employees. Premiums vary with the purchaser's business (they are indexed to several hundred occupational codes) and the insurer. For employees of contractors, where the risk of injury is higher than is the case with, say, office workers, the premiums are higher. Depending on the track record of the employer, premiums can decline or increase. Each state determines how much coverage an employer must buy and what percentage of each employee's salary will be paid if there is an accident or illness. Most states also allow the employer to be self-insured, but this is obviously very risky and it is not allowed under almost all lending institutions' loan policies.

In all cases in which there are contractors or subcontractors on the job, before they are allowed to work on the site, they must produce adequate proof of worker's compensation insurance. This proof should be forwarded to your inspecting engineer and/or to your loan servicer.

Worker's compensation insurance never should be substituted for the borrower's own separate insurance policy because worker's compensation is limited in its coverage. There is always a strong possibility that the borrower will be sued if there is an accident that will not be covered or will be covered only partially (e.g., gross negligence by the employer that resulted in a serious injury). The potential liability, especially with a serious injury, can be very high.

DUPLICATE INSURANCE

With duplicate insurance there are two or more insurance policies covering the same property. Unlike life insurance, in which the more a person pays, the more he gets, in real estate he cannot receive more than the amount of his loss. Therefore, if a borrower has more than one policy on a property aggregating to more than 100 percent of its value, in the case of a complete loss he can receive no more than 100 percent. Depending on the policies and the law, there will be a priority in which one insurer will fund before the other or both will fund proportionally.

AN OCCURRENCE

In the event of an accident or loss the borrower should notify the insurance company and the lender immediately. If the occurrence is significant and has left the property in a state in which further damage can occur readily or can compromise safety if it is not addressed immediately, the insurance company will make a quick advance to enable the borrower to do emergency work as needed. This should limit the possibility of additional costs and a higher insurance claim. The insurance company then will send in a company adjuster who is trained to make a careful and detailed assessment of the property. He will itemize the damage and then assign a dollar value to it. Most borrowers hire their own adjusters, especially since the adjuster often works on a contingency basis.[7] Almost always, the insurance company's adjuster will come in with a lower dollar amount then will the borrower's adjuster. After having a chance to asses the damage further, the insurance company will make one more, usually final advance. Insurance company advances ordinarily come in the form of a check rather than a wire transfer so that a paper trail is produced. The check will be made out to both the borrower and the lender.

The lending institution initially may not be involved because of a lack of awareness. Although the borrower should notify you as soon as possible (this is always required in the insurance section of the loan documentation), he will be preoccupied with a variety of issues that require his immediate attention. However, you can be fairly certain that you will be notified, even if the borrower does not do this, by the insurance company since your institution is named on the binder and the policy as an additionally insured mortgagee.[8]

Once you are notified, you should do the following:

- Call your insurance representative immediately.
- Call your attorney immediately.
- Ask both if you can make an advance without compromising your loan or its position.

---

[7] There is a lucrative industry that consists of independent adjusters who earn a living by contesting insurance companies' payouts. In conjunction with attorneys, on large claims they are compensated by taking a percentage of the difference between what the insurer initially offers and what the final payout is.

[8] Note that some policies indicate that the insurer will give notice to the lender. Others indicate that the insurer only will attempt to give notice to the lender.

- Be prepared to visit the site, talk with the borrower and the inspecting engineer, and make several presentations to senior management that are followed up with written memorandums about the loan and the property's status.

Under the loan documentation, the lender should have the right to receive all of the insurance proceeds and hold them in escrow and have the authority to fund them out just as it would with construction loan advances (the review of all contracts, the filling out of all advance documentation, including AIA forms and lien waivers, etc).[9] Initially, because of the uncertainty and confusion surrounding a major occurrence, you may be called on to make a quick advance to cover emergency repairs that were or will be reimbursed by the insurer. However, by the time the next advance is requested, your inspecting engineer should have a working budget for the additional work to be done.[10] This is crucial because as the lender, you should be careful that the loan remains in balance. That is, when all the insurance proceeds and the loan are fully funded, there should be enough to complete the job as planned.

In the vast majority of insurance claims, it will be determined that it is feasible to repair or rebuild the damaged areas and finish the construction project. The borrower is the one who will fight with the insurance company for the most money in the shortest amount of time. This is his fight, not the lending institution's. Once the initial confusion caused by an occurrence has been resolved and the question of what the damages are has been answered, the work for the lending officer becomes almost routine. Your job will be to make sure that funds are advanced according to the loan documents and that the aggregate amount of money from insurance, your loan, and the borrower is enough to complete the project. From the day you become aware of the occurrence, you should document everything in a working file. Later, when a course of action is determined, you can cull notes, extraneous memorandums, and correspondence.

---

[9] Note that most loan documents contain a provision by which the borrower cannot settle a claim over a certain threshold without the consent of the lender.

[10] It is not uncommon for your inspecting engineering firm to lack the in-house expertise to create a complete and comprehensive budget. The engineer may need specialists to aid him in doing this.

BONDING

Many lending institutions' credit criteria require that the principal contractor or contractors be bonded. Bonding is insurance issued by an insurance company (surety) for the benefit of the owner (and the lender).

There are two types of bonds: completion and performance. Completion bonds are less common because they do not cap expenses. Therefore, an owner probably will be protected with only a performance bond. Performance bonds basically promise that if the bonded contractor does not finish the work under its contract, the bonding company will pay for the completion of the contract up to the face amount of the bond. Ordinarily, the bonding company will have to pay out no more than 10 percent of the amount of the contract because the bonding company's contractor will requisition for and receive the remaining amount of funds available under the development loan. If all the funds under the loan allocated for the particular trade have been advanced, often 90 percent of the work already has been completed.

In addition to the insurance protection, a positive and important aspect of a bond for the owner and the lender is that the contractor is indeed bondable. The bonding company performs an extensive review that includes examining the contractor's tax returns, balance sheet, principals' and firm's résumés, and background checks. Only after a review of the contractor's history, stability, and financial soundness will a surety grant an entity bonding capacity. This provides at least some indication that the contractor can and will perform.

The negative aspect of a bond is the difficulty of obtaining relief from the surety when there is a claim. This is due to several factors, including the number and nature of the parties involved (the owner, lender, contractor, and surety), the often debatable characteristics of performance or lack of performance, and state laws.

The Bond Is a Contract

A bond is a contract that involves the surety, the owner, the contractor, and the lender. To protect the lending institution, the following issues must be dealt with:

- The name of your institution as well as that of the owner (borrower) should be recorded on the bond as an obligee.

The dual obligee endorsement is important for several reasons. One reason is that the coverage provided by the bond will remain intact if your institution steps into the borrower's shoes. It gives and preserves the lender's protection and rights as the new "developer." Another reason is that as a party to the policy, you will be alerted to any correspondence between the surety and your borrower concerning change orders and increases in costs.

- It is important for the developer to make sure the bond allows for increases in costs and modifications of plans and specifications.

  As an obligee and therefore a party to the insurance contract, you should be able to obtain language that allows for up to a 10 percent increase in costs before a bond modification is required (of course, the borrower may have to pay an additional premium).

- You and the surety must approve submissions of change orders.

  Initially, the surety must review and approve the contract, the plans, and the specifications. On the basis of that material, the surety will issue a bond. In regard to subsequent submissions of changes in plans, specifications, and contract amounts, the requirements to the surety should be identical to the requirements to you under your building loan agreement. Holdback amounts (retainage) also should be equal. If the retainage is 10 percent on your loan, make sure the construction contract also has 10 percent retainage. This will prevent confusion and conflict.

- All contractors that are bonded should have fixed-price contracts so that the amount of the bond can be finite and determinable. A time and materials contract is very difficult to put a final number on and easily can exceed your and the borrower's estimates.

- Make sure that the prime contractor is bonded. With the prime contractor bonded, the bonding company has fewer defenses against the developer if it is called on to honor its bond (the reasons for this will be discussed later in this chapter).

A performance bond is not a guarantee. There are often many ways for a bonding company to avoid making a payment. The fact that a bonded contractor does not perform in accordance with its contract provides no real assurance that the borrower (or lender) will recover losses resulting from the contractor's failure. Often the only recourse available to the obligees is to file a suit against the surety. Here are some of the dangers that lead to nonrelief and possible litigation:

- The developer can modify plans and specifications without telling the surety or the lender.[11,12]

  In a construction project, it is extremely rare for a job to proceed without some modifications that can be deemed material in nature. Even a seemingly small change, such as the movement of a chase a couple of feet from its location in the original plans, can cause tremendous changes in a particular contractor's work (a chase is an enclosed space created to run conduit, pipes, and so on, vertically through a structure). For instance, the relocation of a chase may require a plumber to change the size of risers (pipes), add branching (horizontal piping), and add or remove valves. This may affect other trades, such as the electrician, who may have to relocate cables, wires, switches, and lights. The problem is that if later a bonded contractor fails to perform, the surety can use the lack of notification as an effective defense. Essentially, the surety will claim that it insured the completion of a different scope of work.

- The developer or his employees or other trades interfere with the bonded contractor so that it is impossible for it to complete its work under the terms of its contract.

  In the construction industry, there is typically a high level of interdependence among contractors. If there are unusual delays or subpar workmanship on the part of one contractor, that can have ramifications for many of the others. For instance, if the proper electrical service is

---

[11] Although this is not common, even your borrower may not know about significant job changes. This is the case because many changes are made as conditions dictate by the job superintendent and construction personnel at the site level. They are often unaware of or not concerned with the possible negative ramifications of their on-site decisions.

[12] Changes in work and a review by the bonding company should not hold up the project. The work goes forward while the bonding company is doing its review.

not provided for the elevator, the elevator contractor cannot complete its installation. If the masonry contractor building the elevator shaft puts metal plates in the wrong locations, the matter will have to be corrected before elevator installation can begin. The ability of almost all contractors to complete their contracted tasks depends on others. When a project runs into trouble, it is not unusual for contactors to point fingers at one another, claiming that the others are responsible for the job's problems. The surety's defense is that the contractor could not complete its work not because it was negligent or delinquent but because other entities prevented it from doing so.

One way to mitigate this danger is to have only the general contractor and major prime subcontractors bonded. Since the general contractor "controls" all or most of the subcontractors, nobody else is responsible if it fails to complete the project. Therefore, it is much harder for the surety to use the defense that others interfered with the GC, resulting in its inability to complete the project.

• The lender overadvances or underadvances requisitions.

If you underadvance, the borrower may underpay the contractor and state, perhaps rightly, that the lender did not recognize the dollar amount of the contractor's finished work. Later, the surety can defend itself against a claim by charging that the work was not finished because the contractor was not paid its due. It was not the contractor but the borrower that defaulted under its contract. In these cases, the surety may refer to the lender's inspecting engineer's report, among other material, to verify that the level of work performed dictated advancing amounts higher than what actually was funded.

If you overadvance, the surety can use the defense that the lender had less money available than it should have had under the contract to finish the job. Interestingly, the bonding company may agree with the obligee that the contractor has defaulted. However, the reduced amount available for the new contractor to draw against increases the amount that the surety company must pay. If the surety company successfully claims that the owner overfunded by an amount that exceeds the estimated amount needed to complete the remainder of the job, the surety may end up paying nothing.

The bottom line is that you should fund accurately with substantial weight given to your inspecting engineer's report since either underpayments or overpayments to the contractor can give the surety a winning defense.

When the General Contractor Is the Owner

Often the general contractor and the owner are the same entity, especially on smaller projects but increasingly on larger ones in which the owner-borrower came from the general contracting business. If this is the case, it will be impossible for the GC to obtain a bond because it would be an insurance policy against itself: The owner cannot insure against its own actions or inactions. Even when the two entities are the same, some senior lending officers insist on a bond because they do not understand what it is. If institutional policy dictates bonding and the owner is the GC, ask it to obtain bonds from its major subcontractors.

The Costs

The cost of a bond is significant. It is typical for a surety company to charge from 1 percent to 2.5 percent of the full face amount of the bond. For example, if a contractor has a $5 million contract, the bond will add about $100,000 to the cost of the job ($5,000,000 × 2% = $100,000). Noting that in the event of a default by the contractor the bonding company probably will have to pay only about 10 percent of the bond's face amount, the cost against the actual insurance risk will be much higher. In this example using a $5 million contract, the cost of insurance is effectively 20 percent ($100,000 bond premium / $5,000,000 contract × 10% payout = 20 percent).

Although it is paid by the contractor, the cost usually is passed on to the developer in the form of a higher contract amount (although it can be paid by the borrower and listed in the budget as a separate line item). Since the bond is expensive and offers questionable coverage, some developers and lenders look for alternatives.[13]

---

[13] To balance lender protection, practicality, and costs, one lending institution requires bonding only by contractors that have contracts equal to 5 percent of the project's total hard cost budget and exceed a minimum of $750,000. This way, only a limited number of contractors are bonded, usually the major ones, which is what the lender wants.

An Alternative to a Bond

As has been noted in this chapter, requiring bonds from primary contactors has positive aspects, but ironically, collecting on the bond in the case of a contractor's failure to perform is not always a likely scenario. Rather, it provides some comfort to the developer and the lender that the bonded contractor is an entity with a history and status sufficient for a bonding company to take an insurance risk on it.

Many lenders recognize that the value of a bond is limited and typically forgo the requirement that the principal contractors be bonded. Other lenders, desiring some form of protection (particularly banks), in lieu of a bond ask for a clean irrevocable letter of credit (LC). Its face amount is usually equal to 10 percent of the construction contract. The LC is issued by a third party acceptable to the lending institution.[14,15]

Receiving an LC has several advantages:

- The letter of credit can be drawn down immediately, as opposed to a bond, which at best takes weeks or much longer to be honored.

- The probability of receiving funds under the LC is close to 100 percent, as opposed to a bond, where the obligee may receive nothing.

- As was noted above, most bonds pay out 10 percent or less of the face amount. This is the case because the balance of construction funds from the lender is usually sufficient to accomplish 90 percent or more of the construction under the contract. Therefore, an LC for 10 percent of the construction contract is ordinarily sufficient to cover the owner-lender if the contractor fails to perform. Since the LC is for only 10 percent of the contract amount and the fee for an LC is usually about 1 percent of its face amount, the cost to the contractor is very reasonable.

---

[14] The issuer of the LC will receive a fee that will compensate it for its risk. Sometimes the contractor will collateralize the LC with cash or marketable securities or another form of collateral. This of course reduces the issuer's risk if the LC is drawn.

[15] An additional alternative to a bond, if the lender is a bank, is the deposit or a restriction on an existing deposit from the contractor equal to 10 percent of the construction contract. In some cases in which the contractor is well established and maintains high deposit balances, this may not be difficult to obtain. In most cases, however, a contractor will not have the amount needed available or will resist tying up its funds.

- There are many more institutions that issue LCs than there are sureties that issue bonds. An LC may be easier for a contractor to obtain than a bond.

Depending on competitive conditions, the financial and performance strength of the borrower, and his track record with your institution, you may not succeed in getting the borrower to agree to obtain LCs or bonds from the prime contractors. However, if a prime contractor is not bondable, refuses to subject itself to the scrutiny necessary for bonding or obtaining an LC, or refuses to pay the added expense, that should not necessarily be a major deterrent to making the development loan.[16] Since you are proposing making a loan to the developer, you should be fairly confident that he is competent and capable. It is his project. He will be hiring the contractors, and he should be making sure that they perform according to their contractual obligations. If he is prolific, he probably has strong and proven mutually beneficial relationships with many of the project's contractors, reducing his and your risk considerably. Whether contractors are bonded or not, with his equity at stake and his experience, the borrower is a good firewall against any contractor problems that may arise later.[17]

Author's Note
Insurance and bonding can be complex and involve specific knowledge of regulations and law. For developers, they require the use of professionals. For lenders, they may never become an issue or a concern until a problem surfaces. Then, depending on its nature and severity, this still may be an issue to be worked out independently and completely by the borrower. Even with professional help, by knowing the fundamentals, the lender and the developer can avoid costly and avoidable mistakes (misunderstanding coinsurance, for example).

---

[16] This of course is predicated on your institution having a policy that allows development loans to be made without bonding requirements or that allows for flexibility in its bonding policy.

[17] As part of your underwriting analysis, you may want to do some checking of the financial worthiness, experience, credentials, and background of the general contractor and primary contractors, particularly on smaller projects in which names and track records are unknown. Your degree of diligence is a function of your overall comfort level with the borrower and the project.

CHAPTER 14

Title Insurance and Lien Law

TITLE INSURANCE FOR SALES

If I buy a property from Mr. X on Monday morning and Mr. X sells the property again on Tuesday morning to someone else (in effect selling the property twice, which is obviously illegal), and both transactions occurred with attorneys, title companies, bankers, and the like present so that each closing was performed in a professional manner, on Wednesday do I or does someone else own the property? The simple answer is that the new owner is the one whose title company properly recorded the sale at the appropriate recording office first. The buyer who lost out may have closed a day earlier, but what counts is not when the transaction occurred but when it was recorded. Fortunately, it is the title company's responsibility (and risk) to record the sale as soon as possible. The buyer who thought that he owned the property and subsequently found out that he did not should receive full compensation from his title company under the title insurance policy. [1,2]

Because of the complexity of real estate law and the usually significant amounts of money that change hands, almost no sale occurs in the United States without title insurance. The title company

---

[1] Note that this is true in some states but not in others. In several states it is when the transaction is acknowledged, not when it is filed, that establishes priority.

[2] Note that title insurance does not cover closing costs, mortgage costs, attorneys' fees, and so forth. Therefore, the purchaser still will experience a loss.

ensures that the sale of the property to the new owner has been conducted in such a way that the new owner is indeed the new owner. In most transactions, it is the title insurer's responsibility to make sure that there is a "clean" title or, if there is not, that the liens and/or easements are known and addressed by the buyer and the seller. If later there is a claim of ownership on the property by an unknown third party, the title company will insure the owner against that claim. The insurance is for the full purchase price (value) of the property.[3]

LOANS

Title insurance is a must on any loan collateralized by real estate. For the lender, which usually is the senior creditor, the title company ensures that it indeed will have first priority (or second, third, etc., depending on the structure of the transaction) and ensures payment of the amount of the policy, which is equal to the amount of the loan. If there are any liens, claims, or lis pendens[4] superior to the lender's, they will show up in a search performed by the title company and be addressed before the loan closing.

COVERAGE

Title insurance covers illegal activities such as fraud and forged documents. It also covers easements such as access to roads or utility equipment. Title insurance does not cover zoning and use restrictions or governmental actions. If making your loan requires proof or assurances that a project can be developed legally on the real estate in question, you will have to look elsewhere (see Chapter 12).

---

[3] When the size of the transaction on a sale and/or a loan is very large, two or more insurers should share the risk on an allocated basis. A general rule is that the amount of insurance from any single title company should never be more than 25 percent of its assets.

[4] A lis pendens is a legal notice that is recorded to show pending litigation relating to real property and give notice that anyone acquiring an interest in that property subsequent to the date of the notice may be bound by the outcome of the litigation. If the outcome is favorable to the claimant, his claims will be senior in priority to all loan advances made after the lis pendens was filed.

CHAIN OF TITLE

A primary tool of a title insurance company is a review of recorded transfers of property ownership to establish a chain of title. The review may uncover easements and restrictions that can impose practical limitations on the property's use. A chain of title also may reveal clues about the current condition of a property. The name of a former owner that was or is involved in heavy manufacturing, for example, may arouse interest concerning potential environmental problems.

COSTS

Unlike most other types of insurance, title insurance is paid only once, at closing (for either a purchase or a loan). On a loan, the premium always is paid by the borrower even though its purpose is to protect the lender from losing its priority position (first mortgage, second mortgage, etc.). On a development loan, future loan advances are covered by the insurance company (initially free of charge and then for relatively low fees, depending on the number of advances) subject to its being notified and acknowledging that the lender remains insured before each advance.

LIEN LAW

The definition of a lien taken from a building loan agreement, a legal document essential to a development loan, is as follows:

> Lien: Any mortgage, pledge, hypothecation, assignment, deposit arrangement, encumbrance, lien (statutory or other), preference, priority or other security agreement or preferential arrangement of any kind or nature whatsoever (including, without limitation, any conditional sale or other title retention agreement, any financing lease having substantially the same economic effect as any of the foregoing, and the filing of any financing statement under the Uniform Commercial Code or comparable law of any jurisdiction).

Like many other areas of law, lien law is much more complicated than logic would dictate. It is a body of law that specifically addresses the priority of claims against real property by creditors and investors. A creditor can be a lender, a contractor who has worked on the property, a materialman (an entity such as a supply house that has delivered materials to the site such as lumber or kitchen cabinets), a municipality that is owed fees and taxes, a service provider, and virtually anyone who has provided any kind of labor, service, or material in exchange for money or the promise of money. Lien law is an absolute necessity that in most cases is invisible to the lender. One reason for the law's complexity is that it can vary significantly from state to state. These variances are sometimes strong enough to influence institutional lending policy, particularly when a blanket mortgage loan is contemplated on several properties in several states.[5]

Mechanic's Lien

In development lending, you and/or loan servicing personnel may deal with a mechanic's lien. A mechanic's lien (also called a construction lien or another term, depending on which state the lien is filed in) is a claim filed by a contractor or materialman against real property (a lien cannot be filed against a person or legal entity, only against real property). The lien puts on record in the municipality in which it was filed that a claim has been made for a specific amount of money by the filing entity for something it has done to or delivered to the property that has improved it. The work or the delivery of materials must have improved the property. This distinguishes a lien from other legal methods for payment, such as a vendor filing a civil suit in court when the delivery of goods and services has not been paid for. An engineer, for example, cannot file a mechanic's lien but can sue the client (a person or a legal entity) for money owed. A contractor who constructed an HVAC system on the basis of the engineer's specifications, however, can file a mechanic's lien because it physically improved the property.

Subcontractors, who work for contractors, also can file mechanic's liens in certain circumstances. When a contractor has a contractual relationship with the owner, the owner is responsible for paying the contractor. When a subcontractor has a contractual

---

[5] Since lien law is a technical subject and the rules are state-specific, this chapter will focus only on a few elements of New York, New Jersey, and Connecticut law. However, the discussion should give you an appreciation of lien law and how it can affect a lender. An attorney familiar with the laws of the state in which a property is located must be consulted before any transaction is consummated.

relationship with a contractor, the contractor is responsible for paying the subcontractor.

If the owner has not paid the contractor, the contractor may not have sufficient funds to pay its subcontractors. If this is the case, when the owner of the property is in arrears, the subcontractors may file mechanic's liens against the property. However, if the owner has paid the contractor and the contractor has not paid its subcontractors, the subcontractors cannot file mechanic's liens against the property. Instead, the subcontractors must take action directly against the contractor.

This protects an owner from paying for improvements twice: once to the contractor who was paid but did not advance funds to the subcontractors and again to the subcontractors who should have been paid by the contractor, not the owner.

Actions

Since it is the contractor that files the mechanic's lien, its obvious purpose is to protect the contractor. It gives him leverage against the property owner who benefited from his work. Once it is filed, the owner will have to take some action if he wants to sell the property or finance or refinance it or is prompted by a lender to remove the lien to comply with an existing mortgage loan. In a development loan, action may be prompted by the title company before the lender can make its next loan advance. If none of these circumstances are operative, the owner can choose to do nothing.

To avoid abuse of the law by contractors filing spurious liens and tying up a property in perpetuity, there are time limits on the life of a lien. During that life (including any allowable extensions), if the lien is not settled by the owner, the contractor must sue to foreclose on the property. If the contractor fails to sue to foreclose, the lien will expire. Once it expires, it can never be renewed.

Filing, Timing, and Other Matters

Filing a mechanic's lien usually requires that a contractor follow a stringent set of procedures. For instance, in New York a lien must be filed within eight months from the last day the contractor was on the job. A copy of the lien then must be sent to the owner by regular and certified mail within 30 days. Then an affidavit of service must be filed with the county clerk. If the filing is done in the wrong place or the lien is not sent properly, the lien will have no effect since it is deemed to be filed improperly. In New Jersey the filing procedure requires that the proposed lien along with supporting documentation be submitted to the American Arbitration Association for a hearing. At the hearing it is determined whether a lien is warranted and, if it is, the dollar amount. Only then can a lien be filed, but the submission must be made within 90 days from the last day the contractor was on the job. In Connecticut the time frame for filing is the same as it is New Jersey: A lien must be filed within 90 days from the last day the contractor was on the job.

Depending on the state the real property is situated in, the effects of a mechanic's lien can be significantly different. In New York, for instance, a mechanic's lien is filed in the county clerk's office of the county where the property is located, has a term of one year, can be renewed for an additional year, can be filed on the basis of an oral contract, and can be filed without first notifying the owner of the property. In New Jersey a lien is called a construction lien. A construction lien cannot be renewed and can be filed only if there is a written contract. The lienor must file a notice of unpaid balance concurrently with the owner and the county clerk of the county where the property is located. In Connecticut a lien that is filed after work has been completed moves into a position of priority that dates back to the day when the work started, not when the lien was filed (a retroactive lien).[6]

Calling for Title before Funding

Under a development loan, as a rule, loan advances always are made on the basis of a receipt by the loan administrator of a requisition from the borrower. After reviewing the requisition along with supporting material such as continuing proof of no intervening

---

[6] Connecticut laws and those like them can be particularly disturbing to a title company and a lender. A title search may indicate that the property is clear (there are no liens on the property). The lender then funds the requisition. At a later date, however, because a lien is retroactive, the lender finds itself in a subordinate position behind a contractor. Unfortunately, there is little protection in states where liens can become retroactive except to make sure that the title company always is notified and has given its approval to make a loan advance and that lien waivers are executed as part of the borrower's requisition (see Chapter 9 for a discussion of lien waivers). By calling for title, the lender effectively has laid off this risk to the title company.

liens and a report from the lender's inspecting engineer, the administrator (subject to required approvals that are dependent on the lending institution's guidelines but that in most cases include the loan officer), is ready to make a loan advance. One of the last steps in the process is notifying the title company. The title company will perform a title continuation that will uncover any liens that have been recorded against the property. If there are none, the title company will ensure that the advance will take priority over any liens that are filed subsequently or that may surface. If, however, the title search indicates that a lien has been filed, the title company should discuss with you and/or the administrator and the borrower the options available for addressing it. Those options include requiring the borrower to bond the lien, post money in an escrow account against it, or take some other action. Once an approval is received from the title company, the administrator can advance the loan funds.

The Loan Closing

Because a lien cannot be filed on a person, only on real property, after a closing a contractor can file a lien on a property even though it is owned by a different legal entity (the purchaser who is the new owner). Not wishing to postpone a closing, the purchaser's attorney, the lender's attorney, and the title company will take steps to ensure that the property is transferred lien-free to the purchaser. In New York, the seller will sign an affidavit stating that he did not have any work performed in the last eight months before the closing or that if he did, he paid the contractor in full (this effectively closes the eight-month window in which a contractor can file a lien). Then the title insurer will provide insurance to the purchaser against any mechanic's liens that may arise after the closing that are or were the responsibility of the seller. However, if a lien is discovered before closing, which is not unusual, the seller will be required to remove it. The most common way to do that as a closing approaches is to have the lien bonded (insured by a company that specializes in insuring against liens) or to pay the lien off.

In some states it can be crucial if certain types of contracts are signed before the closing of a loan. For example, in New York, brokerage costs, equipment costs, demolition costs, and land-clearing costs will be senior in priority to a mortgage if the contracts are signed before the mortgage is recorded even though work in all those categories may not have started. The borrower may have executed several contracts before the closing and recording of the mortgage. Therefore, before closing, the borrower is required to list all the contracts into which he has entered.

Priority and Timing

Lien law generally favors the contractor. Certain states have gone so far as to give priority to all liens even if only one was filed before a loan advance. If the lien is not satisfied by payment or bonding, it opens a "door," allowing all subsequent liens to move up in priority to the time to when the first lien was filed (which, because it was filed before loan funds were advanced, will be ahead of that advance and all future advances).

A typical scenario occurs when a borrower submits a large requisition. The title company uncovers a small lien, but the borrower puts pressure on the uninformed lending officer or administrator by stressing that the lien is small. He claims the lien is totally unwarranted and insists that the contractor filed it to spite him on the basis of some spurious argument. He needs the money right away to pay off his other contractors, who are doing a very good job. If he does not pay them what they are due, he claims, they may slow down on the job or, worse, walk away and file their own liens. The loan officer or the loan administrator, having formed a trusting relationship with the borrower through the loan underwriting experience and perhaps a lunch or two, agrees to make the advance, thinking that because the lien is small, it will be taken care of by the next advance. Then, a few weeks later, it is discovered that many more contractors have filed liens for much larger amounts against the lender's collateral. Unfortunately, the loan office learns that they are all ahead of his last advance in priority.[7]

The general rule is that all liens must be addressed. The lender never should advance funds unless the title company gives its approval. If a lien is outstanding and the title company agrees to fund, it is the title company's risk, not the lender's.

---

[7] In a situation like this, perhaps the best thing the employee can do is look for another job. Upward mobility in his current firm may no longer exist.

Public Notice of a Construction Loan

In terms of public disclosure, in New York an affidavit called Section 22 is filed with every construction loan. The affidavit puts on public record the amount of money available to fund hard construction costs. Contractors have access to the record and can be assured that there is at least a certain amount of funds available to cover the amounts of their contracts. In practice, very few contractors check the affidavit before entering into a contract.

Although it is a good idea in theory, in certain circumstances the affidavit can create significant potential liability for the lender. This can occur if the amount of available funds in the construction budget declines, something that often happens when the borrower asks that funds saved on a hard cost trade line item be reallocated to a soft cost expense line (e.g., because of unexpectedly high architectural or unforeseen engineering expenses). The borrower in turn promises that if there are hard cost increases, he will cover them with out-of -pocket funds. This is a reasonable request, but it can have unanticipated negative consequences. When funds are moved from hard costs to soft costs, there is a reduction in hard cost funds to an amount which is below what was stated in the filed affidavit. Because of this, if liens are filed after a loan advance, they can have priority over the entire mortgage because supposedly the contractor relied on the affidavit when he entered into his contract. Now he can claim that with hard cost funds reduced, there is not enough money available to pay him when he completes his contract.

Another problem can occur if it is determined that the lender knew about or even should have known about misrepresentations. Again, as punishment, all liens no matter when they were filed can come ahead of its mortgage.

Under laws similar to those of New York if you intend to reallocate hard cost funds to soft costs, you should make sure that your attorney is notified before the reallocation is made so that, if necessary, he can file the changes in the proper manner at the proper office. As a general rule you also should try to make any reallocations at the end of the job when the project is near completion and the job has gone well. Since the value of the property will be higher near completion, the risk of a loss to a lender even if liens have priority over its loan will be reduced because the value of the mortgage collateral should be in excess of the sum of the liens.

Also, if a lien is filed near project completion, the borrower may have a stronger incentive to address it quickly. Failure to do so can hold up the completion of the project and the receipt of sale and/or lease revenues.

Loan Structure

An example of lien law's extensive influence involves New York State. Even though the priority of mechanic's liens is determined to take a first position on the date when they are filed (not retroactively), to safeguard against the potential threat of a lien taking priority over the full mortgage as described in the preceding paragraphs, many New York State real estate attorneys modify the loan structure by bifurcating (divide in two) or even trifurcating a development loan. The attorney employed by the lender often will make a distinction between advances for property acquisition, hard costs, and soft costs (in some states hard and soft costs are defined by statute). Then the attorney will create up to three or a combination of three loans: an acquisition loan, a hard cost loan, and a soft cost loan.

Here is an example:[8]

Let's say there was an agreement between the lender and the borrower to fund a $20 million loan to construct a new office building for a single tenant. The lender made a commitment to contribute $4 million to the land purchase and $16 million to cover hard costs and soft costs. The loan was bifurcated by your attorney into a $4 million land acquisition loan and a $16 million construction loan. Each loan was secured by a separate mortgage. Immediately after the loan closed, $4 million was advanced for the land purchase. Two months after the closing, the lender made a $1 million advance for construction costs. The total outstanding balance is now $5 million. Unknown to the loan officer, after the loan closed, the proper documents were not filed in the correct location. Furthermore, before that last advance, the loan administrator did not notify the title company to confirm that there was clear title.

The borrower now submits a requisition for a new advance. This time, the administrator does perform a title search and discovers that a $500,000 mechanic's lien was filed against the

---

[8] This example is simplified to illustrate the effects of a bifurcated loan more clearly. In practice, the situation would be much more complex.

property before the last $1,000,000 loan advance. Subsequently, it is discovered that because the borrower did not make payments to all of his contractors, more liens are being filed. The aggregate liens reach $3 million. Furthermore, as a result of the unexpected bankruptcy of the future tenant who was to occupy the building after completion and with a general market downturn, it now appears that there will no longer be a strong demand for an office building at the project's location. The projections of rental revenues that were the basis for your making the loan are now highly unlikely, if not impossible. It is surmised that the borrower, realizing the change in the market and having strong doubts about the success of the project, is going to take the money and run.

Obviously, the position of the lender is not good. The loan officer lent the borrower $5 million collateralized by the real property and now discovers that there is an additional $3 million claim on the property. The loan officer also discovers that all the liens, because of an improper filing, come before his loan. Most disturbing is the fact that the value of the property is below the $8 million in claims against it. The current value of the partially completed property is estimated to be $5 million, which is, coincidentally, the amount of the outstanding loan. The question is: With a limited source of funds from the property's sale, who gets paid first and who loses when the money runs out? To answer this question, one must examine the original loan structure.

In this example, in which the loan was bifurcated, the land loan clearly will remain in a first position. If the partially completed property, on a sale, produces a net $5 million in cash, the lender will get back $4 million (the amount of the land loan) and the contractors will get the remaining $1 million. This is the case because the contractors' liens remained junior to the $4 million land acquisition loan but became senior to the construction loan. The lender will lose $1 million, the remainder of the loan outstanding, and the contractors will lose $2 million of the $3 million they are owed.

In the same example, if the loan was not bifurcated but was made as a single mortgage loan combining acquisition and construction financing, the contractors would recover their entire $3 million and the lender would receive only $2 million because the contractors' liens became senior to the lender's full $20 million loan ($5 million of which is outstanding). The result is $2 million less than if the lender's attorney had bifurcated the loan at its inception.

In tabular form the situation looks like this:

Loan request	$20,000,000
The loan is bifurcated as follows:	
Acquisition loan	$4,000,000
Hard and soft cost loan	$16,000,000
Advanced at closing (for acquisition)	$4,000,000
Subsequent advance	
Hard and soft costs	$1,000,000
Loan balance outstanding	$5,000,000
Hard cost liens filed	$3,000,000
The priority of payments looks like this:	
With two loans:	
Lender	$4,000,000
Contractors	$1,000,000
Lender loses out on	$1,000,000
Contractors lose out on	$2,000,000
With one loan:	
Lender	$2,000,000
Contractors	$3,000,000
Lender loses out on	$3,000,000
Contractors lose out on	$0

The difference between a single loan and two loans in this example is $2 million.

Ways to Resolve a Lien

During the course of a construction loan, there are several options for clearing a lien so that the lender can make a timely funding. They include bonding, paying the lienor, and escrowing an amount equal to the amount of the lien. Bonding is the quickest and surest way to get protection and the most commonly used method. One reason it is quick is that the surety company's business is bonding liens. A surety company can bond a lien in a few hours. Also, once a lien is bonded, by law it essentially is removed. This is very important because, as was mentioned previously, if a lien is not removed, in many states liens filed afterward move up in priority to the position of the first lien filed. The sum of the liens then takes priority over your mortgage.[9] Paying the lienor is certainly a way

---

[9] Unfortunately for the borrower, bonding can be expensive. First, the borrower must post collateral in an amount that is often equal to or greater than the amount of the lien. Even if he later wins his case and the lien is removed (by the court, through a misfiling or lateness by the lienor, by the expiration of the lien, etc.), he still must acquire and tie up funds, pay for a letter of credit, or post some other form of collateral, which most likely will create a nonreimbursable expense, usually for many months. Furthermore, he has to pay the bonding company a fee.

to remove a lien, but for many developers it is the last thing they want to do. Unless the lien is relatively small or the borrower truly owes the lienor his claim, it probably is worth bonding it and disputing the claim upon the lienor commencing a suit.

Once a mechanic's lien has been filed, it cannot be waived by the filer but can be removed only upon payment, discharge (this includes bonding), or expiration. Therefore, in lieu of a bond, negotiation between the developer and the lienor may not be timely enough to ensure continuity of funding. There are occasions when the title company, noting the size and nature of the lien and the size and scope of the development, will insure one advance but then ask that the borrower satisfy the lien or bond it before insuring the next advance. At other times, in lieu of a bond, the title insurer may agree to allow the borrower to set aside a cash deposit to be held by the lending institution or an escrow agent.

If the title company gives the loan administrator approval to make a loan advance, you can be assured that the amount funded will be ahead of any filed mechanic's liens. Even if the loan advance's priority slips to a junior position behind mechanic's liens filed later, the title company has insured your institution's position. However, if the title company was not notified about a loan funding, it cannot give you the proper insurance. This, of course, can have a disastrous effect on your principal recovery and you and/or the loan administrator's career. Therefore, never take a casual approach to a loan advance. Always remember that calling for title is an inviolate rule in development lending. You cannot and should not advance any funds without being covered appropriately by title insurance.[10]

What a Lien Means to the Lender

It is important to recognize that if a lien shows up on a search, it is a red flag that should be discussed with the borrower immediately. At the least, it is a small contractor who believes that a lien will blackmail the owner into paying him more money than he

---

[10] If a lien is not removed but a cash deposit is put up in escrow or the borrower pledges additional collateral that includes a clean irrevocable letter of credit from a credit-worthy institution, the lender still needs clearance from the title company before funding (a clean letter of credit has no drawdown conditions and on presentation to the issuer is paid in full). Only on proper clearance by the title insurer can the lender advance any funds.

deserves.[11] At the most, it can be a precursor of serious trouble such as a lack of or misappropriation of funds. Most often, it is the product of a valid dispute between the owner and the contractor that, if taken care of through a bond, deposit, escrow, or agreed-on disposition, should merit proportionate concern and monitoring.

As long as the title company gives notice that it will insure the advance, it is all right to fund. The risk has been transferred from your institution to the title company. If additional liens are filed and move up in priority ahead of the advance, the title company will be responsible for them. However, it is the title company that makes this decision. That is why it is imperative that all advances be preceded by title company clearance.

Author's Note

Title insurance and lien law are complex issues that require the use of knowledgeable professionals. To a lender and a borrower, they are usually invisible until there is a problem. Fortunately, those problems are rare, but when they occur, the money involved can be substantial. Therefore, especially for a borrower who must take initial and direct action, often speedily, it is important to be prepared with at least a basic understanding of what is happening. Then, instead of panicking, the borrower and the lender can do what is necessary to avoid jeopardizing a project's progress.

---

[11] All states have laws that to varying degrees punish a contractor for filing a lien that is spurious or that is for more money than the amount the lienor is owed. In some states, damages against the contractor can be three times the amount of the falsely filed lien. Nonetheless, false or exaggerated claims are hard to prove, especially because it is the contractor who makes the claim and writes the invoices.

CHAPTER 15

Loan Repayment

FORMS OF TAKEOUTS AND REPAYMENTS

Obviously, one of the most important aspects of development loan underwriting is how the lender will be paid back. This is the way out of a loan. A great deal of attention is paid to important credit aspects such as loan collateral, existing and projected cash flows, projected debt service coverage ratios, and the ability of the borrower to perform. Sometimes, except when the loan is paid down through a sale of the property, as in a turnkey situation or the selling off of condominium units, the analyst loses sight of the risks and probability of defined paydown sources. When the borrower plans to continue to retain ownership of the property after construction has been completed, either the borrower or, more often, a third-party source will have to provide all or part of the funds needed to pay down the development loan. Surprisingly, the weak link in many credit analyses is a lack of clarity about final payment.

WAYS OUT

In doing a basic credit analysis, the general repayment rule is to have at least two ways out. On a rental property, the first way out is often a third-party takeout lender. On a turnkey project or a condominium project, the first way out is through the sale of the property at completion. The second way is used if the first way does not work. It usually consists of a restructuring of the development loan to a mini-permanent one (a mini-perm) in which cash flows from the completed property carry the interest on the restructured facility as well as pay down some of the principal. It is hoped that as conditions improve, the loan can be restructured or refinanced by the borrower, allowing the loan to be paid down. A third way out usually involves the repayment of the loan through the sale of the asset. A final way out is from the borrower's resources. This may involve calling on the borrower's guarantee, which, at least in theory, ultimately can be converted into or exchanged for cash.

Takeout

A takeout is a third-party funding source that will take out the development lender before or at the maturity of the development loan. The takeout lender makes a commitment to the developer that after certain hurdles are passed (the receipt of a certificate of occupancy, a certain level of lease-up, etc.), it will make a loan to the developer sufficient to retire the development lender's loan. There are several sources of takeouts. The most traditional and most popular is a permanent mortgage loan. Permanent lenders include insurance companies, commercial banks, savings banks, and public and private investment funds.

Most often, takeout lenders are large institutions that have a predictable cash flow and a stable cost of funds. Their focus is on the long term. To match their long-term horizon, they look for long-term areas of investment. They then can lock in a profit spread between their fixed and projected variable costs (which include their cost of funds, operating expenses, and reserves) and their revenues. Brokers and underwriters spend a great deal of time and energy packaging these long-term loans for sale primarily to institutional investors. The loans must meet very particular and specific criteria before they are placed into pools of similar credits and passed through for sale.

Buy-Sell or Recognition Agreement

A buy-sell agreement is a triparty agreement between the borrower, the development lender, and the permanent lender. A buy-sell agreement is not a development loan requirement, but without one, the takeout is weakened significantly. Generally, a development lender will not accept a takeout without the execution of a buy-sell agreement. That agreement is a legal document that in effect is a modification of or an amendment to the takeout commitment to the developer that includes the development lender as one of the parties.

The borrower enters into a direct contract with the permanent lender that after the achievement of certain milestones within a specified period will allow the permanent lender to fund a loan. The development lender has two concerns in regard to this relationship. The first is the necessity to be aware of all the covenants of the takeout commitment along with all amendments and modifications to ensure that they are being complied with so that a takeout funding will occur. The second is to have the right, if the borrower defaults on its obligations under the development loan, to assume the rights of the borrower or to have the commitment assigned to another entity.

When you enter into a buy-sell agreement, it is extremely important to get as much material and documentation as possible approved by the permanent lender before you close on the development loan. Up front, get approvals of items including lease forms, the forms that will be used to certify completion, and anything else that is specified in the permanent commitment that can be taken care of early. You also want to have the permanent lender acknowledge as many conditions as possible that have been satisfied before your development loan closes. This could include approval of a budget, insurance, leases, contracts, plans, specifications, an appraisal report, engineering reports, and an environmental report. The obvious benefit of this is that it protects you to some extent from surprises from the permanent lender, feigned or genuine, that can impede the takeout of your loan.

Because the buy-sell agreement is such an important document, it is imperative that it be drafted, reviewed, and modified by an attorney who has had direct experience drafting, reviewing, modifying, and negotiating other buy-sell agreements. He should know and call your attention to any rights he believes you should be entitled to as well as pointing out those which have been omitted.

DEVELOPMENT LOAN TAKEOUTS

There are generally two types of takeouts: the permanent takeout and the standby takeout.

Permanent Loan Takeout

A permanent loan takeout commitment is a contract entered into by the borrower and the permanent lender that is often required by the development lender before or at the closing of a development loan. It basically states that the permanent lender will pay down the development lender in full when the borrower passes certain hurdles. Those hurdles typically include completion by a certain future date as certified by an architect or engineer approved by the permanent lender, a permanent or temporary certificate of occupancy for the property, and a specified rental or occupancy achievement. It is standard for the permanent loan commitment to require the borrower to gain the permanent lender's approval of certain items, such as project plans and specifications and all leases.

Review of Takeout Risk

The fact that your development loan has a permanent takeout commitment in place does not mean that it will fund as anticipated. Even if all the requirements of the takeout commitment are met, there is always a risk that the takeout lender, as a result of problems of its own, will look for every possible way not to honor it. Particularly in the downward phase of an economic cycle, a takeout institution may have financial stress that precludes it from stepping up to its contractual obligations. This was seen in the early 1990s when many permanent lenders, even those which remained financially healthy, refused to fund. The results were devastating to many borrowers and development lenders and resulted in years of litigation. That could happen again.

Since the permanent lender is critical to the payback of the development loan, it is important to examine the takeout lender for its financial strength; its past experience and track record in making and honoring its takeout commitments; the level of expertise of its key personnel, including those you will be involved with directly; and its perceived and demonstrated level of flexibility and willingness to create a commitment that is realistic in the marketplace and is structured in a way that will enable you to make your development loan.

It is the borrower who should negotiate the takeout loan commitment, as the loan will be a lien on his project after the development loan has been completely paid down. Before he signs it, though, it is essential that you and your institution's attorney review it.

However, if the borrower comes to you with a deal in which he already has secured a takeout from an unknown or weak institution, you must be very careful about recommending that your institution accept it.

Anticipating that a development lender will require a takeout to obtain a development loan, some borrowers will pay a subprime lender a substantial fee for a commitment even though there is a significant risk that the permanent lender will not fund when required. The borrower "buys" the commitment because he has invested substantial time and money in a project from which he is unwilling to walk away. The borrower believes that by the time the project is completed, he can find another takeout lender, which should be easier since the project will be nearer to completion and thus pose less market risk, or the development lender will extend the loan into a mini-perm. There have been bogus takeout lenders with great-sounding names who have taken a fee from a borrower with no intention of funding the loan or ability to do so. Weak commitments most often materialize when inexperienced borrowers with limited track records and thin capital cannot receive a commitment from an established permanent lender.

The Negative Bias of the Permanent Lender

When a permanent lender issues a loan commitment, the fee is usually 1 to 2 percent of the loan amount. For example, a $10 million loan commitment will result in a fee of $100,000 to $200,000. That money goes directly to the permanent lender's bottom line. It will be earned at the time the takeout commitment is signed, and at least a portion of it is received before or at the development loan closing, which is ordinarily one to two years from the time the permanent lender actually will be called on to honor its obligation. In fact, if the permanent lender does not fund, it still keeps the fee as net income and avoids all the risks of making the permanent loan. Therefore, there is a built-in bias for the permanent lender to issue a commitment for fee income but not to be overly enthusiastic about funding it unless all the commitment terms are clearly met or exceeded.

Some development lenders require the inclusion of a takeout commitment along with a development loan commitment if a takeout is not already in place. The development lender takes itself out. In this case, the development lender can get the additional benefit of an up-front fee and a stable loan at completion. To encourage the borrower to fund its takeout loan and not go elsewhere at construction completion, a back-end penalty fee is written into the commitment. If the borrower chooses to refinance through another lender, he will have to pay the development lender a penalty fee of, for example, 1 percent of the permanent commitment amount. Having the development lender also be the takeout lender makes sense, especially if the borrower is well known for being a capable manager. After all, a loan on the finished product almost always embodies less risk than does one on a project that is under construction. After going through the relatively high risk of the construction loan, why not take advantage of the lower risk of the permanent loan?

Standby Takeout Loan

A standby takeout commitment is issued with the intention that the lender will never be called on to fund. The inducement to make a commitment for this potential lender is primarily the ability to earn an up-front fee.

As was stated previously, development lenders will not, as policy, make a development loan unless a takeout is in place. However, if market conditions are expected to become more favorable or a takeout commitment is delayed, the borrower may choose to obtain a standby commitment. This is done to satisfy the development lender's requirement that a takeout commitment be in place before its funding on the development loan. Features that differentiate a standby loan from a permanent loan include the fact that the standby will have a high interest rate and probably will be for a short term. It therefore encourages the borrower to seek more permanent and less expensive financing before the completion of the project. Since the standby is the least attractive way for the borrower to take out the development loan, you will have to examine it carefully to make sure that if there is a problem, the standby indeed will fund. This means particular attention should be paid to rental achievement clauses, debt service ratios, vacancies, occupancy requirements, time frames, and the definition of completion. Always remember that the standby is a last resort lender. If it is called on to fund, that can mean that the transaction is not attractive to more conventional permanent lenders.

Depending on the experience and risk profile of the lending institution, the development lender may incorporate its own standby into the development loan facility and thus satisfy its own takeout requirement. With the additional up-front fee and the high rate of interest characteristic of all standbys, the lender can receive more income.[1] Often, the risk on the loan has decreased greatly because the property is completed and is income-producing; it is just that the borrower was not successful in obtaining refinancing from a takeout lender. The borrower, of course, remains amply motivated to find a conventional takeout before the development loan is due.

TAKEOUT LENDER STANDARDS

Whether the takeout is a standby or a permanent one, in your development loan commitment it should be stated explicitly that your institution, at its sole and complete discretion, must approve the takeout lender. This will help ensure that the borrower will not enter into a permanent loan commitment with a lender without your assent. Before he signs it, the commitment must be reviewed carefully by you and your counsel. You should challenge certain clauses that are not acceptable. Even when it comes from a recognized permanent lender, there are sections and conditions that can give the permanent lender wide discretion in its decision to fund. This can water down the force of its commitment considerably and increase your risk. There are several things that you should watch out for.

Specific Unyielding Definition of Completion

Although completion of the project is an obvious condition of a permanent loan funding, the definition should be unequivocal. For instance, is the issuance of a temporary certificate of occupancy rather than a permanent certificate of occupancy part of the definition of completion? Is tenant work required? Does the architect have to certify that the work is complete, and if that is the case, will the architect be cooperative when called on to certify?

On almost all construction projects, especially rehabilitation projects, there are changes in design that result from a variety of

---

[1] Usually, when the development lender incorporates a standby, part of the commitment fee is required at funding. For example, a $10 million commitment with a 1 percent fee may require $50,000 at development loan closing and the remaining $50,000 on the development loan funding into the standby. This belated portion of the fee further increases the motivation of the borrower to find a more conventional takeout lender.

factors. Some common factors are undiscovered land and soil conditions, unaccounted for environmental conditions, newly found
physical constraints on existing properties, unclear plans and specifications that require ongoing modifications, and unavailability
of specific supplies and materials. Usually the permanent lender
requires completion according to the initially approved plans and
specifications. However, at the least a clause should be inserted in
the permanent loan commitment indicating that the finished property will be "substantially" in accordance with approved plans and
specifications. Normal and common changes in the plans and specifications never should pose a documented threat to delay or
withhold funding at the discretion of the permanent lender.

Time of Completion

The time of completion is also important. If a fire, a windstorm, or
a public water line breaking and causing a flood creates an unforeseen delay, will there be an extension of the time to complete? The
last thing you and presumably the borrower want is for the permanent lender to walk away because the commitment expires and
the borrower is unable to complete the project in time to trigger
permanent funding. The takeout should have at least a 6-month
and probably a 12-month margin of safety from the anticipated
time of completion to the expiration of the commitment. If possible,
the commitment also should provide an absolute right to obtain an
extension in exchange for a fee.

Appraisal Report after Completion

The takeout lender's commitment is in most cases at least 18 months
in advance of the expected funding date. In return for committing to
fund so far in advance, the takeout lender receives an up-front fee
that includes consideration for economic and market risk for the
promise to fund in the future.

The development lender almost always takes on a greater risk
than does the takeout lender because in addition to the permanent
lender's risks, it is taking on the greater performance risk of construction secured by property that usually is not producing any
income. Allowing the takeout lender to condition its funding on a
new appraisal after completion essentially shifts all the market risk
to the development lender while reducing the market risk to the

permanent lender. At the time it is called on to fund, the permanent lender easily can walk away from its responsibility if the appraised value is lower than what was anticipated when the development loan closed. To add insult to injury, the borrower has paid for a commitment that later may prove meaningless. Since a future appraisal requirement shifts the brunt of the market risk to the development lender, with such a shift, who needs a takeout commitment? A takeout should not be contingent on a new or updated appraisal—period.

Occupancy and/or Rental Achievement

This clause is important to the permanent lender because it demonstrates that the finished product is marketable by providing an objective measure of the property's viability. If it is included by the takeout lender, it is also a strong reason for you to reject any requirement for an appraisal by the permanent lender after completion and before funding, as was discussed in the preceding paragraphs. An appraisal is nothing more than a researched (carefully and objectively, one hopes) opinion of value that always has a degree of subjectivity. Leases and contracts, in contrast, are indisputable.

The rental achievement provides an objective measure of revenues that after projected expenses will provide the permanent lender with a very accurate estimate of the net cash flow available for debt service. In properties in which there will be multiple tenants, rental achievements may be expressed as a percentage of occupancy as well as a minimum cash flow.

The formula is a simple one: a minimum percentage calculated by dividing leased square footage by total leasable square footage with a gross income at or above a benchmark. There may also be a requirement that a minimum number of occupants be in place to help avoid a situation where cash flows are overly dependent on one or a few tenants. This ensures that a cash flow criterion is not met by a few overmarket (inflated) leases with tenants who if they vacate unexpectedly will have a magnified negative effect on the ability of the property to service the permanent debt. The percentage occupancy requirement coupled with a minimum number of tenants requirement helps diversify the risk of a tenant's failure to pay rent by spreading it among many leases.

Note that occupancy can be defined in many ways, such as a certain percentage of overall square footage that is under signed leases, a certain percentage of leasors that are actually paying rent (if there were any free rent periods, they have expired), a certain percentage of space that is physically occupied, or the physical possession of space by a specified tenant. Each of these definitions will affect the timing that can lead to the funding of the permanent loan or, indeed, the expiration of the permanent loan commitment before the rental occupancy requirements are achieved.

Floors and Ceilings

Some takeout loans will fund in increments or stages. A two-staged takeout loan, which is typical, has a floor and a ceiling. After a minimum occupancy and/or cash flow hurdle has been passed, the takeout lender will fund a certain amount of its total commitment. Then, when the project overcomes a higher hurdle, the remainder of the committed amount is funded. This gives the permanent lender some ability to adjust the loan balance to the property's cash flow.

Takeout Lender's Approval of Leases

This condition should be examined carefully. The takeout lender has a right to review leases since they will be the source of the revenues that service its loan. In the takeout commitment, lease restrictions should be broad and reasonable. There may be constraints on what type of tenant may occupy space and also on a prospective tenant's financial strength. The first constraint may include specific retail tenants such as home decorating businesses or negative covenants such as the preclusion of retail food or restaurant tenants. The second constraint may include net worth and cash flow requirements relative to the lease. Other requirements can include a minimum number of years the leasee has been in business, its credit rating and history, and so on.

By reviewing leases, the takeout lender can assure itself that the tenants meet the requirements set forth in the original permanent loan commitment. You, as the development lender, or your institution's attorney must review the leases to make sure they are in accordance with the takeout lender's requirements. Then, if there is a question about a tenant's eligibility or the crafting of the lease, it can be addressed quickly. Ideally, unless the loan is underwritten in a strong market or there are compelling reasons (e.g., a borrower with strong ties to your institution's senior management, a borrower with a very strong track record, expansion into a new strong market, willingness to take on greater lease-up risks), the property should be "preleased" before construction completion and the obtaining of a certificate of occupancy.

Often, as dictated in a development lender's loan policies, before the closing of the development loan or the commencement of construction, a certain amount of preleasing must be in place. This way, the project can begin to generate revenues as soon as possible and the probability of a timely and successful lease-up is enhanced.

No Adverse Change Clause

A no adverse change clause raises many questions that directly affect the development lender and borrower if the borrower or the loan does not perform as expected. This shows up regularly in the buy-sell document and is only for the benefit of the permanent lender. If it is interpreted broadly, it gives the permanent lender the right to walk away, leaving the borrower and the development lender with no rights.

Approval Process for Changes in Plans, Specifications, and Other Significant Modifications

Even the most straightforward construction projects reach surprising levels of complexity that demand a great deal of energy and focus on the part of the developer. It is the rule rather than the exception that as a project evolves, there will be changes in the plans and specifications. This allows the project to be completed with a balance among functionality, cost, and time.[2]

Reporting Changes

Except for those in the loan documents, there are no laws or requirements that compel the borrower to notify the development lender or the takeout lender of construction changes. Therefore,

---

[2] Hopefully, the developer will file with the proper municipal authorities in a timely manner (buildings department, environmental control board, landmark commission, etc.) in order to continue the job unabated and without the risk of delays in approvals, stop-work orders, and/or fines.

you are always at some risk that material changes will not be brought to your attention. To mitigate that possibility, you should maintain a relationship not only with the borrower but also with your consulting engineer. Review his reports from cover to cover. Even if the project is moving along well, call him from time to time and ask a few specific questions. Always demonstrate some involvement, even if it is only casual. You should try to project the attitude that you are actively interested in and are monitoring the job, making it difficult for the developer to avoid and your inspecting engineer to overlook changes that could affect your loan and the borrower's takeout significantly.

There are several reasons why the developer may not notify you. Here are some common ones of which you should be aware:

- *Oversight*. The developer or construction supervisor is too busy and perhaps too poorly organized in his paperwork to alert the lender in a timely way. Inevitably, new job demands decrease the perceived priority of the reporting requirement. The developer postpones reporting with the intention of notifying the lender about current material changes later along with new ones when they occur. When new changes occur, the developer again procrastinates. This creates a cycle in which the borrower never reports any changes.

- *Awareness*. The personnel in the construction office who are performing the day-to-day operations on the job are not cognizant of the requirements of the development loan or the permanent loan. If the developer is not a hands-on individual, he also may not know what changes are taking place and therefore cannot report them.

- *Tension*. Sometimes the development lender's inspecting engineer is not cooperative or is perceived to be adversarial or unsophisticated by the borrower. This perception can be fostered by changes in plans and specifications that can result in the inspecting engineer charging additional fees to the lender for performing extra work which are passed on to the borrower. The inspecting engineer also may need more time to review and approve the changes. This could delay the approval of a requisition when the borrower is eager to receive loan funds to pay contractors and materialmen.

- *Costs.* Sometimes changes are not filed with the proper governmental agencies until the end of the job because of the filing costs and time involved. This is especially true on smaller jobs in which the relative cost of filing against a budget is higher. In many cases, the work progresses with field and shop drawings that do not match the plans in your or the takeout lender's file. The architect and the construction manager track changes until nearly the end of the job, at which time a final "as-built" set of plans and specs is filed with the proper municipal agency. Then the project is inspected by a municipal official, who compares the actual construction with the final filed as-built plans. Although this method of filing at the end of the construction job may work for you, the development lender, it can put the takeout commitment in jeopardy. You therefore must take action to ensure that you and the takeout lender will be notified of any changes in a timely manner. Failure to do this should be a material default under the development loan.

Notification Safeguards

To safeguard against noncompliance by the borrower, intentional or not, you can take certain actions, including the following:

- Make sure that your inspecting engineer is aware that he must alert you to all changes as soon as he becomes aware of them. The buy-sell agreement also may require that each inspection report be sent to the takeout lender. If that is the case, check the inspection report to make sure that it has both your and the takeout lender's addresses.
- Make sure that your borrower's key people are aware of their responsibilities. To put teeth into your reminder, tell them and the borrower that a default under the takeout commitment is a default under the development loan as well. By not reporting properly, they can jeopardize the timeliness of development loan fundings.
- A requirement that is often part of the takeout documentation is the submission to the takeout lender of copies of requisitions, change orders, and the inspecting engineer's

report on a monthly basis. Even if this is not a requirement, sending those documents is a good idea because it shows that you have kept the takeout lender aware of the progress of and any changes to the project. Always obtain proof that materials were sent (e.g., a FedEx or messenger receipt).

- If you are the nervous, overly conscientious type, you should maintain a rapport with the loan officer of the takeout institution. A call from time to time can set up a working relationship and a higher level of cooperation in case things do not go as planned.

Flexibility

When you are reviewing the takeout and buy-sell agreement in conjunction with your attorney, make sure that there is flexibility. For instance, changes in plans and specifications should be material in nature before the takeout lender has to be notified. You also may want to put in a dollar threshold, although it may be hard to quantify. Timeliness should not be an absolute issue. A reasonable time period is preferred. The objective is that the commitment be crafted so that the permanent lender cannot walk away because of a technical issue. Additional questions that should be answered in the affirmative when you are reviewing the takeout commitment are as follows:

- If the borrower goes bankrupt, can someone else step in, and if that is the case, what are the criteria for an acceptable substitute?
- If a substitute steps in for the borrower, including the development lender, will all the rights and protections offered in the permanent commitment be transferred as well?
- Will the development lender have a right to cure clause? This will preserve the takeout commitment even if the borrower has failed to live up to the material conditions of the permanent loan.
- Will the buy-sell agreement give the development lender the right to notify the takeout lender of borrower defaults, and will the takeout lender give the development lender extensions of time in which defaults can be cured?

Commonsense Details and Provisions

Commonsense details frequently are overlooked because they usually are taken for granted. Although many details will and must be reviewed by your attorney, it is not a bad idea to make sure that aspects of the takeout and the buy-sell such as the correct property description, the correct dollar amounts, and the proper articulation of items you negotiated after the initial drafting of the commitment or modifications to it are correct. If the commitment alludes to other documents, what they are, what they contain, and how they affect the lender, the borrower, and the takeout lender obviously are very important. At the very least, make sure you have a good basic understanding of all the legal materials.

Do not rely solely on your attorney. If he makes a mistake or overlooks a critical aspect of the takeout or the buy-sell agreement, he still will receive his fees and almost certainly will not experience career setbacks because of his omissions and mistakes. You and your institution, in contrast, may face a career setback and a major dollar loss, respectively.

OTHER FORMS OF REPAYMENT

Amortization Schedules: Partially Paying Down the Loan

Amortization schedules rarely are used in a development loan because the property is not generating income to pay down the principal. Just the opposite is occurring: Principal is being paid out over time. Also, since amortization schedules usually are spread over a long period, such as 15 to 30 years, the amount of the loan paid down is very small, particularly at the beginning of the loan term, when most payments are apportioned to interest expense.[3] When you are contemplating a paydown of a development loan, amortization payments should not be considered a viable way out and if insisted on will create ill will with borrowers.

Percentage of Sale Method

If you are lending on the construction of a condominium or a fee simple town house type of project, a takeout commitment will not

---

[3] A loan amortizing over a 15-year period with a 7 percent interest rate will have a principal balance of 90.8 percent of its original amount after a 2-year period, which is about the term of an average construction loan.

be part of the repayment structure because the borrower will repay you through sales of the individual units that make up the project. The customary requirement is for the borrower to pay a percentage of the net proceeds on the sale of each unit to the lender or, if the unit sells for a price below a certain predefined threshold value, an absolute minimum dollar amount. The loan can be paid down after some percentage of aggregate sales has occurred.

For instance, you make a $10 million loan to construct a 20-story, 100-unit, 100,000-sellable-square-foot condominium apartment building. The net sellout of the building is expected to be $18,050,000 ($19 million, or $190 per square foot, minus 5 percent for brokerage and closing costs). In your loan presentation and subsequently in the loan commitment, the following terms apply: "Apartment units will be released on the greater of a principal paydown equal to 90 percent of the net sales proceeds per unit or 130 percent of the total debt per square foot of total salable area, multiplied by the salable square foot area of the unit being sold."

If all the units sell at an average of $190 per square foot as predicted, the development loan will be paid down completely after the sale of 62 percent of the units as follows: net sellout of $18,050,000 × 90% release (paydown percentage) = $16,245,000; $10,000,000 fully outstanding loan/$16,245,000 = 62%.

If market conditions improve during the construction of the building and the units sell, for example, at an average net price of $238 per square foot, the loan will be paid down after the sale of only 47 percent of the units: $238 per square foot × 100,000 salable square feet = $23,800,000 net sellout × 90% release (paydown percentage) = $21,420,000; $10,000,000/$21,420,000 = 47%.

If, however, the market declines during the construction of the building and the average price per square foot comes to a net of $115, using the same formula, the loan will be paid down after the sale of an uncomfortably high 97 percent of the units: $115 per square foot × 100,000 salable square feet = $11,500,000 net sellout × 90% release (paydown percentage) = $10,350,000; $10,000,000/$10,350,000 = 97%.[4]

---

[4] Of course, the price per square foot of each unit varies with location, view, height, size, and so on. However, in setting loan terms, the average is used, since it is difficult to ascertain what units will sell, when, and at what price.

Establishing a Minimum Release Price

In the last example, in which units sold for a price below what orig-inally was expected, if the prices slipped further or if there were delays in sales as there may be in a declining market, the sale of the units with a 90 percent release might not be enough to pay down the loan. Therefore, besides dictating a percentage of net sale pro-ceeds per unit requirement, under the percentage of sale method you also must include a minimum release price. In this example, the minimum release price is stated as "130 percent of the total debt per square foot of total salable area, multiplied by the salable square foot area of the unit being sold." Taking the reciprocal of 130 percent, the lender must be paid down on the sale of no more than 77 percent of the project's sales (1/130% = 76.9%). With the same parameters in the example above, let's say there is an apartment for sale that consists of 1,348 salable square feet.[5] The minimum amount the lender will require to release the unit is $219,724, which is calculated as follows: 130% of $10,000,000 loan = $13,000,000/80,000 salable square feet = $162.50 per square foot ($163 rounded to the nearest dollar); $163 × 1,348 square foot apartment = $219,724. Even if the unit sold for below this amount, a $219,724 loan paydown would be required by the lender. The borrower will need to produce additional funds, possibly through equity contributions, to meet the $163 per square foot minimum.

Under the percentage of sale method, a minimum release price never should be omitted. The minimum release price is not trig-gered often because in almost all cases it is well below the projected sales price.[6] A minimum release price protects the lender not only against a soft market but also against the borrower selling units at below-market prices. "Dumping," or severely discounting, units rarely occurs but is more likely to happen when the developer is

---

[5] The total number of square feet and the square footage of each unit can be taken directly from the registered offering for the property.

[6] Often a developer will question the insertion of a minimum release price. The argument is that he may sell some units below the minimum price to prime sales. You should counter this by telling him that the minimum release price is well below the expected price, and so there should be ample room for price flexibility. Furthermore, you should explain that the minimum is a worst-case situation and that if it was anticipated that he would sell units at such a low level, you never would have con-templated underwriting his loan in the first place. Finally, you can add that it is a requirement of your lending institution that a minimum release price be established so that the full principal will be paid down after a certain percentage of sales has been achieved.

able to obtain considerable fees during the construction of the property. This is especially true if the developer has brought in outside investors who have contributed most of the project's equity and who under the partnership or operating agreement will receive a much larger percentage of the profit distribution. If the fees and salary to the developer are substantial, he will have made a good amount of money regardless of the project's success or failure. Therefore, he may have less incentive to put in the necessary time and effort to market and sell units to achieve maximum sales prices over a reasonable market absorption period. A minimum release price also protects the lender against fraudulent sales transactions (including insider sales to owning members for their own use) in which the developer puts some of the sales proceeds into his pocket rather than using them to pay down your development loan and/or distribute profits to his partners.

Determining the Release Percentage

The percentage of the net sale price to release a unit should be based on when you want or expect the loan to be paid down fully. In the example above, it was noted that with an expected sellout of $18,050,000 and a 90 percent release price, the $10 million loan should have been paid down after 62 percent of sales. This is fairly conservative but can be appropriate for a project in a relatively untested market or for a strong borrower that does not need an immediate cash flow and prefers to reduce principal and interest (or a borrower who has received concessions in the loan terms and structure such as a reduced guarantee of repayment or completion in return for a higher release price). If the lender reduces the percentage to 80 percent, the loan should be paid down fully after 69 percent of sales.[7] At 70 percent, the loan should be paid down fully at about 79 percent of sales.

Inexperienced lenders often require the borrower to pay 100 percent of the net proceeds of a sale to reduce the loan. They believe that the loan should be paid down completely before the borrower receives any of his equity or profits. Borrowers who readily agree to this condition may be inexperienced or may have little room to negotiate because they have gone too far in the loan

---

[7] Normally, for most projects a release percentage is in the range of 80 to 90 percent.

process with the prospective development lender and have limited their loan options.

Requiring 100 percent of net sales proceeds is not a good business decision for the lender. Often there will be cost overruns and expenses that are not covered by the development loan, or at completion there can be unanticipated punchlist and touch-up items that the borrower must complete before a sale can be consummated. If the borrower is not allowed to take some money out of a sale, he may not have enough to address these costs, which are essential to the sale of units.[8,9]

A release percentage below 100 percent may enhance the viability of the project, decrease the chance that the borrower will be short of funds to complete the project as intended, and strengthen your collateral.

Sliding Loan-to-Value Ratio

Under the percentage of sale method, on the release of each unit from collateral, the loan-to-value ratio declines. As a simple example (see Figure 15–1), if you have a $10 million loan collateralized by 10 identical units that have an aggregate value of $15 million, each unit has a 66 percent loan-to-value ratio. If you require 90 percent of the net sales proceeds to release each unit and a unit sells net of costs for $1,500,000 (this example excludes closing costs and the like), you, the development lender, will receive back $1,350,000. Now you have a principal balance of $8,650,000 secured by nine

---

[8] Most experienced lenders have been involved in projects that begin with a great deal of effort and expense being put into producing a quality product only to see later on poor execution of trim and finishes and compromises in the quality of appliances, fixtures, and equipment. Buyers do not open walls or floors to see how good a job the developer has done at the beginning and midpoint of a project. They see only the final work and base their opinions on what they see. This can affect the timing of sales and prices, which in turn affects the value of the property. The reason for the falloff in quality, of course, is that the developer ran short of money. Giving the developer a relatively small percentage of each sale (10 to 20 percent) before the loan is paid down completely will enable him, if necessary, to put that money back into the job. This can increase the project's marketability and value.

[9] Another reason to share some of the cash proceeds with the developer is that in many loan budgets the borrower does not take out a developer's or builder's fee during construction but collects those fees only from sales in the form of profit. Putting some money in his pocket before your loan is paid down usually creates an additional and strong incentive for him to sell units and seek the highest prices he can obtain regardless of his net worth.

units with an aggregate value of $13,500,000. Your loan-to-value ratio, which is a measure of risk, has decreased from 66 percent to 64 percent. The difference becomes more pronounced as sales progress. If the developer sells half the project (five units) at an average net sales price of $1,500,000, the lender receives back $6,750,000 and the principal balance drops to $3,250,000. The loan-to-value ratio is now only 43 percent.

FIGURE 15-1

Example of LTV Ratio Reductions through Unit Sales

Reduction of the Loan-to-Value Ratio

Prior to Sales:	
Number of Units	10
Loan Amount	$10,000,000
Aggregate Value	$15,000,000
Loan-to-Value Ratio	66.7%
Value per Unit	$1,500,000
Net Sales Proceeds per Unit	$1,500,000
90% Release per Unit	$1,350,000
One Unit Sold:	
Loan Outstanding after Sale of One Unit	$8,650,000
Aggregate Value of Remaining Nine Units	$13,500,000
Loan-to-Value Ratio	64.1%
Five Units Sold:	
Loan Outstanding after Sale of Five Units	$3,250,000
Aggregate Value of Remaining Five Units	$7,500,000
Loan-to-Value Ratio	43.3%

The decline in risk is particularly important in a revolving or staged development loan, in which after partial paydowns, money will be re-lent to the borrower.

Revolving Loans or Staged Development Loans

A revolving loan or staged development loan is used to finance single-family homes, town houses, and planned unit developments. This type of loan reduces risk for the lender and keeps fees and interest costs down for the borrower. Essentially, it allows the borrower to progress with the development of the project but limits the amount of new construction without presales or actual sales. The primary reason for this loan structure is to reduce market risk (demand for future completed units will be less than originally forecast). Other reasons include protection against development cost increases and delays. The objective is to balance risk against development by limiting the maximum loan outstanding without impeding the progress of critical construction. With less money outstanding, fewer unit sales are needed to pay down the development loan fully. This reduces the chance of losing money or limits the amount of money lost if there are unforeseen adverse events and/or circumstances.

Using an example to demonstrate some of the attributes of a revolving loan (see Figure 15–2), a developer is building seven 9,500-square-foot fee simple homes in a wealthy suburb of Los Angeles. Land development and the construction of all seven homes are projected to cost $41,754,238 (column B). Net revenues from the sale of all seven homes, after deducting 4 percent for brokerage and closing costs, are anticipated to be $53,625,600. The result is a net profit of $11,871,362.

The borrower initially asked the lender for a $31,300,000 loan, which equates to a 75 percent loan-to-cost ratio. He would come up with the remaining $10,454,238 as equity. With this scenario, the lender and the borrower will be at risk for the full project costs. If the units do not sell, the lender can lose a substantial portion of its loan and the borrower is very likely to lose all of his equity.

Instead, the lender and the borrower agreed on a $19,500,000 revolving loan (column C). The borrower arranged with the lender to construct no more than three homes on speculation at any one time. After unit sales, the borrower could redraw on the loan up to the maximum $19,500,000 under the "Each Additional Home Loan" schedule in the figure (column D).

The 1 percent commitment fee, instead of being $313,000, will now be only $195,000. Since the maximum projected loan outstanding will be less, interest expenses are reduced. If the project does not sell as projected, the lending institution and the borrower stand to lose significantly less than they did in the previous scenario. If the project does sell out as planned, the developer should make a better profit than he would have made if the loan had not been structured as a revolver.

FIGURE 15-2

Example of a Revolving Loan Budget

	A Avg. Price per SF	B Total All 7 Homes	C 3-Home Revolving Loan	D Each Addt'l Home Loan
REVENUES				
Expected Total Aggregate Sales	$840	$55,860,000	$23,940,000	$7,980,000
Less Brokerage Fees	($34)	($2,234,400)	($957,600)	($319,200)
Net Sales Proceeds	**$806**	**$53,625,600**	**$22,982,400**	**$7,660,800**
COSTS				
Land Aquisition	$192	$12,800,000	$8,000,000	
Site Development	$11	$759,783	$759,783	
Home Construction	$182	$12,118,041	$5,193,446	$1,731,149
HC Contingency	$12	$807,697	$346,156	$115,385
Landscaping, Grounds, Improvements	$11	$759,783	$379,892	$108,540
ConstructionSupervision	$51	$3,411,737	$0	
Real Estate Taxes	$4	$250,000	$250,000	
Interest on Loan	$51	$3,400,000	$2,500,000	
Appraisal Fee/Environmental Fee	$1	$35,000	$35,000	
Commitment Fee	$5	$313,000	$195,000	
Lender's Construction Consultant	$0	$25,000	$25,000	
Lender's Legal Fees	$0	$30,000	$0	
Permits, Surveys, etc.	$0	$25,000	$0	
Borrower's Architect/Engineering	$12	$777,000	$213,650	$111,000
Title Policies/closing Costs, Etc	$3	$200,000	$200,000	
Builder's Risk Insurance	$7	$450,000	$0	$50,000
Misc/Contingency	$15	$1,000,000	$500,000	$125,000
Legal inc. closing, plan, filing, contracts, etc.	$2	$100,000	$50,000	$25,000
Marketing & Advertising	$9	$630,000	$0	
Office Overhead and Expenses	$22	$1,462,197	$120,073	$40,000
Development Fee	$15	$1,000,000		
Contingency	$21	$1,400,000	$732,000	$167,000
Total Development Costs	**$628**	**$41,754,238**	**$19,500,000**	**$2,423,074**
NET PROFIT TO DEVELOPERS	**$179**	**$11,871,362**		

Funding Infrastructure, Common Elements, and Initial Structures

In a staged development loan, it is often necessary to fund a certain level of infrastructure, such as roads, sewer lines, curbs, and streets. In addition to infrastructure, common elements and amenities such as clubhouses, swimming pools, and perhaps some home models and a sales office must be built. Funding this initial work is particularly risky because it front-loads development loan risk. On staged development loans, it often makes better sense from a risk standpoint to limit infrastructure funding to little more than the essentials needed to entice early buyers. Then, as more sales occur, additional funds for infrastructure and amenities can be advanced since the marketability of units has been proved at least partially.[10]

A different concern with regard to infrastructure occurs when the developer builds too little rather than too much. This is particularly true with many of the "nonessential" amenities that often are constructed at the end of a project (nonessentials include walkways, finished elevator cabs, swimming pools, health centers, boat docks, and so on). This is understandable since it can reduce the net amount of required investor funds. The developer anticipates that proceeds from the sale of units near the end of the project can be plowed back in to complete the remaining infrastructure, or he may be dishonest and after the project sellout walk away without keeping the promises he made to purchasers. This can be a major problem for the lender if it is implicated as a contributor to fraud or negligence.

There is no set and sure rule about how much of the infrastructure should be funded up front. Usually, the borrower's equity supports initial infrastructure work before funds are advanced under the development loan. Subsequent funding should be balanced between infrastructure and units that can be sold.

Second Mortgages and Mezzanine Financing

As little as 15 years ago, mezzanine financing was a mystery for many lending professionals. Since that time its use has mushroomed. This is actually a broadly used term that applies to a variety of capital structures, all of which maintain a subordinate position to the development loan. Mezzanine financing is the input of funds that have elements of a mortgage and elements of equity. Unlike second mortgages, which are fundamentally debt instruments with clearly defined principal and interest components (and

---

[10] Note that there are exceptions to limiting up-front costs when it makes sense to do so. In the previous example, the borrower initially was allowed to draw down for all the infrastructure work even though he was building only the first three of the seven homes. This was done because the borrower was a very financially strong and experienced developer, he materially reduced costs by completing the infrastructure in one phase, and with a very high end product to sell, it was felt that finished infrastructure would enhance the project's pricing and marketability.

are recorded as liens in the municipality where the collateralized property is situated), mezzanine financing almost always is incorporated into the capital structure of the borrower as equity or as a loan to the borrower secured by the equity of the borrower, not the real property. Payouts to the mezzanine lender[11] are made in the form of preferred returns, profits, and capital distributions.

Since mezzanine financing is always subordinate to the development loan, if there is a default, the development lender always has priority over the mezzanine holder. However, there are times when the mezzanine lender can affect the development lender, and when a project does not go according to plan, it may be the source of its takeout.

One instance of this occurs when the mezzanine lender steps into the shoes of the borrower. Here, usually because of a default on the part of the developer in his agreement with the mezzanine lender, the mezzanine lender exercises its right to assume the role of the developer. If the mezzanine lender is a small firm with limited resources and experience, the development loan may be elevated to a substantially higher level of risk. If, however, the mezzanine lender is a large well-heeled investment bank with strong real estate expertise and experience, the development loan may be reduced to a considerably lower level of risk.[12]

If there are problems that cause your institution to foreclose on the development loan and the mezzanine entity is relatively financially substantial, it is highly likely that to protect its position, it will take out the development loan. If it fails to take out the development loan, its entire investment probably will be wiped out (the realized sale price of an unfinished property in a foreclosure sale usually does not return any money to investors or lenders other than the first mortgagee, which is the development lender). By taking out the development lender, the mezzanine lender obtains full control of the property, has a first position on the money used to

---

[11] Mezzanine financiers usually are referred to as lenders regardless of their legal relationship with the borrower.

[12] The way mezzanine financing is structured-more like a loan or more like equity-will determine the rights of the mezzanine lender and its relationship to the development loan. Before the closing on the loan, an intercreditor agreement (triparty agreement) may be executed among the owner (developer), the development lender, and the mezzanine lender; this differs from the triparty agreement discussed earlier in this chapter, which is an agreement among the owner, the development lender, and the takeout lender.

take out the first mortgagee, protects its investment, and can, on completion of the project, perhaps realize some profit.

Author's Note

In the underwriting of every loan, repayment is an obvious consideration. On receiving the initial loan proposal, the loan officer should look beyond the simple ratios of loan to value and debt service coverage. Understanding the way the loan will be repaid, what alternative viable ways of repayment exist, what the likelihood is of the loan being repaid as planned, and when it will be repaid is important in controlling real estate credit risk. No matter how strongly you believe that the planned first way of repayment will occur, you should discuss all the reasonable repayment options in your credit presentation. Then, if the planned method and timing of repayment do not work out, no one can say you did not address all the critical issues properly.

CHAPTER 16

Real Estate Math

ESSENTIALS

As in all types of financial analysis, in real estate there is an abundance of simple mathematical relationships. This chapter discusses key mathematical products and ratios that should be used in the examination of a real estate credit (but not necessarily expressed in a loan presentation).[1]

Loan-to-value ratio = loan amount/perceived value

Perhaps the best-known ratio in lending, the loan-to-value (LTV) ratio needs little explanation. At any given time, the LTV ratio can be calculated by taking the amount of the loan outstanding and dividing it by the property's value. The LTV ratio is an important measure of loan risk.

> Example: According to your lending institution's information system, the current outstanding principal on a loan collateralized by a medical office building is $3,050,000. The value of the property as determined by an outside appraiser is $5 million. The LTV ratio is therefore 61 percent ($3,050,000/$5,000,000 = 61%).

---

[1] Real estate math calculations almost always are performed on a cash basis, not on an accrual basis.

An essential variant of the formula is: loan amount = LTV ratio × perceived value. Benchmark LTV ratios are given in the credit criteria of every lending institution and are based on factors such as the type of real estate, its location, the general economy, and the institution's appetite for risk. The independent variable—the perceived value—determines the maximum amount you are able to lend.

Example: According to a lending institution's credit criteria, the LTV ratio on non-income-producing developed land can be no higher than 65 percent. The value of the property as determined by an outside appraiser is $3 million. The maximum loan amount is therefore $1,950,000 ($3,000,000 × 65% = $1,950,000).

During the construction phase of a project, the loan outstanding increases over time as funds are advanced, but value also increases because the use of the advanced funds improves the property. It can be argued that during the life of a construction loan, the LTV ratio increases until the project nears completion. Then, for each dollar advanced, the marginal value begins to increase by more than a dollar, decreasing the LTV ratio. If this is plotted graphically with the LTV ratio on the vertical axis and the status of completion on the horizontal axis, the line will form a skewed asymmetric bell-shaped curve owing to the fact that a partially completed construction project is worth substantially less than a completed one.

As the outstanding loan grows, the lender continues to take a greater and greater risk of some loss because for every dollar of loan outstanding, less than a dollar of value is created.[2] As the property nears completion, every dollar lent, it is hoped, creates more than a dollar of value so that at completion, the value of the

---

[2] Adding to risk, a development project stalled for even a short period during its middle to final stages can experience major physical damage in a surprisingly short time if its elements are not protected. Add to this the cost of delays caused by unpaid bills, litigation, writing new contracts, bringing workers back to the job, coordinating the job, and so on, and there is an increasing probability that a substantial amount of the funds invested in the project will be lost.

FIGURE 16.1

Relationship between the Percentage of Completion and the LTV Ratio

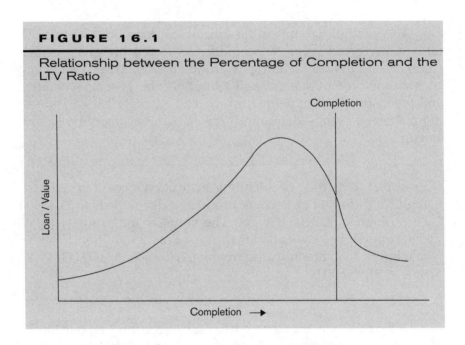

property is easily greater than the loan outstanding. This occurs because near the end of a project most of the work already has been done, the construction risk declines considerably, and the project is close to producing income.[3]

Coverage ratio = net operating income (NOI)[4]/debt service

During the construction loan, the property will not generate any or at most minimal cash flows to pay debt service. Therefore, debt service usually is funded from the construction loan itself. After project completion the property ultimately must produce enough income to support both interest and the repayment of the

---

[3] For a completed, stabilized operating property, the general rule is that over time the LTV ratio decreases. This occurs because the absolute value of the property usually appreciates as a result of rent increases outpacing expenses or because inflation exceeds depreciation and obsolescence. Furthermore, a loan on a completed property usually involves some component of amortization-paydown of principal-which reduces the LTV ratio with every principal payment.

[4] To calculate NOI, sometimes referred to as NI, subtract from total revenues all fixed and variable operating expenses. Not considered in NOI are debt expense, debt amortization, personal taxes (property taxes are considered an operating expense), and depreciation (although a general maintenance and replacement reserve expense should be included).

loan either with the construction lender or with a takeout lender.[5] The coverage ratio determines whether there will be enough (or not enough) expected net income to support the expected debt service and, if so, by what percentage. As in the LTV ratio, the credit criteria of the lending institution usually dictate a benchmark coverage ratio. For instance, for a suburban office building with several tenants, the required coverage ratio may be 1.15×. This means that NOI should be 115 percent of total debt service.

> Example: If your loan requires 115 percent coverage of total debt service and the debt service is projected to be $805,000 per year, the property must produce at least $925,750 per year ($805,000 × 1.15 = $925,750).

The extra 15 percent is the margin of safety that covers contingencies such as vacancies, declines in the leasing market, changes in interest rates on variable-rate loans, and increased operating costs, among others. If in the pro forma the minimum required coverage ratio is not met, the loan amount should be reduced and/or, if your lending institution gives you the flexibility, the amortization schedule should be lengthened.

Mortgage constant = a percentage that is multiplied by the initial loan outstanding

The constant is the amount of total debt service that is paid periodically (usually monthly). Debt service consists of principal and interest, and the varying proportions of those components can be calculated easily on an Excel spreadsheet. Mortgage constants also can be calculated easily on most "financial" handheld calculators (it is doubtful that any professionals today, even old-timers, still use tables). The following example includes the keystrokes using a HP12C calculator to arrive at the correct answer. Other financial calculators or formulas on a spreadsheet program such as Excel will produce the same result.

---

[5] Even if the property is sold, as in the case of condominium apartments, an income analysis will have to be performed in case the first way out-condominium sales-fails and the second way out-sale as rental apartments-has to be employed.

Example: How much will the monthly constant be on a fully outstanding $1 million loan with a 25-year amortization schedule and a fixed rate of 6.5 percent?

On an HP12C, the following keystrokes are inputted:

| F | | CLX | Clears calculator.

| 2 | | 5 | | G |* | N | Enters 300 months.

| 6 | | . | | 5 | | G | | i | Enters 6.5 percent yearly interest rate compounded monthly.

| 1 | | 0 | | 0 | | 0 | | 0 | | 0 | | 0 | Enters $1 million loan amount.

| PMT | Solves for constant = $6,752.07.

*G divides a yearly entry into 12 monthly periods.

On almost all development loans, only interest payments are made. However, the lender needs to make mortgage constant assumptions so that he can determine whether there will be enough operating income to cover debt service after completion to justify the project.

Effective mortgage constant = amortization payment/ remaining principal

On a term loan in which the entire principal is outstanding and constant payments of interest and principal are made, the effective cost of borrowing rises as the principal is paid down. This is the case because constant periodic payments over time will have a higher principal payment component (nondeductible for tax purposes) and a lower interest payment component (deductible for tax purposes). Therefore, it eventually will make sense to refinance the loan if the after-tax cost of a fixed amount of debt can be decreased even if the constant mortgage payments remain the same. Often, the borrower can refinance for a higher loan amount, take money out of the project, and still, with a higher constant payment, have a lower after-tax cost.

Example: A fully outstanding loan of $1 million with an interest rate of 6.5 percent and a 25-year amortization schedule will require monthly debt service payments of $6,752, resulting in a mortgage constant of 0.00675. After the first year, the thirteenth payment will have an interest portion of $5,327 and a principal portion of $1,425. After the ninth year, the 109th payment will have an interest portion of $4,359 and a principal portion of $2,393. Furthermore, the principal outstanding after the ninth year will be $804,704. Dividing the debt service payment by the lower principal amount results in an effective mortgage constant of 0.00839.

Debt service (DS) = loan amount ($) × interest rate (%)

or

Debt service (DS) = loan amount ($) × mortgage constant (%)

Debt service is a fairly obvious number and is known by everyone who has a mortgage on his home. Dividing the debt service by the loan outstanding gives you the debt service ratio. On a construction loan, only interest is charged. On a term or a long-term loan, both interest and principal are charged, usually as a constant aggregate amount each month. On these loans, the proportion of the interest component of the constant decreases and the principal amount of the constant increases with each periodic payment.

Example: A fully outstanding interest-only loan of $1 million with an interest rate of 6.5 percent will have a monthly debt service of $5,417. If the loan includes a 25-year amortization schedule, monthly debt service will be $6,752.

Loan amount = operating income/required coverage ratio/ mortgage constant

The maximum loan amount for a completed project can be determined simply by dividing the amount available for annual debt service by the mortgage constant. You also must factor in a coverage ratio. As was noted above, coverage ratios usually are expressed as a factor greater than 1. For example, a 1.3× coverage ratio means that operating income should cover debt service by 130 percent. When the coverage ratio increases, the maximum loan amount decreases.

Example: An office building with stabilized occupancy is generating $2,675,000 in net operating income per year. The lending institution's required coverage ratio is 1.15×, and the mortgage constant is 6.45 percent. The maximum loan amount is $36,063,364: $2,675,000/1.15/0.0645 = $36,063,364.

The independent variables associated with risk are the coverage ratio and the mortgage constant. The coverage ratio will be higher than the lending institution's benchmark if cash flows are uncertain, are dependent on only one or a few tenants, and/or are related to a project or area where tenancies and economic conditions fluctuate more than the norm. Coverage ratios may be higher if the property is of a higher-risk nature or if the borrower has, for instance, a limited track record.

Breakeven Ratios

Investors and developers have hurdles. That is, they will not invest their money and time in a project unless it meets certain expected targets. Breakeven ratios often are used as yardsticks on which to make a decision to proceed with or abandon work on a potential transaction. They also should be used by lenders to determine quickly whether a project makes sense. Sometimes other ratios, such as debt service coverage and loan to value, may look attractive, particularly when the loan is low in relation to the value. However, the breakeven ratio of the overall project can remain high. If a project does not make enough money to offset the cash investment, work, and risk that you would expect, proceed with caution.

Operating breakeven (BE) ratio =
(operating expenses + debt service)/effective revenue

Generally, if the BE ratio is, say, 85 percent, the project will have a positive cash flow up to a 15 percent loss of expected cash income. Stated another way, at 85 percent of expected income, the property will be at breakeven.

Example: An office building has revenues of $1,347,000 at full occupancy and annual expenses, including debt service, of $949,000. The BE ratio is 70.5 percent ($949,000/$1,347,000). If revenues decrease by 29.5 percent, the property will be at breakeven.

Sales breakeven ratio = total investment/(sales – sales costs)

This ratio is similar to the operating BE ratio discussed above but addresses a project in which income comes from sales, not from ongoing operations.

Example: A developer purchases land and builds 35 town houses at a cost of $8,400,000. The average sale price of each town house is $400,000, which will net him, after subtracting sales costs, $380,000 per house. His BE ratio is 63 percent ($8,400,000/[$380,000 × 35]). He will reach his BE point after the sale of the twenty-third town house (35 × 63% = 22.05).

Payback period = number of periods until capital invested is returned

The payback period is an estimation of how long it will take until investors and/or lenders get back their funds. It is another measure of the risk and success of a project.

Example: A developer builds a 20-unit luxury condominium building for a total cost, including land acquisition, of $10,800,000. He projects net sales proceeds to average $785,000 per unit, for a total of $15,700,000. From the day of completion, he wants to know how long it will take to repay his construction loan and recover all of his investment.

Period:	1	2	3	4	5	6	7	8	9	10	11
	Jan.	Feb.	Mar.	Apr.	May	June	July	Aug.	Sept.	Oct.	Nov.
No. sales:	0	1	2	2	3	4	1	1	2	2	2
$(000s)	0	785	1,570	1,570	2,355	3,140	785	785	1,570	1,570	1,570
Running total	0	785	2,355	3,925	6,280	9,420	10,205	10,990	12,560	14,130	15,700
Total cost/ Running total	13.8	4.6	2.75	1.72	1.15	1.058	**0.98**				

Payback period = 8 months

Expense ratio = operating expenses/stabilized gross revenues

This is the same ratio as the operating BE ratio discussed above except that debt service is not included. It measures the ratio of expenses to revenues and typically is used to gauge the initial attractiveness and reasonableness of a proposal. If the expense ratio of a proposal is low compared with your experience or in comparison to similar projects you have at your disposal to review, the potential borrower may be understating expenses (or overstating revenues) to make the property look better than it is. If the ratio is high, perhaps the proposal is too conservative or there are unusual or unique expenses that should be considered.

On a spreadsheet, forecasting out over several years, operating expenses should increase over time as the property ages and as inflation increases costs. Gross revenues usually are projected optimistically to rise at a rate equal to or greater than that of total expenses. Note that if the revenue growth rate is the same percentage as the expense growth rate, the expense ratio will remain constant, but NOI will increase. This is the case because both the numerator (revenues) and the denominator (expenses) of the ratio are multiplied by the same percentage. However, since revenues start off higher than expenses, the absolute difference between them (NOI) will increase.

Example: A multifamily residential property has effective rental income of $1 million and operating expenses of $800,000, leaving a NOI of $200,000. The expense ratio is 80 percent ($800,000/$1,000,000 = 80%). The next year, revenues and expenses increase equally by 10 percent. Now NOI is $220,000 ($1,100,000 – $880,000), but the expense ratio remains the same ($880,000/$1,100,000 = 80%). The year after that, revenues and expenses again increase by 10 percent. NOI increases to $242,000, but the expense ratio continues to be 80 percent.

Gross rent multiplier (GRM) = property value (or purchase price)/gross rent revenue

This ratio came about as a rough measure of the reasonable value of an income-producing property and usually was associated with its purchase. Before computers, when a purchaser was afraid a property would be taken off the market quickly, all he would do before bidding on it was take a recent rent roll from the seller, add the rents to arrive at a gross rent, and then multiply that total by a rule-of-thumb number.

> Example: If an apartment building throws off $300,000 in gross rents and the multiplier is 8, the perceived value of the property is $2,400,000 ($300,000 × 8 = $2,400,000).

Today the gross rent multiplier still is used extensively as a valid tool by appraisers. Taking the two variables—value, which is assumed in an arm's-length transaction to be equal to the sales price (perhaps adjusted for time), and gross rent, which is usually fairly easy to obtain, since before the property's sale, it was marketed with a disclosure of revenues—and dividing the former by the latter gives you the GRM. The appraiser, seeking out recent sales and gross revenue streams on comparable properties, then can determine a GRM for a type of property in a particular area.

As will be discussed below, the appraiser will estimate expenses, derive an NOI, and choose a cap rate that will result in another measure of value. The appraiser has two checks of value: one determined by using only gross rent and the other, usually more accurate because it is more refined, determined by considering expenses and using a capitalization rate that is nothing more than an expected return. The two methods should produce values that are close. The GRM is a good check and balance.[6]

Capitalization rate (cap rate) = net operating income/property value (or purchase price)

This ratio is similar to the gross rent multiplier but is a bit more sophisticated. It is one of the most widely quoted ratios among

---

[6] Note that expenses often are underestimated in a marketing brochure to make a property seem more attractive. They are not always easy to verify. Rents, however, are more readily subject to verification because the purchaser can examine a lease and, through an attestation by the leasee in the form of an estoppel certificate, feel confident that the lease remains in full force and effect and that the leasee is satisfying its obligations.

buyers, sellers, brokers, developers, investors, and lenders. It subtracts from gross rent all operating expenses to come to an NOI figure. That figure is divided by an estimate of the property value. The final figure is expressed as a percentage.

Example: A purchaser is willing to buy a property with an existing cap rate of 8 percent or higher. The seller of the property gives him a current rent roll and a recent listing of expenses. After making adjustments, he subtracts his expenses from the gross revenue figure and comes up with an NOI. If the NOI is $1,250,000 and the seller is asking for $15,000,000, the cap rate is slightly over 8 percent. It passes the hurdle, and if nothing else comes up in this simple example, he will purchase the property ($1,250,000/$15,000,000 = 8.3%).

For a development lender, the cap rate is an important tool to measure the feasibility of the final product after construction and improvements to the property have been completed. Also, it is important when one is talking with potential borrowers who may be purchasing an income-producing property. Capitalization rates are used extensively in appraisals under the income capitalization method (see Chapter 5) to determine value.

All development lenders should try to get a feel for what the various cap rates are for different types and classes of properties in the marketplaces in which they are lending. This can be done fairly easily by reviewing loan proposals, recent appraisals, and existing loans and talking with borrowers and brokers. Then, using the cap rate, you can make a quick and early judgment about the attractiveness of a project proposal and decide whether it is worth pursuing. Generally, cap rates are inelastic and fall in a fairly narrow range because they are a reflection of the minimum price a purchaser will pay for a particular class and type of property. Higher returns meet resistance in the competitive marketplace. In a sellers' market, in which supply decreases relative to demand, cap rates go down and prices go up. In a buyers' market, in which supply increases relative to demand, cap rates go up and prices go down.

Usually a project will be bought at a cap rate derived from market intelligence. Over time, if NOI increases and the cap rate stays the same, the value of the property will increase. If in the borrower's projections the cap rate is forecast to decrease, the value of the property at some later date may be inflated unrealistically to increase the attractiveness of the proposed transaction. Even a small reduction in the cap rate can have a profound influence on the perceived value.

Example: Using the previous example, the borrower is purchasing the property at an 8 percent cap rate. He expects to hold the property for five years, at which time he plans to refinance it or sell it. In his five-year assumptions, he values the property currently at $15,625,000 ($1,250,000/.08 = $15,625,000). At the end of five years, NOI is expected to grow to $1,595,000, giving it a future value of $19,937,500 ($1,595,000/.08 = $19,937,500). If the borrower, to make the deal more attractive to investors and lenders, drops the cap rate by even one percentage point, the value of the property increases by over 14 percent to $22,786,000 ($1,595,000/.07 = $22,785,714).

Return on investment (ROI) = (operating income before debt expense/total capital investment) – percentage of investment received from sale

Like the cap rate, the gross rent multiplier, and the expense ratio, the ROI is used to gauge the initial attractiveness of a proposal. When it is used as a criterion for investing and lending, it is a hurdle that must be overcome to elicit continued interest in a project. When it is expressed as a percentage, it is used mostly to describe returns at a particular point in time, usually on a yearly basis. It does not take into account the time value of money (the internal rate of return is discussed later in this chapter). It can, however, be calculated in several ways, depending on the time periods used, the life of the investment, and the information supplied. The most common calculation period is yearly. The total operating income is used as the numerator, and the total investment is used as the denominator.

Example 1: A $10 million investment that consists of debt and equity was needed to purchase land and construct an office building. It was a turnkey project in which the end user bought and occupied the completed property for $13 million. The return on investment is 30 percent ([$13,000,000/$10,000,000] − 1 = 30%).

Example 2: The situation is the same as in example 1 except that it will take two years to complete the property and sell it to the end user. In this case, there will be a zero return on investment the first year and a 30 percent return the second year. Without calculating for the time value of money but simply dividing the return over a two-year period, the ROI will average 15 percent per annum.

Example 3: The situation is the same as in example 2 except that the property will be retained by the developer and leased to a tenant. Often a five-year period of ownership is used. The tenant will pay $1,000,000 per year triple net. The initial return on investment is 6 percent per year ($1,000,000/$10,000,000 = 10%/5 × 3 = 6.0%). However, the ultimate sale of the property also must be taken into consideration or the ROI will be understated. With an expected appreciation rate of 3 percent per year on an estimated $13 million value on completion after two years, it is assumed that the property is held for an additional three years, after which it is sold for $14,205,000. The result is an annual return on investment from the sale of 8.4 percent ([$14,205,000/$10,000,000] − 1 = 42%/5 years = 8.4%). Adding 8.4 percent and 6.0 percent gives you 14.4 percent, which is the simple ROI per year.

Return on equity (ROE) = (net cash flow after debt expense/equity investment) − percentage of equity received from sale

Like the expense ratio and the ROI, the return on equity ratio is used to gauge the initial attractiveness of a proposal. It is calculated the same way the ROI is calculated, but the numerator includes debt expense and the denominator does not include the capital component of debt. Debt reduces the borrower's initial capital investment and increases the property's expenses, reducing absolute net cash flow. However, ROE is almost always higher than ROI because of positive leverage (discussed below).

Example 1: An $11 million investment was needed to purchase land and construct an office building. The developers borrowed $8 million. The funds were used to purchase the land ($3 million) and construct the office building ($5 million, of which $1 million was used to cover loan interest). It was a turnkey project in which the end user bought and occupied the completed property for $13 million. The return on equity (ROE) is 67 percent ({[$13,000,000 − $8,000,000]/$3,000,000} -1 = 67%).

Example 2: The situation is same as in example 1 except that it will take two years to complete the property and sell it to the end user. In this case, there will be a zero return on investment the first year and a 67 percent return the second year. Without calculating for the time value of money but simply dividing the return over a two-year period, the ROI will average 33 percent per annum.

Example 3: The situation is the same as in example 2 except that the property will be retained by the developer and leased to a tenant. A five-year period of ownership is used. The tenant will pay $1,000,000 per year triple net. Interest expense per year on an $8,000,000 loan will be $640,000. The initial return on investment is 12 percent per year ([$1,000,000 − $640,000]/$3,000,000 = 12%). However, the ultimate sale of the property also must be taken into consideration or the ROE will be understated. Here, as is often the case, a five-year period of ownership is used. With an expected appreciation of 3 percent per year on an estimated $13 million value on completion after two years, it is assumed that the property is held for an additional three years, after which it is sold for $14,205,000. The result is an annual return on equity of 21 percent ({[$14,205,000 − $8,000,000]/$3,000,000} − 1 = 107%/5 years = 21%). Adding 12 percent and 21 percent gives you 33 percent, which is the simple ROE per year.

Positive Versus Negative Leverage

Related to ROE is the concept of positive or negative leverage. With positive leverage, for every dollar of additional debt, there is an increase in ROE. With negative leverage, for every dollar of additional debt, there is a decrease in ROE.

Example: If an investment of $1 million generates a return of $100,000 cash per year, the return on investment is 10 percent per year. If the owner borrows 80 percent of his investment, he will have contributed $200,000 in equity and will have a loan outstanding of $800,000. If the interest on his loan is at a simple rate of 10 percent, he will pay $80,000 of interest per year and receive $20,000 of income after debt service. The $20,000 of income divided by his $200,000 equity results in a 10 percent return, which is the same ROE that he would get if he did not borrow the money. There is no change in leverage; it is neutral.

However, if the owner borrows the same $800,000 at a 5 percent simple interest rate, his interest payments per year will be $40,000 and he will receive $60,000 of income. The $60,000 in income divided by his $200,000 equity results in a 30 percent ROE. This is positive leverage.

Alternatively, if the owner borrows the same $800,000 at a simple interest rate of 12 percent, interest payments per year will total $96,000 and he will receive $4,000 in income. The $4,000 in income divided by his $200,000 equity results in a 2 percent return. This is negative leverage.

In this example, if the owner, instead of borrowing $800,000, borrows only $200,000 at the same simple interest rate of 12 percent, interest payments per year will total $24,000 and he will receive $76,000 in income. The $76,000 in income divided by his $800,000 equity results in a 9.5 percent return. As the loan amount decreases, the return on equity increases because in this case the loan's interest rate creates negative leverage.

Expressed simply, if the unleveraged ROE (no money is borrowed) is less than the cost (interest rate) of borrowed money, there will be negative leverage. If the unleveraged ROE is more than the cost of borrowing money, there will be positive leverage.

There are two important aspects to consider in regard to leverage.

Small changes in interest rates can have magnified effects on returns. With positive leverage, small increases in debt can have material positive effects on earnings. Negatively leveraged deals, however, eat up the borrower's return for every additional dollar borrowed.

If cash flows decline in a positively leveraged deal, the leverage can turn negative when unleveraged ROE decreases to a point below the cost of borrowed money. The higher the leverage, the less room before debt service cannot be accomplished solely by cash flows from the investment.

The phenomenon of negative leverage raises the question, If negative leverage reduces the investor's return, why will a borrower use it? Following are several reasons:

> Most borrowers have a limited source of funds. They therefore must borrow at least enough to cover the difference between what they are prepared or able to put up as equity and a project's total cost. In spite of negative leverage, if they do not borrow, they cannot take advantage of still profitable projects. Assuming that the investor in the previous example who borrowed $200,000 at a 12 percent interest rate had a minimum required return hurdle on his investment of 8 percent, he could continue to borrow until his return equaled 8 percent. This would be a 50 percent LTV ratio, which equals $500,000 ($500,000 debt × 12% interest = $60,000 in debt service, leaving $40,000 of after-debt cash flow; $40,000/$500,000 of equity = 8.0%). Even with negative leverage, the developer can pursue the project and make his required return assuming that the job is completed and leased or sold as planned.

Borrowers in the construction industry typically have some business infrastructure that has to be supported. This can include an in-house architect, engineers, construction personnel, and a management staff. To continue to support those people and thus assure the developer some baseline ability to seize on new development opportunities, the developer must maintain a continuous cash flow. Even if the return on investment on a particular project is not large, he will be able to draw funds down for construction and operating expenses to support his staff until the next, ideally more profitable project comes along.

A basic tenet of investment is diversification. To reduce risk, a portfolio should be made up of many different classes and different types of investments. A real estate portfolio has significant differences from a cash, stock, or bond portfolio (it is less liquid, requires substantially more management, exists in less perfect markets, etc.), but the principle of diversification is the same. A well-diversified real estate portfolio has less risk than does a portfolio with only a few assets or a concentration of a particular type of asset. With the use of debt, even when negative leverage is experienced, the developer will use less of his investable funds. The remainder of those available funds can be invested in other properties or types of assets. He thus can create some asset diversification and in the process reduce his overall portfolio risk.

One of the dangers for the lender of entering into a negatively leveraged transaction is that the borrower can lose interest in a project when a more lucrative one comes along. However, loss of attention is usually not a major risk because a lower return on equity or even a negative return is only one consideration for the borrower. The borrower's reputation; his continued ability to stay in business through the sourcing of new capital; and penalties, such as the calling of personal guarantees, lawsuits from colleagues, and so on, are all strong and powerful inducements for the borrower to fulfill his obligations.

**Minimum release price = loan amount/
(number of units × release percentage)**

or

**Minimum release price = loan amount × percentage of
ownership interest × reciprocal of release percentage**

In underwriting a development project in which the sale of units (apartments, townhouses, freestanding homes, office condominiums, etc.) will result in a percentage of the proceeds of each unit being used to pay down the principal of the loan, the question of what percentage of each sale should go to reduce the debt must be addressed. This is commonly referred to as the release percentage or the release price.

You should provide a floor or minimum amount that you will accept as a loan principal paydown on each sale. At the same time, you should not limit principal payments if sales prices are higher than expected. Because of the uncertainties of a future market and the inherent different functions and risk parameters of the construction lender and the borrower, you should always strive to be paid down as soon as possible, especially before the borrower reaps a substantial portion of his profits. If the borrower asks for a reduced release price but can give no compelling reason for you to give him one other than that he wants to be able to receive more cash early on, you should hold firm to the original release price in the loan documentation.

Example: A town house development is being proposed as follows:

Number of units	107
Each unit sells for a net average of	$40,000
Total net sellout (107 × $40,000)	$4,280,000
Loan is 70% of net sellout value	$3,000,000

Minimum Release Price

The question the lender faces is what minimum amount of sales proceeds per unit he will take on each unit sale to reduce the debt to zero. The lender's credit policy dictates that his institution is to be paid down completely after the development is no more than 80 percent sold out based on net sales proceeds. Using the 80 percent payoff level, the lender has to receive an average minimum of $35,046 per unit per sale before he will release a unit ($3,000,000/[107 × 80%] = $35,046).

Minimum Release Percentage

Although the formula above works for similar units, it does not account for value differences in units (which occur on the basis of factors such as the size of a unit, its location in the development, its views, and its amenities) but considers only the average. Particularly for condominium projects, it is better to use a minimum release percentage. This is easy to calculate because percentage interests and square footages are listed for all condominium units. Either one can be used to determine a minimum release.

A very simple example concerns a condominium building that consists of three apartments. The loan terms state, "All apartment units will be released on the greater of a principal paydown equal to 90 percent of the net sales proceeds per unit or 125 percent of the total debt per square foot of total salable area, multiplied by the salable square foot area of the unit being sold."

The percentage interest of each unit is as follows:

Unit 1 2,700 square feet = 27% of total salable square feet
Unit 2 3,800 square feet = 38% of total salable square feet
Unit 3 3,500 square feet = 35% of total salable square feet
Totals 10,000 square feet = 100%

A development loan of $3 million is outstanding.

The minimum amounts required by the lender to release units 1, 2, and 3 are as follows:

Unit 1 = $3,000,000 × 27% × 125% = $1,012,500
Unit 2 = $3,000,000 × 38% × 125% = $1,425,000
Unit 3 = $3,000,000 × 35% × 125% = $1,312,500
Total $3,750,000

Note that the total comes to $3,750,000, which is 125 percent of the loan. Taking the reciprocal of 125 percent (1/125%), the 80 percent release percentage is obtained ($3,750,000/$3,000,000 = 125% × 1× = 80%).

Also, note in this example that the lender is requiring a minimum release percentage of "principal paydown equal to 90 percent of the net sales proceeds per unit." Ordinarily, the lender will receive 90 percent of the net proceeds on a unit. The 125 percent calculation above is used when 90 percent falls below the minimum. For example, if unit 3 in the above example sold for a net of $1,800,000, the lender would be paid down $1,620,000, which is above the $1,312,500 minimum. However, if the same unit, because of a downturn in the market, sold for $1,200,000, 90 percent of that amount would come to only $1,080,000. Therefore, the lender would not release the unit. In fact, at the minimum release price of $1,312,500, the borrower would have to come up with $112,500 out of pocket to be able to have the lender's mortgage lien removed from the unit in order to convey it to the purchaser.

THE TIME VALUE OF MONEY

The time value of money is well known but is lacking in many borrowers' and lenders' analyses. This is understandable, since most mathematical calculations used in real estate address discrete points in time. The shortcoming is that pinpoint measures do not account for the real-world dynamics of variable cash flows. Fortunately, calculations that consider only one point in time often can be aggregated and augmented with additional data to adjust for time. Questions that may be worth bearing in mind include the expected time the property will be held before disposition, whether the property is to be refinanced, when that will occur and what the refinancing assumptions are, the amount of anticipated property appreciation, and what the cash flows are after stabilization. The internal rate of return (IRR) helps answer those questions.

Internal Rate of Return

Before entering into a transaction, an investor determines what his required minimum IRR will be for an investment in light of his level of risk aversion and the perceived riskiness of the investment. On coming up with an IRR, he makes projections to determine whether his hurdle is met or exceeded. If it is, he proceeds with his investment. If it is not, he moves on.

The internal rate of return is a percentage that gives a present value to an income stream equal to an initial capital investment.

Calculating an IRR can be cumbersome and prone to error on a handheld calculator but is easy to do on a spreadsheet program such as Excel. Excel will calculate uneven cash flows with one touch of the Enter key, whereas using a calculator involves many keystrokes. The scope of this book precludes an in-depth discussion of IRR; that topic can be reviewed in any good financial textbook. However, to make it easier for you to use Excel, here is the Excel formula for calculating an IRR:

$$= IRR(C1:Cn, 0.25)$$

where cell C1 is the first cell, which is a negative number indicating the initial investment, and Cn is the last cell in the income stream. The cells from C1:Cn inclusive are a periodic stream of inflows and outflows. The 0.25 is a plug IRR that must be used for Excel to carry out its calculations.

Example: A developer with money and capacity is looking for a new project that will give him an IRR of at least 25 percent. An opportunity comes from a broker who represents a client with undeveloped land near a popular highway entrance/exit. He thinks that he can buy the land and construct an office building over an 18-month period. He will need to invest $10 million at closing, with the remainder of the funds provided by a lender. He plans to sell the building in five years. He does a cash flow projection that shows the following:

Year	1	2	3	4	5
Cash flow ($000s)	(10,000)	1,000	2,100	2,163	18,000
	Investment	CF	CF	CF	Sales proceeds

On an Excel spreadsheet you might fill in the following:

	A	B	C	D	E	F
1						
2	=IRR(B2:F2,0.25)	(10,000,000)	1,000,000	2,100,000	2,163,000	18,000,000
3						

The cell A2 will calculate an IRR of 27 percent.

Since the IRR is above his 25 percent hurdle, he should continue to consider the investment.

Sample Spread sheet

The spreadsheet shown in Figure 16–2 was adapted from a project in Manhattan in New York City. Readers who are familiar with real estate math should be able to pick up most of what was discussed by working through the spreadsheet and the calculations that follow.[7]

New York Super Luxury Building

Location: Corner of X & Y Streets		
Desc:	Block 812, Lot 1	
		Res
Total No. Units		10
Total No. of Net SF		24,750
Avg. Rental / SF		$58
Avg. Rental / Unit / Mo.		$10,469

Use of Funds:	Per SF		
Purchase Price:	$125.25	$3,100,000	29.76%
Closing Costs	$18.24	$451,400	4.33%
Const. Costs	$237.98	$5,890,000	56.55%
Other Costs	$0.00	$0	0.00%
Working Capital	$39.39	$974,803	9.36%
	$420.86	$10,416,203	100.00%
Source of Funds:			
	Loan/Cost		
Debt Financing	76.8%	$8,000,000	
Equity Financing		$2,416,203	
		$10,416,203	

		Year	1	2	3	4	TOTAL	
								Inc./Annum
Income			Construction	Const. 6mo				
Rental Income			0	628,135	1,256,270	1,293,959		3.00%
Sale >Cap=	10.0%						12,939,585	
Other			$0	$0	$0	$0		
Gross Income			$0	$628,135	$1,256,270	$1,293,959	$12,939,585	
Vacancy & Collection Loss	3.00%		0	18,844	37,688	38,819		
Effective Gross Income			$0	$609,291	$1,218,582	$1,255,140	$12,939,585	
Operating Expenses (Does Not Include Construction Costs)								Inc./Annum
Real Estate Taxes			$15,000	$101,500	$209,090	$215,363	$540,953	3.00%
Water & Sewer			$10,000	$10,300	$10,609	$10,927	$41,836	3.00%
Professional Fees			$75,000	$25,000	$10,000	$10,300	$120,300	3.00%
Insurance			$35,000	$35,700	$36,414	$37,142	$144,256	2.00%
Fuel			$10,000	$10,000	$10,000	$10,000	$40,000	0.00%
Utilities			$5,000	$5,250	$5,513	$5,788	$21,551	5.00%
Supplies			$3,000	$3,090	$3,183	$3,278	$12,551	3.00%
Repairs & Maintenance				$8,000	$8,240	$8,487	$24,727	3.00%
Management				$7,500	$15,450	$15,914	$38,864	3.00%
Payroll				$22,500	$47,250	$49,613	$119,363	5.00%
Accounting			$5,000	$5,000	$5,000	$5,000	$20,000	
Marketing / Advertising			$0	$50,000	$25,000	$0	$75,000	
Rental Representative				$25,000	$0	$0	$25,000	
Administration			$10,000	$2,000	$2,080	$2,163	$16,243	4.00%
Misc&Reserves			$0	$10,000	$10,000	$10,000	$30,000	
Total Expenses			$168,000	$320,840	$397,828	$383,975	$1,270,643	
Net Operating Income			($168,000)	$288,451	$820,754	$871,165	$11,668,942	
Cumulative Net Operating Income			($168,000)	$120,451	$941,205	$1,812,370	$11,668,942	
Debt Service*								
Interest			$416,000	$619,129	$551,776	$550,988	$2,137,894	
Mortgage Amortization			($0)	$60,125	$126,732	$127,520	$314,376	
Loan Paydown at Sale							$7,685,624	
Total Debt Service			($416,000)	($679,254)	($678,508)	($678,508)	($10,137,894)	
Cum Loan Paydown			($0)	$60,125	$186,856	$314,376	$8,000,000	
CF after Paydown			($584,000)	($390,803)	$142,247	$192,657	$1,531,048	
Working Capital			$584,000	$390,803	$0	$0	$974,803	
Net Cash Flow			$0	$0	$142,247	$192,657	$5,588,864	
Cum Net CF			$0	$0	$142,247	$334,903	$5,588,864	
Equity Return							$2,416,203	
Net Profit Before Dist			$0	$0	$142,247	$192,657	$3,172,662	
Cum Return on TotalCapital			0.0%	1.2%	9.0%	17.4%	112.0%	
IRR on Equity	24%	DSCR	0.0%	0.0%	121.0%	128.4%		
Net Sale Proceeds after Loan Pay Down							$5,253,961	
Net Cash Flow After DS & WC			(2,416,203)	$0	$0	$142,247	$5,446,618	

* 8 1/2% interest only for eighteen months, then 7% fixed with a 25-year amortization schedule.

---

[7] Note that the "Sales Breakeven Ratio," the "Payback Period," and the "Minimum Release Price" calculations were not performed since the example illustrates a rental property, not a housing development or condominium project.

From the spreadsheet, the following values were taken:

a. Loan amount: $8,000,000
b. Cost of project: $10,416,203
c. Appraised value after completion
   (not shown on spreadsheet) $13,800,000
d. Interest rate, floating, 18 months   8.5%
e. Interest rate, fixed, 19–60 months   7.0%
   on a 25-year amortization schedule
f. Effective gross rental income at $1,218,582
   stabilization (third year)
g. Net operating income (third year) $820,754
h. Mortgage constant $678,508

After the fourth year of ownership, the property will be sold for $12,939,585.

The loan principal outstanding at the end of four years will be $7,685,624.

From the spreadsheet, the following values were calculated:

Loan-to-value (LTV) ratio = $8,000,000/$13,800,000 = 58.0%
Loan-to-cost (LC) ratio   = $8,000,000/$10,416,203 = 76.8%
Coverage ratio (year 3)   = $820,754/$678,508 =
                             1.21× (or 121%)
Mortgage constant   = $551,776 + $126,732 = $678,508
(year 3)   yearly, $56,542 monthly
Debt service   = Same as mortgage constant
Operating breakeven   ($397,828 + $678,508)/
ratio (year 3) $1,218,582 = 88.3%
Expense ratio (year 3) $397,828/$1,218,582 = 32.6%
Gross rent multiplier (year 3) $13,800,000/$1,256,270 = 11×
Capitalization rate (year 3) $820,754/$13,800,000 = 5.9%
(cap rate)
Return on   [(-$168,000 + $288,451
investment   + $820,754 + $871,165)/4]/
                             [($10,416,203 − $974,803
                             + $168,000)[= 4.7%
                             ([$12,939,585/{$10,416,203
                             − 974,803 + $168,000}] − 1)/4
                             = 8.7%
                             4.7% + 8.7% = 13.4%

Return on equity	[($0 + $0 + $142,247
	+ $192,657)/4]/$2,416,203
	= 3.5%
	({[$12,939,585 − $7,685,624]/
	$2,416,203} − 1)/4 = 29.4%
	3.5% + 29.4% = 32.9%
Positive versus negative leverage	Positive. Without leverage, the investor's return is 13.4%. With leverage, the investor's return is 32.9%. Therefore, leverage is positive.

Internal rate of return 24%:
Taken from the net CF after DS and WC line on the spreadsheet.
Using Excel, the formula is: = IRR (First Cell:Last Cell, 0.25)

Author's Note

One of the good things about real estate finance is that you can perform most of the mathematical calculations by using basic addition, subtraction, multiplication, and division. With a handheld calculator and a pencil and paper, you can handle most of the work. With a computer, you can do more, but it is still not difficult. Once you master it, you can control and interpret the results in many ways. That is where the art blends with the math.

CHAPTER 17

Pricing

Nothing in the lending business, the real estate business, and certainly the real estate lending business is ever static. This holds true for pricing, in which, depending on the financial markets, institutional profit margins change daily. The all-in price of a loan can attract or lose business and in certain circumstances can contribute to a project's success or failure. Ideally, a lending officer should look for a pricing structure that will bring the required return to the institution and give the borrower something he can say is a good deal.

LOAN PRICING

Loan pricing has two foci: the lending institution's need to make an acceptable profit in light of the perceived risk and the need to create a price structure that will be competitive and realistic in the marketplace.

As is common in large and well-regulated industries, profits are dictated largely by intense competition which limits choices. Profit standardization helps ensure that credit facilities are not underpriced. Pressures to standardize increase when there is a high volume of transactions, senior management does not feel comfortable giving authority for pricing decisions to lower levels of management, the institution perhaps recently experienced past pricing errors and/or fraud, and functionally different departments vie for revenues from the same client.[1]

The problems with a standardized approach vary with the level of inherent institutional flexibility and current market conditions. In a high-demand environment with few real estate lenders, a lending institution has a greater ability to dictate pricing. This situation occurred in the early 1990s when many lenders, after extending credit in a frenzied real estate market, suffered considerable losses when a recession took hold. Public opinion soured on institutions that made irresponsible loans secured by real estate. To satisfy their shareholders, many institutions constricted or essentially closed down their commercial real estate origination divisions. As a result, there were relatively few lenders left in the marketplace. When demand rose, those few lenders were able to dictate higher pricing and earned wider profit margins. The converse occurred in the early 2000s and continues to be the case; in a maturing marketplace, there are many lenders and pricing is much less elastic. To prevent a drop-off in desirable business, lenders have narrowed their profit margins and have adapted more imaginative pricing models to stay competitive.[2]

---

[1] In a bank, senior management may ask for compensating balances as part of the overall pricing structure. Often, those cash balances benefit the branch in which they are deposited. If that branch receives the sole benefit of the deposits, the real estate department will lose the incentive to ask for them. Instead, the real estate department may ask for a higher interest rate or a higher up-front fee even if the acceptance of compensating balances would be more beneficial to the bank.

[2] In the mid–1980s, when the market for secondary single-family residential mortgages was still in its infancy, many mortgage lenders balked at making loans, particularly on cooperative and condominium apartments in New York City. Developers were worried that after the completion of their projects, prospective purchasers of their residential units would not be able to obtain mortgage financing. This had the potential to be catastrophic. One developer approached a Citibank senior officer and voiced his concern. He was so worried by the situation that he told the banker offhandedly that he would pay in advance for the right to have potential purchasers of his project be reviewed for a mortgage to buy units in his project regardless of whether they ultimately qualified for a loan. The banker jumped on the opportunity, and the "Bulk" was born. Under the Bulk, the customer bought a certain amount of purchaser mortgage (end loan) availability for his residential condominium or cooperative project. For instance, if he expected total sales to be $30 million, he might buy a Bulk for $25 million. Then each prospective apartment purchaser could go to Citibank and apply for a mortgage. The fee charged to the project owner for a Bulk was usually 1 percent of the amount of the Bulk (extendable after one year for an additional fee). In the example here, the charge for the first year would be $250,000. Since Citibank was in the market to make end loans, it

COMPONENTS OF PRICING

Pricing models vary widely, depending on the institution, governmental restrictions on regulated lenders, the needs of the borrower, the type and nature of the collateral, and the structure of the credit. Each pricing component can work as an independent variable that can be adjusted to meet the profit hurdles of the lending institution. The components are discussed in the following sections.

Good Faith Deposit

Particularly with the additional work involved in a development loan, it is important that some money be received from the potential borrower almost immediately, beginning with a good faith deposit. The material below, which is part of a term letter to a potential borrower for an $18,500,000 loan, is a typical example of a request for a good faith deposit:

If you are in agreement with the proposed terms, please indicate so by signing and returning the enclosed copy of this letter where required along with a Good Faith Deposit of $25,000 and the additional information requested in Attachment II. If these materials are not received within fourteen (14) days from the date hereof, the conditions described in this letter will be considered null and void.

By executing this letter below, the undersigned requests that Bank ABC proceed with its underwriting and approval process with respect to a request for a Commercial Mortgage, and agrees to furnish all relevant materials which may be requested by Bank ABC to complete its due diligence. THE UNDERSIGNED ACKNOWLEDGES THAT BANK ABC, IN ACCEPTING THE DEPOSIT REQUIRED HEREIN AND CONTINUING TO PROCESS THE LOAN, IS UNDER NO OBLIGATION AND HAS MADE NO COMMITMENT OR AGREEMENT TO LEND ANY MONEY TO THE UNDERSIGNED OR TO ANY ENTITY OR AFFILIATE OF THE UNDERSIGNED. The Good Faith Deposit will be returned, without interest, less $10,000 representing the Bank's application fee and less any expenses actually incurred

---

essentially was able to receive an additional 1 percent fee from the developer without taking on additional risk. Often, much of the Bulk was not used. The Bulk is a great example of taking advantage of limited supply (end loans) by increasing pricing. Citibank took a universal product-a coop or condo mortgage loan-and made millions of additional dollars not from the individual apartment owners but from the developer.

by the Bank in connection with processing this application, including, without limitation, expenses relating to legal services, appraisal reports, environmental audits, and engineering reports, in the event that the Bank does not issue a commitment substantially in accordance with the terms and conditions contained herein. In the event the Bank does issue a commitment in accordance with these terms, the good faith deposit shall be applied as a credit toward the commitment fee.

A good faith deposit has two major purposes:

- It reimburses the institution for out-of-pocket expenses. No matter how successful the institution is or how potentially large the transaction is, something that all institutions are obsessed with is expenses, no matter what the amount. With a good faith deposit, that is no longer a concern.
- It demonstrates at least a minimum level of seriousness on the part of the potential borrower. Although a good faith deposit is not strictly a component of pricing (and is not a significant revenue producer), it increases the probability that your efforts will result in a consummated transaction. Your time is important. Potential borrowers are generally sensitive about walking away when there is something on the table, no matter how small the amount.

Commitment Fee

A commitment fee almost always is expressed as a percentage of the principal amount of the loan. The lender usually requires it to be paid before or at the closing of the loan. Often, though, the commitment fee is paid in two installments. Half of the fee is paid at commitment acceptance, and the remainder at closing.[3]

The commitment always contains language that specifies that when it is signed and returned to the lender, the commitment fee is earned. Particularly for a borrower that has no relationship

---

[3] Sometimes a portion of the commitment fee is taken at the loan paydown. It is called an exit fee, and the logic is that when it is time to pay off the loan, the borrower will have more funds available. A common loan structure is to split a fee in half. For instance, a 2 percent fee will require that 1 percent be paid before or at closing and the other 1 percent concurrently with the loan paydown.

with the lender or is suspected of "shopping" the deal with many other lenders, the whole commitment fee usually is due up front with the return of the commitment letter. By walking away from a loan commitment, the potential borrower gives up the fee. If any of the fee was to be deferred to the loan closing, often the only way the lender can obtain what it is due is to sue the borrower, an action that rarely is taken. With a strong borrower, however, the commitment fee may be paid entirely at the loan closing.

Interest Rate

The interest rate is based on the institution's cost of funds. If the wholesale cost of funds to the lending institution is, say, 5 percent, the interest rate charged to the customer has to be considerably higher for the institution to make a profit after covering operating costs, Federal Reserve requirements if applicable, loan loss and other reserves, and taxes on earnings. Although it is used not as a component of profitability but more as a deterrent and a way of off-setting problem loan costs, most loans incorporate a default interest rate. That rate, which is usually an onerous one near the usury rate ceiling, can boost the overall profitability of a loan considerably.

Deferred Interest

While a project is under construction, it usually cannot generate revenues. If the loan does not have a self-funding line for interest, interest must be paid through an external source (perhaps through a restricted deposit account or equity contributions). Sometimes interest is allowed to accrue until project completion. Then, when the project begins to generate positive cash flows, all or a portion of those flows will be used to pay deferred interest and then the out-standing loan principal. Although deferred interest is infrequently or never employed by depository institutions (banks), private lenders and mezzanine lenders sometimes incorporate deferred interest into their loan structures.

This order of paying interest first and principal second is always the rule for priority of payments. It makes sense because interest always is charged on principal balances. If payments were applied first to the loan principal, interest revenues to the lender would be lower because there would be less loan principal outstanding.

Funding the Loan

Ordinarily, a development loan will fund on a monthly basis with commensurate increases in the loan's outstanding principal. Depending on the negotiation leverage of the lender over the borrower, particularly on smaller loans, there are times when the lender will fund the entire loan at closing into a restricted account. Then the lender will release funds from the account on a monthly basis. Interest is charged on the full loan commitment from the first day, bolstering the lender's profits. Alternatively, funding the whole loan at once is a way for the lending institution to offer a lower rate. It still makes its expected profit by offsetting the lower rate with the benefit of lower cost funds (deposits). Surprisingly, there is usually not much resistance to this type of loan structure because the borrower is characteristically much more sensitive to obtaining the highest loan amount than he is to the rate.

Rate Sensitivity

All borrowers are aware of what interest rates are in the market because they talk with one another and with several lenders.[4] However, slight increases in the rate will not affect a project's profitability outcome materially because the construction loan has a short duration and because only at the end of the job will the loan be entirely outstanding (notwithstanding the rare loans discussed in the preceding paragraph in which all the principal is advanced at closing). During the early part of the loan, the interest charges will be minimal because the principal outstanding will be minimal.

Rate Lock-in Fees

Rate lock-in fees are a type of insurance paid by the borrower to the lender to put a ceiling on the interest rate. This technique is used most commonly to cap a fixed-rate loan. It also can be used to cap a floating-rate loan, but the costs to the borrower usually are deemed too high relative to the rate risk. For a fee, the lending institution will guarantee that if a loan closing occurs within a specified period, the rate will not be higher than what is specified

---

[4] For equity partners, how low the development loan rate is often is perceived as an indication of the managing member's strength and business acumen.

in the rate lock-in agreement. The fee is dependent on the period of time the rate will be fixed, the market cost of money, and the desired lock-in rate. Added to the price are a risk component and a profit markup. The rate lock-in fee is quoted to the real estate loan officer by the appropriate functional area of the lending institution, usually its treasury department.

Compensating Balances

Compensating balances are posted by borrowers in return for lower loan pricing. The deposits are not restricted and can be withdrawn at any time. However, if they fall below a certain amount for specific periods of time, the price of the loan, almost always in the form of its interest rate, increases. When compensating balances are taken, there should be some recognition of balance fluctuations. To smooth things, balances almost always are tracked as monthly or quarterly averages. Then, if average compensating balances fall below a minimum for more than a prescribed period or two, the interest rate on the loan rises. If balances then increase, the rate is lowered. Today, average account balances are tracked routinely. The administration of loans with compensating balance requirements is automatic and painless for the institution. Compensating balances are not very common in a real estate debt structure for several reasons that are discussed below (also see the first footnote in this chapter).

Compensating balances may not be borrowing entity–specific or asset-specific. If the borrower owns several real properties under several legal entities, using deposits from one or several of them as compensating balances so as to reduce a loan's interest rate may be difficult or impossible. For example, if the owning members of the asset that generated the deposit decide to sell that asset, the compensating deposits will evaporate.

Compensating balances, particularly on longer-term loans, can cause borrower resentment. Keeping high balances in a lending institution for short periods may not be difficult. However, in times of economic prosperity, borrowers are eager to invest idle funds in higher-yielding financial assets (this was prevalent in the middle to late 1990s as the stock market soared). Borrowers have sharp pencils. They calculate the expected opportunity cost of keeping compensating balances against the return from other investments.

In bad times, a borrower may need to draw down his balances. Not only is the borrower facing a tougher economic environment as evidenced by the reduction in his liquidity, he also is being penalized when his balance level falls below the minimum required compensating balance amount.

The politics of the institution and the relationship with the borrower may further limit the use of compensating balances.

Escrow Deposits and Restricted Accounts

Escrow deposits and restricted accounts are similar to compensating balances except that they are specific to and have a definite place in the structure of the loan beyond its pricing. With an escrow deposit, the borrower deposits a sum with a third party, usually an attorney, until an event triggers its release back to the borrower or the borrower's designee, or its forfeiture. If the lender is a bank, the deposit can be kept at the bank for additional revenue even though it is controlled by someone other than the lender. With restricted accounts, control is maintained by the lender. Escrow and restricted deposits are a cost to the borrower because the deposited funds cannot generate a high rate of return (even when deposits are interest-bearing, the interest amount is usually relatively low). Also, the borrower can experience liquidity problems if the funds are needed elsewhere in the project or in his organization.

Common reasons for establishing escrow and restricted accounts are to make sure debt service is paid, environmental contamination is taken care of, punchlist items are completed and paid for, a permanent certificate of occupancy is obtained, reserves for maintenance are adequate, utility bills are paid, and tax payments are made. In a development loan, escrow deposits and restricted accounts usually are short term in nature (two years or less).

Letter of Credit

A letter of credit (LC) issued by a bank sometimes is submitted in place of a deposit. It is used by the borrower because it is less expensive. For a fee of typically 0.5 to 2 percent, the LC can be collateralized with marketable securities or other assets that are being used more efficiently. This obviates the need to liquidate investments to fund restricted or escrow deposits. LCs are occasionally issued by the lending bank for the benefit of a future tenant to induce the developer to complete punchlist items, receive a certificate of occupancy by a certain date, or provide assurance against certain adverse contingencies.

Kickers and Participations

In the past, kickers and participations were part of many commercial banks' loan structures. They are now a chief element and a defining factor of mezzanine lenders.

Kickers and participations allow the lender to earn a percentage of a project's profits. For the privilege of being a participant, the lender will lend a higher principal amount (a higher loan-to-value ratio), thus increasing its risk. Unlike commitment fees, interest, and other forms of compensation, which are tied to the loan and are due regardless of the project's success, kickers and participations are based on the project's ultimate performance.[5]

Participations most often are used in transactions in which at the end of the construction process, the property will be sold (e.g., a residential condominium project). This is the case because most development lenders do not want the added risk of participating in a property that after completion introduces a new set of risks: leasing risk and, perhaps more important, management risk. Property management can be difficult to audit and monitor. The borrower, through ineptitude, can operate the property inefficiently, squandering profits, or, worse, can inflate management and other expenses that it receives remuneration for either overtly or covertly (fraudulently). It particularly hurts the lender if the loan principal remains outstanding and interest continues to accrue.

Walkaway Fee

Some development loans include as part of the overall loan terms a takeout commitment as well. A walkaway fee is a contingent fee that is imposed if the borrower chooses not to use the development lender's takeout. It is usually a percentage of the total commitment amount. The takeout can be a standby commitment or a bona fide takeout commitment (see Chapter 15 for a discussion of standby and takeout financing). In some cases the

---

[5] Note, however, that kickers and participations often require that at least some minimum amount be paid to the lender (a floor).

borrower will find a more favorably priced takeout from another lender, but the exit fee negates the pricing advantage. In other cases, such as when a standby is offered, it is not expected that the borrower will use it. Like an exit fee, the primary purpose of the walkaway fee is for the lender to earn additional money at the project's completion.[6]

Extension Fee

A loan extension fee may or may not be included in the initial loan documents. If the project is expected to be completed and the borrower is expected to pay down the loan within a certain period, you may not want to acknowledge the possibility of an extension. Including an option to extend the loan can send an implicit message that the borrower's planned time frame may fail. Perhaps more important, by excluding an extension option in the initial loan documents, if it later becomes necessary to extend, you are able to negotiate not only an extension fee but other terms of the extended loan as well.[7] There are times, though, when an extension fee (and other loan terms) is put up front into the loan documents.

This occurs when the project is complex and/or large and there could be some understandable slippage in completion; when it is acknowledged that there is some uncertainty as a result of external factors such as a contemplated zoning change that can affect the size, type, and scope of the project; or when the borrower is strong and insists on negotiating and addressing the possibility of a loan extension before it is needed. The decision to include an extension fee in the initial loan approval is up to you and your institution's lending criteria and policy.

Interest Rates: Fixed and Floating

The basic rule, at least in theory, is that your institution will source long-term funds to lend at fixed long-term rates to cover long-term stable projects. It will source short-term funds to lend at floating short-term rates to cover short-term projects or projects with

---

[6] Nonetheless, the standby commitment is real and can be drawn down. Therefore, it has some value to the borrower.

[7] Usually the lender has more leverage in negotiations because the loan will mature and, if not fully paid down, will be in default.

principal balances that will vary (a development loan, for example). The interest rate of the loan should be matched to the type and term of the facility.

Development loans are usually for a period of one to three years, with monthly increases in the loan balance as work advances. The time of loan paydown is guessed at; a precise date is impossible in most cases, since it depends on the completion of the project and perhaps the achievement of a certain level of rents, a takeout loan, or the property's sale. From the development lender's point of view, short-term funds will be used to fund the loan and the interest rate structure to the borrower will be some type of floating or short-term fixed rate adjusted on a monthly or trimonthly (quarterly) basis.

As was discussed in Chapter 14, the lender's attorney may use a bifurcated loan structure to protect against the possibility that future liens will gain priority over the aggregate loan amount. Another reason for bifurcation when the development loan involves an acquisition component and a development component is pricing. Since the loan balance of the acquisition portion will remain stable throughout the term of the loan, it may be funded at a fixed rate. The construction portion will vary from month to month on the basis of requisitions and therefore may be funded at a variable or floating rate. Before maturity, the borrower can prepay the floating portion but may not be able to prepay the fixed portion, at least without a penalty.

Mismatched Interest to Loan Term

If the sources and uses of funds are mismatched, the institution may be speculating on future interest rates.[8] To many lenders, this adds an unacceptable level of risk. Using a very simplified example, if an institution gives a borrower a 7 percent fixed-rate loan for three years and the total all-in cost of three-year funds to the institution at the time of the loan origination is 5 percent, the institution will make a 2 percent spread on its loan. However, if the lender does not buy three-year funds but instead uses short-term money to fund the loan and then rates rise sharply and the institution's cost of short-term funds increases to, say, 8 percent, the institution at times will

---

[8] Or it may be forced to take an unaccustomed rate risk position because of competition for the borrower's business or as a concession for a large and profitable borrower relationship.

be losing 1 percent on its investment (the loan). If it had matched its source of funds at the time it originated the loan, it would have locked in the 5 percent cost of funds and, regardless of fluctuations in the short-term capital markets during the term of the loan, would retain a positive 2 percent spread.[9]

Prepayment Penalty, Defeasance, or Mark to Market

With a fixed-rate loan, there is usually a prepayment penalty or a mark-to-market clause in the documentation.[10] This prevents the lender from inadvertently losing money, particularly in an environment of decreasing rates.

As an example, if a lender's all-in cost of funds for a $10 million five-year loan is 5 percent and the loan was made at 6.5 percent, the profit spread for the loan term is 1.5 percent ($150,000 per year) regardless of whether rates increase or decline during the loan term. If the borrower wishes to prepay the loan in the third year, the lender gets its $10 million principal back (an obvious reduction in risk) but no longer receives the $650,000 in yearly interest from the borrower. It still must, however, continue to pay $500,000 per year to cover its cost of funds. Three years from the inception of the loan, it can lend the funds out again, but only at what the market will bear for a similar type of loan. If the interest rate it can lend at is 4.5 percent, for the remaining two years, the institution will experience a negative profit (loss) of 0.5 percent of $10 million, or $50,000 per year.[11]

To protect against prepayment loss, lenders require a fee or penalty that is imposed if there is a prepayment. The fee can be based on a variety of variables, including the amount prepaid, the term of the loan, when the loan will be prepaid, the interest rate of the loan, the rates in effect at the time of repayment, and the

---

[9] Alternatively, short-term market rates could decrease, increasing the spread between the cost of funds and the interest rate on the loan; that would increase the lender's profit.

[10] Although this does not occur commonly, certain loans preclude any prepayments. This occurs when a loan is packaged with other loans into a portfolio and sold to investors with an overall specific risk, rate, outstanding principal balance, and maturity. A prepayment could upset the overall relationship of those variables and the balance of the portfolio.

[11] Note that in an environment of decreasing rates there is more demand to pay off debt early because the borrower can refinance at a lower rate. In an environment of increasing rates the existing loan becomes more attractive to the borrower as the difference between the loan's lower rate and the prevailing market rate widens.

lending institution's characteristics, such as its cost of funds, the mechanisms available and chosen for sourcing funds, and its policies for the reinvestment of prepaid money.

A simple prepayment fee that involves little calculation and continues to be used widely is a specific schedule of charges that is based on when a prepayment occurs. For a five-year loan, for example, the schedule can be a penalty fee equal to 5 percent of the amount of principal prepaid during the first year of the loan term, which is reduced by 1 percent in each successive year to reach a minimum of 1 percent during the fifth year. The advantage of this schedule is that it is simple, and so both the borrower and the lender easily can calculate what the prepayment charge will be at any point in time. Furthermore, it is unlikely that the lender will suffer a loss, since other, more sophisticated methods of calculating prepayment fees usually result in lower charges to the borrower.

A more complicated method calculated by the lender is called a mark-to-market fee or defeasance.[12] Both require the borrower to pay an amount roughly equal to the present value of the lost stream of income that would have been received by the lender. The borrower usually also charges an override fee to cover costs and receive additional profit no matter what the current market interest rates are. Therefore, even if rates are increasing and the lender can relend prepaid money at a higher rate, thus making a profit, there is still a prepayment charge to the borrower.

A PROFITABILITY TABLE

Many lending institutions require an estimate of profitability as part of the credit approval memorandum. For conformity and to reduce the chance of error, all use a form on which to input the chosen variables. The underwriter plugs in the values, and the program (usually Excel) does the rest. Two examples of bank templates are shown below. The first refers to an overall borrower relationship, and the second refers only to meeting a minimum pricing hurdle (see Figures 17–1 and 17–2).

---

[12] In commercial real estate finance, the term defeasance often is used interchangeably with prepayment penalty, mark-to-market, and so on, and is generally a penalty fee for the early repayment of a loan. The term's more precise meaning is the action of a lender that buys high-quality debt instruments (bonds) to replace the real estate collateral of the paid-off loan. The debt instruments provide a source of funds for the lender. The present value (plus additional fees the lender may charge) of the difference between the cash flow from the debt instruments and the loan's interest rate is charged to the borrower as defeasance.

FIGURE 17–1

Borrower Profitability Worksheets
Loan Profitability Worksheet

BORROWER NAME: **ABC Group**
DATE PREPARED: **3/1/200**

EXISTING LOAN FACILITY	(1) AVG. BALANCE OUTSTANDING PAST 12 MONTHS	(2) AVG. LOAN RATE	(3) HISTOR. COF 12 MOS AVER	(4) AVG. SPREAD (2)−(3)	(5) NET INTEREST INCOME (1) x (4)	(6) FEE INCOME	Historical Prime 6.75%
1 823	$2,200,000	7.50%	2.13%	5.37%	$118,140	$1,000	HISTORICAL
2 905	$430,000	6.75%	2.13%	4.62%	$19,866	$2,150	LOAN INCOME
3 422	$3,890,000	6.75%	2.13%	4.62%	$179,718	$22,850	$317,724
4							DEPOSIT INCOME
5							$788
6							FEE INCOME
7							$26,000
8							INCOME
9							$344,512
10							TOTAL YIELD
TOTALS	$6,520,000				$317,724	$26,000	5.28%

EXISTING LOAN FACILITY	(1) AVG. BALANCE OUTSTANDING NEXT 12 MONTHS	(2) AVG. LOAN RATE	(3) BUDGET. COF	(4) AVG. SPREAD (2)−(3)	(5) NET INTEREST INCOME (1) x (4)	(6) FEE INCOME	Prospective Prime 8.50%
1 823	$2,200,000	7.50%	2.37%	5.13%	$112,860	$1,000	
2 905	$215,000	6.75%	2.37%	4.38%	$9,417	$3,225	
3 422	$2,200,000	6.75%	2.37%	4.38%	$96,360	$11,425	
4							
5							
6							
7							
8							
9							
10							
SUBTOTALS	$4,615,000				$218,637	$15,650	

NEW LOAN FACILITY	(1) AVG. BALANCE OUTSTANDING NEXT 12 MONTHS	(2) AVG. LOAN RATE	(3) BUDGET. COF	(4) AVG. SPREAD (2)−(3)	(5) NET INTEREST INCOME (1) x (4)	(6) FEE INCOME	PROJECTED
							LOAN INCOME
11 To Be Deter	$11,160,000	8.500%	2.37%	6.13%	$684,108	$93,000	$902,745
							DEPOSIT INCOME
12							$79,935
13							
14							FEE INCOME
15							$108,650
							INCOME
							$1,091,330
							TOTAL YIELD
TOTAL 1-15	$15,775,000				$902,745	$108,650	6.92%

Deposit Profitability Worksheet

BORROWER NAME: **ABC Group**
DATE PREPARED: **3/1/200**

EXISTING DEPOSIT ACCOUNT	(1) AVG. COLLECTED BALANCES PAST 12 MONTHS	(2) HISTORICAL COF PAST 12 MONTHS	(3) AVG. RATE PAID ON DEPOSIT	(4) NET EARNINGS (2)−(3)	(5) DEPOSIT INCOME (1) × (4)
1 Demand Deposits	$37,000	2.13%	0.00%	2.13%	$788
2					
3					
4					
5					
6					
7					
8					
9					
10					
TOTALS	$37,000				$788

EXISTING DEPOSIT ACCOUNT	(1) AVG. COLLECTED BALANCES NEXT 12 MONTHS	(2) BUDGET COF	(3) AVG. RATE PAID ON DEPOSIT	(4) NET EARNINGS (2)−(3)	(5) DEPOSIT INCOME (1) × (4)
1 Demand Deposits	$1,250,000	2.37%	0.00%	2.37%	$29,625
2					
3					
4					
5					
6					
7					
8					
9					
10					
SUBTOTALS	$1,250,000				$29,625

NEW DEPOSIT ACCOUNT	(1) AVG. COLLECTED BALANCES NEXT 12 MONTHS	(2) BUDGET COF	(3) AVG. RATE PAID ON DEPOSIT	(4) NET EARNINGS (2)−(3)	(5) DEPOSIT INCOME (1) × (4)
11 Construction Loan	$300,000	2.37%	1.20%	1.17%	$3,510
12 Business	$4,000,000	2.37%	1.20%	1.17%	$46,800
13					
14					
15					
TOTAL 1-15		$5,550,000			$79,935

FIGURE 17-2

Pricing Worksheet

ASSUMPTIONS

COST OF FUNDS	5.25%
NOTE RATE MARGIN	1.25%
AFTER-TAX RETURN ON TOTAL ASSETS HURDLE	0.90%
TAX RATE	33.33%
ORIGINATION FEE	0.75%
COF	5.25%
NOTE RATE MARGIN	1.25%
ORIG. FEE	0.75%
TOTAL REVENUE	7.25%
COF	5.25%
ACQUISITION COST	0.50%
SERVICING COST	0.10%
CREDIT LOSSES	0.10%
ALLOC. EQUITY CREDIT	-0.29%
HEDGE (NOT REQUIRED)	0.00%
TOTAL COSTS	5.66%
NET REVENUE	1.59%
TAXES	0.53%
NET AFTER-TAX REVENUE	1.06%
HURDLE	0.90%
EARNINGS BETTER / -WORSE HURDLE	0.16%

Yield and pricing models like the ones mentioned above are normally straightforward and not very complex. They are a tool for quantifying the effect of changes in pricing variables on profitability. Their purpose is to allow the reviewer to get a general and comparative idea of the profitability of a transaction or a relationship and ensure that it meets the minimum profit criteria of the institution.

Author's Note

If you are a lender, you should be knowledgeable about your institution's pricing benchmarks and terms, which are based on objective measures (analytical pricing models) or are determined by more subjective methods that include gauging the strength of the borrower, the competition's pricing, and in certain instances the borrower's celebrity. Pricing always should be considered not only from a bottom-line perspective but also as a tool in negotiations. For lowering a rate or fee, for example, you should get something in return (examples include a 100 percent repayment guarantee rather than a 25 percent one and minimum deposit balances if your institution takes them). If you are a borrower, you should do what the lender does: figure out what the cost of your loan really is by taking into account all the variables, actual and contingent, and quantify them to the present. Then you can determine how good or bad a deal a lender is offering you.

CHAPTER 18

Environmental Concerns

In the 1970s environmental law became a very hot topic. The creation of the Superfund law [the Comprehensive Environmental Response, Compensation, and Liability Act (CERCLA)] and its concurrent threat of potential liability caused a sensation and panic in the lending community, particularly in the construction field. Several lending institutions left the business because of the perceived added risk. Those which remained and those which filled the lending void took a higher return in the form of interest rates, fees, and so forth, as a result of decreased competition in the field.[1]

The original environmental legislation was put in place to address the growing problem of the abandonment of industrial sites by companies that went out of business because of changes in product demand, technology, and/or real property depreciation and obsolescence. Those industrial sites and surrounding areas, which had been contaminated by all kinds of toxic chemicals through the decades, were threatening the health of people and wildlife in the immediate and surrounding communities. Since most of the offending companies were out of business or did not have the monetary wherewithal to make those areas safe, the government put in place a chain of liability, akin to a musical chairs setup, in which the last entity on the chain might be responsible for the entire cost of the cleanup.

---

[1] In light of CERCLA, the seminar business in environmental risk and law exploded, as did the number of environmental start-ups that were poised to perform every task from air and soil tests to the removal of contaminated material and/or remediation projects.

A CLASSIC EXAMPLE

A widely used example of environmental liability involves a manufacturing plant that was at its production peak during World War II. After the war, when demand for its goods declined, the company went out of business and the factory was abandoned. The property later was acquired by a manufacturing company with the help of a mortgage loan obtained from a lending institution. Subsequently, it was determined that the plant and its immediate surroundings were environmentally unsafe and that the cost to clean up the affected areas would be many millions of dollars.

The law was (and still is) that the entity that polluted the site was responsible for cleaning it up. If the culprit entity was no longer in business, the next entity that owned the site was responsible. If that entity was no longer in business, it was the owning entity after that one, and so on. Finally, the current owner, even if it had virtually no responsibility for the contamination, could be responsible for paying for the cleanup.

If a borrower was facing business problems that precluded it from meeting its debt obligations or was facing a huge cost for environmental cleanup and therefore defaulted on its loan and the lender foreclosed and obtained ownership of the property, the lender, which usually had the greatest financial resources to clean up the property (deep pockets), could end up paying several times more in cleanup costs than the original amount of its mortgage. If the current owner did not have the wherewithal to clean up the property and the mortgage lender, sensing trouble with the borrower, the loan, and/or the operation of the property, took what appeared to a court of law to be management control of the property to protect its loan, it could be held fully responsible for the cleanup.[2]

In fact, the cost of the cleanup often greatly exceeded the value of the property, rendering its value less than zero. The property had a negative value because the cost of cleanup and/or remediation was greater than the market price of a similar piece of property with no environmental problems.

The outcome was that the lending institution, having made a good faith loan, was responsible for a defunct company's or a

---

[2] In this example, the lender could have potential liability by being held responsible for the failure of the loan and the failure of the borrower's business as well.

deceased person's actions that had contaminated the property perhaps 50 years or more earlier. The full cost easily could exceed the amount of the lender's loan. In essence, the lender lost the ability to foreclose on the loan or exert any control of its collateral for fear that it would end up responsible for the full cost of the remediation or cleanup.

This very serious problem of cleanup liability led to an amendment of the law in 1986 with an "innocent owner" clause. Essentially, if the owner "did all it could" to check for contaminants and later some contaminants were discovered, it was exempt from liability because it had done all it could. Unfortunately, the question—and the exposure—was whether the owner indeed did all it could to check for contaminants.

Revised Approach

During the last decade major improvements in the law, public perception, experience, and technology have reduced environmental costs and potential liability considerably. The most salient changes are the following:

- In 2002 the law was revised to establish standards for exploring for contaminants and defining the succession of liability.
- Remediation and removal procedures have decreased substantially in cost. In the last 10 years, costs for some procedures have plummeted by more than 90 percent.
- Incentives are well established throughout the country, can be significant, and almost always include tax abatements.
- The perception of environmental hazards has changed from one of an alarmed knee-jerk reaction and a focus on blame to one of pragmatism that tries to balance costs with benefits. Instead of a full cleanup, for many sites remediation is now an allowed method. Contaminants remain on the property and are treated concurrently with its final use. The result is that with lower remediation costs instead of full removal costs, a site is put back into safe productive use.
- Municipalities, developers, investors, lenders, insurance companies, and users now have over two dozen years of

environmental hazard experience. This has reduced the mystery, fear, and risk of becoming involved in environmental issues that are not controllable or have not been predicted.

PRELIMINARY QUESTIONS

When you review a lending proposal and feel there is a good chance you will continue to underwrite a loan actively, you should get answers to several preliminary questions. You then will be in a better position to gauge the likelihood and severity of potential environmental issues. Some basic questions you should be thinking about include the following:

Q: How old is the existing structure on the site?
• Older properties have a higher risk of containing contaminants since knowledge of harmful materials and laws on their containment or disposal were nonexistent or not in place when they were built or modified.

Q: What are the past and the present uses of the site?
• This question has obvious implications. Common sense will guide you in doing your follow-up

Q: Is the property on city water and city sewers?
• This question concerns the runoff of contaminants. A property that draws well water is more likely to be affected than is one on a municipal line. If the property is not connected to a sewer line, where has waste been deposited? Has it been and is it being treated properly?

Q: How was the structure heated?
• If the property was heated with an oil furnace, there may be old tanks that have to be removed or will require that the surrounding soil be removed if oil leaked and leached into the surroundings.

Q: Does the property obtain its electricity from on-site transformers?
• Older transformers were constructed with PCBs, a contaminant that is deadly to wildlife and does not easily break down chemically in nature.

Q: Has an asbestos survey ever been performed? If so, what were the results?

- If asbestos is contained properly, it may never have to be removed. It can be properly contained and checked on periodically. However, if it is friable, minute particles can be released into the air. Asbestos in this state must be removed. Even small quantities can be damaging because once it is in the lungs, asbestos never leaves them.

Q: Is the property on or near an environmentally sensitive area?

- Over time, as a result of natural forces, contaminants can migrate many miles from their source. A property near a contaminated site can be affected by this migration. The owner of a property affected by a contaminated property can face a large cleanup bill even though he was not responsible for the contamination.

What to Do with the Answers

If any of the answers to these questions give you pause, immediately bring your concerns to the potential borrower. At the loan proposal stage, the borrower may not have a good idea of what environmental problems exist if he does not own the property. If he seems unaware of the concerns that you raise or glosses over issues that you know can have a serious negative impact, you should proceed cautiously. If he appears genuinely naive, he probably also is ignorant about other development matters that are important to the success of the overall project. You should expect honest, credible, and informed answers.

Choosing an Environmental Consultant

Before closing a loan, it is standard for a lending institution to hire a third-party environmental inspection firm to review the property for existing, suspected, and potential hazards.[3] Even though the

---

[3] This should not be confused with an environmental impact study, which may be required by the municipality where the project site is situated. Environmental impact studies vary widely and may include projections from increases in car traffic after project completion and stabilization to the effects of development on local vegetation and wildlife. It is important that this contingency be investigated before you make a loan commitment. There are many cases in which a project apparently was approved and set to go only to be crippled by a negative environmental impact study.

borrower is paying for the report, it is you who have to hire the environmental consultant. The consultant's client is the lending institution, not the borrower.

Before hiring a firm to do an examination, you should consult with your institution to see if there is an approved list of environmental professionals from which to choose. In many lending institutions, you may have only indirect control or no control over what firm is selected. That is controlled by loan administration so that there is less likelihood, at least ostensibly, that a lending officer, in collusion with the potential borrower, will encourage reports that fraudulently represent conditions as being better than they are. However, even in these institutions, you usually are informed by the loan administrator about two or three firms' cost quotes and the time it will take to complete the inspection and report. The loan administrator almost always will go along with your choice in the context of cost and time considerations.

Once you choose a firm, depending on the likelihood of an environmental problem, you may want to get opinions from other lending officers who have hired that company. It should be easy to obtain a report from one of them to see how the report is written and judge its quality.

Pricing

The price the consulting firm charges for a report is not a major consideration for a lender because the potential borrower pays for it. As with the cost of an appraisal report, the fee usually is paid up front by the borrower to the institution before it is ordered in the form of a good faith deposit (see Chapter 17). In some institutions, the fee is paid separately. If the borrower has a solid long-term relationship with your institution, you may feel comfortable paying the fee first and then trusting the borrower to reimburse you later. The general rule is that the lender should contract for the environmental report and pay the environmental consulting firm directly with its own check. The borrower should pay the lender before the lender releases the check to the consultant.

Response Time

The turnaround time from giving out the assignment to getting a quick oral report followed up with a written one may be crucial because for the purchase of a property, it is common to have a specific period for the purchaser to perform due diligence. After that period the purchaser risks losing the contract deposit and losing the ability to purchase the property. An oral report can help you and the borrower determine how to proceed to a loan closing or to something more serious, such as a rejection of the loan request and hopefully the quick return of the down payment to the borrower from the seller. If there are no material environmental hazards in an oral report, it is probably not a bad idea to close on the loan, make whatever prudent advance is necessary for the borrower to secure the property, and then make it a condition of the next advance that you get a satisfactory written report.

PHASE I REPORT

In the absence of specific environmental problems that may require a focused, specialized analysis, the first type of environmental report is a Phase I report.

A Phase I report is an assessment of the property to determine the existence or the possibility of environmental contamination. Its major component is an extensive background check. This involves, among other things, a title search at the municipality where the property is located.

The title search lists the prior owners of the property, commonly referred to as the chain of title. Additionally, the search reveals what prior structures, if any, were on the site and what uses they provided to the past owners (as an example, as is common in older cities, a factory was once on a site that is now a parking lot).

The consultant also may conduct interviews with people who could be familiar with the site, the surroundings, and events that might have led to some form of contamination. He also will go to the applicable governmental body or agency for details of groundwater flows, industrial areas near the site, known contaminated sites near the subject site, and other factors that may have an environmental effect.

Perhaps most importantly, the consultant will visit (walk) the property. An older existing building may contain areas that have asbestos, lead paint, a leaky oil tank, unlabeled storage drums, chemical spills, and so on, that can be discovered only by physical inspection.

Finally, the consultant puts all of the data into a written report. A typical report describes the methods and procedures the reporter used, what analysis was performed, what significant findings were revealed, and what actions may be required. The report may include some aerial views and perhaps a description of the area's topography.

The following table of contents and appendixes was taken from a Phase I report on a mid-Manhattan, New York, property. The original written report, including the table of contents with appendixes, totaled over 150 pages, which is typical of a Phase I report.

TABLE OF CONTENTS AND REPORT FORMAT FOR A PHASE I ENVIRONMENTAL SITE ASSESSMENT

A. EXECUTIVE SUMMARY

B. INTRODUCTION
    1. Purpose
    2. Limiting Conditions and Methodology Used

C. SITE INFORMATION
    1. Location and Legal Description
    2. Site and Vicinity Characteristics
    3. Information (if any) Reported by User Regarding Environmental Liens or Specialized Knowledge or Experience (pursuant to Section 5)
    4. Current Uses of the Property
    5. Historical Usage of the Property (to the extent identified)
    6. Current and Past Uses of Adjoining Properties (to the extent identified)
    7. Description of Structures, Roads, Other Improvements on the Site (including heating/cooling system, sewage disposal, source of potable water)

D. RECORD REVIEW
    1. Standard Environmental Record Sources, Federal and State
    2. Summary of Environmental Records Review (Environmental Database Information)

E. INFORMATION FROM SITE RECONNAISSANCE AND INTERVIEWS
    1. Physical Site Inspection
    2. Current Uses of Property
    3. Past Uses of Property

4. Presumed Asbestos-Containing Materials (PACM)
5. PCBs
6. Aboveground Tanks
7. Drums (Interior and Exterior)
8. Stains or Corrosion
9. Pools of Liquid (if any)
10. Odors
11. Interior Wall Coverings (if lead-based paint is an issue)
12. Radon
13. Underground Storage Tanks
14. Solid Wastes
15. Stressed Vegetation
16. Sumps, Pits, Ponds, Lagoons, or Wetlands (if any)
17. Wastewater
18. Wells
19. Underground Injection Control
20. Possibility of Migrating Hazardous Substances
21. Additional Concerns (if any)
22. Interviews

F. FINDINGS AND CONCLUSIONS

G. SIGNATURES OF ENVIRONMENTAL PROFESSIONAL

H. PROFESSIONAL'S QUALIFICATIONS

I. APPENDIXES

The following sources were utilized to determine the physical setting of the subject site and its current and past usage in order to evaluate and recognize environmental conditions that might have an adverse effect on the subject site.

A. USGS 7.5 Minute Topographic Map
B. Zoning/Land Use Records
C. Department of Assessment Records
D. Sanborn or Belcher-Hyde Fire Insurance Maps (if available)
E. Coles Directory
F. Aerial Photographs
G. Local Street Directories
H. Building Department Records
I. Prior Environmental Site Assessment
J. Soils Conditions Report (from the USGS Soil Conservation Service)
K. Groundwater Conditions (USGS Groundwater Flow Map)

In almost all the Phase I reports you will come across, quickly reading the narrative with attention to the findings and conclusions section is all you will need to do to get a grasp of the environmental concerns. If there are any, a follow-up call to the consultant may be appropriate so that you can get a better understanding of the extent and severity of the environmental issues. For instance, if it is not included in the report, you may be able to get an idea of the cost of eliminating, containing, or mitigating the problems and the time it will take to do so.[4]

A major purpose of a Phase I report is to let the reader know if further analysis is needed. If it is, as is often the case, a Phase II environmental report almost always will be recommended. (In certain circumstances, when environmental hazards are found, a Phase II report should not be required, for example, when a small amount of asbestos is identified in a localized defined space.)

PHASE II REPORT

A Phase II report is used to answer the environmental questions raised in a Phase I report. The consultant will focus on those questions, usually by taking samples of the potentially contaminated areas that were reported in the Phase I report. This can include soil samples, water samples, material samples, and air samples, all of which are taken methodically and deliberately. The samples help determine the extent of contamination, its source or direction, and, later, the cost of removing it. Analysis can vary from testing for one or a few contaminants to testing for many. A Phase II study can vary widely in its focus, scope, and methodology, and its turnaround time and cost vary with the amount of fieldwork and analysis needed. For example, if a soil sample shows contamination, a groundwater study may be required to determine whether pollutants have spread to other areas. This can take a lot of time and create significant costs and delays for the owner.

A Phase II report will contain a qualitative section and a quantitative section, have a detailed chemical analysis from a testing lab, make conclusions, and give recommendations. The recommendations should include suggestions about containment, control, or removal of existing or potential hazards, and, if possible, some cost estimates.

---

[4] Note that the consultant is not an estimator. Therefore, his estimates may not be very accurate, especially when there are complex problems.

THE BORROWER'S REPORTS

Sometimes the borrower, as part of his due diligence, hires his own environmental consulting firm before applying for a loan. Since he has reviewed the property thoroughly before closing on the purchase, you can assume that he has a certain level of responsibility and real estate sophistication. If his environmental firm has not been approved by your institution, you should ask for the firm's résumé and qualifications, including names and brief résumés of its key members, a short list of recent assignments and clients, and two or three institutional clients for reference (and perhaps another environmental firm as a reference as well). Whether or not the firm is approved by your institution, you should ask for a letter stating that the report was done in accordance with all the requirements and standards it would exercise if the report had been contracted by and presented solely to your institution.

Some lending institutions will not accept a report from an unapproved firm no matter what licenses, credentials, and endorsements that firm has. In this situation, the report must be reviewed by an approved firm. For the lender, this acts as an additional level of protection (perhaps unnecessary) against slanted, poorly researched, or fraudulent reports. For the borrower, it creates an additional expense.

If a borrower knows the likelihood is strong that he will use a particular lender, before hiring an environmental consultant he should contact that lender for a list of approved environmental firms. That way he avoids the risk of a delay and the expense of a duplicative report of little or no value that was written to satisfy the institutional requirements of the lender.

Another Firm's Statement

A letter by an environmental consultant hired by a potential borrower concerning an investigation of a Manhattan, New York, site follows. Note that the Phase I and Phase II reports were conducted almost a year before the production of the letter. However, no site activity except for a groundwater quality investigation took place after the Phase I and Phase II reports were written. After examining the firm's résumé and references, the lending institution accepted the report and made the loan.

XYZ CONSULTANTS
NEW YORK, NY

July 7, 200_

Mr. B. Lender
National Bank
123 Main Street
New York, NY

Re: Environmental Summary Report
Site Address, New York, NY

Dear Mr. Lender:

In connection with reports prepared by XYZ Consultants, Inc., for
Mr. Borrower:

Phase I Environmental Site Assessment
Site Address, New York, NY
June 20, 200_

Subsurface (Phase II) Environmental Investigation
Site Address, New York, NY
July 17, 200_

Subject to the comments below concerning the Groundwater Quality
Investigation of May 200_, we hereby confirm that National Bank, its successors and/or assigns, may fully rely on the aforementioned reports and
on all matters contained therein, as if such reports were prepared for said
parties and their respective successors and/or assigns in the first instance.

In May 200_, a groundwater quality investigation was intended to determine whether there were any special handling or disposal requirements for
groundwater at the site, should dewatering be necessary for site development. The former on-site buildings had been demolished, and the site was
vacant at the time of this study.

Boring locations were positioned throughout the site to achieve a representative sampling of the underlying groundwater. During the investigation,
refusal was consistently encountered between 10 to 14 feet below surface
grade in the first five borings advanced, which were positioned on the
southern half of the property. It is likely that this refusal was due to former
building foundations located in that area. Following installation of temporary well points, no water was detected in the two wells installed at the site.
As such, the temporary well points were left in the ground for a period of
24 hours to determine whether the lack of water in the wells was due to a
slow groundwater recharge rate. Groundwater was detected in only one of
the temporary well points the next day, at a depth of approximately 16 feet
below surface grade. A groundwater sample was collected from the one
well point and was submitted for laboratory analysis of New York City

Department of Environmental Protection (NYC DEP) regulated parameters for effluent to municipal sewers, which is the assumed course of action for potential dewatering activities for this site.

Based on this study, it appeared that the surface of the water table at the subject property slopes downward to the east, which is consistent with the presumed slope of the bedrock at the site. In general, the water table depth appears to be approximately 12 feet below grade on the western property boundary, approximately 16 feet below grade in the center of the property, and reaches a depth of greater than 21 feet below grade on the eastern portion of the property.

Copper, nickel, and zinc were detected in the sample analyzed, but at concentrations below the NYC DEP effluent limits. Suspended solids and nonpolar material were detected at concentrations well below the effluent limits. No PCBs were detected, and both the pH and ignitability characteristic of the groundwater were within acceptable levels. Methyl tert-butyl ether (MTBE) was detected at a concentration of 96 parts per billion (ppb). This exceeds the NYC DEP effluent limitation of 50 ppb for this compound. No other volatile organic compounds (VOCs) were detected in the sample.

Based on the water table elevations at the site, dewatering may not be necessary during site development activities. However, if dewatering is necessary, based on the concentration of MTBE detected in the ground-water sample collected from the site, groundwater pumped during potential dewatering activities may need to be treated before discharge to the sewer.

Since XYZ's May 200_ study, no major changes have been made to the study site. If you have any questions or comments regarding the enclosed report or any of the work completed at the site, please do not hesitate to contact us.

Sincerely,

XYZ Consultants

If you responsibly select a qualified environmental consultant, review the reports, and get proper advice from additional consultants and attorneys if required, it should be possible to contain and quantify environmental risks acceptably in terms of both time and expense.

WHO PAYS FOR THE WORK?

Today, whenever possible, a lender will not make its first loan advance until all environmental hazards have been removed or controlled.

Ordinarily, this is not a problem because the first step in developing a site is removing or neutralizing its environmental contaminants. Obviously, a new building foundation cannot be built on contaminated soil; the soil must be removed or isolated first. Since in most loan structures the borrower's equity is likely to be contributed to the project before the lender's debt is, the site will be environmentally acceptable before the lender makes its first advance. Therefore, the lender will have very little environmental risk (there is always the risk that some contaminants were not discovered or were contained ineffectively). This is true of rehabilitation projects as well. Workers cannot begin construction or demolition until hazardous materials are controlled or removed.

PROJECT FEASIBILITY

On large and/or complex projects and those in which there is some likelihood of multiple and serious contamination, before a developer removes, contains, or mitigates the problems, he must hire a consultant to perform a feasibility study to determine the time and costs involved. If removal is not practical, he must determine the effects of containment and remediation on his plans for improvements.[5]

In moderately complex situations, a report can run over 100 pages and be extremely detailed. The report must be comprehensive in scope because any omissions can result in a huge economic and/or health issue years or even decades later.

The feasibility study can affect the staging, organization, and coordination of the development process; the modification and placement of the to-be-built improvements; and, in highly contaminated sites, the feasibility of the project itself.

For example, a $1 million cost to remove contaminants from a former factory site that will become an enclosed shopping mall costing $100 million should not in and of itself be a major concern (it may, however, be the final straw for a project's viability). A $500,000 cleanup on a former factory building that will cost $1 million to convert into a low-revenue-producing "incubator" office facility may well kill the project's feasibility.[6]

---

[5] This includes, if applicable, ongoing costs to maintain an environmental maintenance program.

[6] The types of contaminants are very important because substances such as PCBs require relatively stricter cleanup procedures and standards. PCBs must be disposed of at approved centers that can be very far from the development site. Also, depending on the problem and the contaminated site, the developer may have to notify the proper state agencies and an agreed-on action plan may have to be established. This is usually not a major concern, but it is important that it be addressed early, since an omission of this type can result in fines, delays, and, worse, further samplings, demolition of new construction, and postponement of completion.

MOVING FORWARD

In major cleanup and remediation jobs, it is very important that you, the lending officer, be clear about what the issues are. If the environmental problems are significant, you may want to consult with an environmental firm and/or an attorney at the borrower's expense. The attorney or consultant can help you gain confidence that the borrower is on the right track with respect to the legal and regulatory complexities involved in cleanup, remediation, and containment. He also should be able to enunciate the risks clearly in case things do not go according to plan.

Once you are reasonably aware of the particular environmental issues, you should make it clear to your attorney that he will be held responsible for initiating and including the required documentation in the closing package to protect your institution as fully and practically as possible.

For you, the lender, it is important to document conversations with your attorney and environmental expert because if there is a problem later, you will be questioned about it. Having notes and documentation that show that you sought and considered their advice can shed new light on the issues and deflect blame if you are accused of not doing a thorough job that could have prevented or mitigated a problem.

ENVIRONMENTAL INSURANCE

Generally, environmental insurance is of two types. One type provides developers with coverage for cleanup costs for contaminants on the property or adjacent properties if necessary and covers cost overruns over a fixed amount for remediation. The other type covers environmental liability costs that result from the discovery of contaminants and costs from changes in the regulatory environment as well as third-party liability for personal injury. The two types of insurance can be blended and customized to individual situations.

Environmental insurance seldom is required or asked for by a development lender because on most projects, environmental concerns are defined by Phase I and Phase II reports. Furthermore, most or all of the environmental work has to be completed before a lender's first advance. If ongoing remediation is necessary, which is not uncommon, the lender's environmental consultant is the lender's backup to the developer's consultant. Also, environmental insurance is not very common because of its relatively high cost and the sometimes complex, time-consuming, and contentious process of filing and agreeing on a payment stemming from a claim.[7]

ENVIRONMENTAL INDEMNITY

Most forms of guarantees to lenders can be negotiated. However, with rare exceptions, one that cannot be negotiated is an environmental guarantee.[8] Below is a portion of a typical environmental guarantee from a new ground-up development project. It is provided so that you can appreciate its encompassing nature. It puts the full onus of any environmental liability squarely and completely on the borrower. Also note, however, that as discussed in Chapter 7, the strength and therefore the value of a guarantee are often limited.

ENVIRONMENTAL GUARANTEES

NOW, THEREFORE, in consideration of the foregoing and as part of the consideration for the making of the Loan and to make the Loan and advances thereunder, Indemnitor jointly and severally hereby unconditionally covenants and agrees to and with Lender as follows:

The Indemnitor shall protect, indemnify, and save harmless the Lender from and against all liabilities, obligations, claims, damages, penalties, causes of action, costs, and expenses (including, without limitation, reasonable attorney's fees and expenses) that are actually imposed upon or actually incurred by the Lender by reason of (a) the presence, disposal, escape, seepage, leakage, spillage, discharge, emission, or release of any Hazardous Material (as defined in the Mortgage) on, under, from, or affecting the

---

[7] Insurance often is required in situations in which investors condition their involvement on its obtainment. It allows them to avoid what they perceive to be an uncontained risk. On development projects, the developer may purchase insurance when significant environmental problems exist on the site to be developed or on sites near to and adjoining it.

[8] Today, almost all borrowers are aware of this. Those who strongly object to, for instance, a repayment guarantee will sign a full environmental guarantee without much fuss. One of the reasons the borrower will sign an environmental indemnity is that he feels he has done his due diligence, understands the history and surroundings of the site, has budgeted for environmental concerns and understands the risks, and feels in control of the project. An additional reason is that unlike a repayment guarantee, which would be listed as a contingent liability on his balance sheet, an environmental guarantee is not.

Mortgaged Property (an "Occurrence"); (b) any personal injury (including wrongful death) or property damage (real or personal) arising out of or related to an Occurrence; (c) any lawsuit brought, or settlement reached, or governmental order relating to an Occurrence; or (d) any violations of any federal, state, or local law, statute, ordinance, or code relating to health, safety, sanitation, the protection of the environment or governing the use, storage, treatment, generation, transportation, processing, handling, production, or disposal of Hazardous Materials and the rules, regulations, guidelines, decisions, orders, and directives of federal, state, and local governmental agencies, authorities, and courts with respect thereto (collectively, "Environmental Laws"), including, without limitation, reasonable attorney or consultant fees, investigation and laboratory fees, court costs, and litigation expenses.

Indemnitor hereby agrees that its liability hereunder shall be unaffected by (a) any agreement or modification of the provisions of the Note, the Mortgage, or any other instrument made to or with the Lender by the Borrower, or any person who succeeds the Borrower as owner of the Mortgaged Property, which agreement or modification may include, without limitation, an increase to the amount of the Loan, (b) any extension of time for performance required thereby, (c) any sale, assignment, release, satisfaction, or foreclosure of the Note, the Mortgage, or any sale or transfer of the Mortgaged Property, or any part thereof, and Indemnitor agrees that the proceeds of any of the foregoing may be applied by Lender to such obligations of the Borrower under the Note, including, without limitation, the payment of interest, and Mortgage and in such order as Lender may elect without diminishing the liability of the Indemnitor hereunder, (d) exculpatory provisions, if any, in any of said instruments limiting Lender's recourse to property encumbered by the Mortgage or to any other security or limiting Lender's rights to enforce a deficiency judgment against the Borrower, (e) the release of the Borrower, the Indemnitor, or any other person or entity from performance or observance of any of the agreements, terms, or conditions contained in any said instruments by operation of law, whether made with or without notice to the Indemnitor, (f) any bankruptcy, insolvency, reorganization, arrangement, assignment for the benefit of creditors, receivership, or trusteeship affecting the Borrower, the Mortgaged Property, and/or the Indemnitor or any of its respective successors or assigns, whether or not any notice thereof is given to the Indemnitor, or (g) Lender's failure to record the Mortgage or file any UCC–1 financing statements or to otherwise perfect, protect, secure, or insure any security interest or lien given as security for the Note.

Indemnitor hereby waives any and all legal requirements that Lender shall institute any action or proceedings at law or in equity against Borrower, or anyone else, as a condition precedent to bringing an action against the Indemnitor upon this Environmental Indemnity. All remedies afforded to Lender by reason of this Environmental Indemnity are separate and cumulative remedies, and it is agreed that no one of such remedies, whether exercised by Lender or not, shall be deemed to be an exclusion of any of the other remedies available to Lender and shall not limit or prejudice any other legal or equitable remedy which Lender may have.

It is understood and agreed that the Indemnitor shall not be released by any act or thing which might, but for this provision of this instrument, be deemed a legal or equitable discharge of an indemnitor, or by reason of any waiver, extension, modification, forbearance, or delay or other act or omission of Lender or its failure to proceed promptly or otherwise, or by reason of any action taken or omitted or circumstance which may or might vary the risk or affect the rights or remedies of Indemnitor or any of them or by reason of any further dealings between Borrower and Lender, whether relating to the Loan or otherwise, and the Indemnitor hereby expressly waives and surrenders any defense of its liability hereunder based upon any of the foregoing acts, omissions, things, agreements, waivers or any of them and hereby expressly waives and relinquishes all other rights and remedies accorded by applicable law to indemnitors; it being the purpose and intent of the parties hereto that the obligations of Indemnitor hereunder are absolute and unconditional under any and all circumstances.

In the event that the Indemnitor shall advance or become obligated to pay any sums for any purpose in connection with the Mortgaged Property, or in the event that for any reason whatsoever the Borrower or any subsequent owner of the Mortgaged Property, or any part thereof, is now, or shall hereafter become, indebted to the Indemnitor, the Indemnitor agrees that the amount of such sums and of such indebtedness and all interest thereon shall at all times be subordinate as to lien, time of payment, and in all other respects to all sums, including principal, interest, and other amounts at any time owing to the Lender under this Environmental Indemnity, and that the Indemnitor shall not be entitled to enforce or receive payment thereof until such sum owing to the Lender has been paid in full. Nothing herein contained is intended or shall be construed to give the Indemnitor any right of subrogation in or under the Loan, the obligations evidencing same or the Mortgage or any right to participate in any way therein or in the right, title, or interest of the Lender in or to the Mortgaged Property or other mortgaged property, notwithstanding any payments made by the Indemnitor under this Environmental Indemnity, all such rights of subrogation and participation being hereby expressly waived and released.

The Indemnitor shall promptly notify the Lender in writing if such Indemnitor, or, to such Indemnitor's actual knowledge, any person or entity now, hereafter, or heretofore occupying, owning, operating, leasing, subleasing, possessing, using, or controlling the Mortgaged Property or any part or aspect of the Mortgaged Property, receives any written notice or written request from any governmental agency, entity, or person, concerning any actual, suspected, or threatened Occurrence, or any pending or threatened actions, suits, proceedings, investigations, or other actions, of any type or nature, that relate to or arise out of an Occurrence or threatened Occurrence on, above, within, in the vicinity of, related to, or affecting, the Mortgaged Property.

The Indemnitor, at its sole cost and expense, shall allow, participate in, and otherwise assist in (including, without limitation, granting full access to the Mortgaged Property) the conduct and completion of any inspections, investigations, studies, sampling, testing, removal, containment, or other remedial action or other cleanup related to Hazardous Materials on, above, within, or in the vicinity of the Mortgaged Property, as may be required by any applicable Environmental Law.

The Indemnitor shall undertake and complete all inspections, investigations, studies, sampling, testing and all removal, containment, or other remedial action necessary or appropriate to contain, remove, and otherwise eliminate and clean up all actual, suspected, or threatened Hazardous Materials on, above, within, related to, or affecting the Mortgaged Property.

The Indemnitor acknowledges that Lender is not an environmental consultant, engineer, investigator, or inspector of any type whatsoever. Receipt, review, and/or approval by Lender or any of its agents of any information, reports, studies, audits, or other materials concerning the environmental condition of the Mortgaged Property, and the delivery of any such information, reports, studies, audits, or other materials to Lender shall in no event be deemed to be a representation or warranty by Lender or any of its agents as to the content or conclusions of such information, reports, studies, audits, or other materials or the accuracy or sufficiency thereof. The responsibility for compliance with all environmental laws and regulations rests solely with the Indemnitor or any present or previous owner or user of the Mortgaged Property.

All notices, requests, and other communications pursuant to this Environmental Indemnity shall be in writing, delivered by hand or overnight mail, or sent by certified mail, return receipt requested.

Author's Note

For the lender and the developer, environmental issues are an evolving area of laws, regulations, constraints, politics, technology, money, and emotions. Development lenders will see more and more proposals to build on environmentally contaminated land or protected land because of decreases in the time and cost of environmental work and pressures caused by population increases and migrations.

The key to addressing environmental problems is to follow the procedures prescribed by your institution (e.g., a Phase I environmental study followed by a Phase II if required). Remain objective. Do not take any shortcuts on behalf of yourself or your borrower. Follow the suggestions and steps in the studies and reports, and make sure the borrower does what is required. If necessary, have the right professional review the work the borrower is performing or has performed. Finally, if any issue or even the suggestion of an issue surfaces, take notes for your own file to protect yourself in case problems emerge later.

CHAPTER 19

Marketing: Searching for Loan Prospects

The type of financial institution you work for will have a strong influence on your approach to marketing, from not doing any marketing to taking part in a cold calling program. In larger institutions, the policy will lean toward the former. The real estate lending group will be focused primarily on the large tasks involved in evaluating and underwriting transactions, closing them, administering them, and getting repaid. Even so, during your lending career, no matter what size lender you are working for, you may be forced to take a more aggressive approach to marketing than you are accustomed to or prepared for. This can occur when there is a change in departmental management, the real estate department is below its expected profit levels, your institution is taken over by an institution with different business philosophies, or competition between lenders increases.

GOALS AND CONTAINMENTS

Every lending institution is constrained by its regulatory environment (bank, insurance company, investment bank, private lender, offshore entity, etc.), financial capacity, geographic location, and geographic reach (multistate presence, city presence, etc.). These constraints are usually slow to change and are largely outside your direct control; they are often outside the control of your lending institution. Within these constraints you will have to contend with institution-wide goals as well as the real estate department's subobjectives. Furthermore, the department's goals may not be enunciated except on a very general basis. They also may be out-dated and therefore of little use.[1] In spite of these potential difficul-ties, it is important to get a quick but firm idea of what objectives your lending institution and real estate department are moving toward so that you can decide whether you need to create an effective personal marketing plan.

In many institutions a marketing program is not needed. The reputation of the lending institution is such that there are more than enough proposals coming through the door. Those opportunities come from existing relationships, word of mouth, and recognition in the marketplace. In other institutions, especially those which are changing strategies or facing tough competition for loan growth, there may be considerable pressure to find new business. It is always important to know where you stand. Knowing the business goals of your employer can be critical to your early and continued success. Also, having knowledge of implicit unstated goals can be extremely helpful because they may be more powerful than the stated ones.

Because this is a guide to commercial real estate development, the discussion of marketing will be brief. Most likely, it will be ben-eficial to lenders who are finding the pipeline[2] running thin. It also should benefit borrowers in their search for efficient and productive ways to find a lender to help finance their projects.

GETTING PREPARED TO MARKET AND SELL

The best way to begin to set up a personal marketing program is to become familiar with your lending institution's credit and proce-dures manual. In banks that take deposits, a manual is a regulatory requirement. It may be general and outdated, but it will give you an idea of your lending institution's focus. Topics outlined in the pro-cedures manual should include geographic target markets, preferred property types, preferred customer profiles, preferred types of loan products, loan structure, and pricing.

Concurrently with a review of the credit and procedures manual, you should review recently written and approved credits.

---

[1] Many organizations tactfully avoid defining goals too carefully because they often are perceived as a constraint on flexibility and as potentially threatening if not used properly and counterproductive if not achieved.

[2] A pipeline is a list of potential loans usually categorized by type, location, expected loan amount, pricing, and possibly the probability of occurrence.

This should give you a better idea of the types of deals that have passed institutional scrutiny and the direction of senior management's credit focus.[3]

Once you have a grasp of the kinds of facilities your department will consider, what it might consider, and what it definitely will not consider, you can begin to create project and borrower profiles. This should incorporate both the institution's goals and your subgoals. The profiles can be anything from the minimum to the maximum loan size, key ratios such as loan to value and debt service coverage, pricing, loan durations, minimum personal net worth, and guaranty requirements. This is crucial because without at least some general knowledge of what each of your credit products are, what you want most to concentrate on within one or many products (large deals versus small deals, office buildings, residential buildings or hotels, etc.), what the constraints are and what ability you have to modify and customize each one, you will not be able to sell them effectively.

As your product knowledge increases in breadth and depth, you can develop and enhance your marketing and sales techniques. By using several of the sources discussed in this chapter, you can identify potential borrowers and match your institution's products with their needs.

Bear in mind, though, that no matter how much a potential borrower likes, respects, or wants to do business with you, if he does not have a project ready for a loan or if he or his project does not fit your business profile, he cannot be a borrower. Even a small real estate development can take a great deal of time. Assuming that

---

[3] Depending on the person and the institution you work for, obtaining copies of credit memorandums can be very easy or very difficult. One reason it may be difficult is that your institution fosters a climate that encourages its lending officers to be possessive about their work. This can be especially true of small lenders with only a few account officers.

Generally, it would be in the best interest of all for each employee to learn as much as he can so that he can do a better job and increase institutional productivity. However, petty jealousies, mismanagement, and poorly designed reward systems can work against you. For example, an account officer may feel rightly or wrongly that after reviewing his work, you will be in a position to steal his customer relationship, or he may fear that you will criticize his work to others. Essentially, the department may suffer from a universal lack of trust.

You can determine the level of information sharing quickly by asking your supervisor or your colleagues for samples of recent credits. Either they will be forthcoming or you will have to do some digging on your own. In any case, try to establish an ongoing dialogue with your colleagues and senior management about what new deals are being considered seriously in the pipeline and are moving through the approval process.

the average project lasts 24 months from the instant it is identified to its completion and that the average capacity of a developer is three projects at once, a potential borrower will consummate on average a transaction only every eight months. Including resistance on the part of the prospect to changing lenders, the time frame from the first contact with a prospect to the time when it bears fruit can be several years. Do not be discouraged by rejection. At the time of your call, he did not have a need for your services or your criteria eliminated him from proceeding with a loan. Often after several misses there is a hit that results in the formation of an excellent relationship.

Listed in order of overall preference and the likelihood of success, these borrower sources are described in the following sections.

Existing and Past Customers

By far, the best source and the easiest one to leverage is your existing and historical customer base. By keeping in touch with your past borrowers (including those from earlier employers if you have moved to a new lending institution), you are putting yourself in the immediate consciousness of your most likely customers. This is an opportunity to take a prospect you have had a relationship with and make that prospect a borrower again.

If you are new to real estate lending or have run out of past contacts and borrowers to call on, try to find out which relationships your predecessors or colleagues threw away because of lack of attention or poor judgment. You may be able to do this by going through old, inactive, or dormant credit files, memos, call reports, and other material throughout your department. If you are able to uncover past relationships that are dormant in your institution, you may have a legitimate claim to call on them even if you have not had a prior personal relationship with them.[4]

---

[4] If you have moved from one institution to another, you may be forced to give up relationships that you thought you could bring with you because lenders in your new department have existing relationships with several of your contacts. In this case, unless there is a reassignment of accounts by senior management, you have no justification for approaching those past borrowers since they already are doing business with your new firm. Also, if the climate and incentive programs of the new institution do not breed a fair amount of trust and openness, even continuing relationships with customers from your former institution can be a problem if, for instance, a lending officer of your new employer made overtures in the past to bring in a customer. You should be aggressive in seeking new business but also remain alert, sensitive, and prudent in regard to the environment around you. If in doubt, hold back until you can assess the situation.

Real Estate Brokers

Brokers are a natural source of business because they share a goal with you: placing the loan at your institution. They get paid only if they are successful. Therefore, they are usually eager and receptive to your initial overtures. Once a broker gets a basic understanding of your lending posture, he will pursue you with deals or will ignore you, often for long periods. Since brokers ordinarily are compensated only through closed deals, they can be aggressive and at times unrealistic in their assumptions as well as apt to skew facts and figures toward the more attractive features of a potential project. They also are primarily salespeople and therefore may lack the depth of understanding and experience needed to answer questions beneath the surface of a loan proposal. Since you will be dealing directly with the potential borrower soon after the initial introduction by the broker and exclusively with the borrower during the term of the loan, it is not important and sometimes is irrelevant whether the broker is cognizant of the many nuances of a transaction. Some of the best brokers have very good contacts in the real estate field but know little about real estate–secured lending. They step back quickly and let the borrower and lender interact from the beginning.

It is up to you to determine if a broker will be effective. If you decide he will not be effective, remember the "silver rule"—never burn bridges, especially with a broker. The world is ever-changing, as is the real estate industry and all who play in it. Call brokers regularly and let them know that you want their business. Try to reach a point where the broker thinks of calling you whenever he receives a prospect or client to whom you may be able to lend. Never take a broker for granted.[5]

Other Functional Areas of Your Lending Institution

Other areas of your lending institution can be sources of business through cross-selling. A cross-selling program is created and instituted at senior management levels, with deliberate consideration

---

[5] In lending institutions that focus their business on urban areas, it is not unusual for brokers to account for about 80 percent of all new loan originations. In one mid-size metropolitan lending institution, the head of the commercial real estate department goes out of his way to court brokers. He then takes all the submissions and divides them among the lending teams that report to him. He and his subordinates claim that the results have been very good. The institution's pipeline consistently has been more robust than those of its competitors. Brokers want to send him packages and deal with him.

given to structuring controls, compensation, and recognition. The experience in most institutions is that the cross-selling idea sounds good and from time to time is given lip service, but almost always is implemented poorly and never is very effective. The main reason for failure is the fact that often the benefits of cross-selling are unable to surmount its negatives. This is especially true in light of the potential time commitment needed to make cross-selling successful and the tendency of people to mistrust one another, particularly in a competitive environment.

In lending institutions, customers are typically proprietary to a specific lending officer or department, based on function, type of transaction, geographic area, and the like. It is normal and perhaps healthy for a loan officer to have some suspicion and concern that an important customer of his will not be treated properly by another person. Handing a client off results in some loss of his control of the lender-borrower relationship. Furthermore, if the institution offers little or no practical recognition and inadequate monetary compensation for cross-selling for the time and risk involved, the process is inherently negative. At worst, the lending officer will lose a profitable customer.

In spite of all the negatives and the barriers, you should form strategic relationships with other lenders and service providers in your institution whenever possible. Even one referral on a casual basis can result in a tremendous amount of business later on.

Professionals Related to the Real Estate Industry (Contractors, Lawyers, Attorneys, Title Personnel, Accountants)

On the surface, it would appear that professionals in the real estate industry would be a prime source for referrals. Because this group is easily approachable, you do not have to go far out of your way to begin an informal dialogue aimed at generating new business. Generally, they have a high level of sophistication and are acquainted with a large number of potential borrowers.

On the downside, they are generally not very aggressive in selling you to clients because they have little incentive to do so and perhaps fear being perceived by a developer as having an ulterior motive (a brokerage fee) for making an introduction. Also, they often see a deal very close to or after its capital structure has been determined. The lender already has been chosen.

Trade Groups and Professional Organizations

Trade groups and professional organizations are one of the less likely areas for finding new borrower relationships because the members of these groups are like you: They are looking for new loan business. It is unrealistic to assume that you will get new borrower contacts, but you may receive some intelligence on potential relationships and relationships you already have or have had when they span two or more institutions. The occasional slip of a tongue can be very beneficial. There are many benefits you can get from these groups, ranging from camaraderie, to education, to networking for your next job.

Trade, Internet, and Newspaper Leads

Obtaining leads from newspapers and magazines, both from objective stories and from public relations (PR) stories, can be fruitful. Most prospective borrowers love to see their names in print or on television. They are flattered that they have gained some attention and usually will be receptive to your initial call. In the Sunday *New York Times*, for example, there is a real estate section which regularly features articles on projects under new construction or under renovation. A call to the developer named in the article can be productive. It may get you in the door to compete on the project the article highlights if financing is not in place and on new financing opportunities that will be coming up in the future.

Promoting Yourself and Your Institution: Newspapers, Magazines, Discussions, Teaching

Advertising yourself through PR stories, teaching, lecturing, panel discussions, and the like is not for everyone. First, you need to have a story, a personal quality, experience, knowledge, or position that will enable you to attract an audience. Then, if you are fortunate enough to be asked to give an interview or perform in some other way, you must be able to deliver. If you are a boring lecturer, for example, the probability of winning new business as a result of your presentation may not be high. In the worst case, if you perform below the audience's expectations, you may hurt your reputation and perhaps your career. A further risk is that if you do not do as well as you expect, your self-confidence will suffer. Self-promotion, even if done well, often gets varying results. Its effectiveness often is limited because in many public real estate venues, your exposure is limited to small audiences. Also, your name in public is ephemeral. In a world of incessant bombardment of information and message sending, a week after a presentation or an interview it might as well never have taken place.[6]

Aside from the marketing perspective, teaching, presenting, and self-promotion can be a wonderful personal and professional experience that gives you energy and elation. These activities also require you to know your subject, and that can motivate you to brush up or learn new material that can make you a more knowledgeable professional.

Reconnoitering Development Sites and Taking Down Information

If you have passed by a lot of construction sites, you are aware that each one has a sign with the developer's name, the contracting company, telephone numbers to call in case of emergency, and perhaps the names of the architect, the engineer, and other players, including the lender. Calling from site signs is a technique used by many real estate brokers to find out who is doing what and to ask if they can be of service after the project has been completed. On completion, if the property is not 100 percent presold or leased, there can be broker opportunities.

For a lender, the probability of landing a loan is not high because the project probably has been financed already. Surprisingly, though, there are times when the developer has begun construction without becoming locked into a financing package. He may be using his own funds, the funds from equity partners, or funds from expensive "hard money" lenders to develop the project while simultaneously negotiating a development loan. This happens, for instance, when a developer enters into a lease for a piece of land. The developer must pay the lessor rent regardless of the development stage of the project. The sooner construction is completed, the sooner income can be generated to cover leasing

---

[6] It pays to be aware that particularly with foreign banks and large institutions, there are policies against promoting yourself or the company in regard to its business without consulting and obtaining approval first. Even if the publicity is favorable, if you have broken with policy, you can get in trouble. A positive PR piece may have surprising and unintended negative affects on your career. It is therefore always best to check with your institution before giving interviews, sitting on panels, and so on. The only exceptions would be if you are certain there will be no negative consequences or if the public exposure would outweigh any potential negative consequences.

costs. Even a month's delay can be very expensive. As the project is continuing through the approval process, demolition or site development often can proceed. The developer will use his own funds to shorten the time to realize income generation. Another example occurs usually in metropolitan areas that wish to encourage growth. They offer developers incentive programs such as tax abatements, tax credits, and additional size, height, and bulk allowances for finite periods. However, the developer must perform some preliminary site construction that will lock in those benefits before the program expires. Since site work must be performed by a certain date whether or not financing is in place, the job may be proceeding without a construction loan commitment.

Public Records

Although public records can be a source for prospecting, because of their broad and general nature, the difficulty of accessing them, and the inconvenience of using them, they are not a productive place to find new borrowers.[7] However, public records can be a very useful tool to augment your knowledge of an existing relationship or a particular property. For instance, you can find the names of both the purchaser and the seller of a property, their addresses, the date the sale took place, the amount of any recorded mortgage, and the name of the lender.

In several metropolitan areas that generate a high volume of real estate transactions, there are private firms that package and sell public and proprietary information either through a single purchase or through subscription. They offer services to target audiences in the real estate industry principally in three ways: choosing relevant information and arranging it in a usable format, delivering information so that it is conveniently available, and alerting the subscriber of changes or new information on a very timely, often nearly instantaneous basis. All this information may not be a great help in finding borrower prospects, but it can help a great deal in the underwriting process. Especially in the beginning stages of reviewing a loan proposal, when you are determining underwriting feasibility, the checking of basic

---

[7] Many large cities in the United States have put great amounts of useful information and data on Web sites, making its retrieval efficient and easy. However, because of the expense required to transfer information to a more convenient medium, most municipalities still have their records on paper and microfiche, requiring a visit to the town hall, the clerk's office, or another central location. The time, cost, and aggravation of retrieving public records this way make it an impractical way to find new borrowers.

facts available in the records can save you considerable time whether or not you choose to continue exploring the transaction.

Lists of Prospects from Trade Publications, Newspapers, and Magazines

Cold calling from a list is difficult and discouraging and may be frowned on or prohibited by your lending institution. It may call into question where your career path is headed: toward lending or toward marketing. Although the former cannot take place without some of the latter, cold calling is an aggressive tactic that should be practiced only by those who are not faint of heart. Do not expect a high success rate and be prepared to face lots of rejection.[8]

Word of Mouth

Word of mouth is one of the best ways to increase business, but that does not necessarily result from your efforts. After being in the business for a short time, you probably will witness word-of-mouth successes time and time again. Put a group of developers together, and when they start talking about financing, they will mention their favorite institutions and who they know and deal with at each one. Mention that you are a lender in the real estate field, and your prospect often will mention who he deals with. Word of mouth from a satisfied borrower can have exponential effects in the industry. If you have a good relationship with a borrower, it does not hurt to ask him to talk you up.

MARKETING AND SELLING: PATIENCE, PLANNING, AND PERSISTENCE

To obtain new borrowers in the real estate field, you often must have a great deal of patience. This may be particularly difficult in an institution that is demanding and seemingly unreasonably pushing to increase its real estate business without considering lead times or its ability to support the effort through staffing, credit, and marketing policies.

As important as it is to be persistent in your calling so that when an opportunity develops, you are in a good position to exploit

---

[8] Most stockbrokers begin their careers by cold calling; that is why the brokerage industry has such high employee turnover. Over time, though, a few cold callers have become extremely successful.

it, it is just as important to know when to stop calling a prospect. You should maintain a list on your computer or personal planner so that after each conversation with a prospect you can put down a future date to call him again. Make notes so that you will know where you left off when you last talked. If the prospect is inactive, place his name on the calendar six or nine months out. If you suspect the prospect will be doing a new project soon or has an upcoming credit need, put his name on the calendar 30 or 60 days out. If the prospect has a slim chance of becoming a borrower, call him once a year or so. If the prospect is very unlikely to ever bear fruit, do not hesitate to drop him from your calling list.

Knowing when to drop a prospect or severely reduce calling frequency can save you a lot of time and frustration. Many new account officers naturally gravitate to those prospects that are the friendliest and seem the least threatening. You can spend a great deal of time talking about the real estate business, viewing projects, and going out to lunch and never move any closer to your main objective, which is to get new business.

It is often beneficial to step back from time to time to evaluate your relationships. By understanding what those relationships are, you will have more realistic expectations of where and how each one will develop. Some turn into strong friendships; others turn into good business associations. Ideally, only a few will turn into major disappointments.

BASIC MARKETING MECHANICS

This may be stating the obvious, but before you make the first call, you must go through some preparation. If the prospect is well known to you, you already have some knowledge about his general business needs, perhaps more than enough to make the first call.

If the prospect does not know you, your approach must be different. First, you have to be able to speak to him directly. If he has a secretary or an assistant, you have to have a message that will allow you to get through that person to your target. Often, stating your name and the institution you are with and mentioning a project that the prospect is involved in will get you to the next level. It is a good idea to be succinct and to the point. The go-between may not be sophisticated or motivated to understand all that you are saying, and you will not have much time to get your message across. Try to keep the message simple. You want to leave something on the table (the name of a project, an event, a mutual acquaintance, etc.) that the assistant can convey easily to your target. If you provide too much information, you may give the assistant a reason not to allow you access or for the target not to take your call.

When you speak to the prospect, you should have a story or hook that will get him interested in you. One of the best ways to introduce yourself to a prospect is to talk about him. Do some quick research on the prospect. This can be as simple as having a casual conversation with a real estate associate, reviewing an article in a newspaper, researching the prospect's name on the Internet, or going over an old loan file. Write the information down, but not too much of it. You want to be able to refer to a few points quickly and easily while sounding extemporaneous. Remember, the objective is not just to call people and hope for the best; it is to start a rapport with the prospect that leads to results. A small amount of planning is very helpful.

FACE-TO-FACE CONTACT

It is almost impossible to get any business without a face-to-face meeting with the prospective borrower. If you meet a prospect at a social event (a golf or tennis outing, a wedding, etc.), it should not ordinarily be considered a real face-to-face because you usually do not have a chance to address what you do or learn what the prospect does in detail. A face-to-face is when you and the prospect get to know about each other and each other's business and business parameters and each one conveys his needs. Before meeting the prospect in person, just as you would on any call, do some preliminary due diligence. Try to learn something about the prospect's reputation, track record, associates, and general financial status. The amount of time you put into preliminary due diligence is up to you. Basically, it should be determined by the size of the potential relationship, its complexity, the probability of bringing it to fruition, the potential benefits for your institution, and the benefits, tangible and intangible, that will come to you.

Author's Note
The most important thing you should do in your marketing pursuits is maintain and project a positive attitude. You ultimately will do well even in the face of adversity if you put your rejections and disappointments in perspective. Remember that if you can establish even a few significant borrower relationships, you will have a great chance of being successful either with your present institution or at your next one.

CHAPTER 20

Loan Participations

ADVANTAGES FOR THE LEAD AND THE PARTICIPANT

For a lending institution to enter into an agreement with another lending institution, there must be advantages for both parties. Two incentives for lead lenders and participants[1] are diversification and higher profit margins.

LOAN PORTFOLIO BALANCE AND DIVERSIFICATION

Just as in a stock and bond portfolio, in an institution's loan portfolio there has to be a rebalancing of loan assets from time to time to reduce risk. Concentration in a particular type of collateral or a limited geographic area can be dangerous. If there is a market downturn in a product sector or a region in which a lender has heavy exposure, it can have a severe impact on earnings. Participations in loans collateralized by desirable projects and areas can mitigate concentration risk. Even for an institution with considerable construction lending experience, a participation may be the easiest and most expedient way to diversify.

---

[1] A lead lender is the institution that actually makes the loan. Usually, the obligation of the borrower is solely to the lead lender. The lead "participates the loan" to other lenders by allowing them through binding agreements to fund a portion of the lead lender's loan. In return, participants receive compensation chiefly from interest and fees.

PRODUCT TYPE

As this book is being written, most lenders have come off a historical peak of multifamily loan activity because low interest rates have fueled demand for new housing. Conversely, office vacancies throughout the country remained stubbornly high, generally as a result of strong increases in productivity which until recently have resulted in very little new office construction. A lender looking to mitigate its dependence on residential loan revenue may be eager to participate in an apparently sound office construction transaction and, after completion, perhaps take itself out by participating in the funding of a term loan. A few participations can help rebalance real estate loan revenue sources.

GEOGRAPHIC AREA

Most lenders do business in a relatively small geographic area. Lacking market and business familiarity with other regions they deem desirable, they are receptive to participations with lenders who have a successful track record and are knowledgeable in those different regions.

If a participant is versed in construction lending, a reciprocal relationship can be established. A lender participating with a lead lender in one part of the country may become the lead lender on transactions in its own part of the country, with the former lead becoming the participant. The result is a mutually beneficial partnership. Through participations, lenders can extend their reach nationally or even internationally.

PROFITABILITY

Loans secured by stabilized income-producing real estate collateral with marked similarities are subjected to higher degrees of standardization so that they can be bundled, packaged, and efficiently sold to investors (e.g., commercial mortgage–backed securities). The level of standardization has been highest with multifamily residential properties. An owner of a multifamily building with 20 units or more that is in good condition, is operating within budget, has manageable deferred maintenance, and is generating a good net operating income can expect quotes on loan fees, rates, and terms among many lenders to fall within a very narrow range.

The growth of efficient capital markets has made profit margins for this type of product relatively inelastic.

In contrast to a loan collateralized by a completed stabilized property, a development loan is usually far more complex and variable in structure. With greater risk and lender attention, construction loans can be difficult or even impossible to package and sell. They therefore generally command higher fees and interest rates. Also, since the typical construction loan has a short duration (usually 18 to 36 months) and the outstanding loan amount and concurrent interest payments grow incrementally over time, borrowers are not as sensitive to interest rates. They are willing to pay more for flexibility, for professional service, and in many cases to get a binding loan commitment in the shortest possible time. The greater profits from construction loans can be apportioned among participants so that both the lead and the participants benefit.

THE PARTICIPANT

Advantages for the Participant

In addition to mutual benefits, in all transactions there are unique advantages and disadvantages to either the lead or the participant. Let's start with the participant.

A Firsthand Education

Perhaps the easiest way for a lending institution to get involved in construction lending is to participate with another institution that has experience, stability, and a successful track record. The less experienced lender can take advantage of professional and administrative expertise not available in its own house. This can be an excellent method for obtaining an in-depth insider's experience. To receive the most value, the participant should try to negotiate opportunities for involvement in the processes that are unique to development lending, such as visits to the construction site; examination of documentation and reports related to the loan, including plans and specifications, engineering reports, monthly requisitions, and change orders; and inclusion in some construction-related meetings. After a few participations, participation lenders may gain enough comfort and justification to begin making or expanding their own development loan production.

If you are employed by a lender or are in a department that generally does not make construction loans or makes them on a scale or for a product type that is not in line with your career objectives, the chance to get a piece of a loan as a participant on a deal that interests you can be rewarding. Not only do you get a guided inside look at the process, you generally do not have to take on the lead lender's responsibilities. You can ask the lead lender "dumb" questions that you would never ask a member of your own organization. As point man for your institution, you can position yourself to receive new solicitations from the lead and other participants. Over time, as your experience with participations grows, you can become involved in more challenging transactions. You then can use your experience as a participant to leverage your career to a higher level either within your firm or with a new lender that is seeking development lending professionals.

Building a Portfolio with Limited Human Resources

When you are a participant, underwriting a loan is always easier because the lead lender has done much of the work for you. Its solicitation package and follow-up material outline all of the deal's facts and the lead lender's relevant observations. Often, on large participations, the material is several inches thick and slickly produced. Everything you need to underwrite the loan, or at least everything concerning a written loan presentation, is usually available. For an institution that wants to expand its real estate loan portfolio but cannot underwrite enough loans because of manpower constraints, participations can be an efficient way to increase credit originations quickly.

Efficiencies

Participants usually enter into an agreement with the expectation that the lead lender will take care of the loan mechanics and inform the participants from time to time as spelled out in the participation agreement. In most situations, the level of the participant's day-to-day involvement is very low. This is the norm and can be a considerable benefit when a lender does not plan to enter into or ramp up and spend money on construction loan servicing. The participant essentially is outsourcing the loan administration to the lead. Only when there are problems with the loan or dissatisfaction with the lead lender will the participant's activities increase markedly.[2]

---

[2] One major investment bank active in construction lending outsources virtually its entire loan servicing, whether a loan is participated or not, to a third-party firm that specializes in loan servicing.

Accommodating an Existing Relationship

Sometimes an institution may enter into a participation because the borrower has a relationship with it that is very important, for example, when the customer keeps high deposit balances with a bank. If the borrower is using another lender for its development loan, by participating it can, at least on some level, continue the relationship and ideally retain the customer's business.

On occasion, because a lender does not have the in-house capability to make a loan (e.g., the loan exceeds the institution's loan limits, the project is outside the lender's geographic limits, or the in-house staff does not have the specialized expertise to analyze the specific project type confidently), the relationship lender will fall back to the role of a participant.

When a lender refers a relationship borrower to another institution that will act as a lead lender, it often plays a larger role in the initial underwriting process. It has reviewed the loan proposal before deciding to refer it, and that should expedite the review and approval process of the lead lender.

The introduction of the transaction to the lead and extra work by the participant should be used as a leveraging tool whenever possible to gain a more meaningful involvement in the decision-making processes. The institutional participant may even be able to structure the agreement so that it is named as a co-lead. One advantage to this is that it has greater visibility with the borrower.

Reduced Risk

When you are invited to review a transaction as a potential participant, the loan ostensibly has been reviewed, underwritten, scrutinized, and approved by another lender. This should encourage you to give the solicitation serious attention, since the loan's risk already has been deemed acceptable. If other lenders are participating, there is additional comfort in knowing that two or more lenders have deemed the risk acceptable. The probability that a negative fact or circumstance was overlooked is lessened considerably.

However, you should not be lulled into false confidence and reliance on the lead lender's underwriting thoroughness and ability. At the very least, you should do a random check of claims and facts in the proposal. During your underwriting, make sure to ask for backup material that may not be in the presentation, such as a copy of a complete appraisal or the consulting engineer's report. If in doubt, ask questions.[3]

Size Counts

A case can be made at most lending institutions that senior managers are always looking for bigger challenges. This is evidenced by the high level of growth and consolidation in the lending industry. In development lending, the trophy project is the one that is talked about. The smaller, more difficult, more complex, and more creative transaction often is forgotten. It is human nature to strive for bigger things.

Participations can allow you and your institution to take part in very large transactions. Besides giving you bragging rights, being involved in something big can be used to market you and your institution as experienced, sophisticated, and capable underwriters for all sizes and types of projects. Your experience can be used to market not only your institution but yourself.

Disadvantages for the Participant

The disadvantages of becoming a participant are usually not material. They can, however, become significant if the facility gets in trouble.

Limited Effective Control

The typical agreement gives the participant very limited control in ordinary circumstances. Depending on how much money your institution committed to the participation, how many participants there are, and the structure of the agreement, you may have very

---

[3] When you are going though the approval process, make sure you know the transaction as well as you would if you were the sole original underwriter. One of the worst things you can do when presenting a proposal to senior management is to suggest that because it passed scrutiny with another institution, it should pass scrutiny with yours. The implications are that you have not done your homework, have avoided your underwriting responsibility, are ceding your decision-making authority and capability to someone else, and may not have the expertise necessary to form a valued credit judgment. Do not let this happen. Study and stay on top of the pertinent business and credit details.

little and possibly no practical say in the management of the loan. You essentially can be little more than a passive investor.[4]

Loss of a Customer Relationship

If you referred a customer to another institution or if your institution entered into the loan to maintain contact with a customer in hopes of future business, you are in a weakened position. Since a construction loan requires a lot of hands-on involvement with the borrower and/or the borrower's development team, the opportunity for the lead to establish a strong rapport with the borrower represents a business risk. You may not be able to overcome the new relationship established between the lead lender and your old customer.

The best way to mitigate this risk is to stay in touch with the borrower as much as you can. Work on a participation agreement that gives you access to the borrower and during the term of the loan, get regular updates from the lead lender, stay visible to the borrower (e.g., visit the construction site and try to attend meetings), and try to get involved in the decision-making process.

Loss of Status

Associated with loss of control and the possible loss of a customer relationship is a loss of status. The degree of loss depends on the size and style of your lending institution, the size of the transaction, the number of participants and their overall reputation, and

---

[4] In the early 1990s, the United States was experiencing a recession allegedly led by a collapse in the real estate industry. A branch of a foreign bank the author was familiar with had taken a $10 million participation in a $300 million loan secured by the Plaza Hotel in New York City. There was a general participants meeting across the street from the hotel at the former General Motors building. Attending were at least 50 people representing over a dozen lenders. The guest speaker, Donald Trump, suggested repaying the loan by converting the Plaza Hotel into a residential condominium. The loan would be paid down through condominium sales. Fortunately for all who attended, including Mr. Trump, the economy picked up and the loan worked itself out. (Later, Mr. Trump, through an alliance with a now-bankrupt insurance company, bought the General Motors building as well and put his name on it. He subsequently sold it for $1.4 billion in 2003.) Throughout the process, the foreign bank had virtually no control over any loan decisions. In absolute terms, a $10 million loan is significant. In relative terms, the lender had only a 3.3 percent stake in the overall transaction. (Today, much of the Plaza Hotel has been converted into residential condominiums that are being sold, even by New York standards, at fabulous prices.)

the professionalism of the lead. It is human nature to think of the lead as the more experienced and more competent entity. This, of course, may not be the case.

The risk of serious status consequences, especially on smaller transactions with limited participants, depends almost entirely on the objectives, personality, and ethical standards of the lead's point men. Your institution may be maligned as small, unsophisticated, unable to provide services properly, lacking flexibility, and so on. You personally may be cast as inexperienced, unknowledgeable, unintelligent, and the like. These accusations can be conveyed discreetly by a lead and thus be impossible for you to discover. They usually are motivated by the lead representative's desire to increase his customer base and, more often, the unfortunate tendency of many people to make themselves appear more competent by putting down, justly or unjustly, others who are current or potential competitors. If these rumors spread, they can persist for a long time even if they are unfounded. The way to mitigate this danger is to know the reputation and track record of the lead institution and, more important, know the lead's key players who will be directly involved with you and the borrower.

Par or Subpar Performance of the Lead

The fact that the lead lender did a good job on the underwriting and presentation of the loan proposal does not mean that it did a good job on performing due diligence or will do a good job on the administration of the loan. The lead's representative may just be a good participation marketer and salesman.

The development process is fraught with surprises and exceptions that can occur at accelerated speeds. Normally, only an experienced and knowledgeable lender can manage the many unexpected and challenging situations.

The performance of a lending institution, much like the performance of a loan, is likely to depend on only one or two individuals. If they are not up to the job or if the lead institution experiences the loss of key personnel, political departmental infighting, or reorganization, by the time the participant is able to exert control, it may be too late to stem credit damage. As was stated in the section on loss of status, the best way to guard against subpar performance is to know not only the lead institution but the lead's key players who will be involved in the loan.

THE LEAD LENDER

Advantages for the Lead

For the lead lending institution, there are many advantages. Some were touched on in the discussion of the participant.

Status and Name Recognition

For you to be the key representative of your institution on a loan in which it its the lead, your colleagues whose institutions are taking participations in the loan must think that you are able to carry out the lead function. If they did not think that, they would not participate. Your lead status gives you the opportunity to establish and strengthen personal relationships with the point men of each participating institution. This can have a snowball effect. Real estate is replete with industry seminars, meetings, cocktail hours, dinners, conventions, and outings. If you know a few commercial lenders through working relationships, your name and reputation will spread. Assuming you are a knowledgeable and conscientious performer, you may be able to enjoy a small measure of celebrity. Being favorably known in the industry can help you obtain a better position within your institution or to move another institution.

New and/or Strengthened Borrower Relationships

For most borrowers, the fact that their loan will be participated is not a concern. From a servicing perspective, the functional contact between the borrower and the lenders will be solely through the lead. Therefore, in the marketplace, it can appear that the lead lender is the sole lender on a much larger loan than it normally would have the dollar capacity to lend against. This can be a competitive advantage in seeking new business opportunities.

New and/or Strengthened Lender Relationships

As a known lead lender, you occasionally can get a desirable deal that you otherwise would have missed. Lending institutions do not exist in a vacuum. A lead lender attracts business not only from borrowers but also from other lenders. If your participants are treated professionally, a few may refer you to valuable borrowers from time to time if, for example, a loan officer was turned down on a loan proposal that he believes has merit, his institution does not have the in-house capacity to administer the loan, or the size of the loan requires that it be shared. It also does not hurt to let lending officers know that you are seeking new participating opportunities.

Size

Participations are a good way to get around size constraints imposed either internally or through government regulation. However, unlike a participant, the lead maintains a high level of control and visibility with the borrower. For some lending institutions, only a lead role is an acceptable one. With their in-house experience and expertise, they will not allow themselves to be participants because it may increase their risk.

Profit Margin

As was mentioned above, construction loans should command a higher pricing structure because of their service-intensive nature and generally higher risk. Since many lenders avoid construction loans because of those factors, there is generally less lender competition. Less competition allows more flexibility in setting prices.[5] Although the lead and participants almost always have the same level of risk, the lead often negotiates a revenue premium for the additional work and responsibility. On larger loans, this can be a significant amount of money.

Revenue distribution depends on several factors, such as the relative and absolute size of participants' contributions, the number of participants, the relationship with the borrower of the lead and/or participants, the various institutional pricing guidelines, and the negotiating ability of each participant's representative. If you know your participants' constraints and appetites, you have a better chance of negotiating a higher share of the revenues.

---

[5] The argument that less competition allows greater price flexibility and profit does not always translate well into practice in the marketplace. As this book is being written, there are burgeoning capital markets and a wave of lender consolidations. This has led to intense competition among a few strong players who offer borrowers razor-thin pricing. These large institutions have sophisticated construction loan-servicing operations (some are outsourced) and huge amounts of capital. They are attracted to larger deals, but with the competition to book those deals and intense pricing pressure, the loan size these players are involved in has decreased steadily as they have looked for higher profit spreads. They now regularly lend against projects previously left to smaller, more localized institutions. Although there are fewer competitors, with their large amounts of lower-cost investable capital, price competition has become greater.

Information and Action

As the lead, you receive all news, good or bad, first. Therefore, you have more time to review, question, understand, and react to it. This is important for two reasons.

The first reason is that your participants most likely are not as attuned to the nuances of the particular transaction the way you are. This makes sense since you may be the only one with whom the borrower interacts. You probably also have been involved with the loan from its inception and therefore have studied the transaction the longest. Additionally, in relation to your participating lenders, you may be the most experienced and sophisticated in the construction lending realm (your perceived knowledge may be a major reason they became involved in the transaction in the first place). For these reasons, it makes sense that you should be in the best position to make expeditious decisions and take action by making well-founded recommendations to the participants or, more likely in day-to-day situations, taking unilateral action. Most participation agreements give a good deal of authority to the lead because it is recognized that it is best able to exercise that authority in a manner that will be favorable to all. The lead and the participants in almost all cases have similar or identical interests.

The second reason is that if the loan is not performing up to initial expectations, you are having a communication or relationship problem with your participants, or you believe in a course of action that may be controversial; you can prepare yourself before addressing the participants. With a loan that is not moving along as planned, having the time to adjust your presentation to the issues can have obvious advantages not only for your professional standing but for your institution's.

If you receive negative news or are the cause of it, you must manage it objectively and efficiently. Do not let it become a personalized issue that can cloud your judgment. First talk to your manager, your credit person, or anyone who has the authority to advise or dictate to you how to react to the situation. If you have the authority to react unilaterally, you still may want to consult with your colleagues to get their opinions about how to handle the situation and cover yourself if the problem can cause the credit to deteriorate materially. Then, after talking with the right people in your institution, you can proceed to contact participants with confidence and assurance.

Disadvantages for the Lead Lender

As with participating positions, lead positions have disadvantages. If you or your organization is not up to the task of leading on a facility, even if a loan is performing well, there will be issues that can become problems quickly. If a loan gets in trouble, inability to act nimbly on multiple fronts and levels can be a serious problem.

Paperwork

If you have made development loans before, you know that the quantity of paperwork to service the loan can be very large. The amount of written material that the servicer receives for a routine monthly requisition can be several inches thick. On big transactions, if the servicer is inexperienced and does not know what to look for, the information can be overwhelming.

With a participation, all information and material that must be distributed per the participation agreement has to be organized, copied, and sent to each participant. If your servicing staff lacks experience, you will have to guide and monitor them, and that can be time-consuming.

Every bit of information and material that is sent out is a reflection on the quality of your institution and perhaps you. If there are mistakes or if information that you do not want to be sent is sent, you may have to spend time explaining yourself or the status of the loan. At best, this can be time-consuming. At worst, it can open you up to criticism that goes well beyond information distribution. It is a good idea from the beginning to dedicate a person to the facility who is capable and responsible, has a good understanding of the information distribution process, and has the time to make copies and distribute paperwork and reports.

Reporting Current Events

Participants get most of their information from you, the lead lender. If you regularly convey to them that the loan is performing satisfactorily and there are no unusual occurrences, they have no reason to ask for more. This is expected since most participants are reactive. Perhaps the only time you will have to provide more detail is when a participating loan officer must complete an annual review required by his institution or when auditors have asked to review his loan file. Unfortunately, if a problem is developing or if the lead is stuck with an unusually inquisitive or troublesome participant, reporting can mushroom into a chore and the degree of servicing and hand-holding can be significant. You must be careful to respond to your participants in a levelheaded, objective, and professional manner. Reacting emotionally can cause a situation to spin out of control.

Control

Participants react to the lead representative on a personal level as well an objective one. If you appear to be arrogant or aloof, do not return telephone calls, or seem to be too busy to respond to participants' requests in a reasonable manner, they will be willing to believe the negative rather than the positive side of a situation. Therefore, you must take the time and make an effort to pay attention to each participant on an individual as well as a collective basis. If your institution participates the loan to many lenders, the span of control may become too great. As a result, you will have a harder time giving each member the attention he needs. This can become a concern if problems or issues occur that require consensus.

If participants for whatever reason are not in sync with the lead, they may choose courses of action or inaction that can be detrimental to the lead and to the other participants. If an inopportune situation is felt to be getting out of control, in virtually all participation agreements there will be a mechanism for the participants to wrest control from the lead or at least have additional involvement in the loan administration. The lead lender may be overruled on key and major issues, especially if the trouble is perceived as being the lead's fault. This can cause embarrassment to your institution and could cost you your job. At the least, you will be working on the loan for long hours without much positive reinforcement from others.

Legal Action

Although this occurs only rarely, if the loan does not pan out as projected or if there are accounting irregularities or poor communication that leads to participants' suspicion, depending on how the participation agreement is written, the lead lender may be sued by participants for negligence, fraud, and the like. As was noted earlier in this chapter, before taking on the responsibility of a lead lender, make sure your loan servicer or servicing department has the required knowledge, experience, and attention to detail. Also, make sure you have an ongoing rapport with your loan servicer. From time to time ask to see a loan requisition. Go out with your inspecting engineer at least every few months to check on construction progress firsthand. Do not let a third party's inattentiveness or lack of ability become your problem. If something is wrong with your team, the rule is to fix it fast. If there is any chance that a problem will become significant, address it quickly. If there is a chance that your participants may find out negative news through a source other than yourself, make sure that you give them the news first. Then tell them how you are going to address the problem. Then give them frequent updates on your progress until the problem is fixed.

OVER YOUR HEAD

Before taking a position as the lead point man on a transaction, make sure that you have knowledge and experience in development lending. If you are uncertain or lack confidence on routine matters, the chances are good that this will be understood by your participants. With their institutions' money at stake, they will not be forgiving.

If you are not sure you can handle a position as a lead point man but your career dictates that you have little choice about accepting the assignment, do whatever you can to move up the learning curve quickly. Make sure to memorize and understand all the terms of the loan transaction and then do your best to get your hands on other project files, preferably those for a similar type and size of development. Study requisitions and their backup so that you know what is expected before each construction funding. Try to find a loan that had some issues. Read the memorandums so that you know how to structure them and who to address them to. Read the correspondence sent to participants so that you can get an idea of how the underwriter disseminated news. Become friends with your loan servicer; if he has experience, he will be a very valuable resource. Also, seek advice from your inspecting engineer and, if you are comfortable doing so, your colleagues. Finally, buy some basic books on development and real estate finance and study them.

Author's Note

Participations can be used to great advantage for both you and your institution. Whether you are the lead or the participant, take an active approach. You will become a better lender, make potentially valuable professional contacts, and possibly increase your borrower base. However, like any other credit facility, do an analysis of the transaction and make sure to assess its risks, both personal and institutional.

CHAPTER 21

Problems and Issues

During the development process it is extremely unlikely that even the most straightforward project will go according to plan. Depending on how conservative the original estimates were, as often as not a project will be over budget, will be completed late, and will need follow-up for punchlist items and defects after completion. It is the lender's art and responsibility to determine which problems are "natural" and are not cause for alarm and which ones are major or can become major and therefore threaten the quality of the loan.

Ultimately, even the best real estate lender makes a loan in which the probability of interest and principal recovery degenerates. Along the way, there is increasing risk not only to the institution's money but, depending on the politics of the lending institution and the nature and severity of the problems, also to the careers of the originating lending officer and more senior personnel.

VISITING THE PROPERTY: VISUAL INSPECTIONS

One of the most effective ways to monitor a development project is to visit the construction site. Begin by asking the developer and/or members of the development team general questions. As the lender, you will get their immediate attention. Key construction personnel usually will be willing to give you basic understandable answers, both because they do not want to upset you (or their employer) and because they will enjoy showing off their knowledge. Since you are not expected to be an expert in construction, you can start with very general questions and, based on the answers you receive, become more specific.

WHEN THERE IS A PROBLEM

When you are told about a problem or deduce one from your visual inspections and/or conversations, you must assess its impact on the job and on your loan. To make this assessment you must know something about timing, coordination, and construction costs. Unfortunately, this is knowledge that most lenders do not have. If you have limited knowledge in these areas, you must rely on help. The first source probably should be the developer. The adage that every story has two sides is true here. What you might see as a major problem may not be, or it may be in the process of being fixed.

Giving the developer a first chance to address your concerns can be the most efficient initial course of action. Sometimes, though, the developer may not be aware of the problem. If this is the case, you want to know why. Perhaps it just surfaced or was not deemed serious enough to be brought to his attention. Perhaps it is a sign of a slippage in supervision, oversight, and/or communication. Just as important, whether he is aware of the problem or not, does he think it is as serious as you do once you are certain it is indeed serious?

A good developer and certainly his project manager will be cognizant of what is going on with regard to their project. They also should have a plan for correcting a problem fairly swiftly after it surfaces.

QUESTIONS AND ANSWERS

If there is a recognized problem, the critical questions you should be asking yourself and continually following up on are the following ones:

Is the borrower doing what should be done about it?
Is there an action plan in place?
Is the action plan being followed?
Is the plan being reviewed constantly, and is it flexible
    enough to meet the current challenges and problems?
Is the plan working?

If it is a construction-related issue, your inspecting engineer also may have picked up on it during his regular inspections and paperwork review; perhaps he was the one who alerted you to it. He should be able to give you a balanced view of the situation, including its severity, its expected ramifications in terms of cost and time, and ways it can be corrected.

Once you are aware of an existing or potential problem and have a reasonable amount of information from the borrower, your inspecting engineer, and possibly other sources, you need to ascertain how it can affect the progress and cost of the job. If you believe that it will affect the project materially, you should get as clear an understanding as possible of how. Is there a chain reaction involved? Who is responsible for the problem? Is it the developer, or is it a force out of the developer's control? Finally, you should consider what should be done by the borrower and what should be done by you.[1]

Most important, you should review the situation with senior personnel. However, it is important that you be as informed as possible before speaking to institutional management because they inevitably will hold you responsible for making a clearly and intelligently presented report on the situation.

The most important rule is that if a problem is grave at the outset, if the developer seems unable to cope, if he refuses to act, if his plan is not working, or if you have any doubts about what is going to happen next, make sure senior management and your institution's attorney is aware of the situation, and then take action.

COMMON PROBLEMS

Several problems have been discussed throughout this book. Some common ones are highlighted below, along with possible results and solutions.

Problem: Contractor Leaves the Job without Warning

Result

This can lead to delays caused by the need to find and hire a replacement contractor. A replacement contractor almost always

---

[1] If a situation is complex, you may want to list the potential outcomes on a worksheet. You then can evaluate what could go wrong as a result of the situation and focus on the most likely or severe scenarios.

will charge more to do the work. The delays probably will throw the job off schedule and out of sequence. Rescheduling can result in further delays as some subcontractors may not be available at the rescheduled date. Any advances paid to the subcontractor are usually irretrievable. This occurs particularly with small subcontractors, who may ask for and receive funds in advance to purchase materials.

Solution

The obvious solution is for the developer to find a new contractor as quickly as possible, bite the bullet on increased costs, and plead with other subcontractors to appear on the rescheduled dates. Most often, it is a smaller subcontractor who will act irresponsibly, and so the impact on the job will be less severe. The remedy for the developer may involve litigation that could take months or even years before payback. Therefore, with small subcontractors, litigation may not be worthwhile. With a large job and substantial work, potential overruns can jeopardize project completion. The solution is for the borrower or, if the borrower is unable to, the lender to fund the additional costs.[2] With larger subcontractors, the situation should be watched closely.

Problem: Poor Workmanship, Poor Installation, Defective Materials, or Defective Equipment

Result

Generally, poor workmanship and installation or defective materials or equipment are very similar problems with the same remedies.[3] They can lead to delays because work has to be redone. The problem can be compounded if subsequent work obscures subpar work or defective materials. As was mentioned in the last section, the job can be thrown out of sequence. Whenever there is work out of sequence such as the replacement of materials or equipment, it can throw other trades out of sequence. Rescheduling can result in further delays as some subcontractors may not be available on the rescheduled dates. Unfortunately, in some work the defects surface only after the

---

[2] Instead of increasing the development loan, most lenders will make a new loan with different terms (e.g., a higher interest rate, additional collateral if possible. and personal guarantees).

[3] Note that material and equipment defects in buildings are unusual today because almost all are well tested. More often, these defects are due to materials being misapplied or improperly installed.

contractor is long gone. If the contractor was fully paid, it may be difficult or impossible to bring the contractor back to the job site.

Solution

If the contractor bought materials or equipment and installed them, unless stated otherwise in the contract, the contractor is responsible for replacing defective materials or equipment and performing all the labor involved at its own cost. If the developer bought materials or equipment for the contractor, the developer not only will be responsible for replacing defective materials or equipment but also will have to pay the contractor to reinstall them. Contracts that include labor and materials (and/or equipment) put the risk of defective materials and installation with the contractor, whereas those which involve only labor shift the risk of defective materials and the labor to replace them or correct the defects to the developer.[4]

If the contractor is reputable and the developer is strong with ongoing business, there is a high likelihood that the contractor will honor its contract.[5] Alternatively, if the contractor does not come back and the developer retains a construction and/or maintenance staff, depending on the nature of the work and the problem, the developer may be able to have his own men do the work. Otherwise the developer may have no choice but to find a new contractor. As in the example above, the developer will have to find a new contractor as quickly as possible, bite the bullet on increased costs, and plead with other contractors to appear on the rescheduled dates to do the ancillary repair work. The remedy for the developer may involve litigation which could take months or even years before payback. With small subcontractors, litigation may not be worthwhile. With large jobs and substantial work, potential overruns can jeopardize project completion and may force the lender, if the developer is unable to, to fund the additional costs. With larger subcontractors, the situation should be watched closely.

---

[4] Although several different members of a development project can hire a contractor (see Chapter 8), in this chapter, for clarity, the developer is the one entering directly into contracts with the contractor.

[5] The developer most likely still will have to pay for work done by other contractors whose work was affected by the faulty workmanship, improper installation, or defective material used by another. For example, poor air-conditioning ductwork insulation can allow ducts to throw off condensed moisture that soaks through ceiling drywall and drops onto hardwood floors. Not only will the insulation have to be replaced and properly secured, the ceiling and floor will have to be repaired as well.

Problem: Unapproved Deviation from Municipally Approved Plans or Work Done without Full Approvals

Result

The consequences here include delays and expense from work that has to be redone. The problem can be compounded if the unapproved work involves several trades. For example, replacing unapproved windows with landmark board–approved windows in a 10-story occupied building may require the erection of a street bridge, the manufacturing of new windows, some demolition work to remove existing windows, the fitting of the new windows, the fitting of trim, new drywall, taping, and painting. A deviation in unapproved plans may require, for instance, the relocation of wall partitions. This in turn may require that electrical wiring be removed or rerouted, along with telecommunications lines. Also, it may involve the removal of and reinstallation of plumbing, depending on what is in the wall.

The job almost certainly will be delayed and could be thrown out of sequence. Rescheduling difficulties can result in further delays as some contractors may not be available on the rescheduled dates.

Solution

Generally, the solution is the same as the solution for poor workmanship. However, the situation is more complicated, time-consuming, and costly. First, the developer will have to file amended drawings and specifications with the applicable municipalities and agencies. Then there will be a wait while they are reviewed. If they consider the developer a troublemaker, municipalities or agencies can hold up approvals for weeks or months. Since the developer can begin to correct the work previously done only after the receipt of approvals, the result can be devastating. Depending on the circumstances, it is not uncommon for the developer to give up a substantial amount of profits and in some cases even capital from what otherwise would have been a very lucrative project.[6]

---

[6] In all municipalities, certain agencies and departments are easier to work with than others and some have more power and authority than others. Usually, practitioners in the area know each agency, its quirks, the personalities of its key staff members, its speed of processing, and the difficulty of getting the desired results. Having worked in the municipality before or hiring someone who has experience and the right contacts can be the key to success in obtaining favorable and timely approvals.

For the lender, the question of competence becomes an issue because receiving approvals is a fundamental step in the development process. This situation also calls into question the ability of the developer to get final sign-offs and approvals for a temporary or permanent certificate of occupancy since that can be an arduous and time-consuming process. Questions to ask include the following: Was the problem the result of negligence on the part of the developer, the architect, an engineer, or a contractor? Is the project being supervised properly? When did the developer know that work was being performed (or completed), and was he trying to cover up unapproved work or did he quickly move to correct it? Obviously, the situation should be watched closely.

Problem: Accident at the Site That Injures People

Result: The two major variables in an accident are the seriousness of the accident and who was determined to be negligent. Usually the job will continue without any major or even minor consequences. If there is a serious injury, though, the job may be shut down by the local municipality while a safety check is performed and action is contemplated.

Solution
It goes without saying that the developer, the contractor, and the subcontractors on the job should be insured adequately. It is important that the lending institution's inspecting engineer receive certificates of insurance for each major contractor and subcontractor and that advances not be made or portions of advances should be held back until proof of insurance is provided. On subcontractors' insurance certificates, usually on a standard ACORD form, the contractor who hired the subcontractor should be named as an additional insured. General contractors should name the owner of the property and the lending institution as additional insureds.

On larger jobs, the developer should employ a safety consultant to make periodic inspections and recommendations. Most of the consultant's recommendations will seem obvious, but all should be taken seriously and acted on promptly. This is the case because when there is an accident, an investigation may prove that the conditions that resulted in the accident were known or caused by the developer or his responsible party, establishing a certain level of negligence that can result in a costly judgment. More important, with the use of a safety consultant, the probability of accidents should decline because potentially dangerous conditions are likely to be identified and corrected more quickly. Accidents always happen. The goal is to reduce to as close to zero as possible those which in hindsight were preventable.

In almost all accidents, there will be litigation that will require active participation by the developer, parties that have or may have been involved or possibly responsible for the accident, the person who was injured, the insurance company, and all of their attorneys. The lender rarely will be involved in litigation. Nonetheless, the lending officer should document the facts of the accident as he knows and understands them. In the future, often a year or more from the date of the accident, he may be called on to discuss them.

Problem: Property Damage from Fire, Flood, and the Like

Result

The major variables here are the severity of the damage, the point in the construction process when the damage occurred, and how it was caused. As in the case of a personal injury, who is determined to be negligent is an important issue. If the damage was the result of, say, a hurricane, negligence is probably not an issue. If the damage resulted from a fire, how the fire started and the conditions surrounding it may be an important issue. Fire and flood damage can set back a construction job to a state worse than the one before the project began since there may be more demolition, salvage, and carting. For a project that has advanced for some time, there is more at risk since more time, material, and labor have been invested.

Solution

The first thing a developer should do is call his insurance broker or an adjuster recommended by the broker and, depending on the extent of the damage, a structural engineer and the job's architect. The first thing the loan officer should do is learn as much as he can from the developer and then call his institution's lawyer. The lending institution should have language in the loan documentation describing what rights it has and what actions it can take. The loan officer should review this section to understand the institution's rights and remedies. The documentation should include, among other things, a provision that allows all insurance proceeds to be held by the lending institution and be released on the basis of the submission of requisitions and work completed. If damage is significant, some insurance proceeds may be received in a matter of hours or days to pay for emergency work. However, further advances usually are preceded by the scoping out of necessary work and a new budget, the drafting of new plans and specifications by engineers or the architect and approval by the proper municipal agencies, the bidding out of the work to contractors, the creation and approval of shop drawings, and the performance of the work.

Understandably, the developer often is concerned that he will lose a considerable amount of money because of the damage. He also may feel that the damage was not his fault and therefore feel victimized. You, as the loan officer, must make sure that you, not he, receive and have control over the insurance proceeds. When the insurance check is sent by the insurer to the developer, it names the developer as the payee along with the lending institution. Despite the requirement that both the developer and the lender endorse the check, it is relatively easy for a developer to deposit the proceeds without the lender's knowledge. (If the lender is a bank, it is particularly easy for the proceeds to be deposited in the project's checking account as if the funds already had been advanced by the lender because a teller or clerk accepting the check will see that it is endorsed by the developer and that the payee on the check has the bank's name on it. He may not be aware that the bank has to endorse it also.) The result is that the lender does not have any control of the funds or know that the borrower received them. There is a potential for the insurance proceeds to be used for other project expenses, as a "loan" to the developer for outside purposes such as funding other projects, or even for a distribution of equity. This can jeopardize the project and the primary collateral on which the loan was made. To avoid this possibility, you or your institution's attorney should contact the insurance company immediately with a notice that all insurance proceeds checks should be sent to the lender's attention with a copy to the borrower. If insurance proceeds must be sent to the borrower, ask the insurer to give you notice. Finally, if you have any suspicions, you may want to contact the insurer independently to determine how much money was advanced at any particular time.

Problem: Money Is Diverted from the Job and Not Paid to Contractors

Result

This situation is usually a very serious one since the borrower, the entity you have put your trust in, has taken someone else's money, only temporarily, one hopes. Failure to pay outstanding invoices can result in slowdowns, lien filing, and/or work stoppages. This can have magnified negative affects since the sequencing, organization, coordination, and performance of workers and trades and the delivery of materials are involved.

Solution

You need to understand the situation as quickly as possible. The first thing to do is contact the borrower for an explanation. Since the borrower has breached his contractual obligations actively, information probably will not be forthcoming. Therefore, you will have to have a dogged and perhaps aggressive attitude. After a talk with him, no matter what his explanation is, the next step is to notify senior management immediately and then call your institution's attorney. In fact, whenever the loan deteriorates to a level that may necessitate action by your institution, your attorney should be aware of the situation and be in a standby mode. The next steps you and/or your institution take can have considerable range. They begin with watching the loan closely if it is expected that the situation will be resolved quickly (this includes making regular reports to senior management and your attorney about the loan's status and possibly classifying the loan, as discussed later in this chapter) and can escalate to suspending loan advances, declaring the loan in default, and taking legal action.

Problem: Borrower Has Run Out of Money and Cannot Finish the Job

Result

For any lender and of course for the borrower, this can be a nightmare since the ultimate decision is whether to increase the amount of the loan or take some other action. At the least, you will have to give explanations and write reports to senior management. There is also a possibility that you will face some level of professional embarrassment, especially if you pushed hard to convince management to make the loan.

Solution

After quickly reviewing the loan file and making sure you understand what went wrong, contact senior management immediately. Let them know about the problem, including why you think it happened. Depending on your institution's functional organization, its culture, your senior manager's personality, and your level of confidence, it may be helpful to come up with and advance preliminary suggestions about how to proceed.

In this situation, you should review and reevaluate the development budget (if hard cost increases are a factor, they should be reviewed by the consulting engineer). Some of your determinations and actions will be similar to the ones mentioned in the discussion of the diversion of funds including the immediate notification of your institution's attorney. Even if you refuse any increase or reallocation of loan funds and the developer is able to obtain funds elsewhere, your institution's attorney may have to modify the loan documentation to include a new capital structure and retain lender's rights (allow subordinate financing, recognize a new managing member, draw up a recognition agreement, etc.).

In this case, the borrower did not divert funds but came up short. This is not uncommon in development projects and often is due to exogenous factors such as a rise in interest rates, an unforeseen delay caused by an event beyond the developer's control, and an increase in the cost of labor and/or materials. In most cases, if the job has advanced to the final stage and there apparently are no other material negative circumstances, it is probably best to increase the loan so that the project can be finished and your institution can be repaid. If possible, though, do not just give the money away. Try to take something extra such as additional collateral in the form of a mortgage on another property or a full guarantee of repayment if you do not have one already. Monitor the situation closely.

Problem: Material Delays and/or Shortages

Result

In this situation, the project can be delayed and coordination and sequencing among contractors may be jeopardized. The significance of the problem can vary widely, depending on how critical the material is at the particular stage of development, how long a delay there is, and what can be done to reduce the impact. When a contractor is buying the materials per his contract, the developer may have little choice but to suffer until delivery (or perhaps even reimburse the contractor for his loss if a deposit has been made to encourage the contractor to seek another source).

Solution
This situation is a developer's headache but is not unusual. Your borrower must use his experience and skill to mitigate the situation so that delays, if there are any, are lessened and subsequent work can be accelerated, For example, a shortage or delay in a shipment of precut steel will stop a high-rise office project in its tracks. However, a delay in a shipment of high-end bathroom fixtures may be offset by the installation of cheap "throwaway" fixtures that will make it possible to obtain a certificate of occupancy and allow rents to begin, followed by the installation of the high-end fixtures on their arrival. The usual remedies include moving workers and construction to other areas of the job that are not as advanced and therefore have more lead time before the missing materials are needed. The developer also should scramble for other sources of materials and weigh the possible cost increases of buying from another supplier against a job delay. For you, the course of action is to watch the situation closely.

Problem: Union Disruptions

Result
Depending on the nature,[7] size, and scope of a project; its location (urban, rural, suburban, etc.); and the status of the construction labor market, the developer may or may not need or want to use union labor. The general difference between a union job and a nonunion job is usually not quality, although the unions would disagree, but cost.[8]

---

[7] The nature of a project covers a myriad of situations. For instance, if a union is providing a portion of the financing, one of the conditions will be that the project use union labor. If the project is sponsored by a municipality, a requirement may be the use of union labor since unions have political influence. Perhaps the developer will use union labor because the end user requires it (this is common with larger institutions due to their high public and political profiles).

[8] During the planning phase of a job, the lending officer should ask if the job will be performed by union or nonunion labor. When a developer has estimated the cost of the job on the low side, he may say nonunion to convince you that his budget is realistic. In reviewing the budget, if you have any doubts, ask your consulting engineer to comment on the reasonableness of performing work with nonunion labor. For certain trades, such as concrete, it is almost impossible in some areas to do nonunion work. For demolition work, it is often easy to use nonunion workers.

Unionized contractors generally cost more because their workers are paid more per hour (some of that money goes to pay union dues) and union rules generally allow them to work fewer hours. In many situations, it is almost impossible to avoid hiring nonunion contractors, for example, in the delivery and assembly of steel. In other trades, such as hanging drywall, there are many nonunion contractors.

On small developments and most moderate rehabilitation projects, it is easier for the developer to employ nonunion workers since the project is not as visible to the public as is the case on larger jobs. To satisfy the institutional and large project markets that require union employees but stay competitive with smaller jobs in which bids are made by nonunion companies, some contractors will have one company with union employees and another with many of the same employees who will agree to work nonunion.

When unions strike a project, it usually causes disruption for an indeterminate amount of time. Depending on the strength of the union and its organization at the site, the strength of the developer, and general economic conditions in the market, the union's effectiveness can vary widely. The developer's choice of actions includes using nonunion labor, negotiating with the union, shutting down the project for an indefinite period, or hiring a security detail as a show of force to workers on the job and to make sure that union activists are kept at a distance from the site. Today union demonstrations are rare and not very effective. At the job sites where they occur, a hard-line defense by the developer (security guards and the like) can be fairly effective.

Solution
This situation is a developer's headache but not one in which a lender should get involved. The developer must use his experience and skill to resolve the situation. Often, the work progresses and the project is completed on time or is delayed only slightly. For the lender, the course of action is to watch the situation closely.

EXOGENOUS FACTORS: SUPPLY AND DEMAND AND CYCLICALITY

During the ramp-up of an economic growth cycle, money is readily available for construction purposes; a large number of projects are being undertaken; business spending, capital expenditures, and consumer spending are usually on the rise; and projected demand for real estate is high. In some cases, several categories and types of properties may not have been constructed for over a decade.[9] Then, over a relatively short period, there is a flurry of activity in which construction projects begin simultaneously to meet pent-up demand. This quickly raises development costs since resources are stretched. The cost of materials and labor increases, along with delivery times. Also, coordinating the various construction activities is more difficult since contractors may be booked on several jobs and are short of trained personnel. The point in the cycle where a project begins will determine how severely it is affected by these limited resources.

Since real estate development is a highly capital intensive undertaking, each project requires a great degree of planning and deliberation. Because the lead time to create product is relatively long, their completion can exceed the duration of a rising and stable economy. Construction projects begun in good times may be completed in bad times. As a result, the expected first and second ways out of a loan may be insufficient to pay down the development loan. The lending institution is forced to take measures that exceed what was expected when the loan was made.

Two Examples

Below are two examples in which good projects become not so good projects because of the ever-changing balance of supply and demand. One involves the economic cycle; the other involves a product with a perceived demand that never materialized.

Cyclicality

Several examples of cyclicality took place in the late 1990s. One involved hotels in New York City. After the end of a recession in the early 1990s, there was virtually no construction of new hotels in New York. As the global and domestic economies grew, there was a tremendous influx of foreign and domestic tourists. The demand led to high occupancy rates and soaring ADRs (average daily rates) that

---

[9] Augmenting periods of positive growth, with new methods and technologies being incorporated in new structures, older existing properties may exhibit accelerated states of functional obsolescence. This reduces supply.

encouraged many developers to create new and convert existing structures into flag hotels and boutique hotels.[10]

With slick interior decorating and designs and heavy marketing, the new hotels were directed at market segments that all seemed to be growing. Of course, the excitement of being in the same business as Donald Trump and Ian Schrager (a partial owner of Studio 54 in Manhattan) led investors to pour great amounts of cash into those projects, encouraged by optimistic financial projections. The result was that everyone wanted to develop and/or own a hotel.

In New York, the major and critical hotel season begins in September and ends in December. The summer months are slow because potential visitors prefer the beaches to the hot asphalt, and in January, the lowest visitor month, people apparently are recovering from the December holidays. In the summer of 2001 demand was slightly off, but that was not a major concern because hotel owners were expecting that the season from September through December would follow the course of prior years. The economy, although showing signs of slowing, was still in a growth phase, and globally there were no major crises. Then the destruction of the World Trade Center on September 11, 2001, devastated not only the lower Manhattan landscape but the travel and transportation industries, and that affected the city's hotel occupancy and financial landscape. It had the direct and immediate effect of cutting off virtually all foreign tourists, a substantial portion of domestic tourists, and almost all convention and business travelers to New York City.

From September 12 on, hotel construction in New York City was no longer an attractive investment. New hotel projects were scrapped, and existing hotels became potential workout candidates. September 11 was only a trigger to the hotel industry's precipitous downturn. Hotels already were arguably overbuilt in New York,

---

[10] Broadly defined, hotels that are managed by third-party management firms that take fees for their services are called flag hotels. Examples include the Hyatt, Marriott, and Hilton chains. Hotels without any affiliation to hotel management firms are independent and usually smaller. If they offer some special services or cachet, they are called boutique hotels. The major perceived advantages of independent and boutique hotels are direct management control, the saving of considerable management fees, and the ability and flexibility to differentiate a hotel radically from its general competition. The major perceived advantages of flag hotels are their extensive reservation systems, extensive marketing and advertising budgets, competitively positioned well-known branding, economies of scale, and proven management capability.

and the softened economy would have led to problems in any case. Then, in late 2002, as the effects of the tragedy wore off and the domestic and international economies improved, travelers once again began to come back to New York City. The result was that occupancies increased modestly at first and then accelerated. During the writing of this book, New York City occupancies per week have consistently been greater than 80 percent and average ADRs per year broke the $250 barrier. New hotels are again being built in the city. The New York hotel industry has come full cycle and then a half cycle more.

Supply and Demand

An example involving supply and demand concerns the telecommunications industry. As one of the cutting edge industries of the 1990s, the telecom "hotel" had enormous appeal for developers for several reasons:

- Initially, developers could buy properties cheaply in depressed industrial areas or underutilized areas where fiber-optic cables were in close proximity. Later, when owners and brokers caught on, property prices increased, but they were still perceived as attractive.
- The structures were relatively easy to build, although they were indeed expensive.
- The needs specified by end users were precise and exact. Fixtures and equipment were needed to accommodate rows of computers and telecommunications equipment whose size, temperature, and placement had to be measured accurately. The result was the development of structures with floors that were free of vibration with state-of-the-art heating and cooling instruments to control building temperatures; ceiling heights that allowed for equipment, cables, and ductwork; flexibility to accommodate equipment and floor plan configuration upgrades and backup electrical generating systems that could sense power drops and outages and supply backup power in milliseconds; and very close proximity to fiber-optic cables or "highways."
- Expensive and more subjectively chosen fixtures for people were required only on a very limited basis since only a handful of people would be at a facility at any particular time.

- On completion, the tenant was responsible for all maintenance, which was minimal in light of the final use of the property: the housing of machines with few or no moving parts.

Demand for the centers was perceived to be insatiable as experts on the future, outdoing one another in their praise of the electronic telecommunications world, expected that telecommunications technology would force demand. Unfortunately, the demand never materialized. Instead, there were some spectacular telecommunication company failures along with those dependent on them for major portions of their business.

The Lending Officer and a Bad Loan

Institutions that made loans collateralized by hotels and telecommunication-related companies that later got into trouble probably made what appeared to be reasonable and sound lending decisions. When a good loan turns into one that needs watching or worse, it is usually not the lending officer's fault. He did not act unilaterally but had to go through the institution's loan process and therefore received approval of the loan from other officers.[11]

However, if a loan you have underwritten develops problems, you may be criticized at some level for your poor individual judgment. If you pushed strongly to make the loan, you may be blamed outright. You also may lose much of your autonomy because others will become more directly involved in the loan and periodically will want updated information about the progress of planned solutions (this is not necessarily a criticism of your judgment or a lack of confidence in you; it is senior management's job to monitor problem loans more carefully). In many institutions, depending on the degree and severity of the problem, the loan will be taken out of your control and reassigned to a workout officer or workout department.

What to Do

With problem loans, because of a higher possibility that the loan file will be taken from you and assigned to another person, in addition

---

[11] If nothing else, this should help the lending officer maintain his perspective and self-esteem.

to the official loan file, make sure that you establish and maintain a personal backup file and update it frequently. Particularly in dealing with a problem loan, having a private source you can refer to can make the difference between defending yourself properly and capitulating to a charge because of your inability to review the facts weeks or months after they occurred.

Keep the official loan file current and organized and remove any erroneous and/or personal material. Anything that does not belong in it is an invitation for someone to criticize or second-guess your decisions.[12]

Since the loan and, by extension, you may get a lot more institutional attention, review the loan file and perhaps some of the legal documentation that discusses the lender's rights and remedies. Try to memorize as much of the core transaction as possible as well as any relevant facts that can be used in oral presentations. You usually get only a limited amount of time to voice an opinion or make an argument. If it seems that you know what you are talking about, you may be able to turn a problem loan into a career advantage by making a good impression on senior management.

Make an effort to speak with others to get their advice. Most important, confer with your institution's real estate attorney or, if that proves difficult, with the attorney who closed the original loan. Strategizing with someone who has experienced a similar situation and/or knows the law almost always helps by providing new ideas or a validation of your ideas.

Cooperate as much as possible with your institution's credit people, auditors, workout department personnel, attorneys, and senior management. Keep them apprised of the situation on a regular basis so that they know you are giving the loan ongoing attention.

Do not overreact to the problem situation, but do not underreact either. Be as objective as possible with both the borrower and your institution's personnel. Your job is not to become directly

---

[12] There have been instances in which destroying documentation has gotten people into regulatory and even legal trouble. To avoid this possibility, make culling the official file a routine activity, not one that can be called an attempt to hide or destroy derogatory material. Also, keep your personal file personal and try to limit its content to facts, not opinions. Although this occurs only rarely, the file may be requested by legal authorities or attorneys conducting an investigation (usually the request is for "all" documentation, notes, etc., pertaining to a particular loan, not specifically for personal files).

involved as the manager of the problem situation (this can result in lender liability). Always retain a balanced approach from the perspective of a lender, not an active developer or equity investor.

Do not resist losing control. If it has been determined that the loan should be managed by someone else, the decision was a deliberate one. It may be due to institutional policy, in which case the choice to move it was almost automatic. Alternatively, there may be more experienced personnel who do nothing but deal with problem loans every day. Whatever the reason, the prudent action is to turn over the file in a cooperative manner.

If you are asked to give up control, cooperate with the new loan and/or credit officer as much as possible but keep your guard up. Since part of the credit officer's job is to be critical, chances are that he will cite you in some way. He is paid to identify problems. The more negatively he portrays a situation, the more he is absolved of responsibility if the situation gets worse. This allows him to establish a low benchmark for measuring his performance, thereby increasing his chances of claiming success.

CLASSIFYING LOANS ACCORDING TO PERCEIVED RISK

All institutional lenders track their loan portfolios according to a variety of variables. The goal is to establish a gauge that is as objective as possible and that therefore provides a good measure of each loan's overall risk. If a loan is perceived to have a diminished credit quality, it is downgraded to a lower classification. If a downgraded loan later displays enhanced quality (something that is relatively rare), it is upgraded to a higher classification. Classifications are important to the lending institution because they can determine whether expenses are recognized for losses of accrued interest, loan loss reserves or loan write-downs; affect the ratings of the institution by analysts, which can have a direct bearing on its cost of funds in capital markets and its stock price; and result in the imposition of restrictions by governmental agencies. For the loan officer, it can dictate the degree of control he has over a loan and may be used as an indicator of his underwriting skills which include his ability to recognize and properly address risk.

For a borrower, the way his loan is classified can affect who he will be interfacing with and what negotiating power he has. Sometimes a downgrade of a loan can benefit the borrower. For instance, if a loan is classified to a level at which a reserve for loss has to be taken by the lending institution, it must recognize the reserve as an expense on its income statement. The institution, already having suffered the loss of income, may sell the loan at a discount to its face amount back to the borrower. If the borrower is deemed competent and the problems were not attributed to his actions, the borrower may be able to negotiate a reduced interest rate or an extended loan term.

Determining the place of a loan in the classification hierarchy can help both the borrower and the lender. Following is a basic example of risk classification definitions adapted from a commercial bank.[13]

LOAN CLASSIFICATIONS

Satisfactory: Assets at risk that meet the bank's quality standards in every respect. A realistic source of repayment that was identified before final approval exists. All necessary documentation, especially pertaining to collateral, is in proper order.

Watch list: Essentially sound credits but with declining trends or other aspects that make more frequent examination desirable. Relatively new borrowing entities without a useful history of operation and fairly sound borrowers in distressed industries are among the types of credits classified here. Loans so classified are not considered to be criticized by loan review.

Deficient: Credits rated deficient are items that, because of weakened financial strength, otherwise would receive a satisfactory classification if not for the fact that documentation or other administrative deficiencies exist. When the cited deficiencies are corrected to the satisfaction of loan review, the loan will be reclassified to the satisfactory category.

Special mention: Assets in this category are currently protected but are potentially weak. The credit risk may be relatively minor yet constitutes an unwarranted risk in light of the circumstances surrounding a specific asset. Potential weaknesses exist in the credit that, if not checked or corrected now, may in the future weaken the asset or inadequately protect the bank's position as a creditor. Although loans so designated are considered to be criticized, they are not classified to a degree requiring a specific allocation to the loan loss reserve.

Substandard: An asset inadequately protected by the current worth and paying capacity of the obligor or of the collateral pledged, if any. Such assets have well-defined weaknesses that jeopardize the liquidation of the debt.

---

[13] Note that the example given is generic in nature. Most lending institutions classify their loan portfolio based on more precise benchmarks which are beyond the scope of this book.

The real possibility exists that if these deficiencies are not corrected, the bank will sustain some loss.

Doubtful: These assets have all the characteristics of assets classified as substandard but also have weaknesses to a degree that make collection of the debt to the bank in full highly questionable and improbable. In some cases, this category could include assets that might otherwise be deemed a loss but might be recoverable because of a specific event that, if consummated, would result in repayment. Examples of such events could include pending mergers or possible infusions of capital from identified, interested sources. In the case of the anticipated liquidation of the assets securing the bank's loan, if there is no other specific, identifiable source of funds to repay the obligation, any shortfall between the book value of the loan and the estimated sale value of the asset(s) to be sold should be classified as a loss.

Loss: Assets so classified lack any realistic source of repayment to a degree that they can no longer be justified as bankable assets. Included here are loans where the possibility of at least some recovery exists, though without certainty. It is better to classify these items as loss and recognize any recovery when actually, if ever, realized.

Essentially an adverse classification is intended to initiate attention and supervision at a higher official level than would have been required without such classification.

Loan Charge-Offs

Loans classified as doubtful should be placed on a nonaccrual basis and previously accrued and unpaid interest must be reversed. It will then be the responsibility of the credit department to collect the principal or face amount of the debt remaining. Based on known factors, or the likelihood of additional adverse factors, consideration should be given to establishing a loss reserve.

When classified as a loss, the obligation must be placed on a nonaccrual basis, all previously accrued and unpaid interest must be reversed, and the loan principal must be charged off or fully reversed.

Author's Note

Although this is not a book about loan workouts, it is inevitable that problems will occur with loans from time to time. Unfortunately, there are many unenlightened managers who are not prepared for negative news. Others in your institution may try to capitalize on credit problems even though those problems are part and parcel of the lending business. Borrowers and a host of other key personnel in the development process can turn from being cooperative to being adversarial. You should be prepared for these possibilities. Fortunately, though, the great majority of people in the real estate finance and development industries are professional, objective, and to a great extent cooperative.

Loan problems usually surface with little or no warning, often require uncomfortable decisions, and can take up a lot of a loan officer's time and energy with little or no positive reinforcement. The best loan officers are those who keep a cool head, remain nonjudgmental, focus on the problems, are objective, establish goals, and stay on track to achieve them. Simply put, you should try to be one of the best.

INDEX

ABOUT THE AUTHOR

Ira Nachem has over 25 years of progressive commercial real estate experience in finance, investment, development, construction, and management. His experience in commercial real estate finance includes involvement in all types of credit and equity transactions, the maintenance of several diverse credit portfolios, and the administration and working out of problem loans throughout the United States and Canada. He has advised, invested in, and been involved in all aspects of the real estate development and construction process for several projects in the New York metropolitan area. Mr. Nachem has given seminars on credit, real estate finance, investment, and development. He currently lectures on real estate and construction finance at New York University.